MW01000213

SAP® SuccessFactors®

Amy Grubb, Luke Marson

SAP® SuccessFactors®

An Introduction

Editor Megan Fuerst
Acquisitions Editor Emily Nicholls
Copyeditor Rachel Paul
Cover Design Graham Geary
Photo Credit Shutterstock.com/1069528964/© Longchalerm Rungruang
Layout Design Vera Brauner
Production Hannah Lane
Typesetting III-satz, Husby (Germany)
Printed and bound in the United States of America, on paper from sustainable sources

ISBN 978-1-4932-1818-9

3rd edition 2020

Library of Congress Cataloging-in-Publication Data
Names: Grubb, Amy, author. | Marson, Luke, author.
Title: SAP SuccessFactors : an introduction / Amy Grubb, Luke Marson.
Description: 3rd Edition. | Boston : Rheinwerk Publishing, [2019] | Revised edition of the authors' SuccessFactors with SAP ERP HCM, [2015] | Includes index.
Identifiers: LCCN 2019017620 (print) | LCCN 2019019564 (ebook) | ISBN 9781493218196 | ISBN 9781493218189 (alk. paper)
Subjects: LCSH: SAP ERP. | Personnel management--Data processing. | Personnel management--Computer programs. | Manpower planning--Computer programs. | SuccessFactors (Firm)
Classification: LCC HF5549.5.D37 (ebook) | LCC HF5549.5.D37 G78 2019 (print) | DDC 658.300285/53--dc23
LC record available at https://lccn.loc.gov/2019017620

Contents at a Glance

Dear Reader,

What are the key factors—you might call them *success factors*—for publishing a good book? It's a long list.

First, you need dedicated authors who are experts in their field, aware of information needs in the community, and committed to putting that content to paper. Then, the manuscript needs to be honed and polished by its editor. Everything from selecting an appealing cover to sharpening hundreds of screenshots to binding the book depends on a dedicated production department. A savvy marketing team connects the book to its readers through social media and promotional events. And let's not forget the customer service and HR representatives who ensure both the customer-facing frontend and administrative backend are running smoothly.

It's not surprising that all of these success factors have one thing in common: people. And if you're looking to manage, support, and empower the people that drive your organization forward, then this book on the SAP SuccessFactors HCM Suite is where your journey begins.

What did you think about *SAP SuccessFactors: An Introduction*? Your comments and suggestions are the most useful tools to help us make our books the best they can be. Please feel free to contact me and share any praise or criticism you may have.

Thank you for purchasing a book from SAP PRESS!

Megan Fuerst
Editor, SAP PRESS

meganf@rheinwerk-publishing.com
www.sap-press.com
Rheinwerk Publishing · Boston, MA

Contents

8 Recruiting 297

17 Administration 631

Foreword

The nature of work is changing rapidly. Businesses everywhere continue to be disrupted by social change, globalization, the impact of new technologies, and the need to adapt to volatility and acceleration. The one thing we know for sure is that the way we approach and manage work in the future will be very different from the way we handle it today.

But what is the one thing that remains constant? People. No matter how much technology helps us automate processes, it's people who make the difference. To thrive in this new world, we all need to tap into our collective humanity. Human resources (HR) is at the heart of that effort. We are truly embarking on a human revolution, a moment when HR leaders are reimagining their function to create an inspired workforce that improves both profit and performance.

SAP SuccessFactors solutions enable HR teams to run at their best, lead a people strategy for the next chapter of their business, and help organizations become a best-run workforce. SuccessFactors Inc. was acquired in 2012 by SAP. At the time of publication, SAP SuccessFactors solutions now reach 6,700 customers with 125 million users. Business leaders around the world have told us that harnessing the changing workforce and having a laser focus on talent are critical to scaling their companies and competing in the future.

What's also critical is engagement. When you turn employees into ambassadors and fanatics of your culture, brand, and customers, you will see business results. It can mean 21% greater profitability, 17% higher productivity, and 10% higher customer ratings (Gallup 2016, 2018).

People experiences matter.

It's not only about workplace experiences—it's about human experiences: family, health, job, finances, and time. These are life events that many of us have experienced. Feelings of high stress or burnout. A new role or a new team. Unexpected expenses. A new child or an aging parent.

How we address events such as these can make or break an employee's relationship with a company. By tending to the well-being of the whole person —both inside and outside the work environment—we can positively impact employee performance and productivity.

So how can a company support its people in such a targeted, personal way?

SAP SuccessFactors: An Introduction gives readers an inside look at the capabilities we've been building for more than a decade. We offer an extensive human capital management (HCM) suite that brings together a global platform combined with powerful people analytics and experience management solutions, enabling you to deliver exceptional experiences that fundamentally improve the moments that matter. The book highlights key areas of the SAP SuccessFactors solution portfolio—core HR, payroll, talent management, learning, recruiting, compensation, and mobile—and covers some of our latest offerings such as diversity, inclusion, and wellbeing. It describes what is today just the start of our journey to use the power of SAP SuccessFactors solutions and experience management solutions from SAP to deliver the ultimate talent experience.

A special thanks to authors Luke Marson and Amy Grubb, along with contributors Mick Collins, Eliza Dash, Sven Ringling, and Joelle Smith for sharing with readers their expertise and passion for the HR market. They've produced a valuable asset for our customers as they look for new ways to prioritize and invest in their most important asset—their people.

Amy Wilson
Senior Vice President, Products
SAP SuccessFactors

Preface

Welcome to the third edition of this introduction to SAP SuccessFactors. SAP acquired SuccessFactors in early 2012, and the first edition of this book was published in late 2013. The second edition followed in 2015. Since the acquisition, the pace of change in the SAP SuccessFactors HCM Suite has been astounding.

With four releases per year, there have been more than fifteen releases since the last edition of the book. In that time, the suite has seen a raft of functionality, architectural enhancements, and a new user interface. And even in the coming months after this book is published, there will be more changes still to come. Based on this, it was clear that a new edition was needed.

With this edition, we have tried to create a solid overview book that includes key processes and features, the pertinent technical aspects, and insights into implementing and administering the system. We hope this continues to act as the SAP SuccessFactors "bible" and can further help educate the ecosystem of customers, consultants, SAP employees, and more.

Objective of This Book

This book is intended to be a source of information for anyone interested in learning more about what SAP SuccessFactors is and how it can transform business's human resources (HR). Whether you are an HRIS analyst, a chief HR manager (CHRO), a configuration consultant, or a sales executive, this book should be able to help you understand what the suite offers.

The intention has been to provide a comprehensive overview of each module in the suite, alongside implementation, integration, administration, and other aspects of using, implementing, and managing the suite. We have also introduced Qualtrics, a recent acquisition by SAP for managing the employee and customer experience.

This book should provide you with the grounding to be able to understand and talk about what the suite offers and can do for HR transformation programs. With this knowledge as a foundation, moving onto an implementation project or taking a certification will provide valuable insights that can help you gain expertise when applied.

One thing this book is not intended to do is reinvent the wheel. Since the last edition, SAP has published and continues to publish a wealth of information and resources for customers, partners, and consultants. We cover a lot of these resources in Appendix A and reference them throughout the book. We do not aim to repeat technical or other information that SAP provides elsewhere.

Target Audience

For customers, this book aims to provide an understanding of how you will execute your processes using SAP SuccessFactors, how data is managed, how integration can be achieved, how you will manage a live system, and how you will implement it. The book covers tips and tricks for when you implement any module of the suite and also gives you a chance to learn about other areas that you might not have been previously exposed to.

For partners and their consultants, the book can be a valuable tool to get up to speed with SAP SuccessFactors and all of the implementation-related areas.

New and Changed in This Edition

With so much change over the last few years, it is not possible to list all of the new content and changes we have made. However, there are certainly a number of changes that are well worth mentioning. The release of the SAP Fiori-based user interface has been a major change since the last edition, as well as the new Admin Center and redesigned SAP SuccessFactors Mobile app. We've also updated information around implementation; SAP have since released the SAP Activate methodology to replace the BizXpert methodology covered in the last edition, and they have begun to release implementation design and architecture best practice materials to provide recommendations and safeguards during implementation.

Some of the modules have grown significantly, and the increased page counts for modules such as SAP SuccessFactors Employee Central and SAP SuccessFactors Employee Central Payroll reflect this. There is also a significantly larger body of integrations and technology available.

SAP Jam no longer features in the book, as it has since become a crossfunctional social collaboration software in its own right. You will find an SAP Jam E-Bite available from SAP PRESS that covers this topic.

As noted previously, Qualtrics is a new addition. SAP acquired Qualtrics to help customers manage the customer and employee experience, and we wanted to show how Qualtrics can be used as part of your employee engagement and experience strategy. Only time will tell if Qualtrics stays as close to SAP SuccessFactors as SAP Jam once did.

How to Read This Book

We have attempted to order this book logically, starting with an introduction to the suite, implementation, running through each of the modules, the mobile app, integration, administration, and an appendix of useful resources to help you along your SAP SuccessFactors journey.

While we think it is good to read the book sequentially through each chapter, it is also perfectly fine to focus on just the chapters that are relevant to you. For some of the modules, SAP PRESS offer dedicated titles, such as Employee Central, SAP SuccessFactors Recruiting and SAP SuccessFactors Onboarding, SAP SuccessFactors Learning, and integration. SAP PRESS also offer E-Bites for individual aspects of the suite, including the Admin Center, data migration, an introduction to Employee Central Payroll, and the related Payroll Control Center. If you want to dig deeper beyond the overview we provide, then we recommend that you take a look at the range of titles offered by SAP PRESS to see if they cater to the module or area you are seeking. Otherwise, this title should give you a sufficient introduction to each module.

How This Book Is Organized

Let's review what is covered in each chapter of this book:

- **Chapter 1**
  The first chapter in the book gives an overview of the SAP SuccessFactors suite. It briefly looks at each module, walks through the deployment models, and walks through some core cloud concepts focused on SAP SuccessFactors, such as localization and quarterly releases.
- **Chapter 2**
  Chapter 2 walks through considerations when implementing SAP SuccessFactors, the roles and responsibilities of the project team, the standard SAP Activate methodology, and how project delivery works for cloud implementations versus traditional on-premise implementations.

- **Chapter 3**
  This chapter looks at the SAP SuccessFactors platform and the foundational functionality it provides to configure and manage the system. This includes walking through the technical architecture, security, and user interface. It also includes other core platform functionality, like the Metadata Framework (MDF) to build extensions, the Job Profile Builder to manage competencies and job descriptions, and picklists to control the selection of field values. Alongside this, we also cover other topics such as the Employee Profile and Org Chart.
- **Chapter 4**
  In this chapter we look at Employee Central—the core HR system in the SAP SuccessFactors HCM Suite—and how it can help manage your HR processes; provide you with manager and employee self-services; and assist with time management, benefits, management of global employees, and more.
- **Chapter 5**
  Chapter 5 sees us walk through Employee Central Payroll and what it offers to manage and run payroll, including the innovative Payroll Control Center.
- **Chapter 6**
  This chapter covers the Performance Management and Goals Management applications and how they combined to create a goal-oriented performance management process that can also leverage continuous, real-time feedback.
- **Chapter 7**
  The Compensation module is the focus of Chapter 7. Here we introduce how the module can support various types of compensation planning, such as merit and bonus. We also take a look at the Variable Pay module and integration between Compensation/Variable Pay and Employee Central.
- **Chapter 8**
  This chapter introduces the recruiting applications in the suite: Recruiting Management, Recruiting Marketing, and Job Posting. We also look at managing candidates and the candidate experience.
- **Chapter 9**
  In this chapter, we look at the Onboarding module and how it supports employee onboarding, crossboarding, and offboarding. We also look at how the key features can help with employee engagement and retention.
- **Chapter 10**
  In Chapter 10 we turn our attention to the learning management system in the SAP SuccessFactors HCM Suite. Learning is a robust solution that covers a wide

breadth of functionality, and as such this chapter contains a comprehensive overview of all of the features, functionality, and processes supported by the market-leading solution.

- **Chapter 11**
  Succession planning and career development planning (CDP) are the focus of Chapter 11. We take a look at each of these modules and how they work in tandem to support talent identification, succession plans, and long-term development planning for your top-performing and high-potential employees.
- **Chapter 12**
  In this chapter, we take a look at analytics solution in the suite, Workforce Analytics. Workforce Analytics is rich in functionality to assess, view, and drill down into your data and understand the trends and stories that can help you make better decisions about your workforce.
- **Chapter 13**
  Sitting on top of the data in Workforce Analytics is the Workforce Planning solution. This builds on your analytics data to enable you to create strategic workforce plans and better understand your skills and workforce gaps, as well as predict what is needed in the future.
- **Chapter 14**
  Chapter 14 introduces Qualtrics and how it can be used as part of your employee engagement strategy. We take a look at experience management and the surveys offered by Qualtrics to assess employee experience.
- **Chapter 15**
  In this chapter we run through the functionality offered in the mobile app. We cover the key features available for the relevant SAP SuccessFactors modules, as well as the embedded SAP Jam functionality.
- **Chapter 16**
  Integration is a hot topic in the SAP SuccessFactors world, and we take the opportunity to walk through the different integration technologies, standard-delivered content, application programming interfaces (APIs), and other functionality and resources that SAP provides to enable you to integrate SAP SuccessFactors with other systems.
- **Chapter 17**
  In the final chapter of the book, we take a look at the administrative side of the suite and what is available for you to administer and maintain the system. This chapter builds on some of the functionality introduced in Chapter 3 and subsequent chapters.

- **Appendix A**
  Appendix A provides a detailed look at the different resources available to support you in your SAP SuccessFactors journey, including SAP Community, SAP Learning Hub, LinkedIn groups, social media, and more.

Now with all that said, let's move onto Chapter 1 and get a first look at SAP SuccessFactors.

Chapter 1
Introduction

A leader in human resources (HR), payroll, analytics, and social collaboration software in the cloud, SAP provides a full range of human capital management (HCM) solutions that are suitable for organizations of any size, any industry, and any geography.

SAP SuccessFactors is SAP's go-to solution for HR. It's a multitenant software-as-a-service (SaaS) solution that is hosted by SAP and licensed through an annual subscription. While the fundamentals of HR have not evolved much since the early days of electronic record keeping and manager approvals, today's HR systems have moved toward being intelligent systems of engagement and automation that open up possibilities to provide HR processes and services not previously possible.

The SAP SuccessFactors HCM Suite covers the spectrum of HR processes, including core HR, talent management, workforce planning, and analytics. Within core HR, SAP SuccessFactors offers a core human resource information system (HRIS), payroll, time management, benefits, shared services management, and wellness management. All of this is supported on a mobile application for smartphones and tablet devices.

Originally, SAP SuccessFactors had a particular strength in talent management and social collaboration, but in the past five years we've seen significant growth of SAP SuccessFactors Employee Central; in days gone by, customers tended to start with talent applications, but we're now seeing a strong trend of customers starting with core HR before moving to talent. The suite's range of talent management solutions covers all of the key process areas: performance management, recruitment, onboarding, compensation management, learning management, succession planning, and career development planning. The vendor-agnostic analytics solution has 30 years of experience behind it and provides more than 1,000 predefined analytics.

This book has seen many changes to the SAP SuccessFactors HCM Suite of solutions, the adoption of SAP SuccessFactors, the market, and the ecosystem since the first edition was published back in 2013. At the time of writing (fall 2019), the SAP SuccessFactors HCM Suite now handles in excess of 12 billion transactions by more than 100 million users at more than 6,500 customers in 26 different industries. More than 85 of these customers have more than 100,000 employees. SAP is implementing more than 2,000 regulatory updates per year and has upward of 19,500 pieces of predelivered content. These statistics speak volumes about the growth and adoption of SAP SuccessFactors.

In this updated and expanded edition, we'll look at the latest processes and features released since the last edition of this book, as well as the updated user interface (UI) and new features like Intelligent Services, Digital Assistant, and Work-Life (focused on health and well-being). In addition, we have added content to show how SAP SuccessFactors applications can add value to your HR processes.

We'll now take a look at a brief history of SAP SuccessFactors before taking a high-level look at the modules of the suite, SAP's strategy and roadmap, and then a few core concepts of the system.

1.1 History of SAP SuccessFactors

SuccessFactors was founded in 2001 as an SaaS performance management software vendor. It quickly evolved its strategy to focus on providing "business execution" software and, thus, expanding its offering to cover talent management and analytics.

SAP announced its intention to acquire SuccessFactors on December 3, 2011, and the acquisition was formally completed in February 2012. SuccessFactors became "SuccessFactors, an SAP company" shortly thereafter, before eventually becoming "SAP SuccessFactors" as SAP's family of cloud applications were given the "SAP" moniker before their name.

The acquisition was significant for SAP in a number of ways: it provided SAP with access to genuine cloud expertise and enabled it to offer a full cloud-based HCM suite. It also gave both SAP and SuccessFactors significant exposure within and outside the SAP ERP Human Capital Management (SAP ERP HCM) ecosystem.

Both SAP and SuccessFactors announced their unified product direction in February 2012, shortly after the acquisition had closed. For core HR, customers had a choice of either Employee Central or SAP ERP HCM. For talent management, SAP

SuccessFactors was the "go-forward" solution available to customers. This meant that unless specifically requested, customers would always be offered SAP SuccessFactors when they wanted to discuss buying any talent management applications.

Over the years, SAP SuccessFactors added recruiting marketing, recruiting posting, onboarding, workforce analytics, and social collaboration through acquisition of specialist vendors. The SuccessFactors Jam collaboration solution was eventually morphed into the cross-domain SAP Jam solution.

1.2 SAP SuccessFactors HCM Suite

The SAP SuccessFactors HCM Suite covers core HR, talent management, analytics, and social collaboration. Content, integration, and extensibility underpin the suite. SAP SuccessFactors has more than 19,500 pieces of standard content, covering skills, competencies, and goals. The suite contains the following solutions:

- Platform
- Employee Central
- Employee Central Service Center
- Employee Central Payroll
- Work-Life
- Performance & Goals
- Compensation
- Recruiting
- Onboarding
- Learning
- Succession & Development
- Workforce Planning
- Workforce Analytics
- Mobile

Figure 1.1 is the graphic used by SAP and SAP SuccessFactors to visualize the HCM suite.

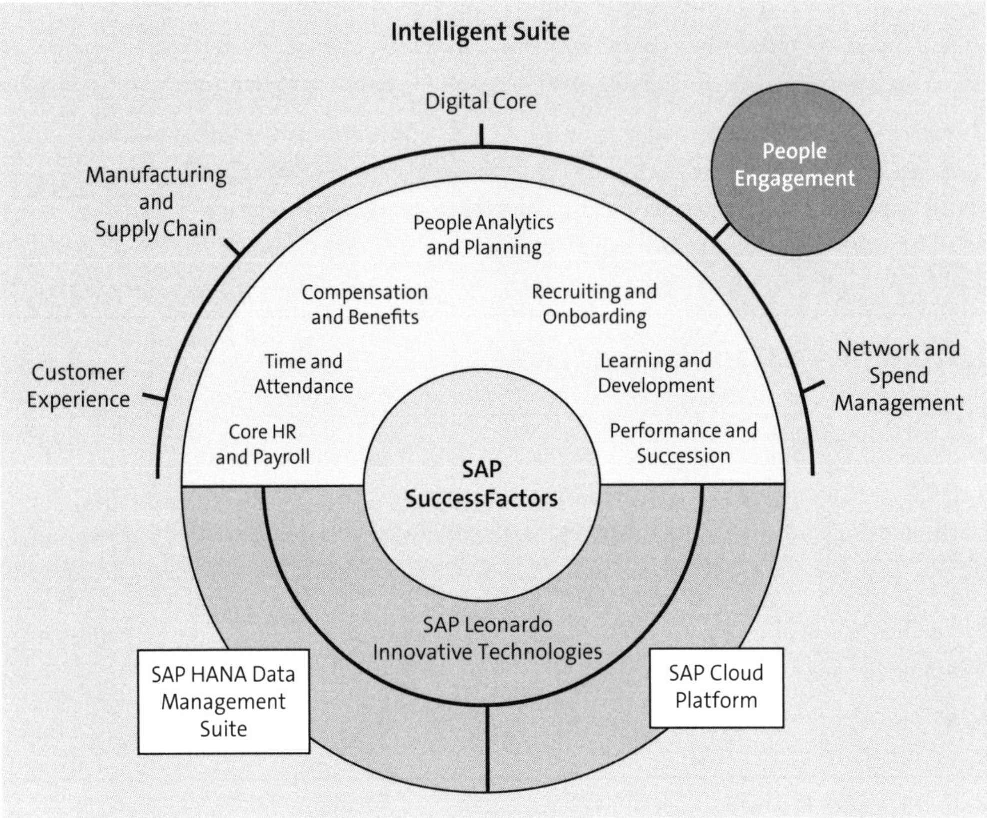

Figure 1.1 The SAP SuccessFactors HCM Suite

Let's walk through the key components of the SAP SuccessFactors HCM Suite.

1.2.1 Platform

The SAP SuccessFactors platform is the technical foundation for the entire SAP SuccessFactors HCM Suite. It provides core functionality, such as the home page, Admin Center, People Profile, Org Chart (shown in Figure 1.2), badges, email notifications, Metadata Framework (MDF), Extension Center, Integration Center, Upgrade Center, theming, permissions framework, and more. It's required when the first SAP SuccessFactors application(s) is configured and provides all prerequisite technical elements required to run any suite applications.

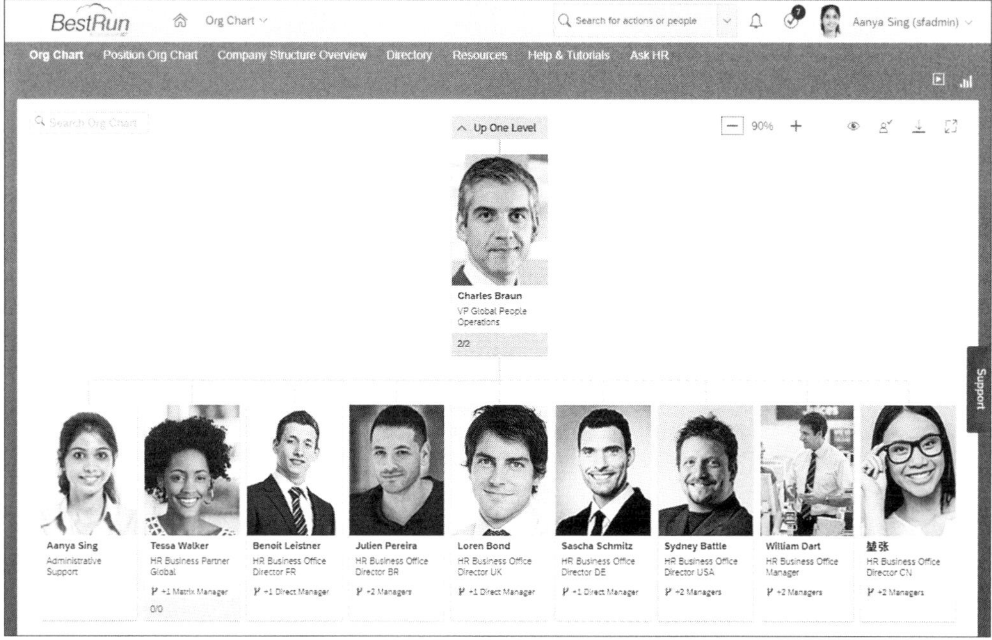

Figure 1.2 The Org Chart

More information on the SAP SuccessFactors platform can be found in Chapter 3.

1.2.2 Core HR

In this section, we'll cover the four applications in the core HR lifecycle, which enable management of employee data, self-services, payroll, time management, benefits, ticketing and issue management, and health and well-being. We'll start by looking at SAP SuccessFactors Employee Central, the core HR solution of the SAP SuccessFactors HCM Suite.

Employee Central

SAP SuccessFactors Employee Central is the core HRIS of the SAP SuccessFactors HCM Suite. It provides configurable enterprise-level HCM processes and functionality in an intuitive UI for HR professionals, executives, managers, and employees. It allows users to view, maintain, audit, and report on employee and organizational data across different countries, cost centers, legal entities, and employee types. Event-based transactions, workflows, and HR processes are available to fully manage everyday HR operations and activities. The solution is localized for 98 countries (at the time of writing, fall 2019), which covers address formats, national ID validations, country-specific fields, reports, and more. Figure 1.3 shows the profile of an employee.

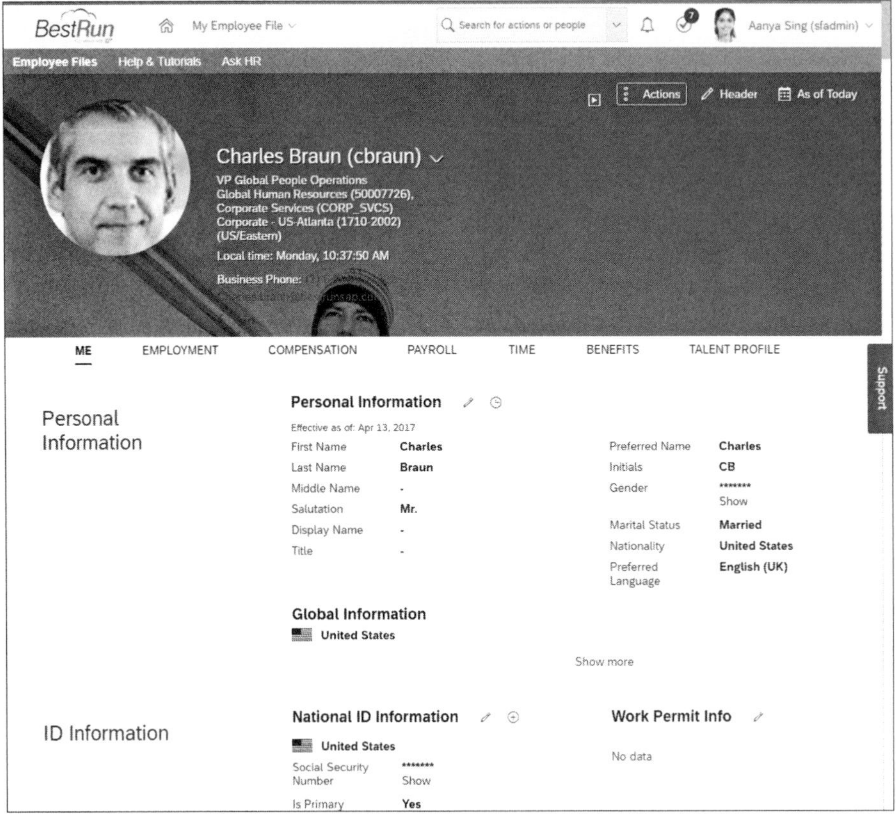

Figure 1.3 An Employee's Profile in Employee Central

Employee Central also offers the ability to perform time management, manage employee benefits, track contingent workers in the workforce, and much more. More information on Employee Central can be found in Chapter 4.

Employee Central Payroll

SAP SuccessFactors Employee Central Payroll provides the combination of the world's premier payroll engine with the power of advanced UI-driven payroll (pre- and postprocessing). With the backbone of SAP ERP Payroll and the modern Payroll Control Center solution—coupled with regulatory localizations for 43 countries (at the time of writing, fall 2019)—customers can be confident that they have the ability to run their entire payroll process, no matter what the complexity of their processing rules and whether they run payroll in-house or outsource. Figure 1.4 shows an employee's pay slip in Employee Central Payroll.

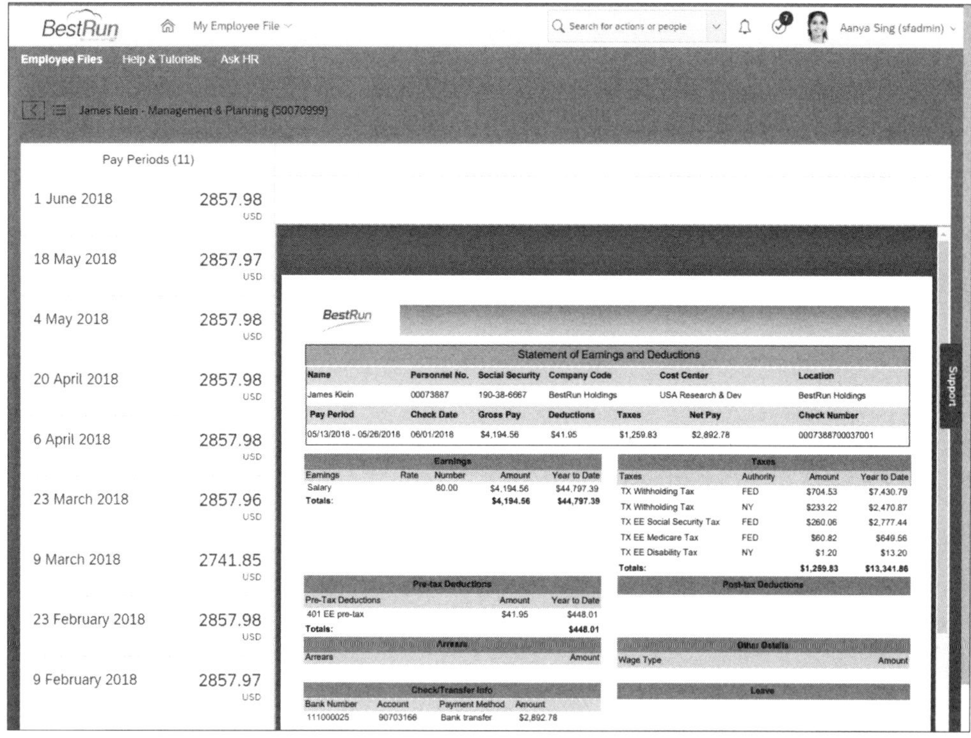

Figure 1.4 Pay Slip in Employee Central Payroll

More information on Employee Central Payroll can be found in Chapter 5.

Employee Central Service Center

For managing HR shared services and knowledge bases, SAP SuccessFactors offers Employee Central Service Center. The solution is split into two core areas: *Ask HR* and *HR Ticketing*.

Ask HR can be accessed from anywhere in the SAP SuccessFactors HCM Suite and provides employees with the ability to research topics in their knowledge base, open a ticket for more information (see Figure 1.5), place a call with the helpdesk, email the helpdesk, or initiate a chat session. HR Ticketing enables shared services representatives and HR professionals to review tickets, access information as needed, route tickets to the appropriate individual or group, and action and resolve tickets.

Employee Central Service Center also includes dashboards and analytics on service-level agreements (SLAs), frequently raised issues, employee interactions, bottlenecks, and the quality of the resolutions provided. Customer-specific reports can be built to cover those KPIs not delivered out-of-the-box.

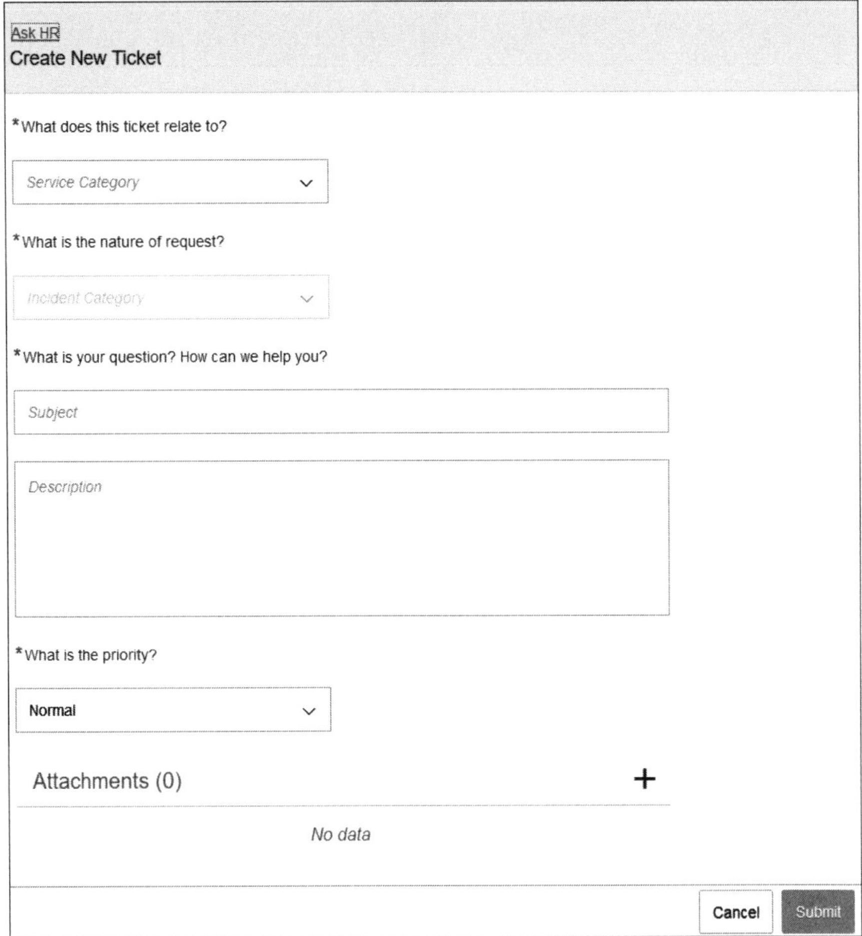

Figure 1.5 Raising a Ticket in Employee Central Service Center

Employee Central Service Center is not widely used, due to the availability of other solutions in the market that also offer functionality beyond the scope of Employee Central Service Center. Therefore, we'll not cover it further in this book.

Work-Life

Health and well-being is a fairly recent HR trend that SAP SuccessFactors is able to support with SAP SuccessFactors Work-Life. Work-Life enables employees to conduct assessments of their well-being, view content that can enable them to improve their well-being (see Figure 1.6), receive proposals on how to improve their well-being, perform activities, and track their progress. Employees and managers can also have activity-related conversations with each other. Managers can create quick polls to get feedback from employees and can view various anonymized reports to compare data from different groups within their company.

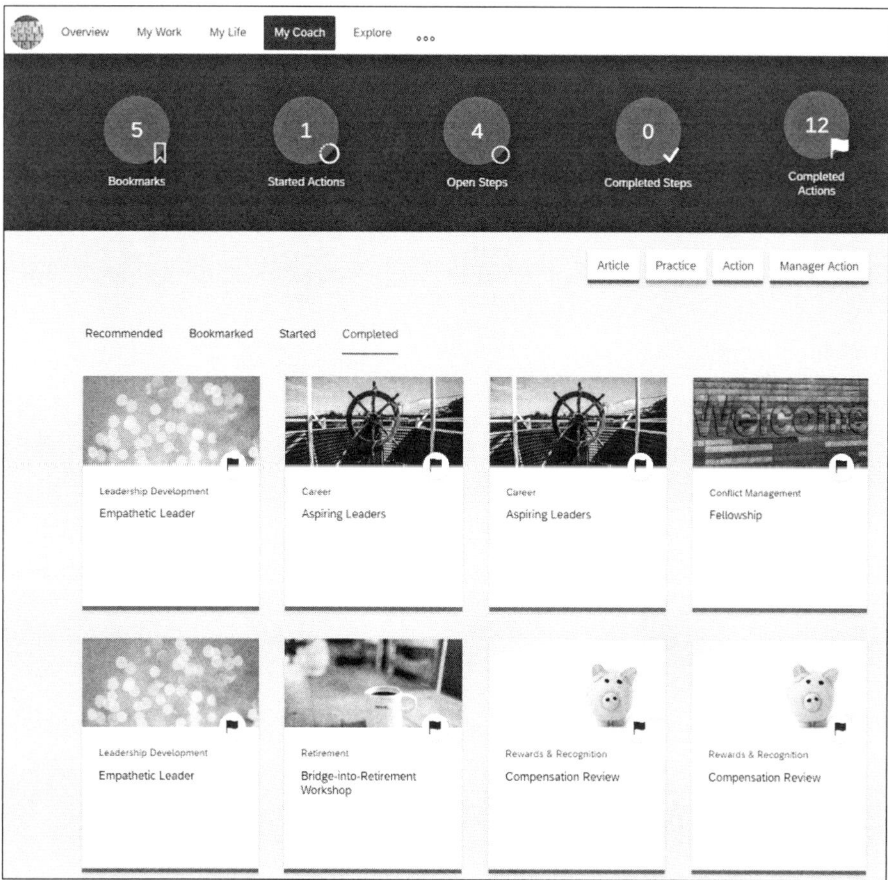

Figure 1.6 My Coach Screen of Work-Life

Work-Life is a brand new solution with many features still in development and, therefore, we'll not cover it further in this book.

1.2.3 Talent Management

We'll now take a look at the SAP SuccessFactors Talent Management solutions. The talent solutions provided by SAP SuccessFactors cover the entire lifecycle of talent processes, meaning you can manage integrated end-to-end talent management programs in the suite.

Performance & Goals

SAP SuccessFactors Performance & Goals is the performance management and goal-setting solution. One of the strongest modules of the SAP SuccessFactors HCM Suite, it's feature-rich, supports organizations to deliver more meaningful employee reviews, and aligns employee goals with business goals by using management by objectives (MBO) principles. The solution also delivers continuous performance management capabilities for ongoing feedback and development.

To help users assign appropriate goals to employees and cascade those goals back to the managers and departments that assigned them, the application comes with a SMART wizard and library of more than 500 goals. While completing performance review forms, it's easy for managers to add ratings and comments using the writing assistant, coaching advisor, and legal scan to ensure meaningful, legally robust, and compliant remarks.

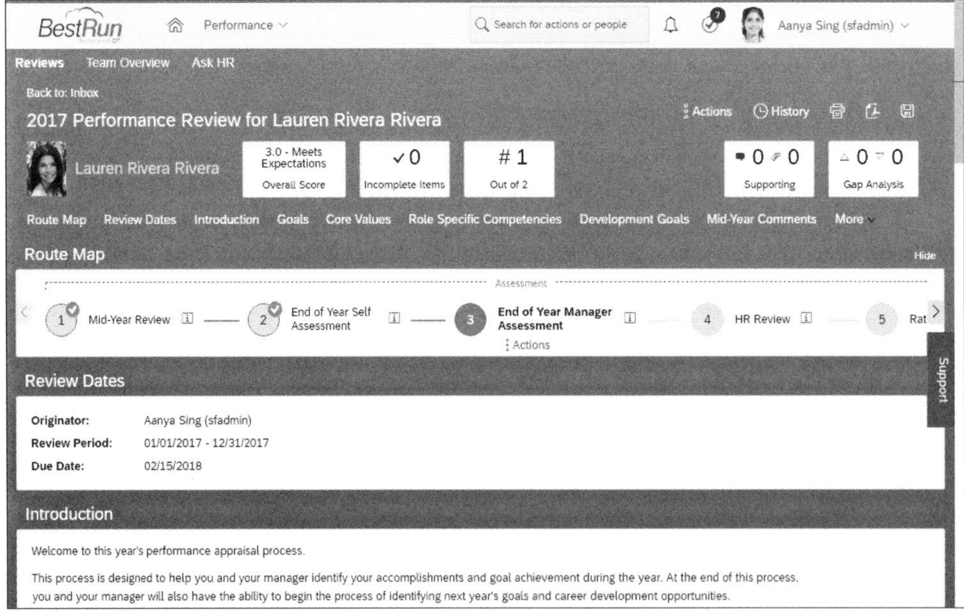

Figure 1.7 A Performance Evaluation in Performance & Goals

Other functions available to managers during the assessment process include team overview, team evaluation (as shown in Figure 1.7), calibration, 360 Multi-Rater assessments, competency gap assessments, and dashboards.

More information on Performance & Goals can be found in Chapter 6.

Compensation

SAP SuccessFactors Compensation, shown in Figure 1.8, covers the compensation management processes and provides a range of functionality expected in an enterprise-level compensation management solution. For managers, there is a wealth of functionality in compensation planning, including the following:

- Access-controlled compensation plans
- Budgeting
- Calibration
- Variable pay options
- Pay for performance

Compensation also features hierarchy-based approvals, departmental budget roll-ups, promotions, and total rewards statements. Dashboards and analytics measure the impact of compensation measurements and adjustments on budgets in real time.

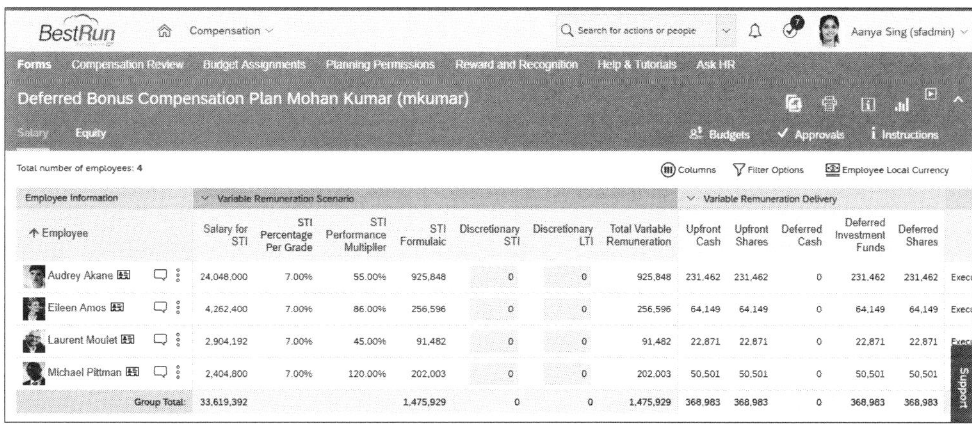

Figure 1.8 Compensation and Bonus Plan in Compensation

Variable Pay is a module offered within the Compensation solution that facilitates the administration of complex bonus programs impacted by business and employee performance measures.

More information on Compensation and Variable Pay can be found in Chapter 7.

Recruiting

SAP SuccessFactors Recruiting supports attracting, engaging, and selecting hires more efficiently. It's a solution composed of several modules that can be implemented together or separately. The solution comprises three core modules:

- Recruiting Management: A mobile and collaborative recruiting management platform
- Recruiting Marketing: A social recruiting marketing platform with a full-fledged and SEO-optimized career site builder
- Recruiting Posting: The ability to post jobs to various job boards

Together, these solutions provide holistic end-to-end recruiting capability.

By using techniques such as search engine optimization (SEO), customizable job landing pages, and social network integration, Recruiting can offer a truly attractive, modern recruiting platform to engage applicants. Career site optimization, Social-Matcher, and the use of QR codes help further support the social aspects of recruiting.

Analytics dashboards help recruiters and managers identify the number of visitors, source of visitors, and areas where the recruiting process needs to be adjusted. Integration between candidate sourcing and Employee Central enable accurate evaluation of candidates versus position requirements. Figure 1.9 shows a job requisition in Recruiting.

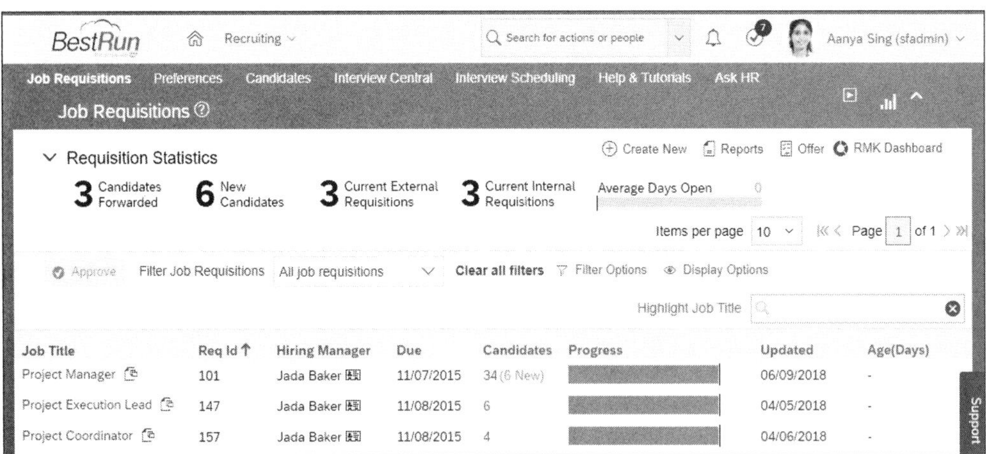

Figure 1.9 A Job Requisition in Recruiting Management

More information on Recruiting can be found in Chapter 8.

Onboarding

SAP SuccessFactors Onboarding provides onboarding functionality for new hires, crossboarding for transfers, and offboarding for leavers. It allows new hires to gain access to the online portal, where they can access and complete required documentation, get an overview of their new team, view their learning plan, see and interact in SAP Jam groups, and ask questions of their new colleagues.

In addition, it gives managers and HR professionals an easy way to ensure that new hires get access to the right information, the right documents, and the right people, so they can hit the ground running at their new company. Figure 1.10 shows the dashboard for an Onboarding administrator.

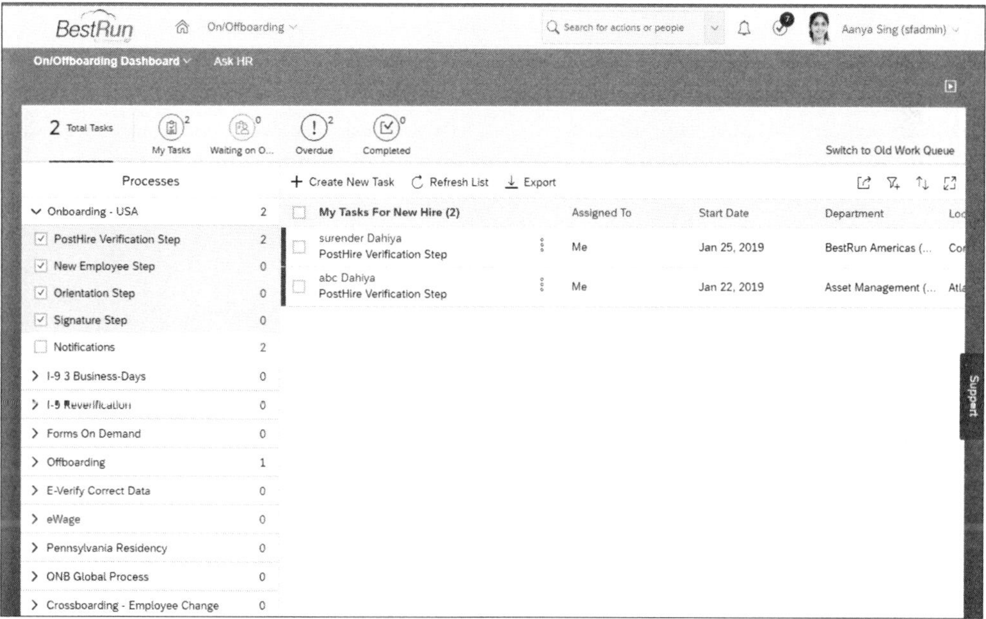

Figure 1.10 The Onboarding Dashboard

More information on Onboarding can be found in Chapter 9.

Learning

SAP SuccessFactors Learning is a learning management system (LMS) that features the heavy use of social and mobile features to enhance the learning experience.

With Learning, courses and programs can be created, delegated automatically or by supervisors, and employees can search the course catalog. The to-do list, easy links, and status pods allow employees to track their learning activities and visit their most frequently performed tasks. Managers can track due and overdue courses (as shown in Figure 1.11) and identify skills gaps for their employees.

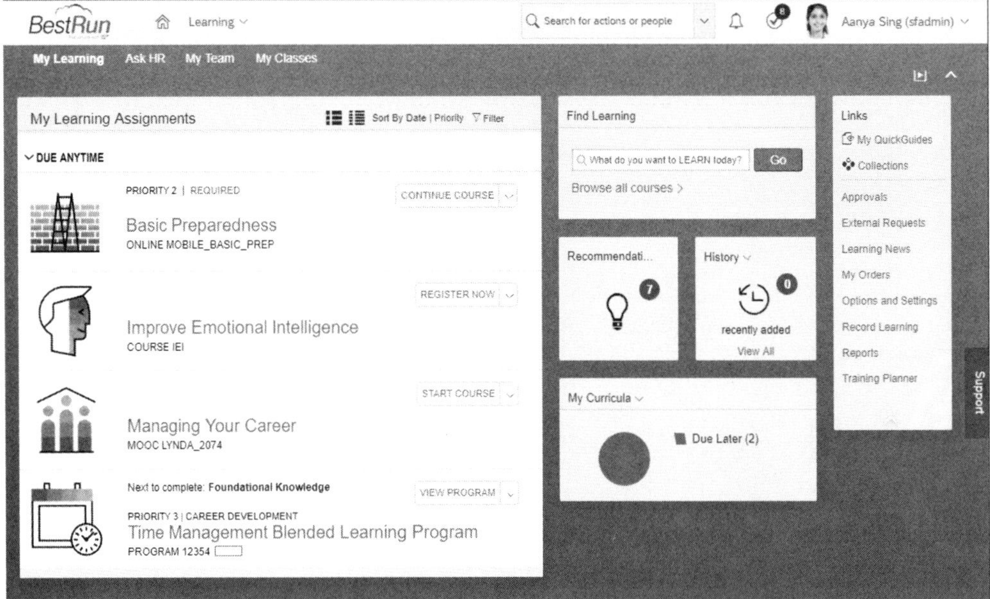

Figure 1.11 Learning Plan

Learning administrators have a wealth of options for creating and managing different types of courses and course content, in addition to managing overall learning activities across the organization. Analytics dashboards and reports also let them track the benefits of learning activities to the organization in relation to overall goals. E-learning content can be created, managed, and delivered using iContent, which is a content-as-a-service (CaaS) platform. Aviation Industry CBT Committee (AICC) and Sharable Content Object Reference Model (SCORM) content is supported in Learning.

More information on Learning can be found in Chapter 10.

Succession & Development

SAP SuccessFactors Succession & Development is a succession planning and career development solution to help objectively identify high-potential individuals, assign successors to key positions, and create development plans for successors.

The Succession Org Chart—built on top of the standard Org Chart functionality—allows an overall view of health of positions, employee risks, and successor readiness. As shown in Figure 1.12, you can highlight key positions, identify the risk and impact of loss of position holders, assess successors' readiness, and make nominations.

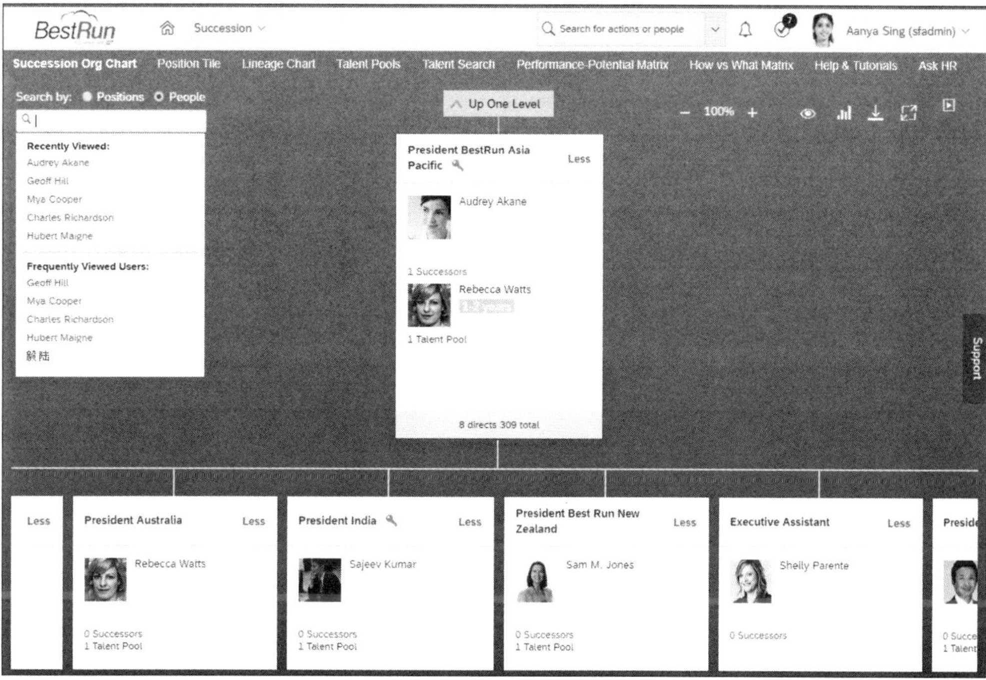

Figure 1.12 The Succession Org Chart

The competency-based **Talent Search**, **Talent Pools**, side-by-side comparison, and **Performance-Potential Matrix** (nine-box grid) enable talent specialists to find the best employees and successors across the organization. You can use calibration to ensure that performance and potential ratings are adequate for a selection of employees. The Presentations module enables you to build out talent review meetings with interactive and auto-refreshed data.

You can create development plans to track career development activities for employees and successors. Career worksheets enable employees to track favored positions and identify the competencies needed to progress toward those roles. Identified competencies can be assigned as development goals.

More information on Succession & Development can be found in Chapter 11.

1.2.4 People Analytics

SAP SuccessFactors offers customers built-in reporting capabilities, including embedded analytics, ad-hoc reporting, and dashboards. However, for deeper analytical insights and workforce planning, SAP SuccessFactors offers two solutions:

- SAP SuccessFactors Workforce Analytics
- SAP SuccessFactors Workforce Planning

We'll look at these now.

Workforce Analytics

SAP SuccessFactors Workforce Analytics is a comprehensive, vendor-agnostic analytics and reporting solution that comes with more than a thousand predefined analytics and key performance indicators (KPIs). Because it can connect to various systems simultaneously, Workforce Analytics provides a complete and unified view of how various talent-based activities, such as recruiting and learning, impact metrics such as retention, engagement, and performance. Analytics such as headcounts, retention, mobility, diversity, and profit per employee can be measured and correlated with business KPIs focused on revenue, profitability, and costs. Figures can also be examined further and deeper with drilldown and slicing capabilities.

The solution also features built-in industry benchmarks so that users can compare various analytics and metrics from their own businesses with like-for-like organizations of similar size, industry, and geographical locations. By using the Questions functionality, organizations can spot trends and then use the interpretation guides to understand data, identify issues, and find resolutions. Ad hoc reports can be built based on on-the-spot requirements, and automated, personalized reports can be set up for a set frequency with predefined format and content for each target user, such as managers or executives. Figure 1.13 shows various charts within Workforce Analytics.

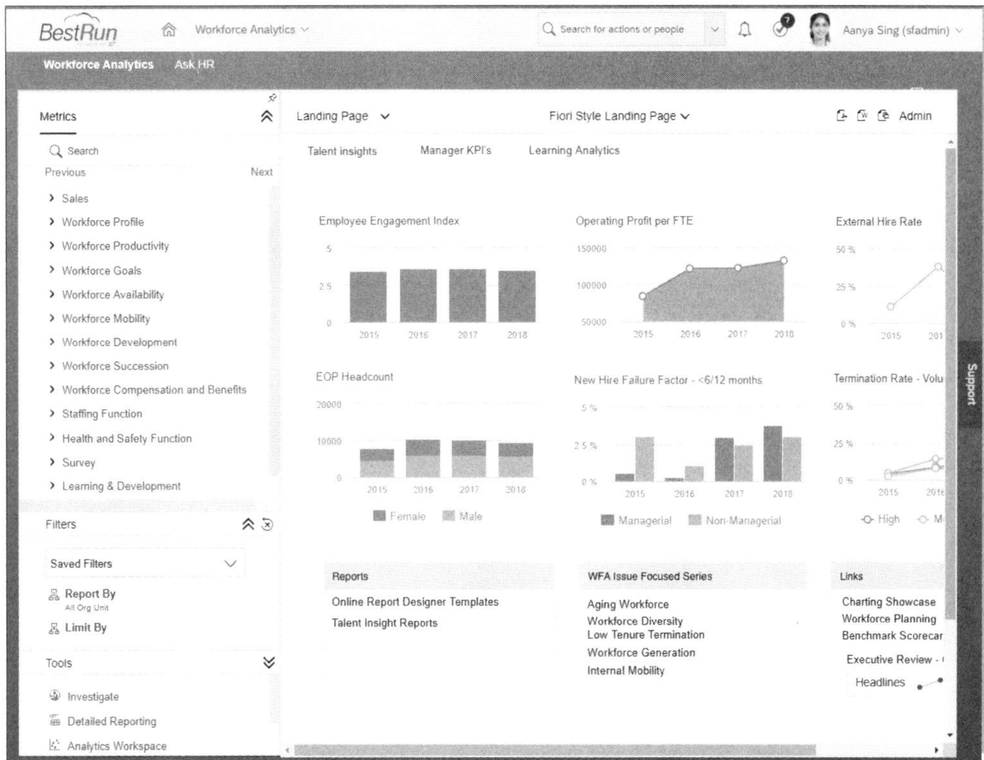

Figure 1.13 Home Page of Workforce Analytics

More information on Workforce Analytics can be found in Chapter 12.

Workforce Planning

SAP SuccessFactors Workforce Planning enables organizations to match workforce supply to workforce demand in the long-term future. It helps organizations predict long-term workforce needs and forecast the costs and skills associated with meeting those needs.

Figure 1.14 displays the **Headcount Planning** component of Workforce Planning, which enables you to strategically plan your organizational head count.

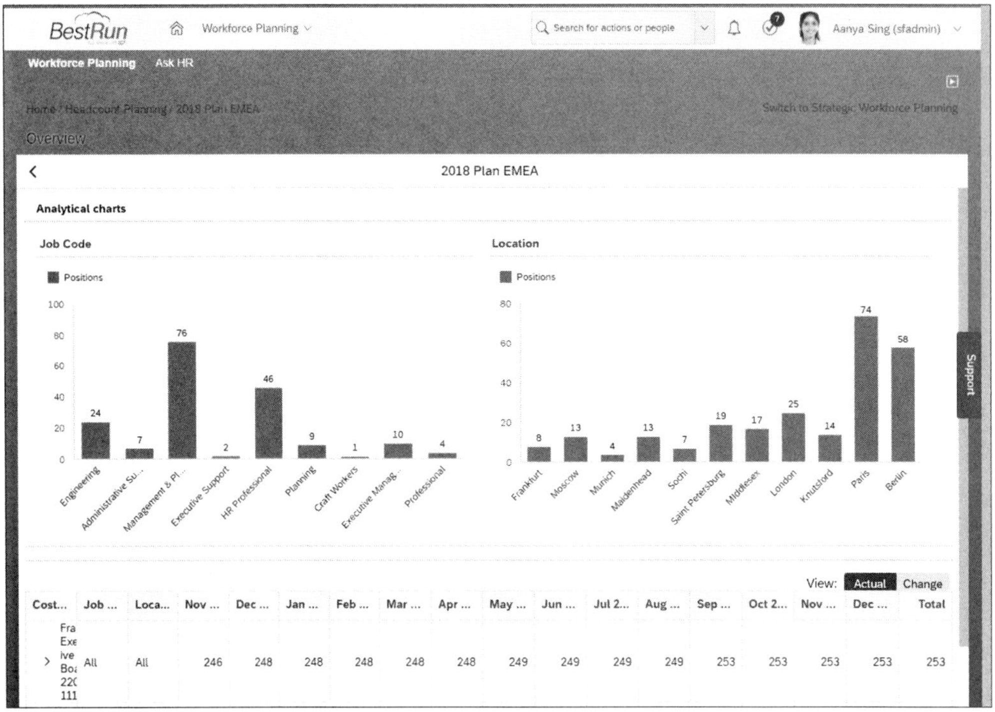

Figure 1.14 The Headcount Planning Part of Workforce Planning

Strategic workforce plans can be created that forecast demand, supply, and gaps in workforce requirements. You can generate "what-if" scenarios using various data and models made to simulate the cost impact of different scenarios. Predictive capabilities allow Workforce Planning to forecast how the future supply will look if present trends continue, and different variables can be set to produce forecasts and gap analyses of employees and competencies.

More information on Workforce Planning can be found in Chapter 13.

1.2.5 SAP SuccessFactors Mobile

SAP SuccessFactors Mobile is the mobile solution to view notifications, arrange and review meetings, view and manage open to-do activities, view direct reports, update personal information, display the Org Chart, and much more while on the go. The mobile app is available on various Android and Apple iOS devices. Figure 1.15 shows the Org Chart in the mobile app on Android.

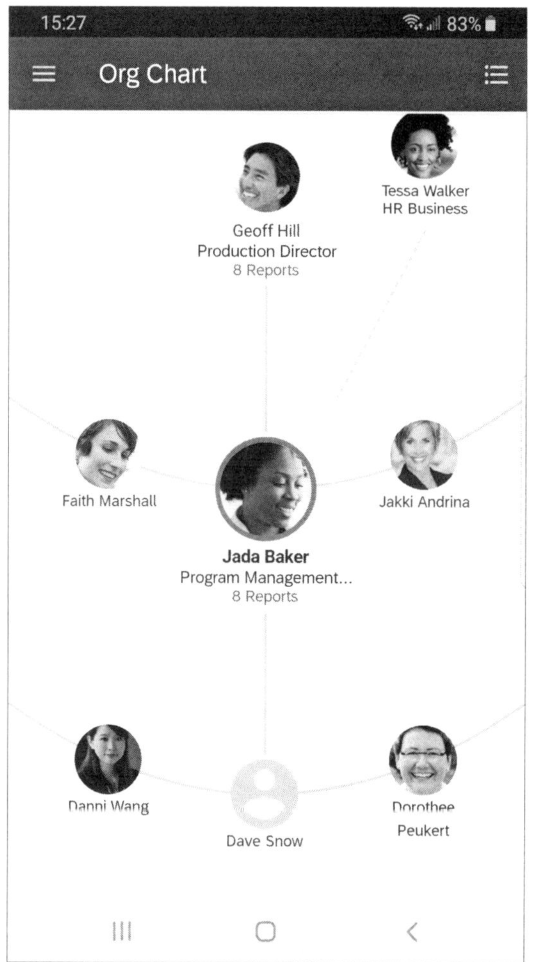

Figure 1.15 The Org Chart in the SAP SuccessFactors Mobile App

More information on SAP SuccessFactors Mobile can be found in Chapter 15.

1.2.6 SAP Solution Extensions

In addition to the applications provided within the SAP SuccessFactors HCM Suite, SAP resells several applications as SAP Solution Extensions (commonly referred to as SolEx applications). These are full-blown applications by major software vendors that SAP resells on their price list to provide complimentary functionality to the SAP

SuccessFactors HCM Suite. Often SAP provides packaged integrations to integrate SAP Solution Extensions with SAP SuccessFactors. The most common solutions include:

- SAP U.S. Benefits Administration application by Benefitfocus
- SAP Time Management by Kronos
- SAP Time and Attendance Management application by WorkForce Software
- SAP SuccessFactors Extended Enterprise Content Management by OpenText
- SAP Signature Management by DocuSign
- SAP Data Encryption by CipherCloud

SAP Solution Extensions are supported by SAP the same way that SAP SuccessFactors and other SAP solutions are supported.

We do not cover SAP Solution Extensions in this book due to the extensive nature of these applications.

1.3 Deployment Models

SAP offers customers four deployment models for some or all of the SAP SuccessFactors HCM Suite: talent hybrid, cloud hybrid, full cloud HCM, and side-by-side. Some of these models use packaged integrations from SAP to enable connectivity; we'll discuss these integrations in Chapter 16. For now, let's take a quick look at these models:

- **Talent hybrid**
  When a customer uses SAP ERP HCM on-premise or SAP S/4HANA on-premise for core HR processes (personnel administration, organizational management, payroll, etc.) and SAP SuccessFactors HCM Suite for talent management, they are using the talent hybrid model. Workforce Planning and Workforce Analytics are also considered part of the talent hybrid model.
- **Core hybrid**
  When a customer uses Employee Central (with or without other SAP SuccessFactors HCM Suite applications) and uses payroll or time management in SAP ERP or SAP S/4HANA, then they are using the core hybrid model.
- **Full cloud HCM**
  The full cloud HCM model refers to using the entire SAP SuccessFactors HCM Suite and can include Employee Central Payroll. Customers new to SAP often use the full

cloud HCM model if they have no other SAP on-premise footprint. When SAP SuccessFactors is used with SAP S/4HANA Cloud, this is sometimes referred to as the all cloud model.

- **Side-by-side**
  The side-by-side model allows customers to run SAP ERP HCM and Employee Central side by side as dual systems of record. Each system is the master system for a defined group of employees (referred to as "mastered" employees), and data is synchronized between SAP ERP HCM and Employee Central. Standard integration is provided by SAP, and UI mashups mean that WebDynpro applications from SAP ERP HCM can be run within Employee Central for those employees mastered in SAP ERP HCM.

1.4 Core Cloud System Concepts

Being a different delivery model, SAP SuccessFactors leverages some concepts not so familiar with on-premise customers. We'll look at a few of these in this section.

1.4.1 Globalization and Localization

While *globalization* and *localizations* are not necessarily new topics, they are a big focus for SAP SuccessFactors—especially with Employee Central and Employee Central Payroll. In an SAP SuccessFactors context, these are defined as:

- Globalizations: Refers to the ability to use a particular solution in multiple countries (e.g., currencies, time zones, languages, address formats, etc.).
- Localizations: Dynamic services and content offered by the software provider that proactively enable the maintenance of local legal requirements (e.g., legal reporting, legal changes, mandatory data capture fields, dropdown values, etc.).

SAP provides these for more than 95 countries in Employee Central and more than 40 countries in Employee Central Payroll.

The **Upgrade Center** in the **Admin Center**, shown in Figure 1.16, provides a one-stop shop to review and apply legal changes and other localization content released. Typically, globalization content is pushed into SAP SuccessFactors when it's released and then enabled/used as needed.

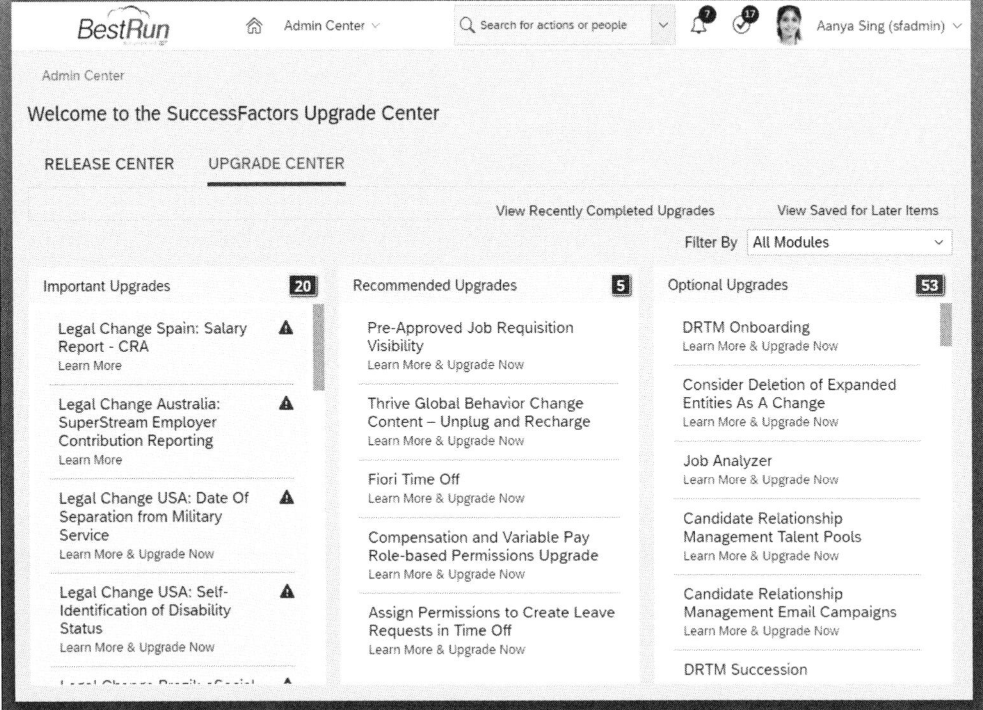

Figure 1.16 The Upgrade Center

1.4.2 Quarterly Releases

SAP SuccessFactors has four releases per year, called *quarterly releases*. They are typically released into preview instances in February, May, August, and November, and production instances in March, June, September, and December each year. Each release is referred to by its quarter and year—for example, the release in the first quarter of 2020 is called the Q1 2020 release. Sometimes releases are referred to by their old internal name, which is formatted with the letter *b*, the two-digit year, and the two-digit month; using the previous example, the release would be the b2001 release.

SAP SuccessFactors' typical release cycle is shown in Table 1.1.

Activity	Days Before/After Release
Release summary is released	60 days before
Release information webinars are delivered	35 days before

Table 1.1 SAP SuccessFactors Release Cycle

Activity	Days Before/After Release
Preview release	28 days before
Production release	0 days
Training content	28 days afterward

Table 1.1 SAP SuccessFactors Release Cycle (Cont.)

SAP SuccessFactors have two types of release:

- Q1 and Q4 releases, which focus on system stability and security
- Q2 and Q3 releases, which focus on major feature upgrades and new functionality

Patch updates to fix defects and bugs are provided on a biweekly basis.

Further Resources

Further details on quarterly releases and patch updates can be found on the SAP SuccessFactors Community website.

1.4.3 Licensing

Like most SaaS applications, SAP SuccessFactors is licensed on a subscription basis. Each SAP SuccessFactors HCM Suite solution is licensed for a single fee on a per-user, per-year basis, with no additional maintenance costs. In contrast, SAP ERP HCM is licensed for a one-off fee on a per-user basis in perpetuity, plus maintenance at a rate of around 20 percent. Additional applications, such as the Employee Interaction Center or SAP Talent Visualization by Nakisa, are charged additionally on the same basis plus maintenance.

The SaaS licensing module reduces the large capital expenditure for licenses, meaning that customers are charged only for what they use. This is often considered an operational expense (OpEx). In the on-premise model, a customer buys a fixed number of licenses at a fixed cost, and if fewer users employ the system, the price does not change. This is usually a capital expenditure (CapEx). In the subscription model, a customer can cancel the contract at the end of the term, which tends to be a year, without incurring any additional costs. In an on-premise scenario, the customer will likely lose that license investment.

1.5 Summary

SAP SuccessFactors provides a full HCM suite in the cloud to meet the needs of HR departments and HR professionals of customers of all sizes and types, across any industry and any geography. Its range of processes, features, and functionality—along with its integration and extensibility capabilities—enables customers to transform their HR processes and digitize the employee experience.

In the next chapter we'll take a look at implementing SAP SuccessFactors and what you can do to prepare and manage your implementation project.

Chapter 2
Implementation

SAP SuccessFactors can be designed and configured to support customers' processes, and tested and deployed in weeks rather than months. Orienting yourself to the difference between configuration and development is the key to understanding the implementation of SAP SuccessFactors.

The SAP SuccessFactors HCM Suite is a highly configurable, cloud-based system that can be implemented successfully in a compressed timeline and in a remote manner. SAP SuccessFactors has worked for years to develop and hone its project methodology to support customers in implementing best-in-class human resources (HR) solutions for millions of users in the cloud. By choosing to implement the SAP SuccessFactors HCM Suite, you are embarking on a new adventure that will present you with a different way of approaching a systems implementation than you may be accustomed to.

As a cloud technology, SAP SuccessFactors can be implemented from wherever an Internet connection and web browser are available. By leveraging built-in best practices and focusing on system configuration and business process changes, rather than developing functionality to close system requirement gaps, you can implement SAP SuccessFactors in a much shorter timeframe than an on-premise solution.

This chapter will discuss important topics for you to consider when embarking upon a SAP SuccessFactors implementation, provide an overview of a typical project structure, take a look at the methodology used to implement SAP SuccessFactors, review some of the resources SAP SuccessFactors provides, and offer insight into how SAP SuccessFactors projects are delivered.

2.1 Implementation Considerations

There are many things to consider when planning to undertake any system implementation, and these considerations are no different if you plan to implement a cloud solution or an on-premise solution. Use this opportunity to review the applicable business processes, taking care to revisit why you do things the way you do and evaluate how they can be improved. Understand whether the processes exist because they are best practices, because they supported the legacy system, or because that is simply the way business has always been done. This is your chance to adequately prepare the organization for the change that is coming. When you implement SAP SuccessFactors, this change may have the biggest impact on the business process owners in HR, rather than on the employee end users.

We'll walk through the key steps and points to consider as you plan your implementation in this section.

2.1.1 Setting the Strategic Objectives of the Project

The success of any project, especially a system implementation, depends upon aligning the project with the strategic objectives of the company. By developing a strong business case for making the move from on-premise to the cloud, you set your success criteria from the beginning.

If you're engaged with an implementation partner in these early stages of the project, they can assist you with business case development and should be able to provide resources to perform live demonstrations of system functionality for your key stakeholders. Demonstrations often help facilitate buy-in and foster enthusiasm for the change you are about to make. Whether in the business case or in the first weeks of the project, take time to identify the business objectives of the project. This is critical for ensuring that all project team members, key stakeholders, and partners are on the same page from the beginning. Once business objectives are identified, agree to the success criteria that will be used to evaluate the overall success of the project. These should be closely aligned to the business objectives. The most successful system implementations are those for which project objectives and success criteria are set at the start and used for measurement throughout the project.

2.1.2 Choosing an Implementation Approach

When planning an implementation, there are a couple of approaches to consider. While these mostly apply to SAP SuccessFactors Employee Central, when implementing multiple talent modules on a multinational or global basis, a number of elements of the approaches can apply. There are several factors that impact which approach you should take.

When implementing Employee Central and/or multiple modules in the SAP SuccessFactors HCM Suite, it's important to consider whether you will take a *big bang* approach or a *phased* approach to the rollout.

A big bang approach is when all countries and/or modules go live at the same time. There are different factors that determine whether this works for you, and we'll look at those shortly. An example of how a timeline would look for a big bang approach for Employee Central across multiple countries can be seen in Figure 2.1. Likewise, in Figure 2.2, we can see how this is similar for multiple different modules. These, of course, can be combined together.

Months →	2	4	6	8	10
Country A/Region A					
Country B/Region B					
Country C/Region C					

Figure 2.1 Big Bang Approach for Employee Central

Months →	2	4	6	8	10
Recruiting and Onboarding					
Performance & Goals and Compensation					
Learning					

Figure 2.2 Big Bang Approach for Multiple Modules

A phased approach is when different countries/regions and/or modules go live in different phases. There are times when this is much more manageable and feasible than a big bang approach. Again, we'll look at these shortly. In Figure 2.3, we can see what a phased approach for Employee Central looks like, and in Figure 2.4 we can see how this could look for multiple modules.

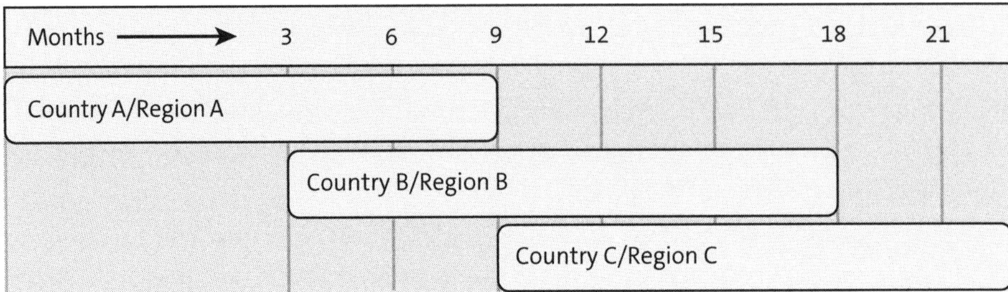

Figure 2.3 Phased Approach for Employee Central

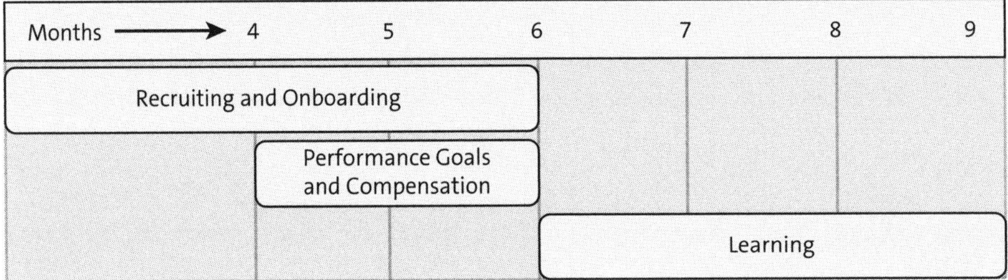

Figure 2.4 Phased Approach for Multiple Modules

There are technical and operational reasons to consider when choosing the type of rollout. We'll look at the advantages and disadvantages of each now.

There are different advantages for taking one approach versus the other, as shown in Table 2.1.

Big Bang	Phased
▪ Get everything live together ▪ All data is in the new system together and one can report on all HR data ▪ No temporary integrations ▪ Legacy system(s) can be retired sooner ▪ Design decisions aligned across other modules ▪ Can prevent project fatigue	▪ Fast time to value ▪ More manageable change management ▪ Smaller workload ▪ Incrementally get to learn the new system and the changes it creates ▪ Lower risk than big bang approach, with more distributed risk ▪ Issues from a previous phase can be rectified in a subsequent phase

Table 2.1 Advantages for the Big Bang and Phased Approaches

Naturally, with advantages there come disadvantages, as shown in Table 2.2.

Big Bang	Phased
■ A large workload and project team to be managed ■ Challenges with multiple time zones, countries, cultures, etc. ■ Greater governance and standards needed ■ Higher risk than phased approach	■ Temporary integrations may be needed to some legacy systems ■ Double-entry in multiple systems is possible ■ Maintenance of legacy systems ■ Potential rework of previously implemented modules ■ Additional regression testing

Table 2.2 Disadvantages for the Big Bang and Phased Approaches

There is also the cost factor to consider. A phased approach will see your implementation investment spread over a longer period, but the overall cost will also increase as you lose synergies of a big bang implementation and potentially have temporary integrations and legacy system operational costs.

In general, a big bang approach is optimal, but in many cases it just isn't feasible and shouldn't be tried if the risk of failure is high.

For a phased approach for Employee Central, there is also the potential need to assess the deployment model. Based on your approach, employees can be mastered in Employee Central or mastered in a legacy system until a later phase of a rollout. Two deployment models support this:

- Side-by-side deployment model
- Multiple feed deployment model

For the side-by-side deployment model, this works the same way as we discussed in Chapter 1, Section 1.3. Ultimately, this requires having a master in your legacy human resource information system (HRIS) and a master in your Employee Central system that has to be integrated to keep updates in both systems. This can be more complex, because it requires not just employee data, but all of the foundational object data needed to support Employee Central processes.

The second option is used when you are also implement one or more talent modules and integrate a legacy HRIS with Employee Central. In this scenario, you would have one population mastered in Employee Central and other populations mastered in other systems. However, the user data file (UDF) would need to be populated with a mini-master of data from these legacy systems, which would be done through a temporary integration. These employees would be visible in the Org Chart and have a

People Profile, but they would not have the complete dataset that those mastered in Employee Central would have.

The architecture of the first phase of a multiple feed deployment model is demonstrated in Figure 2.5.

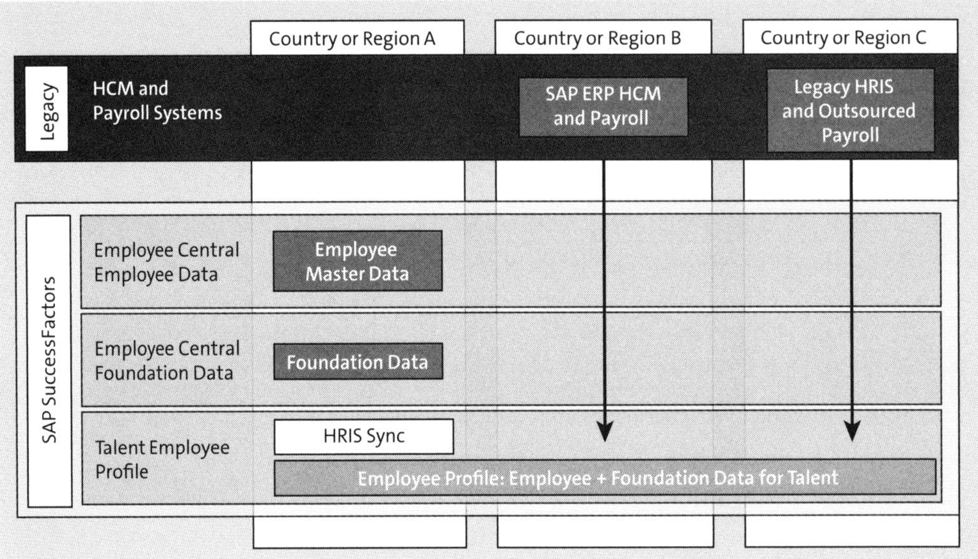

Figure 2.5 The First Phase of a Multiple Feed Deployment Model

In Figure 2.6, we can see how this might look after the second phase of a phased approach rollout. In this, we can see that the first two countries/regions are both now mastered in Employee Central, while the third country/region is still mastered in a legacy HRIS.

The challenges with this are that organizational hierarchy links can break if a manager changes in Employee Central but the change is not made in the legacy system. The challenge with workflows that need to span different business units, divisions, or departures is that they can get stuck if an approver does not have an Employee Central dataset. You also need to pay attention to user IDs and other key field data to avoid running into issues with overwriting other employees or needing to manage mapping tables. Additionally, transfers between parts of the business that operate in different systems (e.g., from Employee Central to a legacy HRIS) can be difficult to manage and involve manual interventions. Full reporting will not be possible until the end of the phased approach rollout.

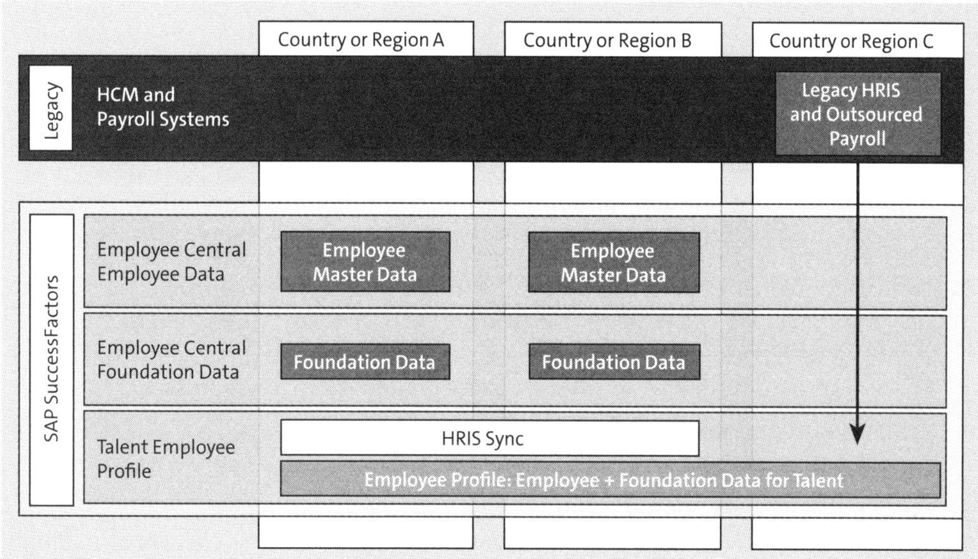

Figure 2.6 The Second Phase of a Multiple Feed Deployment Model

Now let's move onto looking at planning an implementation.

2.1.3 Planning for the Implementation

Are you looking to implement the full SAP SuccessFactors HCM Suite? Not sure where to start? Although there is no set order to implement the modules within SAP SuccessFactors, you should keep some considerations in mind when planning how to approach the implementation. Several modules are very complementary and are usually implemented together as a kind of bundle. Others are more suited to being implemented on their own. We'll walk through some examples of how you might bundle the implementation phases of your full-suite project from a process viewpoint, after we've touched on a few points to consider when implementing SAP SuccessFactors. Keep in mind that implementing the SAP SuccessFactors Platform module is necessary for any modules that you implement and is always included in the first project phase. The SAP SuccessFactors platform includes a minimum level of configuration for business rule settings within the instance, including the Employee Profile, single sign-on (SSO), and role-based permissions (RBPs).

Timeline

The length needed to implement a module will depend on the modules being implemented, the number of countries, your employee size and geographical distribution, and your overall complexity. Whether you can handle multiple modules will depend on whether your project team can handle the additional workload. This is usually true for smaller HR teams and change management, both of whom can get stretched for time with too much going on. Project delays can hit these types of projects hard if there are not enough resources assigned to the project.

Project Team

The team you assemble for your implementation is key to success. You will need enough resources and adequate availability from each resource. Likewise, your partner team will also need to be skilled and experienced in the type of project you are undertaking.

If you do not have sufficient people allocated to the team, then there is a possibility of delays and increased cost. This is particularly important when implementing SAP SuccessFactors Employee Central Payroll in certain countries.

Educating the project team prior to the kickoff of the implementation can be invaluable as the team make critical design decisions. SAP provides project team orientation (PTO) training and administrator training that can be taken prior to the beginning of the project.

In some cases, implementation partners offer training prior to design workshops.

Change Management

The success of your project will heavily rely on the change management and adoption strategy that you define during the implementation and the level of resourcing that you provide to execute that strategy. Despite the potential high cost, it's recommended to invest in change management that runs the duration of the project. See Section 2.2.7 for more details.

Performance Review Process

The performance review process most often includes reviewing performance for the previous review period and setting objectives for the coming performance period. In this way, the Performance Management and Goal Management modules of SAP SuccessFactors are intricately integrated and almost always implemented together. Goal plans can be pulled into performance review forms so that employees can be rated on their performance toward the goals from the previous year. Also, it's possible to link the coming year's goal plan in the performance review form so that goal setting can be accomplished at the same time the performance review is completed. Additional integration with the Development module includes adding a development plan section to the performance review template so that development goals can be created when they are most often identified: during the performance review.

Complementary to Performance Management and Goal Management, the 360 Multi-Rater module is often implemented. Results from the 360 Multi-Rater review can be accessed from within the performance review, giving any manager completing an employee review easy access to third-party reviewers.

Performance and Salary Planning Process

Additional complementary modules are Performance Management and Goal Management with Compensation and Variable Pay. Because the merit and bonus planning cycle follows the performance or focal review process, the Compensation and Variable Pay modules are often implemented at the same time as Performance Management and Goal Management. Performance forms can be integrated into the compensation form so that managers can view an employee's performance review rating on the salary planning sheet, as well as access the details by clicking the hyperlink and opening the performance review in a new window.

Succession Planning Process

The scorecard is accessed from the People Profile of SAP SuccessFactors, and many companies opt to implement these two modules together. If the People Profile was implemented at an earlier project phase, the Succession module implementation is a good time to review the configuration of the People Profile and make any changes or updates. Succession is also a good candidate for implementation in conjunction with Performance Management and Goal Management.

Another module often implemented in conjunction with Succession is the Development module. Many companies use the succession process to identify development areas or goals for successors nominated to certain positions, so it makes sense for them to implement Development with Succession to support their process.

Development and Learning Process

The Development module is very similar to the Goal Management module and includes defining a development plan whereby employees and managers can create and maintain development goals. Development goals can be linked with learning activities that are pulled from the learning catalogs assigned to employees in the learning management system (LMS). Consequently, customers often choose to implement the Development module and LMS together.

Recruiting Process

SAP SuccessFactors offers two recruiting modules: Recruiting Marketing and Recruiting Management. These two modules are now offered as SAP SuccessFactors Recruiting. While the Recruiting Marketing module is always implemented with or after the Recruiting Management module, customers often choose to implement Recruiting Management on its own.

Both the Recruiting Management and Recruiting Marketing modules contain a tremendous amount of functionality, so implementing one or both of these in an environment of high-volume sourcing or detailed processes is quite an undertaking. Because these business process owners are often different from those who own the performance and merit processes, implementation of the Recruiting module can also be undertaken in parallel with any other modules, but will have a longer project life due to the complexity of the product and all of the configuration decisions involved.

2.1.4 Business Processes

Before you embark on an implementation, we advise you to spend some time reviewing the business processes involved. Although business process review should be included during the implementation, understanding the weaknesses or limitations of your existing processes facilitates a more robust kickoff meeting and expedites the system configuration decisions post-kickoff. Because SAP SuccessFactors can be configured but not developed, it's possible that not all system requirements are met by existing system functionality and configuration possibilities. This is typical of a cloud-based solution, so be prepared to use a combination of system configuration and business process change to address outstanding system requirements. A good understanding of the as-is processes and any legal or corporate requirements becomes key in these situations.

2.1.5 Competencies and Job Roles

Revising or adopting a competency model can be one of the most time-consuming activities you can undertake when implementing any performance management solution; in fact, it's fair to say that you cannot begin this preparation soon enough. If you have not adopted a competency model for the organization, SAP SuccessFactors offers more than 80 best-practice behavioral competencies that can be used in the performance and development processes. If your company already has a behavioral competency model, SAP SuccessFactors lets you create and maintain custom competencies as well.

Another critical activity is determining how to manage job roles within the organization and how these are represented within SAP SuccessFactors. This should include a thorough review of how your jobs and positions are defined and organized today, so this activity may also require some modification in your legacy HCM system before bringing these over to SAP SuccessFactors. Although your implementation consultant can assist you through these reviews and decisions, this is something that should be undertaken during the initial planning phases of the project to ensure adequate time before you go live.

2.1.6 Employee Data

If you use or implement Employee Central, then this is the master repository for your employee data. However, when you use a different HRIS than Employee Central, SAP SuccessFactors will leverage a set of employee data that is brought over from that legacy HRIS. This enables you to run talent management processes without being forced to implement Employee Central as your HRIS.

Numerous standard fields such as name, manager, address, job title, and others are supported; up to 15 custom columns may also be defined to house additional data that is necessary to support the talent management processes completed in the talent modules in SAP SuccessFactors. This is covered in detail in Chapter 3. As with competencies and job roles, the sooner you begin reviewing the employee data requirements, location, and cleanliness of the data, the less impact there is on the overall project schedule.

2.2 Project Team Structure

Although the project team structure of an SAP SuccessFactors implementation varies depending on the number of modules undertaken at one time, you can expect to see some baselines. Implementation can be as varied as the partners in the ecosystem; however, you should ensure that your consultants have product expertise in the implemented module(s), coupled with process and best practice expertise.

The project team can comprise the following types of resources:

- Lead consultant(s)
- Project manager
- Project sponsor
- Technical resource
- Functional/business resource
- Stakeholder group representatives
- Change management resource

Let's look at each of these resources.

2.2.1 Lead Consultant

The lead consultant is your product expert. They should have the requisite certification issued by SAP SuccessFactors and product experience in the modules they are implementing so that they can configure the system and guide the customer through process discussions, offering best practices where applicable. Ideally you should be looking for consultants who are certified professionals or who have completed at least three implementations as a lead consultant.

You may have several consultants implementing on your team, but it's also normal for one consultant to implement multiple modules. For example, you could have one consulting resource implementing Goal Management, Performance Management, 360 Multi-Rater, and employee profiles.

Implementation consultant responsibilities include the following:

- Conducting the kickoff meeting
- Conducting regular (usually weekly) project meetings by module
- Addressing customer questions on functionality, best practices, and system functionality
- Guiding the customer in completing the configuration workbook
- Configuring the system to customer requirements, as defined in the configuration workbook
- Testing the configuration to ensure completeness and functionality
- Leading the customer through testing each iteration configuration

- Conducting administrator training for customer administrators
- Maintaining project plan, issues log, and risks for their respective module(s)

2.2.2 Project Manager

As with any project, the project manager's role is to manage the work plan, project issues, and risks, and keep resources aligned and on track. You may have both a consulting project manager and a client project manager working together to manage the entire project. If there is not a consulting project manager, the lead consultant may serve in a project management capacity, keeping the work plan updated and assisting the project manager in understanding the SAP Activate methodology phases and deliverables. It's not uncommon for implementations of a single talent module (e.g., Compensation or Succession) to be managed by the lead consultant.

If you are implementing the entire SAP SuccessFactors HCM Suite, you likely have a project manager dedicated by your implementation partner who will remain consistent across all modules. This resource will work closely with the client project manager throughout the life of the project and through all project waves until all modules have gone live and are in support.

2.2.3 Project Sponsor

Project sponsors champion the project within the client organization and assist with issue resolution, when appropriate. They serve as key stakeholders in the change management and communication plan and are often a delivery channel for key messages. They also ultimately sign off on the business processes and system configuration. Often, the project sponsor is the one who signs off on the configuration workbooks and other project milestone sign-off gates.

2.2.4 Technical Resource

One or more technical resources are involved with various aspects of implementation, mainly related to data migration and integration. Traditionally, the technical resources are engaged to provide an extract of employee data to feed SAP SuccessFactors and set up the automated feed. They are also involved with setting up SSO and any data migration that might be undertaken. For customers moving from on-premise solutions to SAP SuccessFactors, the technical resources are involved with setting up the various data connectors and integration packages.

2.2.5 Functional/Business Resource

The functional and business resources are possibly the most critical members of the project team because they define the end-state business processes and corresponding system configuration. They often bring the knowledge of the business and how it works, and in many occasions know where improvements need to be made.

Numerous resources are usually involved per module implemented. We recommend that you keep project-dedicated resources to a minimum while keeping a larger pool of functional/business resources involved for input, validation, and testing. Your core team of functional resources will prove critical to providing business process knowledge and context when you are working with the implementation consultant in fleshing out system capabilities to arrive at a satisfactory configuration that meets system and business process requirements.

Functional/business resources should be engaged early in the project planning so that they can begin working on the previously mentioned competency and job role work, review the applicable business processes, and assist with communication and training strategies.

2.2.6 Stakeholder Group Representatives

Stakeholder group representatives play a key role in project communication and training strategies and execution. Like project sponsors, they deliver key project messages and drive user adoption after the project is live. Key stakeholders should be involved in various times throughout the project to help validate the to-be business processes, participate in testing, and provide input to training plans. These are your change champions within the organization.

2.2.7 Change Management Resource

The key to any successful systems implementation is a solid and well-executed change management strategy. To ensure adoption of the system, consistent and frequent communication with stakeholders and employees is a must, along with appropriate, just-in-time training for all end user groups. Even though SAP SuccessFactors is an intuitive solution with "toy-like" qualities and easy-to-use features, the training plan should not be overlooked. Training gives end users the opportunity to touch the system before it's live and get to understand why you are implementing the system.

Often, you roll out SAP SuccessFactors in conjunction with significant process updates; ensuring that your employees and managers are informed and prepared for the change is just as important for an SAP SuccessFactors implementation. Involve the change management, training, and communication resources early in the project and keep them engaged through to post-go-live.

Now, let's shift our focus to how SAP SuccessFactors modules are implemented by discussing project methodology.

2.3 Project Methodology

SAP provides a single methodology for implementing all of their cloud applications—the *SAP Activate* methodology. The SAP Activate methodology is therefore SAP's implementation methodology for SAP SuccessFactors.

The SAP Activate methodology draws from the strengths of the existing project methodologies and includes best practices from industry standards (such as PMP, PRINCE2, and Agile) while leveraging best practices from SAP's experience of implementing cloud products. The focus of the methodology is using SAP Best Practices content to give you a starting point for your implementation. SAP Best Practices content provides a baseline system configuration, alongside workbooks and other project documentation. For customers who wish to start without a baseline, there is no need to leverage the SAP Best Practices content.

Further Resources

More information on SAP Best Practices can be found at *http://s-prs.co/v485800.*

At the time of writing (fall 2019), SAP is in the process of rolling out their SAP Model Company methodology. SAP Model Company is much like the name suggests—it provides model configuration and company data with which to start your project. You gain a design based on best practices coupled with test data and project documentation.

As shown in Figure 2.7, the SAP Activate methodology includes six phases: discover, prepare, explore, realize, deploy, and run.

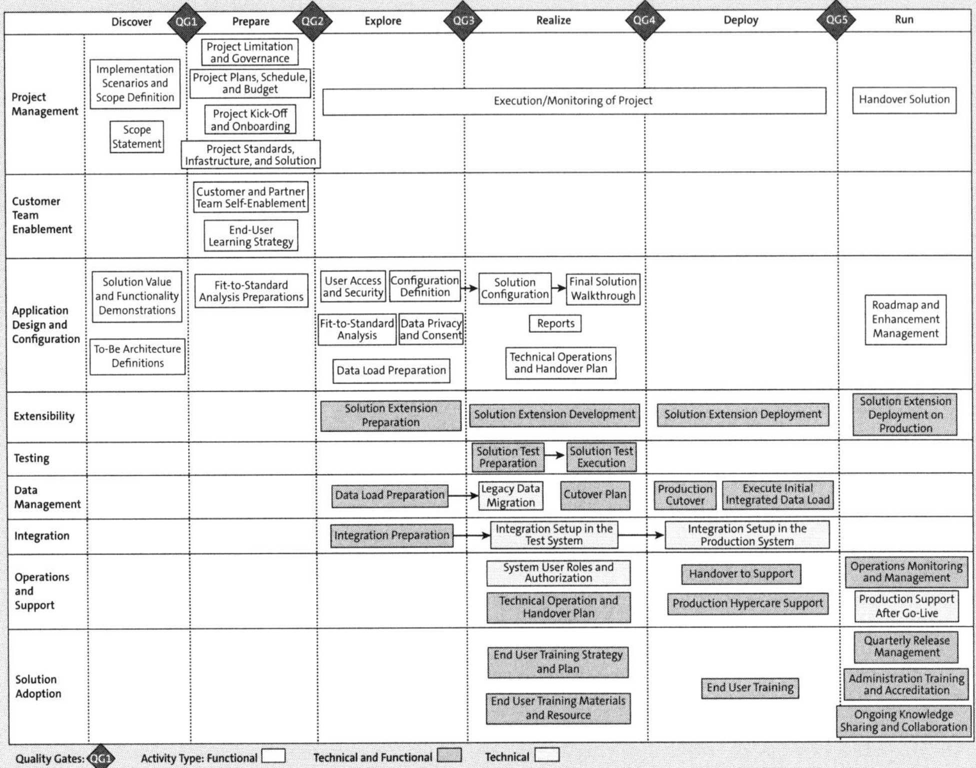

Figure 2.7 SAP Activate Project Methodology Phases

> **Further Resources**
>
> SAP SuccessFactors partners can access information on the SAP Activate methodology on SAP PartnerEdge.

We'll now take a high-level look at each phase.

2.3.1 Discover Phase

The *discover phase* focuses on defining the HR transformation initiative that is being undertaken. Here, customers define the HR strategy, key drivers and measurements for success, implementation scenario, scope, and to-be architecture, along with seeing the baseline solution. It's where you can understand what SAP SuccessFactors can do and open up the possibilities available in the solutions being implemented. In some cases, this part of the methodology occurs as part of the finalization of the sales process.

2.3.2 Prepare Phase

The *prepare phase* lays the groundwork for a successful implementation. Tasks are focused on kicking off the project and developing the project plan, as well as ensuring that the customer is prepared for the implementation process and the key differences in a cloud-based implementation. Key tasks in the prepare phase include the following:

- Project team orientation
- Kickoff meeting
- Definition of project governance and standards
- Development of project plan and tracking documentation
- Project scheduling and budgeting
- Preparation for analysis of the ability to fit to the standard-delivered processes and functionality
- Definition of roles and responsibilities for the project team
- Assignment of project team members

Project team orientation includes orienting the team to the project framework, guidelines, and schedule. It may also include some project team tool training on the particular module(s) being implemented.

The kickoff meeting focuses on the following:

- Project scope
- Methodology
- Key project business drivers
- Initial timeline/project plan
- Customer resources, such as the customer community
- Project team roles and responsibilities

2.3.3 Explore Phase

The *explore phase* is focused on the start of the execution of the project. The focus here is on activities such as:

- Analysis of the ability to fit to the standard-delivered processes and functionality
- Solution validation
- Define solution design
- Requirements gathering
- User access and security definition
- Data migration preparation
- Integration preparation
- Data privacy and protection strategy and consents
- Solution extension design and preparation

The focus of the explore phase is the consulting team working with the customer to analyze their fit to standard-delivered processes, define the processes that the system will support, design the solution, and collect the system requirements. These activities typically take the form of a series of workshops. Depending on the module, these might take a few hours to a few days to a few weeks and, in some cases, even longer. The pace at which these are conducted depends on the breadth and/or complexity of the module, the availability of the project team, the number of decisions that need to be made, and many other factors. Many of these factors are specific to each customer.

The entire project team, consultants, and business stakeholders work together to identify the processes, design, and system configuration required to meet the customer's needs.

For modules such as Performance Management and Goal Management, these workshops can likely be covered in a day. But for modules such as Employee Central, Learning, and Recruiting, it may take several days or more to talk through the processes and configuration options and to document the decisions. While many process and design decisions can be made during the workshops, the workbooks should be completed over a span of days or a few weeks. The end result is the completion of a detailed configuration workbook, which consultants then use to configure the system. Typically, the longer it takes to document the first iteration, the more complete it is, and the fewer changes are made in later iterations.

Table 2.3 lists the estimated duration of the workshop meetings by module, not including detailed process mapping. Naturally, these are a baseline and may be significantly longer for some customers that go through more complex scenarios or multiple countries.

Module	Kickoff Meeting Duration
Employee Central	4 – 15 days
Employee Central Payroll	10 – 15 days
Goal Management	2 – 3 hours
Performance Management	3 – 4 hours
360 Multi-Rater	1 – 2 hours
Employee Profile	2 – 3 hours
Succession Planning	3 – 5 hours
Recruiting Management	8 – 12 hours
Recruiting Marketing	8 – 12 hours
Onboarding	8 – 12 hours
Learning	1 – 3 days
Compensation Management	8 – 12 hours
Variable Pay	8 – 12 hours
Workforce Planning and Workforce Analytics	2 days

Table 2.3 Workshop Meetings by Module

Data migration and technical workshops (if applicable) are centered on ancillary implementation work, such as migrating legacy data and implementing packaged integrations, custom connectors, or other third-party integrations. These are conducted on an as-needed basis; the length of the workshops is determined by the services required, the number of integrations, the amount and type of data to be migrated, and the complexity of the scope of work. Data migration work should start as early as possible to enable cleansing, mappings, and definition of transformation rules to be performed.

Project plan development is also completed during this phase, outlining key tasks, deliverables, and milestones necessary for project success. As with any implementation, project planning is an ongoing task throughout the project.

2.3.4 Realize Phase

During the *realize phase*, the focus is on iterative system configuration, data migration (if applicable), and testing of the solution. The following activities make up the realize phase:

- Solution configuration
- Walkthrough of the final, configured solution
- Definition and configuration of reports
- Operations, post go-live support, and internal transition planning
- Test preparation and execution
- Data migration
- Cutover planning
- Training preparation, materials development, and execution

The processes, system design, and requirements identified during the prepare phase are built in the customer's test instance. The implementation consultants are responsible for configuring all modules, with the exception of Learning. For this module, the customer is heavily involved in configuration, guided by the implementation consultant. Configuration for these modules is heavy in administrative tasks and can be done directly via the Admin Center in the instance.

Let's take a closer look at key components of the realize phase.

Configuration Cycles

The configuration is completed in the test instance, with the exception of Employee Central, which is completed in a development instance. The following is a simplified process for most modules:

1. Consultant completes configuration per the requirements identified during the explore phase.
2. Configuration is made available to the customer for testing.
3. Customer tests the configuration to the business processes impacted and provides feedback to the consultant on necessary changes.

Depending on the modules being implemented, you could have up to three cycles of configuration updates and testing. This depends upon the complexity of the requirements and the business processes impacted. Each cycle of configuration consists of smaller requirements-gathering sessions. These are typically conducted virtually and can occur over a series of meetings. Configuration workbooks are updated and given back to the consultant to update system configuration. The customer then retests the updated configuration, and the cycle repeats itself until complete. Traditionally, there are three iterations of configuration and testing.

In the case of the Learning module, the customer provides feedback on the configuration, and the consultants work closely with the customer administrator to refine the system configuration. With Learning, the majority of the configuration is master data that is controlled directly in the instance. When the customer administrator is involved from the beginning, training and knowledge transfer occurs throughout the project, resulting in a fully capable customer administrator by go-live.

Data Migration or Other Technical Services

If the customer is migrating data from a legacy system or has included other technical services, integrations, or custom connectors in the project scope, data migration or other technical activities run parallel to the configuration cycles during the realize phase. Much of the data migration activities focus on getting the customer up to speed on how data is brought into the SAP SuccessFactors HCM Suite. Many self-service tools, videos, documents, and sample files are available to the customer team in the Customer Welcome Kit.

If the customer is migrating data into Learning, a small sample file is created so that the customer can test the upload via the Admin Center or via the Secure File Transfer Protocol (SFTP). Data cleansing and validation are critical during this testing phase. After the sample file loads cleanly, the larger data file can be prepared. It's advisable to load the full file into the customer's test instance toward the end of the realize phase and before the deploy phase.

Testing

The customer executes the testing plan developed during the prepare phase to prove that the system is configured as designed and is "fit for purpose." Because the test plan and script development are a key customer deliverable, samples are available in the Customer Welcome Kit, and the implementation consultant can provide input based on project experience, as well.

The types of testing included in the test plan are familiar as the same testing that occurs in most systems implementations. The customer can determine which testing activities to conduct, but the following are typically included:

- **Unit testing**
  Confirms that each item identified in the configuration workbook has been configured and is working as expected. Unit testing is the responsibility of the implementation consultant.
- **Application testing**
  Confirms that the system configuration meets the customer's functional requirements. It's critical to confirm that the system is ready for end-to-end testing. The customer project team is responsible for application testing.
- **Integration testing**
  Required if other systems will be integrated with SAP SuccessFactors. If integration testing occurs, it's the responsibility of the customer project team, usually focused on IT personnel and key stakeholders representing the systems integrating with SAP SuccessFactors. Because integration deals with existing customer systems, the customer bears the responsibility to develop detailed testing scripts. At the conclusion of integration testing, there is often a customer sign-off before moving forward.
- **User acceptance testing (UAT)**
  Confirms that the system is configured to meet the end-to-end business requirements and is the responsibility of the customer UAT team. The most successful user testing includes testers from outside the core project team and has representation from the key business areas impacted by the system.

Sometimes other testing is performed, such as regression testing for existing modules or negative testing to determine if the system stands up to negative or unintended actions.

Preparing the Organization

While testing is underway, the communication and training plans begin execution. Any successful systems implementation hinges on clear communication and preparation of end users. These tasks are typically owned by the customer, so it's advisable to engage any customer teams that provide change management and training services. Because SAP SuccessFactors modules touch on employee performance, compensation, and career development, it's critical that any change in process or system is deployed with the utmost care and planning. Although SAP SuccessFactors is an intuitive system that can be picked up with minimal training, it's often accompanied by radical process change. These changes, and the business reasons driving them, should be "over-communicated" to employees and management alike.

2.3.5 Deploy Phase

The *deploy phase* is all about preparing to go live, launching the system, and transitioning to support. After all testing activities are completed, identified issues are addressed and retested, and final sign-off of testing is achieved, the implementation consultant begins cutting over configuration from the test instance to the customer's production instance.

The *cutover checklist* is a critical deliverable of this phase that is used to monitor progress of all cutover activities, responsibilities, and statuses. The implementation consultant prepares the cutover checklist, and tasks are determined by the modules implemented. Cutting over can take from one day to many days, depending on the complexity of the modules, configuration, and business processes impacted. For example, a Recruiting Marketing cutover of moderate complexity with no data migration takes approximately four days, while a Performance Management and Goal Management cutover can be completed in one day. Cutover also includes enabling the production SFTP and final user connector for employee data, as well as enabling SSO, if applicable.

At the completion of cutover, including data migration as applicable, the customer begins production validation. After that is complete, the transition to the SAP SuccessFactors support organization Customer Success begins. The final deliverable of the project is the production readiness sign-off document, which is submitted to Customer Success when submitting the case to have customer accounts created. This process not only provides the customer access to the SAP SuccessFactors support portal, but also notifies SAP SuccessFactors that the customer has successfully transitioned into the production instance and is now live.

2.3.6 Run Phase

The *run phase* is used to further optimize the operation and support of the solution. It's also an opportunity to plan the roadmap for further enhancements to the solution and put in place a process to manage quarterly releases.

Further Resources

More information on the SAP Activate methodology can be found in the SAP Roadmap Viewer at *http://s-prs.co/v485801* and in the Empowerment Center on the SAP SuccessFactors Community website. Partners can find a range of documents and resources on SAP PartnerEdge.

2.4 Project Delivery

Recall that a big difference between implementations of SAP SuccessFactors HCM Suite and legacy on-premise systems is that the emphasis is on configuration rather than development. As an SaaS solution, SAP SuccessFactors offers a series of configuration options that can be deployed as needed to support a customer's business processes. If the system cannot be configured to a specific requirement, the applicable business process needs to be changed accordingly or extension applications should be built. Customers can then submit enhancement requests through the customer community to request functionality that they would like to see added to the roadmap and worked into the solution.

Because the project focuses on configuration rather than development, the customer project team can get its hands on the system almost immediately. To support the kickoff meeting, the implementation consultant often performs some best-practice, baseline configuration in the customer's test instance, so that the customer project team can log in and "play" in a sandbox environment while discussing and making configuration decisions. This is an excellent way to confirm iteration 1 configuration decisions before submitting them to the implementation consultant. In this way, the system configuration is being continually tested throughout the entire realize phase.

A new concept to most customers is *virtual project delivery*. As a cloud-based solution, SAP SuccessFactors can be configured anywhere an Internet connection and web browser are available. After an onsite kickoff meeting, most of the implementation has traditionally been done in a virtual manner, with implementation consultants working from their home offices and supporting the customer project team over regular web conferences.

The main objective of the SAP Activate implementation methodology is to empower customers to own their solutions, so activities are designed to give them the tools to do just that. Implementation consultants work with the project team on a mutually agreed upon, regular basis (not less than weekly) to review system configuration questions and decisions. The features in the Admin Center of SAP SuccessFactors are covered in detail as they apply to the implemented modules.

SAP SuccessFactors provides a variety of resources to be used during implementation, such as the SAP SuccessFactors Process Library, Implementation Design Principles (IDPs), and those found in the Empowerment Center on the SAP SuccessFactors Community website. These are covered in Appendix A.

While project delivery varies depending on the implementation partner and complexity of the customer's business processes and scope, the days of teams of consultants camping out in client offices for months on end are no longer necessary. SuccessFactors had more than 10 years of successful implementations using this model with some of the largest companies in the world prior to being acquired by SAP.

2.5 Summary

Implementing your SAP SuccessFactors HCM Suite solutions should be an opportunity to review existing business processes and add efficiency while providing enhanced system functionality.

By selecting SAP SuccessFactors, you have taken the first step toward a best-practice core HCM or talent management landscape in your organization. The SAP Activate methodology provides the structure, milestones, and deliverables necessary to ensure a successful project. Staffing your project team appropriately and providing them with the tools to deliver a fully configured system is critical to ensuring that your resulting system meets the needs of the organization and stakeholders. You can ensure a successful go-live by teaming up with an experienced implementation partner who has deep business process knowledge and who can provide best practices, along with deep knowledge of the SAP SuccessFactors modules you are implementing. Lastly, preparing your organization for the new system and processes that will drive their performance and career planning is crucial to ensuring user adoption. The importance of this element cannot be overstated.

In the next chapter, we'll look at the SAP SuccessFactors platform.

Chapter 3
Platform

The basis of the SAP SuccessFactors HCM Suite is the platform. It provides the basic data and functionality framework required by each of the applications in the suite. The underlying platform now serves integration and extensibility that make the suite flexible for many customer needs.

As the basis of the suite, the platform provides the fundamental cross-suite functionality required by all applications in the SAP SuccessFactors HCM Suite. The platform's functionality is highly configurable and, with the Metadata Framework (MDF)/ Extension Center and extensions offered on SAP Cloud Platform, it is now possible to create custom objects, screens, business rules, logic, and even applications.

In this chapter, we'll walk through an overview of the key pieces of provided platform functionality before taking a look at extensibility options with the MDF, the Extension Center, and SAP Cloud Platform. To begin, we'll take a look at the technical architecture and various technical aspects of SAP SuccessFactors and how it differs from SAP ERP Human Capital Management (SAP ERP HCM). We'll also look at some of the security aspects of SAP SuccessFactors. Although application programming interfaces (APIs) are part of the platform, these are covered during our discussion of integration in Chapter 16.

Note

While we introduce the Admin Center briefly in Section 3.4 and the Upgrade Center in Section 3.6, we will cover them in detail—along with various administration activities—in Chapter 17.

3.1 Platform Basics

The platform provides a host of the foundational functionality required by the system:

- System configuration and administration
- User management
- Authentication and password policy
- Permissions framework
- User interface
- Home page
- Email notifications
- Theme and logo
- Picklists
- Data imports
- Upgrade Center
- Release Center
- APIs

In addition, it also provides some applications that are either cross-suite or not specific to any SAP SuccessFactors application. These include the following:

- Employee Profile
- Org Chart
- Presentations
- Skills and Competencies
- Job Profile Builder
- Diversity and Inclusion
- Upgrade Center
- MDF/Extension Center
- Integration Center

All features and applications that form part of the platform are inclusive in the SAP SuccessFactors subscription; no additional licensing is necessary to use features such as Org Chart or Presentations.

The first time that any SAP SuccessFactors application is implemented, the platform must be implemented. This requires configuring the Employee Profile, importing user data to create user accounts, setting up role-based permissions (RBPs), and defining password policies. There are many optional configurations that can be made, such as email notifications and the tiles used on the home page.

3.2 Technical Architecture

SAP SuccessFactors HCM Suite follows a fairly common multitenant architecture. This enables SAP SuccessFactors to keep technical maintenance and feature release simple and regular for all customers. The architecture allows for very fast, stable, and customizable solutions that perform well and allows SAP SuccessFactors to maintain highly scalable and effective procedures not only to store and run data, but also to maintain data security and protection while keeping applications fast and stable.

The approach for examining the technical architecture of SAP SuccessFactors varies greatly from other HCM solutions, particularly compared to SAP's on-premise HCM offering, SAP ERP HCM. The days of creating custom tables from scratch and implementing completely custom functionality in house using specialized skill sets are no more. Furthermore, because SAP SuccessFactors is a cloud solution, everything from security to moving configuration from one system to another system is different.

However, that's not to say that SAP SuccessFactors HCM Suite is not flexible. SAP SuccessFactors delivers significant functionality by default and uses the MDF and the Rules Engine to customize your own objects, rules, behavior, and screen elements. The flexibility of the architecture allows for endless customization. Extensibility with SAP Cloud Platform enables entirely customizable applications to be built and integrated into the SAP SuccessFactors HCM Suite from both a visual and data perspective.

In Figure 3.1, you can see that the overall architecture of the SAP SuccessFactors application landscape runs similarly to many other software-as-a-service (SaaS) multitenant applications. There are the core application and database in the SAP SuccessFactors data center, and then there is the client-side web browser that consumes the application from the data center. Architecturally, SAP SuccessFactors is split into three layers: two are within the data center, and one connects the data center to the client:

- Within the data center, the *database layer* contains the underlying application metadata configuration and the customer data.
- The *application layer*, also within the data center, contains the actual application and overall logic of the SAP SuccessFactors HCM Suite.
- The *communication layer* lies between the application layer and the client web browser.

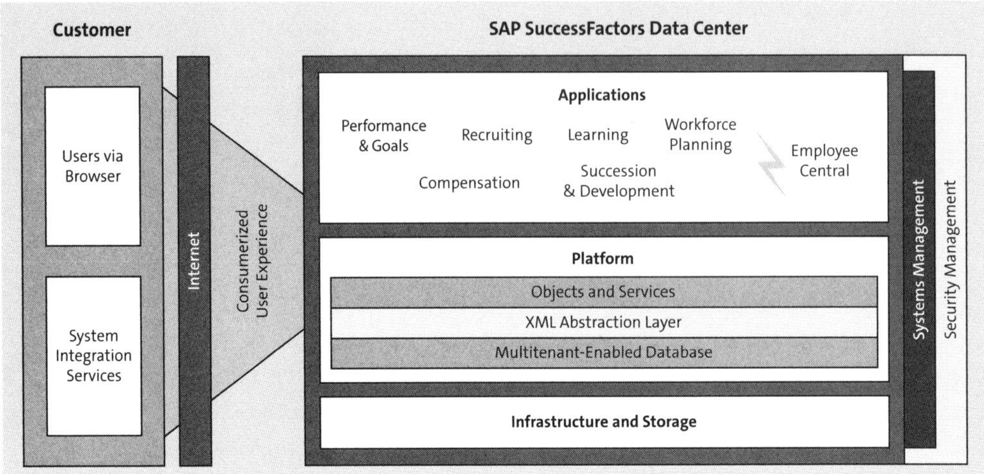

Figure 3.1 SAP SuccessFactors Architecture

As with all cloud applications, data security is a concern for customers—especially with the introduction of the General Data Protection Regulation (GDPR) in the European Union (EU). We'll cover security in depth in Section 3.3. First, we'll briefly look at each of the layers.

3.2.1 Database Layer

SAP SuccessFactors HCM Suite houses all customer data in SAP HANA databases.

Because the SAP SuccessFactors HCM Suite is a multitenant SaaS suite, customers share infrastructure, web servers, database instances, and the application itself. For storage of customer configuration and data, SAP SuccessFactors HCM Suite uses SAP's proprietary SAP HANA database. Each customer has their own partition in the database, along with the customer-specific database schema. They also have their own configuration of the software (called a "tenant"). This allows for high flexibility, use of the software and data, and the export of any data from the database at any time with no effect on any other customer. Because the database partition is separated from other customer data and linked specifically to the customer's tenant, data cannot be accessed from any place except the customer's SAP SuccessFactors tenant. This also means that configuration in one customer tenant does not affect any other customer tenant running on the same instance of the software.

Of course, sharing database space with another customer's sensitive HR data raises some obvious security concerns to those not familiar with the technical architecture of the database landscape. We'll address how SAP SuccessFactors rigorously tests each level of the stack to ensure data security in Section 3.3.

3.2.2 Application Layer

One of the most important aspects of a SaaS solution is that it is multitenant. Because of the multitenant architecture, all of the users share the same core code base of the application, but they each have their own tenant of configuration. This differs from on-premise solutions, wherein each instance of the system requires a separate installation of the software on different instances of hardware. Having all users on the same code base has many advantages:

- **Scheduled releases**
  The SAP SuccessFactors development team is constantly updating the software to improve performance and increase functionality. Users get regular, scheduled updates automatically every quarter. Many of the new features that are delivered must be proactively activated by the customer to be used (opt-in), so there are no "nasty surprises" for customers. In some cases, SAP SuccessFactors do make mandatory changes and functionality retirements, although these are communicated well in advance.
- **Latest version across all customers**
  With the scheduled releases, all customers are up-to-date on the latest version all the time. This means that there are no more costly upgrades, creating different versions for different customers. It also means all customers get all bug fixes.
- **No hardware, operating systems, or database licenses**
  A single subscription licensing fee is paid to use SAP SuccessFactors and includes all necessary costs for hardware, database, and support.
- **Optimal hardware and software combination**
  SAP SuccessFactors resides on hardware that is optimized for its own software.
- **Consistent performance and stability**
  All customers use the same software and hardware, so the fast, stable, and secure experience is shared by all customers.
- **More manageable and efficient support and maintenance**
  SAP SuccessFactors can easily support and maintain its software because it is standardized.

- **Data mining and aggregation for analytical benchmarking**
  Analytics can easily be pulled with maximum efficiency due to the standardization of software and hardware.

Now, let's take a closer look at the application architecture itself. Figure 3.2 shows a more in-depth overview of the SAP SuccessFactors components within the application engine.

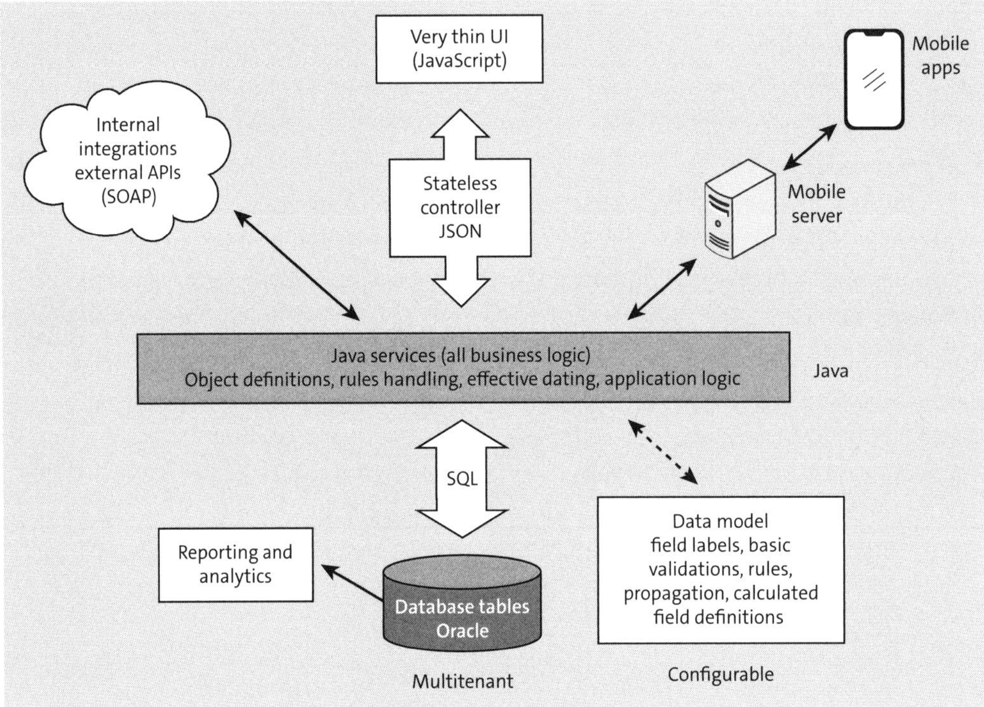

Figure 3.2 Technologies Used with SAP SuccessFactors

The applications are written in the Java programming language using Java Platform Enterprise Edition (J2EE) specifications, so they conform to a standard set of programming logic. The user interface leverages SAP's UI5 SAP Fiori technology (SAPUI5).

We'll cover the UI itself in Section 3.8.

Also, within this layer are the APIs and connectors to other web services (for example, SAP SuccessFactors Recruiting can connect to job boards), mobile application services, and all the logic that drives the entire application.

3.2.3 Communication Layer

The communication layer transports the data for the application to the web browser for rendering and communications data calls to and from the data center. This is important from an architectural perspective because this layer is sending sensitive application and personal HR information across the Internet. As a result, SAP SuccessFactors has implemented well-known standards for data transfer, including Secure Shell (SSH), VeriSign-certified Secure Sockets Layer (SSL)/Transport Layer Security (TLS), and Secure File Transfer Protocol (SFTP).

Now that you understand the various layers of the application, let's take a look at how SAP SuccessFactors secures data within the application.

3.3 Security

SAP SuccessFactors takes security and protecting its customers' sensitive data very seriously. Because its systems store sensitive HR data from multiple customers, every aspect of technology used is thoroughly tested and includes many security standards to ensure proper security. Data is secured in two ways: through authentication and through security applied to each of the layers described previously in this section. Additionally, SAP has implemented functionality to enable customers with operations within the European Union to be fully compliant with GDPR.

3.3.1 Authentication Security

SAP SuccessFactors has many different levels of security on all layers. It supports the SSL and TLS encryption languages that are leveraged by standard web providers. In addition, there are following authentication methods:

- **Internal authentication**
  Using an internal repository of user profiles, this authentication occurs on the SAP SuccessFactors side when customers choose not to integrate their own identity management system.
- **Federated authentication (SSO)**
  Single sign-on (SSO) implementation requires users to first be authenticated through their own authorization systems (LDAP) using tokens (MD5, SHA-1, HMAC encryption, DES, 3DES) or Security Assertion Markup Languages (SAML 2.0). The user is then redirected to the SAP SuccessFactors instance using HTTPS.

- **SSO without federation**
  This method uses a public encryption key that is sent to the customer's authentication server from SAP SuccessFactors. By using this key, users can connect to SAP SuccessFactors by using a preestablished authentication method.
- **Separate security applications**
  Because authorization is usually deeply integrated in source code in standard solutions, SAP SuccessFactors uses a separate authorization and authentication application from that of the data and functions. This allows for future growth of security throughout the application, as needed. This security application logs every action of the user and validates each request to prevent cross-site scripting (XSS) attacks.
- **Password protection**
  Strong passwords with regular password changes are required by SAP SuccessFactors. Administrators can also set custom rules for passwords that users must abide by.

3.3.2 Layer Security

The SAP SuccessFactors environment is made up of multiple layers of security. The security layers and accompanying encryption and technology are shown in Figure 3.3.

The data center itself also conforms to many security standards:

- EU 95/46 EC
- PCI-DSS
- ISO 27002
- BS7799
- ASIO-4
- FIPS Moderate
- BS10012
- SSAE-16/SOC2

Because of these safeguards, customers' information is encrypted and protected, so even if the data is stolen, it is inaccessible and unusable.

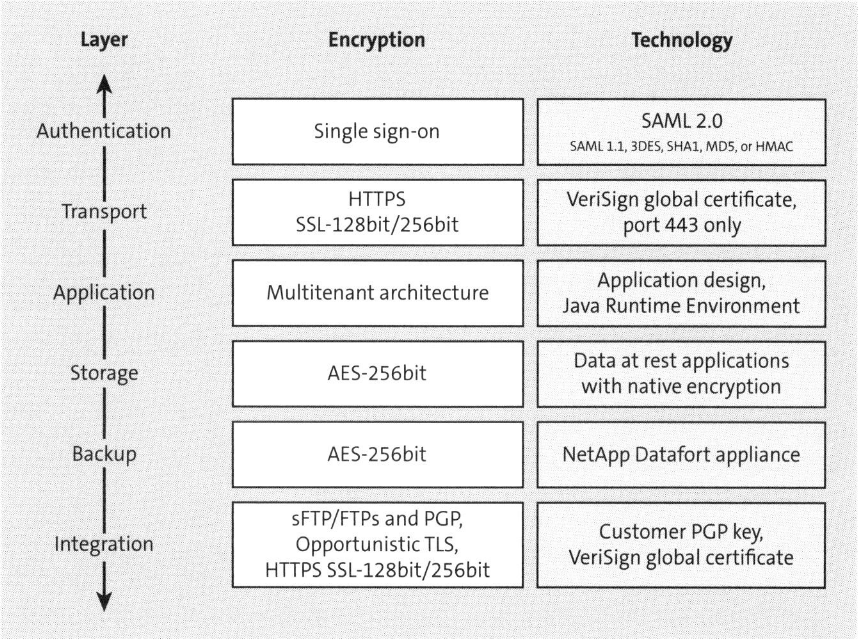

Figure 3.3 The Security Layers of SAP SuccessFactors Applications

3.3.3 Role-Based Permissions Security

The RBP framework in SAP SuccessFactors provides a flexible, robust, and granular approach to securing data and functionality to the right groups of users for specified target groups of employees. It allows authorizations and security to be managed at all levels, including the function, transaction, field, and data levels. Field-level permissions can also be set so that data can be hidden, viewable, or viewable and editable for specific roles. We will discuss RBPs further in Chapter 17, Section 17.5.

Now that you understand how the data and layers are secured, let's explore some of the key components of the SAP SuccessFactors platform.

3.4 Admin Center

Administrators within SAP SuccessFactors have many powerful tools at their fingertips, including the Admin Center, which enable administration of features such as employee and organizational data, forms used in various SAP SuccessFactors HCM Suite solutions, picklists, and notification emails. Figure 3.4 shows the Admin Center.

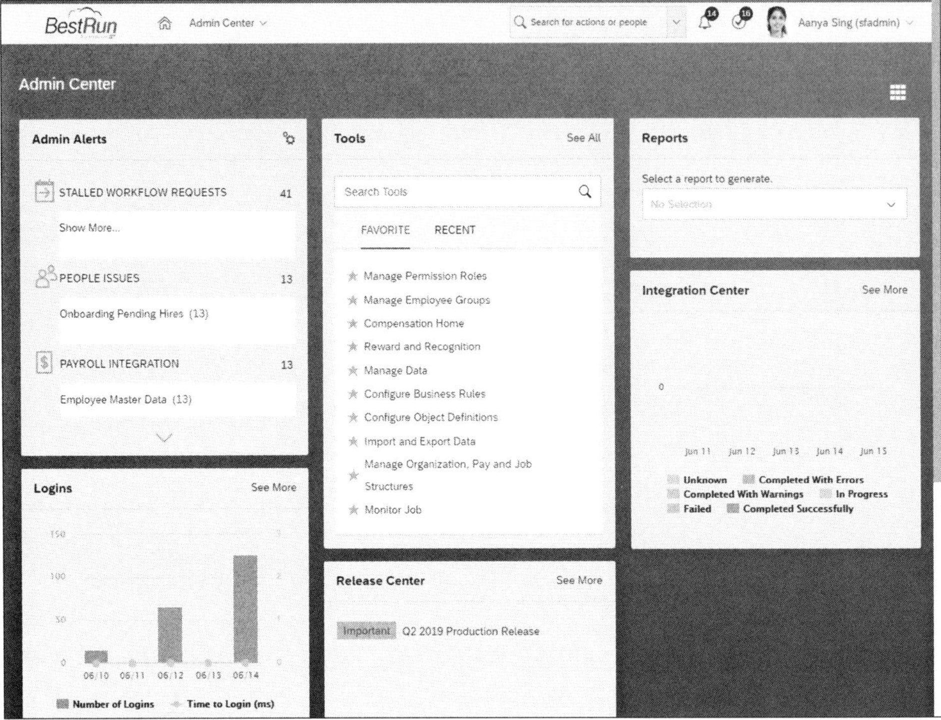

Figure 3.4 The Admin Center in SAP SuccessFactors

We will cover some of the practical administration activities in the Admin Center in Chapter 17, Section 17.2.

3.5 Picklists

Picklists are the dropdown lists of input values a user must choose from when entering data. They are used throughout SAP SuccessFactors and are defined in a central location. Picklists are managed in the Admin Center, in Picklists Management. We will cover this in more detail in Chapter 17, Section 17.9.

> **Note**
>
> MDF picklists differ from standard picklists, in that they are used only with generic objects and are configured in a different part of the application. We will cover MDF picklists in Chapter 17, Section 17.9.

3.6 Upgrade Center

The Upgrade Center allows customers to apply certain enhanced features and functionality to their instances without having to log a customer support ticket or engaging an implementation partner.

We will cover details of the Upgrade Center in Chapter 17, Section 17.3.

3.7 Release Center

The Release Center enables customers to discover details of SAP SuccessFactors quarterly releases. Here, customers can view each feature that is part of a quarterly release by type (universal or optional); you can also filter them by module. For each feature, you have the option to navigate to the SAP SuccessFactors Community or to the SAP Help Portal for additional information and documentation. You can also navigate to the Upgrade Center from the Release Center so that you can view further details of a feature and—if desired—enable that feature.

We will cover details of the Release Center in Chapter 17, Section 17.4.

3.8 User Interface

The SAP SuccessFactors UI has been designed to provide an engaging and enriching user experience for the end user. The simple design provides powerful benefits to employees and managers who have minimal training or exposure to SAP SuccessFactors. The UI is built on SAPUI5 technology.

SAP SuccessFactors has leveraged their SMART design principles in every aspect of the UI: social, mobile, analytical, rich, and toy-like. The modular and easy-to-use UI provides enhanced productivity through intuitive navigation and data presentation. The aesthetics of the UI provide a much richer visual user experience than SAP ERP or other on-premise applications.

The UI is designed to conform to the needs of organizations of various sizes that operate in a wide array of industries and territories. Unlike traditional software applications that target one level of user in an organization, this solution is designed to adapt to the different needs of various types of users, from C-level executives to HR business partners, line managers, and even entry-level employees.

Now, let's take a look at some of the aspects of the UI.

3.8.1 Navigation Menu

Each of the applications that the user is permissioned to access can be reached via the navigation menu in the top-left corner of the application. Figure 3.5 shows the navigation menu in SAP SuccessFactors. This is where each of the licensed applications in the suite can be accessed.

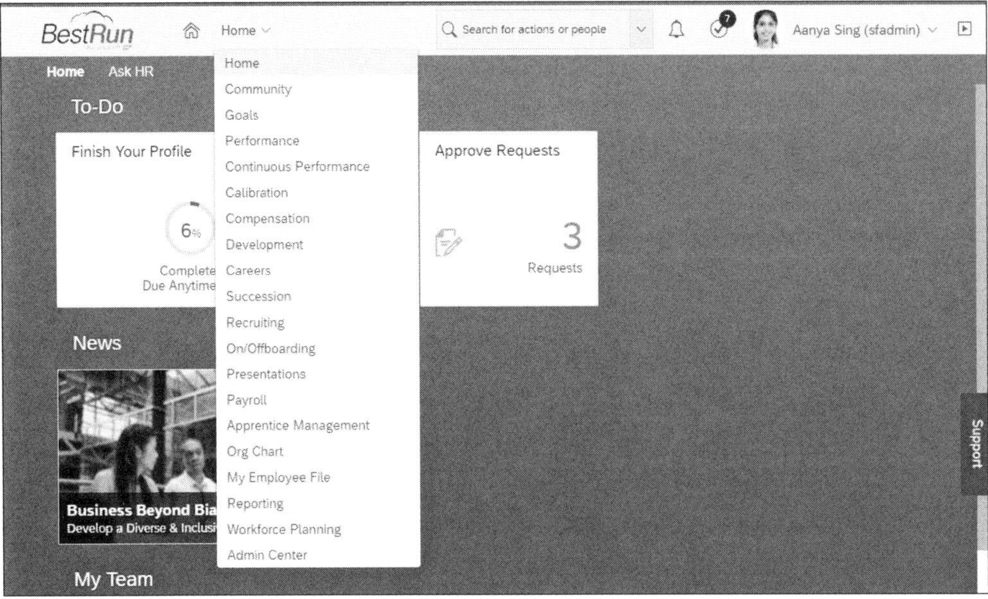

Figure 3.5 The Navigation Menu in SAP SuccessFactors

Depending on the number of licensed modules and the permission design, the menu in Figure 3.5 may be much smaller for some or all audiences in your organization.

3.8.2 User Menu and Options

The user menu provides the user with access to options and—depending on user permissions—the proxy feature and/or Admin Center. The user can also log out of the system here.

The user accesses the user menu by clicking their name at the top of the screen, as seen in Figure 3.6.

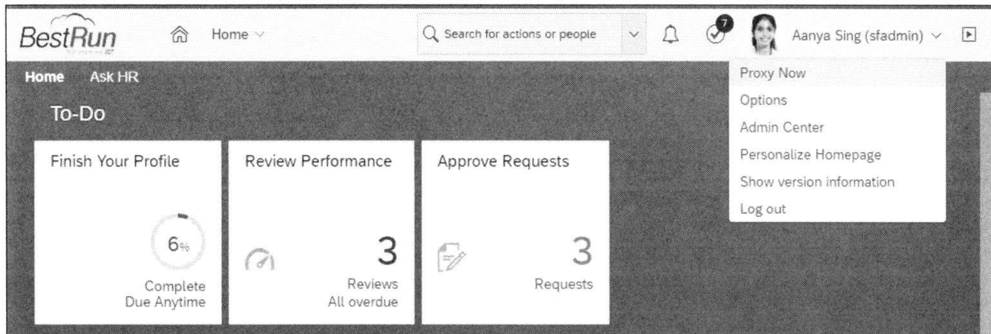

Figure 3.6 User Menu

The **Options** page allows the user to personalize the user experience. It contains features such as the following:

- Change password
- Set start page when logging into SAP SuccessFactors
- Configure notifications
- Change language
- Enable accessibility
- Configure proxy settings
- Create groups
- Enable SAP SuccessFactors Mobile functionality

The proxy feature allows the user to log in on behalf of another user if the appropriate permissions have been assigned. For example, a manager could proxy in as a direct report during the direct report's annual vacation to approve a stalled workflow.

3.8.3 Notifications

Located to the right side of the header bar is the notifications icon. The bell icon shows the number of notifications relating to such things as the user having a new manager or notifications from SAP Jam (when the customer uses and integrates SAP Jam with SAP SuccessFactors). This will depend on what functionality is configured and permissioned for the user. Selecting the icon brings up the most recent notifications and provides a link to view all SAP Jam notifications (see Figure 3.7).

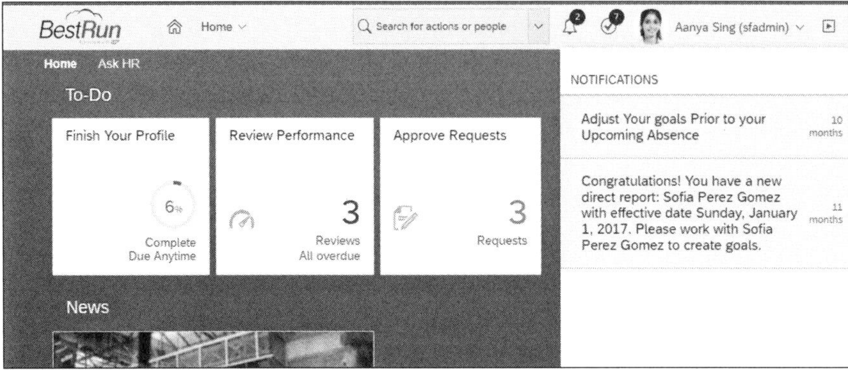

Figure 3.7 The Jam Notifications Icon

3.8.4 To-Dos

Next to the notifications icon is the to-dos icon. The tick icon—similarly to the notifications bell icon—shows the number of to-dos that the user has, as shown in Figure 3.8. These to-dos include activities such as workflow approvals, requisition approvals, onboarding activities, and so forth. These to-dos will depend on what functionality is configured and permissioned for the user.

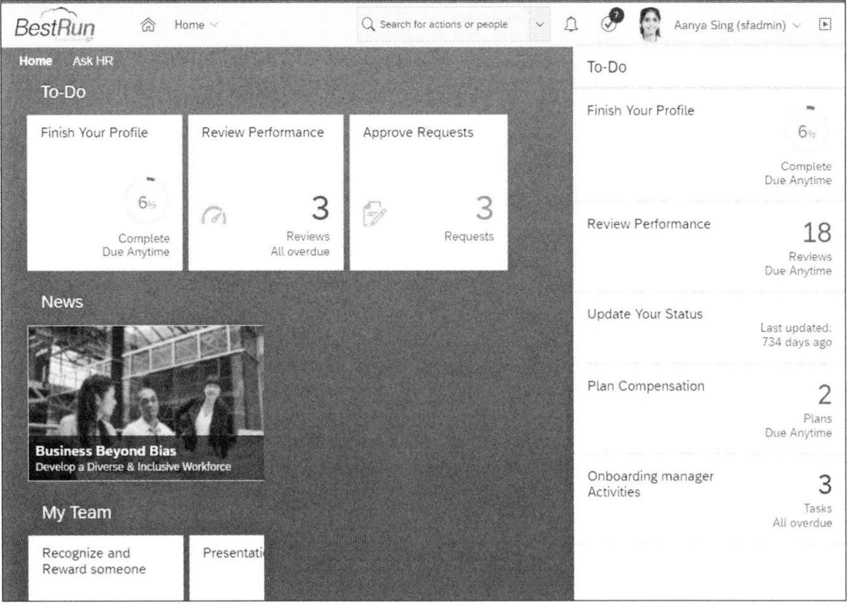

Figure 3.8 The To-Do Menu

3.8.5 Action Search

The action search is the way to search for people in the system, launch processes or functionality, or perform specific actions. It is located on the right side of the header by the notifications and to-dos icons, as seen in Figure 3.8 to the left of the notifications icon.

To get going, simply start typing in the box and results will show in a dropdown box. What happens next depends on whether you type an employee or an action. We'll cover these separately.

Search for an Employee

If you type any part of an employee's name, any matching results will be shown. You can click on an employee to go to their profile, or if you hover over an employee, you will see their quick card, on which you can see some basic information and their contact details, and from which you can perform the following actions:

- Launch an email to them
- View them in the Org Chart
- Navigate to their profile
- Navigate to their manager's profile
- Navigate to various module-specific processes, forms, or actions (e.g., go to performance form, terminate, give a spot bonus to, etc.)

Figure 3.9 shows the quickcard of an employee found in the action search.

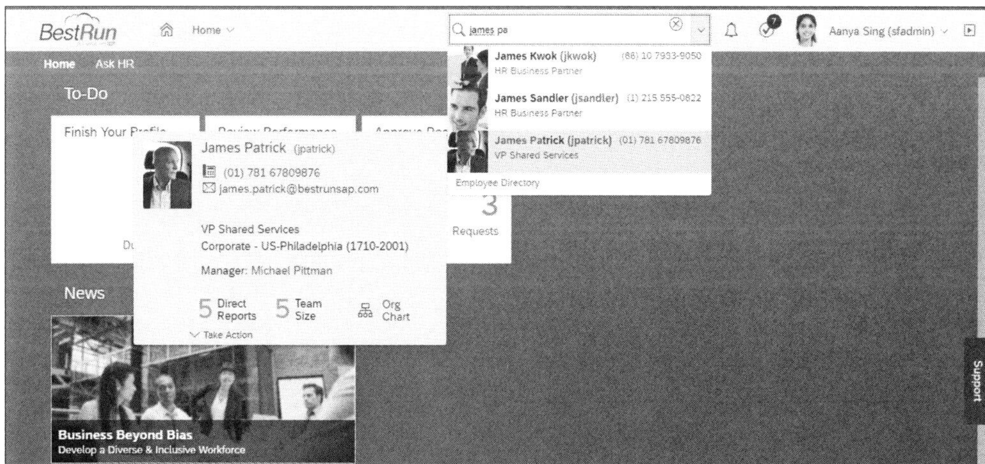

Figure 3.9 The Quickcard of an Employee Found in the Action Search

Search for an Action

If you type an action into the action search box to launch a specific process, you will see a list of matching results in a dropdown box. Selecting any action in the list will launch that action. In Figure 3.10, we can see a search for actions that include "assign" in the name of the action.

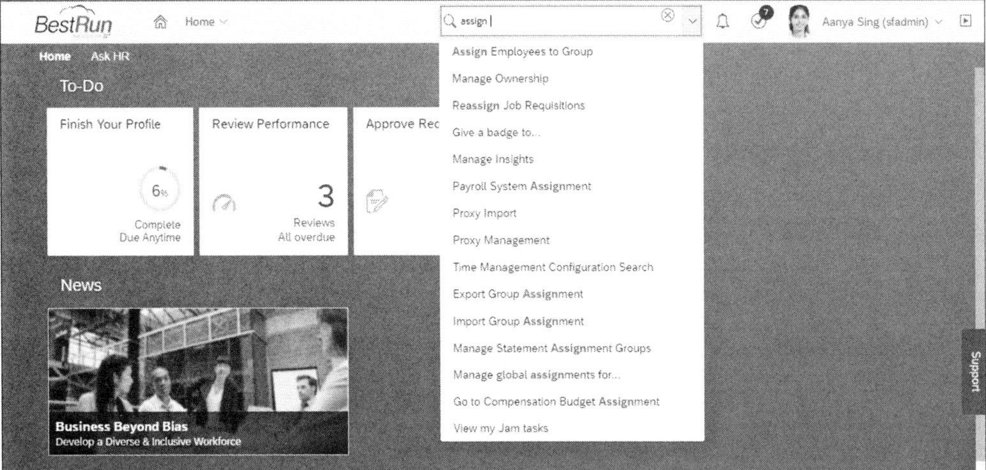

Figure 3.10 Using the Action Search

3.8.6 Theme

You want SAP SuccessFactors to adopt your theming and your name, right? Well, the good news is that that configuration of the theme, logo, and wording is extremely flexible and can adhere to most corporate branding themes. Different themes can also be assigned to different user groups. You can also have multiple themes based on different brands your company may have.

The company logo can be defined by an administrator by searching for "Upload Company Logo" in the action search, or by clicking **Upload Company Logo** in the Admin Center. The logo displays in the top-right of the application and on the logon screen.

You can also configure the theme of the instance by searching for "Theme Manager" in the action search, or by selecting **Theme Manager** in the Admin Center.

Multiple themes can exist in the system, but only one default theme can be set. Depending on which setting is made in provisioning, different themes can be assigned to specific divisions, departments, or locations. Hovering over a theme gives you three options:

- Try it out
- Duplicate
- Delete

Selecting a theme brings up the **Edit Theme** page, which looks similar to Figure 3.11.

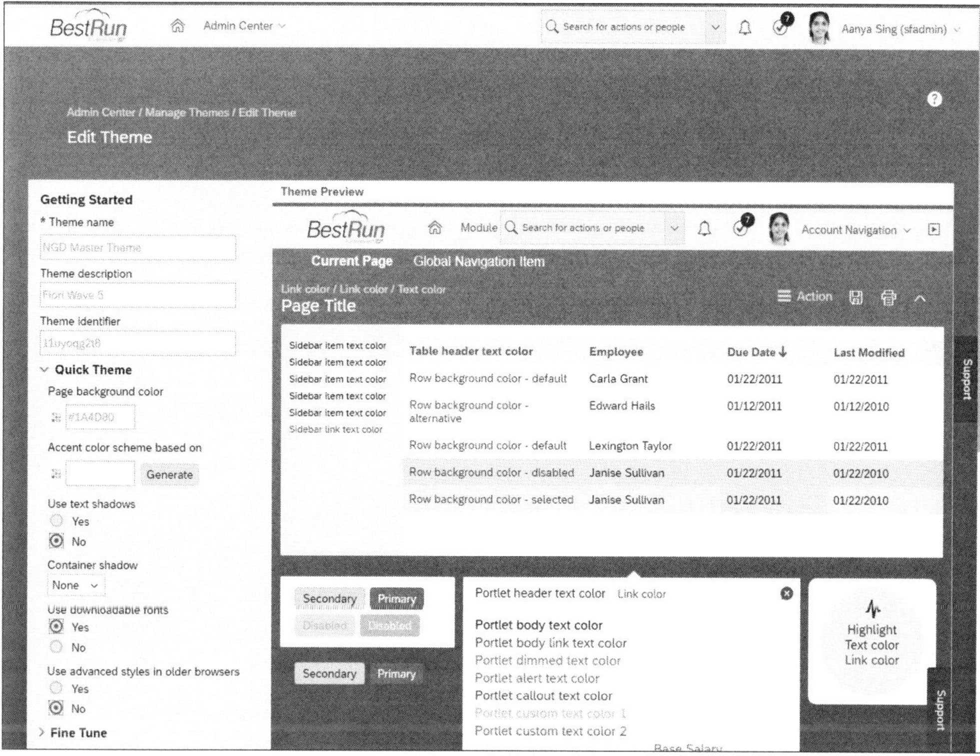

Figure 3.11 The Edit Theme Page

Here you can edit all aspects of the theme and preview how it looks.

3.8.7 Languages

The SAP SuccessFactors UI supports multiple languages across the suite. Each module supports a number of languages, with translations provided across the application as standard. Right-to-left (RTL) languages are also supported for some modules.

SAP SuccessFactors are able to provide the most up-to-date list of languages available for the applications you are using or considering using. At the time of writing (fall 2019), around 44 languages are provided. The latest list of languages available can be found in SAP Note 2269945.

Next, we will explore the SAP SuccessFactors home page for employees.

3.9 Home Page

The home page is the main landing page for employees when they log on to the SAP SuccessFactors system. It is the default landing page, although employees have the option to change their default landing page in the **Options** menu that we discussed in Section 3.8.2. Figure 3.12 shows a typical home page.

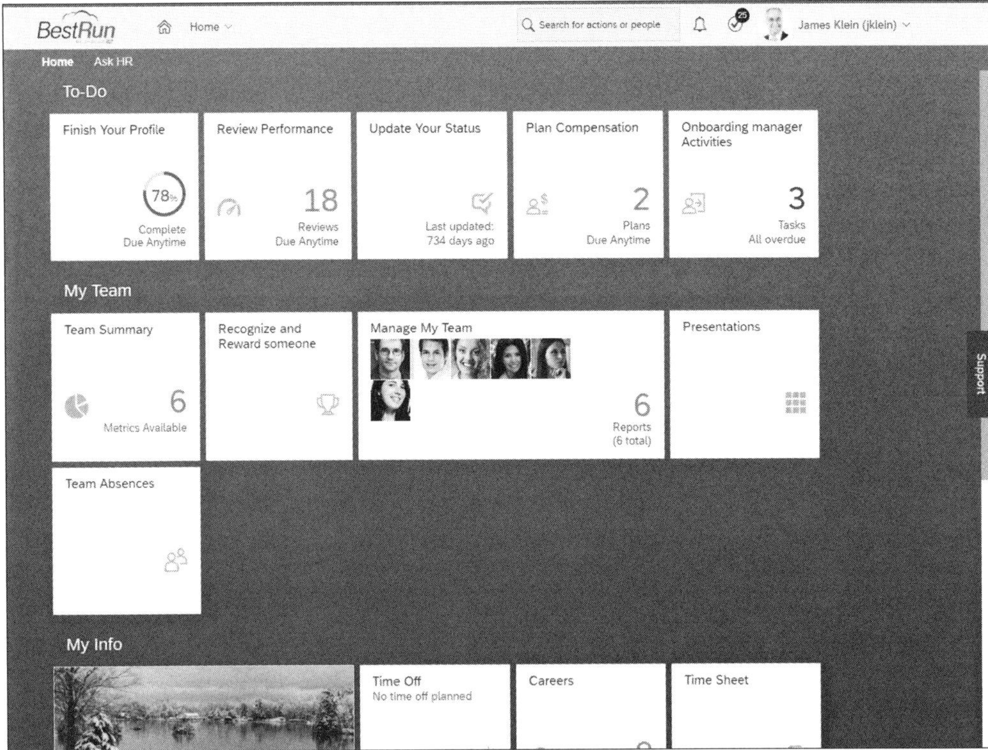

Figure 3.12 The SAP SuccessFactors Home Page

The home page consists of a number of *tiles*. Tiles show a snapshot of information and allow the user to perform certain actions, depending on the tile. Selecting a tile will navigate you to the process or application that is the focus of the tile. Tiles are grouped into *sections*. Sections are groupings of similar tiles, such as **To-Do** or **My Team**.

3.9.1 Standard Delivered Content

SAP SuccessFactors provides a number of standard-delivered sections and tiles, which cover the applications that are enabled in the system. In addition to the standard-delivered tiles, custom tiles can be added. We'll cover those in Section 3.9.3.

Several tiles come delivered in the system. They are split into several sections, which you can also edit; this is covered shortly. Some of the delivered sections and tiles are:

- **To Do**: Lists all of the outstanding actions and activities of the user, such as workflows to be approved or performance evaluations to be assessed
- **Links**: Provides a list of links to different applications and processes, such as the Org Chart and the People Profile
- **My Team**: Displays the user's direct reports and allows actions to be launched for team members, such as:
  - **Manage My Team**
  - **Team Summary**
  - **Birthday/Work Anniversary**
  - **Recognize and Reward someone**
  - **Presentations**
  - **Team Absences Calendar**
- **My Info**: Displays basic info about the user and enables self-service actions to be launched by the user, such as:
  - **My Profile**
  - **Time Sheet**
  - **Time Off**
  - **Careers**
  - **Manage Pending Requests**
- **My Specialty**: Displays tiles for some module-specific activities, such as payroll activities

The home page and its sections and tiles are managed by selecting **Manage Home Page** via the action search or in the Admin Center.

3.9.2 Managing Sections and Tiles

Sections are managed by navigating to **Manage Home Page** and selecting **Edit Sections**. Here you can add new sections, edit existing sections, delete sections, and change the permissions for each section.

Once all of your sections are defined, you can add tiles to those sections.

Tiles are managed in Admin Center in **Manage Home Page** under **Company Settings** (which can also be accessed via action search or the Admin Center search); this is shown in Figure 3.13. Here, all tiles are accessible, including both standard-delivered and custom created tiles. Each tile can be defined to be removable and be moved to a different section. Certain tiles have additional settings that can be configured by clicking on the pencil icon on the row of the tile.

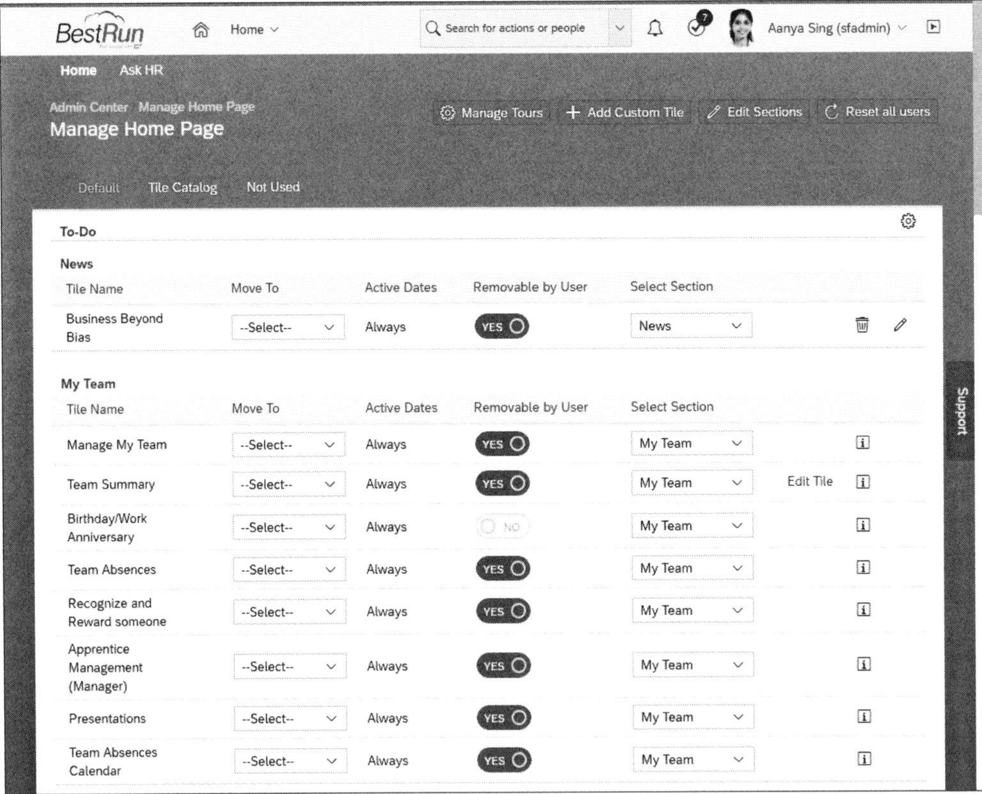

Figure 3.13 Manage Home Page Screen

3.9.3 Adding Custom Tiles

Custom tiles can be added by selecting **Add Custom Tile** in **Manage Home Page**. This opens the **Create Custom Tile Wizard**, which guides you through the process of creating a new tile. Here, you can create tiles for different groups of employees with static or dynamic content in one or more languages. Tiles can also be set to be triggered based on business rules (business rules are covered in Section 3.18.3).

The content editor allows a variety of different content types, including HTML code, Flash objects, images, and hyperlinks. Text can also be formatted in common methods, such as font face and size, color, alignment, bold, italic, underline, and so forth. This enables flexible types of content to be added to reflect a number of use cases and scenarios.

3.10 User Data File

The *user data file* (UDF)—also known as the *basic user import*—is the basic user data required by the SAP SuccessFactors HCM Suite to run talent applications. When you run Employee Central in your SAP SuccessFactors instance, it automatically populates and updates the UDF based on data changes in Employee Central using *HRIS sync*, which we cover in Section 3.10.4.

In an integration concept, the data stored in the system is called the *user entity*. If you run the talent hybrid integration scenario (you use SAP ERP HCM on-premise and use SAP SuccessFactors for talent processes), then the packaged integration from SAP populates the UDF with data from SAP ERP HCM.

Let's unpack the key components of the UDF, before moving on to managing users, importing and exporting data, and walking through the HRIS sync feature.

3.10.1 Components

The UDF is made up of the 49 standard elements from the Succession data model: 34 fields, plus 15 customizable fields available for any use. Nine of these fields are mandatory in SAP SuccessFactors and must be defined. The standard elements used in the UDF are defined in the view template *sysUserDirectorySetting* in the Succession data model. We recommend that you leave the standard fields, as they are provided in the data model. The standard fields are as follows:

- **STATUS**: Employee status (active or inactive)*
- **USERID**: Unique identifier*

- **USERNAME**: Employee's user name for login*
- **FIRSTNAME**: First name*
- **NICKNAME**: Nickname
- **MI**: Middle name
- **LASTNAME**: Last name*
- **SUFFIX**: Name suffix
- **TITLE**: Job title
- **GENDER**: Gender
- **EMAIL**: Email address*
- **MANAGER**: Manager*
- **HR**: HR administrator*
- **DEPARTMENT**: Department
- **JOBCODE**: Job code
- **DIVISION**: Division
- **LOCATION**: Location
- **TIMEZONE**: Time zone of user*
- **HIREDATE**: Hire date
- **EMPID**: Employee's ID
- **BIZ_PHONE**: Telephone number
- **FAX**: Fax number
- **ADDR1**: Address line 1
- **ADDR2**: Address line 2
- **CITY**: City
- **STATE**: State/Province
- **ZIP**: Zip Code/Postal Code
- **COUNTRY**: Country
- **REVIEW_FREQ**: Performance appraisal frequency
- **LAST_REVIEW_DATE**: Date of last performance appraisal
- **MATRIX_MANAGER**: Dotted line (matrix) manager
- **DEFAULT_LOCALE**: Default locale of employee
- **PROXY**: Proxy user
- **CUSTOM01** through **CUSTOM15**: Customizable field 1 through customizable field 15

Fields marked with * are mandatory and cannot be left blank. Although **MANAGER** and **HR** cannot be left blank, an entry can be made to define that the user does not have a manager or HR administrator by using values **NO_MANAGER** *and* **NO_HR**, respectively. If you are defining a manager or HR administrator, that user's **USERID** field value is used.

The values for the **TIMEZONE** field are predefined, and the correct values must be used. These can be obtained from an SAP SuccessFactors implementation specialist or from SAP SuccessFactors professional services.

All date formats are stored in format MM/DD/YYYY.

How you manage the UDF depends on whether you use Employee Central or not, as follows:

- When you use Employee Central and hire a new employee in the **Hire New Employee** transaction, a UDF record is created automatically. When an employee is rehired, their UDF record status is changed from **Inactive** to **Active**. When any employee data is changed, it is synchronized automatically to the UDF.
- If you don't use Employee Central, then the UDF needs to be updated via the Manage Users transaction, by importing users, or via integration.

We'll now look at all of the ways that you can manage the UDF.

3.10.2 Manage Users

When you are not using Employee Central, adding a UDF record for an employee is performed through Admin Center, through the **Manage Users** option under **Update User Information**. Here, the user has the option of doing a quick add for the required fields, or entering a full record. Both options are found under the **Add New User** button.

Figure 3.14 shows an example of an exported UDF with some data.

	A	B	C	D	E	F	G	H	I	J	K	L
1	STATUS	USERID	USERNAME	FIRSTNAME	LASTNAME	SUFFIX	TITLE	GENDER	EMAIL	MANAGER	HR	DEPARTMENT
2	active	54645	awan	Adam	Wan		HR Administrator	M	aadmin1@ACECompany.com	65324	122326	Industries
3	active	8324	abagot	Alain	Bagot		Program Manager	M	ABagot@ACECompany.com	65324	43789	Client Service (SVCS)
4	active	123123	achin	Alan	Chin		Recruiter - HC	M	AChin@ACECompany.com	43535	34349	Talent Management (TALENT)
5	active	8253	alake	Alan	Lake		VP, Operations	M	ALake@ACECompany.com	NO_MANAGER	22455	Operations (OPS)
6	active	84543	aanderson	Alex	Anderson		Sr. Manager, Analytics	M	AAnderson@ACECompany.com	74545	5938	Talent Management (TALENT)
7	active	27857	athompson	Alexander	Thompson		President	M	AThompson@ACECompany.com	23777	6477	Alliances (ALNCE)
8	active	58677	afong	Alice	Fong		Recruiter	F	AFong@ACECompany.com	54555	24667	Talent Management (TALENT)
9	active	73782	amick	Alison	Mick		Director, IT Support	F	AMick@ACECompany.com	92133	NO_HR	IT (IT)
10	active	42421	akohne	Amanda	Kohne		Director, IT	F	AKohne@ACECompany.com	123331	NO_HR	IT (IT)

Figure 3.14 The UDF with Data

3.10.3 Importing and Exporting Data

The UDF can be imported by searching for **Import Employee Data** in the action search, searching for it under Tools in the Admin Center, or selecting **See All** under **Tools** and selecting **Import Employee Data**, which can be seen in Figure 3.15. Exporting data can be done similarly by searching for **Employee Export**.

No matter whether Employee Central is used, the UDF can be exported using the option **Employee Export**.

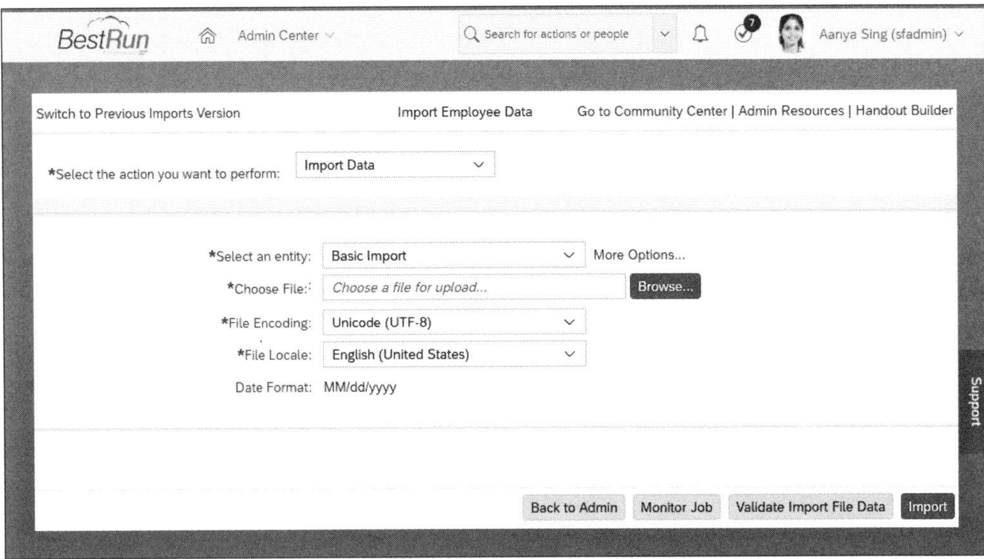

Figure 3.15 Employee Import Screen

3.10.4 HRIS Sync

When using Employee Central, data is synchronized to the UDF automatically and in real time when changes are made to employee data in Employee Central. This is called *HRIS sync*. The synchronized fields include the following:

- First name
- Last name
- Division
- Department
- Job code
- Manager
- HR administrator
- Email address

Other Employee Central fields are mapped to UDF fields in the Succession data model. These are synchronized by a daily job that must be set up in provisioning. Typically, Employee Central data is mapped to the customizable fields in the UDF so that they can be displayed in the Employee Profile or used in filters. Employee Central fields can also be synchronized to user-info elements.

3.11 Employee Profile

The Employee Profile is the foundation for many of the talent applications in SAP SuccessFactors. It is where an employee's basic information, history, accomplishments, employment performance details, and other data are stored. The Employee Profile helps encourage employee engagement by providing employees with a place to connect with their colleagues and actively participate in their personal careers and development planning. It should be noted that the Employee Profile is not intended to be used as a human resource information system (HRIS) or system of record keeping of full employee HR data.

The Employee Profile enables customers to create a continuously updated, easily searchable directory of employee skills, interests, and expertise. Employees can maintain their own data, find colleagues with relevant or similar skills and interests, and publicly recognize their peers. Managers can view workforce information to identify skill gaps in their organization and ensure that they are working with the right people and on the right things, aligning them with team and company objectives.

The Employee Profile comprises numerous elements that work together to provide a complete picture of an employee's profile. These elements are used by many people in an organization to view data about an employee. Managers use the data stored in the Employee Profile as data points for the performance management, succession planning, and career development planning processes. Other employees can view the Employee Profile to quickly get contact information for their colleagues.

Data in the Employee Profile is synchronized from three places: SAP SuccessFactors Employee Central, if the customer is utilizing it for HR data; the Candidate Profile, if Recruiting is used and this integration is configured; or the source HRIS (e.g., SAP ERP HCM, PeopleSoft, and so on) via the UDF import or via web service-based integration. This includes data from commonly used fields such as **Name**, **Job**, **Division**, **Department**, and **Manager**.

When a customer uses Employee Central, then other data that is part of Employee Central is combined with Employee Profile data in the employee's profile. This is part of the People Profile, which we'll cover next.

3.11.1 People Profile

The People Profile is the UI that displays the Employee Profile. It provides an attractive, usable view for employees to access data on colleagues and also provides all employees with a snapshot of anyone in the organization, along with that person's contact information, such as job title, department, phone number, and email address, as shown for James Klein in Figure 3.16. Colleagues can also view details such as a brief description about the employee and the employee's interests, contact information, organization chart, local time, badges, and so forth. Each of these types of information are grouped together in what are called *blocks*, which technically are called *background elements* in the data model.

When configuring the People Profile (performed using the **Configure People Profile** transaction in the Admin Center), you can add different blocks to build out the type of information you want to be displayed for employees on the People Profile. We'll touch on this in the next section.

The People Profile provides employees the opportunity to visually express themselves to their colleagues by choosing a background photo. They can choose from images already provided by SAP SuccessFactors or upload their own personal photo—depending on company guidelines of course! This provides a personalized feel that allows employees to stand out to their colleagues.

It is also possible to take actions from the People Profile by using the **Actions** button. Here you can navigate to the Org Chart to view the employee, add a note, give a badge, print the profile or export as a PDF, or navigate to processes in Employee Central or talent applications, such as to give the employee a bonus or to view the employee's goal plan. These settings all depend on what features are enabled and what the user is permissioned to see/do.

When you also use Employee Central, People Profile allows you to build a profile that mixes the data from Employee Central, Employee Central Payroll, Employee Profile, Job Profile Builder, and other modules as you see you see fit.

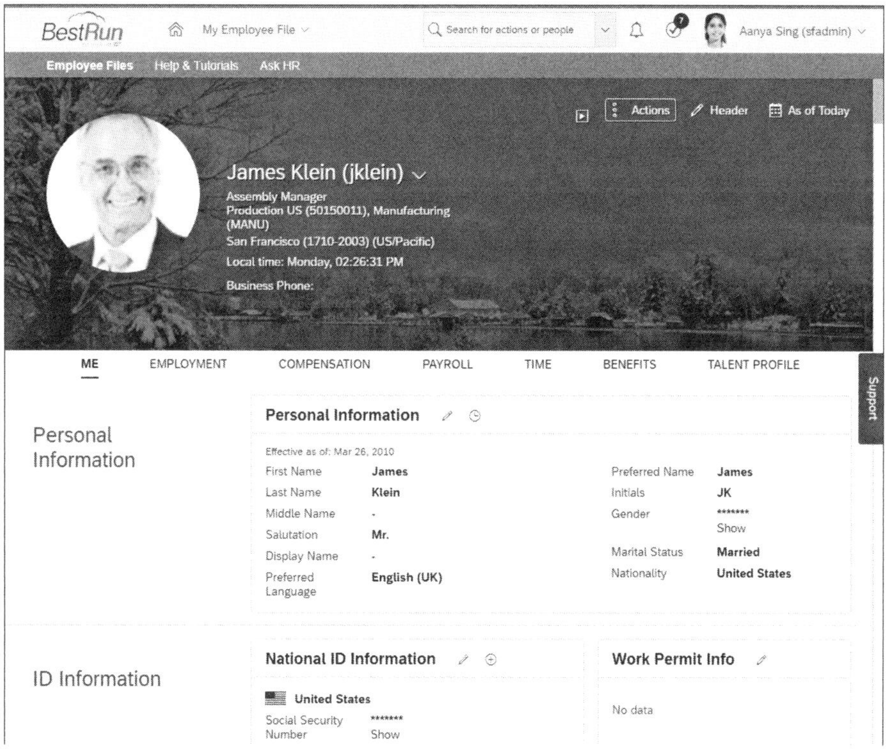

Figure 3.16 People Profile for James Klein

We'll now look at some specific blocks and features of the People Profile that you might find useful. We've grouped together some of the blocks into related categories in the next few sections.

Employee Overview

From a scorecard perspective, several blocks can be used to give a snapshot of the employee and provide an overview of the employee's succession data, such as performance and potential rating and placement on the nine-box report. The **Overview** block is generally visible only to the manager, upline managers, HR representatives, and the custom manager (if that role is utilized in succession planning).

Experience

An employee's experience is captured across numerous blocks that are designed to reflect the roles employees have held within the company, the type of functional experience they've had in those roles, any leadership experience they have had, and previous employment. This information can be captured in the following standard background elements (see Figure 3.17):

- **Work Experience Within Organization**
- **Functional Experience**
- **Leadership Experience** (not shown)
- **Previous Employment**

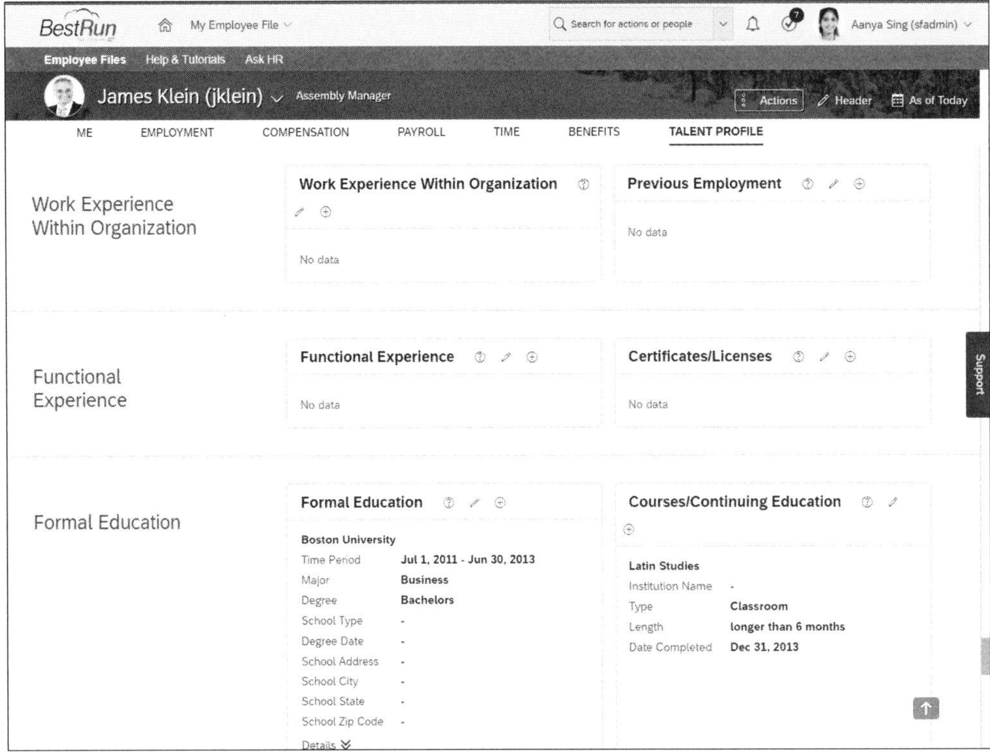

Figure 3.17 Work/Experience Background Elements

Education and Interests

An employee's educational background and specialty interests can also be captured in standard blocks. Along with gathering information on whether an employee is open to relocating, these blocks capture their career goals and interests to assist managers and HR in career planning for the employee.

Finally, this section also documents any special assignments, roles, or projects the employee has participated in that aren't directly tied to their role but are relevant to their experience and development. This information can be captured in the following standard blocks:

- **Formal Education**
- **Career Goals**
- **Geographic Mobility**
- **Special Assignments/Projects**
- **Certificates/Licenses**
- **Courses/Continuing Education**

Talent Information

The **Talent Information** block, shown in Figure 3.18, captures data that can be used as flags and icons on the Succession Org Chart. Talent flags like the following are determined by each customer during implementation:

- **Risk of Loss**
- **Impact of Loss**
- **Reason for Leaving**
- **Bench Strength**
- **Future Leader**
- **Key Position**

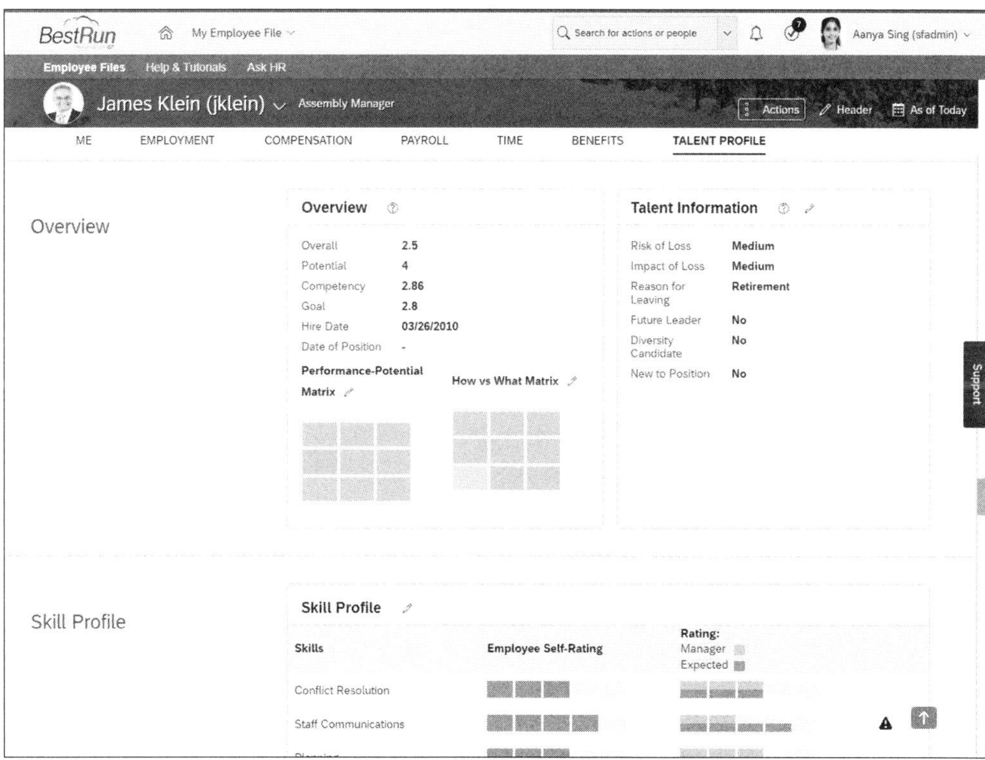

Figure 3.18 Talent Information Portlet

Skills Profile

The Skills Profile block lists skills of the employees and shows their self-rating and their manager's rating, as shown in Figure 3.18. You can click on each skill to see its description and the description of each of its proficiency levels.

By selecting the **Find other people with these skills** option, you can get a list of employees who have similar skills to the employee.

Competency and Objective

Companies can choose to use standard blocks that display an employee's competencies, objectives, and related ratings. This information may be relevant and helpful during the talent review and succession planning process by providing ready access to how employees are developing and performing against their core and job-specific competencies. Easy access to the **Competencies** and **Objective** blocks prevents managers and talent planners from navigating away from the Talent Profile to the **Reports** tab or pulling up the employee's past performance reviews to get this data; these are shown in Figure 3.19.

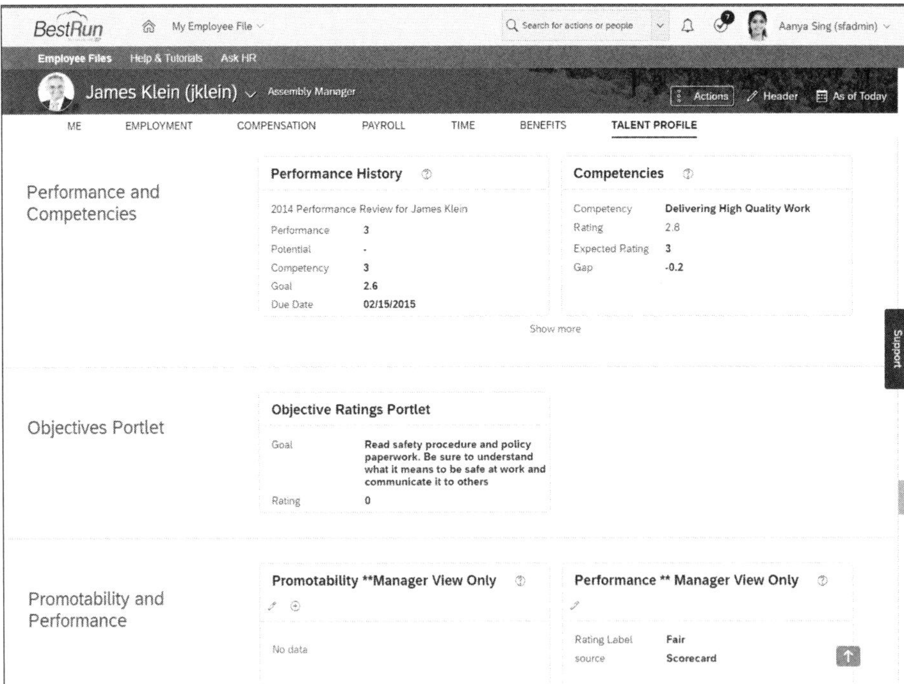

Figure 3.19 Competency and Objective Blocks

The **How vs. What Historical Matrix Grid Placement Trend** block (not shown) is a nine-box grid that displays competencies versus objectives, much in a similar way to the more well-known performance versus potential nine-box grid.

Performance and Potential

Several blocks are available to display current and historical performance and potential rating information (see Figure 3.20). These include:

- **Performance History**
- **Goal Ratings**
- **Performance **Manager View Only**
- **Potential **Manager View Only**
- **Promotability **Manager View Only**
- **Performance-Potential Historical Matrix Grid Placement Trend**

The blocks are not available to employees. These are intended to store historical performance/potential ratings relevant to succession planning and career development planning, and are an input into the **Overall** rating in the **Overview** block. These two blocks can be permissioned so that managers or custom managers can add both performance and potential scores directly during the succession planning process.

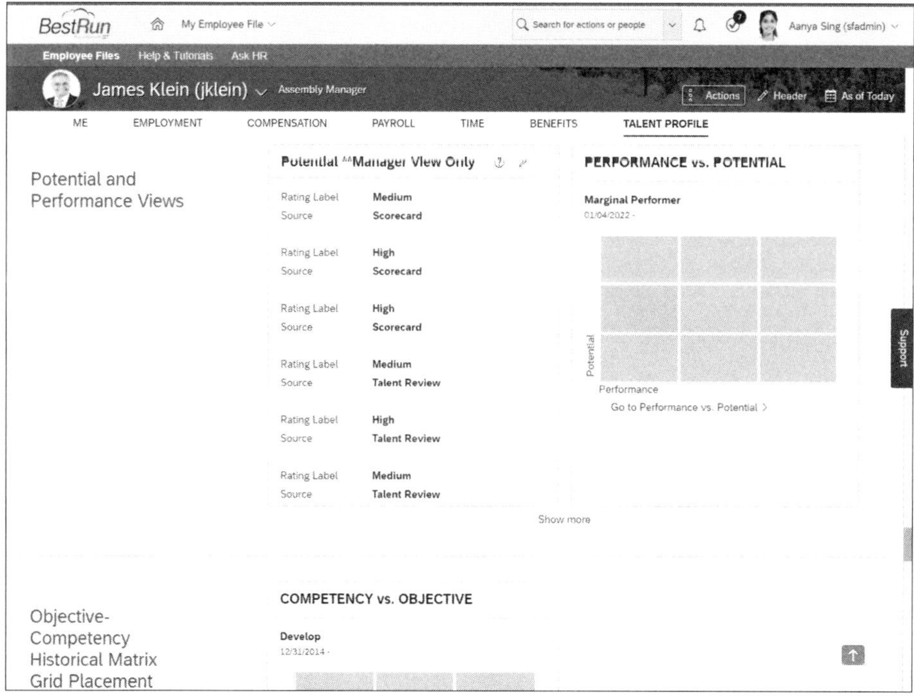

Figure 3.20 Potential **Manager View Only Block

Succession Planning

Succession planning data is typically considered highly confidential and is not made available for viewing to a wide population. Whether you wish to go down this route or not is a configuration decision that is made according to the company's process and data requirements, but the system allows a great amount of flexibility and a granular level of security through RBP and adding permissions to data and background elements in the Succession data model. Your implementation consultant will help guide you through considerations for making these critical configuration decisions.

There are two core succession planning blocks that are used by managers (not taking into account those mentioned in the previous sections of this chapter):

- **Successor Portlet**
- **Nomination Portlet**

The **Successor Portlet** block displays successors assigned to the employee's position, while the **Nomination Portlet** block displays positions to which the employee has been nominated as a successor and any talent pools the employee has been nominated to. Managers can add new nominations directly in these blocks. Both blocks can be seen in Figure 3.21.

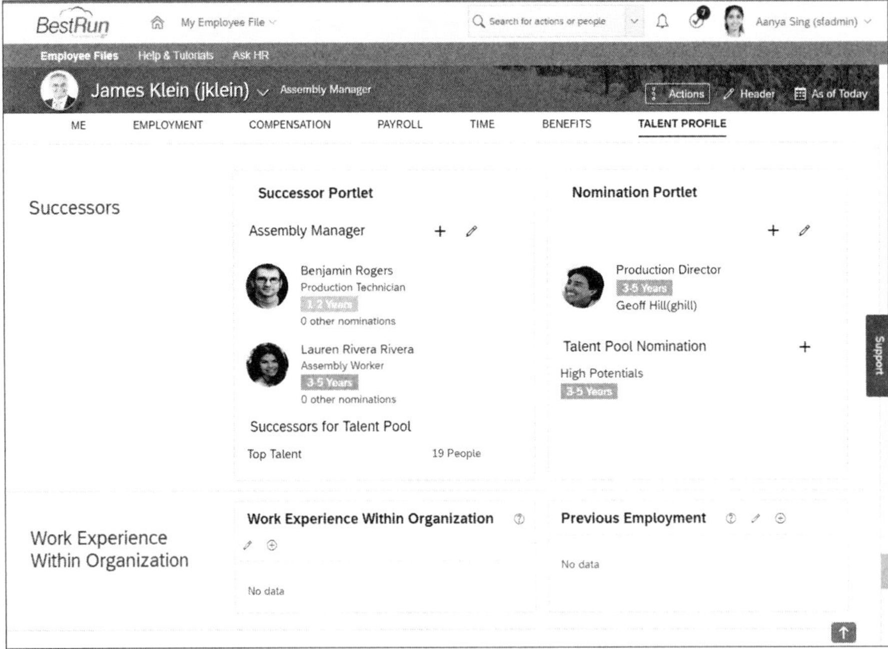

Figure 3.21 The Successor Portlet and Nomination Portlet

Miscellaneous

Companies are able to gather data around outside training and certifications that employees have obtained, as well as languages spoken. An employee's professional memberships, honors, and community involvement can also be documented in various blocks. This information can also be critical to the talent and development processes because it underscores the qualifications employees have for future positions and other roles within the company. This information can be documented in the following blocks:

- **Language Skills**
- **Memberships**
- **Awards**
- **Community/Volunteer Involvement**

> **Note**
>
> While all of the blocks (and more) that we've discussed so far in this chapter are available for use, it is important to keep in mind that you don't need to use all of them. You can decide which blocks to deploy while implementing People Profile. These can be used as is, modified at the field level per requirements, or custom configured by your implementation consultant. Also, the People Profile can be edited in the Admin Center, so companies have the option to add or remove blocks at any time.

Badges

The People Profile allows you to give employees badges, which are used to recognize colleagues' achievements and efforts. Badges allow employees and managers to recognize each other outside of the normal performance and compensation management processes, which are often private. Badges are meant to be awarded by others; employees cannot award badges to themselves.

Badges are selected from by using the **Give a badge** button in the **Badges** block on the employee's profile. You can also define custom badges that reflect your company values and branding. Administrative users can control the use of badges by enabling or disabling default badges and custom badges or localizing badge names in Admin Center. Figure 3.22 provides an example of the **Badges** block displaying one of the default badges. Permissions for viewing badges have the same configuration and behavior as other data elements, and are governed by the RBP model created in the instance and permissions defined in the Succession data model.

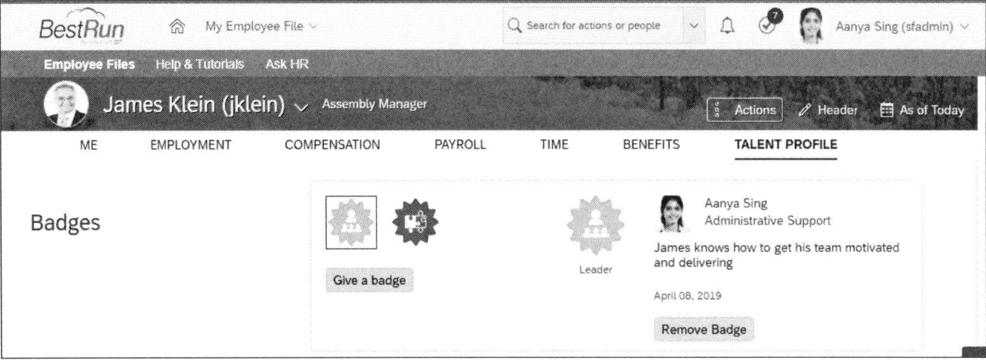

Figure 3.22 Badges Background Element

Permissions for adding or deleting badges have the same configuration and behavior as the edit permissions for any other data elements, except that you must be the creator or recipient of a badge to delete it—that is, employees cannot delete other employees' badges at will. Editing of existing badges isn't supported.

Tags

Tags provide a way for users to self-identify group affiliation such as professional associations/organizations and community activity groups, both internally and externally. You are able to see all employees who have selected certain tags and leverage the system to stay connected to those in the tag group. Unlike badges, users can add tags to their own profile to identify with groups or interests within the organization with which they want to be affiliated. Tags can also be assigned by other users.

Because tags are displayed on the **Company Info** page when you are searching the directory and on the People Profile, you can more easily find other employees who share the same tags, thereby increasing company cohesiveness and fostering a greater sense of community and collaboration.

Tags are enabled by adding the **Tags** block to the People Profile.

Notes

The **Notes** block enables you to add notes about an employee. Notes can be created, edited, and deleted, and can also be shared with other users (including the subject of the note themselves). By default, the employee who is the subject of the note cannot see it unless it is shared with them.

Facebook

Facebook integration allows you to easily look up an employee in the Facebook application. You can click the **Facebook** icon to search for all users on Facebook with the same first and last name as the employee that you are looking for. If you sign up as a Facebook user and accept the Facebook cookie, you experience seamless integration between SAP SuccessFactors and Facebook.

LinkedIn

LinkedIn integration allows you to easily look up an employee on the LinkedIn application. You can click the **LinkedIn** link to search for all users at *http://www.LinkedIn.com* with the same first and last name as the employee that you are looking for.

3.11.2 Configuring the People Profile

The beauty of People Profile and all of its components is that it's highly configurable directly from the Admin Center interface, putting the control in the hands of the customer. After the requisite data and background elements are configured in the Succession data model, the customer may add, remove, and reorder the blocks on the People Profile. This can be seen in Figure 3.23.

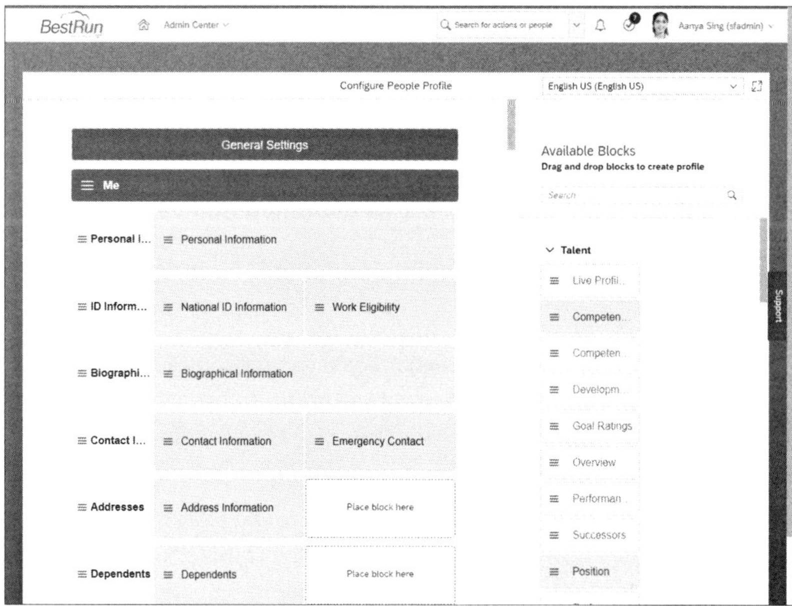

Figure 3.23 Configuring the People Profile

Any system administrator with the appropriate permission may choose to configure the People Profile directly from the Admin Center page by clicking **Configure People Profile**. Any changes made to the People Profile are effective immediately upon saving the changes, so it's critical that this administrative privilege not be widely dispersed and that care be taken to make changes that don't impact users during business hours.

Changes to the People Profile are easy to make. There are several actions an administrator can perform when configuring the People Profile:

- Configure general settings
- Add new section
- Configure sections
- Add, reorder, or remove blocks
- Configure blocks
- Add custom generic objects as blocks

General settings for the People Profile can be changed by clicking on **General Settings** at the top of the screen. This enables configuration of the following:

- People Profile header fields (which fields to show)
- Whether to allow employees to edit the background image
- Background image library
- Whether to allow employees to record the pronunciation of their name
- Whether to allow employees to record an "about me" video
- Whether to allow employees to enter introductory text
- Whether to show the completion percentage of the People Profile
- The name format to use
- Talent data date range to use
- Talent data source processes

Blocks can be grouped in sections. In the **General Settings**, you can modify an existing section to set whether it is shown on the People Profile and changing the name (in each language available in the system).

Blocks can be added, reordered, or removed in each section, and blocks can be moved between sections. This is all done by dragging and dropping blocks, either from within a section or from the list of available blocks on the right side of the screen. Depending on the block, selecting it allows you to make some changes to the block.

All blocks are predelivered, aside from the Live Profile MDF Information block. By using the Live Profile MDF Information block, you can add a generic object as a block in a section of the people profile.

3.12 Company Info

The **Company Info** application provides employees with the ability to access organizational information, such as the Org Chart, directory, and general help and resources. We will cover each of these in the next few sections.

3.12.1 Org Chart

The Org Chart is a central component of the platform and variants form a core component of succession planning and Position Management. The Org Chart enables users to have a visual view of the organization's reporting structure and shows a manager their direct and indirect reports, as shown in Figure 3.24. It is accessed by selecting **Company Info** in the navigation menu. Some basic configuration can be performed in Admin Center via **Org Chart Configuration** under **Company Settings**.

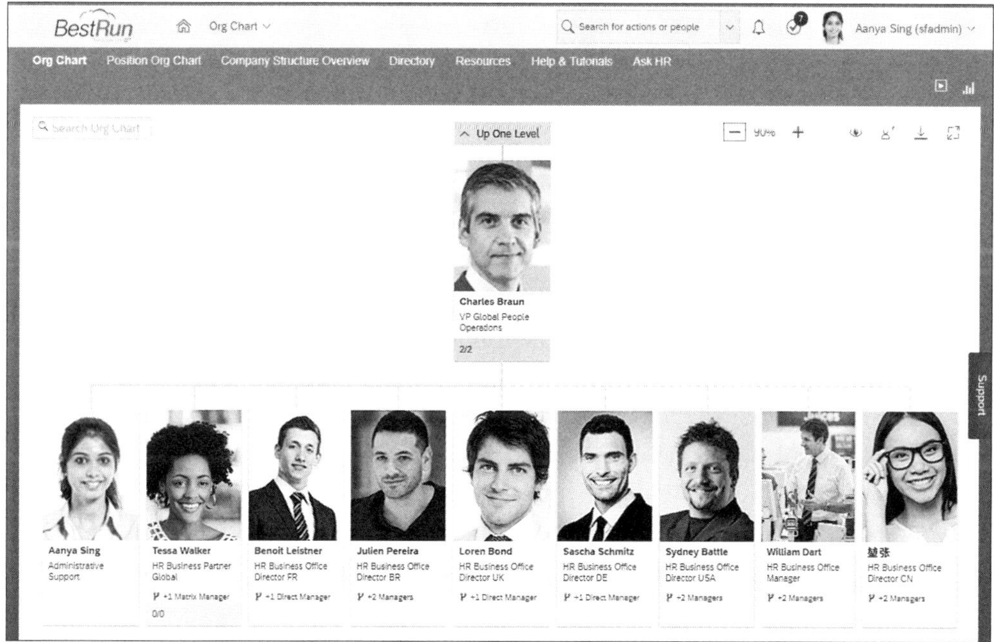

Figure 3.24 The Org Chart

When accessing the Org Chart, the user always sees their own team. They can view the team of another employee by searching for that employee in the **Search Org Chart** box, which can be seen in the top-left of the **Org Chart** screen in Figure 3.24. In the top-right of the **Org Chart** screen, the user can zoom in or out of the Org Chart, access options to display direct or matrix reports, toggle whether to see contingent workers (if Contingent Workforce Management in Employee Central is configured), add a new employee (if Employee Central is used and the user has the appropriate permissions), export the Org Chart, and hide the top navigation panel of the screen.

By clicking the box of an employee, users can access that employee's quickcard. If an employee has direct reports, a small section at the bottom of the box displays the number of direct and indirect reports. Clicking this expands the Org Chart to show the direct reports of that employee. In a similar location in the box of an employee, it will specify whether an employee has more than one employment.

Employees who have a matrix relationship show under their matrix manager with a dotted line. In Figure 3.24, you can see a dotted line to several employees.

Employees who have a concurrent employment, have a global assignment, or who are a contingent worker will have a colored bar across the box, indicating as such. You can see an example of these in Figure 3.24.

3.12.2 Position Org Chart

If you use Position Management in SAP SuccessFactors (see Chapter 4, Section 4.1.4), then you will be able to access the Position Org Chart—shown in Figure 3.25—by clicking **Position Org Chart**. This shows the position reporting relationships that are stored in SAP SuccessFactors.

From the Position Org Chart, it is possible to perform a number of actions, including viewing the incumbent history of a position, adding other positions, or, if enabled, launching requisitions in Recruiting. Each position shows the target full-time equivalent (FTE) and actual FTE, if configured. You can also toggle whether to see child positions, matrix positions, and/or inactive positions. Additionally, it is possible to create a position or to export the Position Org Chart.

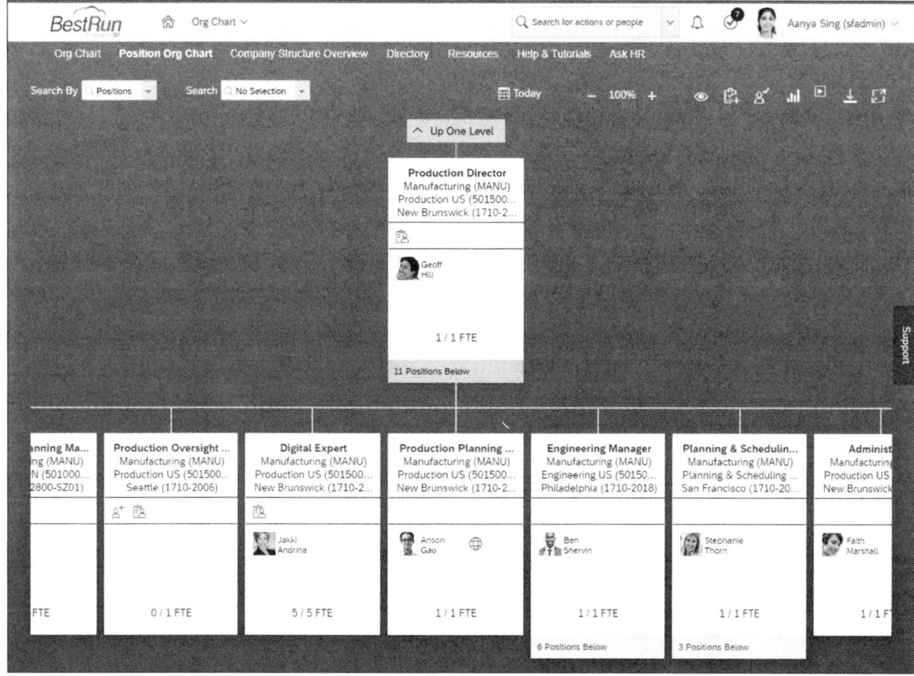

Figure 3.25 Position Org Chart

3.12.3 Company Structure Overview

The **Company Structure Overview** enables you to view the org structure based on the foundation objects configured in Employee Central, as shown in Figure 3.26. Typically, this would be made up of business units, division, and departments, but the objects you see would be based on your specific configuration.

Various **Company Structure** views can be configured to show different objects in the structure. These can be toggled between as needed.

Each object shows data on it, as configured in the **Company Structure** view. This can include several bits of information that can also be used by selecting an object, such as the following:

- Name
- Code
- Head of unit (where applicable)
- History of changes
- People in the hierarchy of the object
- Positions in the hierarchy of the object
- Details and number of entities in the hierarchy of the object

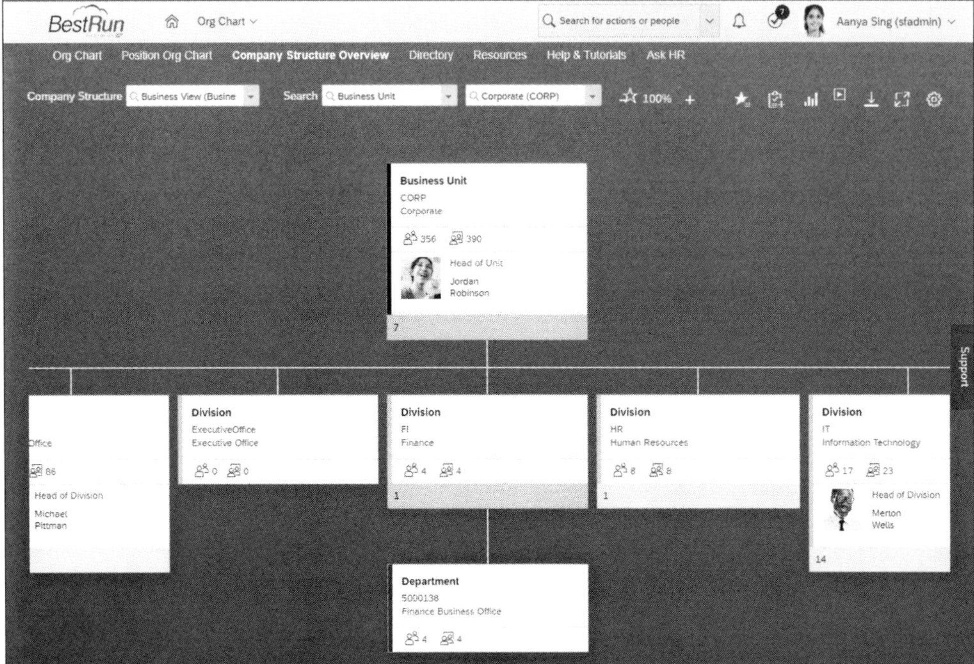

Figure 3.26 Company Structure Overview

Users can create favorite combinations of **Company Structure** views and starting objects, as well as zoom in or out, add entities, and export the structure to PDF.

While usually employed for viewing the org structure, it is also possible to use the **Company Structure Overview** to view hierarchies like the pay scale structure or a cost center hierarchy.

3.12.4 Directory

The directory is where employees can search for other employees. There are two different types of search: people search and skills search. The people search enables a free text or attribute-based search for employees. The skills search enables you to find employees by searching for skills. We'll look at both briefly.

People Search

A search can be performed by typing some or all of a name and executing the search. You will then see the results, which will be covered very shortly. When searching, there are also a variety of different options available to use to search for employees, including:

- First name, middle name, and last name
- Nickname
- Username
- Type of employee (manager, individual, or either)
- Division
- Department
- Location
- Person ID
- Tags
- Start date
- Include inactive employees or not

Figure 3.27 shows the people search in the directory.

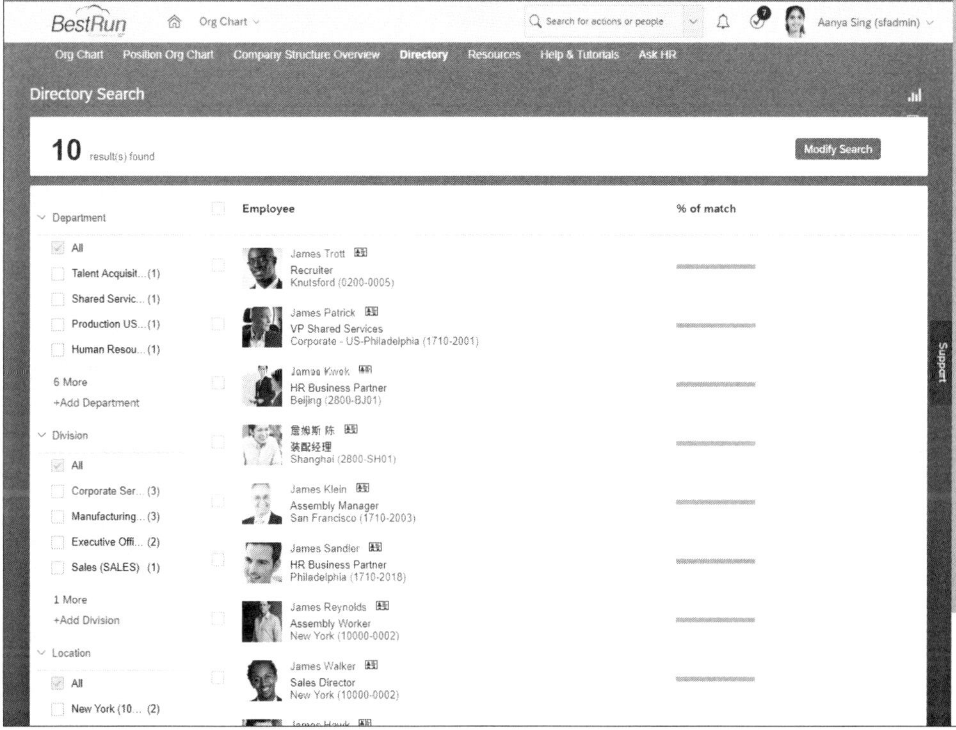

Figure 3.27 The Directory

The search results show all of the employees with a match percentage (e.g., what percentage the employee matches the search criteria). Results can be searched by division, department, or location.

Skills Search

The skills search enables you to search for skills and showing all employees that have one or more of those skills. When you start typing a skill's name in the search box, the system uses an autocomplete to enable you to select the skill to search for. Multiple skills can be searched on at one time. You are able to toggle whether to allow results for unrated skills.

The result shows the employee and all the skills assigned, with the searched skill(s) shown in bold (see Figure 3.28).

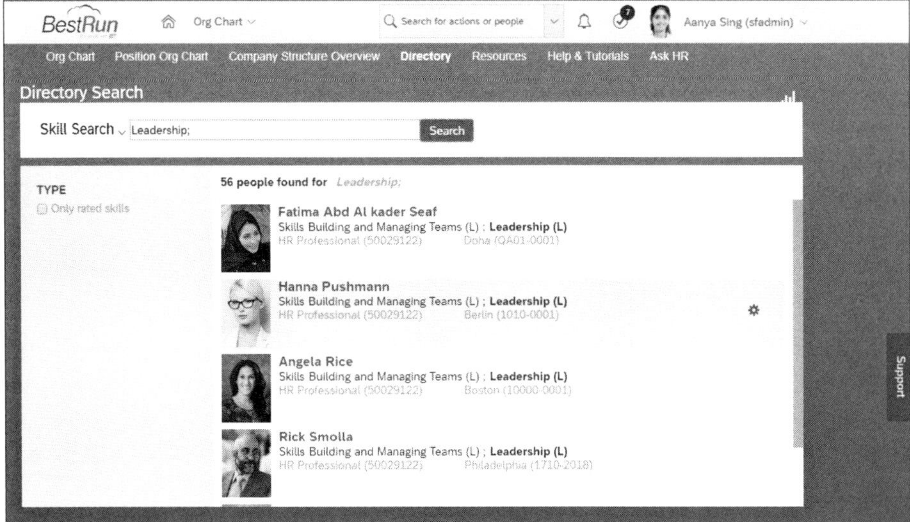

Figure 3.28 The Skills Search in the Directory

For each search result, you can either send an email to that employee or find similar employees.

3.12.5 Resources

The **Resources** page is where an organization can provide information and resources to its employees about the system and topics such as HR processes, guides, reference documents, and videos. The **Resources** page also features the **Directory Search** that is found on the **Directory** page. The **Resources** page is a configurable page and has the same editing options as when adding custom tiles, which we covered in Section 3.9.3. Company resources can be added in each of the languages enabled in the system.

3

3.13 Talent Card

The *talent card* is an overview of an employee's talent information from their profile, such as organizational information, badges, talent information, and work experience. It is highly configurable and is used within the Presentations application (which we'll cover in Section 3.15) and the Position Tile view in the Succession Org Chart. Only one talent card can exist per application. Figure 3.29 shows an example of a talent card on the far right side.

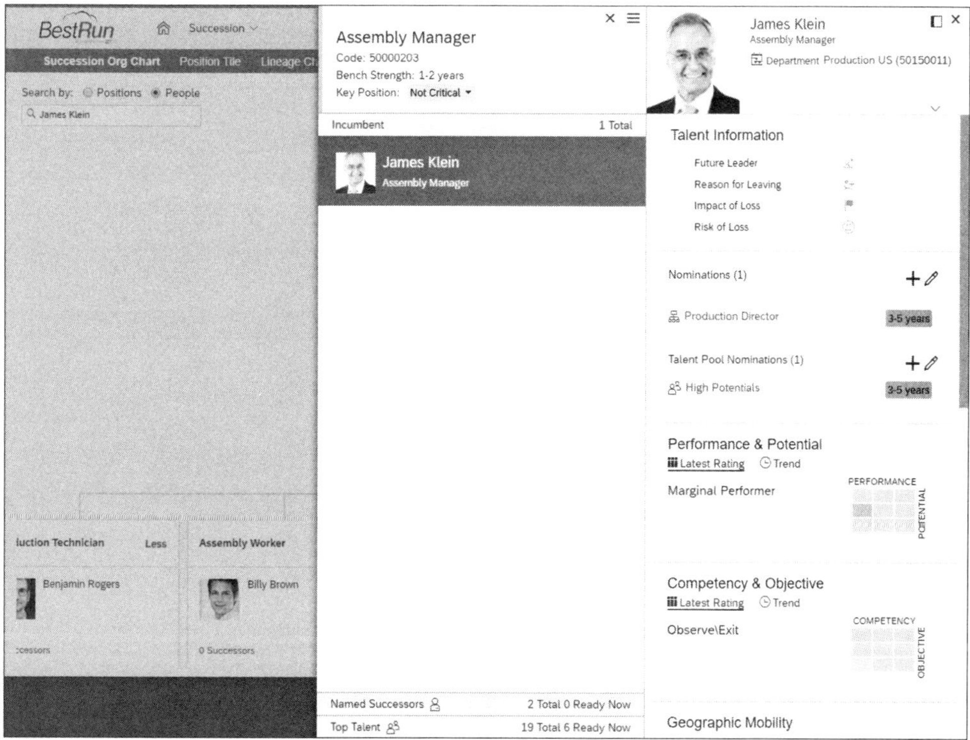

Figure 3.29 A Talent Card

Talent cards are configured in Admin Center, in **Manage Talent Cards**. Here, a blank talent card is provided with an overview prefilled. The overview is standard, but each field can be disabled, and the department field can be overridden with any piece of data from the UDF.

The main body of the talent card can be configured to include the following information:

- Internal work experience
- Previous work experience
- Education
- Performance and potential matrix
- Competency and objective matrix
- Badges
- Custom section

Five fields can be added to each section, and the available fields depend on what has been configured for the Employee Profile already.

3.14 Insights

Each application in SAP SuccessFactors has the Insights feature, which enables a selection of real-time analytics to be displayed that pertain to the application you are using. You do not need to use SAP SuccessFactors Workforce Analytics to leverage the power of Insights. These analytics—called *tiles*—can be accessed by selecting the **Insights** icon to the top right of the screen you are on. Figure 3.30 shows an example of Insights being displayed for the Succession module.

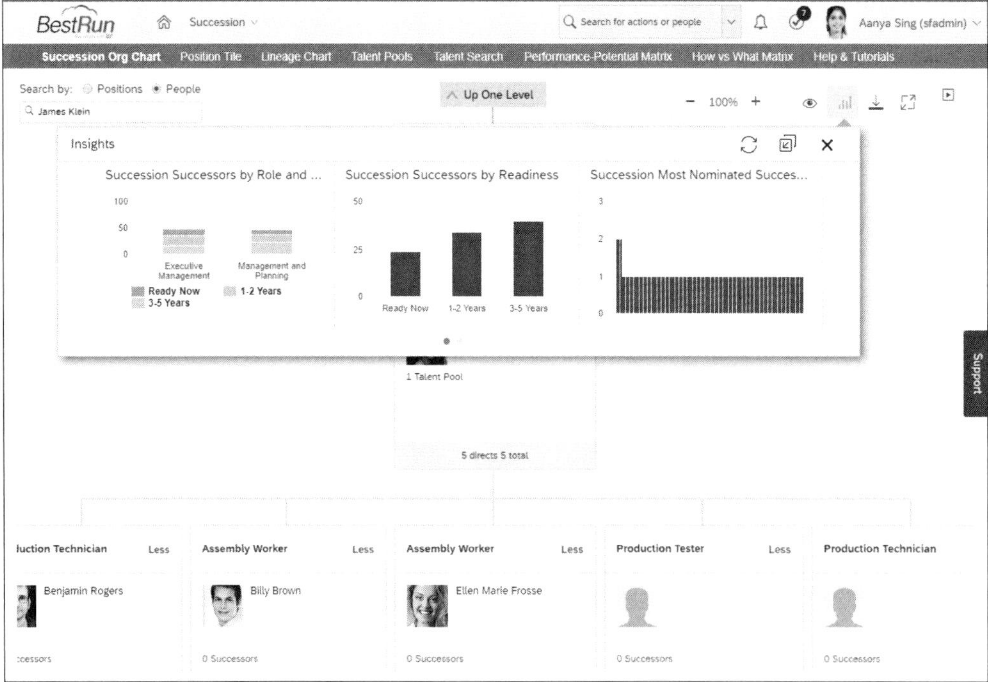

Figure 3.30 Insights for the Succession Module

The different analytics are shown horizontally, although when viewing Insights, you can switch them to be viewed vertically. You can also "undock" the Insights, which means you can move them to another area of the screen than the default location where they pop up.

Insights are configured in **Manage Insights** in the Admin Center. Insights can be turned on or off for each application, and which tiles you want to display can be managed. Each application has more than 50 different tiles available to choose from. In theory you can add all available tiles, but naturally this would not make it easy to view the key analytics for each module.

3.15 Presentations

Presentations is an application designed for quickly producing interactive talent review presentations that can be used in a variety of meetings. Typically, a significant amount of time is spent creating meeting presentations and compiling data and visuals for them. With Presentations, this can be done in an hour or so by uploading a Microsoft PowerPoint template to SAP SuccessFactors and adding a variety of different types of dynamic content that is both interactive and displayed in real time. Because the dynamic content and data come directly from the system, they are already prepared and ready to be used in a meeting.

Presentations can be used to support a number of use cases, particularly talent review meetings. However, they can also be used for compensation reviews, succession planning, and recruiting talent pool reviews.

You access the Presentations application by selecting **Presentations** in the **Navigation** menu. This takes you the **Presentations** screen that is shown in Figure 3.31. Here, any existing presentations are displayed, as well as any that have been shared with the user. Each of these presentations can be run, edited, renamed, shared, moved to a new folder, or deleted as required.

Presentations can be put into folders, which you can create by clicking on the **+ Create New Folder** button on the left side of the screen (shown in Figure 3.31). Presentations themselves can be moved by clicking the icon of three dots on a presentation and selecting **Move To**.

A new presentation can be created by clicking the **+** button on the top right side of the screen (as shown in Figure 3.31). This opens a pop-up window for naming our new presentation, which appears on the **Talent Review Meeting** screen that is shown in Figure 3.32.

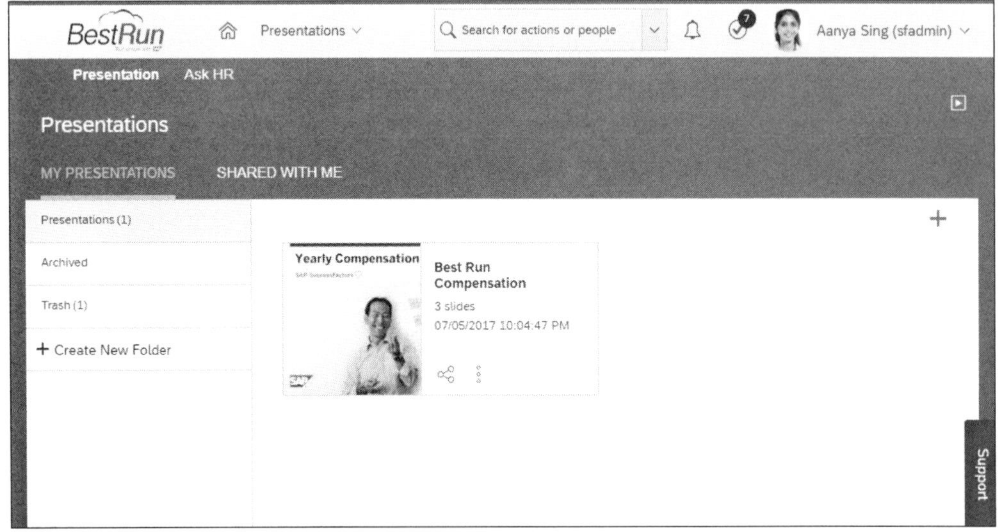

Figure 3.31 The Presentations Application

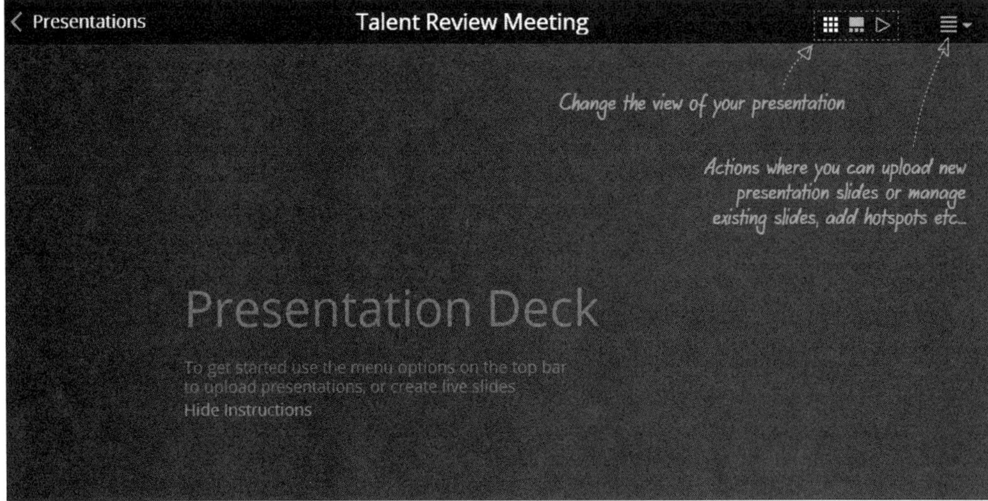

Figure 3.32 Talent Review Meeting Screen

The **Menu** button in the top-right corner of the screen is used to upload Microsoft PowerPoint slides, add a live slide of dynamic content, edit details of the presentation, or delete the presentation. Figure 3.33 shows the menu.

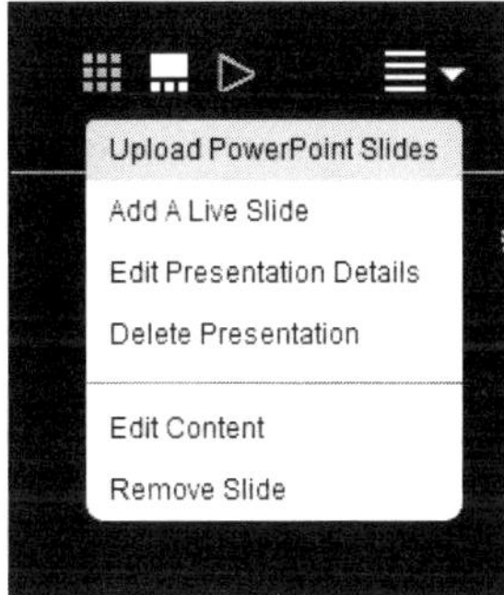

Figure 3.33 The Options Menu

Let's walk through the dynamic content available in the Presentations application, before taking a look at creating and running a presentation.

3.15.1 Dynamic Content

Different types of dynamic content can be added to a presentation by selecting the option **Add A Live Slide,** as shown in Figure 3.33. These options—which can be seen later in Figure 3.36—are:

- **Performance-Potential Matrix**: Adds a Performance-Potential Matrix slide for a definable team and date period
- **How vs. What Matrix**: Adds a How vs. What Matrix slide for a definable team and date period
- **Succession Org Chart**: Adds a Succession Org Chart showing a manager's direct reports, matrix reports, and their successors
- **Team View**: Adds a view of a manager's direct and matrix reports
- **Talent Pool**: Adds a list of one or more MDF-based talent pools
- **People Grid**: Adds a grid of grouped employees
- **Compensation Review**: Adds a compensation executive review template
- **Position Tile**: Adds a position tile
- **People Profile**: Adds the People Profile of an employee, team, or group of employees
- **Performance History**: Adds performance history of an employee, team, or group of employees
- **Analytics**: Adds analytics tiles (choose up to four tiles)

Each type of content reads data from SAP SuccessFactors in real time and can be inserted anywhere within the PowerPoint presentation that is uploaded to the system. Now that we've taken a look at the application and dynamic content, let's create a presentation to see how this might look.

3.15.2 Creating a Presentation

To create a presentation, we first need to upload a Microsoft PowerPoint presentation. This is done by selecting **Upload PowerPoint Slides** in the top-right menu—as shown in Figure 3.33—and uploading the file in the pop-up window. Once this is done, we see our presentation in the **Slide Holding Area** at the bottom of the **Talent Review Meeting** screen, which you can see in Figure 3.34.

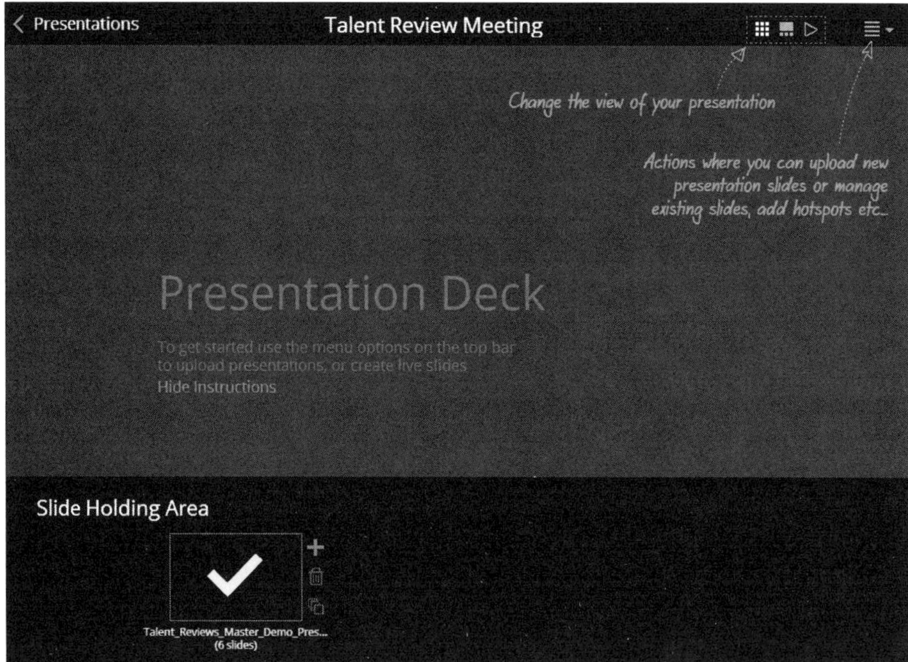

Figure 3.34 Slide Holding Area in the Talent Review Meeting Screen

Selecting the **Expand** button (the bottom of the three buttons on the right side of the presentation in the **Slide Holding Area**) shows a preview of all of the slides in a film strip-style view. Figure 3.35 shows the slides preview. This becomes useful when we begin to build the presentation later.

Now, we're going to add a live slide to the presentation. We do this by selecting the option **Add A Live Slide**. This shows us the different dynamic content options, which you can select for your slide, as shown in Figure 3.36.

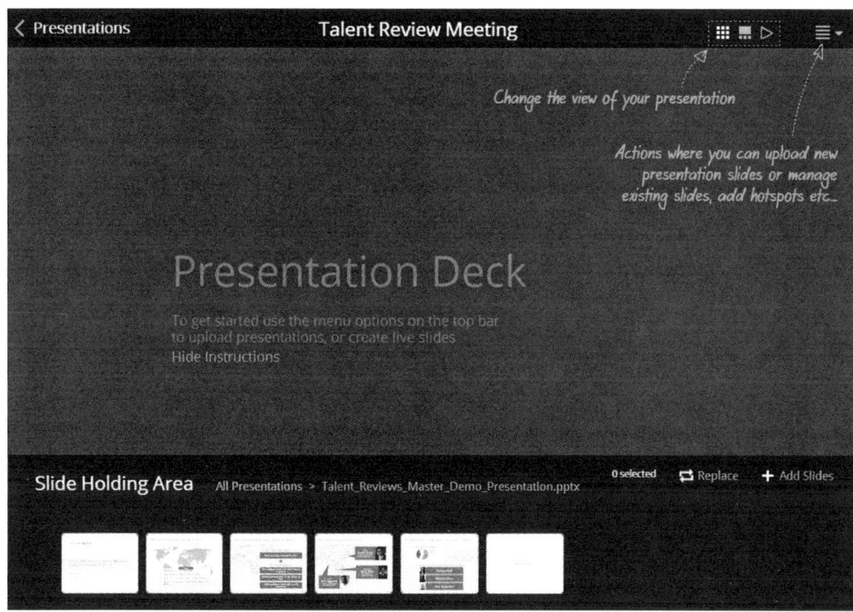

Figure 3.35 Presentation Slides Preview in Slide Holding Area

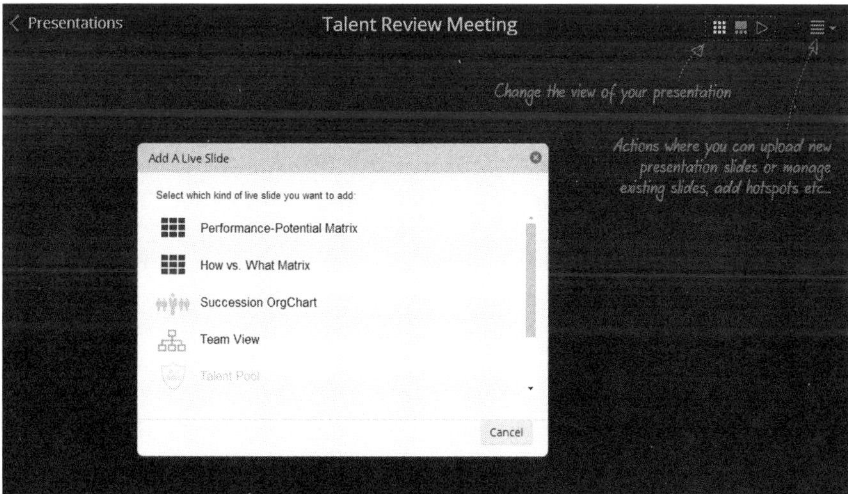

Figure 3.36 Dynamic Content Options for a Live Slide

Once the slide has been configured and we return to the **Talent Review Meeting** screen, we can now compile our presentation using the PowerPoint presentation that we uploaded earlier and our new live slide by dragging each of the PowerPoint slides from the **Slide Holding Area** into the main area where our live slide is.

Each slide can be previewed by selecting the **View Slide Timeline** button in the top-right of the screen (the middle of the three buttons located to the left of the options menu).

A feature for static slides (i.e., those slides from an uploaded PowerPoint presentation) is the ability to add *hotspots*. Hotspots allow part of a static slide to be linked to dynamic content, such as a talent card or an external link. These hotspots can then be selected during the actual presentation.

It is also possible to create a customized slide from your static slide deck. This is done by selecting the slide to use as a template, clicking the menu icon in the top-right corner, and selecting **Create Customized Slide**. Here you can drag and drop various fields available for an employee onto the slide. These fields will then be populated when the slide is run in the presentation.

Now, if we return to the main **Presentations** screen, we can see our presentation, along with a preview of the slides that we added, as shown in Figure 3.37.

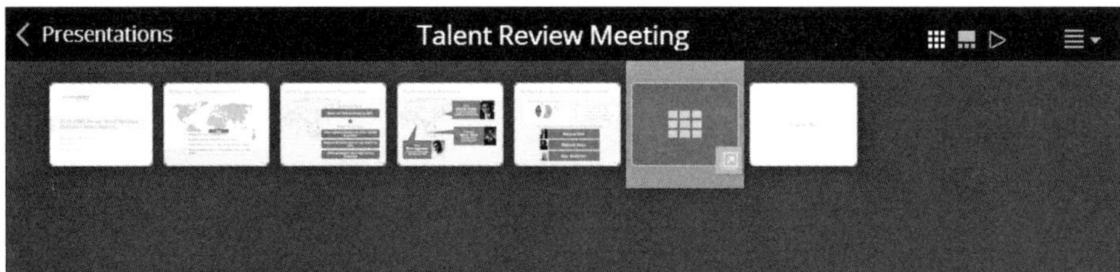

Figure 3.37 Our Presentation in the Presentations Application Screen

Created presentations can be shared with colleagues by using the **Share** button on the right side of the presentation. Once presentations are shared, the number of users that the presentation is shared with displays next to the **Share** icon. Now, let's take a look at conducting our presentation.

3.15.3 Running a Presentation

Presentations are conducted by selecting the presentation on the **Presentations** screen that we showed in Figure 3.31 and then selecting the **Start Presentation Mode** button in the top-right of the screen (the rightmost of the three buttons located to the left of the options menu). Now our presentation can begin, as we see in Figure 3.38.

During our presentation, it is possible to view the Talent Card for employees in a live slide by simply clicking them. Talent cards can also be opened for side-by-side comparison.

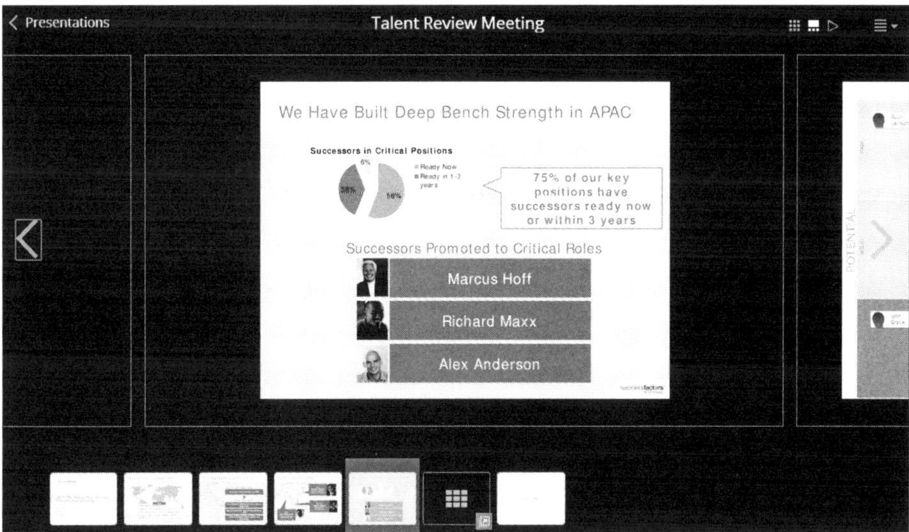

Figure 3.38 A Presentation in Action

3.16 Job Profile Builder

SAP SuccessFactors provides a framework for managing Job Profiles for using talent applications such as Performance & Goals, Succession & Development, and Recruiting. These Job Profiles allow the assignment of job families and job roles, which in turn are linked to job codes and competencies, as well as providing job descriptions and other related job content. Essentially, Job Profiles help organizations have the right person in the right job at the right time.

Job families are used to define job categories, such as sales or engineering, and contain a number of *job roles*. Each job role can have one or more associated job codes, which are used to map role-specific competencies to users for use in performance management, succession, and development.

As part of the Job Profile Builder, more than 13,000 industry-verified skills in more than 250 predefined job families are provided. Each job family comes with 4–7 job roles with skills premapped, each with five levels of proficiency. This is a significant amount of content and enables the use of skills to be almost instantaneous once the Job Profile Builder is used.

The Job Profile Builder enables administrators to build content repositories for the various types of content required for a Job Profile, as well as Job Profile templates that are used to provide robust formats from which to create the Job Profiles. The following content can be created and managed in the Job Profile Builder and used to build Job Profile templates:

- Families and roles
- Certifications
- Competencies
- Employment conditions
- Education (degree and major)
- Interview questions
- Job responsibilities
- Physical requirements
- Relevant industries
- Skills

Let's walk through some key processes associated with the Job Profile Builder.

3.16.1 Managing Job Profile Content

Job Profile content can be created in SAP SuccessFactors or imported into the system, both of which are performed in Admin Center. Job Profile content is created in **Manage Job Profile Content**, and data is imported or exported in **Manage Job Profile Contents Import/Export**. The date import/export uses the same engine as importing and exporting MDF data, and covers all types of Job Profile content.

Figure 3.39 shows the different content options that can be created in **Manage Job Profile Content**. The option **Set Up Families and Roles** lists all of the job families in the system and enables new job families to be created using the **Create Family** button or imported from the SAP SuccessFactors SuccessStore, using the **Add Families from SuccessStore** button, as shown in Figure 3.40.

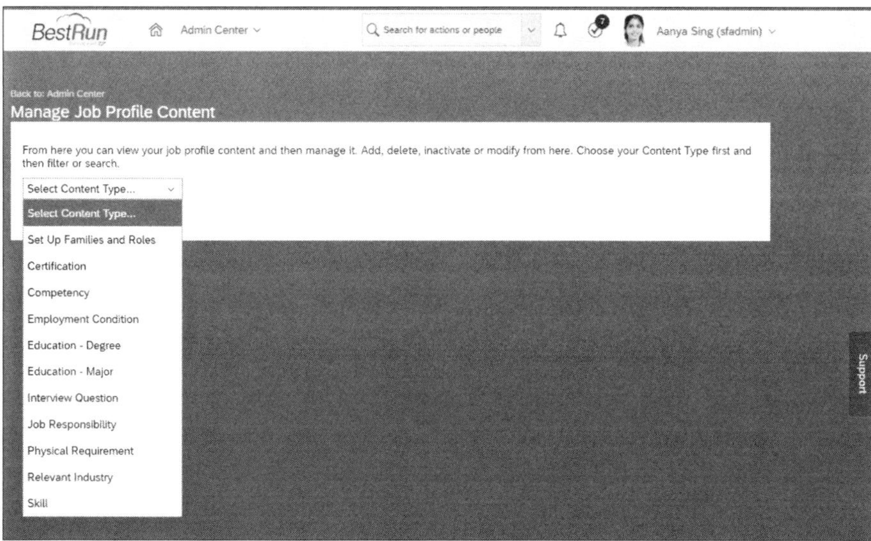

Figure 3.39 Manage Job Profile Content Screen

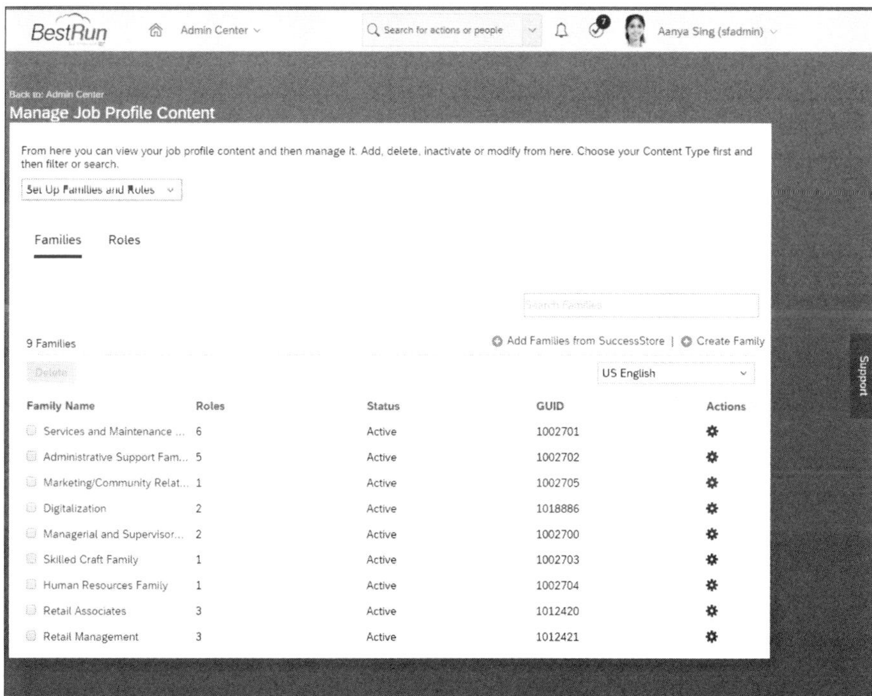

Figure 3.40 Job Families within Manage Job Profile Content

The two tabs at the top of the screen enable the user to switch between the **Families** (the default option) and the **Roles**. Switching to the **Roles** provides a list of all of the roles in the system, similar to the list of families. Roles can be created or imported from the SuccessStore in a similar fashion as the families can.

By clicking a **Family** or **Role,** the user can see more details about each object. Selecting a **Family** shows all of the roles associated with it. Similarly, **Skills** and **Competencies** assigned directly to the family can also be viewed by switching between the tabs.

Selecting a role within a family or within the **Roles** tab displays details about that role. Here, the user can view the family that the role is assigned to, as well as the mapped job codes, skills, competencies, and talent pools. Additional mappings can also be made here. Skills can be assigned with a proficiency level, while competencies can be mapped with a **Weight** and **Rating**.

Now that we've taken a brief look at families and roles, let's take a look at creating some job responsibility content. On the **Manage Job Profile Content** screen that we saw in Figure 3.39, we select **Job Responsibility** from the dropdown menu. We then see all of the job responsibility content listed, as well as options to filter the list and create new job responsibility content.

3.16.2 Creating Job Profile Templates

Job Profile templates define the structure and layout of the Job Profiles. They do not contain data on the Job Profile; rather, they have content types, specify the order of the sections, and define what sections are required and the formatting of Job Profiles, among other things. Companies may have one Job Profile template that is used for all Job Profiles, or they may create multiple Job Profile templates.

Job Profile templates are created and managed in Admin Center, in **Manage Job Profile Templates**. Here, you can manage existing templates or create new ones from a default template. Figure 3.41 shows some Job Profile templates in SAP SuccessFactors.

Job Profile templates are created in a two-step process by clicking **Create Template** on the Job Profile templates screen, which you can see in Figure 3.41. The first step is to define the name of the Job Profile templates and the job families to associate with it. The second step is where the template itself is designed.

Fourteen different types of sections can be added to the Job Profile template using the **Add Section** button. These fourteen types include all of the Job Profile content plus **Short Description**, **Long Description**, **Header**, and **Footer**. Sections can be added and deleted easily, reordered via drag and drop, individually formatted, set as required, set to show in a job requisition, and, if required, set to be viewable only by administrators. Figure 3.42 shows an example of a Job Profile template.

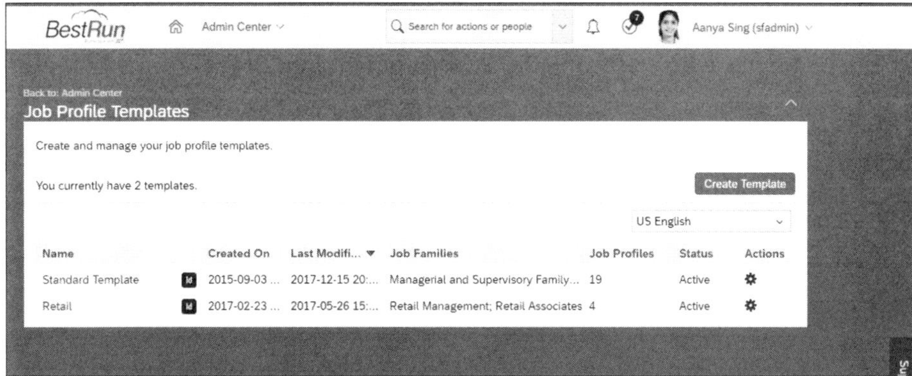

Figure 3.41 Job Profile Templates

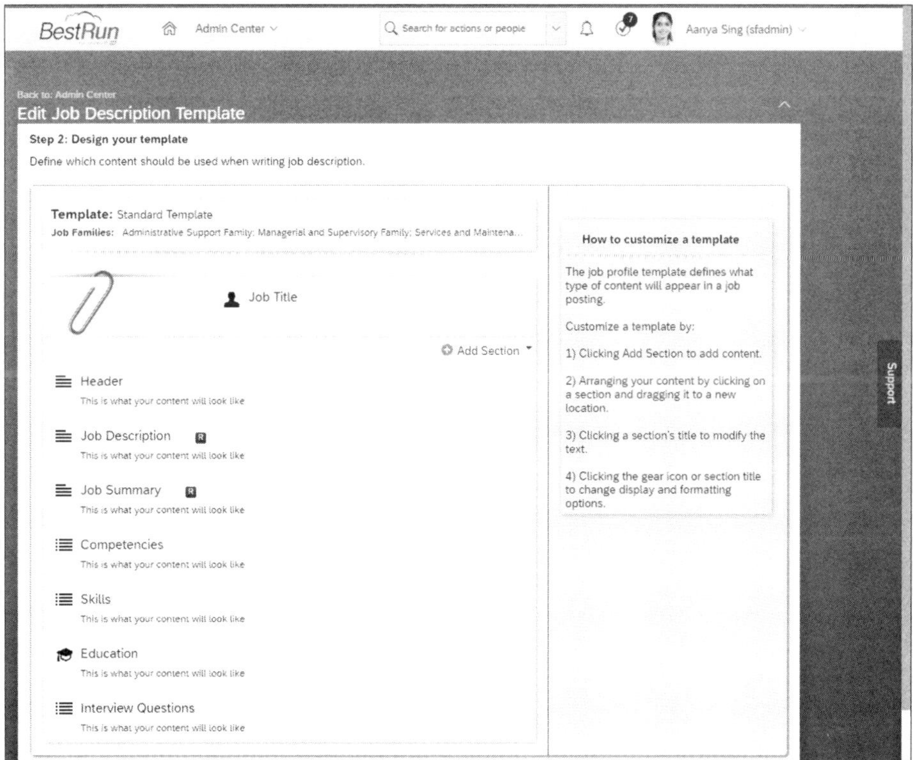

Figure 3.42 Designing a Job Profile Template

3.16.3 Creating Job Profiles

Once Job Profile templates have been defined, you are ready to create the Job Profiles in the Admin Center, in **Manage Job Profiles**. The first thing you'll see are all the existing Job Profiles within the system, similar to Figure 3.43.

Job Profiles can be searched and filtered, and clicking any Job Profile displays that Job Profile. Job Profiles also subject to an approval workflow can be viewed in the **In-workflow Job Profile** tab.

The first step of creating a Job Profile is to select the job family, role, and job position for which you want to create a Job Profile. Once these have been selected, click the **Next** button, and then the Job Profile template associated with the job family and role is displayed. Figure 3.44 shows the **Craft Workers Job Profile**.

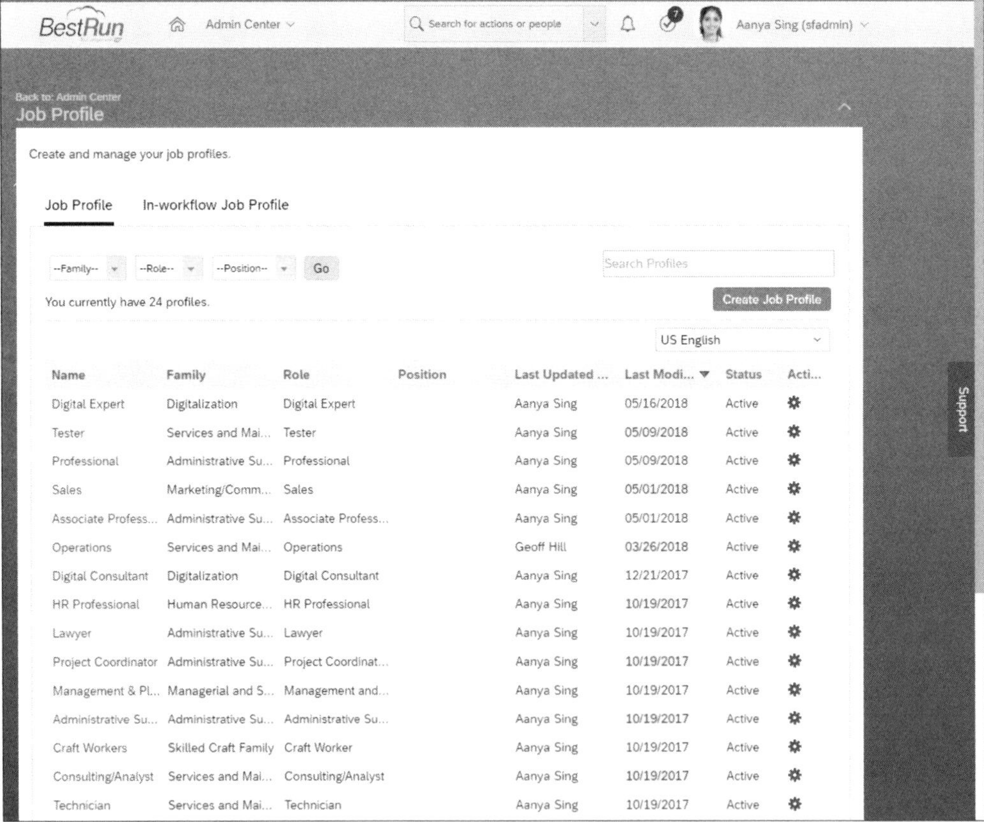

Figure 3.43 Job Profiles

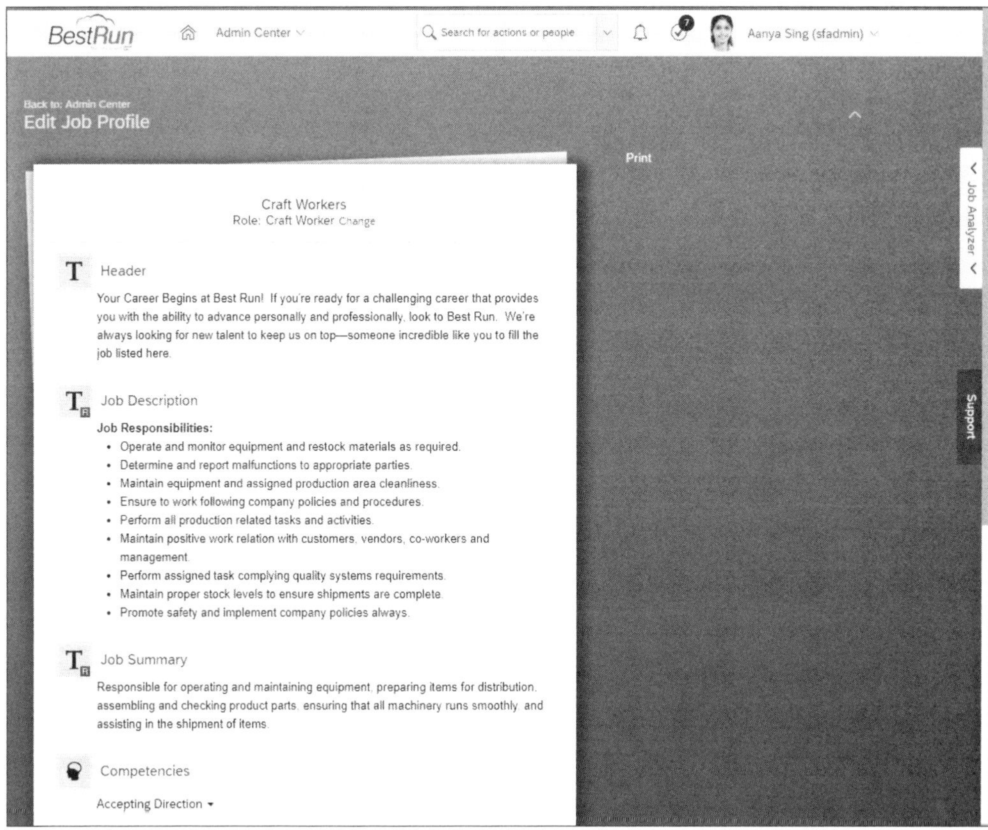

Figure 3.44 The Job Profile for Craft Workers

Job Profile content can be added either as free-form text or by selecting from the content libraries that we mentioned earlier in this section. Once we have added the appropriate content, our Job Profile is complete.

All Job Profiles are saved as drafts until they are made active, which is done by clicking the **Action** icon (the cog icon to the right side of the row of the Job Profile) of the Job Profile in the main **Job Profile** screen (see Figure 3.43) and clicking **Activate** in the menu. Draft Job Profiles are not visible to end users.

Job Profiles can also be created and edited via workflow, if this is enabled. Workflow enables a collaborative process of creating Job Profiles among several team members. If workflow is enabled, it is still possible to create Job Profiles in the Admin Center. However, if a Job Profile is then edited, it goes through workflow, even though it was initially created without workflow. When a Job Profile is created or edited in workflow, once approved, it immediately impacts all users in that role, regardless of whether the final approver is the manager or HR business partner of all the users. For this reason, it is important to think through who has access to create or edit Job Profiles.

3.17 Diversity and Inclusion

Diversity and Inclusion is part of SAP's Business Beyond Bias initiative to promote diversity, inclusion, and equality, and to provide fairness in everyday business processes for all employees, no matter their background, race, gender, sexuality, or physical or mental challenges. In order to help customers be able to break down barriers for all employees, SAP SuccessFactors has developed the Diversity and Inclusion functionality.

Diversity and Inclusion provides a range of functionality that touches many of the applications in the SAP SuccessFactors HCM Suite, such as hiring, Job Profiles, language input into assessment forms, salaries, and more. The aim of Diversity and Inclusion is to provide capabilities that guide the user to make fair actions and decisions and remove any unconscious bias from these actions and decisions.

We'll now take a look at a couple of areas where Diversity and Inclusion functionality helps achieve this.

3.17.1 Recruiting

For supporting recruiting processes, Diversity and Inclusion provides the Job Analyzer, which combines machine learning techniques job market data and text and number recognition to identify when language used in Recruiting and the Job Profile Builder may be unsuitable or when salary offers may not match the ideal market value.

The Job Analyzer is accessed when creating or editing a Job Profile in the Job Profile Builder or when creating a job requisition in Recruiting. Simply select **Job Analyzer** on the right side of the screen, as shown in Figure 3.45.

The Job Analyzer can then be run to highlight any language or salary discrepancies.

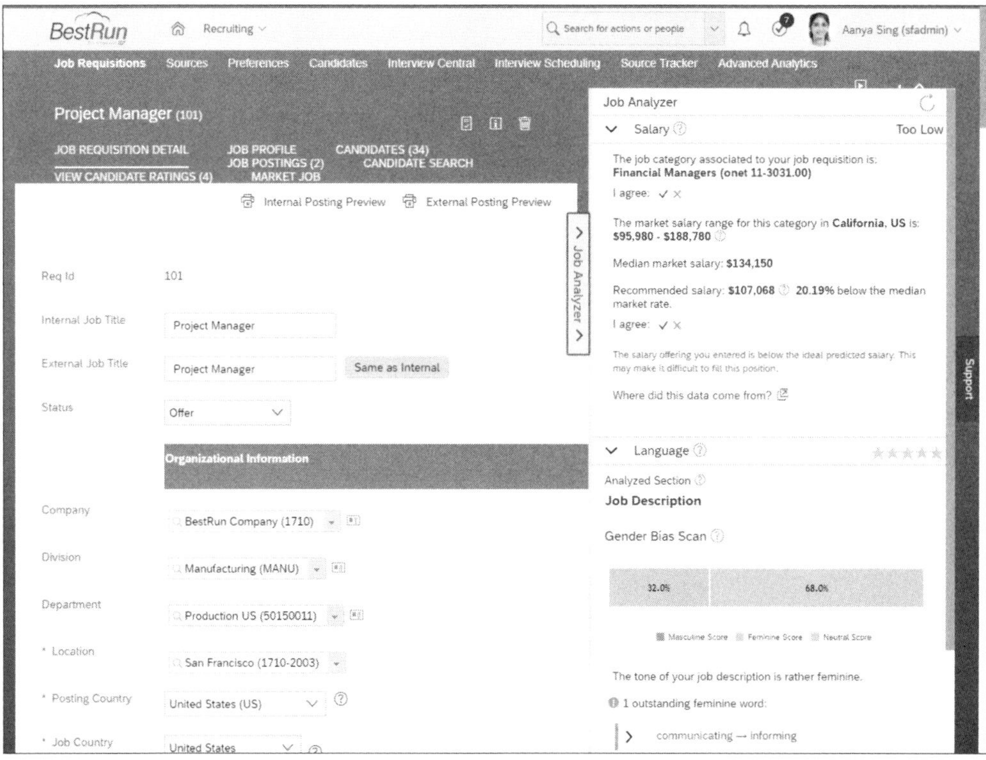

Figure 3.45 The Job Analyzer in a Job Requisition

Additionally, you can also proactively build your career site messaging in the Career Site Builder to be more diverse and inclusive.

3.17.2 Analytics

Although there isn't any specific functionality provided in the reporting and analytics applications (as of the time of writing, fall 2019), it's worth thinking about how you can leverage what is provided by SAP SuccessFactors to identify areas of improvement in your processes. For example, you can look at the gender of promotions or salary raises, or the percentage of applicants from specific ethnic background or disability areas.

3.18 Extensibility

Although SAP SuccessFactors is highly configurable, the focus of extensibility is extending beyond the standard configurability. Extensibility really is about creating new functionality where it does not exist in the system. There are three focus areas for Employee Central extensibility:

- MDF/Extension Center
- Business rules
- SAP Cloud Platform

We will discuss each in the following sections.

3.18.1 Metadata Framework

The MDF is an extensibility framework that allows users to create, modify, and maintain custom objects, screens, and business rules within the SAP SuccessFactors UI. Although it contains enough complexity to handle complicated requirements, it's also simple enough for customers to learn and use without needing outside expertise. The MDF requires no coding, because everything is created via the UI. The Extension Center is the UI frontend for the MDF, although MDF transactions are still available for technical users in the SAP SuccessFactors system.

The beauty of the MDF is that it enables customers to create objects without risking the safety and stability of their own and other customer instances within the data center. Because the MDF uses metadata to influence a central set of technical system components instead of creating new technical components, the system is safeguarded and future-proofed to enable quarterly releases to be installed without adversely affecting customer functionality or operation of their instances.

Custom objects created using the Extension Center are called *extensions*, although the underlying object is called a *generic object*. The standard enterprise subscription provides 25 generic objects for customer consumption. This figure does not include objects delivered by SAP SuccessFactors in quarterly releases. Only the top-level object counts within the limit of 25 objects. If there are child objects—for example, for country-specific fields or for detailed data—they are not considered against the overall count.

The MDF consists of a framework that uses metadata to allow easy creation and maintenance of objects using a generic set of components that are reused by all objects. As a result, nothing related to new objects or the enhancement of existing objects is hard-coded within the SAP SuccessFactors system, and no programming or coding is required—even for objects introduced by SAP SuccessFactors. In fact, it is easier for SAP SuccessFactors to introduce new objects and functionality into the system. Functionality such as Time Management, Job Profile Builder, Position Management, and support for GDPR are built on the MDF. The specialized nature and design of the MDF means that you can create multiple objects while retaining a high level of performance within the system.

The objects created in the MDF are called *generic objects*; they can be new objects, new screens for existing objects, new rules, or new fields—for example, an employee asset or a work center. A screen and a set of rules could also be configured through the MDF—for example, to support administration of a company car plan. Generic objects are easily configurable through the Admin Center interface without programming or editing XML files, although more complete MDF extensions can be created using the Extension Center (we'll touch on the Extension Center in Section 3.18.2). Some applications within the SAP SuccessFactors HCM Suite do not yet leverage the MDF, although SAP SuccessFactors aims to finish rolling this out across the entire SAP SuccessFactors HCM Suite in the future.

MDF offers some advantages as a way of customizing the standard delivered system beyond "simple" configuration:

- Reliance on technical or external assistance to add new objects or fields is no longer required.
- Stability and upgradability are maintained because standard objects and components are not changed.
- There is a consistency across objects, such as the look and feel of the UI, searching, and auditing.
- A minimal level of training is required to use MDF or Extension Center because it has an easy-to-use GUI, and it isn't necessary to understand the technical aspects.
- The performance of generic objects is superior to the performance of standard SAP SuccessFactors objects.
- The standard UIs delivered by SAP SuccessFactors are fully compatible with the MDF and can leverage generic objects.

Technical Aspects

Each object within the SAP SuccessFactors is made up of a number of components, including an API, controller, UI, workflow implementation, database table, set of Java services, and reporting integration. Each of these objects has its own instances of these components. Within the MDF, only one instance of each of the components exists; this single instance of each object is used for *all* generic objects. Through the definition and structure of the metadata, these generic components can operate without error, no matter how the objects are created and what metadata is used.

Because the components required for generic objects already exist, only their behavior needs to be configured. For example, the name of the fields, the field data type, and the rules used for validation must be configured. However, you don't need to take the UI, object controller, and database tables into consideration when configuring the object. This means that the overall complexity of creating new or extending existing objects in SAP SuccessFactors is reduced significantly through this framework.

The objects created in the MDF are also automatically exposed via the OData APIs, so they can be integrated with other systems, such as an ERP system or other HCM. As a result, data can be replicated to or from generic objects through API-based integration. Import templates for new objects are automatically generated.

Generic Object Definitions

Generic object definitions are created in Admin Center, in **Configure Object Definitions**. When creating an extension in Extension Center, a generic object is automatically created.

Generic objects definitions have a number of fixed attributes that must be defined during creation; some are mandatory, and others are optional. In addition to these attributes, up to 200 custom fields can be configured for each generic object. A number of attributes are required for each generic object, including the object code and whether it is effective-dated. Optional attributes include label, workflow configuration, whether data should be displayed before or after a workflow has been approved, the to-do category to use for workflow, whether the generic object is visible to the API, and additional fields. Labels can be maintained in multiple languages for systems that have more than one language enabled. These can be seen in Figure 3.46.

Standard fields exist for a generic object, including the code and name. If the object is effective-dated, a **Start Date** field is added to the definition. A number of fields are automatically assigned by the system once a generic object is saved.

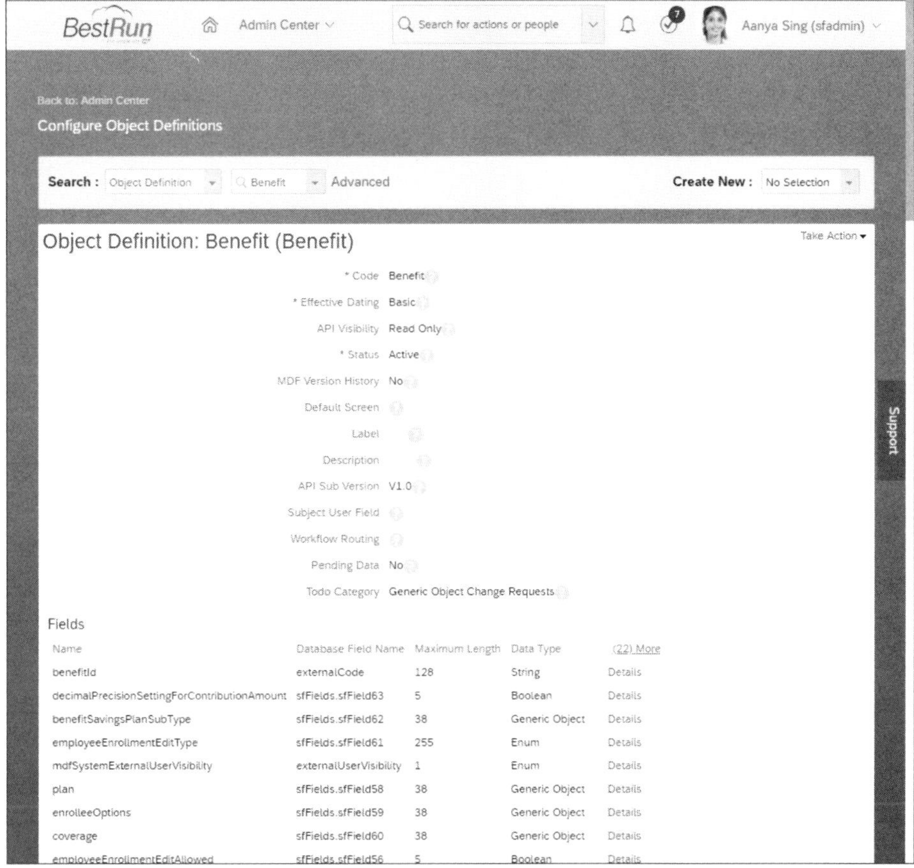

Figure 3.46 Creating a Generic Object Definition

Like standard objects and foundation objects, generic objects can have associations assigned to them. Associations designate a relationship with another object and define attributes of these relationships. Associations have several attributes that can be configured, including:

- **Type**
  - Composite (the associated object can exist only as a child of the object)
  - Valid when (valid with or without the existence of the associated object)
- **Multiplicity**
  - One-to-one (one object can be related to only one object)
  - One-to-many (one object can be related to many objects)

- **Required**
  - Yes (at least one child record is required)
  - No
- **Visibility**
  - Editable (users can view, add, edit, or delete child records)
  - Not visible (users cannot see the child records)
  - Read only (users can only view the child records)

Each generic object can have searchable fields assigned, just as standard objects do. As the term suggests, these are fields of the object that can be searched upon.

Once a generic object has been created, data for the object is maintained in the Admin Center, in **Manage Data**, as shown in Figure 3.47.

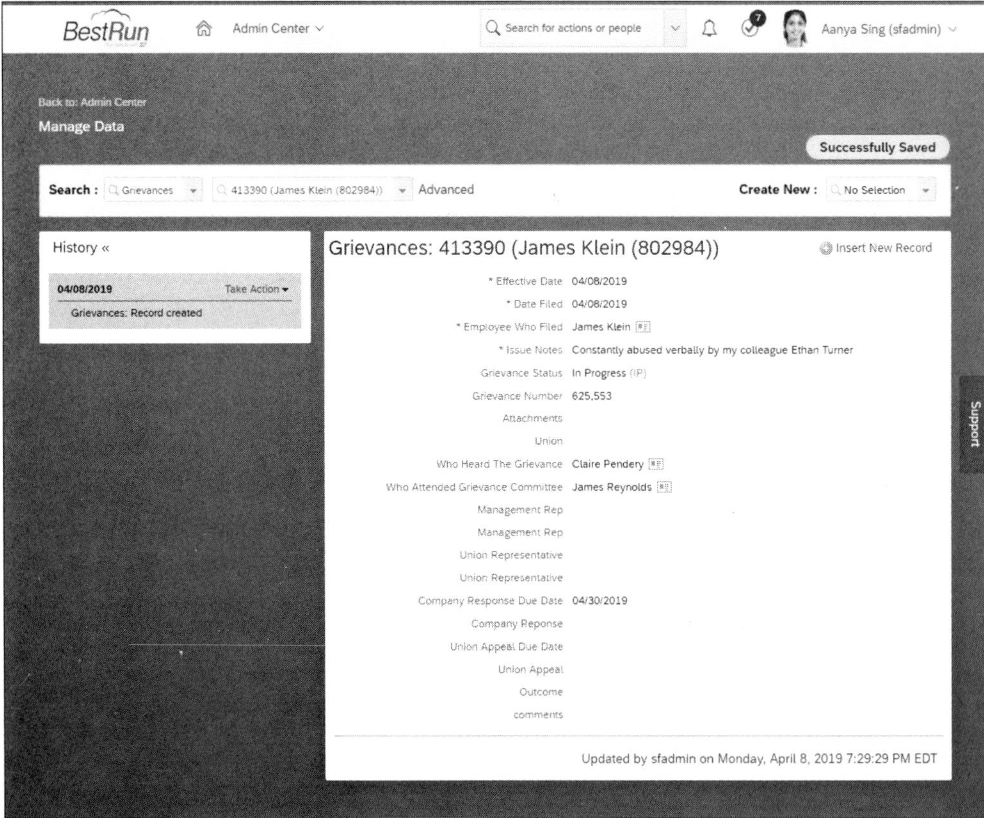

Figure 3.47 Data Record for a Generic Object in Manage Data

Configuration UIs

A configuration UI enables a generic object definition to be configured and formatted for display to employees in the People Profile, so that data can be viewed and maintained as part of an employee's profile. An example of this—**Grievances**—is shown in Figure 3.48.

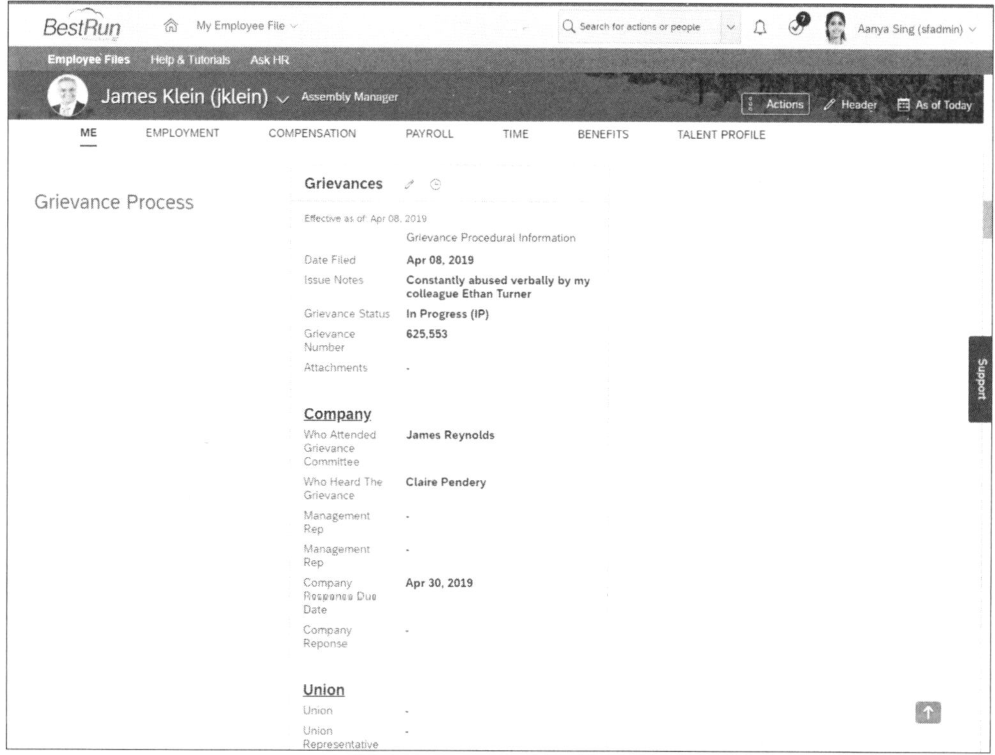

Figure 3.48 A Configuration UI in the People Profile

Because the self-service user experience is important, the layout of the generic object fields that you wish to display for employees—and how you want to display those fields—may differ from the layout and configuration of the object definition that was created. Configuration UIs present a variety of options to enable a flexible object layout when displayed in the Employee Central UI. It also means data can be maintained without needing access to the Admin Center.

Configurable UIs are configured in the Admin Center in **Manage Configuration UI** or in the Extension Center under a newly created or existing extension. The Manage

Configuration UI designer is a what-you-see-is-what-you-get (WYSIWYG), drag-and-drop UI editor that lets users style the UI for a generic object exactly as they require.

By default, the designer creates the UI layout with the same design as in the **Manage Data** screen. The user can then modify this screen as required by moving fields, changing the layout of the fields, adding new fields, hiding fields, and adding rules that only trigger when the object is maintained in self-service (e.g., by an employee and/or a manager). Groups of fields (called *groups*) can also be added to separate a group of fields with its own header. Groups can be assigned titles, have borders, and be collapsible. Figure 3.49 shows a new UI being created in the designer.

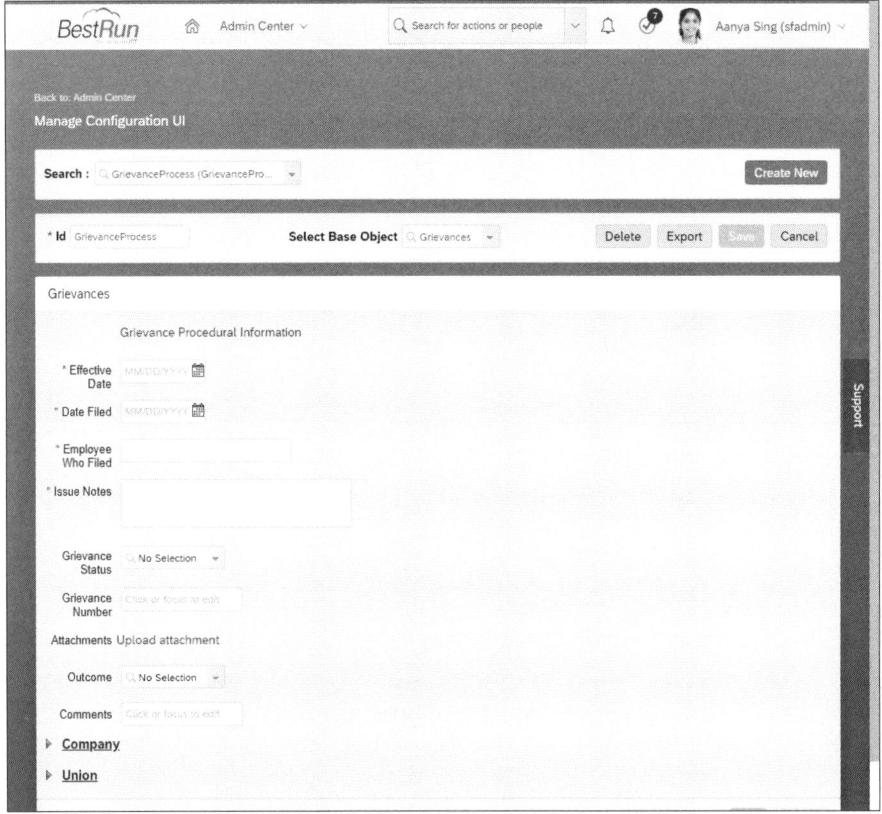

Figure 3.49 Manage Configuration UI Screen

Once a configuration UI has been created and you have permissioned your extension, your extension is ready to be added to the People Profile. This is performed in the Admin Center in **Configure People Profile**.

To do this, drag the **Live Profile MDF Information** block from the list of available blocks to the section where you want the block. In the right window, select the configuration UI you just created and click **Save** at the bottom of the screen. Figure 3.50 shows how this should look.

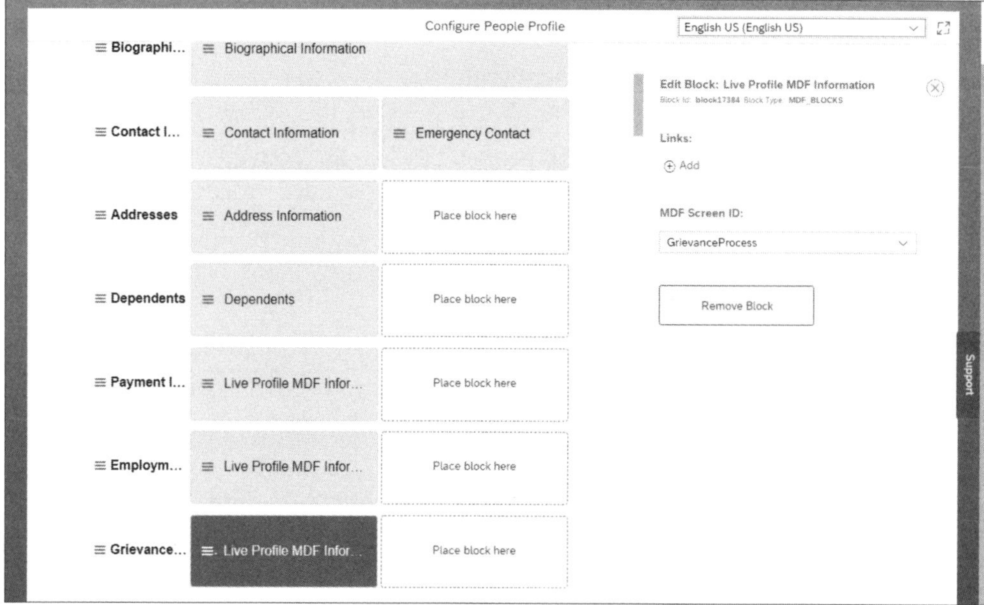

Figure 3.50 Live Profile MDF Information Block

MDF Picklists

MDF picklists are similar to but configured slightly differently from standard picklists. You create them in the Picklist Center within the Admin Center. MDF picklists must be created before they can be assigned to generic object fields.

We'll cover administering picklists in Chapter 17, Section 17.9.

Data Import and Export

Through **Import and Export Data**, in the Admin Center, it is possible to import or export generic object data, including generic object definitions and business rule definitions. You can also import and export data stored in generic objects. Blank template files can be downloaded to populate with data to be uploaded.

You can also download SuccessStore objects in **Import and Export Data**.

3.18.2 Extension Center

The Extension Center reduces a large proportion of the technical aspects required to create new objects and processes in the SAP SuccessFactors system and puts control in the hands of business users and system administrators. The possibility to extend the SAP SuccessFactors system is no longer reliant on technical consultants or deep knowledge of complex structures or procedures; now, customers can benefit from a flexible system that can be adjusted at will to meet the ever-changing demands of the business.

Let's walk through an overview of key processes in the Extension Center, from navigation tips to creating extensions, picklists, object definitions, and publishing.

Navigating the Extension Center

The Extension Center is accessed in the Admin Center from the **Company Settings** menu. Figure 3.51 shows the home page of the Extension Center. The home page displays all extensions in the system, which can be displayed as tiles (the default view) or as a list. Both MDF extensions and SAP Cloud Platform extensions are managed here.

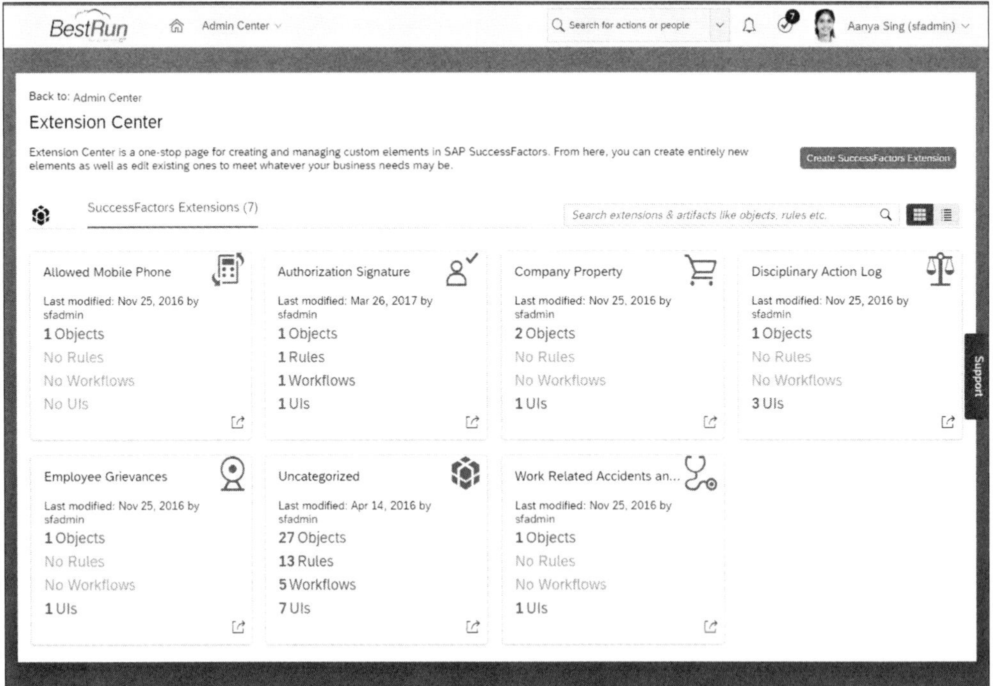

Figure 3.51 Extension Center Home Page

Additionally, it is possible to search through your extension and their components using the search box.

To view details of an extension, simply click the tile of that extension to go to the **Extension Detail** screen for the extension, as shown in Figure 3.52.

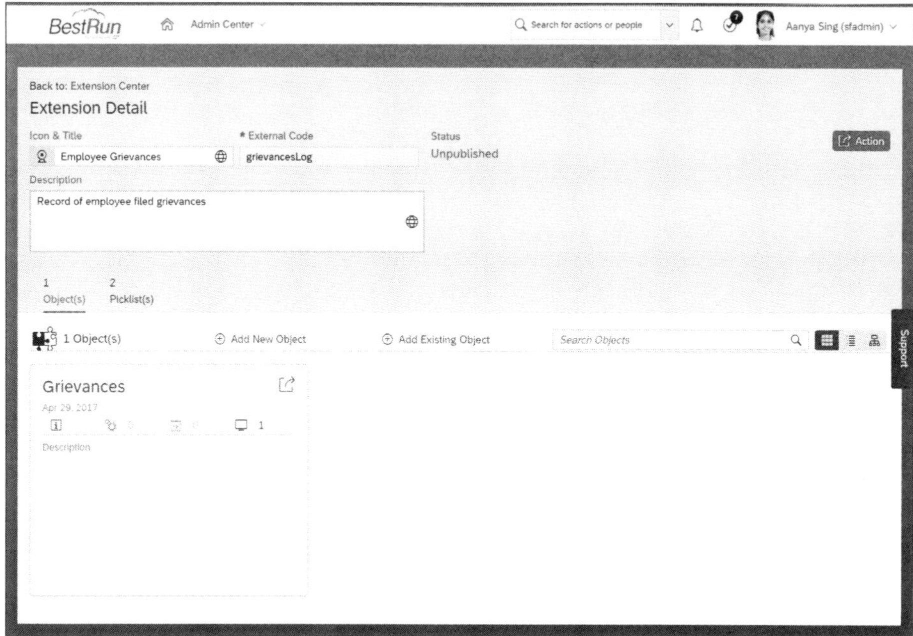

Figure 3.52 The Extension Detail Screen

As well as viewing details of the extension, you can also make changes here and publish or republish the extension so it can be used in the instance. We'll cover some of these topics as we go through creating an extension in the next section. Figure 3.53 shows the details of the fields of generic objects.

There are two tabs located below the description box that enable you to view all of the generic objects (**OBJECTS**) or all picklists (**PICKLISTS**) that are part of the extension. You can then select any of those generic objects or picklists to view more details about them.

For all of these generic objects and picklists, you can view them as tiles or a list, as with the extension on the home page of the Extension Center. However, there is also a third option called the **Entity Relationship Diagram**, which displays the relationships of all generic objects and picklists in the extension.

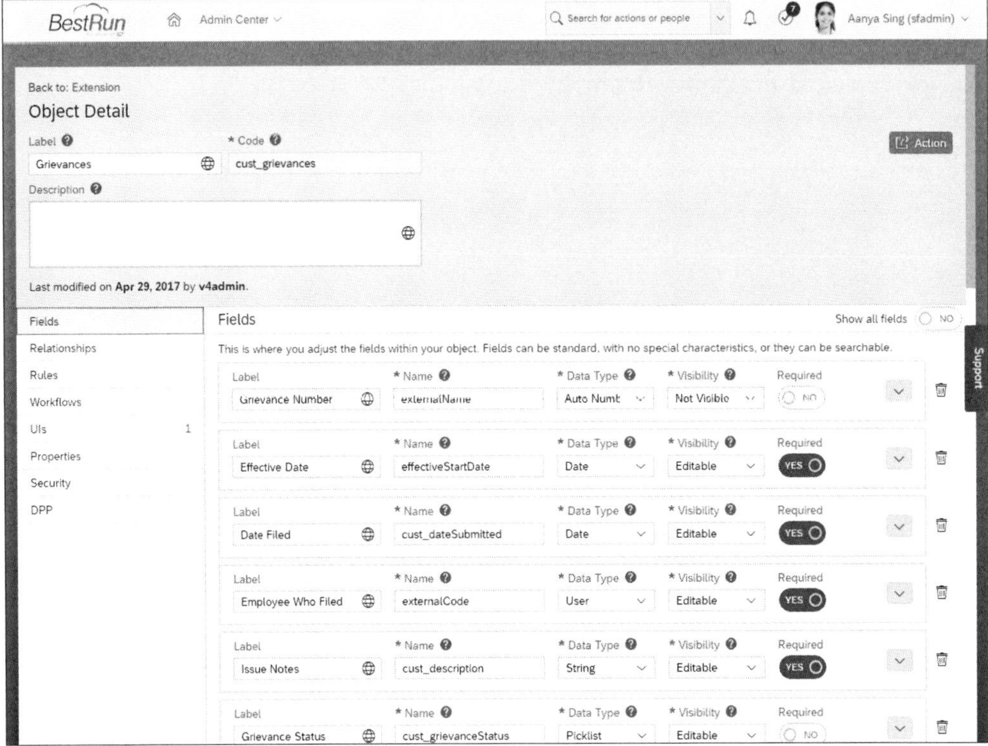

Figure 3.53 Generic Object Details

Now let's take a quick look at the process of creating an extension in the Extension Center.

Creating Extensions

Creating an extension is a relatively straightforward activity and uses a guided configuration wizard to support the creation process. Generic objects and picklists can be reused across multiple extensions, so you do not have to reinvent the wheel when creating your extension.

> **Note**
>
> Create the picklists you need before you create your extension so that they are already available to select when you define the fields of your extension.

To create an extension, click the **Create SuccessFactors Extension** button in the Extension Center home page (as shown in Figure 3.51 earlier in the chapter). You'll be taken to the **Extension Detail** screen where you can create your extension, shown in Figure 3.54.

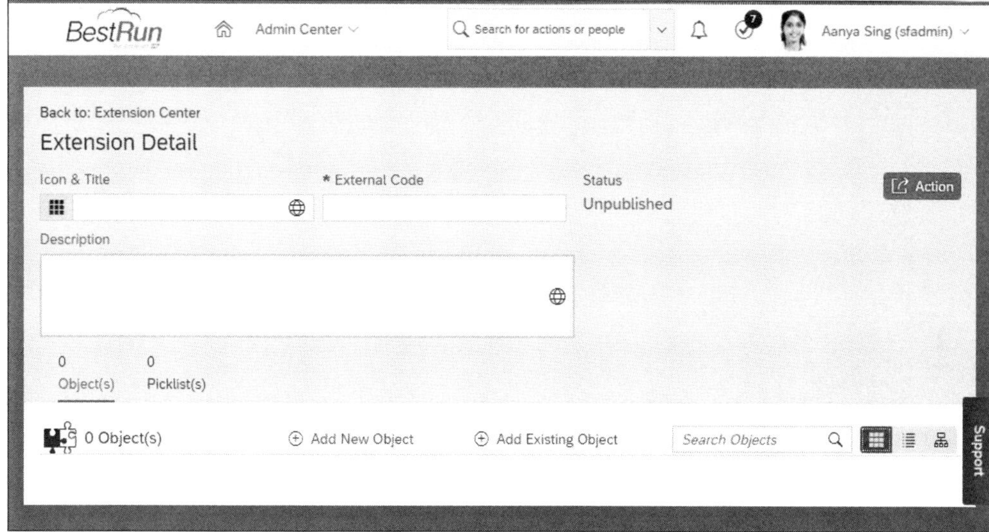

Figure 3.54 Extension Detail Screen when Creating an Extension

Once you have entered some basic information about your extension (i.e., name, code description, and icon), then it is time to create any picklists that you are going to use in your extension. Remember, you can use any existing picklists in your extension, so you do not need to re-create any picklists that already exist.

We'll now walk through the different steps you need to take to create a simple self-service or similar application.

Creating Picklists

Picklists can be created or existing picklists added to the extension by clicking the **Picklist(s)** tab and then selecting one of two options: **Add New Picklist** or **Add Existing Picklist**. Picklists can also be created in the Admin Center, in the Picklist Center, which we cover in Chapter 17, Section 17.9.

To create a new picklist, select **Add New Picklist** to open the **Edit Picklist** screen and then enter the details needed to configure your picklist. Once you have filled in the fields, the screen should look like Figure 3.55.

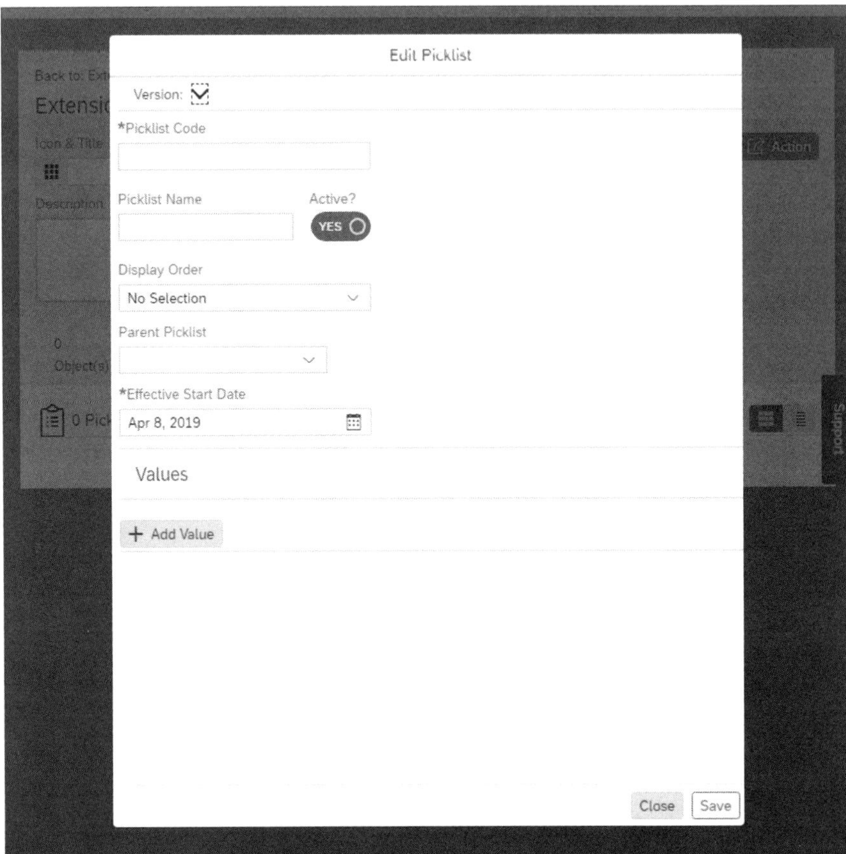

Figure 3.55 A New Picklist Being Created

Once your picklist is finished, click the **Save** button to save it. The effective date of the record will then appear as the version of the picklist at the top of the screen, and the last modified date will be shown at the bottom of the screen along with your user name. Click **Close** to return to the **Extension Detail** page.

You can now create additional picklists, or you can add an existing picklist to your extension. To add an existing picklist to your extension, click **Add Existing Picklist**, as previously seen in Figure 3.54. This will take you to the **Add Existing Picklist** screen, where you can select one or more picklists to add to your extension.

Once you've selected the picklists to add, click the **Save** button. You will then return to the **Extension Detail** screen, where you can see all picklists added to your extension.

Creating Object Definitions

Like with picklists, you can either create a new object definition or add an existing object definition. To create a generic object, select the **Object(s)** tab and then select **Add New Object**; you will be taken to the **Object Detail** screen, which we saw back in Figure 3.53.

An existing generic object can be added to your extension by selecting the **Add Existing Object** button on the **Extension Detail** screen.

> **Note**
>
> You can only maintain the **Fields**, **Relationships**, **Workflows**, and **Properties** sections before saving the generic object. Once you've saved the generic object, you can maintain the **Rules**, **UIs**, and **Security** sections.

There are a number of standard fields provided on a generic object—most beginning with *mdf*—and many of them are system fields that should be left as is. Bear in mind that the name for some of these fields in generic objects delivered by SAP SuccessFactors may vary from those used when creating a generic object. You can change the value in the **Name** field, but the system automatically provides the value in the **Database Field Name** field.

After the fields have been defined, you can create any associations to other generic objects as required in the **Relationships** section. If a child generic objects has not yet been created or added to the extension, then skip this part and come back to it once you have created or added a child generic objects. To create an association, click the **Add Relationship** button. The association can be either one-to-one or one-to-many, depending on whether the generic object record is related to only one other child or can have multiple other child generic objects.

Additional attributes are available after selecting the **Advanced Options** button to the right (the down arrow).

After adding any associations, you can add workflows by selecting **Workflows** in the left-side menu. Here you can open the workflow engine (where you can search, create, edit, or delete a workflow foundation object as per the standard process), create a new workflow configuration, or select an existing workflow configuration. If your generic object needs some form of conditional workflow, you should add that via a business rule in the **Rules** section. Remember that we cannot add any business rules yet (in the **Rules** section), as we need to save our object first, which requires us to complete the definition.

Once you've added any workflows, you can configure properties of the generic object in the **Properties** section, which is used to define the core attributes of the generic object, such as the effective dating, history handling, API visibility, and status. There are two sections of properties: **Basic Properties** and **Advanced Properties**.

Once properties have been defined, you can save the object to go back to the **Extension Detail** page. You can now create/define any business rules, configuration UIs, and security requirements for your generic objects. These are configured using the requisite menu items (**Rules**, **UIs**, and **Security**) in the left menu.

Adding an Extension to the People Profile

We covered this earlier in Section 3.18.1.

Publishing your Extension

Once your extension is finished, you need to publish the extension to make it live in the system.

> **Note**
>
> Before you can publish the extension, you'll need to make sure that an instance synchronization connection is set up between the source and target instances. For details on instance synchronization, see Chapter 17, Section 17.11.1.

3.18.3 Business Rules

SAP SuccessFactors features a robust and comprehensive *Rules Engine* that can be used to design complex rules so that you can apply your own rules and business logic to different areas of SAP SuccessFactors. They can be used in a variety of different use cases, such as defining default field values, changing the values of fields based on the values of other fields, prepopulating ID fields, showing or hiding fields based on other field values, performing numerical field calculations, identifying groups of employees for program eligibility, and much more. Rules are configured in the Admin Center, in **Configure Business Rules**.

Rules can be used across Employee Central objects, in Recruiting, and for Compensation planning eligibility. In addition, many of the Employee Central objects have a version called the *model* that allows field attributes to be set (e.g., visibility or required). For example, the Job Information model allows any field on job information to have its attributes changed by a rule.

Rules are modeled with statements (using conditions such as AND and OR) and flow logic to define the business logic used; once created, they can be assigned to fields or objects. Through this functionality, you can easily modify standard system behavior or add your own business rules or logic to a host of actions or data fields throughout the SAP SuccessFactors system.

Rules have a standard logic flow and are configured with three sections:

- Rule attributes: Attributes such rule name, ID, type, base object type, effective date, and description
- If logic: The logic to trigger the rule
- Then logic: The action to execute if the rule is triggered

Additional logic can be added, should the rule require it, using Else If and Else logic, similarly to the If and Then logic:

- Else If: The If logic to trigger and the Then action to execute if triggered.
- Else: The action to execute if the Else If logic isn't triggered

Figure 3.56 shows an example of a simple rule.

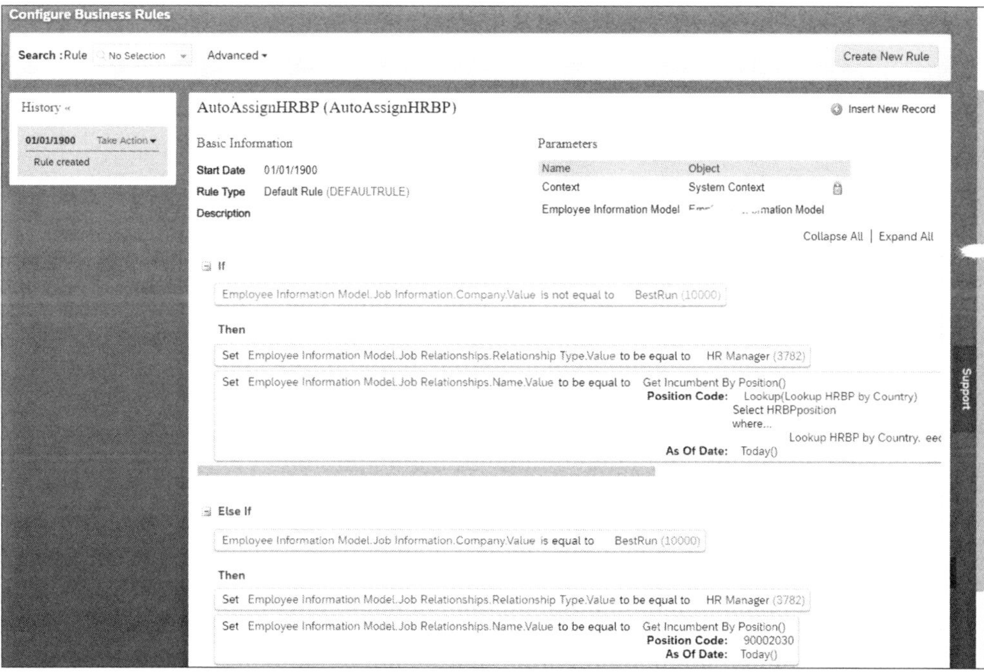

Figure 3.56 Example of a Rule

For If logic, AND and OR conditions are used to model statements that can reference any object field or object field attribute of the base object that is selected. These statements determine the action to take, which is defined in the Then logic. With Then logic, an object field, object field attribute, or system variable can be set to a specific value. The If logic can be set to **Always True**, which means that the Then logic is always executed when the rule is triggered.

In the example in Figure 3.56, the rule **AutoAssignHRBP** is triggered if the value of the **Company** field value is not equal to **BestRun**. The logic to be executed assigns the HR manager to the employee's **Job Relationships** portlet.

Once rules have been created, they need to be set to their trigger points. We'll now look at these trigger points.

Trigger Events

Rules can be triggered at the object or field level for generic objects, Employee Central foundation objects, personal information portlets, and employment information portlets. For rules triggered at the object level, the following trigger events are available:

- **OnInit**
  Triggers the rule when a portlet or the New Hire transaction is loaded
- **OnSave**
  Triggers the rule when the portlet or screen (e.g., **Add New Employee**, **Employment Information**, or **Personal Information**) is saved after the user has modified it
- **OnView**
  Triggers the rule for values that are calculated on the fly when a portlet or screen is loaded
- **OnEdit**
  Triggers a rule to default the values for editable field in the *paymentInfo* object in Employee Central
- **saveAlert**
  Triggers a rule for a workflow alert

At the field level, the *onChange* trigger is available. This triggers a rule when the field value is changed.

Rules can be configured to only trigger for specific screens. For example, you may only wish for a rule assigned to an onInit trigger to trigger when the screen is accessed in the New Hire wizard.

Rules can also be triggered by configuring in the Admin Center. Typically, this is for Compensation eligibility, Recruiting rules, and some Position Management rules.

Assigning Rules

Rules are assigned to objects either in the XML configuration files or in the Manage Business configuration UI. Other rules—as mentioned previously—are assigned in the Admin Center. For generic objects, rules are assigned directly to the generic object definition.

3.18.4 SAP Cloud Platform Extensions

With SAP Cloud Platform, a platform-as-a-service (PaaS), it is possible to create custom applications to embed within SAP SuccessFactors HCM Suite solutions.

SAP Cloud Platform is a cloud-based platform for developers to create scalable applications that can leverage the speed, power, and scale of SAP HANA and can integrate into cloud-based applications, such as SAP SuccessFactors or applications within SAP's other cloud pillars. It also leverages the MDF and integrates with mobile and SAP Jam. One of the key platform services is the SAP Cloud Platform Portal, which enables the quick creation of mobile-ready, highly brandable sites without coding.

Extensions can be built for any purpose and can integrate with any SAP SuccessFactors application via API. The Employee Central extension package was released to allow applications to be built for Employee Central on the SAP Cloud Platform. Applications built on the platform integrate with Employee Central using SSO and leverage the SAP SuccessFactors APIs to fetch employee details. These applications also integrate with the home screen (so they can be shown as tiles) and the theme and navigation of SAP SuccessFactors HCM Suite. Figure 3.57 shows an Enterprise Alumni application that has been created on SAP Cloud Platform and is integrated into the SAP SuccessFactors HCM Suite.

The SAP App Center enables customers to browse, test, and buy applications from across the SAP portfolio. Within the SAP App Center there is a section for SAP SuccessFactors applications, which includes extension applications and SAP Solution Extensions (such as SAP Time and Attendance Management by WorkForce Software and SAP Benefits Administration by Benefitfocus). The SAP App Center can be seen in Figure 3.58.

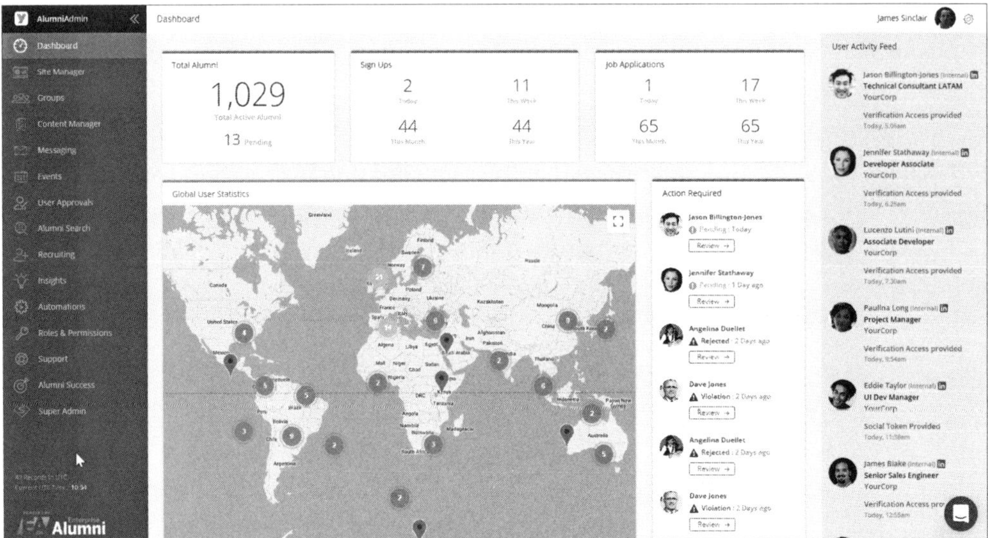

Figure 3.57 Enterprise Alumni Application

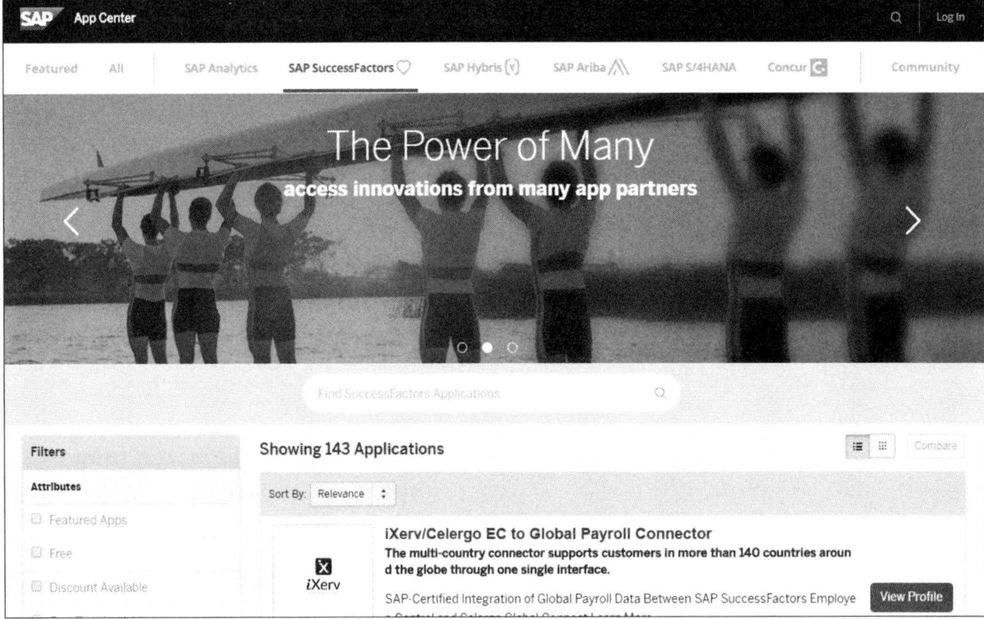

Figure 3.58 The SAP App Center

Each extension app or solution extension listed on the SAP App Center can be viewed, with several details provided for each app. Figure 3.59 shows an extension app listed on the SAP App Center.

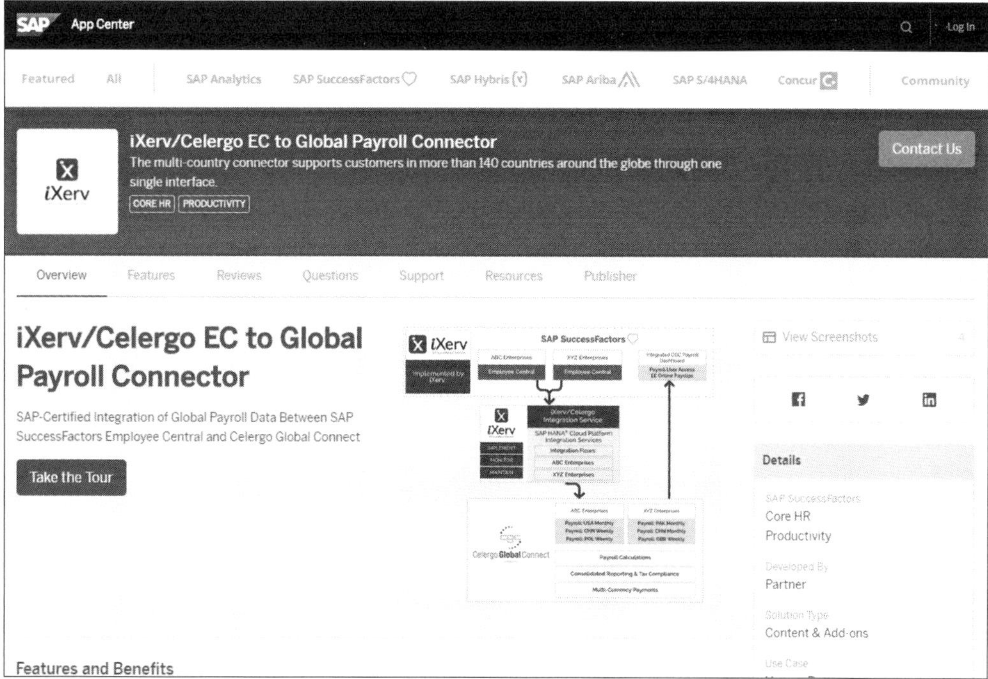

Figure 3.59 An App Listed on the SAP App Center

The SAP App Center can be accessed at *http://s-prs.co/v485802*.

3.19 Summary

We started this chapter with the technical architecture of SAP SuccessFactors and the various layers of the architecture. Because this is a cloud solution, the architecture must be light, scalable, and powerful. SAP SuccessFactors delivers this by using a dynamic backend technology, coupled with an intuitive frontend that creates a very powerful architecture. Security is of the utmost importance to SAP SuccessFactors. Therefore, every layer of technology within SAP SuccessFactors contains its own strong security and is independently penetration-tested to ensure that the data, code, and connections are secured every step of the way.

We then covered the various features and components that are part of the SAP SuccessFactors platform before discussing extensibility and how it can be used to create extension applications, data objects, screens, and rules that are future-proofed against future upgrades and releases.

Now that you understand some of the technology and functions that make SAP SuccessFactors run, let's jump into Employee Central.

Chapter 4
Employee Central

SAP SuccessFactors Employee Central is a robust, innovative, and evolving solution for managing the enterprise. Coupled with its attractive user interface and powerful capabilities, Employee Central is an excellent foundation for the entire SAP SuccessFactors HCM Suite.

Organizations large and small are undergoing people and process transformations now more than ever before. They require a true human resource information system (HRIS) that streamlines processes and data flows to achieve efficiencies while allowing them to build strategic human resource (HR) programs and manage the enterprise efficiently and cost-effectively.

SAP SuccessFactors Employee Central achieves all of this and more through its organic and robust design and superior user interface (UI). Built from the ground up with modern design principles and based on the needs of mature organizations, Employee Central is a continuously evolving HRIS based on the dynamically changing needs of global organizations and SAP's global co-innovation partners.

Employee Central is a global system of record that supports localizations for 98 countries and 42 languages (at the time of writing, fall 2019). These localizations cover country-specific company and job fields, validations and dropdown values, localized regulatory compliance reporting, advances and deductions, global benefits, global assignments, and more. For example, national ID card options and validations are provided for each of these 98 countries, as well as country-specific address formats.

In this chapter, we'll examine the key features of Employee Central, and the pivotal roles it plays in transforming organizations with the value of an efficient people- and process-centric core HRIS. We'll look at the basics of Employee Central, objects that lay the foundation of organizational and personnel data in Employee Central, HR processes and transactions supported by the system, and some of the key functionalities that can be implemented to further enhance your HR business processes. We'll conclude with a look at Employee Central administration, reporting, and some implementation tips.

Note

There are many features and processes available in Employee Central that we won't cover in depth in this book, which can be used depending on your needs. Here is a selection of some of the more commonly used features and processes:

- Dependents management: Allows management of dependents, who can then be used in other processes.
- Pay scale progression: Allows for pay scale progression for unionized workers or workers with collective bargaining agreements.
- Advances and deductions: Provides a process to give employees an advance against future compensation and recoup the advances with deductions, as well as deduct other amounts from an employee's salary.
- Alternative cost distribution: Allows multiple cost centers to be assigned to cover up to 100 percent of an employee's cost.
- Pensions payouts: Manage pensioned employees and former employees.
- Document generation: Set up document templates and generate documents, either as an administrator as an employee or manager through self-services.
- Apprentice management: Set up apprentice programs and manage apprentices.

4.1 Employee Central Basics

Employee Central has an agile and easy-to-adapt design for customers' changing HR business requirements. In this section, we'll begin with the Employee Central basics, namely data objects and organization and fundamental features, including events, Org Charts, and more.

Further Resources

SAP has published a large number of guides on Employee Central. These can be found on SAP Help Portal under the SAP SuccessFactors Employee Central product page.

You can also read more about Employee Central in the book *SAP SuccessFactors Employee Central: The Comprehensive Guide* by Luke Marson, Murali Mazhavanchery, and Rebecca Murray (2nd edition, SAP PRESS, 2018).

4.1.1 Data Objects

Employee Central's data model consists of a set of foundational data objects that drive employee employment information. The data model is also extendable using the tools provided in the Admin Center, including the Manage Business configuration UI and the Extension Center (which we discussed in Chapter 3, Section 3.18). The data model consists of a few different types of objects that are used to configure, manage, and propagate data in Employee Central, which we'll discuss in this section.

Foundation Objects

Foundation objects are objects that define the company data for an organization. They are a combination of database objects and generic objects (see the following section) that hold information about enterprise-level objects, such as a business unit or cost center. The foundation object tables capture detailed information about a company's organization, pay, and job structures. Each object has a set of standard fields, 80 available custom fields (200 for generic object-based foundation objects), and country-specific fields to house country-specific data. Of course, you are not expected to remember any table names or transactions to access the information housed in these objects.

Let's look at each of these structures and understand their importance in building your core HR system through a few examples:

- **Organizational structures**
  Organizational structures are the building blocks that organizations can use to structure their organizations to custom fit their needs. Eight standard organizational structures are delivered (legal entity, business unit, division, department, location group, geo zone, location, and cost center), but generic objects can also be created to act as custom foundation objects if the standard delivered objects need extending for your needs. For example, a division may have an additional level of subdivision in the organizational hierarchy.
- **Job structures**
  Job structures' functionality is used to create job codes and job functions in your organization. The two job structures objects are job classification and job function.
- **Pay structures**
  Pay structures are used to store the compensation components of any employee. These objects include pay group, pay component, pay component group, pay grade, pay range, pay calendar, and frequency. Pay structure objects can be easily configured in the UI when elements of the structure change, such as when new pay incentives or pay grades are introduced.

In addition to these, there are also some other foundation objects, including dynamic role, workflow configuration, event reason, and currency exchange rate.

Foundation objects, in addition to storing data about organizational elements, are used to populate aspects of an employee's profile and can also be used to propagate data from that object to the employee's profile using business rules.

Propagation allows data to be transferred from fields of an object onto the employee' profile, such as their job information or compensation information. A widely used example that you most likely will encounter is the propagation of fields from the job code object to the position object when creating a position (e.g., the grade, working hours, or job level, etc.). Likewise, when selecting a position on the employee's profile, fields in the employee's job information will populate with data from the position.

Country-specific data can also be stored on foundation objects. For example, perhaps you need to store country-specific fields such as a Federal Employer Identification Number (FEIN) for a US-based legal entity or company code, but you need to keep the remaining fields applicable to all countries.

Figure 4.1 shows an example of the country-specific fields configured for France on the legal entity foundation object **BestRun France**.

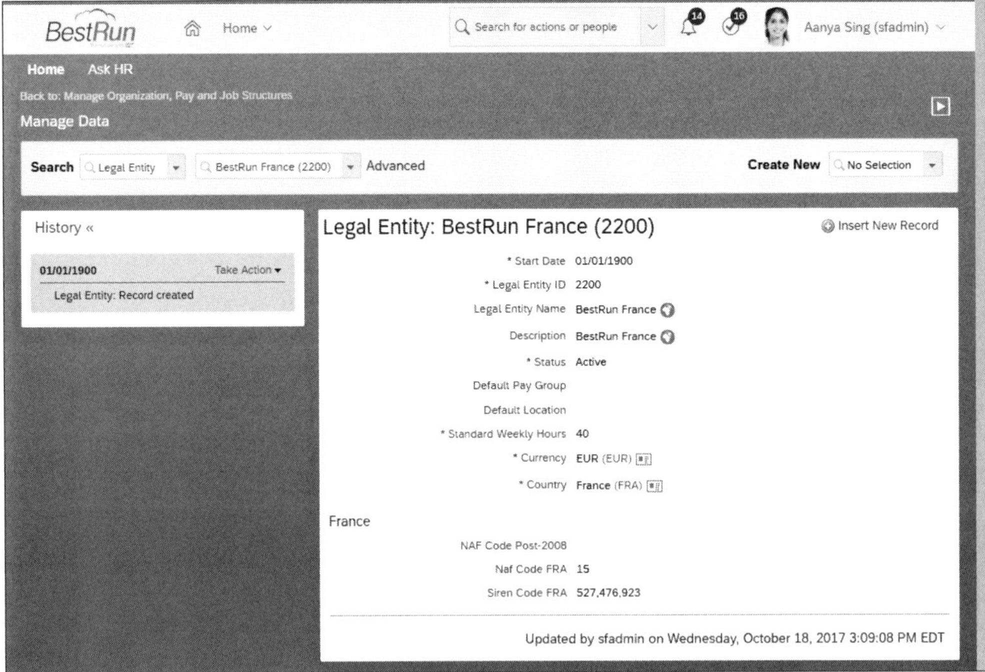

Figure 4.1 Country-Specific Fields on a Legal Entity

Generic Objects

Generic objects—which we covered in Chapter 3—are the foundation of custom objects and new functionality from SAP SuccessFactors. They enable customers to add custom foundation objects, new objects, and new People Profile blocks to cover requirements that are not catered by the core product. SAP SuccessFactors uses generic objects in functionality such as Position Management, Time Management, and Global Benefits.

Adding custom object enables customers to add their own functionalities into Employee Central. This is especially useful for industry-specific capabilities. Figure 4.2 shows a generic object for grievances in the People Profile. As you can see, it fits right into the UI, alongside standard and custom objects.

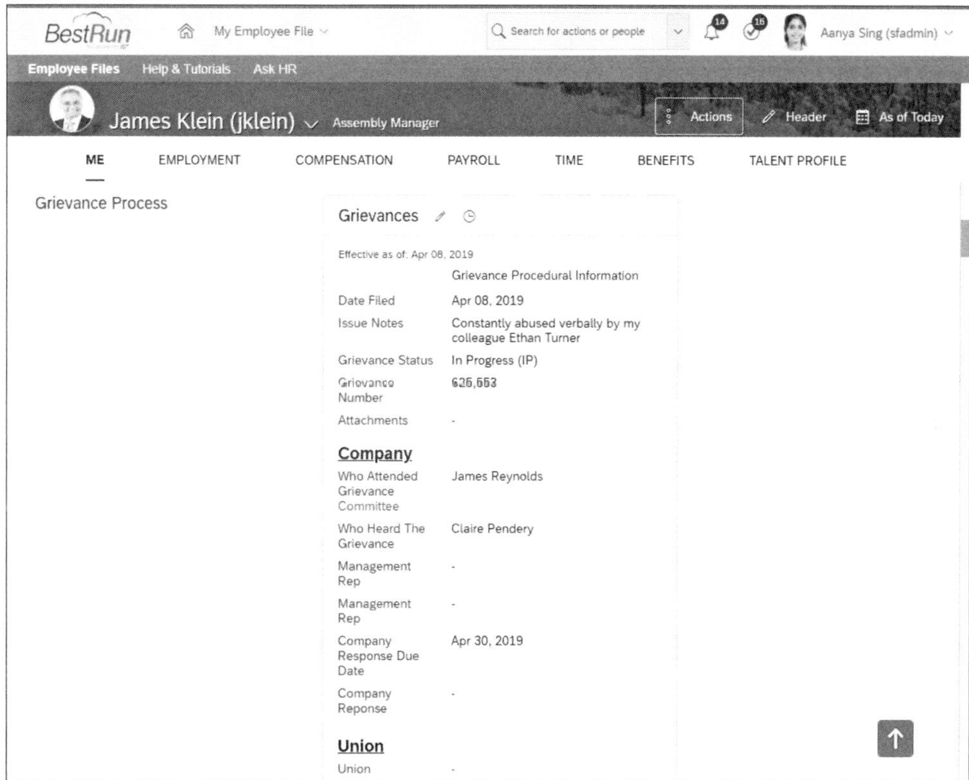

Figure 4.2 A Generic Object Screen in Employee Central

Now, let's take a look at employee data and how it is displayed and managed in Employee Central.

4.1.2 Employee Data

Employee data is accessed in the People Profile, as we discussed in Chapter 3, Section 3.11. Data is grouped into logic blocks of data, such as visa and permits, dependents, job information, and compensation information.

All of the blocks can be extended with additional fields and have rules applied on the block level or field level.

HR users can edit data in each block if they have permission to access either edit access or actions in the **Actions** menu. Users may also be given access to the additional **History** icon, where they can see and edit historical data records. The option(s) that you can access depend on the role you have assigned.

Additionally, you can display past or future data on screen by clicking **As Of Today** and selecting the date you wish to use.

There are multiple blocks delivered as part of Employee Central, which include:

- **National ID Information**: Information about national IDs
- **Home Address**: Home and other addresses of the employee
- **Personal Information**: Information such as first name, last name, marital status, native language, and so on
- **Biographical Information**: The employee's user ID, date of birth, country of birth, and so forth
- **Work Permit Info**: Any work permits issued to the employee
- **Contact Information**: Email, phone, and social media contact information
- **Primary Emergency Contact**: Details about emergency contacts
- **Dependents**: Information about dependents of the employee
- **Payment Information**: Direct deposit and payment details
- **Job Information**: All information about the organizational assignment, job, and position of the employee
- **Employment Details**: Details about hire date, service dates, stock options, etc.
- **Alternative Cost Distribution**: Any alternative cost distributions (the Alternative Cost Distribution feature must be enabled before it is available)
- **Job Relationships**: Any job relationships, such as HR manager or matrix manager
- **Compensation Information**: All details relating to the employee's compensation
- **Eligibility For Advances**: Any advances to the employee (the Advances feature must be enabled before it is available)

- **Recurring Deduction**: Any recurring deductions (the Deductions feature must be enabled before it is available)
- **One Time Deduction User**: Any one-off deductions (the Deductions feature must be enabled before it is available)

4.1.3 Events and Event Reasons

Many events occur during the employee lifecycle, and Employee Central enables events and event reasons to be selected. The event reason foundation object is used to define the different reasons. A fixed set of events is provided with Employee Central, which cannot be modified. However, an unlimited number of event reason objects can be defined for each event.

Employee Central provides the following events in the system:

- **Add Global Assignment**
- **Additional Job**
- **Assignment**
- **Assignment Completion**
- **Away on Global Assignment**
- **Back from Global Assignment**
- **Completion of Probation**
- **Data Change**
- **Demotion**
- **Discard Pension Payout**
- **End Global Assignment**
- **End Pension Payout**
- **Furlough**
- **Hire**
- **Job Change**
- **Job Reclassification**
- **Leave of Absence**
- **Obsolete**
- **Pay Rate Change**
- **Position Change**
- **Probation**
- **Promotion**
- **Rehire**
- **Return From Disability**
- **Return to Work**
- **Start Pension Payout**
- **Suspension**
- **Termination**
- **Transfer**

Occasionally, SAP SuccessFactors introduces new events. For example, **Add Global Assignment** was introduced for the Global Assignment feature.

Employee Central enables the status of an employee to be controlled via event reasons. Event reasons can have an employee status value assigned, to change the status of an employee when the associated event takes place. For example, an event reason tied to the hire event would have the employee status of **Active**. Likewise, event reasons for the termination event would have the employee status of **Terminated**.

Events do not have to have an employee status assigned. For example, a change in compensation does not change the status of an employee. Their existing status—whether **Active**, **Terminated**, **Paid Leave**, and so forth—does not change based on the event that takes place and the event reason selected. The following different employee status values are available in the system:

- **Active**
- **Unpaid Leave**
- **Paid Leave**
- **Retired**
- **Suspended**
- **Terminated**
- **Furlough**
- **Discarded**
- **Dormant**

Event reasons are used only for changes to the **Personal Information**, **Job Information**, and **Compensation Information** blocks. Although the event reason is selected automatically with event derivation, it can be manually changed in the **History** screen of each portlet if a user has the appropriate permissions.

4.1.4 Position Management

Position Management gives you the ability to manage your organization through positions. It gives you a structured way of managing roles and head count, launching job requisitions, and propagating data across objects and employees. These positions are also used in other processes, such as recruiting and succession planning. There are a number of features available in Position Management, including:

- Storing and tracking position attributes, such as regular, part-time, job description, and related organizational entities
- Enabling positions to inherit attributes from the assigned job code
- Enabling employees to inherit attributes from the assigned position
- Defining an employee's manager when their direct manager leaves the organization or is transferred
- Configuring headcount management (strict position control versus non-budget-driven process)
- For vacant/to-be-hired positions, launching requisitions in SAP SuccessFactors Recruiting with the required position information

- Using positions in SAP SuccessFactors Succession & Development so that the successors are planned based on the existing positions hierarchy
- Viewing the position reporting structure in the Position Org Chart

The position object definition is configured as any other generic object, and position records are created in the same way that other generic object data is created. This means that various rules that enable field value defaulting, propagation, autogeneration of the position code, full-time equivalent (FTE) management, workflows, and synchronizations can be applied to the position object. Figure 4.3 shows a position.

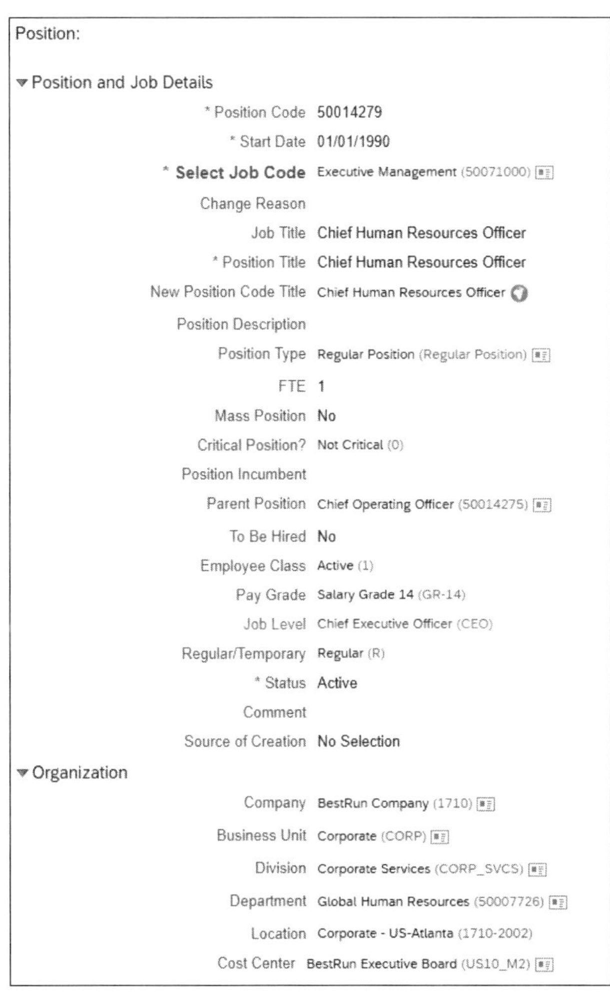

Figure 4.3 A Position

Matrix relationships can be defined for a position, such as HR manager, matrix manager, custom manager, and so forth. This enables you to propagate position holders as job relationships of an employee, which can be viewed in the **Job Relationships** block of an employee's People Profile.

Position Management settings are configured in the Admin Center in **Position Management Settings**, as shown in Figure 4.4.

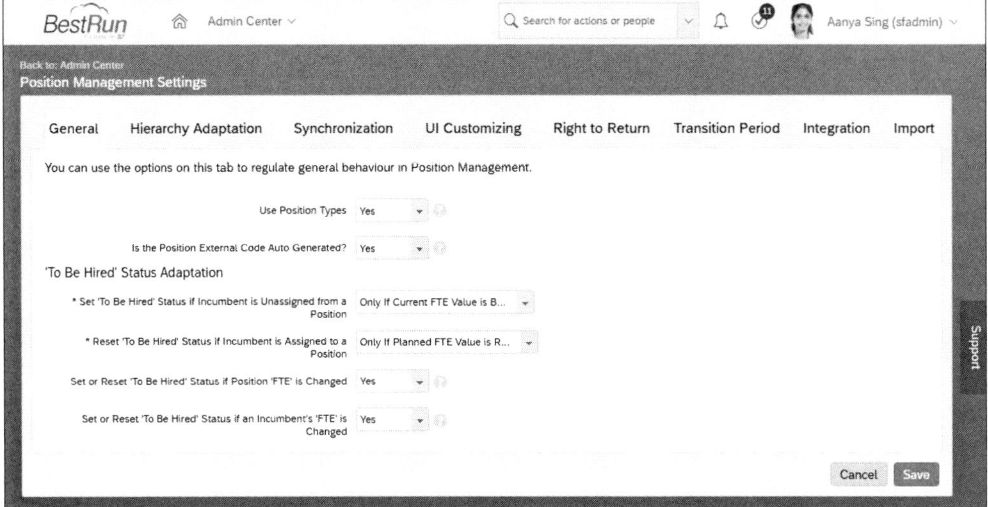

Figure 4.4 Position Management Settings

Specific settings that can be made for Position Management include:

- How the **To Be Hired** field is treated during assignment and transfer of employees
- The leading hierarchy
- Position searching during reclassifications and transfers
- The field for determining position headcount control
- If the position code is auto-generated
- The rules for defining fields during position copy and synchronizing position data position data with job information
- UI behavior
- Right to return
- Transition period

- Integration with Recruiting
- Position management data import settings

The *leading hierarchy* is a concept that affects various actions in the system that involve positions. There are two options for leading hierarchy: **Position Hierarchy** and **Reporting Hierarchy**. This selection affects how higher-level managers are selected for employees during position assignments, the new hire process, and position changes in the Position Org Chart. It also impacts how positions are found when a position reclassification takes place.

Positions are assigned to an employee's job information, usually during hire or when there is a position transfer (see Section 4.2).

> **Further Resources**
>
> Further information can be found in the guide *Employee Central Position Management* found on the SAP Help Portal under the SAP SuccessFactors Employee Central product page.

4.1.5 Org Charts

Org Charts form one of the of access points to see employees and access their data. Managers and employees can view the Org Chart of their area and see employees in their team and other teams. They can also launch actions from the Org Chart, such as a job change, or access a performance form. See Chapter 3, Section 3.12.1, for more details.

For organizational management, the Position Org Chart is used to view and manage positions and head count. See Chapter 3, Section 3.12.2, for more details.

4.1.6 People Profile

The People Profile is the screen that contains all information about an employee that a user is allowed to see. We introduced the People Profile in Chapter 3, Section 3.11. The People Profile is where users view data about employees and implements changes to employee data, as either an HR professional, manager, or employee. We'll cover this in Section 4.3.

Now let's look at hiring, rehiring, transferring, and terminating employees in Employee Central.

4.2 Hiring and Firing

It is inevitable that you will have employees joining and leaving your organization periodically, and for many organizations it is common to rehire former employees.

Further Resources

Further information can be found in the guide *Managing Employment in Employee Central* found on the SAP Help Portal under the SAP SuccessFactors Employee Central product page.

Let's look at the different hiring and firing processes in Employee Central.

4.2.1 New Hires

New employees can be hired into Employee Central through a hiring wizard. Employees that have been hired through Recruiting, have been onboarded through SAP SuccessFactors Onboarding, or are contingent workers from SAP Fieldglass can also be hired through the same wizard, but with prepopulated data from those modules.

Employees are hired through the **Add New Employee** transaction. The transaction has a four-step route map to enter details of the new employee. It can also match against previous employees who are not currently active in the system; we'll discuss rehiring former employees in Section 4.2.2. The **Add New Employee** transaction has a standard set of blocks to enter data. These are the same blocks that are seen in the People Profile. The **Add New Employee** wizard can be launched through the Admin Center or in the Org Chart.

If new hires were processed through another SAP SuccessFactors application or from SAP Fieldglass, they can be hired through the **Manage Pending Hires** transaction (shown in Figure 4.5), accessed in the Admin Center. This launches the **Add New Employee** transaction with data populated from those modules. As mentioned, the **Add New Employee** wizard—seen in Figure 4.6—is split into four steps:

1. **Identity**: Personal, biographical, and ID card information (for example, name, date of birth, and social security number)
2. **Personal Information**: Personal data, contact information, emergency contact, and dependents
3. **Job Information**: Employment data, organizational data, job data, job relationships, and work permit

4. **Compensation Information**: Salary and bonus data

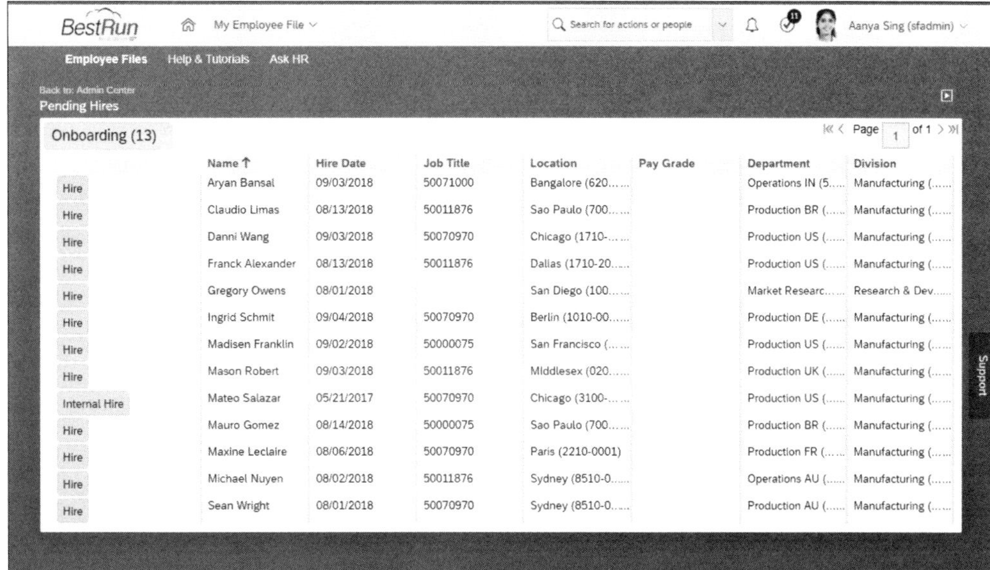

Figure 4.5 Manage Pending Hires

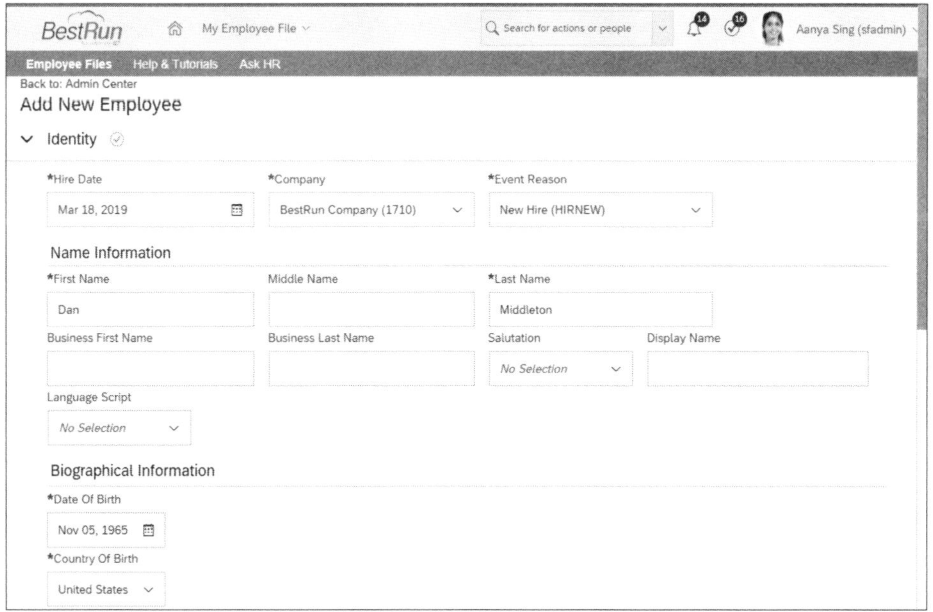

Figure 4.6 The Add New Employee Wizard

The first thing you must do when launching the transaction is select the hire data, company/legal entity, and event reason. Only event reasons that have the **Hire** action assigned are available to select.

After completing all necessary fields, you can navigate from one step to the next. Once all steps are filled, you can submit the hire. Depending on the system setup, there may be a workflow triggered to approve the new hire before they become active in the system.

The ID of the employee can be generated automatically by the system or entered manually. If a **Person ID** or the **First Name** and **Last Name** combination entered on the **Identity** screen already exists, the system validates it and informs the user of the duplicate entry, as shown in Figure 4.7. You can choose to go back and enter new credentials. If you click **Ignore Matches**, the system gives you an error and prompts you to enter a unique value for the **Person ID** field. This is the same way a rehire can be triggered, which we'll cover in the next section.

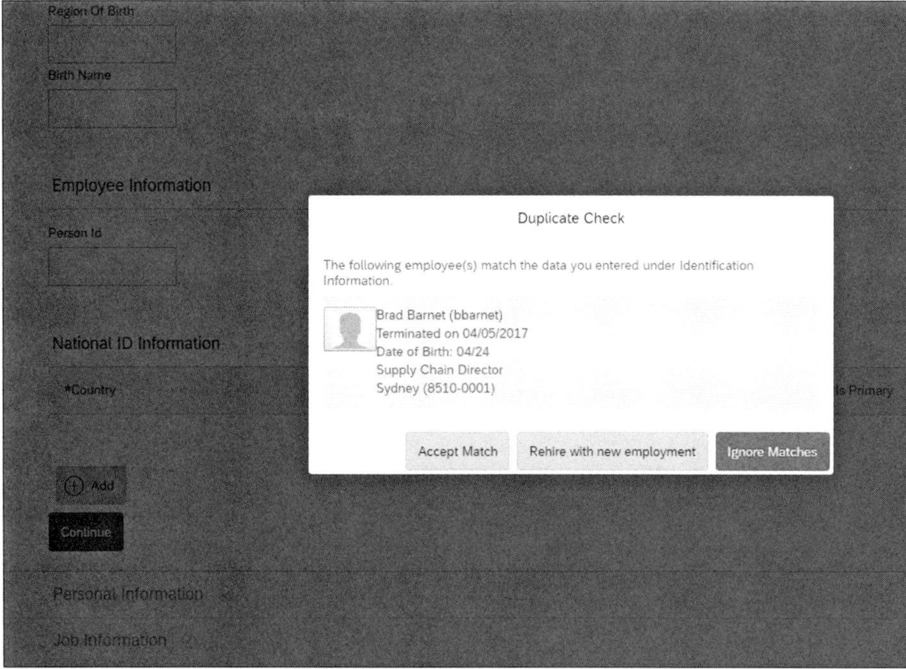

Figure 4.7 Duplicate Match for a New Hire

4.2.2 Rehires

Employees who have left your organization and are coming back can be rehired using previous data stored in Employee Central. If a previous employee was not ever in Employee Central or data protection rules required an employee to be removed from the system, then you can't rehire them.

It is possible to rehire employees using their original employment details or with a different employment, so that you can shield previous employment details from the user rehiring the employee. This is also useful for legal purposes when an employee moves to a different legal entity or when there is a requirement with your payroll system to have a different employment.

Employees are rehired through a number of methods:

- **Rehire Inactive Employee** transaction in the Admin Center: Search for a former employee and launch the **Add New Employee** wizard for this employee.
- **Manage Pending Hires** transaction in the Admin Center: Former employees that have gone through recruiting or onboarding can be hired from **Manage Pending Hires**, as with new hires.
- **Add New Employee** wizard: If you enter certain criteria that matches to a terminated employee, then the system will notify you and you can rehire that former employee.

When rehiring former employees, only event reasons that have the **Rehire** action assigned are available to select.

Like with hiring an employee, once the hiring wizard is completed, a workflow can trigger to have the hire approved.

4.2.3 Transfers

The transfer of employees within the organization can occur in the Employee Central system in two ways:

- A transfer is triggered on an employee's profile by a user with the appropriate permission (e.g., a manager, HR administrator, HR business partner, etc.).
- An employee is hired for a new job through the Recruiting module (see Chapter 8).

The first of the above options is performed through self-services, which we'll cover in Section 4.3.2. The second option enables an employee that got hired to a new internal role through the Recruiting module and may also have gone through the onboarding process in the Onboarding module. These employees are transferred in **Manage Pending Hires** (they have **Internal Hire** specified instead of **Hire** on the button to launch the hiring action, as shown previously in Figure 4.5) and are taken through the **Internal Hire** wizard. The **Internal Hire** wizard is simpler than the **Add New Employee** wizard, since during a transfer only the main data such as employment, job, and compensation information is changed, rather than entering all data from scratch.

It is possible to force Employee Central to terminate and hire an employee again as part of a transfer. This is typically due to local country legislation or because certain payroll systems enforce this kind of change.

4.2.4 Terminations

Employees are terminated through the **Termination** wizard, which is accessed by navigating to the employee, clicking the **Actions** button, and then selecting **Terminate**. Here, details about the termination can be included, such as termination date, event reason (which must be selected irrespective of whether event derivation is used), salary end date, whether it's acceptable to rehire the employee, whether you regret the termination, and notes. Any custom fields would also be displayed here. If the employee has any direct reports, then once the termination date is selected, the option to select a new manager appears, along with the transfer date. The new manager is defaulted to the to-be-terminated employee's current manager, as shown in Figure 4.8.

Once the termination action is completed and the termination date is reached, the terminated employee's employment status changes to **Terminated**, as shown in Figure 4.9.

If a user has permissions, they can search for terminated employees in People Profile to view the People Profile of a terminated employee. Terminated employees cannot be found using the people search.

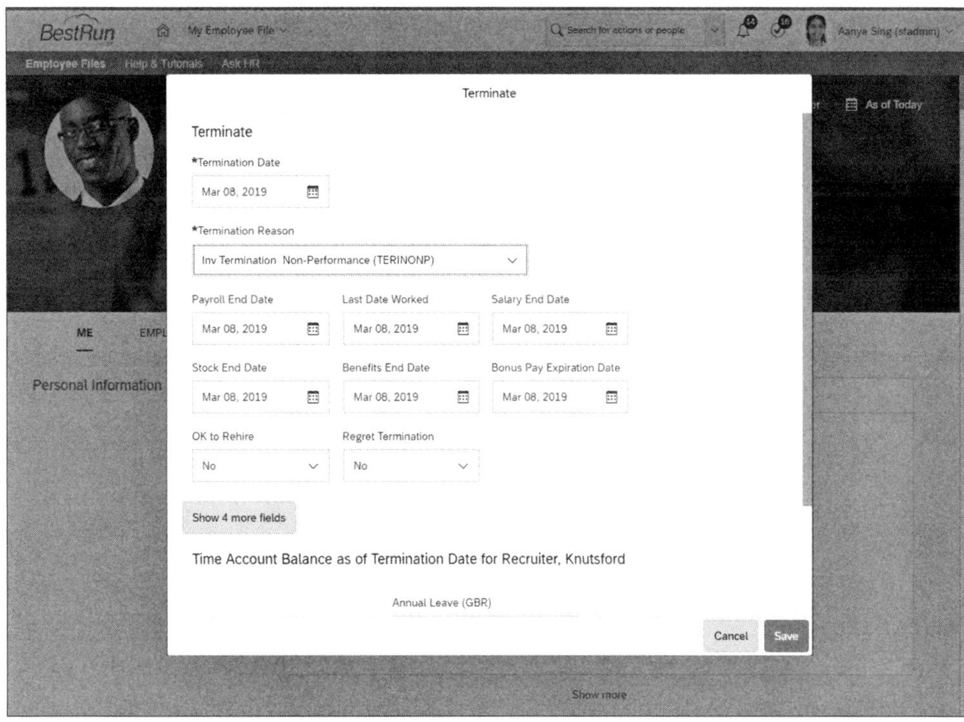

Figure 4.8 A Termination Transaction

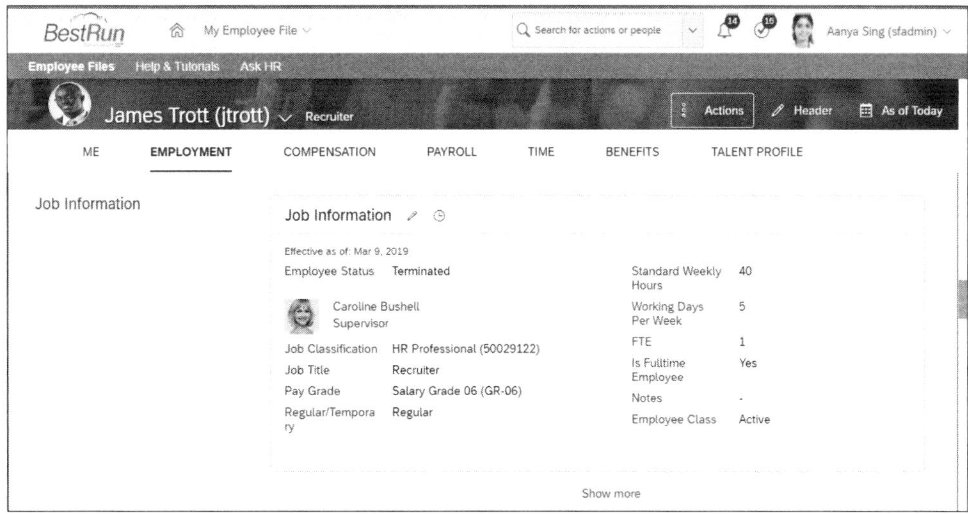

Figure 4.9 Termination Details on the People Profile

4.3 Data Access and Maintenance

Employee data can be viewed and maintained in a few ways. HR administrators can view and edit employee data and history directly in the People Profile, while managers view it in the People Profile and use the **Actions** menu on the People Profile to edit data. Employees have access to their data in the same way as managers and HR administrators, and they can edit the data that they are allowed to change (for example, address or dependents) here too. We'll cover data viewing and maintenance by HR as well as manager and employee self-services in this section.

4.3.1 Human Resources

HR administrators can make data changes through the edit or history icon in each block on the People Profile. Figure 4.10 shows an administrator editing the history of an employee's job information. In some instances, you may want them to make changes through the **Actions** menu on the People Profile, like managers or employees do. This is controlled via permissions.

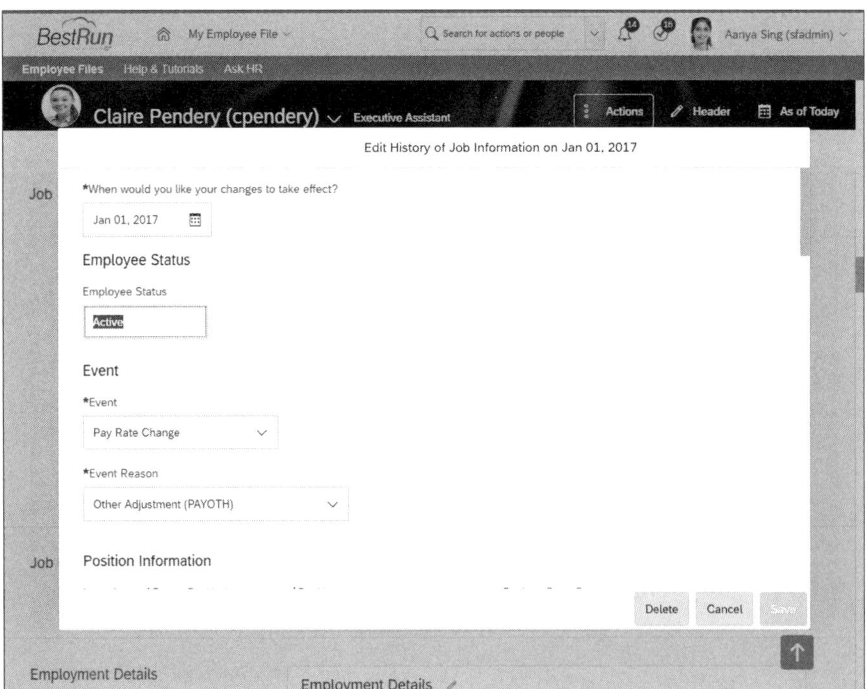

Figure 4.10 Editing Job Information History

Generic object data can also be edited through **Manage Data** in the Admin Center.

4.3.2 Self-Services

A core feature of Employee Central is built-in self-services functionality for managers and employees. The Employee Central architecture is designed so that the only functional difference between what a HR administrator or power user can do and what a manager or employee can do is what you allow them to do via the permissions framework. This gives you flexibility to control whatever type of access you want users to have and to control what users can see and do. Through this framework, self-services can be designed to allow visibility and changes by managers and employees to only the data that they should be allowed to access.

The Org Chart and People Profile are the focus of self-services, as we mentioned back in Section 4.1.5 and Section 4.1.6. Employees can be found in the Org Chart, and their data can be viewed in the People Profile, where changes can also be implemented. Data changes where an event and event reason need to be selected can have the selection of the event and event reason automated based on the changes being made. After changes have been made, the changes can go through a workflow approval process, with the approval process configurable based on what changes are being made.

Let's take a look at employee and manager self-services and see how those types of users both view and manage data in Employee Central, as well as the event derivation and workflow functionality that supports self-service data consistency and approvals.

Employee Self-Services

Employee self-services (ESS) allows employees to view their own data and perform a number of activities or make requests within the system. These could be such things as making an address change, adding or editing dependents, viewing pay slips (when using SAP SuccessFactors Employee Central Payroll), requesting an employment verification document, booking a vacation, or electing a benefit.

Employees typically edit data using the pencil icon in the top-right corner of the block where they wish to change information. It is possible that an employee sees some blocks but cannot edit data in that block, such as with a national ID card.

Figure 4.11 shows an employee editing their home address in ESS.

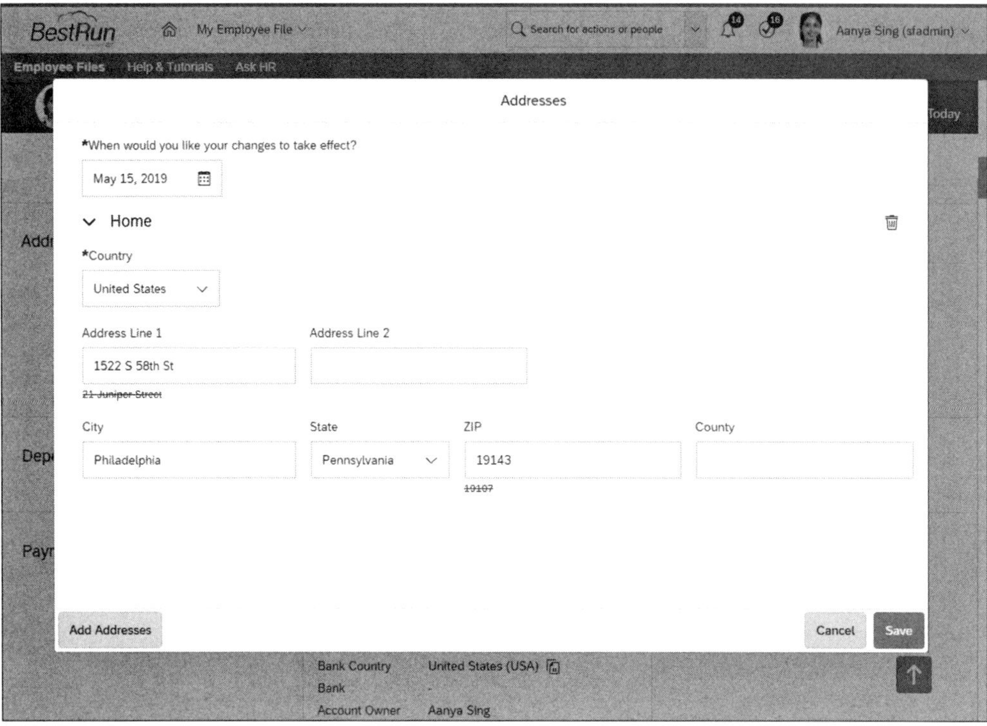

Figure 4.11 Editing a Home Address in ESS

Some transactions are initiated using the **Actions** menu in the header of the People Profile, such as generating forms or documents. Some requests made from blocks in the People Profile may take the employee to another screen, such as making a vacation request or making changes to benefits elections.

Manager Self-Services

Managers will see the People Profile similarly for their reports as they would for themselves. However, they are likely to see more data and have more actions available to perform for their reports than on their own profile. Typically, a manager will be able to launch a number of different actions, such as a job change or a change in compensation.

There are a number of actions that a manager can launch from the People Profile of a report or from the **My Team** tile on the home page. These are launched by selecting the appropriate action in the **Actions** menu on the People Profile. These options include:

- **Change Job and Compensation Info**
  Change the employee's job information and/or compensation information.
- **Add: Concurrent Employment**
  Add a concurrent employment.
- **Add: Global Assignment Details**
  Send the employee on a global assignment.
- **Terminate**
  Terminate the employee.
- **One Time Deduction**
  Set up a one-time deduction for the employee.
- **Manage Recurring Deduction**
  Add, edit, or end a recurring deduction.
- **Manage Alternative Cost Distribution**
  Assign additional cost centers.
- **Generate Document**
  Generate a document for the employee (MSS) or request a document (ESS).

Note that some of these options only occur if you have those features enabled. If the manager selects **Change Job and Compensation Info**, then they have three other options available:

- **Job Information**
- **Job Relationships**
- **Compensation Information**

Each of these changes—with the exception of **Job Relationships**—is effective dated and, once approved, may trigger a workflow approval prior to being visible on the employee's People Profile.

Figure 4.12 shows a manager maintaining alternative cost distribution information for a report from the **My Team** tile on the home page.

A manager is able to change any fields for which they have permission. It may even be that they do not have permission to see all of the above options, or your company may not use all of the functionalities (for example, document generation or concurrent employment).

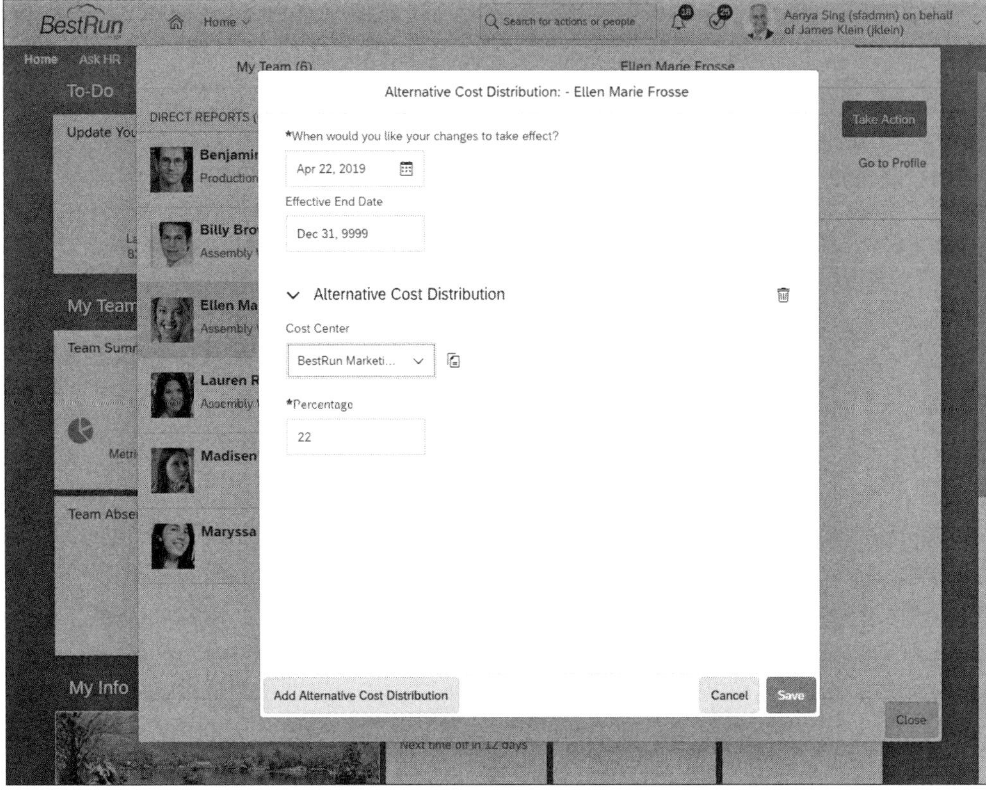

Figure 4.12 Adding Alternative Cost Distribution to a Direct Report from the My Team Tile

Event Derivation

When making a change in **Change Job and Compensation Info**, the system can automatically select the event of the manager's action based on the data that is changed. This is called *event derivation*. Event derivation enables the system to automatically select an event and an event reason based on the event derivation business rules that are configured in the system. This significantly reduces user error, which can impact data accuracy and integrity.

Workflows

Workflows provide an approval path for self-service actions and data changes to be approved. Workflows can also be used for some data changes not performed as self-service, such as hiring an employee, due to the flexibility of the workflow framework. In Employee Central, workflows also provide participants in the workflow the ability to provide comments or to receive notifications. Workflows ensure that the necessary approvals and authorizations are provided for important and sensitive data changes.

A workflow is a foundation object (which we covered in Section 4.1.1), and system administrators can easily create and maintain workflows in the Admin Center. Workflows are triggered using business rules, so, again, these can easily be created and maintained in the Admin Center. Figure 4.13 shows a typical workflow configuration.

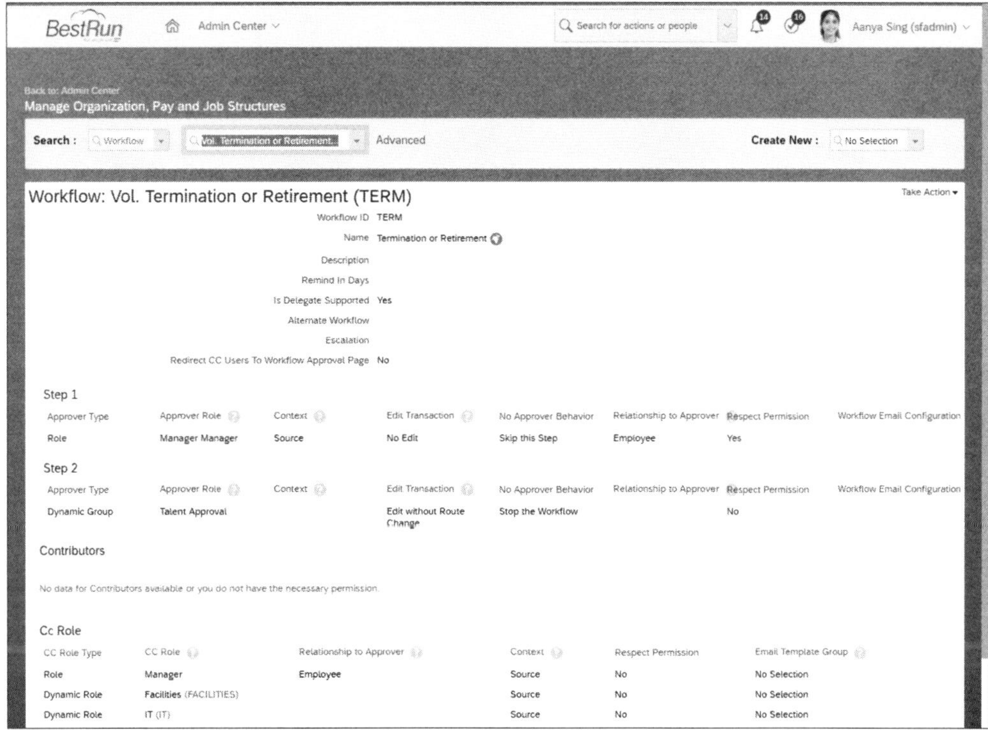

Figure 4.13 A Workflow Configuration

Workflows have the following features:

- Multiple participants, including the following:
  - Approver: Users who are required to approve the workflow
  - Contributor: Users who are able to add comments to an active workflow
  - CC roles: Users who are notified once a workflow has been approved, which can also include an email address

- Delegation (either manual or automatic)
- Reminders
- Escalations for unapproved workflows
- Changes to data in in-flight workflows
- Different email notification templates for each workflow step
- Ability to respect or not respect permissions for data in workflow approval steps

When a workflow is triggered, the approver(s) will receive an email notification and will receive a notification in the **To-Do** menu and **To-Do** tile on the home page. Selecting the workflow will take the user to the **My Workflows Requests** screen, which you can see in Figure 4.14.

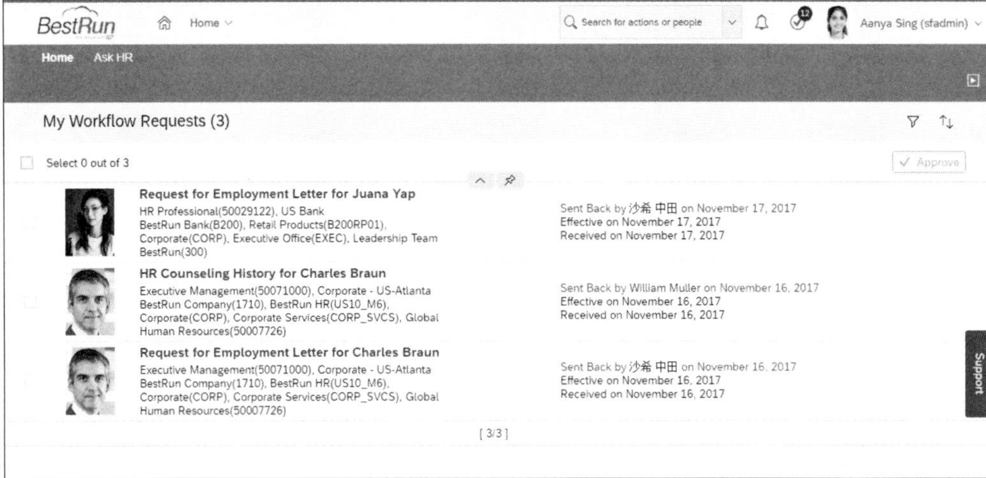

Figure 4.14 My Workflow Requests Page

Selecting a workflow opens the workflow approval page. Here, the details of the initiation, workflow participants, employee, data change(s), and workflow activity can be seen. A comments box is also available. The approver has the option to approve the workflow, update it, or send it back to the initiator.

Once an approver approves the workflow, it moves along to the next approver. A contributor can make comments on a workflow at any point before it is approved by the final approver. Once approved, any users assigned as **CC Roles** in the workflow will be notified about the approved changes. Changes only become active in the system once the workflow has been fully approved. Figure 4.15 shows a workflow being approved.

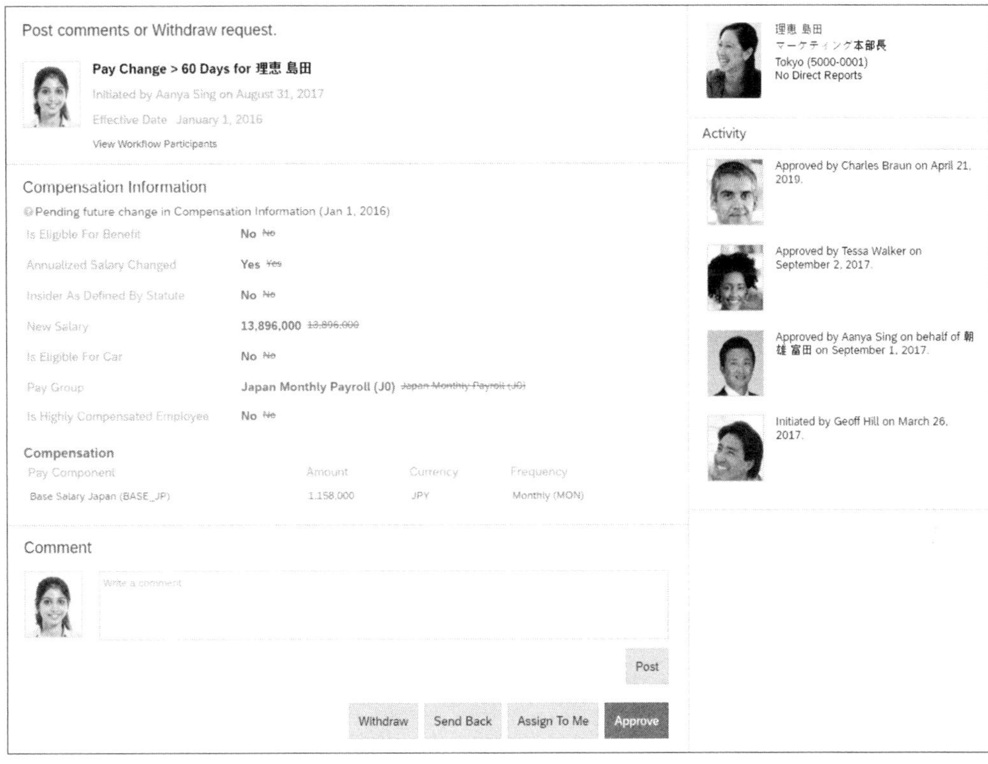

Figure 4.15 Workflow Approval Screen

Workflows are triggered using business rules. Once a rule is created, it is then assigned to a trigger point; the method of assignment depends on the object for which the workflow will trigger. For employee data, workflow trigger rules can be set to only trigger within certain contexts, such as MSS/ESS, the **History** UI, data imports, the New Hire/Rehire wizard, and so forth.

Workflows are triggered when data changes are made by using the **Edit** icon on a block in the People Profile, through the **History** UI (accessed with the **History** icon on a block in the People Profile), or through a transaction (e.g., new hire, termination, time off request, and so on).

When changes that trigger a workflow are being made, a pop-up window appears that shows the event reason for the workflow and a comments box. Selecting the **View Workflow Participants** hyperlink expands the window to show all the participants for the workflow, as seen in Figure 4.16.

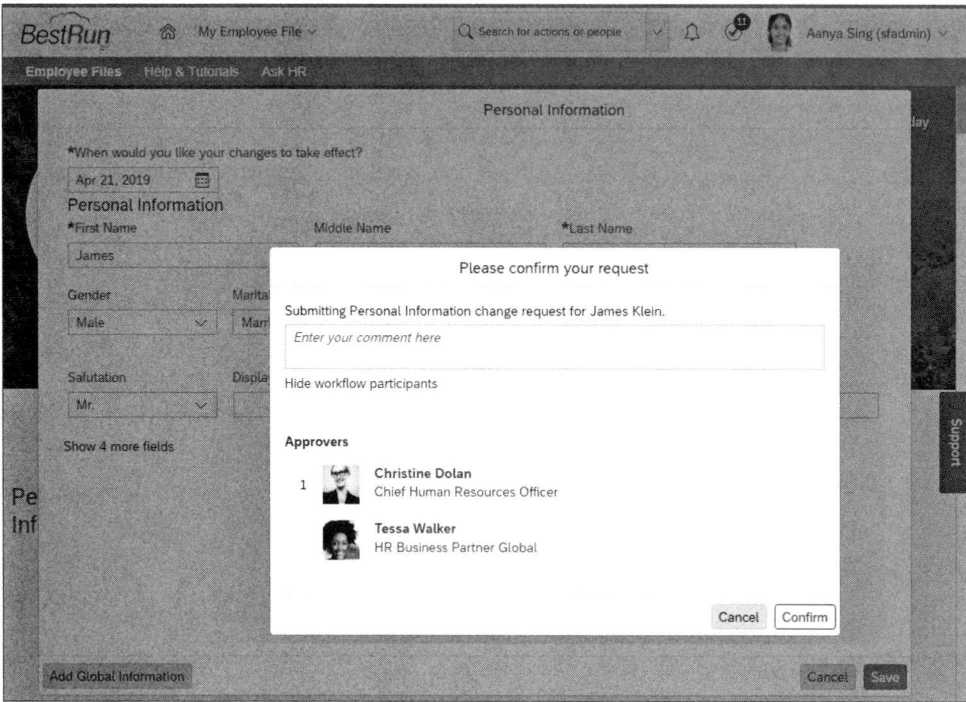

Figure 4.16 Workflow Pop-Up Window

Note that the workflow window does not open if the employee does not have any users' approvers assigned (for example, they have no manager or no HR manager) or the workflow has no approvers assigned. Also, the initiator of a workflow does not show if they are the first approver of a workflow. Once a workflow is submitted, it is routed to the first approver and any contributors. If the user has permission, they see a pending approval notification within the data changes, as shown in Figure 4.17.

In the **History** page of an effective-dated block, the workflow approval history can be displayed by selecting the **History** icon, selecting the appropriate record, and then selecting the **View Approval History** button. You can see this **Approval History** in Figure 4.18.

Further Resources

Further information can be found in the guide *Using Workflows in Employee Central* found on the SAP Help Portal under the SAP SuccessFactors Employee Central product page.

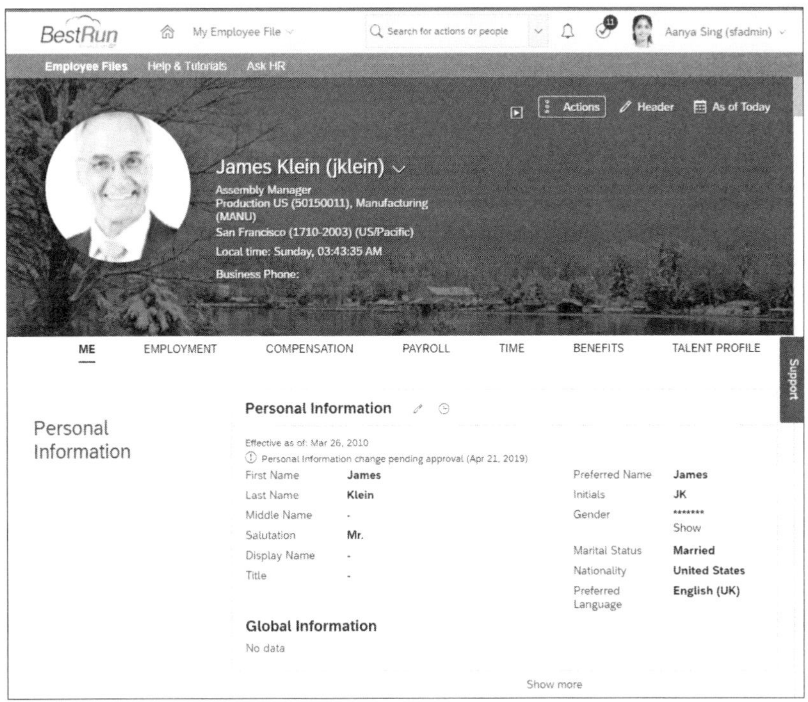

Figure 4.17 Pending Workflow Approval Notification

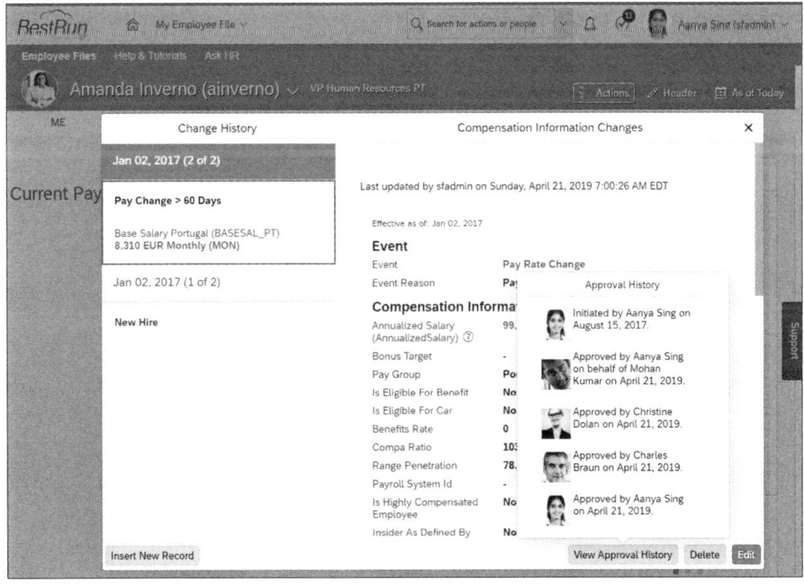

Figure 4.18 Workflow Approval History for a Record

4.4 Benefits

The Global Benefits module enables you to manage your benefits programs in each country inside the Employee Central system. It also allows organizations to create country-specific and global benefits programs and benefits for employees. Employees can enroll in benefits programs, and HR, managers, and employees can manage benefits in the system. Global Benefits also supports country-specific actions and benefits features, such as open enrollment in the United States or marriage gift reimbursement in Switzerland.

Global Benefits currently supports reimbursements, allowances (including deductible allowances), insurance plans, retirement savings plans, benefits-in-kind benefits, and a range of country-specific benefits. Several predelivered benefits are provided in the standard system, which customers can leverage.

Integration can be created between Global Benefits and third-party benefits providers. A standard integration template is available in the Integration Center (see Chapter 16) to export an Electronic Data Interchange (EDI) file of benefits data, and SAP Cloud Platform Integration contains a benefits integration template.

Let's walk through key benefits processes and features such as enrollments and claims.

4.4.1 Creating and Managing Benefits and Benefit Programs

Benefits and benefit programs are created and managed in the Admin Center in **Benefits Admin Overview**. Figure 4.19 shows a **Benefit Program** that has three **Benefits** associated with it. Multiple benefit programs can be created, and multiple benefits can be added to a benefit program.

Benefits contain a large number of configurable details that define all characteristics, such as benefit type, entitlement amount, enrollment details, workflow, associated pay components, policy documents, forms, and useful links. Pay components should be created prior to creating a benefit that will use them. Different rules can be created to manage eligibility to different benefits and benefit programs. Figure 4.20 shows an example of a benefit assigned to a benefit program.

Admins can also create dependencies between benefits and benefits plans for a specific time period. This enables you to define benefits that are contingent on other benefits for enrollment or lack of enrollment. An example might be where enrollment into a medical insurance plan in the US gives the ability to then enroll in a health savings account (HSA) or flexible spending account (FSA).

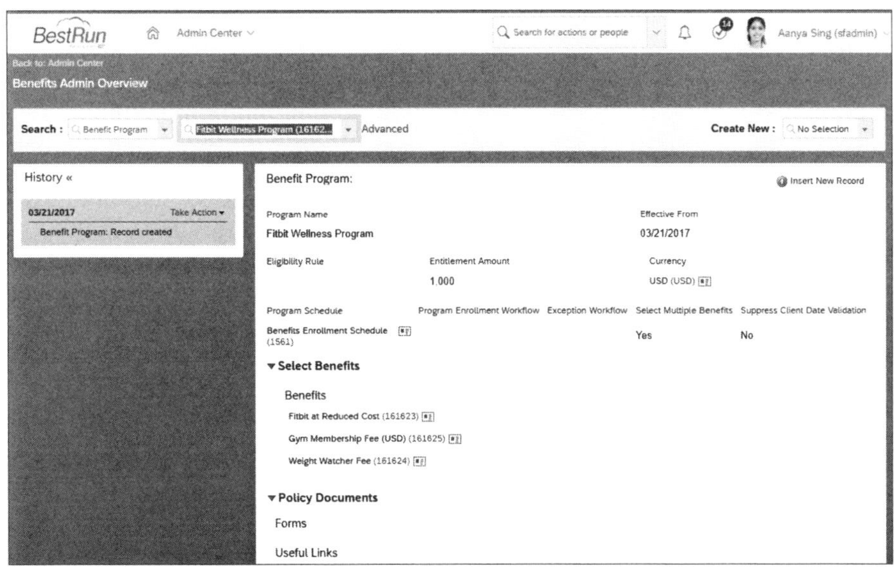

Figure 4.19 A Benefits Program in Benefits Admin Overview

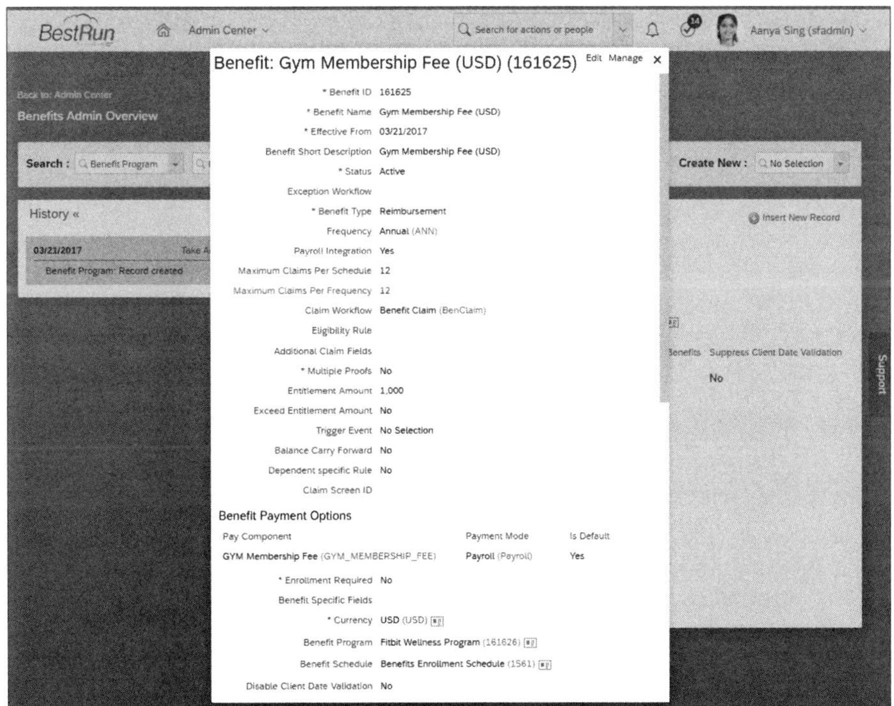

Figure 4.20 A Benefit in Benefits Admin Overview

The sections available on the **Benefits Overview** page, which we'll cover next, can be configured for such attributes as visibility of the section, names, and order.

4.4.2 Enrollment and Claims

Employees can access their benefits, enroll in benefits or benefits programs, or claim a benefit in the People Profile. They can go directly to their benefits overview through the People Profile or via the action search. Figure 4.21 shows benefits blocks on the People Profile.

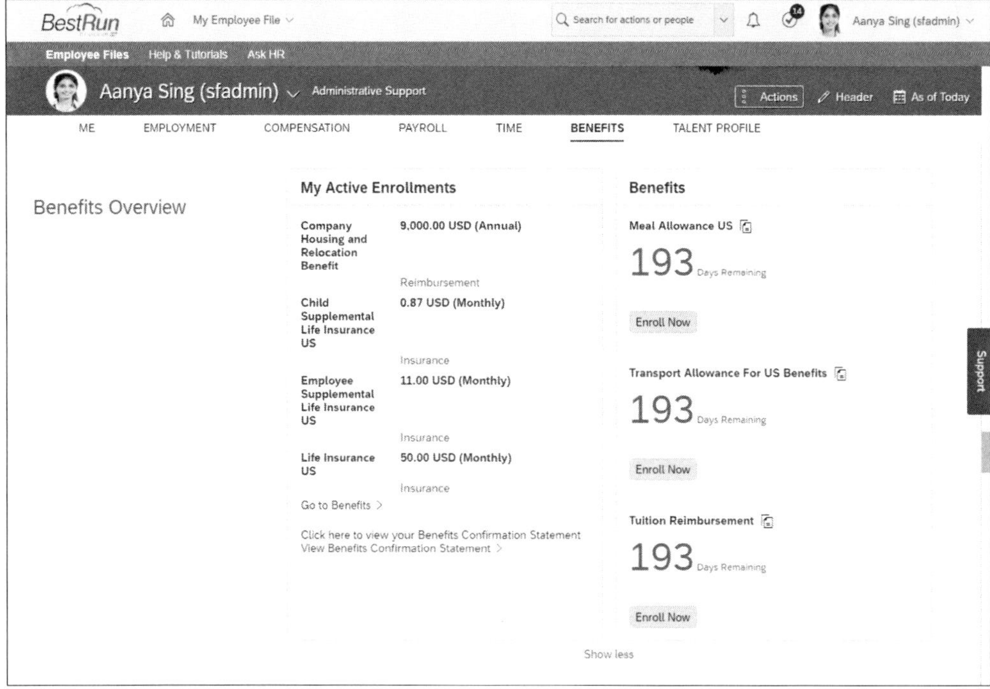

Figure 4.21 Employee Benefits Overview in the People Profile

Employees can view their enrollments in the **My Active Enrollments** block, as well as go to the benefits overview screen and view their **Benefits Confirmation Statement**. Employees can enroll in benefits in the **Benefits** block by selecting **Enroll Now** under the benefit that they wish to enroll in.

The overview screen—shown in Figure 4.22—gives employees a complete overview of their benefits information and allows them to enroll (including open enrollment in the United States) in benefits programs and benefits; it also allows them to make claims.

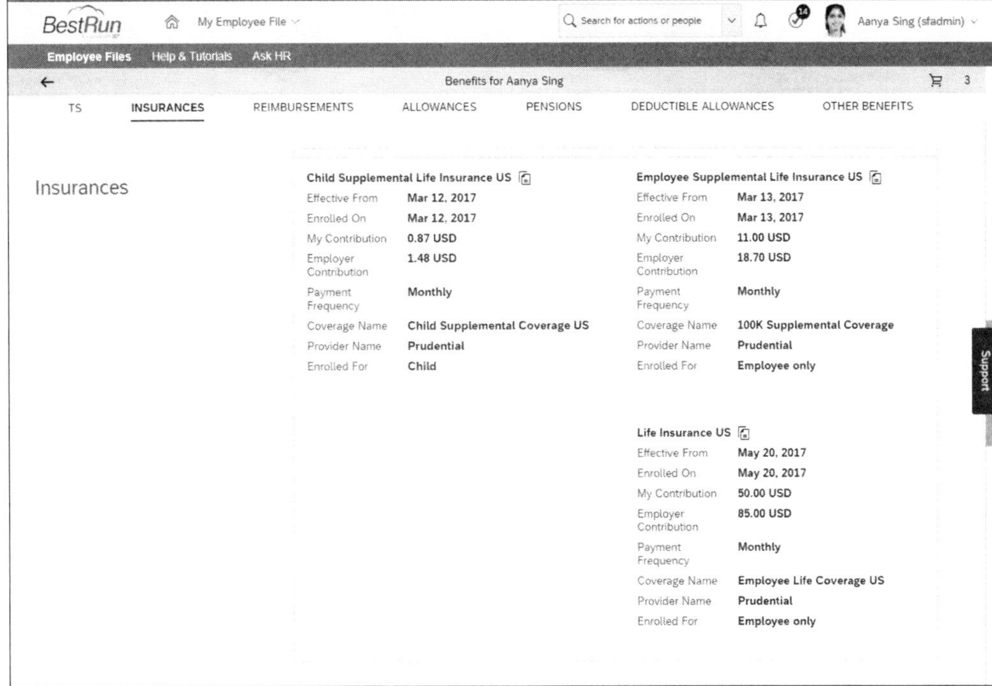

Figure 4.22 Benefits Overview Screen

Where a claim can be made for a benefit, employees use the **Start a Claim** button on the benefit block for which they want to make a claim. The claim process will vary based on the type of benefit and the configuration of the benefit.

The **Benefits Confirmation Statement** is a summary of benefits that employees can use to confirm they are enrolled in certain benefits. It typically contains details of benefit elections, any dependents or beneficiaries, costs, contributions, and more. Figure 4.23 shows a **Benefits Confirmation Statement**.

Further Resources

Further information can be found in the guides *Implementing and Configuring Global Benefits in Employee Central* and *Using Global Benefits in Employee Central* located on the SAP Help Portal under the SAP SuccessFactors Employee Central product page.

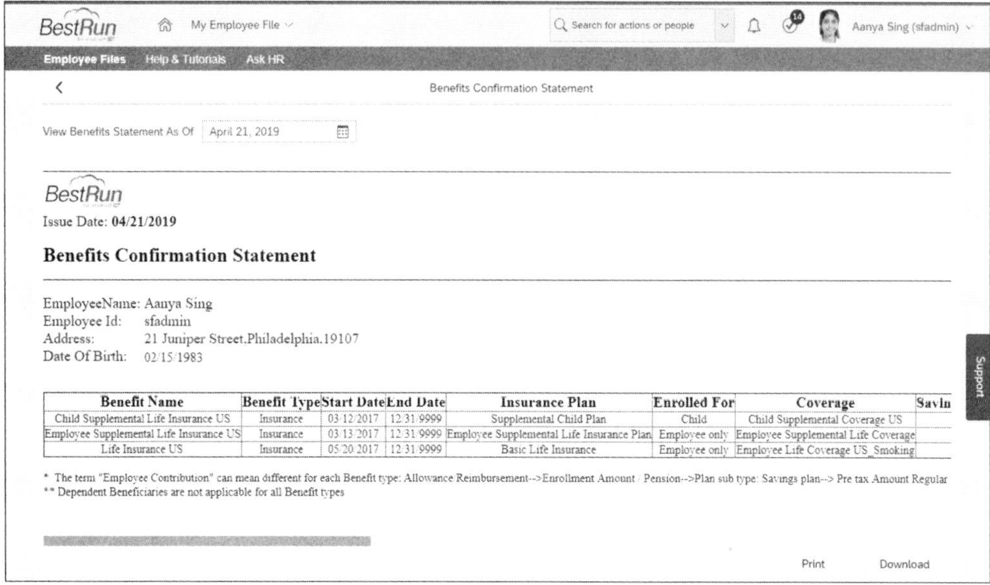

BestRun

Issue Date: **04/21/2019**

Benefits Confirmation Statement

EmployeeName: Aanya Sing
Employee Id: sfadmin
Address: 21 Juniper Street,Philadelphia,19107
Date Of Birth: 02/15/1983

Benefit Name	Benefit Type	Start Date	End Date	Insurance Plan	Enrolled For	Coverage	Savin
Child Supplemental Life Insurance US	Insurance	03/12/2017	12/31/9999	Supplemental Child Plan	Child	Child Supplemental Coverage US	
Employee Supplemental Life Insurance US	Insurance	03/13/2017	12/31/9999	Employee Supplemental Life Insurance Plan	Employee only	Employee Supplemental Life Coverage	
Life Insurance US	Insurance	05/20/2017	12/31/9999	Basic Life Insurance	Employee only	Employee Life Coverage US_Smoking	

* The term "Employee Contribution" can mean different for each Benefit type: Allowance/Reimbursement-->Enrollment Amount / Pension-->Plan sub type: Savings plan--> Pre tax Amount Regular
** Dependent Beneficiaries are not applicable for all Benefit types

Figure 4.23 Benefits Confirmation Statement

4.5 Time Management

Employee Central features a robust Time Management module. It provides two modules:

- *Payroll Time Sheet*: Time recording and valuation
- *Time Off*: Vacation and absence booking

Both solutions provide country-specific requirements for a number of countries. Typically, these are specific requirements that can't be handled by the standard-delivered modules. There are a significant number of rule scenarios and rule functions provided to enable you to build a variety of complex rules for eligibility, processing, and calculations. SAP also provides integration of time data to SAP ERP and Employee Central Payroll.

Employees view their time balances and access their timesheet and request time off from the People Profile. Figure 4.24 shows an employee's time information.

Where Employee Central Time Management cannot meet your needs, you have the opportunity to subscribe to a time management extension from SAP Solution

Extensions. It is recommended to have an in-depth evaluation of your needs prior to making a selection about which system(s) you will use for time entry.

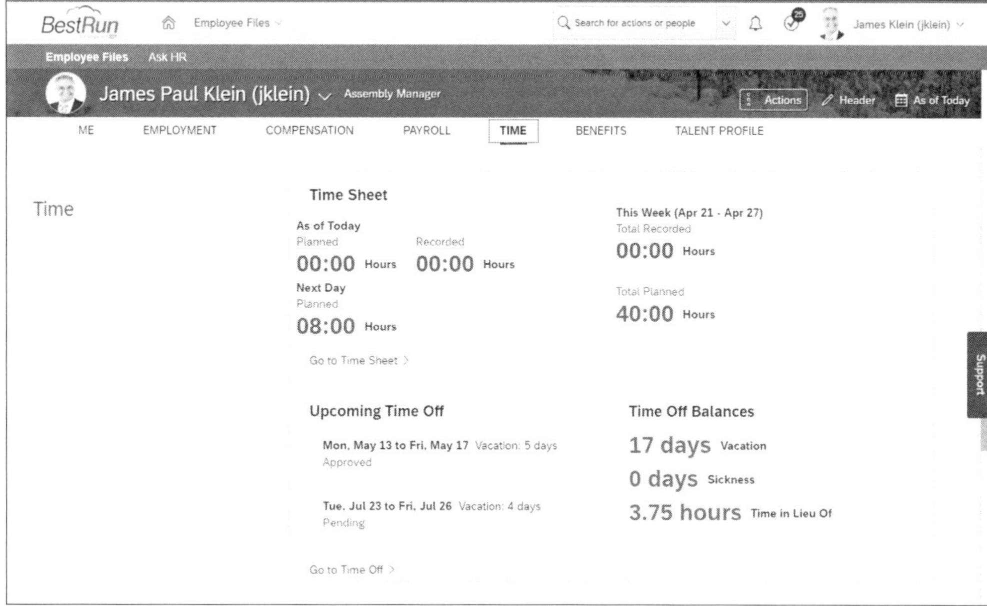

Figure 4.24 An Employee's Time Information on Their People Profile

Let's take a look at each module now.

4.5.1 Payroll Time Sheet

Time recording is performed in the Payroll Time Sheet module. The Payroll Time Sheet module provides a time sheet for employees, a valuation engine, and integration into Employee Central Payroll and SAP ERP, to use when running payroll in SAP ERP Payroll.

Timesheets are on a weekly basis and enable employees to enter their time worked each day in an hours and minutes format against one or more time types. Time recorded against a time type can be assigned to a cost center. On-call time, allowances, and absences can also be recorded. Workflows are used to allow approval of time after a timesheet has been submitted. Figure 4.25 shows a time sheet with entered time.

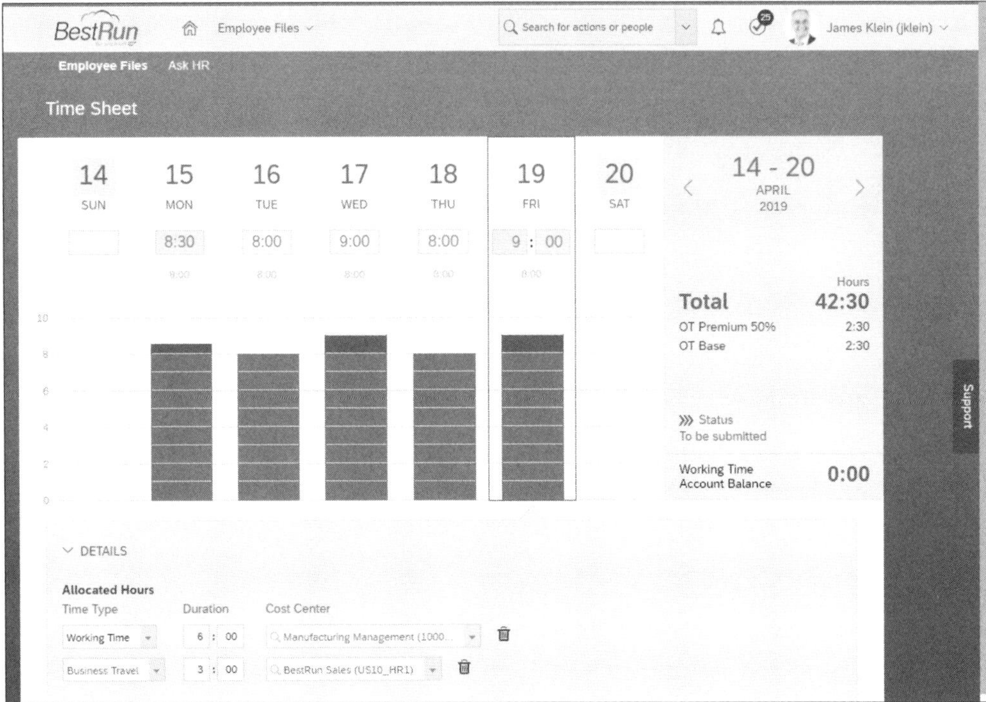

Figure 4.25 An Employee's Time Sheet

Once time has been approved, it is evaluated and then converted in pay components in an employee's compensation information.

Payroll Time Sheet allows time entry for three different scenarios:

- **Positive time recording**
  All time worked is entered into the timesheet. The entries are compared to the employee's planned work time to determine base pay, any overtime, or any holiday pay. Typically, positive time recording is used by hourly employees.
- **Overtime recording**
  Employees only enter hours worked beyond their standard work schedule. Overtime hours are then tallied and then overtime calculated. Business rules can be used to determine the type of overtime and what rates are to be applied. Typically, overtime recording is used by salaried employees.
- **Negative time recording**
  Employees only enter deviations from their standard work schedule, such as absences. The system assumes that, unless something is entered in the timesheet,

the employee is working their standard work schedule. Typically, negative time recording is used by salaried employees.

Time is entered on a daily basis in minutes and hours. Time can either be entered for an entire day at the end of the day, or it can be entered into one or more time types. Each time type entry can have a cost center assigned. Employees can also enter on-call time, any allowances provided, and any absences.

The time entered will be totaled up and displayed on the right side. Any overtime or other types of time that are not considered to be the employee's regular worked time are listed below the total. Once a timesheet is completed for the work, it is submitted. A draft can be saved so an employee can enter time periodically over the week.

Depending on the rules configured, if an employee enters more time than has been defined, then the employee will get an error message specifying this.

Employees who have specific defined breaks can have these as part of their timesheet, although it is also possible to configure dynamic breaks. *Dynamic breaks* essentially mean that employees take and enter their break after a certain number of hours.

Although timesheets are weekly and independent of each other, it is possible to evaluate data from multiple timesheets over a period. For example, a vacation accrual may be based on the number of hours worked over a four-week period. The time collector would assess the timesheets over a four-week period to determine the accrual that needs to be applied to the time type for the relevant vacation.

Employees may be able to amend past timesheets, depending on the time recording admissibility rules that are configured.

Further Resources

Further information can be found in the following guides on the SAP Help Portal under the SAP SuccessFactors Employee Central product page:

- *Implementing Employee Central Payroll Time Sheet*
- *Using Employee Central Payroll Time Sheet in Employee Central*
- *Recalculation in Employee Central Time Management*
- *Employee Central Time Management: Rules and Concepts*

4.5.2 Time Off

The Time Off module enables employees to book vacation or a leave of absence. Employees can request time off in SAP SuccessFactors via the browser-based application or via a mobile or tablet device, and managers can approve time off requests in the same way. HR and managers can also create leave of absence requests for employees who may need to take unplanned or long-term absences outside of their vacation.

Employees view their vacation balance on People Profile and request time off by selecting the **Go to Time Off** link. The **Time Off** page is shown in Figure 4.26. Here, employees can book time off for the different vacation time accounts that they have, including leave of absences.

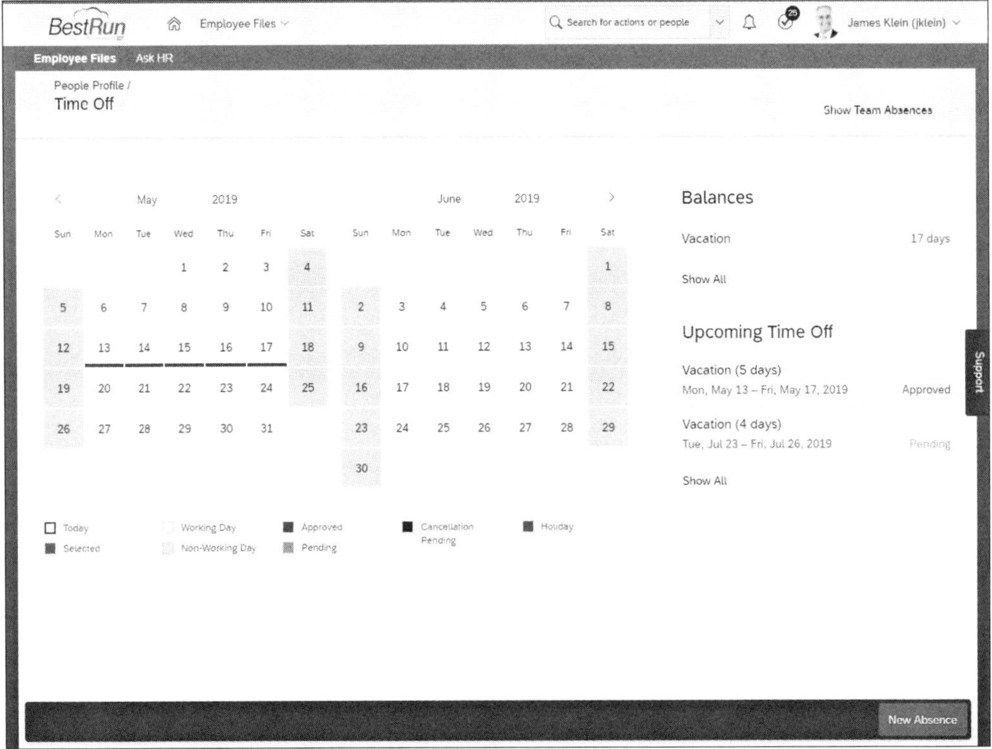

Figure 4.26 The Time Off Screen

Once a leave request has been submitted, then it will route for approval using a workflow. It will show as pending until it is approved.

Negative balances are allowed in Time Off. These can be used if an employee goes over their balance, is taking days against a future balance, or to clear old accounts at period-end processing. A limit can be placed on time accounts to prevent employees from going below a certain balance.

Managers have access to the **Team Absence Calendar**, which displays all of the absences in their team. This is shown in Figure 4.27.

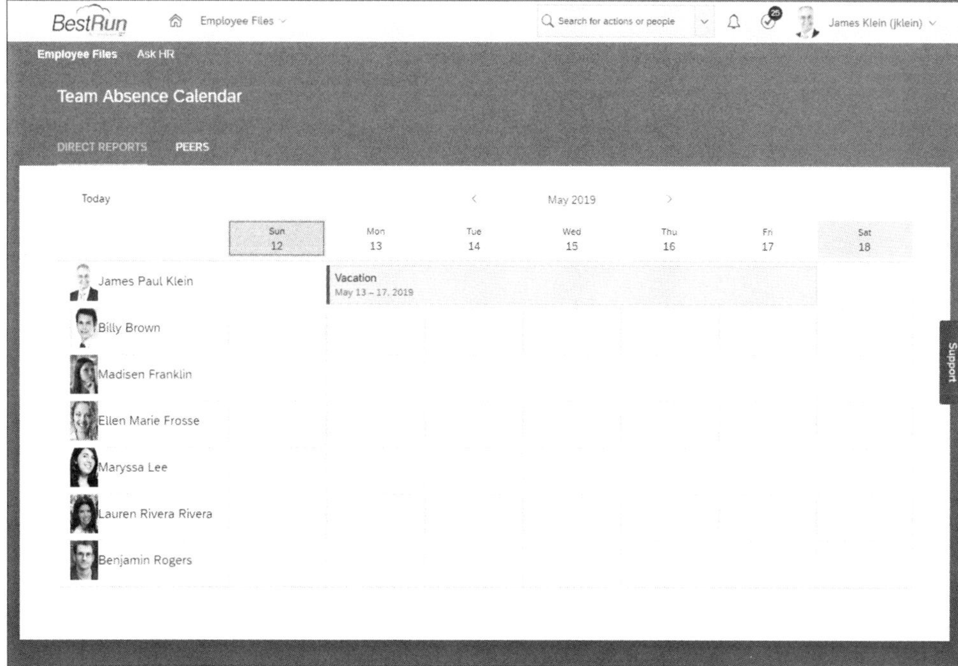

Figure 4.27 The Team Absence Calendar

Administrators have the ability to administer time directly for employees from the People Profile. The **Time Information** page—shown in Figure 4.28—enables administrators to view details of an employee's time records, time accounts, payouts, work schedule, alerts, and time collectors. Administrators can also make manual adjustments to employees' leave requests and time accounts.

Further Resources

Further information can be found in the following guides on the SAP Help Portal under the SAP SuccessFactors Employee Central product page:

- *Implementing Employee Central Time Off*
- *Using Employee Central Time Off in Employee Central*
- *Country-Specific Features in Employee Central Time Off*
- *Recalculation in Employee Central Time Management*
- *Employee Central Time Management: Rules and Concepts*

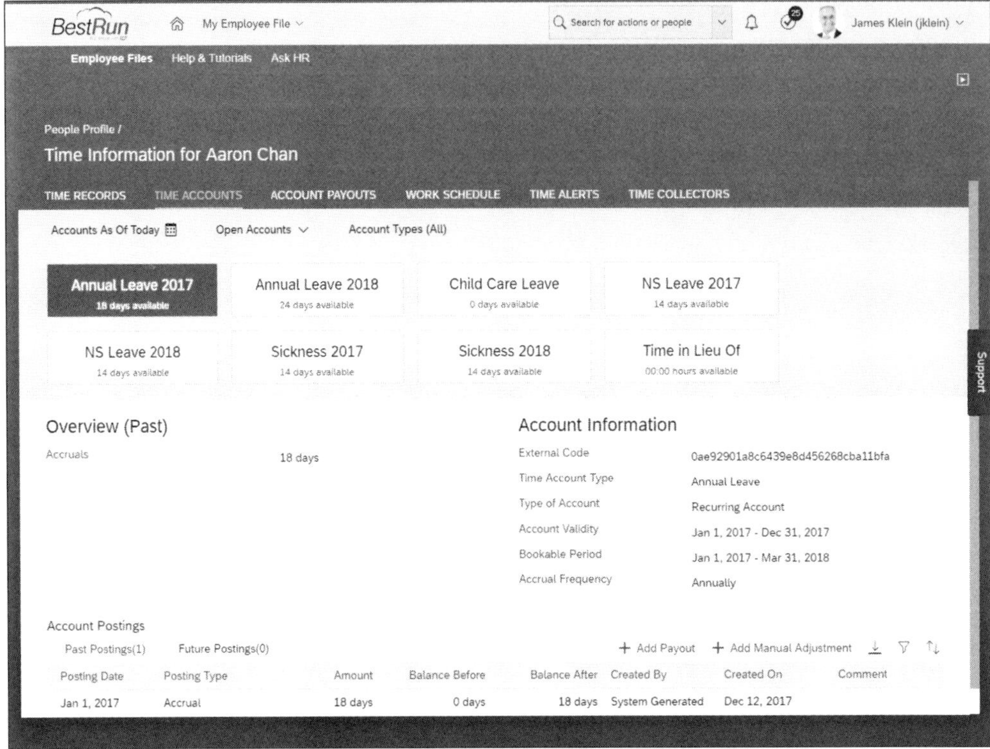

Figure 4.28 The Time Information Screen Available for Administrators

4.6 Global Assignment

The Global Assignment module enables employees to be sent on assignment to another company within their organization, with a home and host employment record to cover both the home employment and the expatriate employment.

Global assignments have several components and actions:

- The global assignment in the People Profile
- Events and event reasons
- Adding, editing, ending, and deleting a global assignment

When an employee is sent on an assignment to another company, this is considered another employment in Employee Central. The global assignment employment is referred to as the host employment, while their main employment is referred to as the home employment. You can toggle between these assignments. We'll cover this a bit later in this section.

Employees can only have one global assignment at any one time. In order to go on global assignment, any existing global assignments must be ended. A global assignment can be converted to a permanent employment. It is important to note that concurrent employment must be configured to perform this conversion. We will cover concurrent employment in Section 4.7.

A global assignment is added through the **Actions** button on the People Profile header by selecting the **Add: Global Assignment Details** option. Here, you define the event reason, start date, assignment type, planned end date, and the company of the assignment, as shown in Figure 4.29.

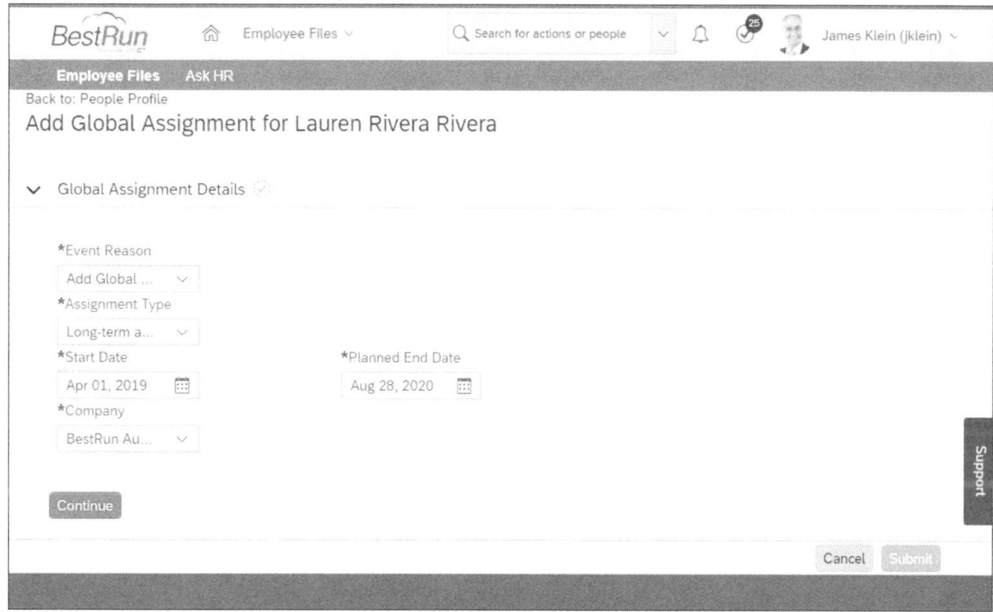

Figure 4.29 Adding a Global Assignment

You then define the details of the assignment job attributes in the following blocks:

- **Job Information**
- **Job Relationships**
- **Work Permit Info**
- **Compensation Information**

After the details have been entered and submitted—and any workflow has been approved—then the global assignment can be seen on the employee's People Profile and can be accessed using the toggle radio button. Depending on your configuration, the employee's home assignment will be set using an employee status that is dormant.

The global assignment can be viewed on the employee's People Profile in the header. A radio button for each assignment (home and host) is displayed in the People Profile header and acts as a menu to toggle between the People Profile of each assignment; the host assignment is selected by default when it is active.

The home assignment has the highlighted text **Home Assignment - Paused** next to it. The host assignment has the highlighted text **On Global Assignment** next to it, along with the planned end date of the assignment next to the text. In Figure 4.30, you can see the People Profile after an employee has gone on global assignment.

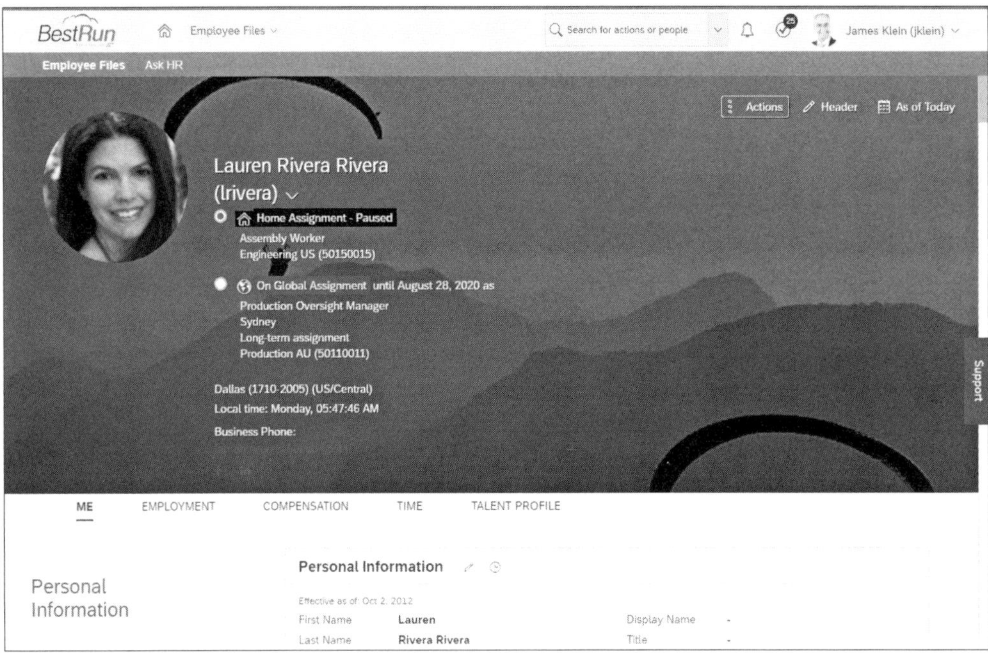

Figure 4.30 The Radio Buttons to Toggle between Assignments

The host assignment button always remains on the People Profile header, as long as there has been at least one global assignment in the past or there will be one in the future. For past assignments, the highlighted text **Past Assignment** is shown next to the radio button. For future assignments, the highlighted text **Future Assignment** is shown, as you can see in Figure 4.31.

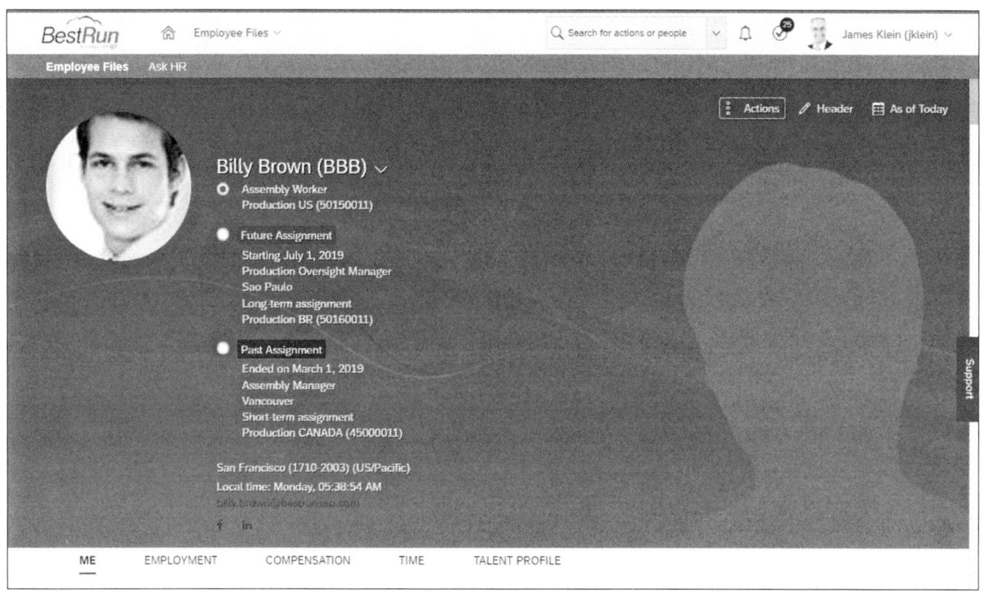

Figure 4.31 The Radio Buttons to Toggle between Past and Future Assignments

The People Profile displays the same background element data for both assignments, such as performance data or succession planning data.

On the People Profile, the host assignment shows mostly the same details as the home assignment, although the **Employment Details** block is replaced by the **Global Assignment Details** block for a host assignment, as shown in Figure 4.32. The **Global Assignment Details** block contains the details entered in the first step of sending an employee on a global assignment.

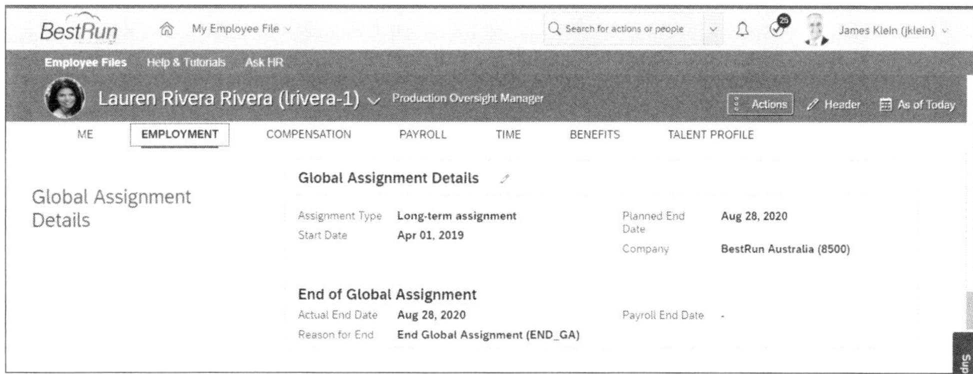

Figure 4.32 The Host Assignment

The global assignment can be edited, ended, or deleted by selecting **Actions** in the People Profile header and selecting the **Manage Global Assignment Details** option. Here, you will see the status of the assignment (**Active, Ended**, or **Future**) and have the option to either edit or delete the assignment. When you choose to edit the assignment, you are presented with the option to edit the details entered during the creation of the assignment or you can enter the actual end date on which the assignment ended or is to end (this could be the same as or different from the planned end date entered when the assignment was created).

Once the global assignment has ended, the **Global Assignment Details** block will display the **End of Global Assignment** section that displays the actual end date and the event reason for ending the assignment. This was seen back in Figure 4.32.

It is possible to set up automatic ending of global assignments using the Rules Engine. Additionally, alerts and notifications can be created to support the global assignments processes.

When searching for employees using the action search, the employee will show **Multiple Assignments** under their name, and their quickcard will show both assignments with the host assignment color-coded, as shown in Figure 4.33. On the Org Chart, employees on global assignment will show the text **Paused Assignment** on their home assignment, and for their host assignment a colored bar under their name that will specify that they are on global assignment (also shown in Figure 4.33).

When employees who are on global assignment login to SAP SuccessFactors, they will see a **Global Assignment** button next to their name in the header panel. This enables the user to switch between each assignment so that they can perform different processes for each assignment.

Performance and compensation forms can be created for either or both home and host assignments. However, forms that have already been created for one assignment cannot be transferred or linked to the other assignment. Depending on how permissions are setup, a manager may only be able to see objectives (if the form created against the home assignment) but not performance (if the form was created against the host assignment). Additionally, an employee could have forms launched for both their home and host assignments if the criteria within the form is configured to enable it (for example, if a common field like **Employee Class** or **Job Code** is used).

The employee's address while away on global assignment can be added to the **Home Address** portlet of the employee's host assignment. This address will be visible for both the home and host assignments, but adding, editing, or deleting an address for global assignment should be only be performed in the **Home Address** portlet of the host assignment.

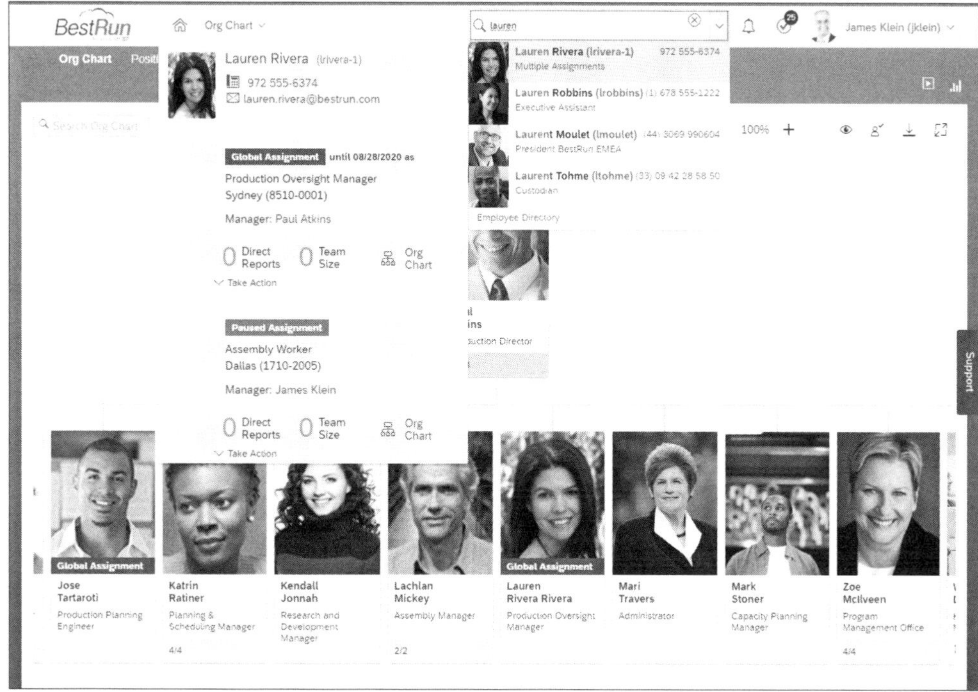

Figure 4.33 Assignments on the Quickcard

Further Resources

Further information can be found in the guides *Implementing and Configuring Global Assignments in Employee Central* and *Managing Employment in Employee Central* located on the SAP Help Portal under the SAP SuccessFactors Employee Central product page.

4.7 Concurrent Employment

The concurrent employment feature enables employees to have multiple employments concurrently. This may be needed if an employee has two or more roles or employment contracts in the same company or a different company of the organization that differ in terms of, for example, location, responsibilities, and/or compensation. A concurrent employment is referred to as the *secondary employment* while their main employment is referred to as the *primary employment*. Concurrent employment works very similarly to the global assignment process that we covered in the previous section.

To add a concurrent employment, select **Actions** in the People Profile header and then select **Add: Concurrent Employment**. Here you define hire date, company assignment, event reason (which is based on a hire event), and other fields, as defined in the **Concurrent Employment Details** block on the People Profile, which is shown in Figure 4.34.

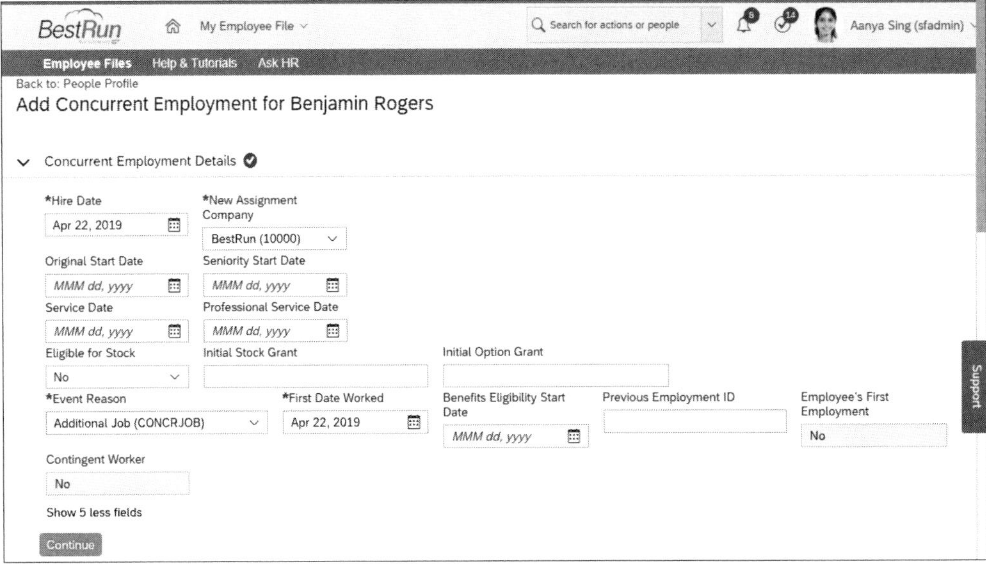

Figure 4.34 Adding a Concurrent Employment

Once these details are entered, four further blocks appear:

- **Secondary Employment Information**
- **Job Information**
- **Job Relationships**
- **Compensation Information**

After the details have been entered and submitted—and any workflow has been approved—then the concurrent employment can be seen on the employee's People Profile and can be accessed using the toggle radio button.

The concurrent employment can be viewed on the employee's People Profile in the header. A radio button for each employment is displayed in the People Profile header and acts as a menu to toggle between the People Profile of each employment; the main employment is selected by default and is indicated with a star next to it. This radio button (shown in Figure 4.35) always remains in the People Profile header, as long as there has been at least one concurrent employment either in the past or there will be one in the future.

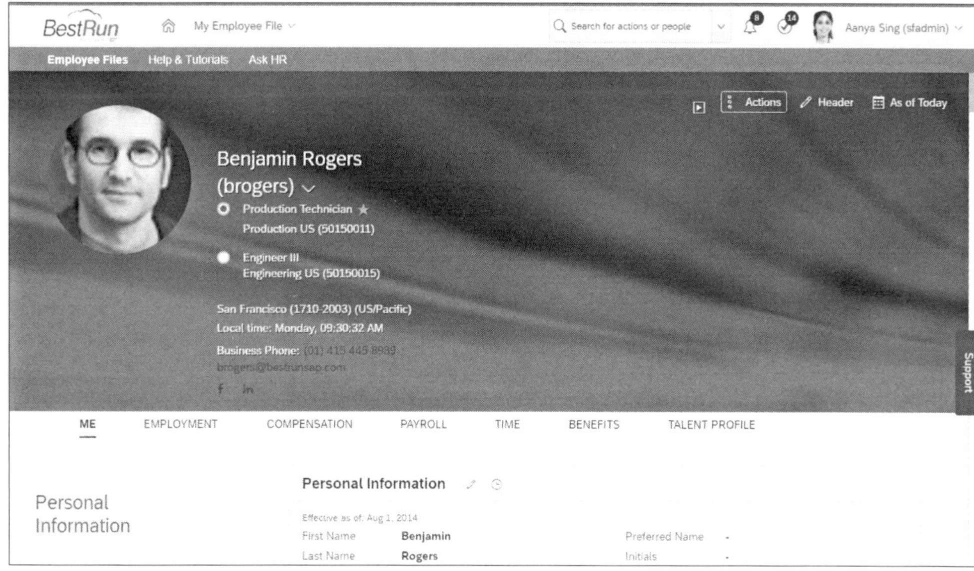

Figure 4.35 Radio Buttons to Toggle between Employments

For past employments, the text **(past)** is shown next to the radio button. For future employments, the text **(future)** is shown. They are both shown in Figure 4.36.

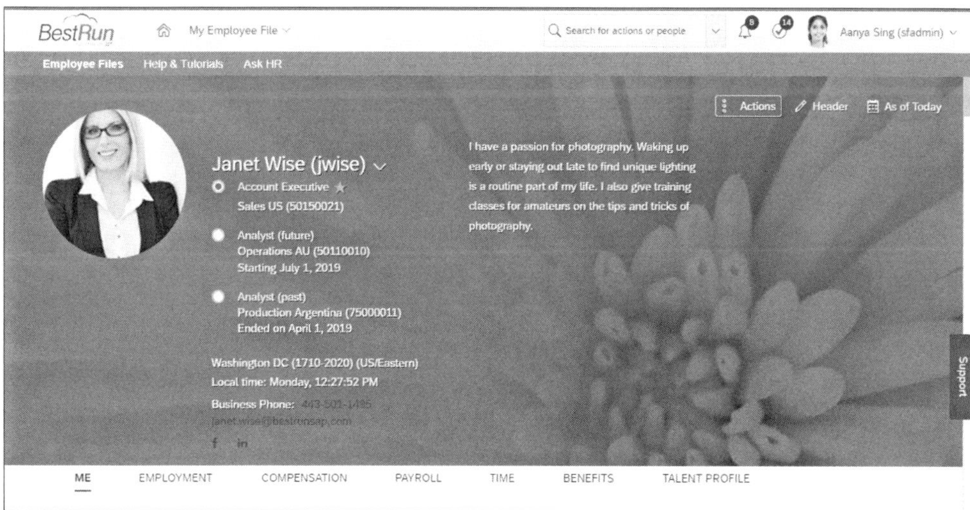

Figure 4.36 Radio Buttons to Toggle between Past and Future Employments

Employments are ended by using the **Terminate** option in the **Actions** menu on the People Profile of the employment you wish to end. You will be asked to confirm if it is the current employment or all employments that you want to terminate.

It is possible to convert a secondary employment to be the sole main employment or to swap a secondary employment to be the main employment.

Alerts and notifications can be set up to alert certain employees about the expiration of concurrent employments.

When employees who are on concurrent employment login to SAP SuccessFactors, they will see their main employment listed under their name in the header panel, just as with a global assignment. As with that functionality, this enables the employee to switch between each of their employments to perform the different processes for each employment.

Performance and compensation forms can be created for concurrent employments. Depending on how permissions are set up, a manager may only be able to see objectives (if the form was created against the primary employment) but not performance (if the form was created against a concurrent employment). Additionally, an employee could have forms launched for employments if the criteria within the form is configured to enable it (e.g., if a common field like employee class or job code is used).

Further Resources

Further information can be found in the guides *Implementing and Configuring Concurrent Employment in Employee Central* and *Managing Employment in Employee Central* located on the SAP Help Portal under the SAP SuccessFactors Employee Central product page.

4.8 Contingent Workforce Management

Contingent Workforce Management allows you to display details of contingent workers in Employee Central. Contingent workers are typically contract labor, temporary workers, freelancers, consultants, and so forth. If using SAP Fieldglass, you can replicate contingent workers from SAP Fieldglass to Contingent Workforce Management and launch requisitions in SAP Fieldglass from the Position Org Chart.

Contingent Workforce Management is not a replacement for a vendor management system (VMS) like SAP Fieldglass, but it compliments a VMS in being able to allow you to visualize contingent workers in the Org Chart and view details about a contingent worker in the People Profile. Naturally, the data and views you see of a contingent worker differ somewhat from what you see about employees. Because contingent workers are not employees, you won't see such things as national ID information, compensation information, or talent information on their People Profile. You will, however, see information about the work order the contingent worker is procured under and any custom blocks added to the People Profile that users are permissioned to see for contingent workers.

In addition to adding a contingent worker, Contingent Workforce Management provides the following capabilities:

- Create and maintain list of vendors
- View contingent workers in the People Profile
- View contingent workers in the Org Chart (and toggle them on or off)
- Hire a contingent worker as a full-time employee
- Convert a full-time employee to a contingent worker
- View reports with or without contingent workers included
- Allow contingent workers to be part of talent management processes

Contingent workers are added to Employee Central in one of two ways:

- The Add Contingent Worker wizard
- From SAP Fieldglass

The Add Contingent Worker wizard (shown in Figure 4.37) is similar to the New Hire wizard, although it contains fewer sections because the employee-specific blocks are naturally not part of the wizard. Business rules can be used to further hide fields not needed in the Add Contingent Worker wizard.

Contingent workers can be viewed in the Org Chart, as seen in Figure 4.38. From here you can navigate to the contingent worker's People Profile, which we can see in Figure 4.39.

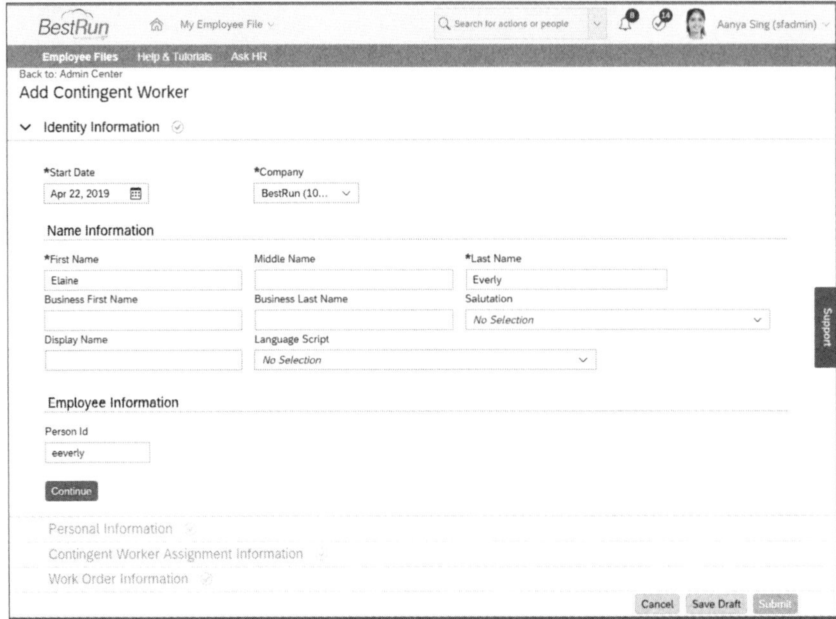

Figure 4.37 The Add Contingent Worker Wizard

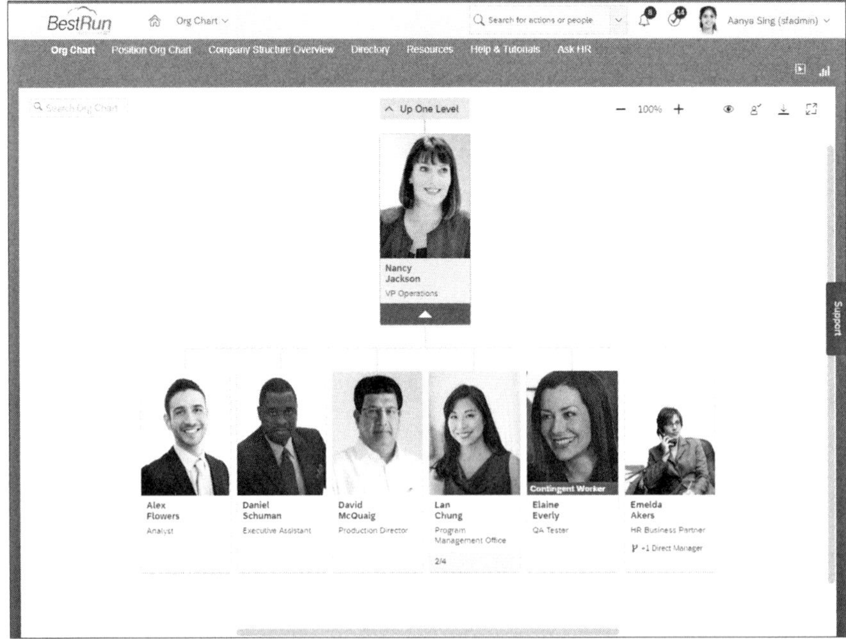

Figure 4.38 Viewing a Contingent Worker in the Org Chart

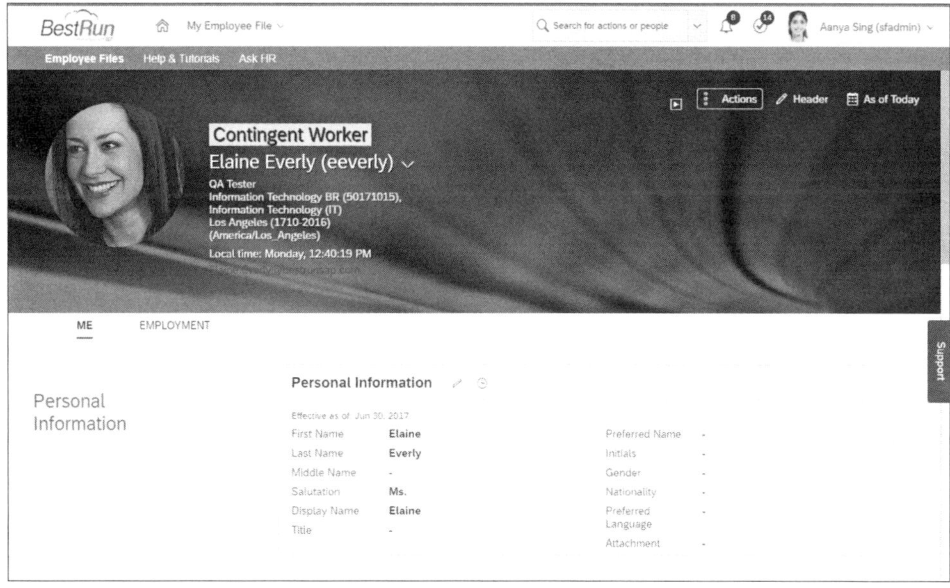

Figure 4.39 Viewing a Contingent Worker's People Profile

When searching for employees in the action search, contingent workers will be highlighted with the words **Contingent Worker** in a colored bar, as shown in Figure 4.40.

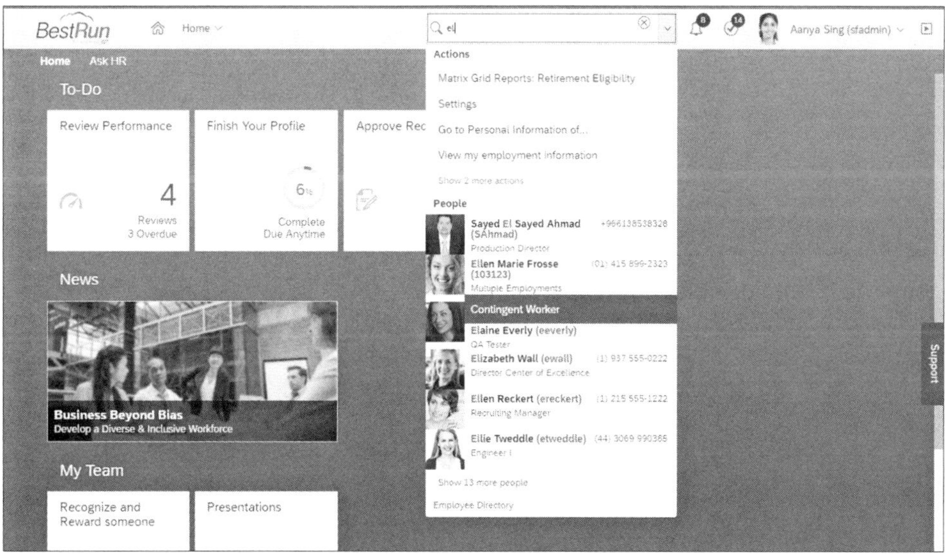

Figure 4.40 A Contingent Worker Highlighted in the Action Search Results

Further Resources

Further information can be found in the guides *Contingent Workforce Management* and *Using SAP Fieldglass with Employee Central* found on the SAP Help Portal under the SAP SuccessFactors Employee Central product page.

4.9 Administration

There are a number of key Employee Central administrative activities that may need to be performed on a regular basis, and thus should be addressed. We'll cover them now.

4.9.1 Invalid HR Data

Employees who have invalid data can be identified using the **Employees Associated With Invalid HR Data** application in the Admin Center, as shown in Figure 4.41.

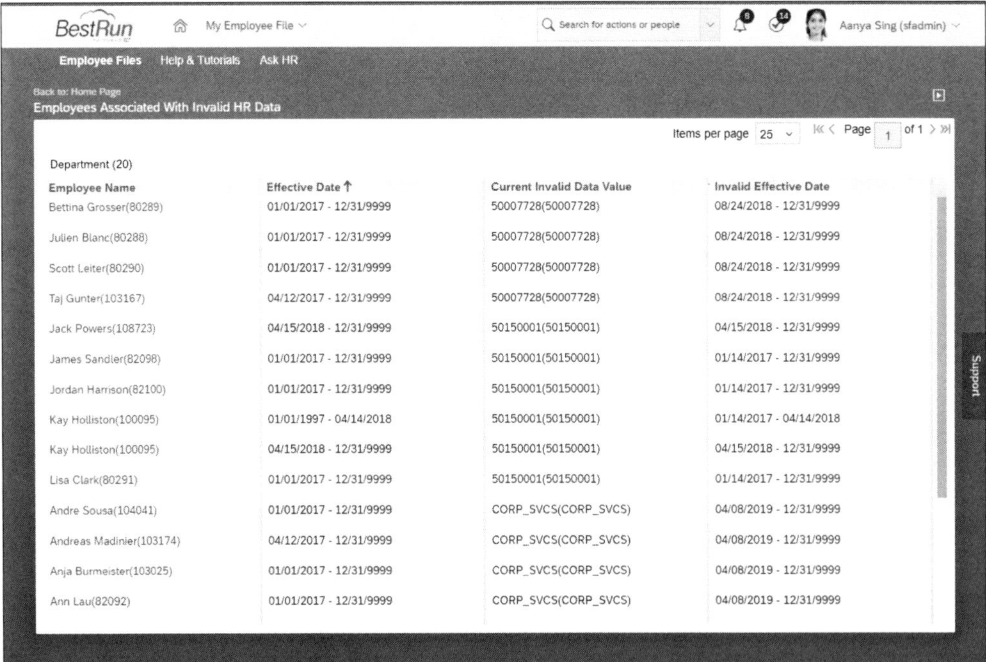

Figure 4.41 Employees Associated with Invalid HR Data Application

The application shows a horizontal list of fields at the top of the application portlet with values in brackets next to them; these represent the different types of invalid HR data that have been detected and how many instances have been detected. The number of fields varies based on the amount of data issued in the system. Each field is a hyperlink, and if you select one of them, you are shown a complete list of employees with the effective date and invalid value.

Clicking an employee takes you to a screen showing the history screen and which records and fields have invalid data. You can then correct this by using the **Take Action** button and selecting **Make Correction**. Figure 4.42 shows an invalid **Department**.

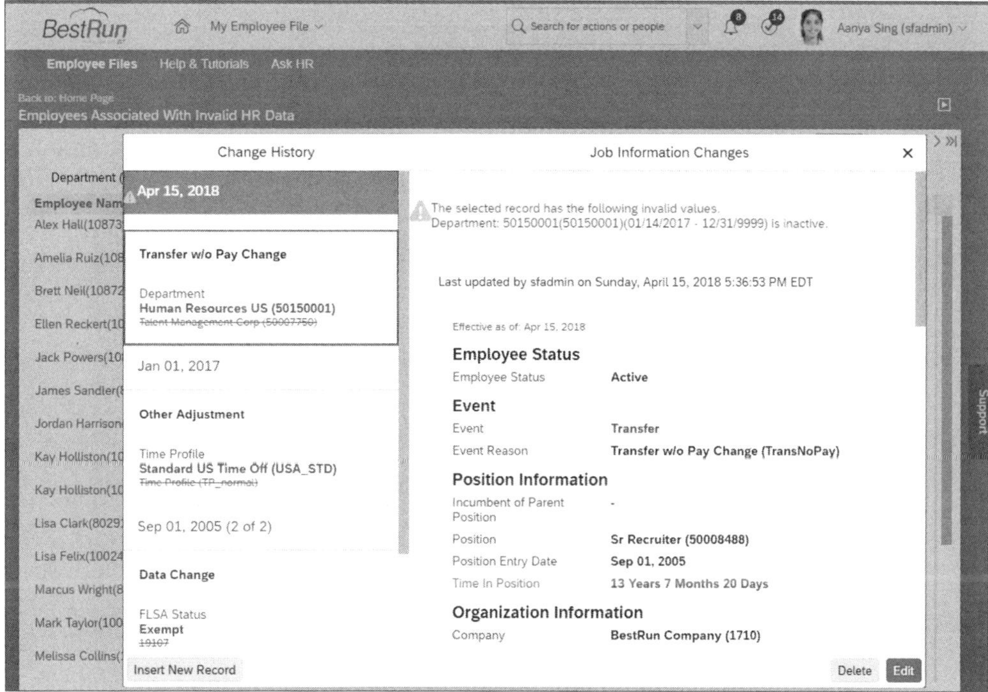

Figure 4.42 Invalid Data for an Employee

4.9.2 Manage Workflow Requests

There are two features available that allow the management of workflow requests. These are used to perform all sorts of activities on workflows, as well as to identify workflows with invalid approvers. We'll take a brief look at each of these now Workflow requests can be managed through the option **Manage Workflow Requests** in the

Admin Center. Here, workflow requests can be displayed based on a number of search criteria, including the initiator, subject employee, workflow configuration, workflow request status, effective date range, and requested date range. Figure 4.43 shows a list of workflow requests with status **SENTBACK**.

Each workflow can be displayed and also have one of the following options performed: lock the workflow request, add another approver, change approver(s), remove approver(s), reroute the request, or decline the request. You perform these by selecting the **Take Action** button in the **Actions** column for the appropriate request. If the button does not exist, no actions can be performed on that particular workflow request.

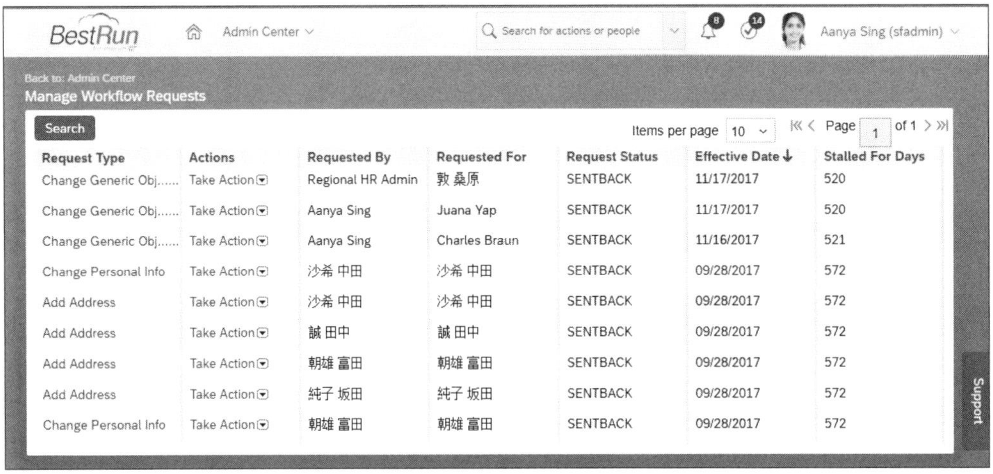

Request Type	Actions	Requested By	Requested For	Request Status	Effective Date	Stalled For Days
Change Generic Obj......	Take Action	Regional HR Admin	敦 桑原	SENTBACK	11/17/2017	520
Change Generic Obj......	Take Action	Aanya Sing	Juana Yap	SENTBACK	11/17/2017	520
Change Generic Obj......	Take Action	Aanya Sing	Charles Braun	SENTBACK	11/16/2017	521
Change Personal Info	Take Action	沙希 中田	沙希 中田	SENTBACK	09/28/2017	572
Add Address	Take Action	沙希 中田	沙希 中田	SENTBACK	09/28/2017	572
Add Address	Take Action	誠 田中	誠 田中	SENTBACK	09/28/2017	572
Add Address	Take Action	朝雄 富田	朝雄 富田	SENTBACK	09/28/2017	572
Add Address	Take Action	純子 坂田	純子 坂田	SENTBACK	09/28/2017	572
Change Personal Info	Take Action	朝雄 富田	朝雄 富田	SENTBACK	09/28/2017	572

Figure 4.43 Workflow Requests for SENTBACK Status

Workflow requests with invalid approvers can be managed through the option **Manage workflow requests with invalid approvers** under **Employee Files** in the Admin Center. This feature is very similar to the **Manage Workflow Requests** feature, although it does not have search criteria. In the list of workflows, the same columns are shown as in **Manage Workflow Requests**, with an additional column for the invalid approver. The same actions can be performed on these workflows as in **Manage Workflow Requests**.

4.9.3 Mass Changes

Administrators can create mass data changes, such as organizational changes, job relationship changes, and so on. Mass changes are created in the Admin Center via

Manage Mass Changes, as shown in Figure 4.44. They can be initiated for any field in the **Job Information** or **Job Relationships** portlets from the **Employment Information** screen.

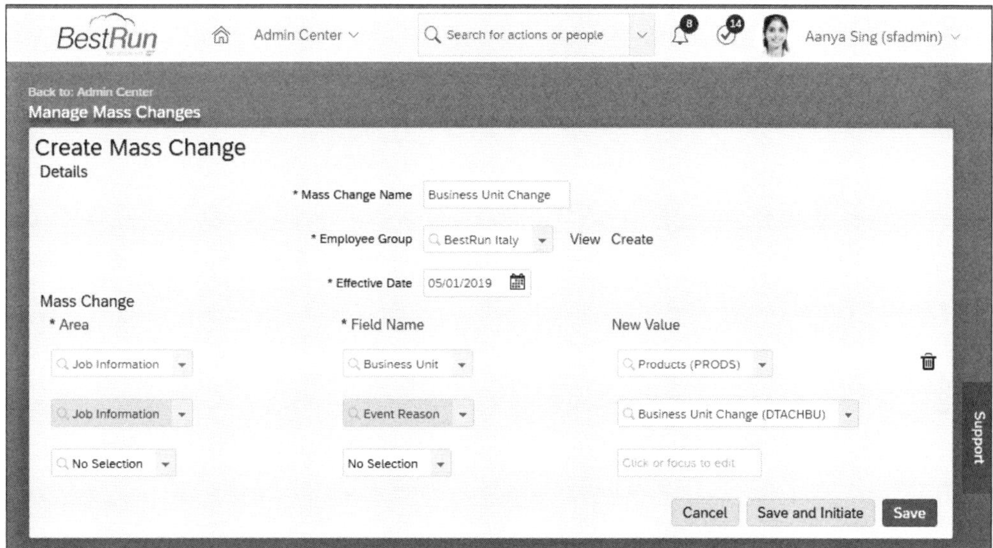

Figure 4.44 Creating a Mass Change

Once the **Manage Mass Changes** application is opened, a list of all created mass changes requests is shown. A new mass change can be created by clicking the **Create New** button. Existing mass changes can be viewed (and when viewed, executed) or copied.

Mass changes are created for specific employee groups—which are defined during the mass change creation process—on an effective date for one or more fields. For **Job Information** changes, an event reason must always be defined, and this field displays in the list of fields automatically.

When you're creating a mass change, the name, employee group, effective date, and fields to be changed need to be defined. After a mass change action is created, the system gives you two buttons: **Save** and **Save and Initiate**. **Save** creates the mass change action but does not execute it, while **Save and Initiate** both saves the mass change and also executes it immediately. Once executed, the mass change shows in the list of mass changes on the main screen with status **Initiated**. Once it starts, the status changes to **Started** until execution is completed; then, it changes to either **Complete Successfully** or **Completed with Errors**.

4.10 Reporting

Like with other applications, Employee Central data can be reported on with ad hoc reporting. However, Employee Central also features advanced reporting. At the time of writing (fall 2019), Employee Central's advanced reporting provides more than 96 standard reports that can be used and adapted as required. These reports also include more than 30 country-specific reports.

Advanced reporting is accessed through the Report Center. Figure 4.45 shows the **Headcount and FTEs** report.

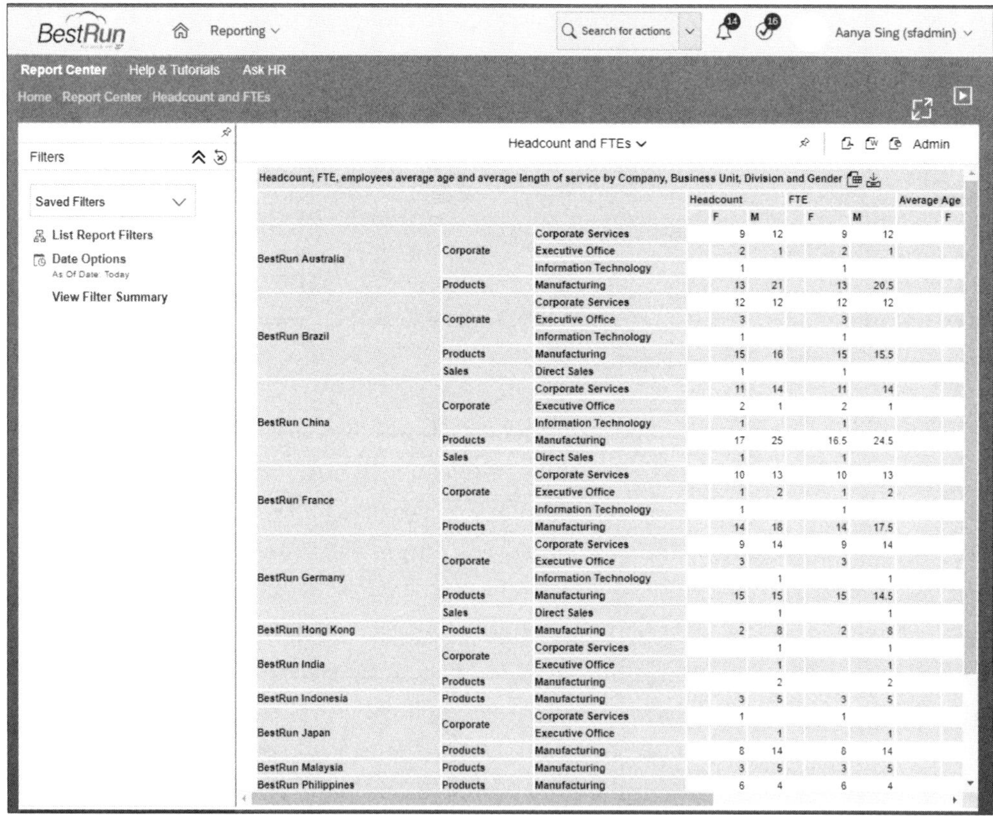

Figure 4.45 Headcount and FTEs Report in Advanced Employee Central Reporting

The Report Designer is a tool offered in the Report Center that can be used to create reports based on those from advanced Employee Central reporting.

Further Resources

Further information can be found in the guide *Employee Central Advanced Reporting: Standard Reports* located on the SAP Help Portal under the SAP SuccessFactors Employee Central product page.

4.11 Implementation Tips

Implementing Employee Central can be a hefty process. Your core HR system touches every employee, a number of different systems, and various end-to-end processes. Let's run through a few useful tips when undergoing an Employee Central implementation:

- **Start with understanding the system**
  It's hard to design a system you're not familiar with, so before you can make design decisions about your processes and new Employee Central system, you should have the opportunity to experience the system and get some basic training on the fundamentals of the system. SAP provide customers with basic administrator training, but your implementation partner should offer or be able to provide a comprehensive demo and/or this type of training.
- **Data migration**
  No matter how much time and effort you budget for data migration and data conversion, it will take more time and effort than you think. Even if you have a tool that accelerates the process, cleansing the data and understanding how the SAP SuccessFactors import templates need to be filled and how data imports work can take time.
- **Design and functionality**
  Implementing Employee Central is an HR transformation and will provide an opportunity to revamp and reinvigorate your HR business processes. While some of your current processes may work fine, there is plenty of opportunities to do things a bit differently and to optimize every business process.

  Likewise, not all new systems will have the same or more advanced functionality than the legacy system. There will always be situations where your legacy system does something better or HR members are fond of an old process, but that shouldn't be the reason to configure Employee Central to behave in the same or a similar way.

The bottom line is that "That's the way we've always done it" or "We can't go backward in functionality" are not valid rationales for making important business decisions.

- **Documentation**
  It is important to document your processes, design, and configuration choices. SAP provides consultants with workbooks for the core system configuration, but to document your processes, business rules, any customer objects, or nonstandard functionality, then you or your partner consultants will need to produce documentation that covers all processes and requirements.
- **Org structure**
  The org structure in Employee Central drives many features and processes and is usually different from the org structure in other systems. The org structure in Employee Central is very flexible and can provide granular management and visibility of your organization. You should take time to understand the Employee Central functionality and walk through how your organization looks before finalizing your org structure design.

  One point to note is that this flexibility and granularity can complicate the integration of employees and/or organizational data to other systems, depending on how your organization is designed in Employee Central or the target system.
- **Self-services**
  With native built-in self-services functionality, workflows, and event derivation—coupled with an impressive user experience—Employee Central offers the ideal opportunity to provide managers and employees with the ability to perform transactions, implement data changes, and document requests (such as leaving requests or employment documentation) directly.

  Consideration should be given to what capabilities are given to managers and employees, as well as the change management effort needed to ensure the workforce understands how and why the additional activities that they will have to undertake will benefit them. Self-service and workflow approvals should be kept simple and easy-to-use, and enable execution of data changes without the need to refer to a guide or manual.
- **Keep workflows simple**
  Simplicity is key for approvals. The more approvers there are in a workflow, the more workflows that won't be approved. Ensure approval paths are simple but

allow the right authority to approve what is being performed. Think about who would need to approve a decision if no system existed, and how senior managers and executives would feel about getting multiple approval requests.

- **Stick to best practice where possible**
  While there are endless possibilities to configure Employee Central to do what you need, it's important to remember that an Employee Central implementation is a transformation project and that you should be looking to add maximum value with lowest complexity. There are a number of common and best practices that your partner can help you apply to your implementation, and they can help guide you to keep your processes simple yet effective.

  SAP SuccessFactors provides some tools to help with this, including:
  - SAP SuccessFactors Process Library
  - Implementation Design Principles (IDP)
  - Architectural Leading Practices (ALPs)

  Both of these sets of resources can be found on the SAP SuccessFactors Community website.

4.12 Summary

Employee Central is the foundation of the entire SAP SuccessFactors HCM Suite. It is an excellent core HR system that can be used to manage the entire employee lifecycle and can be integrated to multiple systems.

In this chapter, we introduced the unique features and functionalities of Employee Central that offer a competitive advantage to customers looking for a global core HRIS integrated with the Talent Management solutions of the SAP SuccessFactors HCM Suite. We explored the data models that form the spinal column of the Employee Central framework and the Admin Center interface that empowers customers with a configurable UI. We also looked at the many transactions and processes that Employee Central supports, as well as the numerous other features included.

In the next chapter, we will examine the features of Employee Central Payroll.

Chapter 5
Employee Central Payroll

Payroll is a fundamental business process that every organization of any size needs. It is complex and has to be highly functioning and reliable. Consolidation of existing payroll systems into a robust, global payroll system can offer a lot of value for your organization when moving to the cloud.

SAP SuccessFactors Employee Central Payroll is a cloud-hosted payroll system available for Employee Central customers. It gives you the advantage of managing your payroll within the convenience of the cloud while taking advantage of new features not available with SAP ERP Payroll.

Employee Central Payroll combines the payroll capabilities of SAP ERP Payroll with the benefits and advantages of Employee Central in an integrated, hosted, cloud system. With Payroll Control Center, integrations to third-party systems, and user interface (UI) integration with Employee Central, Employee Central Payroll is a viable payroll option for Employee Central customers.

In this chapter, we will cover how Employee Central Payroll fits with Employee Central, which features are exclusive to this payroll scenario, and how employees and managers can run self-service payroll transactions in Employee Central, before ending with implementation tips.

Let's begin by looking at some of the basics for Employee Central Payroll.

5.1 Employee Central Payroll Basics

Employee Central Payroll is a cloud-hosted payroll system that is only available for Employee Central customers and is built using the SAP ERP Payroll engine. Employee Central Payroll is available for 45 countries at the time of writing (fall 2019), but SAP hopes to eventually bring the number of Employee Central Payroll countries in line with SAP ERP Payroll. SAP can provide a current list of country versions for Employee

Central Payroll, or you can review the list in SAP Note 2438150 or at *http://s-prs.co/v485803*.

Employee Central Payroll features a comprehensive set of payroll processes for managing and processing payrolls of all levels of complexity. These processes include the following:

- Gross pay calculation based on time entered in the Payroll Time Sheet module or third-party time systems
- Gross-to-net calculation of paychecks
- Retroactive pay calculation
- Garnishments
- Paychecks and deposit advices (viewable in Employee Central and SAP SuccessFactors Mobile)
- Check printing
- Direct deposit of paychecks
- Payroll tax forms to be filed using a tax report
- Quarterly and year-end reports and forms
- Pre-payroll error checking and resolution
- End-to-end payroll process interfacing with Financial Accounting and Controlling with SAP ERP
- Advanced reporting

Like with software-as-a-service (SaaS) applications, Employee Central Payroll has upgrades, patches, legal changes, and tax updates applied to the payroll engine as part of the hosted service. Employee Central Payroll integrates directly with Employee Central using point-to-point (PTP) integration, although older customers may be integrating the two systems with Dell Boomi AtomSphere.

Employee Central Payroll integrates with BSI TaxFactory SaaS and BSI eFormsFactory, and packaged integrations are provided for this purpose.

Employee Central Payroll data is stored in infotypes, which will be familiar to any SAP ERP Human Capital Management (SAP ERP HCM) or SAP ERP Payroll customer. *Infotypes* are tables that stores related employee data. Many Employee Central Payroll infotypes can be updated by employees and managers in Employee Central using *mash-ups*. Mash-ups are screens in Employee Central Payroll system that connect directly to the payroll infotypes so that they can be updated in real-time. Payroll managers may often make changes directly in the Employee Central Payroll system using the SAP GUI or through the Payroll Control Center (which is embedded into the SAP SuccessFactors UI).

Access to Employee Central Payroll varies by user role. Typically, different users access Employee Central Payroll processes and data in different ways, as shown in Table 5.1.

User Role	Access Point	Process/Data
System administrator	Admin Center	Change frontend configuration, monitor integration, apply legal changes or upgrades
System administrator	SAP GUI	Change backend system configuration or view logs
Payroll manager	Payroll Control Center	Run pre-payroll processes, run payroll, monitor payroll, etc.
Payroll manager	SAP GUI	Maintain payroll data, run reports
HR administrator	People Profile	View payroll data
Manager	People Profile	View payroll data of reports
Employee	People Profile	View pay slip, maintain tax information and forms, etc.

Table 5.1 Access Points in Employee Central Payroll

Logging directly into the Employee Central Payroll system is via the SAP GUI using a virtual private network (VPN) connection.

Further Resources

You can read more about SAP ERP Payroll in *Practical SAP US Payroll* by Satish Badgi (2nd edition, SAP PRESS, 2012). For more information about the Payroll Control Center and its implementation, refer to *The Payroll Control Center for SAP ERP HCM and SAP SuccessFactors* E-Bite by Imran Sajid (SAP PRESS, 2016). For an expanded discussion on Employee Central Payroll, refer to *Introducing SAP SuccessFactors Employee Central Payroll* E-Bite by Satish Badgi, Dries Smit, and Imran Sajid (SAP PRESS, 2019).

Now that we've reviewed what Employee Central Payroll is, in the next section we'll discuss the key pre-payroll processes that can be performed within Employee Central Payroll.

5.2 Pre-Payroll

The Payroll Control Center provides a large amount of functionality for payroll managers and payroll processors. It provides the ability to control, monitor, and take corrective action on payroll, prior to running the payroll. You will have the ability to see what the results will look like prior to starting your production payroll run. In the Employee Central Payroll backend, you only have the capability to run a payroll simulation and master data audits. And even then, a payroll simulation will only identify employees whose master data records cause an error due to incorrect or missing data.

As part of the pre-payroll process, you can create alerts based on certain policy deviations or payroll errors, so that these can be resolved quickly ahead of payroll being run. The Payroll Control Center event listener for pre-payroll monitoring enables data changes to be identified periodically and to run these data changes against payroll alerts to see if the changes impact the alert results. You can also run these manually. If a data change corrects an error, then the alert result will be removed for that error.

The aim of the pre-payroll functionality is to enable ongoing monitoring and alerts that enable error resolution without manual intervention in the monitoring process. This means that during the period between payroll runs, errors can be resolved without the need to scramble for fixes during the payroll run itself.

5.3 Payroll

The Payroll Control Center is a one-stop shop for running the end-to-end payroll process, including releasing the payroll data, triggering the payroll run, posting the simulation, running checks, and exiting the payroll. Payroll managers can perform the following activities:

- Plan, execute, and monitor payroll processes and each process step
- Monitor the progress and status of each payroll process and confirm successful completion of each step
- Execute validation rules and route issues to payroll administrators for correction
- Enable audit processes using an automatically filled log file

The Payroll Control Center is accessed via the **Payroll** option in the navigation menu. After accessing the Payroll Control Center, there are several different screens available to manage the payroll activities:

- **My Processes**: Gives you access to view your active processes, upcoming processes, upcoming off-cycle processes, and completed processes (shown in Figure 5.1)
- **My Alerts**: Lists all of your alerts
- **Unassigned Alerts**: List of alerts that are not assigned to a user
- **Manage Processes**: View and edit the different payroll processes in the system
- **Manage Policies**: View and edit the different policies in the system
- **My Off-cycles**: View the different off-cycle processes assigned to you
- **Manage Teams**: Manage the different payroll processing teams in the system
- **My Teams**: View your teams

You will be taken to the **My Processes** screen by default, which we can see in Figure 5.1. By clicking the system, a dropdown of all available systems will be displayed, whereby you can select the system for which you want to perform activities.

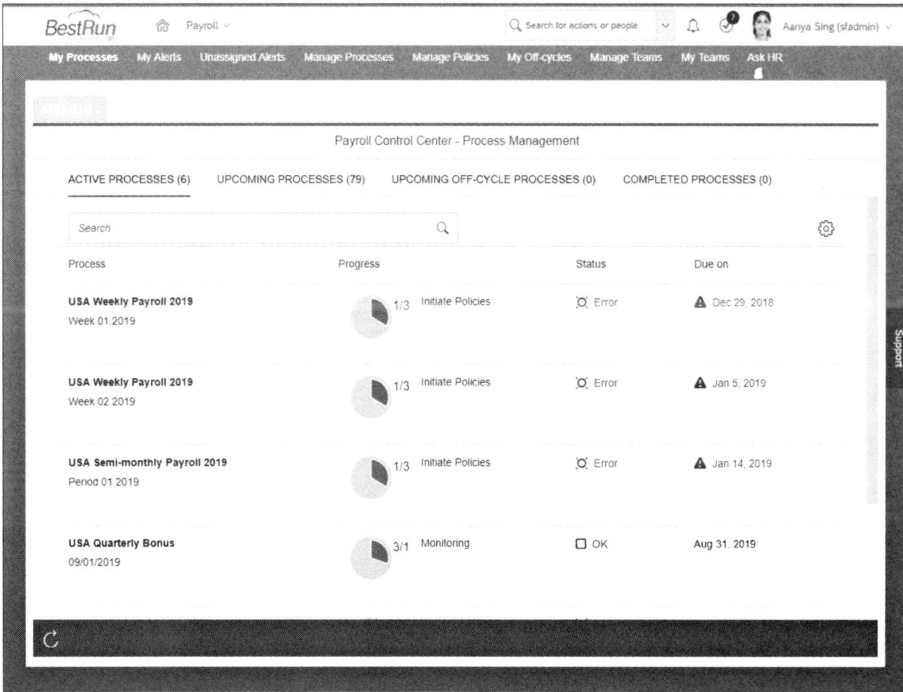

Figure 5.1 The My Processes Screen Showing Active Payroll Processes

The **My Processes** screen gives you access to view active processes, upcoming processes, upcoming off-cycle processes, and completed processes. You can click on a process to be see details of that process, as seen in Figure 5.2. From there, you can execute the process, create test payroll data to test the process, see the details of any errors, and monitor the process.

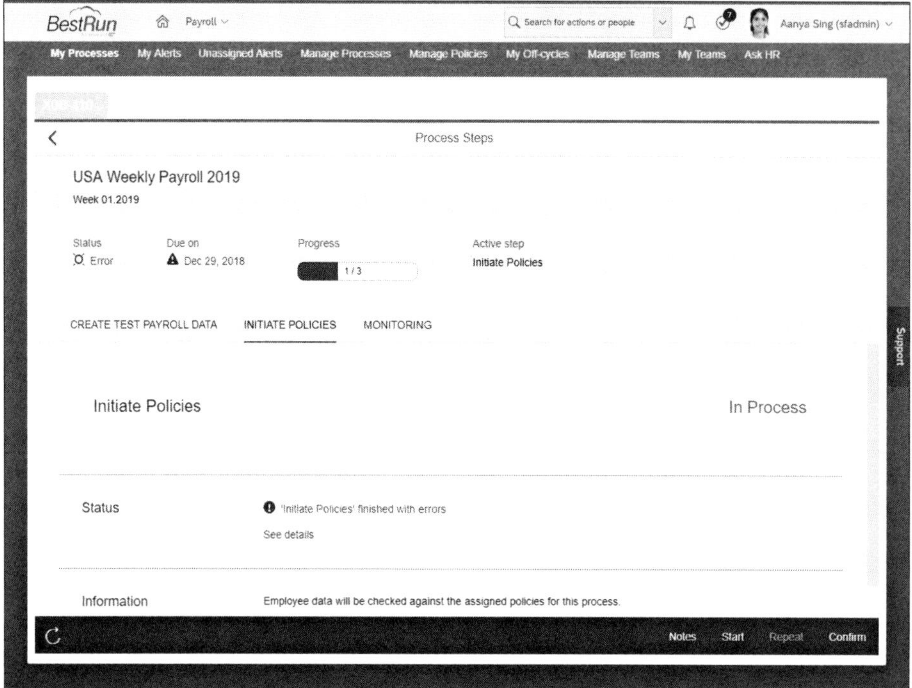

Figure 5.2 Details of a Payroll Process

5.4 Post-Payroll

Once payroll has been run, the Payroll Control Center enables you to perform activities such as post the payroll results to the general ledger in your finance system, pay vendors via the third-party remittance functionality, print checks, create direct deposit files, review key performance indicators (KPIs) from the payroll run, and close out the payroll cycle.

KPIs that can be viewed include such metrics as total gross payroll, total taxes, total net pay, and so on, as shown in Figure 5.3. You can also compare the numbers between periods.

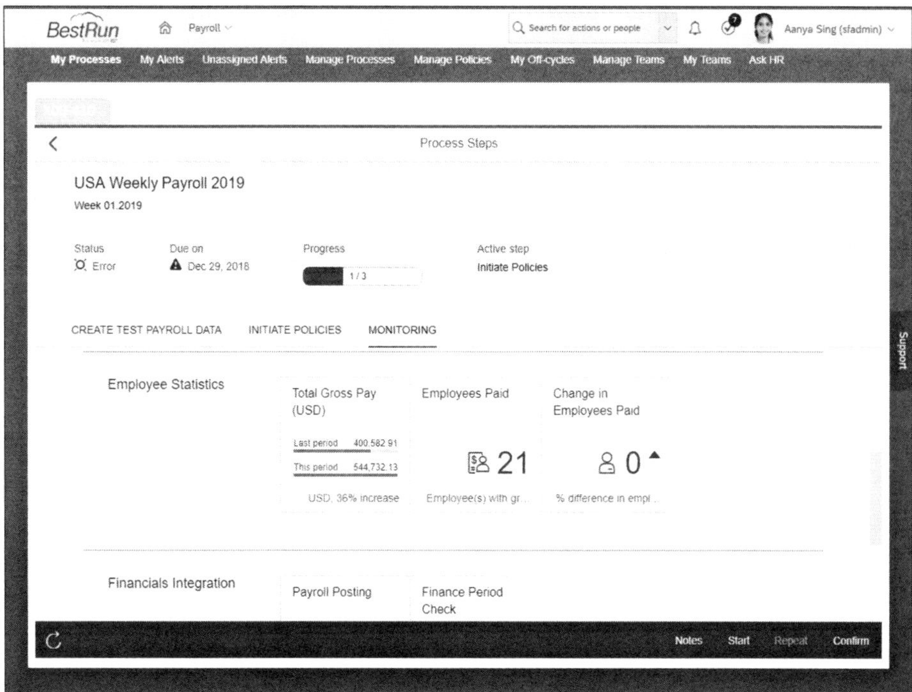

Figure 5.3 KPIs for the Payroll Process

5.5 Payroll Maintenance

Employee Central Payroll is configured in the Employee Central Payroll backend system through the SAP GUI and in the Admin Center. Since the backend Employee Central Payroll system is an SAP ERP Payroll system, the configuration is performed via the Implementation Guide (IMG) and the other places in which SAP ERP applications are typically configured. Any SAP ERP Payroll consultant will have a solid understanding of how to configure Employee Central Payroll. The technical configuration of the entire payroll system is made in this way.

The frontend configuration is performed in the Admin Center. There are a number of configurations to make, including the following:

- **Payroll System Assignment**
  Each user who needs to access Employee Central Payroll processes must be assigned one or more Employee Central Payroll instances.

- **Payroll Configuration**
  The payroll system for each payroll country is configured here, along with which portlets will be used for each country.
- **Payroll Control Center Configuration**
  For each payroll instance, the Payroll Control Center is enabled where it is intended to be used.
- **Payroll Unified Configuration**
  Configure payroll system information, create or edit portlets for the **Payroll Information** page, and create or edit tasks for the **Complete Payroll Tasks** tile (as shown in Figure 5.4).

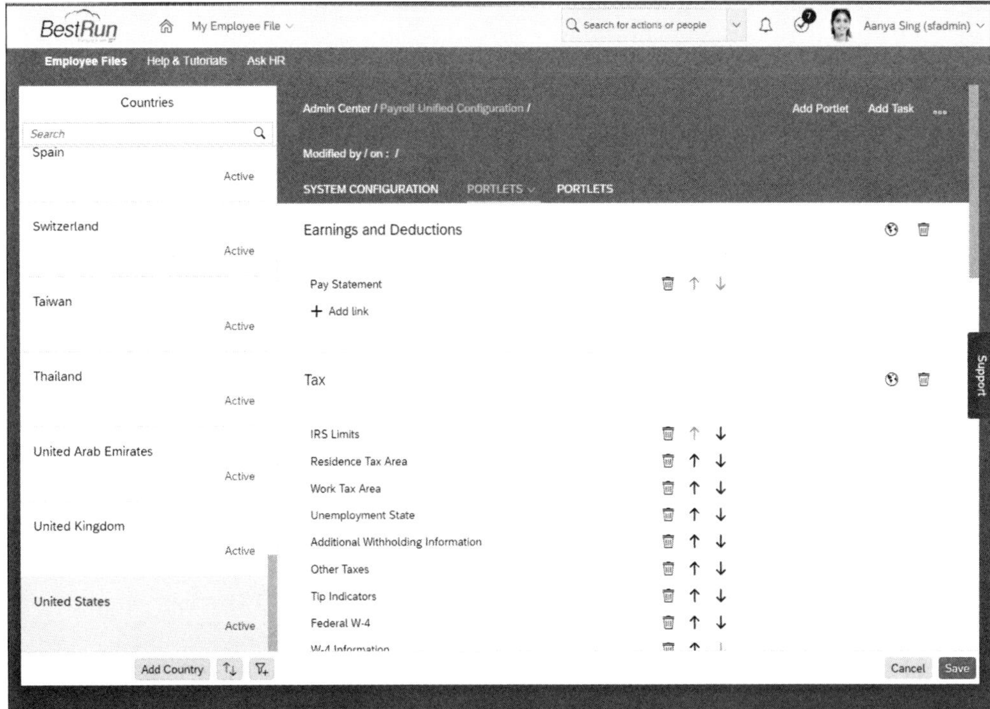

Figure 5.4 Payroll Unified Configuration

The **Payroll System Information** screen enables you to view your current, upcoming, and available support packages. The screen provides the description, affected countries, availability dates of packages, status, and action to be taken. The screen also enables you to create a ticket to have an available upgrade applied.

5.6 Self-Service Access

Employees and their managers access and maintain payroll information in **People Profile** in the **Payroll Information** block. In this section, we'll explore employee self-services (ESS) and manager self-services (MSS) for payroll.

5.6.1 Employee Self-Services

In **Payroll Information**, employees can view their gross and net salary, taxes, view and maintain tax various tax data and documents (depending on their locations), and access their pay slips and other pay and benefits statements, as shown in Figure 5.5.

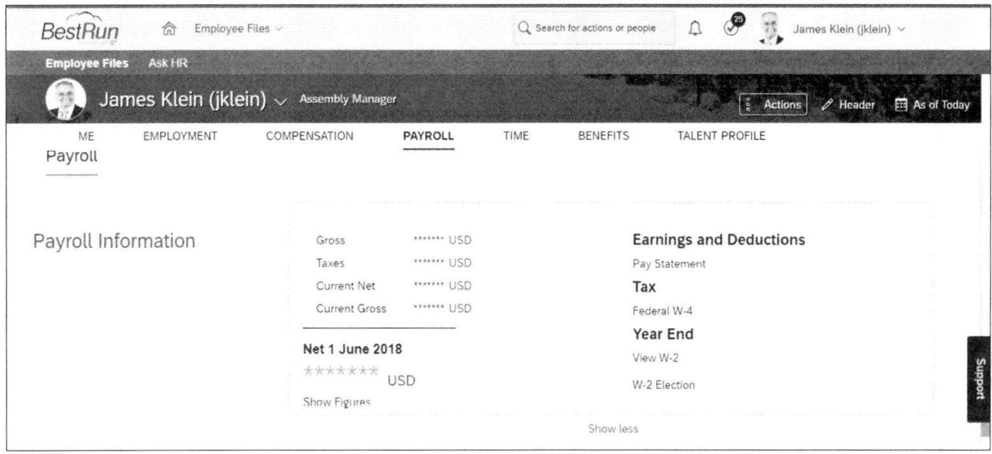

Figure 5.5 Payroll Information for an Employee in People Profile

By default, the gross and net salary and taxes that are seen in Figure 5.5 are hidden but can be displayed by selecting **Show Figures**.

Figure 5.6 shows the screen for entering tax information for the United States federal W-4 and W-5 tax withholding forms. You can access this screen through **Withholding Information W4/W5** in the **Tax** portlet. The screen inside the **Tax** portlet may be familiar to SAP ERP customers because it's a Web Dynpro screen shown directly from the Employee Central Payroll system inside Employee Central.

Employees also can view their pay slips in Employee Central. They are generated and displayed directly from the Employee Central Payroll system, as shown in Figure 5.7.

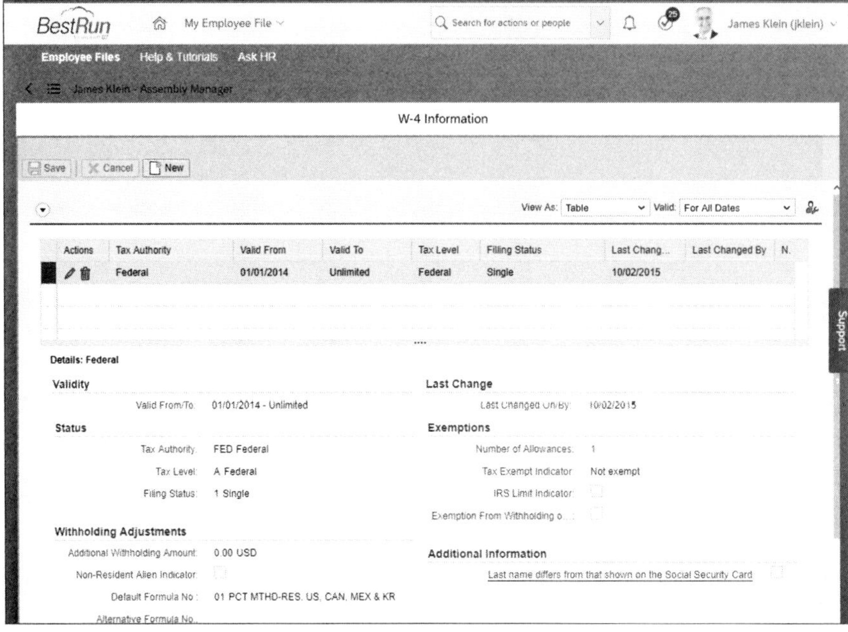

Figure 5.6 Tax Withholding Forms for US Employees

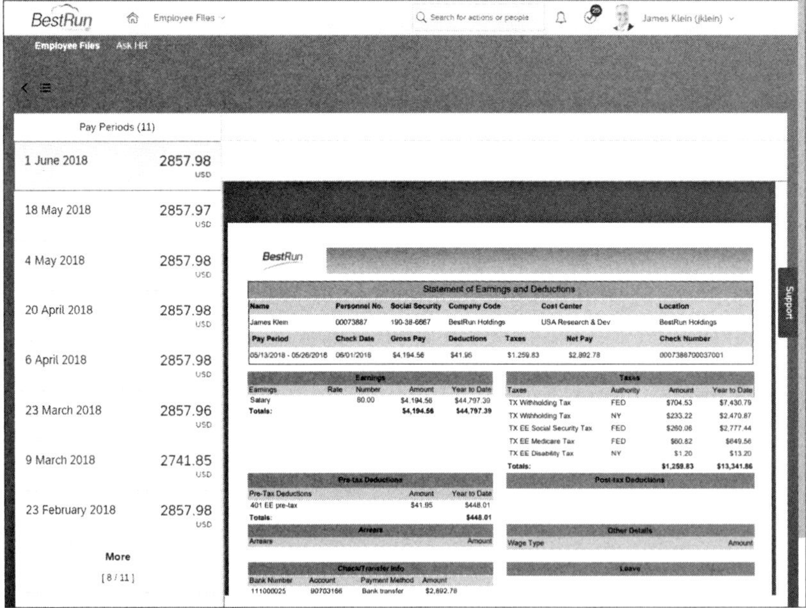

Figure 5.7 Employee's Pay Slip

5.6.2 Manager Self-Services

In **Payroll Information**, managers and HR administrators can view and maintain the following data for their reports or employees in their area of responsibilities, depending on their countries:

- Social insurance and social security information
- Work and residence tax areas
- Working hours information
- Reduction of working hours
- Unemployment state
- Tax withholding information
- Garnishments information (in the United States)
- Additional employer benefits
- Pension and retirements information
- Earnings and deductions
- Pay and benefits statements
- Other tax and payments information

5

Figure 5.8 shows an example of the **Payroll Information** screen that managers can see for their employees.

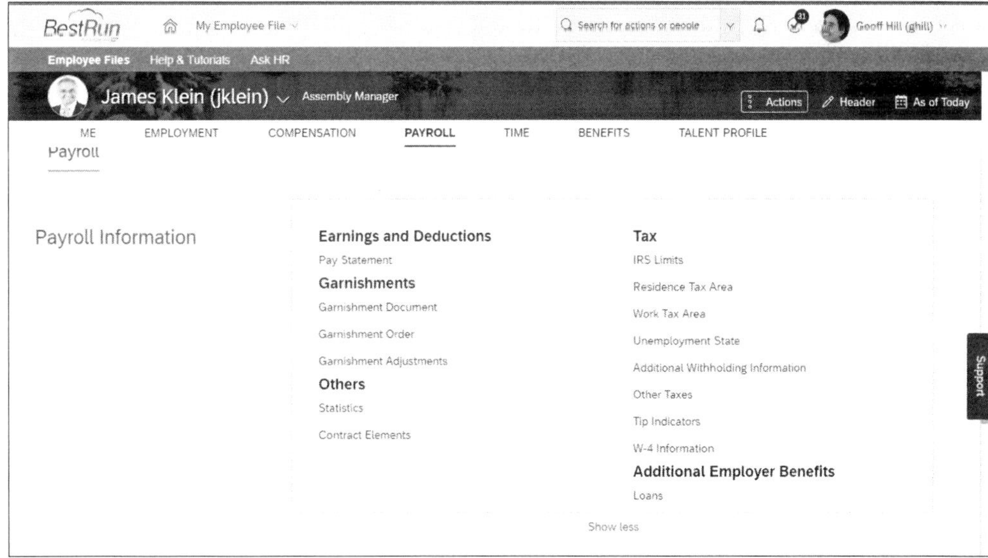

Figure 5.8 Manager's View of Payroll Information in People Profile

Figure 5.9 shows the **Additional Employer Benefits** screen, where managers and HR administrators can maintain any payroll-related benefits for employees. You can add new employer benefits by clicking the **New** button, followed by one of the available options.

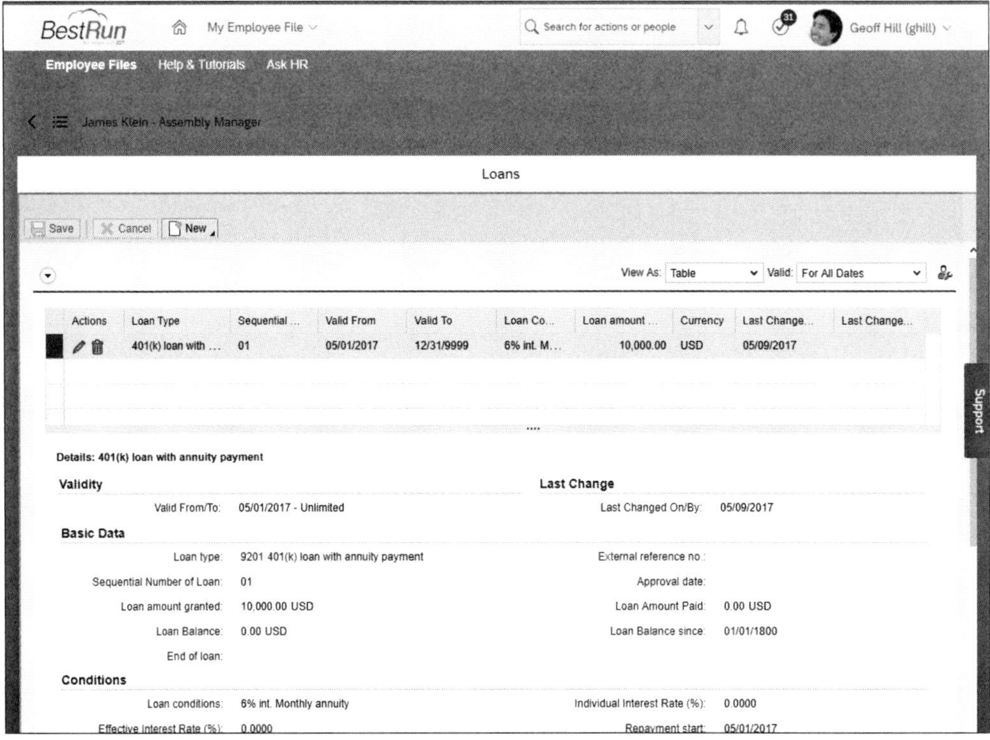

Figure 5.9 Additional Employer Benefits

5.7 Implementation Tips

Payroll can be extremely complex, so it is important to set your implementation up to be well managed and successful. There are several tips customers and consultants can use to better prepare and execute an Employee Central Payroll implementation project:

- **Resourcing**
  It is critical to have the right resources leading your implementation and working on your team from both a consulting and business perspective. While it can be fine

to have an experienced SAP ERP Payroll consultant leading the implementation, there are nuanced differences in Employee Central Payroll that will not be known to a consultant with little-to-no experience in this specific solution.

Similarly, the Payroll Control Center is a critical part of Employee Central Payroll, and customers should ensure that not only is this included in the statement of work or contract for their project, but also that their payroll consulting team understands how it works and how it is implemented. It can be challenging to design payroll processes if the Payroll Control Center is an afterthought.

Multiple different types of resource profiles are needed to deliver an Employee Central Payroll implementation, such as:

- Employee Central Payroll consultant (with knowledge of Employee Central, BSI applications, mash-ups, and the PTP replication)
- Payroll Control Center consultant
- ABAP development
- Basis consultant
- Integration consultant

Additionally, customers need to ensure they have the right number of resources available to help with design, review, testing, and more—while still being able to keep the current payroll running until go live.

- **Connectivity**

  Access to Employee Central Payroll requires VPN to access the system. Customers should ensure that they setup the SAP router and VPN from their network to SAP during the early stages of the implementation. In some situations, it can be more difficult to setup and get working for some customers more than others. Any delays in getting it setup can impact the ability for the partner consultants to get access to the Employee Central Payroll system.

  Additionally, customers need to think about how their partner consultants will access the system. The SAP GUI is required for some configurations, such as HRFORMS for pay slips and ABAP for business add-ins (BAdIs). Security conscious customers may not want to provide public access to their SAProuter and so have to consider how consultants who may often work remotely are going to get access.

- **Hardware for check printing**

  If checks, pay advices, or US form W-2s will be printed from Employee Central Payroll, then the check printer hardware and SAP spool functionality needs to be set up. While this is not necessarily complicated, if not done, then it can cause delays at a later date. Additionally, it is worth noting that this work often requires a Basis consultant.

- **Testing**
  Testing is important in any project, but with a system that directly impacts every member of your workforce, it is critical to ensure your payroll system works perfectly from the first payroll run. It is recommended to have a dedicated and experienced testing lead who can build a testing strategy, manage the entire process, and ensure that in-depth testing takes place across all scenarios.

  Parallel payroll testing is the most critical aspect of your payroll testing strategy, since its success determines whether your payroll systems is functioning as planned and will provide the confidence needed that the correct payroll results will be generated by the system once live. Parallel payroll testing involves running payroll in the legacy system and new system and comparing the results. Two parallel tests are typically run.

- **Updates**
  When your Employee Central Payroll system is provisioned, you should raise tickets to have the latest support packages added. In the Upgrade Center, you should look to add all the necessary features.

- **Reporting**
  Reporting options in Employee Central Payroll can be somewhat limited, and it is important to understand what limitations exist while you are in a position to fully understand your options. Reporting in Employee Central Payroll is only for data inside the system, so any Employee Central data not replicated to Employee Central Payroll cannot be reported on. This typically includes organizational objects.

  Some add-on solutions—such as Spinifex IT's tools—can provide a lot of value without a heavy investment, but you have to arrange to acquire these tools sooner rather than later in your project lifespan.

- **Integration**
  Some of the standard integrations delivered to integrate SAP Solution Extensions with Employee Central Payroll sometimes require additional configuration, even though the intention is that they are fairly ready to use. Complex or global customers will definitely need to plan additional review, design, configuration, and testing of integrations. Planning some time and effort to review and configure these integrations will save unplanned effort and prevent potential post-go-live issues.

5.8 Summary

Employee Central Payroll is a world-class payroll engine that can process even the most complex payrolls across multiple countries. It supports ESS and MSS—as well as HR administrator access—through the Employee Central UI and Payroll Control Center. Available in more than 40 countries, it is a comprehensive solution that can suit any organization.

In this chapter, we provided an overview of the solution, what processes it offers, how it is accessed, and what transactions are available. In the next chapter, we'll look at SAP SuccessFactors Performance & Goals.

Chapter 6
Performance and Goals

Performance Management has evolved from twice per year formal reviews to a focus on ongoing communication between employees and managers. In this chapter, we'll walk through the functionality provided by SAP SuccessFactors Performance & Goals to support this ongoing communication.

6

The latest trend in Performance Management is to foster ongoing communication between managers and employees throughout the year with less focus on a formal review process. Many organizations have ceased collecting performance review "scores" and have moved more toward quality feedback that encourages an employee's performance and overall development. Other organizations are maintaining a review process but eliminating ratings in favor of comments that encourage discussion about permission and development, while still other organizations are holding fast to traditional performance reviews and putting effort into improving the experience for employees and managers, providing tools that produce better results. The good news is that SAP SuccessFactors Performance & Goals can support all of those trends.

Through the Performance Management and Goal Management modules in the SAP SuccessFactors HCM Suite, a company can drive alignment across the organization through a series of goals that are cascaded to every employee. Progress toward these goals can be tracked from the top; executives can be sure that their entire team of employees is aware of the corporate strategy and the role each individual plays in executing that strategy. This helps drive focus toward the right things, provides visibility of progress of the entire organization, and heightens accountability. This is a key foundational element of the SAP SuccessFactors HCM Suite and has existed since the product's inception while continually being enhanced to support employees in setting and achieving goals. With the addition of learning activities to the Goal Management functionality, employees and managers can now track training and other nonformal training that help employees achieve their goals. Also, the linkage between goals and continuous performance achievements provides visibility across these valuable tools in the suite.

The Performance Management module continues to offer robust tools such as the Stack Ranker (or Team Rater) and Writing Assisting and Coaching Advisor to support both employees and managers in providing thoughtful, well-formed feedback on competency reviews. The 360 Multi-Rater continues to provide the ability to capture robust feedback from peers and customers that can feed into the performance review or ongoing conversations. Calibration allows managers, HR, and executive leadership a high level view of performance that can be "sliced and diced" any number of ways. Trends have seen increased utilization of the Calibration component in SAP SuccessFactors to analyze how ratings are falling out across organizations, while fewer organizations are engaging in formal 360 reviews, instead favoring more informal feedback from others.

While Performance Management and Goal Management are two separate modules within the Performance & Goals solution, they work hand in hand to support talent development processes. In this chapter, we will discuss features of Goal Management and look at key elements of the Performance Management module that enable organizations to effectively manage employee performance. Specifically, we will discuss goal setting and maintenance, performance evaluation, calibration, and implementation tips. First, let's begin with the Performance Management and Goal Management basics.

6.1 Performance and Goal Management Basics

Since its origins, SAP SuccessFactors HCM Suite has helped organizations develop high performing teams by providing tools for employees and managers to focus on the right activities and assessing performance against those activities at various points along the way. While the ways in which organizations develop their people have changed and evolved, SAP SuccessFactors is still the market leader in bringing best practice-rich functionality to its customers for supporting their Performance Management programs. Today, Performance Management is less about formal review check points and more about a continual conversation between employees and managers all throughout the year. Ease of use and getting the best feedback in the least amount of time are what both employees and managers are looking for. SAP SuccessFactors is known for helping align an organization with company-wide goals. This is an area that remains critical to the development of the SAP SuccessFactors HCM Suite because of its foundational importance to the ways businesses operate.

Successful businesses set corporate objectives and link division, department, team and individual performance to those objectives so that everyone in the organization is rowing in the same direction. Executives and HR have visibility to those goals at any time needed. Setting goals can sometimes be more of an art than a science, but providing employees and managers with guidance on how to set effective goals will increase the likelihood of success. This is where the SAP SuccessFactors SMART Goal wizard and the goal library can provide a tremendous amount of value, as seen in Figure 6.1. While the SMART Goal wizard walks employees and managers through how to create a goal that is specific, measurable, achievable, relevant, and time-bound, the goal library allows users to browse already developed goals (based on the SMART principle) that they can personalize and add to their goal plan. Beginning with a sound goal sets employees off on the right foot at the beginning of the performance year.

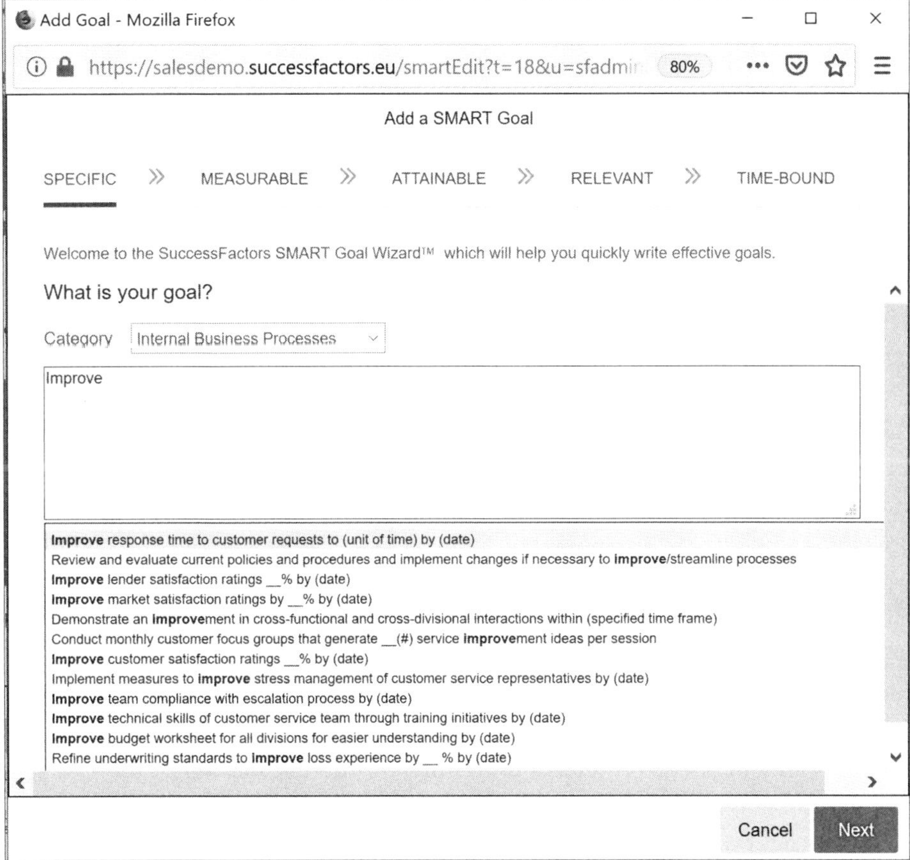

Figure 6.1 The SMART Goal Wizard

For those organizations that maintain a formal review process, the SAP SuccessFactors Performance & Goals modules provide flexibility to create a review form that incorporates numerous elements. A well-designed performance review form will often include any combination of the following:

- Performance goals
- Core competencies
- Role-specific competencies
- Development objectives
- Comments on strengths and development opportunities

The Manage Templates tool in the Admin Center provides an easy to use interface for administrators to create performance review forms and goal plans to meet their organization's requirements at any time, incorporating the sections above as well as custom sections that may be required. The result is a user-friendly yet powerful tool to support a company's performance program.

In this chapter, we will look at the tools SAP SuccessFactors provides to support organizations in setting and maintaining goals, as well as review the feature-rich tools in Performance Management that support formal reviews and ongoing conversations about performance, along with tools such as Calibration and 360 Multi-Rater forms. Let's begin with a look at setting and maintaining goals.

6.2 Goal Setting and Maintenance

SAP SuccessFactors has long provided a host of tools to enable employees to set performance goals and maintain them throughout the year. Most organizations begin their performance year with a goal-setting exercise, where employees and managers agree on what the employee will focus on throughout the upcoming year. The SAP SuccessFactors HCM Suite facilitates the creation, alignment, monitoring, and measurement of both organizational and personal goals. The *goal plan* is the basis for Goal Management in SAP SuccessFactors, as represented in Figure 6.1. The goals that appear in the goal plan are easy to create and edit throughout the year, by both the employee and manager. The goal plan provides visibility and transparency of goals for employees, managers, upline management, and HR.

Goals are often evaluated during a formal performance review and can be presented to employees and managers in the review form for rating and comments. The synchronization between the goal plan and the performance review allows additions, deletions, and modifications in either location to be represented at all times.

Let's take a closer look at key features of the goal plan and how SAP SuccessFactors supports organizations in setting and maintaining goals.

6.2.1 Goal Plan Features

The goal plan comprises the following elements:

- **Goal categories**
  Categories are used to organize goals on the goal plan. Standard goal categories are based on the Balanced Scorecard methodology and include:
  - Financial
  - Customer
  - Internal business process
  - Learning and growth

  Customers can adopt the Balance Scorecard categories or create their own categories to meet their tracking and reporting requirements. There must be at least one category, but there are no other restrictions to the number of categories that can be defined. Categories can be useful in reporting, as the categories can be defined as report filters. Their main feature is to organize goals on the goal plan, as illustrated in Figure 6.2.

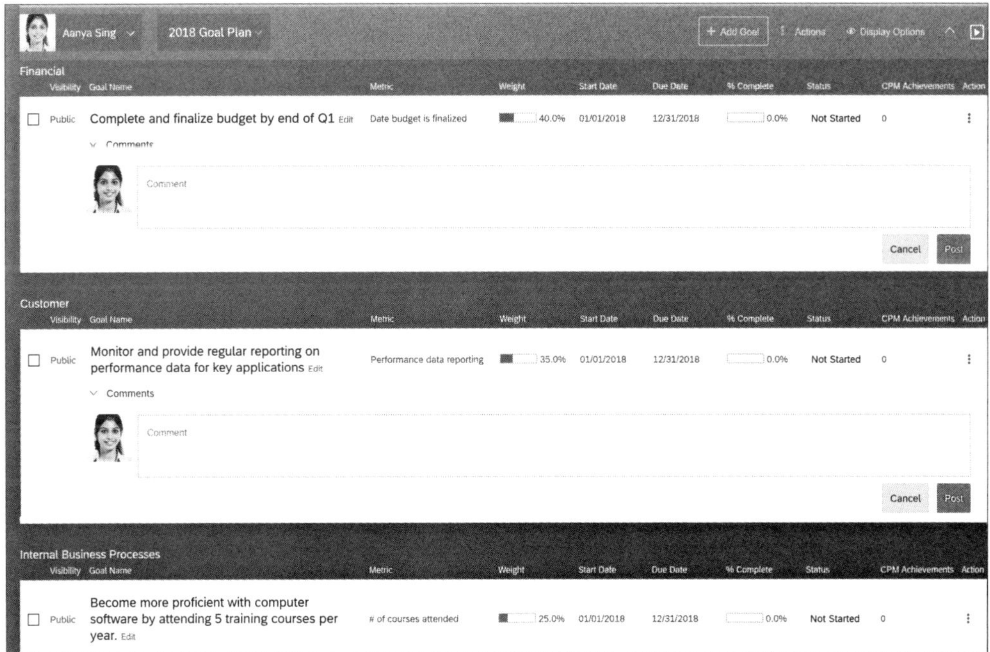

Figure 6.2 Categories Organize Goals on the Goal Plan

- **Align and link**
  This functionality encourages organizational goal adoption throughout business units, departments, and other organizational groups. Cascading goals from the top of the organization down through the organizational structure ensures company alignment to individual and group objectives. Linking goals allows alignment and tracking across the organization. Goals may be aligned at any level, so for example, a manager can align their goals to the goal plans of their direct reports to facilitate goal visibility among teams. It's important to note that aligning can be up or down, meaning that it's possible to allow employees to align their goals to their manager's goal plan.
- **SMART Goal wizard**
  As mentioned in Section 6.1, the SMART Goal wizard is one of the most popular features of Goal Management. This powerful tool provides employees with a step-by-step wizard to walk through creating goals that are specific, measurable, attainable, relevant, and time-bound. This tool enables both employees and managers to create well-formed goals based on the SMART framework.
- **Best-practice goal library**
  This best-practice collection of goals provides more than 500 ready-to-use, function-specific goals that customers can leverage as corporate or individual goals, as illustrated in Figure 6.3. This goal library comprises a part of the nearly 20,000 pieces of content that come with the SAP SuccessFactors HCM Suite. This goal library can be modified by customers, enabling customers to remove the goals that are not applicable to their business and adding company specific goals as well.
- **Goal alignment spotlight**
  What use is goal alignment if you have no visibility? This feature provides full line-of-sight visibility to goals across and down through the organization. As goals are aligned down and across the organization, the alignment spotlight provides management and HR with visibility to those goals.
- **Dashboards and spotlights**
  Throughout the SAP SuccessFactors HCM Suite, information is provided to users in dashboards that help focus their attention on the right places. There are standard dashboards that present goal information to managers, leaders, and HR, so they have visibility into progression of the organization against corporate and other aligned goals. From dashboards, managers can track how their team is performing against corporate strategies.

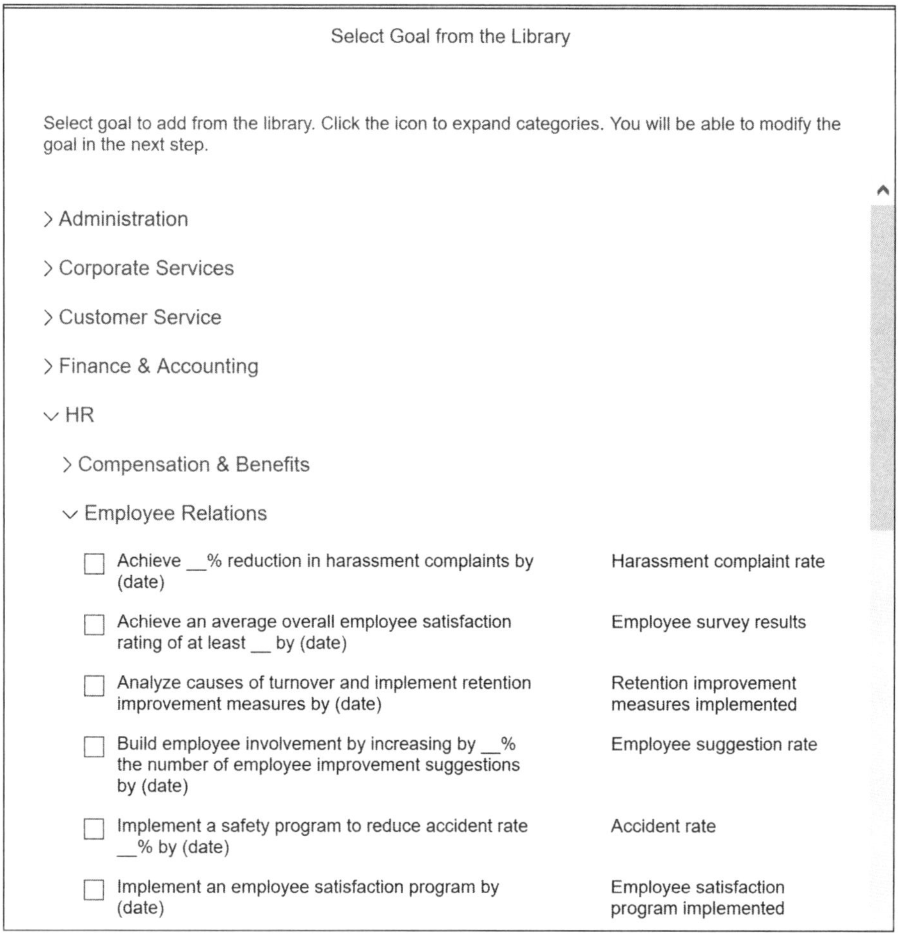

Select Goal from the Library

Select goal to add from the library. Click the icon to expand categories. You will be able to modify the goal in the next step.

> Administration

> Corporate Services

> Customer Service

> Finance & Accounting

∨ HR

> Compensation & Benefits

∨ Employee Relations

	Goal	Metric
☐	Achieve __% reduction in harassment complaints by (date)	Harassment complaint rate
☐	Achieve an average overall employee satisfaction rating of at least __ by (date)	Employee survey results
☐	Analyze causes of turnover and implement retention improvement measures by (date)	Retention improvement measures implemented
☐	Build employee involvement by increasing by __% the number of employee improvement suggestions by (date)	Employee suggestion rate
☐	Implement a safety program to reduce accident rate __% by (date)	Accident rate
☐	Implement an employee satisfaction program by (date)	Employee satisfaction program implemented

Figure 6.3 The Goal Library

Goal plans are structured for ease of use by employees and managers. Each category is clearly labeled with corresponding categorized goals that are numerically ordered under each category. Display options are user defined, so each user can display the information that is most pertinent and helpful to achieving the goals of that particular user, as shown in Figure 6.4. Managers may easily navigate to their team's goal plans with a single mouse click. You can track aligned (cascaded) goals directly from the user's goal plan by selecting the **Aligned Up** or **Aligned Down** display options to the left. Outlook calendar integration is available so that goal-related due dates can be added to a user's calendar. The **Status** of the goal is clearly labeled with a colored bar to indicate goal progress.

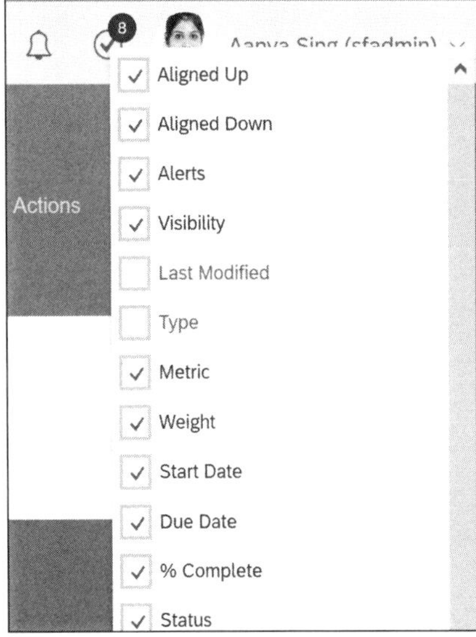

Figure 6.4 User-Specific Goal Plan Display Options

6.2.2 Maintaining Goals

You can create or edit goals at any time. New goals can be created in several ways:

- Create a custom goal by defining fields from a blank template
- Use the goal library to browse categories of goals and example goals
- Use the SMART Goal wizard to step through the elements of a SMART goal
- Copy the goal from another goal plan and modify it as needed

Figure 6.5 shows an example of a goal plan. You can create your own goal by selecting the **Add Goal** button, which allows you to populate all fields in the goal plan. Or, you can choose **Create a Library Goal**.

Regardless of which option is selected, you end up at the same screen. The appearance of the **Add Goal** dialog layout depends on the design decisions made during implementation. Two critical features to note are the **Visibility** and **Category** fields.

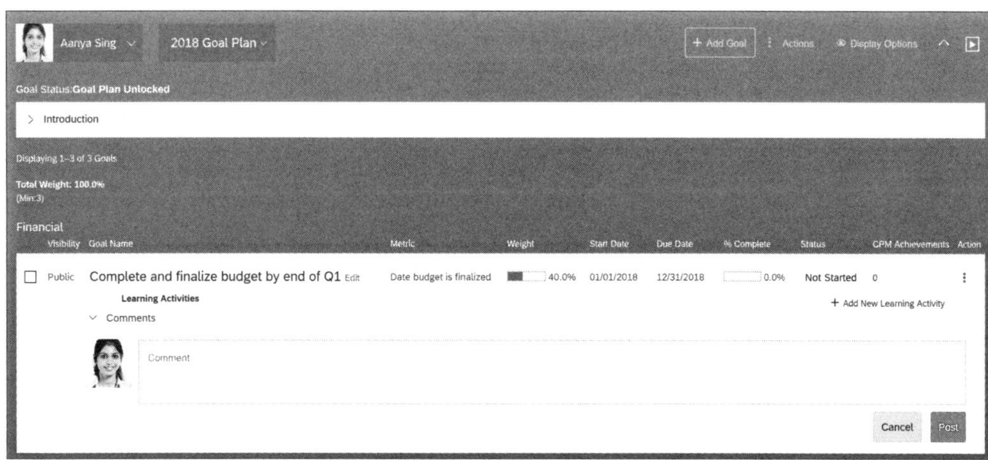

Figure 6.5 Maintaining Goals in the Goal Plan

Visibility, as you might imagine, controls who can see a goal. Goals can be either public or private, and each customer determines what this means by the permissions in each goal plan template. For example, if a customer has two goal plan templates (Performance Goals and New Hire Goals) they may decide that for Performance Goals, public means that the employee, the manager, and the second level manager can see the goal, while private restricts goals to just the employee and manager. In the New Hire Goal template, they may define public as granting visibility to the employee, the manager, the upline management, and HR. Default visibility is configured in the goal plan template, but employees may choose to change this after the goal is created. Many customers opt to remove this feature from the user interface (UI) and decide instead that all goals will have the same visibility. This can eliminate confusion and apprehension about who has access to an employee's goals, as "public" can seem quite transparent.

As discussed in Section 6.2.1, categories are used to organize goals on the goal plan. Each goal is assigned a category when created, and can be reassigned, if needed, when editing the goal. If categories are used as report filters, it is important that goals are assigned to the correct category to avoid negatively impacting downstream reporting, alignment spotlights, and dashboards.

Users unfamiliar with the SMART goal framework may opt to utilize the SMART Goal wizard and have the system guide them through creating a SMART goal. The goal library is also leveraged in the SMART Goal wizard so users can select a library goal as a starting point by typing their goal in the **Goal Name** box. They are offered possible matches based on what they are typing. Users are taken through each step of a SMART goal until they have met all elements and are then presented the **Add Goal** dialog box, as displayed in Figure 6.6. Here, they can add any additional details that may be required and then save the goal.

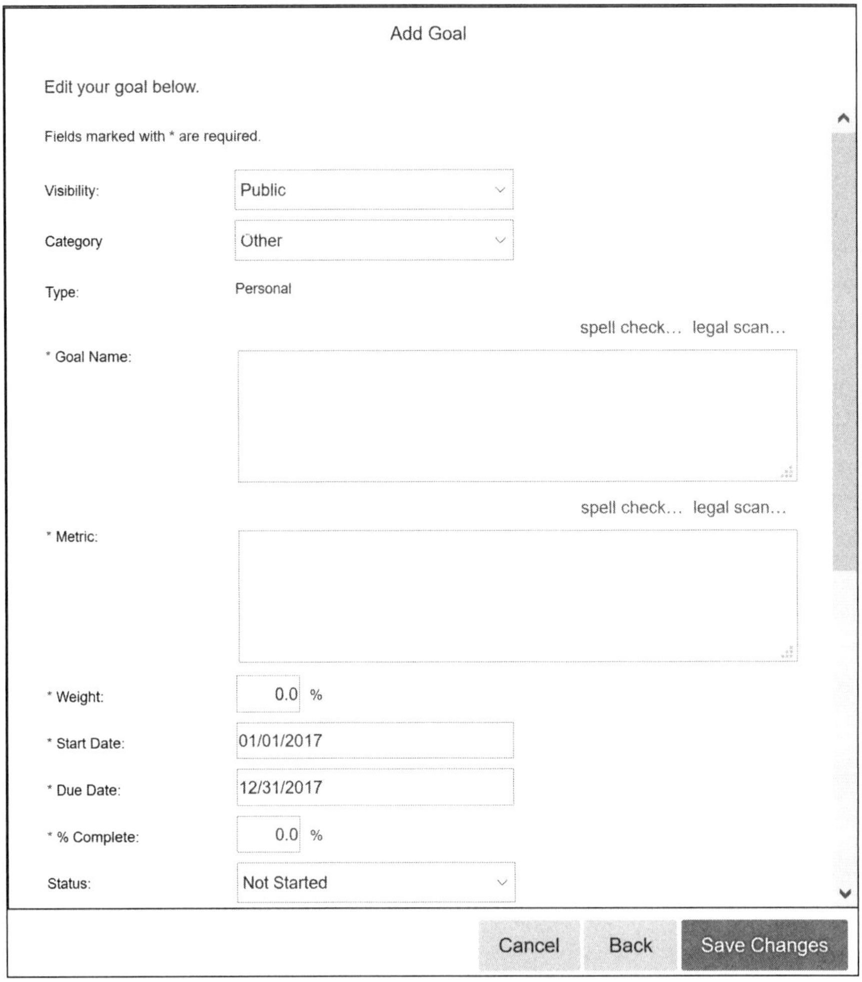

Figure 6.6 The Add Goal Dialog

6.2.3 Aligning and Cascading Goals

After goals are created, they can be cascaded up or down the reporting chain, depending on alignment permissions. Through this alignment of goals, a company has visibility to the goals that employees are working toward, as well as whether they are corporate or personal goals. Anyone with direct reports may cascade a goal down to their team or matrix reports. If goal plan permissions allow, goals may also be cascaded up. It's possible for mangers to cascade a goal up to themselves from their direct report's goal plan, or for employees to cascade a goal up to their managers.

Cascading or aligning goals creates a relationship between goals on different goal plans, so that progress on the goals is visible from the plan the goal is cascaded. For example, if a manager cascades a goal from their goal plan to three of their direct reports' plans, the manager can view progress on that goal from their goal plan as updates are made. This increases visibility to delays and other issues, and can assist the manager in following up, as shown in Figure 6.7.

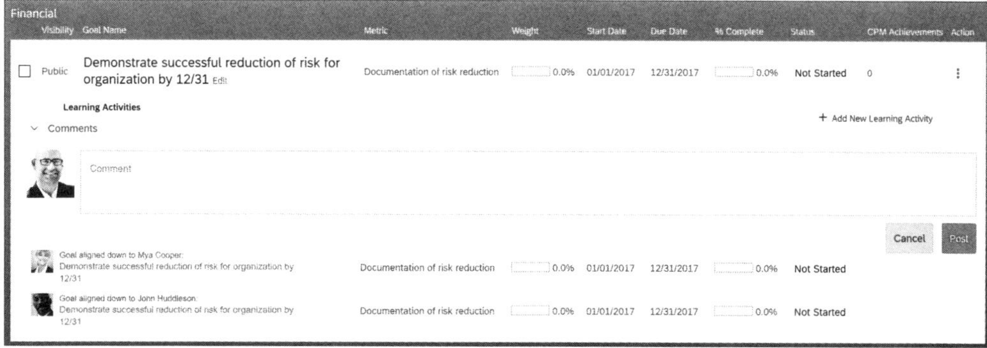

Figure 6.7 Cascaded Goals Visible from the Manager's Goal Plan

Goals may be cascaded individually or in a group to one or more team members. The Cascade Goal wizard walks through the steps necessary to cascade the goal(s) to the appropriate people. After they are cascaded, display options keep the user up to date on progress of aligned goals, as demonstrated in Figure 6.7.

6.2.4 Learning Activities

Long available on the development plan, learning activities are now also available on the goal plan. A learning activity is tied to a goal, to track any training or other type of learning that will support the employee in achieving the goal. Learning activities can be added from the SAP SuccessFactors Learning catalog (if the customer has Learning implemented) or custom learning activities can be added. One or more learning activities can be created for each goal, as suits the needs of the employee.

The learning activities are then available to view and track directly from the goal plan, either from the **Goal Management** tab or from the goal plan embedded within a review form, as shown in Figure 6.8.

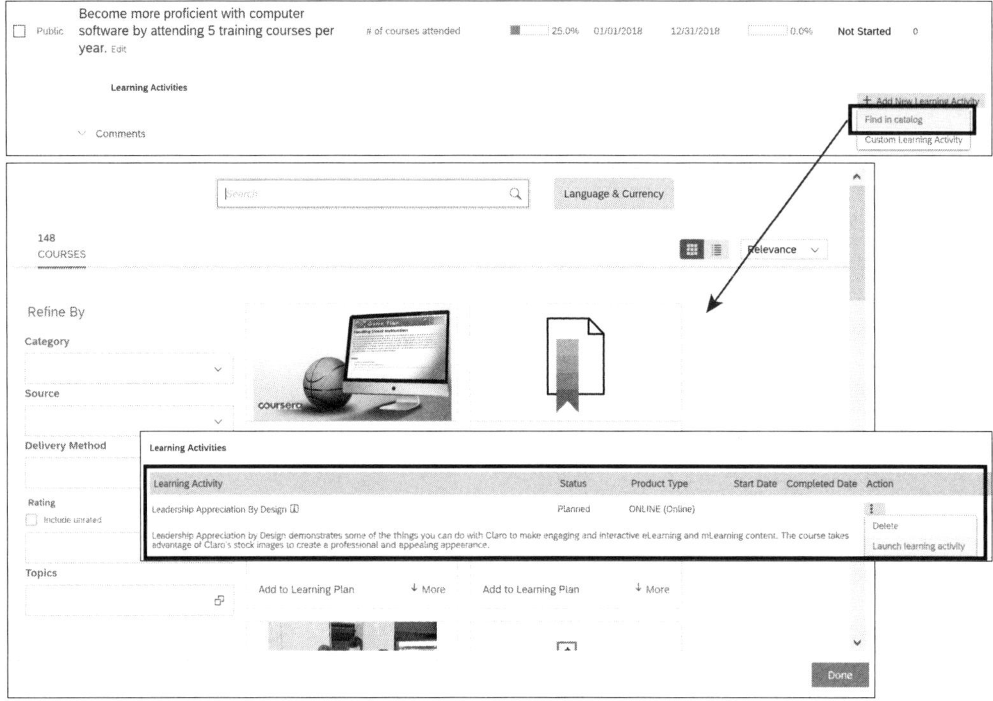

Figure 6.8 Add Learning Activities to Goals

If the learning activity is added from an item in the Learning catalog, once that item has been completed in Learning, the status will show as complete on the learning activity. This is a great feature that ensures data is up to date and reflects the learning the employee is undertaking in relation to their performance goals. The learning item can also be launched directly from the learning activity on the goal plan. Custom learning activities can be added to track learning interventions that are not in the Learning catalog. Customers that do not have Learning will use custom learning activities.

> **Note**
>
> For customers that also have SAP SuccessFactors Succession & Development, learning activities can be accessed from the **Learning Activities** tab in the Development module.

6.3 Evaluating Performance

As mentioned at the start of this chapter, there is a growing trend among organizations to move away from formal performance reviews toward more ongoing performance conversations between employees and managers. Other organizations continue to leverage performance review exercises to capture goal and competency ratings for employees and generate overall performance ratings. Regardless of where on the spectrum an organization falls, Performance Management has robust tools that enable employees and managers to participate in the performance process, while maximizing their time and the quality of feedback and communication.

In this section, we will discuss a few of the tools that Performance Management provides to support organizations in this area. Specifically, we'll discuss:

- Performance reviews
- Continuous performance
- 360 Multi-Rater assessments

Let's begin by looking at how SAP SuccessFactors supports formal performance reviews.

6.3.1 Performance Reviews

Performance reviews in Performance Management assist companies in measuring individual performance against company objectives and competencies, as well as personal objectives and competencies. This information feeds into any number of other talent processes, such as compensation management, succession planning, learning, and career development planning (CDP). Performance reviews are designed on best practices and provide numerous tools to assist all participants in the process to produce the best possible performance feedback. The latest version of Performance & Goals product provides many best practice design features and tools that customers can leverage to easily improve the quality and effectiveness of the feedback captured on reviews. A few of these tools include the following:

- **Team Rater**
  The ability to rate all competencies on all forms in the Team Rater screen is a huge time saver for managers. Here they not only can rate competencies, but can also provide comments (making use of the Writing Assistant and Coaching Advisor) and see how their individual team members are falling out against each

other, as illustrated in Figure 6.9. This provides an informal Calibration view of the competency ratings within a team.

Figure 6.9 Team Rater Interface

- **Writing Assistant and Coaching Advisor**
  This powerful tool provides best-practice content for commenting on competency feedback. It's available to both employees and managers, and greatly increases the effectiveness of meaningful feedback in the performance process.
- **Flexible workflows**
  Each form has a route map that determines who touches the performance review, what they can do with it, and when each step is due. Tools such as iterative steps, to allow the form to go between two users before moving forward, and collaborative steps, wherein the form resides in two users' inboxes simultaneously, help increase the completeness of performance reviews.

- **Legal Scan**
  This tool works much like a spell check and reviews and flags potentially inappropriate language in a performance review.
- **Team Overview**
  This interface gives managers a dashboard-like view of their team's review status. Review feedback and workflow steps can be managed from this view and action taken to confirm 1:1 meetings and sign the forms.
- **Ask for Feedback**
  Soliciting feedback from others as input to a performance review is effortless with the enhanced Ask for Feedback functionality. Requests are sent and respondents can reply via email, and the responses are visible from within the performance review form. Recent enhancements make this feature, previously only available to managers, now available to employees, with the ability to add role-based permissions (RBPs) so employees do not see the feedback requested by managers.

Although performance reviews can be configured to include items specific to customers' needs, the best practice performance review includes three main content sections:

- The goal plan
- Core competencies
- Role-specific competencies

Each section is given a weight of the overall performance score or selected to be excluded from the overall score. Ratings can be given easily by hovering over the start or circle, and clicking to save. Competencies are still available to rate in the **Team Overview** Team Rater screen. Comments can be collected at the goal or competency item level, for the entire section, or both. The Writing Assistant (see Figure 6.10) is available for competencies. Each comment box can have spell check and legal scan available for use. The Writing Assistant provides "teasers" for users to aid in developing comments for competency assessments. It is available for employees and managers, and can describe behavior or give advice in the Coaching Advisor.

Customers may choose to also include an **Individual Development Plan** section in the form; this is common for customers who are not implementing the Development module. Note that any development goals created in this section are available in the form only if linked to the *development plan* in the Development module. The Development module will be covered in detail in Chapter 11.

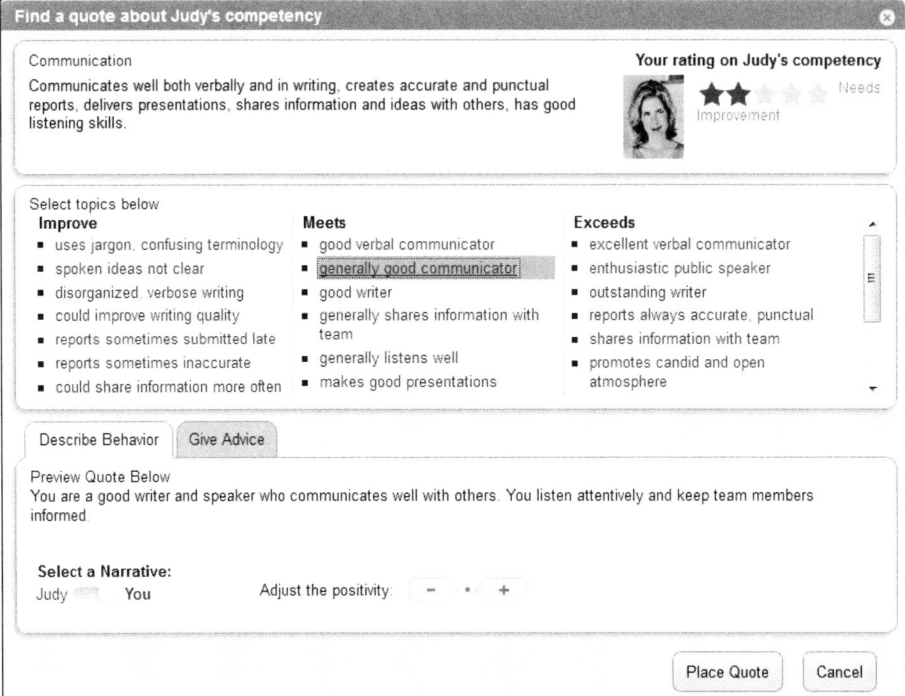

Figure 6.10 The Writing Assistant Providing Teasers

Finally, the form has an **Overall Performance Summary** section. This is usually visible to the manager and displays a summary of the rated items in the form, although it can also be permissioned for read access for employees. The **Overall Score** is also displayed at the top of the form in the **Score Pod**, making this information readily visible to the manager. Other available pods track the number of incomplete items in the review and where the current employee ranks in the overall team (Stack Ranker), as shown in Figure 6.11.

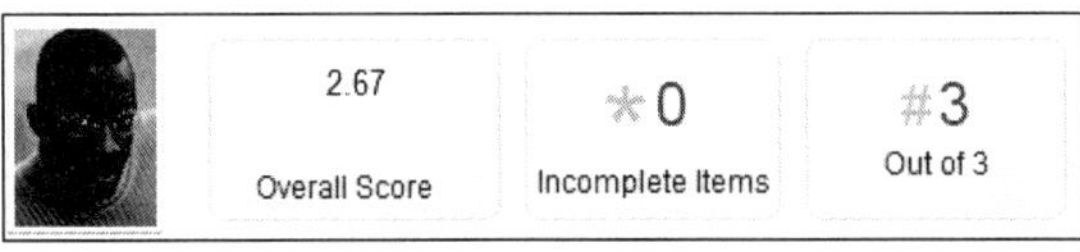

Figure 6.11 The Overall Score, Incomplete Items, and Stack Ranker Pods

The **Team Overview** subtab is available for managers and is where they can manage all performance reviews in one view. On the **Team Overview** subtab, they can see who has completed a self-review and which team members still need to be rated, and also use the **Ask for Feedback** functionality (see Figure 6.12), which allows managers to request informal feedback from others that is accessible in the performance review form. You can then track the form along the workflow until it's completed.

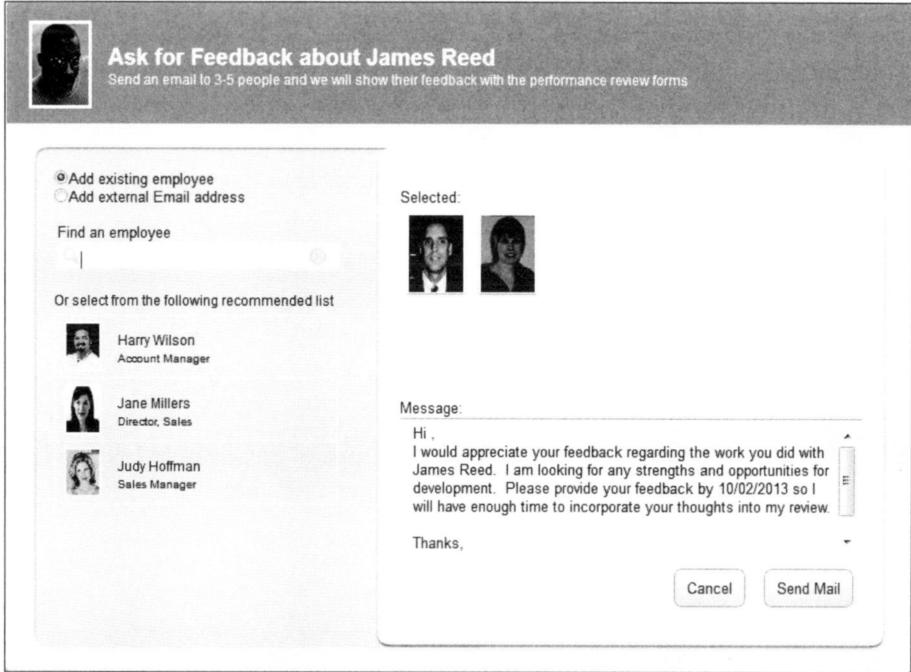

Figure 6.12 The Ask for Feedback Feature

6.3.2 Continuous Performance

As more and more companies move toward a culture of going conversations and feedback throughout the year, the Continuous Performance Management module provides a set of tools to capture critical conversations, set meeting agendas, and track achievements that are accessible by both employees and managers in their browser or from their mobile device. Used in conjunction with formal performance reviews, or as organizations move away from a review exercise, Continuous Performance is designed to help employees, managers, and executives make critical business decisions related to performance and development of their human resources (HR). Companies that introduce a culture of continuous performance can realize the following:

- Better relationships between employees and managers
- More effective performance review cycles
- Greater recognition of employee performance and their potential
- Focus on future development, not past behavior

Beyond any technology, the key to achieving successful Continuous Performance Management is communicating and setting clear expectations around coaching and feedback behaviors to managers. That includes defining what "effective feedback" means, how frequently managers should be having conversations with their employees, and, most especially, holding managers accountable for engaging in those conversations.

The tools SAP SuccessFactors provides around Continuous Performance Management support employees in documenting activities and accomplishments, as illustrated in Figure 6.13, that provide their managers with the insight needed to have the coaching conversation and help guide employees with regard to performance and development. Employees can request feedback from their peers at any time. They can also capture the results of these coaching and feedback sessions by documenting a one-on-one meeting.

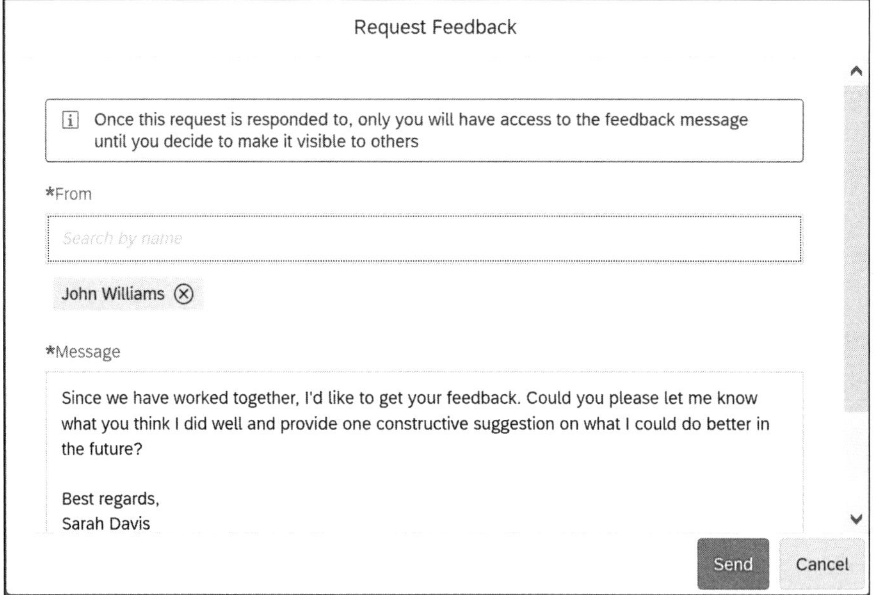

Figure 6.13 Request Feedback Screen

Notifications can be enabled to remind managers to have one-on-one meetings, and these can be seen as "overdue" in the system, helping foster a culture of ongoing conversation. Additionally, employees may request, provide, or receive feedback at any time, as shown in Figure 6.14. This can be provided to or requested from anyone and is fully mobile enabled. This can help foster a culture where employees feel encouraged and empowered to give and receive feedback regularly.

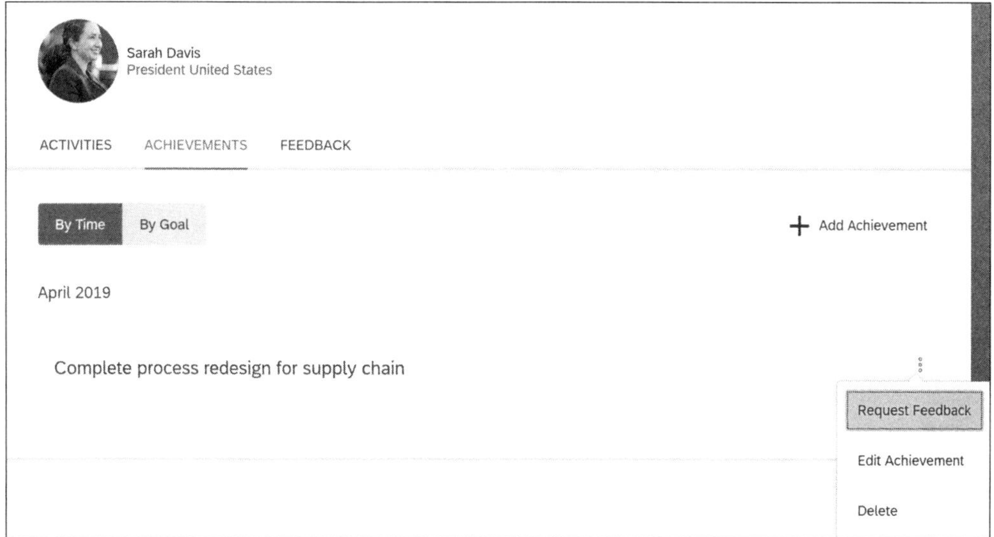

Figure 6.14 Activities and Achievements Request Feedback

6.3.3 360 Multi-Rater Assessment

The 360 Multi-Rater assessment facilitates gathering performance feedback on goals and competencies from a full spectrum of participants. True 360 assessments include the employee, manager, peers, direct reports, and other colleagues in the organization. Performance Management also supports gathering assessments from external participants external to the organization. This is ideal for those roles that have customer-facing roles. The 360 Multi-Rater assessment is different from the Ask for Feedback feature in that it's an actual form, allowing raters to provide feedback and even rate an employee, usually against the role-specific competencies assigned to that employee. This mechanism can collect quantitative and qualitative data from all the "raters." While it's typical to gather feedback on role-specific competencies, it is absolutely possible to include additional items such as goals and core competencies, and ask for narrative feedback on strengths and development opportunities, as well as other types of feedback in custom sections.

The 360 Multi-Rater assessment supports adding internal and external raters and has a configurable workflow, just like the performance review. As this is a performance template, the Writing Assistant and Coaching Advsor is available to help respondents provide meaningful feedback to the form subject. If a rater receives multiple 360 forms to review, they can utilize the Stack Ranker functionality to evaluate the competencies included in each form. This is basically the Team Rater tool we discussed in Section 6.3.1, and it allows respondents to rate all competencies on all forms in one screen. This feature works exactly as it does on performance forms, with one exception: the rater is always excluded from the list of those being evaluated. As you might imagine, gathering peer feedback in this manner can often be a sensitive subject, so the 360 Multi-Rater assessment can be anonymous if you so choose. This is the most common method of gathering feedback, and encourages the frankest feedback from colleagues and direct reports.

Detailed reporting that accompanies this feedback can be made available to the employee, the manager, or both; however it's most typical that this report is only accessible by the manager. The detailed report, displayed in Figure 6.15, breaks down the ratings by rater category (for example, peer, direct report, and so on) and provides all raters' comments in one consolidated view, broken down by rater category. This report can be accessed by managers from within the performance review form and can provide additional input into competency ratings and comments for performance review. The **Detailed 360 Report** button is accessible from the **Form** page, in the top toolbar section. This is helpful, as it makes the information accessible in the fewest mouse-clicks.

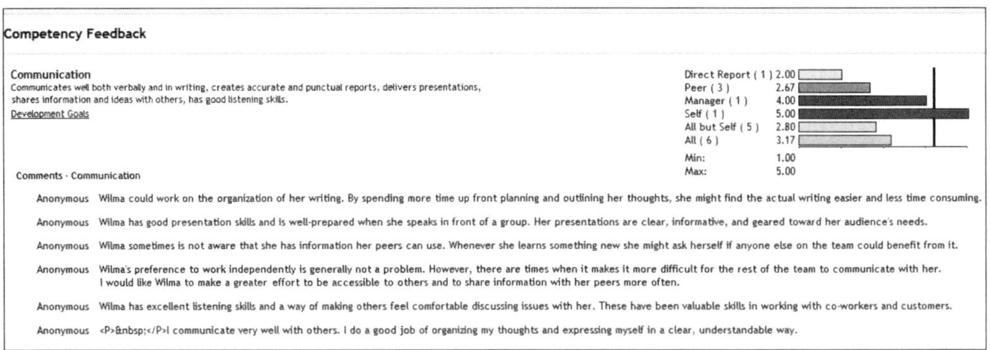

Figure 6.15 The 360 Detailed Report

A few other features in the 360 Multi-Rater assessment to note include:

- **Validate start date**
  The ability to validate that the start date of the form is earlier than the end date, and to prevent the start date from being edited erroneously after the form is launched.
- **Enforce maximum number of raters**
  The Forms Launch tool and **Modify Participants** interface support enforcing the form setting limit for the number of times a user can be selected as a rater; administrators can choose to show a warning in the **Modify Participants** list or to disallow the addition of a user when the limit is reached.
- **Manager transfer**
  You can automatically add the new manager as a 360 participant when an employee is transferred to a new manager.

Note

The 360 Multi-Rater assessment is one of the original tools in Performance Management, and it still has the look and feel of the legacy Performance v11 form UI. Look for it to get an update to a new UI very soon!

6.4 Calibration

Many organizations that generate performance ratings will undertake a calibration exercise to see how ratings are falling across the organization. This can provide valuable information but is often a very manual and time-consuming effort. Performance Management allows customers to calibrate the data that resides in the system easily and provides visibility any number of ways, depending on how the calibration sessions are set up. Calibration helps make employee calibration a simpler and more efficient exercise, bringing objectivity to a process that can often be too subjective. This is critical when the outcome influences an individual's career growth, compensation, and succession planning decisions.

To assess performance accurately, the Calibration feature, shown in Figure 6.16, provides a visual comparison of employees, much like the Stack Ranker view for rating competencies. It allows managers in calibration sessions to compare their team members against each other and make the most informed decisions, eliminating variability across managers. They can see performance ratings, compensation, and potential distributions in both bin and grid views.

The easy-to-use UI allows you to drag and drop employees from one bin to another to calibrate the ratings. This tool identifies a company's true high performers because all employees are viewed together. Managers are trained to assess performance more objectively and accurately when they see the results their ratings have on downstream processes, such as compensation and succession.

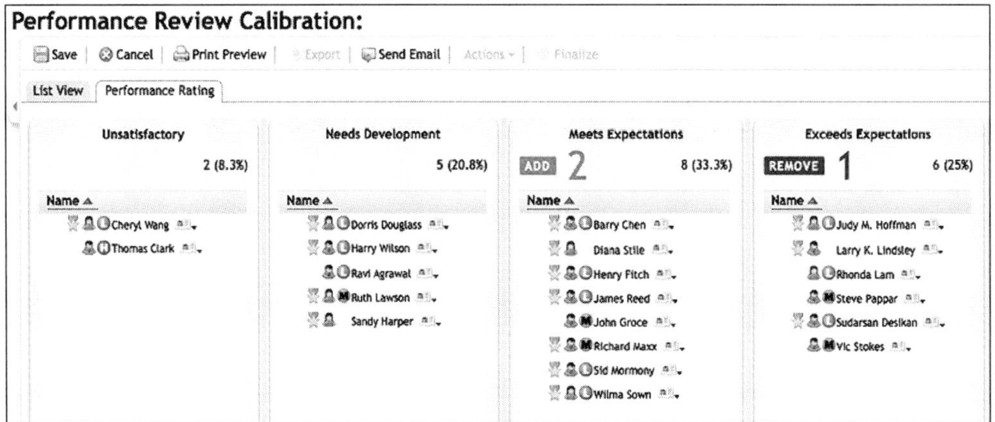

Figure 6.16 Calibration View

6.5 Implementation Tips

When implementing these Performance Management and Goal Management modules, it is important to understand all of the features available within the modules and think through how you will introduce them into your process and landscape. Here we will touch on a few tips you can keep in mind while planning for the implementation of Performance & Goals:

- **Time management**
  Give yourself plenty of time prior to the beginning of the performance review event to get the modules implemented and your population trained. While these modules can be implemented more quickly than, say, SAP SuccessFactors Employee Central or SAP SuccessFactors Recruiting, customers often wait until far too close to the beginning of their performance event to start. You want to give yourself time to design and test your goal plan and think through how Continuous Performance Management may be rolled out in the organization.

- **Best practices**
  Adopt the best practices that are entrenched in the modules, even if it means making a change in how you do things today. Don't limit the product by going in with preconceived ideas of how you want the system to work or shy away from features because you don't think your employees or managers would be able to adapt. The functionality in the system today represents more than 15 years of research and customer input on performance and goal management trends, and they are all available for you to take advantage of. Yes, it may represent a big change from how you do performance reviews today, but sometimes change is a good thing!
- **Gradual adoption**
  Phase in the different components of the system to ensure good adoption. As you have seen in this chapter, there is *a lot* of functionality available to utilize, from goal plans, to performance reviews, to 360 Multi-Rater assessments, to Calibration, and beyond. That can be overwhelming to your employees and managers and can negatively impact their adoption of the system. While SAP SuccessFactors is very intuitive and user-friendly, and none of these modules are difficult to learn, you must keep in mind that these tools are meant to make peoples' lives easier, while fostering higher quality feedback and results.

6.6 Summary

The Goal Management module provides a manager with a robust set of tools to accurately develop and track corporate, team, and individual goals and ensure that progress is on track and aligned with the overall corporate strategy. Adding one or more learning activities allows employees to track learning interventions that can help them achieve goals. The goals flow into the performance process with the linkage to Continuous Performance Management, syncing goals to the performance review to capture ratings and/or comments. With 360 Multi-Rater assessments, companies can collect formal feedback on any number of elements, such as goals, competencies, and narrative feedback, all of which can be fed into the performance review results. Continuous Performance Management provides the ability to track and document ongoing feedback conversations throughout the year. Finally, Calibration provides visibility to ratings across the organization to ensure managers are providing ratings and feedback consistently throughout the organization.

With a host of other tools, such as Ask for Feedback, the Writing Assistant and Coaching Advisor, and full mobile access all combining to enable the completion of the performance process, your employees and managers will be well equipped.

In Chapter 7, we will look at the SAP SuccessFactors Compensation module and how it facilitates managing merit, bonuses, and stock plans.

Chapter 7
Compensation

Designing an effective compensation system is crucial to an organization's talent management and total rewards strategy because compensation management plays a big factor in attracting and retaining talented employees. The SAP SuccessFactors Compensation module provides the toolsets to design, automate, and launch a solid compensation program.

Economic trends are forcing organizations to adopt pay-for-performance strategies because tying workers' pay to actual business results provides more visibility and control into the compensation payout, improves budget accuracy, and reduces risk. This helps enforce a culture in which everyone in the organization is awarded fairly according to individual contribution and organizational performance in areas such as teams, projects, and business units. It provides incentives for the workforce to align and deliver on the goals of an organization in a tangible way. This enables organizations to drive toward profitability and thus provide a bigger pool to reward employees who helped create that additional profitability.

SAP SuccessFactors Compensation is a comprehensive solution that enables an organization to streamline the following planning components:

- **Base pay**
  Merit, salary, promotion, and lump sum planning
- **Long-term incentive pay**
  Restricted stock, stock options, performance units, and cash awards
- **Short-term incentive pay**
  Bonus and spot awards
- **Variable pay**
  Bonus based on variable pay components (through the SAP SuccessFactors Variable Pay module)

Some common methods of calculating employee compensation are leveraging spreadsheet tools or deploying custom software. This complex and nonintegrated approach is inflexible to an organization's changing dynamics and introduces data inconsistencies between human resource information systems (HRISs) and compensation systems.

Compensation provides a single source of all employee data to be utilized for calculation of compensation components. Data from SAP SuccessFactors Employee Central or SAP ERP Human Capital Management (SAP ERP HCM) is integrated, providing a single source of truth for the compensation process.

The Compensation solution has two component offerings:

- **Compensation**
  This is an engine for calculating merit, stock, and bonus data in relation to employee performance and guidelines.
- **Variable Pay**
  This complex and robust bonus calculation engine allows you to tie business goals and individual results to the payout amount.

Further Resources

For further information, refer to the SAP SuccessFactors Compensation product page on the SAP Help Portal.

We'll look at these solutions as we go through the chapter. First, we'll take a look at the basics of employee compensation with the Compensation solution, before we discuss the compensation process, reporting options, and implementation tips.

7.1 Compensation Basics

Compensation provides a standard configurable framework that enables you to perform various types of compensation planning processes. Whether you are performing merit or bonus planning—or another form of compensation planning—the Compensation module enables compensation planners and HR professionals to access information quickly, make required changes, and complete the compensation cycle in an efficient and simple manner.

An out-of-the-box and configurable workflow provides flexibility to launch the compensation cycle, whether you're using standard approval hierarchy or a custom compensation hierarchy. The Admin Center provides configuration flexibility for each step of the compensation cycle. Approval of the compensation cycle is also a seamless process for both planners and HR professionals in the organization. As the compensation cycle progresses through the workflow steps, Compensation notifies the appropriate planner or administrator through emails and dashboard alerts if an action is required on their part.

To successfully launch a compensation cycle, you must set up a Compensation Plan template and perform the configuration and setup activities that meet the design needs of your organization. These activities are performed in **Compensation Home** found under the Admin Center, as shown in Figure 7.1.

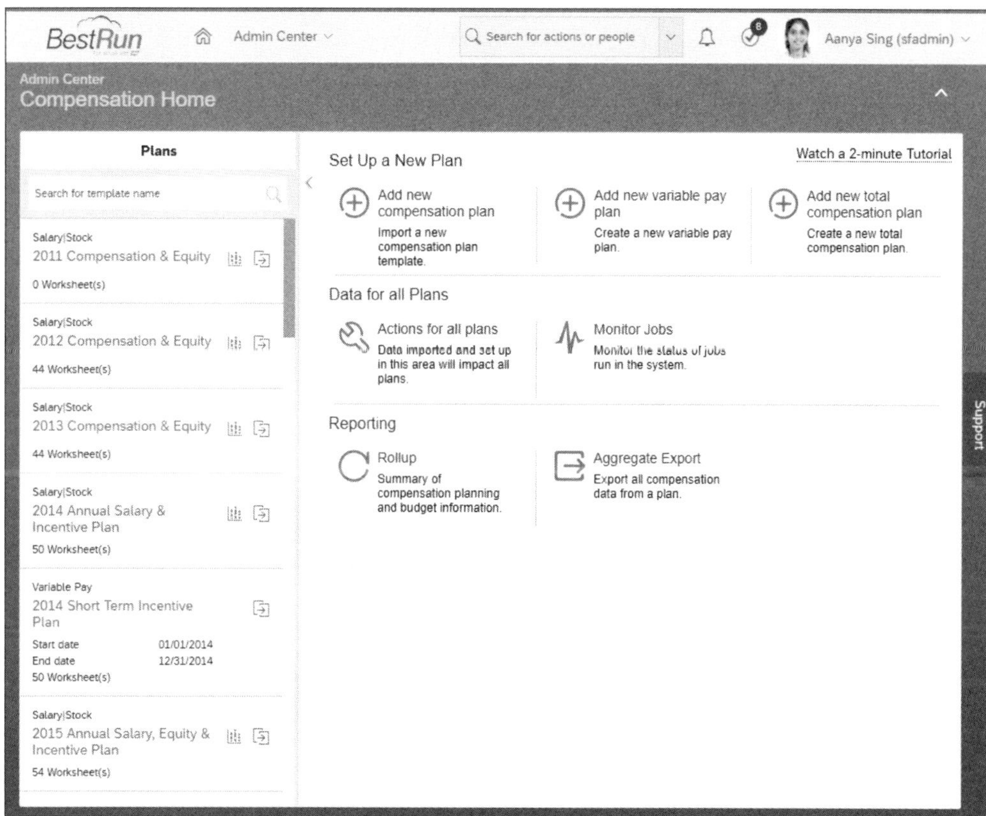

Figure 7.1 Compensation Home

The next step is to generate compensation worksheets (forms), which are created based on current data in the system. As the compensation cycle progresses toward completion, compensation forms require updates based on certain data elements that may have been updated during the compensation cycle.

The final step is to review and approve all of the compensation worksheets by the respective planners. Once this is completed, data is ready to be consumed by your HRIS for further action. Rewards statements and reports are generated after approval of the compensation forms.

In this section, we'll walk through the foundational components of Compensation, including plans for both Compensation and Variable Pay.

7.1.1 Compensation and Variable Pay

With Compensation, you can configure the following three compensation components:

- **Salary**
  You can configure any combination of merit increase, promotion, adjustment, lump sum, or bonus calculations. Performance ratings can be leveraged from the Performance Management solution or uploaded into the solution as required per the compensation guidelines. You can prorate bonus calculations based on the employee hire date and end date for the year. Standard and custom fields set up for this component leverage the lookup tables, salary pay matrix, and job code and pay grade mapping tables to perform functions and calculations that are reflected on the compensation form.
- **Bonus**
  Management by objectives (MBO) can enforce a pay-for-performance bonus configuration, as opposed to a formula-based bonus. Goal attainment data is integrated from Performance Management, and the bonus amount is calculated as a percentage of bonus targets.
- **Stock**
  You can configure stock options, restricted share units, performance units, and cash. Standard and custom fields set up for this component leverage the lookup tables, stock value, and stock factor tables to perform the calculations.

Variable Pay, meanwhile, is a robust solution that calculates employee bonuses based on quantitative business performance and individual performance measures.

An organization can decide whether to use the bonus calculation feature of the Compensation solution or the Variable Pay solution as part of the compensation planning cycle design.

The following are key features of the Variable Pay solution:

- Proration of bonus calculation for an employee who has held two or more positions in the organization, has had two or more pay grades, has had a salary change, or is associated with multiple scorecards
- Management of several bonus plans with weighted business goals
- Modeling of "what-if" scenarios to forecast bonus payout
- Integration of employee performance in bonus calculation
- Support for additive or multiplicative formulas
- Multiple time-based payout cycles such as monthly, quarterly, and annually

Compensation leverages standard functionality from the SAP SuccessFactors HCM Suite that is essential in delivering a complete end-to-end compensation process. The following are key features of Compensation that you would use during your compensation planning processes:

- **Calibration**
  "Nine-box" sessions review compensation data across teams, departments, and the entire organization to ensure fairness in the compensation process. Performance data from SAP SuccessFactors Performance & Goals can be leveraged to align performance and goals with compensation. Compensation data can be leveraged during the succession Calibration session; Figure 7.2 shows an output of a Calibration session.
- **Live metrics**
  As shown in Figure 7.3, live metrics offer graphical visibility into employee and compensation data, such as performance distribution by employees or pay versus performance matrix.
- **Rewards statement**
  You can generate compensation and variable pay statements for employees using standard fields and custom text.
- **Executive review**
  This provides visibility into all compensation and variable pay data. Employees can be viewed according to security permissions, reporting structure, organization levels, and views.

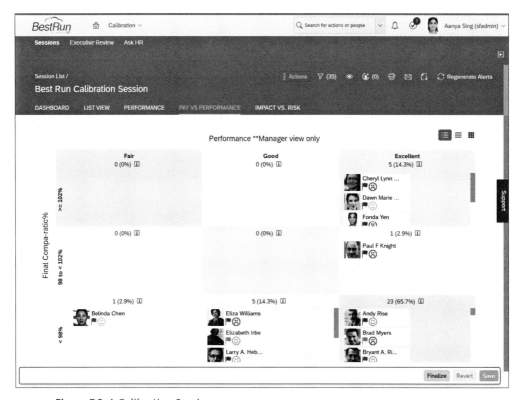

Figure 7.2 A Calibration Session

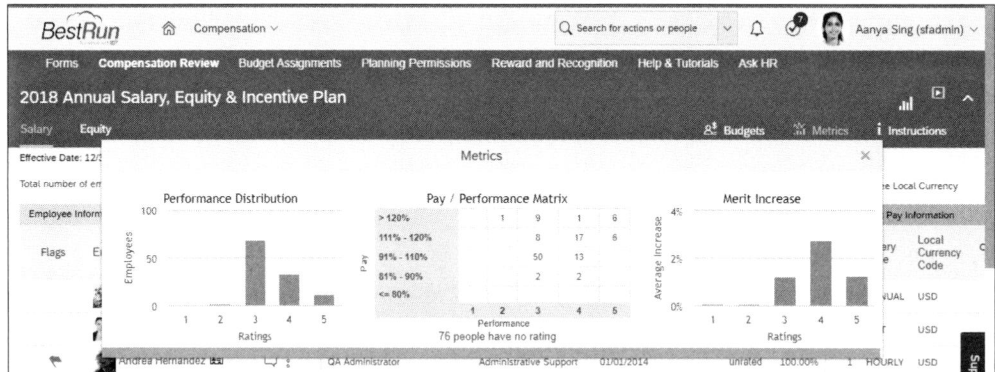

Figure 7.3 Live Metrics in a Worksheet

- **Compensation Profile**
  This lets compensation planners make recommendations while viewing employee history and graphical views of positions. Figure 7.4 shows a planner's view of an employee Compensation Profile.

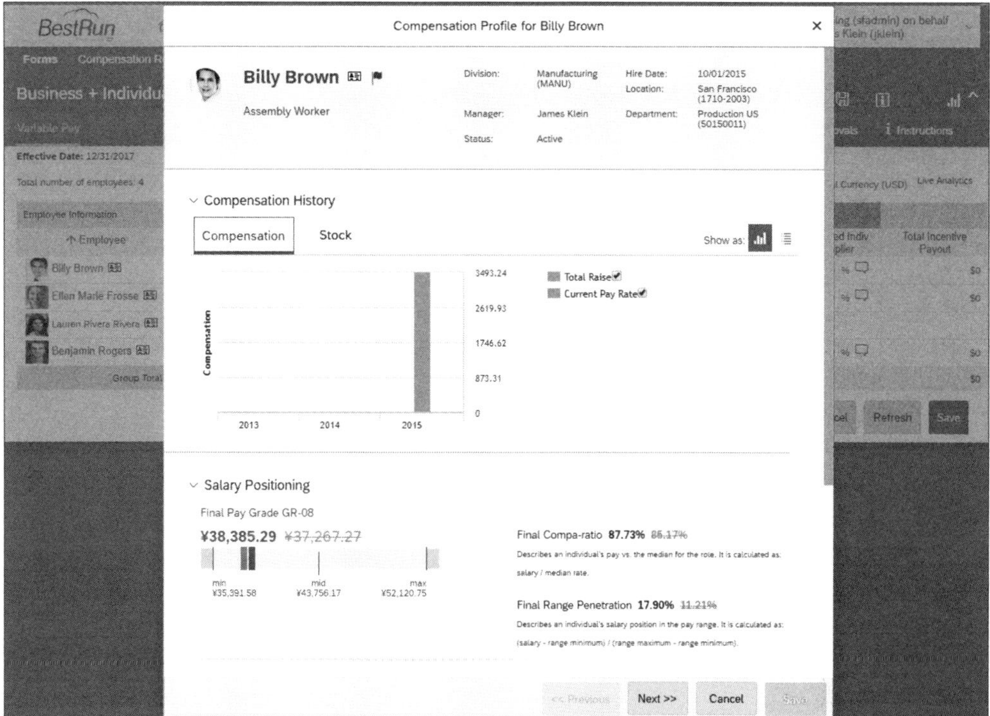

Figure 7.4 A Compensation Profile

- **Decentralized administration**
  This allows global companies with unique local requirements for compensation components to have their administered locally with governance provided by the centralized administration team. The elements currently available for decentralized administration include Compensation and Variable Pay guidelines, Variable Pay bonus plans, business goals, and business goal weights.

Let's take a look at how compensation plans work.

7.1.2 Compensation Plans

Most organizations have an annual compensation cycle; each compensation cycle should have a corresponding plan in the system. Figure 7.5 illustrates the summary of a sample compensation plan for all eligible employees. Plans are generally not personalized and represent an entire population of the organization under a specific hierarchy.

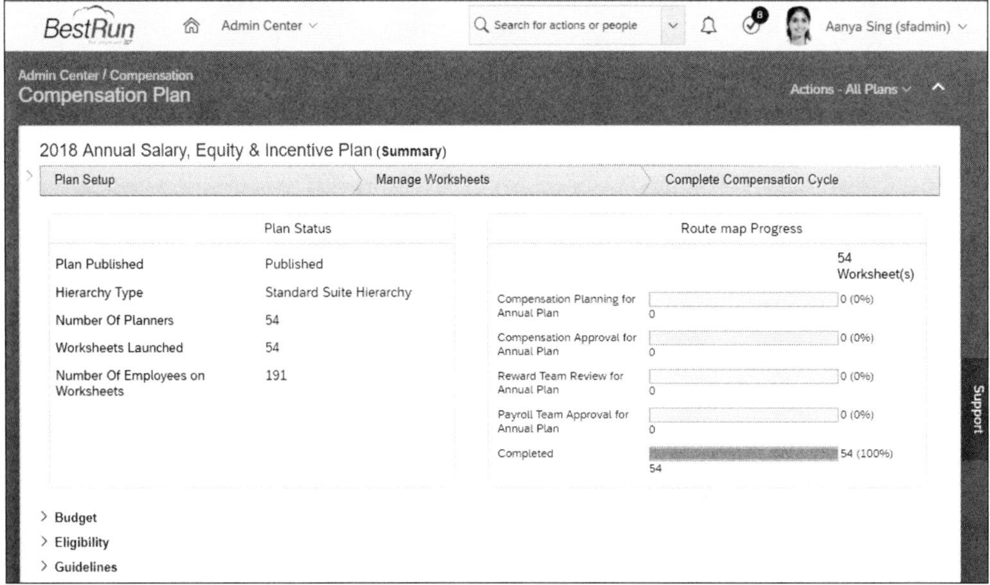

Figure 7.5 Summary View of the Compensation Plan

The **Plan Status** section on the left provides a high-level summary about the plan; the **Route map Progress** section on the right illustrates the progress of the compensation cycle.

Under the plan details—shown in Figure 7.6—you can see the **Budget** status for each compensation component within the plan, such as **Merit**, **Promotion**, **Lump Sum**, and so on.

At the bottom of Figure 7.6 you can also see the employee **Eligibility** statistics—comparing the number eligible and ineligible employees—for the plan components.

Below **Eligibility,** you'll find the **Guidelines** assignment statistics for employees, seen in Figure 7.7. This provides a quick analysis of how many employees meet the guidelines configured for the compensation plan template.

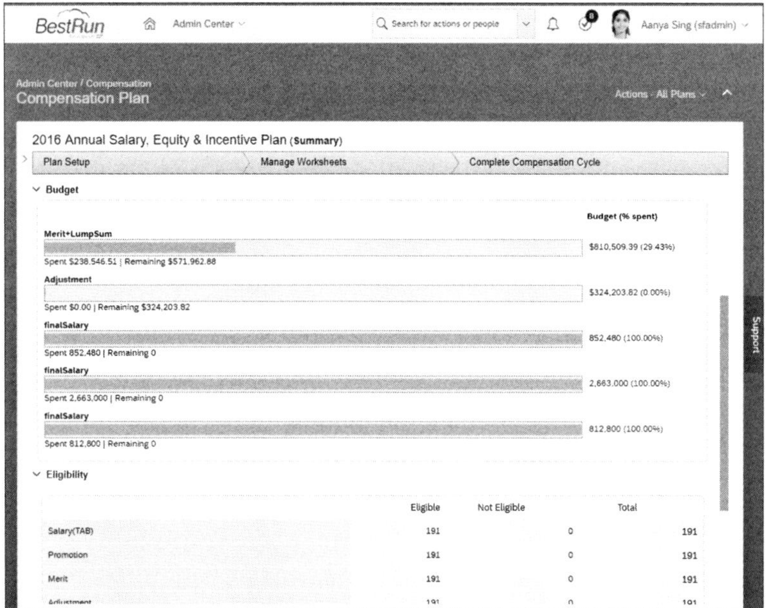

Figure 7.6 Budget Overview of the Compensation Plan

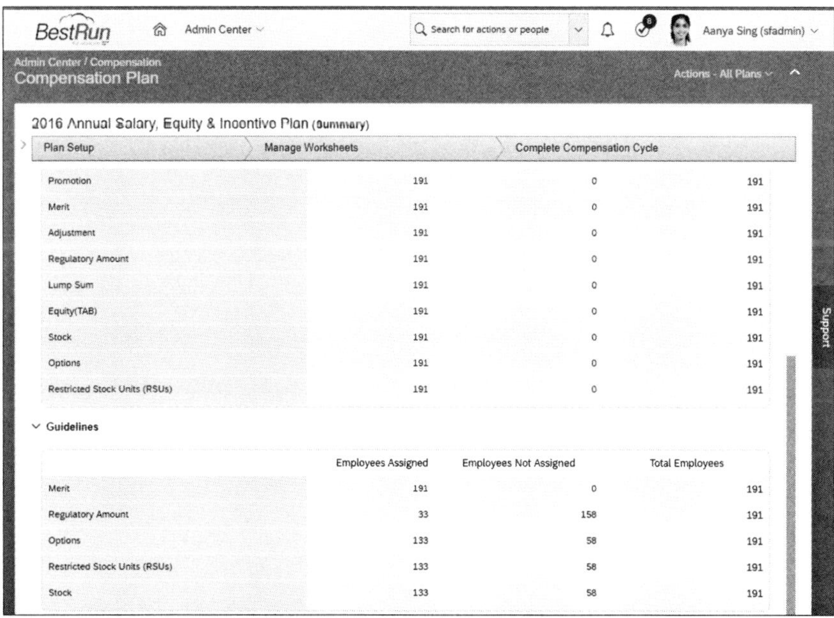

Figure 7.7 Guidelines Analysis of the Compensation Plan

7.1.3 Maintaining Compensation Process Data

Before you initiate the setup of the compensation plan, you must populate the required base setup tables with data. These data elements are accessed on the **Compensation Home** page by selecting **Actions for all plans**. You will be taken to the **Import/Export Data** section by default, where you can populate this data for the first time or maintain data that has been populated before.

In the **Import/Export Data** section, you use the **All Plans** menu to export employee data (which is useful for troubleshooting employee data issues), import and export the currency conversion table, and create lookup tables to be used in the compensation and variable pay forms.

Lookup tables are used in custom formulas to map data to an employee based on certain attributes if the required information is not contained in one of the compensation worksheet columns. Your compensation plan design includes gathering any requirements for setting these tables. Input and output columns form the structure of the lookup table, which is then referenced in the formula box of the compensation plan template. Figure 7.8 shows an example of a lookup table.

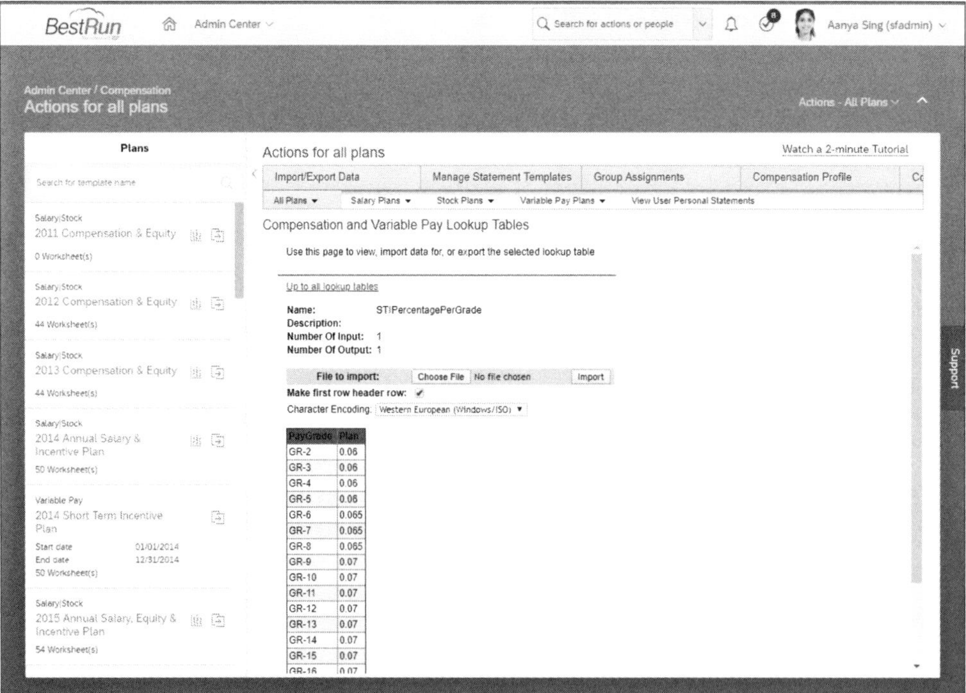

PayGrade	Plan
GR-2	0.06
GR-3	0.06
GR-4	0.06
GR-5	0.06
GR-6	0.065
GR-7	0.065
GR-8	0.065
GR-9	0.07
GR-10	0.07
GR-11	0.07
GR-12	0.07
GR-13	0.07
GR-14	0.07
GR-15	0.07
GR-16	0.07

Figure 7.8 A Lookup Table for STIPercentagePerGrade

The **Salary Plans** menu of the **Import/Export Data** section is where you can upload or export salary pay matrices and perform job code and pay grade mapping. If you use Employee Central, then the pay ranges you have set up in Employee Central can be used. However, a number of customers do not use pay ranges in Employee Central, and so this integration is optional.

Salary pay matrices contain the salary ranges for each distinct value of pay grade. Values in the salary pay matrix are set up in functional currency and also drive the comparison ratio (compa-ratio; i.e., the employee's salary divided by the market rate salary) and range penetration (the employee's salary minus the pay range minimum, divided by the pay range maximum minus the range minimum) calculations on the compensation form for each employee. As part of the salary matrix, you can define whether the pay grade is eligible for promotion and add up to three different attributes for each pay grade. Figure 7.9 shows an example of a salary pay matrix.

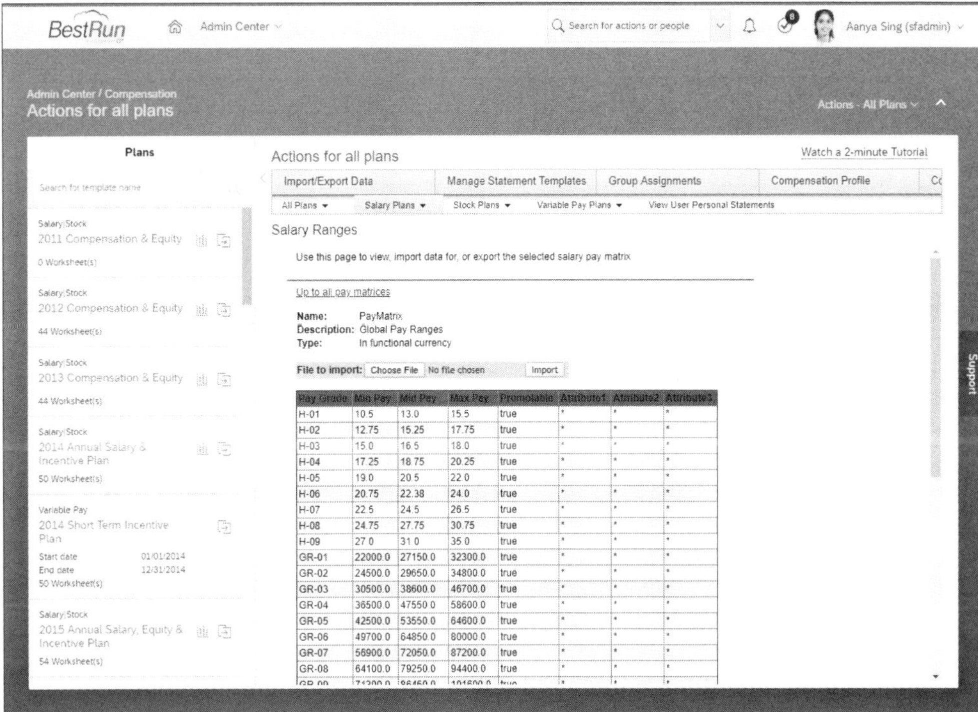

Figure 7.9 Salary Pay Matrix

The **Stock Plans** menu of the **Import/Export Data** section is where you maintain stock values tables, stock factor tables, and stock participation guideline tables.

The stock value tables are used to define a numerical value for each type of stock. Depending on your requirements, this numerical value can represent the purchase price of the stock or price per unit of a stock. The stock factor tables are used to automatically calculate the appropriate mix of stock types for your employees. You can define the various guidelines for stock participation guidelines table in a stock participation guideline table.

7.1.4 Creating Plans for Compensation

Compensation plans and variable pay plans are created in **Compensation Home** by selecting either **Add new compensation plan** or **Add new variable pay plan**, which was shown back in Figure 7.1. Creating a plan template requires setting a number of settings, defining the layout and field for your plan worksheet, setting details of your plan, and then defining the planners that will use the plan. We'll go over these steps in the following sections.

When creating a plan template, you have to define the name and upload a template or select one from the SuccessStore. As a best practice, you should choose a template name that reflects the year of the compensation cycle and the compensation components being planned against.

Plan Setup

The **Plan Setup** section (see Figure 7.10) is where you configure the settings for your plan template. The main settings to configure include:

- **Starting Point for Eligibility**
  Whether the starting point for eligibility is all employees or no employees. This impacts how your eligibility rules will work.
- **Route Map**
  The route map is the sequence of workflow steps associated with all forms that have been generated based on this compensation plan template. Routing maps are configured to generate compensation forms with employees and their respective planners or HR administrators. Each route map has several steps; each step type can be assigned to a single role, be iterative between two people to exchange feedback, or be collaborative to allow for group review.
- **Currency Settings**
  For your plan you need to select the currency conversion template and the functional currency. If your organization has planners that plan in multiple currencies,

the **Currency Conversion Rate Table** converts the functional currency to the default currency of the form.

- **Salary Pay Matrix**
  If you are an Employee Central customer, you can choose to use the salary pay matrix as defined in the Employee Central solution. For non-Employee Central customers, you must select a salary pay matrix.
- **Enable Salary Proration**
  This setting enables salary guidelines to be adjusted for employees whose salaries are subject to proration.
- **Enable Guideline Optimization**
  By default, this option isn't checked. If your organization has many compensation guidelines that are slowing down the performance of your system, check this option to improve performance.

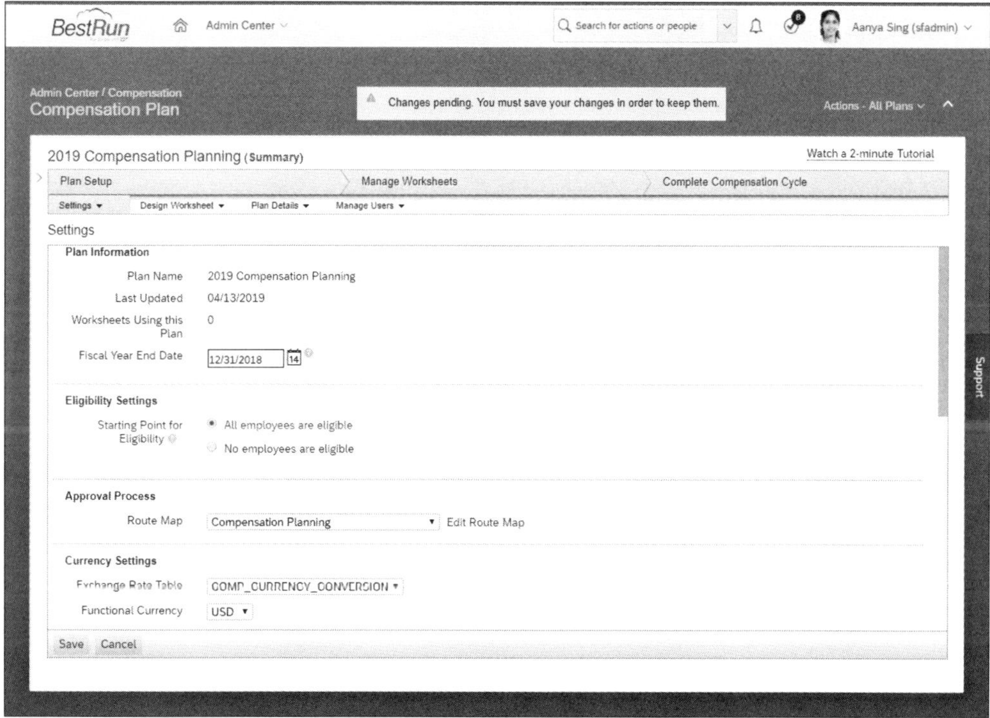

Figure 7.10 The Plan Setup Screen for a New Compensation Plan

The **Advanced Settings** subsection—accessed in the **Settings** dropdown—is the central location for managing the compensation plan template settings, such as form behavior, workflow, security, and functions.

> **Note**
>
> After the compensation forms are generated, settings changed on the compensation plan template don't take effect unless the compensation forms are deleted and generated again.

Design Worksheet

The **Design Worksheet** subsection (see Figure 7.11) is where you design the layout of your compensation form and configure the fields for the compensation components that are required as part of the compensation plan template. It is accessed from the **Design Worksheet** menu.

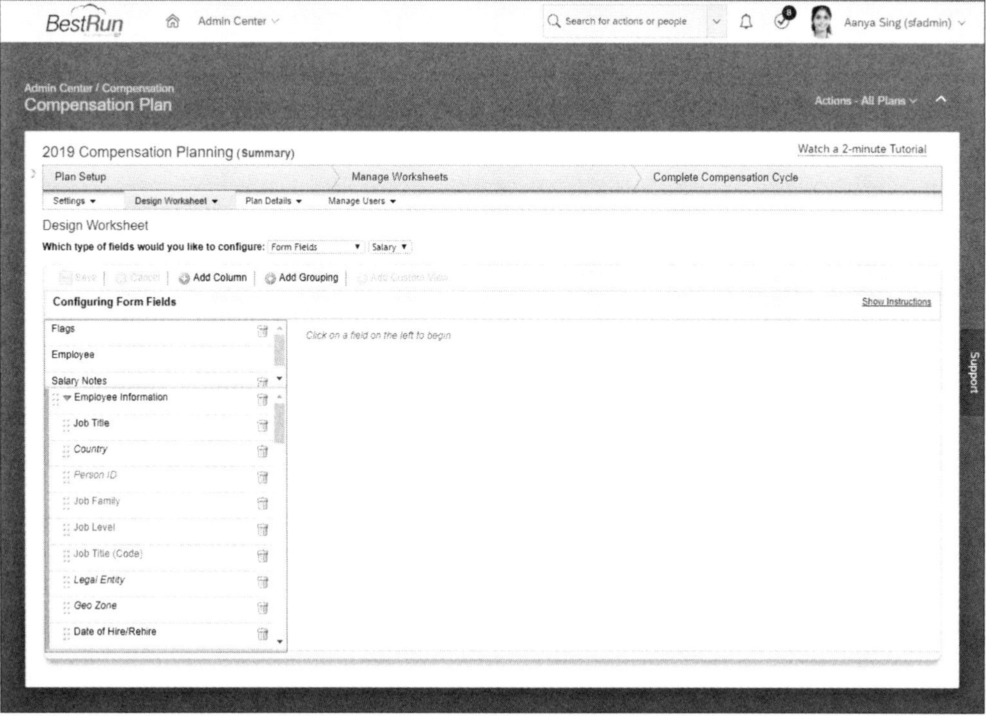

Figure 7.11 Compensation Plan Template Designer

A number of standard fields (called *columns* in Compensation) are available to add to the plan template. These columns are based on the instance configuration for your organization. Custom columns can also be added to the plan template. Various properties can be modified for custom columns, such as title, read-only, visibility, type, format, formula, and so forth. In the **Formula** box, you can enter mathematical calculations, If logic, conversions, and reference lookup statements pointing to the lookup tables. Each custom columns can also be hidden if it is not required to be visible for the planner, be reloadable if data in this field will change frequently based on data import, be reportable to make available in reports and extracts, and have a unique import key associated with it.

Columns can be grouped together into relevant, logical groups that can be color-coded for easy on-screen identification. This helps the compensation planner identify employee and planning information easily on the compensation form.

Note

Field permission groups can be used by compensation administrators to restrict field visibility to both standard and custom fields.

Custom messages can be added to the top of the compensation form.

Plan Details

The **Plan Details** menu is where you configure the budget, eligibility, guidelines, and rating sources for your plan template.

For budgets—accessed via the **Budget** option on the **Plan Details** menu—you can configure the following:

- **Budget calculation**
  The budget calculation status on the compensation form can be configured to be viewed by compensation planners. The configuration options available include the budget calculation mode shown on the form, the planning components the budget is used for, the default budget value, and whom to base the budget calculation on. Multiple budget calculation options can be configured within the compensation plan template.
- **Budget rules**
  Budget rules allow you to setup rules for budget calculations. You can choose to allow, warn, or disallow planners from exceeding budget calculations and to save

the compensation form if the budget is exceeded. You can set up multiple rules for each compensation plan template.

- **Budget groupings**
  You can group fields together to create combined budgets.

The eligibility of employees to be part of the compensation planning process is configured in the **Eligibility** menu option. Here, multiple eligibility rules can be configured for the compensation plan template. It is important to undertake designing each eligibility rule carefully because it affects the planner's ability to enter planning details against each employee on the compensation form. Rules can be anchored on standard fields available on the compensation plan template, such as pay grade or performance ratings.

Guidelines are the rules a planner follows to effectively plan employee compensation for each component on the compensation form. You can configure guidelines in the **Guidelines** menu option. Multiple rules can be set up per compensation plan template. Each guideline rule has a large number of options available for configuration.

The sources of performance ratings to be used in the plan template can be configured in the **Rating Sources** menu option. You can import these ratings or leverage them from other SAP SuccessFactors HCM Suite solutions.

Manage Users

The **Manager Users** menu has one option: the **Define Planners** subsection. Here you can define the hierarchy structure compensation forms that are generated for planners to plan employee compensation. The default option is to use the **Standard Suite Hierarchy**, which is based on the employee and the employee's manager that is set up in the SAP SuccessFactors HCM Suite. Another option, the **Rollup Hierarchy**, allows for planning responsibilities to be assigned to managers higher up in the organization. A custom hierarchy can also be configured as required to meet your organization's needs. This subsection is also leveraged for troubleshooting employee and planner hierarchy setup.

7.1.5 Creating Plans for Variable Pay

As mentioned at the start of Section 7.1.4, variable pay plans are created in **Compensation Home** by selecting **Add new variable pay plan**.

Within the **Plan Setup** section, the menu options you saw when creating a compensation plan template are there, along with additional menus that do not exist for compensation plan templates. Looking further, you'll find the options within each menu are different from the same menus that are used when creating a compensation plan template.

For variable pay plans, the settings to be configured differ from what you've seen in Compensation. The settings that you can configure include:

- A background section for variable data in the data model.
- A start date and end date for the bonus calculation.
- Calculation settings, which give you multiple options to configure how your variable pay process works, including the use of a flexible payout curve, proration, and multipliers for sections.

In addition to the currency conversation table and functional currency to select, there are options to control which currency is used (either the functional currency or the local currency) and which users can have currency views during the compensation planning process.

Some of the other menus that you will need to consider when configuring variable pay plan templates include:

- **Settings**
  In the **Settings** menu, you can find your advanced options, which are similar to the compensation plan templates. You can also configure calculation formulas used for bonuses, goal plans, pay components, and so forth, and create number formatting rules that are referenced for each value in the variable pay calculation.
- **Design Worksheet**
  In this menu, you configure the visibility of variable pay sections, fields, and label names. You can also access the Column Designer, which enables you to configure what fields will appear on the worksheet as columns, and set the number format for values in the variable pay calculation.
- **Manage Plan Details**
  The various options in the **Manage Plan Details** menu enable you to create, import, or export various data needed to run the variable pay process:
  - Business goals and bonus plans: Create, import, and export
  - Business goal weighing: Import and export

  - Eligibility rules: Created with business rules
  - Guidelines: Create or export
  - Budgets: Create
- **Manager Users**
  The same **Define Planners** option exists for variable pay plan templates, but the **Manager Users** menu also includes options to import and edit employee history data.
- **Forecast Bonus**
  Here you can generate forecasts of your bonus spend, based on selecting a calculation method.
- **Calculate Bonus**
  The only option here allows you to configure paying out bonuses.
- **Reports**
  You can run validation reports for eligibility and proration, business goal performance, individual preview, and other reports.
- **Bonus Assignment Status**
  Enables you to manage, generate, and recall bonus assignment statements.

Now let's look at running the compensation process.

7.2 Compensation Forms

Compensation planning with either Compensation or Variable Pay is performed using worksheets, where the compensation planner makes the required salary and compensation adjustments for their reports. Worksheets are forms that planners use to evaluate, assess, and change compensation. The first step of this process is to generate compensation worksheets. After the compensation planning has taken place, the worksheets can be submitted for approval. Worksheets are based on the templates that we talked about in Section 7.1.4 .

The **Manage Worksheets** section shown in Figure 7.12 is the central location to launch compensation forms and manage the lifecycle of the forms generated for the related compensation plan template.

Let's walk through how to create and launch worksheets, and go over considerations for those who use Variable Pay, before we look at performing compensation planning with the worksheet.

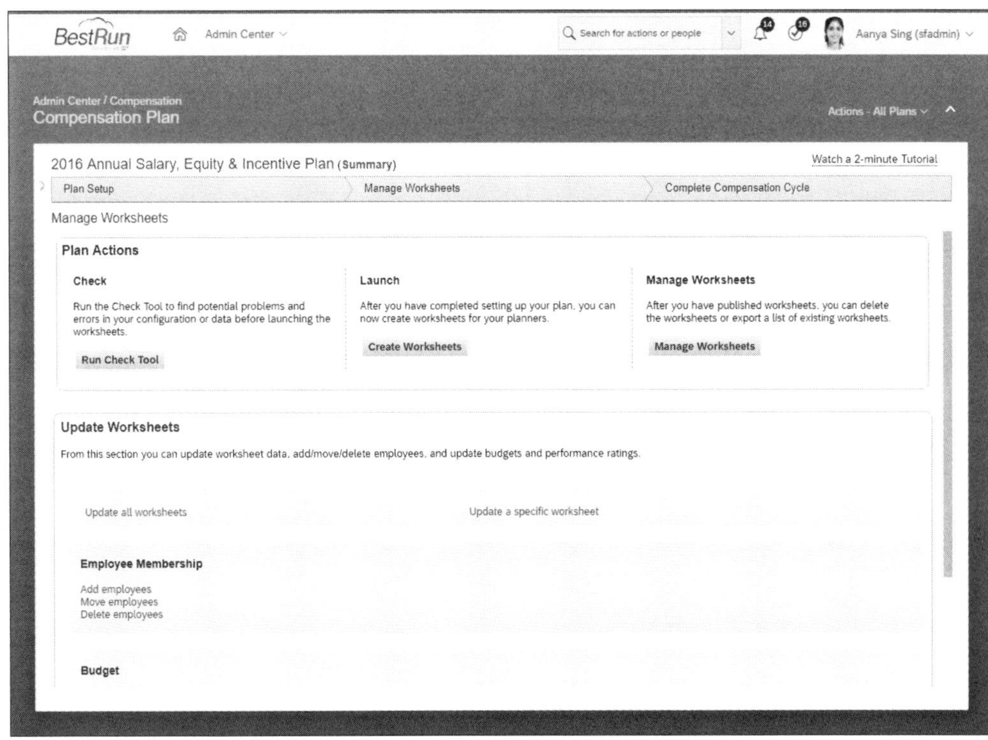

Figure 7.12 Manage Worksheets Section

7.2.1 Create and Launch Worksheets

The **Create Worksheets** option under the **Launch** subsection opens the panel, as shown in Figure 7.13, to provide step-by-step details for form generation.

Generating a worksheet is quite straightforward. The following steps are involved:

1. **Name Your Worksheet**
   Enter the worksheet name visible to the planner. The planner's name is appended to this name automatically.
2. **Set Plan Dates**
   Choose the start and end dates of your organization's planning cycle. The **Due Date** controls the workflow activity of the form, such as when to notify planners based on date criteria.
3. **Select Worksheets to Create**
   Select the topmost planner in your organization hierarchy. This launches forms

for all planners in the organization per the hierarchy configuration setting of the compensation template. You have the option to generate forms only for the specific planner. You can choose to notify planners of compensation form availability by email.

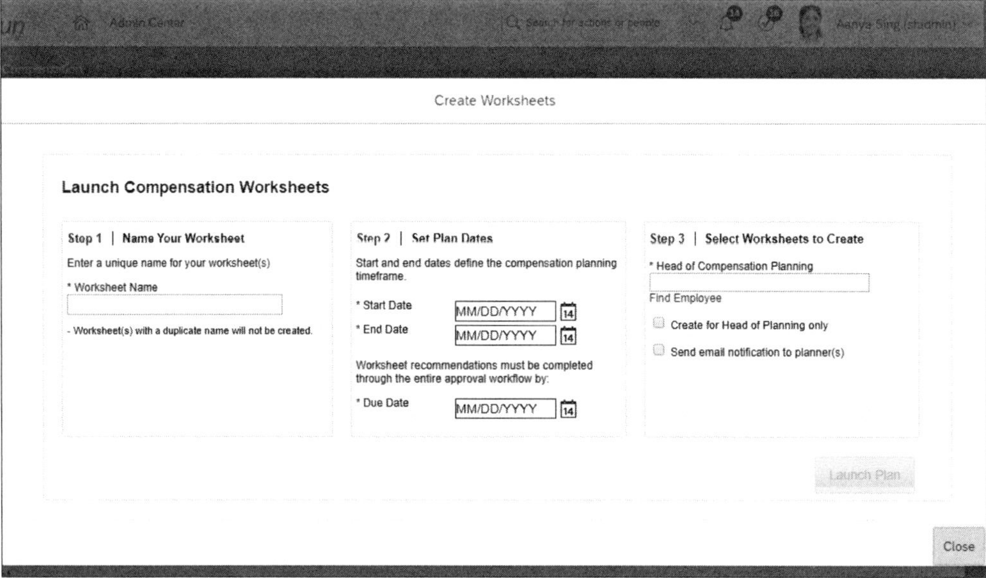

Figure 7.13 Launch Compensation Worksheets

After all of the details are entered, click the **Launch Plan** option to start the request for the form-generation process. Upon completion of the process, an email notification is sent with details about how many compensation forms were generated. At this stage, the compensation forms are considered in progress and are shown in the **Compensation** section we just mentioned. Planners can view and access the compensation form, as shown in Figure 7.14, by selecting **Compensation** in the navigation menu.

7.2.2 Administering Worksheets

Once worksheets have been created, as a compensation administrator you can further manage the worksheets throughout the process by using the **Manage Worksheets** option under the **Manage Worksheets** section. As shown in Figure 7.15, this gives you visibility into the individual forms generated as part of the compensation plan template.

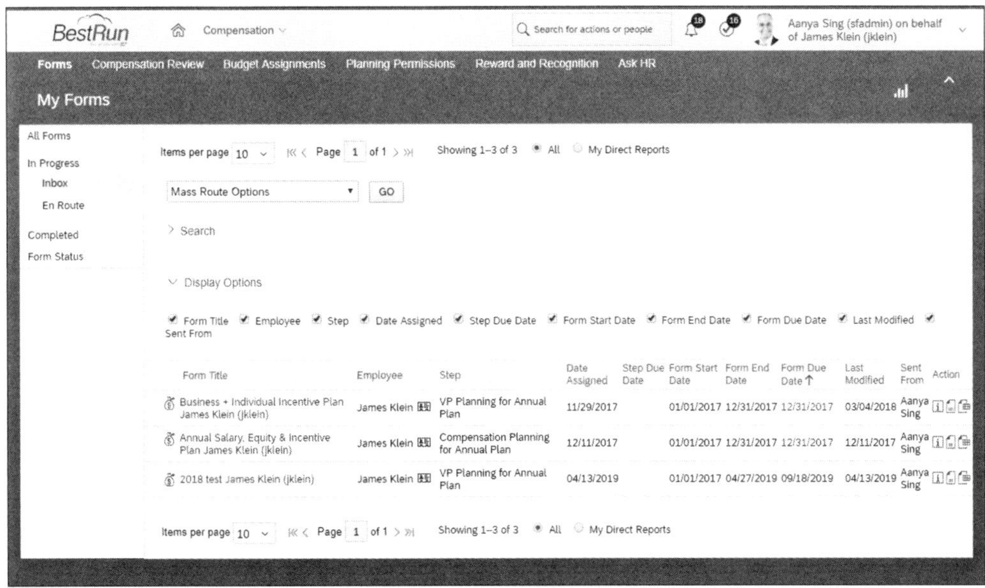

Figure 7.14 Manager's View of the Compensation Home Screen

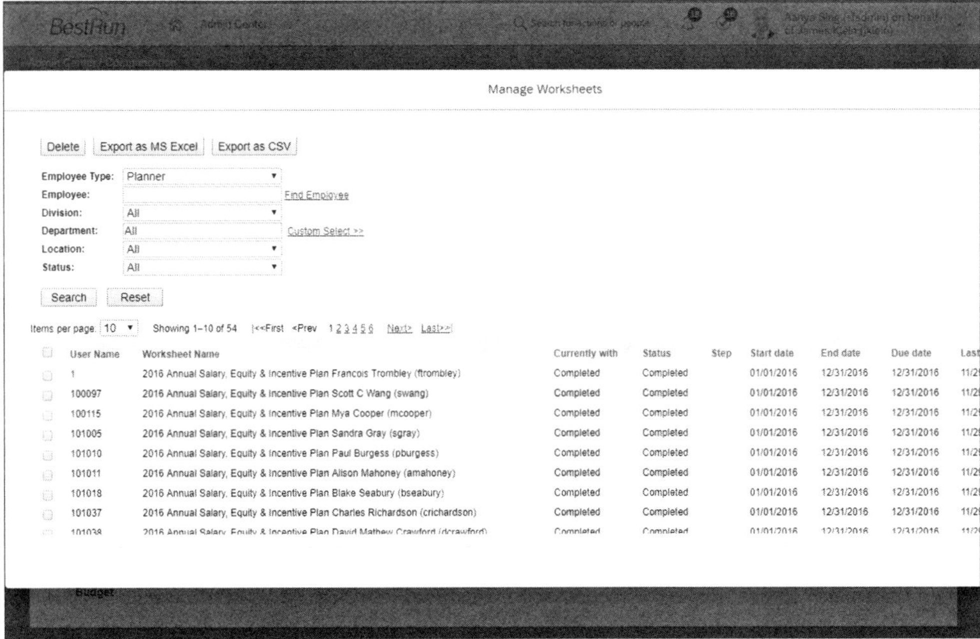

Figure 7.15 Manage Worksheets Option

In this example, there are forms for Francois Trombley, Scott C Wang, Mya Cooper, and their colleagues. From this option, you can choose to **Delete** the form, **Export as MS Excel**, or **Export as CSV**.

During the compensation planning process, the forms that have been generated may need to be periodically updated. These updates are typically activities such as updating compensation form membership or accounting for budget changes until the compensation planning cycle reaches completion. These activities are performed under the **Update Worksheets** panel under the **Manage Worksheets** section, as shown in Figure 7.16.

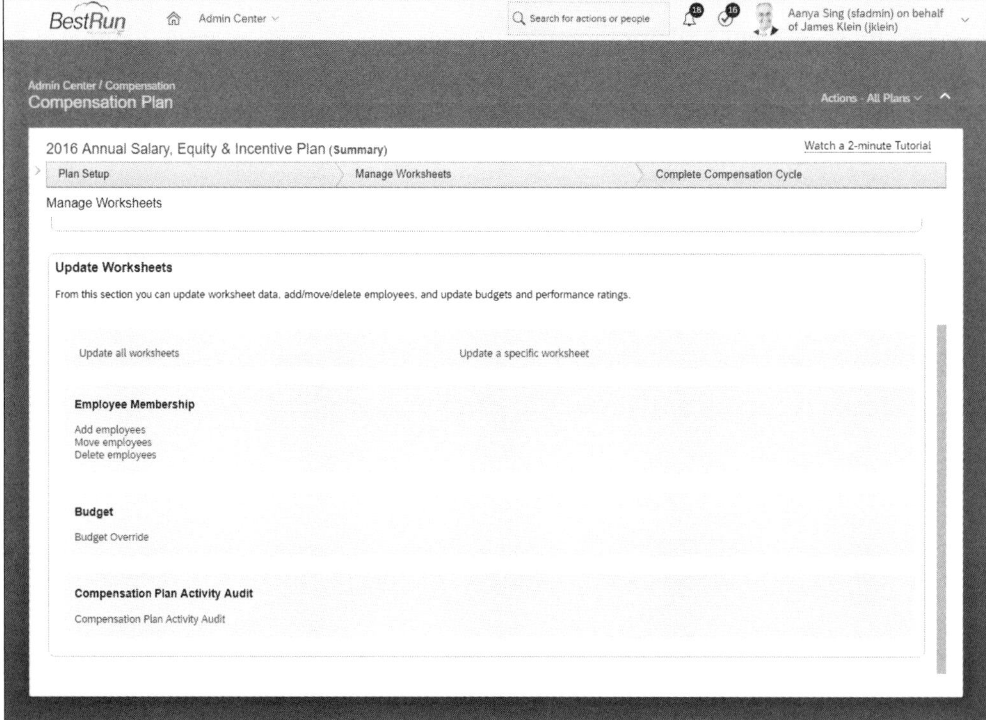

Figure 7.16 Update Worksheets Options

The following options are available in this subsection:

- **Update all worksheets**
  Clicking this option opens the panel shown in Figure 7.17. You can choose the settings that reflect the data change being applied, such as hire of a new employee, termination of an employee, budget changes, or change in organization hierarchy

structure. Any changes in compensation eligibility criteria can be updated through this option. This option allows for updates to completed compensation forms, as well.

- **Update a specific worksheet**
  This enables you to update a specific worksheet, including synchronization of bonus data with performance management forms and the People Profile, adding a new employee to compensation worksheet, removing inactive employees, and updating the budget.
- **Add employees, Move employees, and Delete employees**
  Add employees to existing compensation forms, move employees from one compensation form to another form, and delete employees from a form.
- **Budget Override**
  Update the budget pool available for the compensation cycle. Additional budgets can be propagated and distributed to planners in the organization. Cascading budgets can't be propagated if the amount spent exceeds the new budget amount.

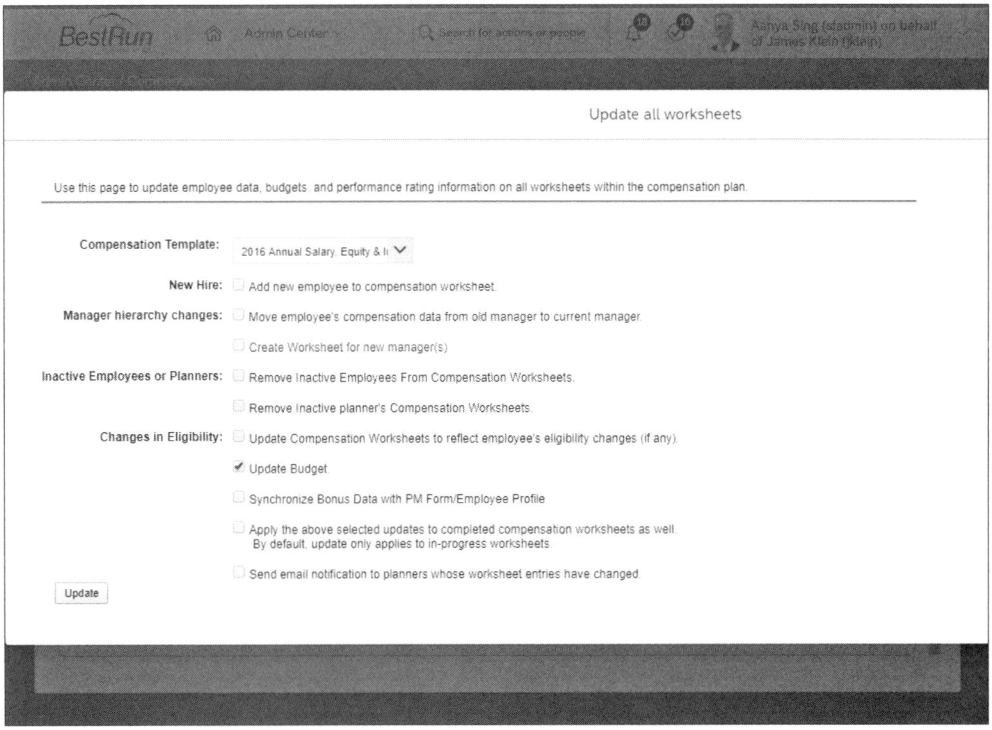

Figure 7.17 The Update All Worksheets Options

7.2.3 Variable Pay Form Specifics

After the Variable Pay setup is complete, the process to generate variable pay forms is exactly the same as for generation of compensation forms discussed in Section 7.1.4.

On a form, if the planner wants to view detailed calculations for an employee instead of the overview, the planner can click the **Action** icon next to the employee's name and select **View Details**. The plan details include, for example, target amounts, proration, goals, weighting, and payout amounts. Alternatively, the planner can expand the Compensation Profile to conduct further analysis on the employee result, as shown back in Figure 7.4.

The planner can also view summary results of the variable pay worksheet by clicking the **Live Analytics** link located on the top-right section, as shown in Figure 7.18.

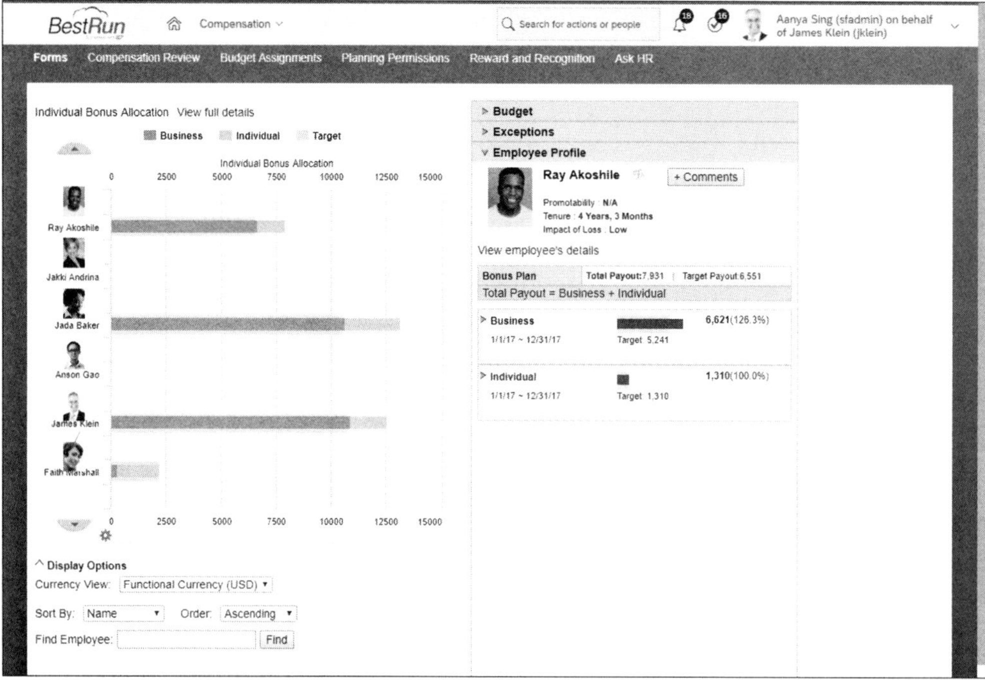

Figure 7.18 Live Analytics on Variable Pay Worksheet

7.3 Compensation Planning

Compensation plans are typically merit, bonus, or equity plans, but there can be other types of compensation plans used, and you may be running a different type of compensation plan. Whatever type of compensation plan you are running, the process to run them is the same.

Each planner in the organization is responsible for timely recommendations for employees as part of the compensation planning cycle process. These activities are performed on the compensation forms generated for each planner. Figure 7.19 shows a sample compensation form with the salary compensation component configuration.

Planners can adjust the display options on the form to get the desired information about the employee and also filter employee information on the worksheet.

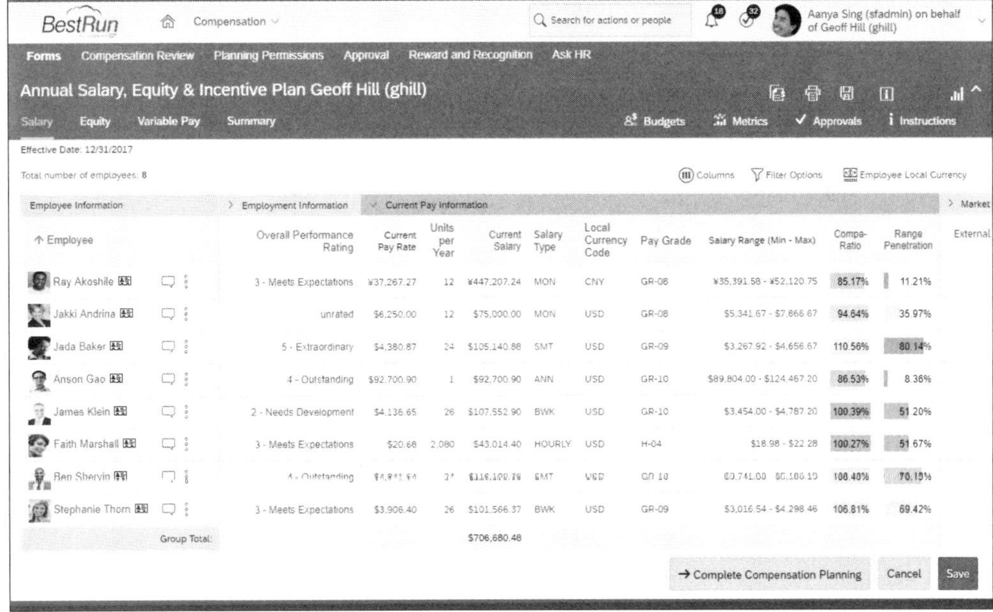

Figure 7.19 Planner's View of the Compensation Worksheet

When calculated recommendations are provided in the compensation form, planners can choose whether to accept the calculated recommendations for the employees based on the compensation plan template setup or override the system-calculated recommendations. Planners also have the flexibility to view the compensation guidelines as a percentage value or numerical value by adjusting the toggle available in the appropriate column.

Depending on how the compensation plan template is configured, a planner can also view multiple compensation planning components as separate tabs by clicking the appropriate link on the top-left section of the compensation worksheet. The **Summary** tab is shown in Figure 7.20.

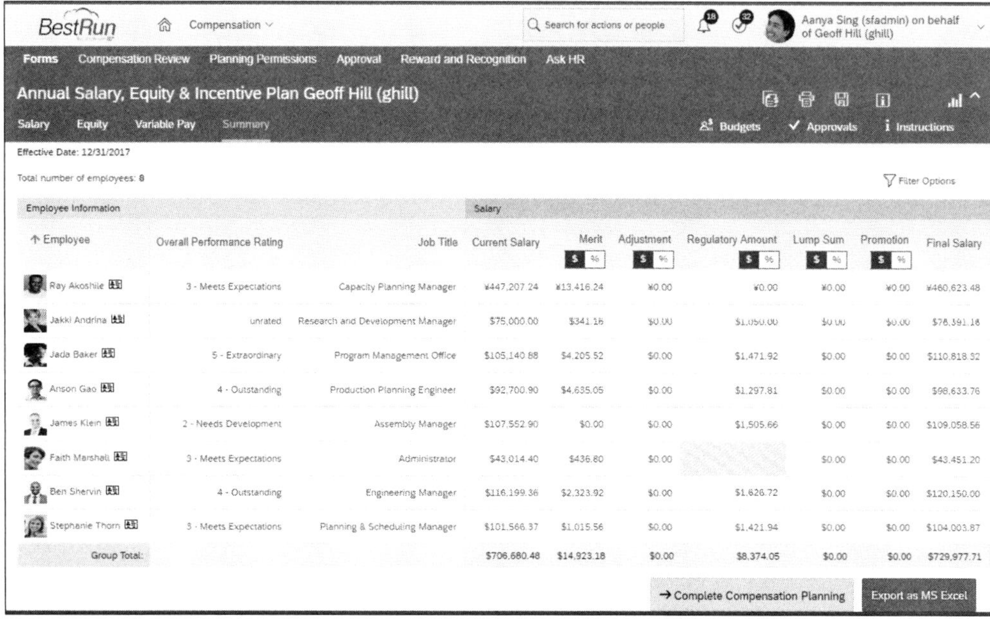

Figure 7.20 Summary Tab View on the Compensation Worksheet

After a planner has finished making their recommendations on the compensation form, the logical next step is to move the form to the workflow process for approval. To perform this, a planner must click the **Send to Next Step** button at the top of the compensation form.

Another option available in Compensation for approving the planner recommendations is to enable *hierarchy-based approval* as part of your solution design. It provides a simple approval model based on tree structure navigation that is built on the organization hierarchy; approvals move up the structure and rejections move downward. This configuration option eliminates the need to generate forms or send forms to the next step in the approval process.

> **Note**
>
> The hierarchy-based approval configuration for approving compensation forms isn't available for the Variable Pay solution. Otherwise, the compensation planning process is the same for both modules.

7.4 Promotions

When you use Employee Central, Compensation offers the ability to promote employees during the compensation planning process. This integration with Employee Central enables a change of job information in Employee Central directly from Compensation, although changes don't become effective until the compensation planning results are published to Employee Central.

> **Note**
>
> The promotions integration is not available for Variable Pay, as Variable Pay only covers the bonus process, which doesn't include promotions.

Promotion of an employee is triggered from a worksheet by selecting the menu for the employee and selecting **Promote**, as shown in Figure 7.21.

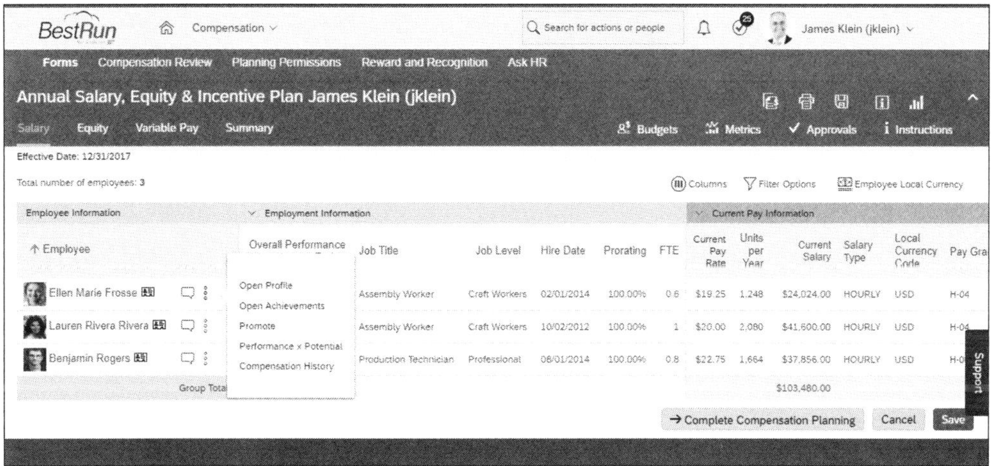

Figure 7.21 The Promote Option on the Worksheet

After clicking **Promote**, the **Employee Details** window will appear (shown in Figure 7.22). Here, you can make the necessary changes to the employee's job information to initiate a promotion for the employee.

Once the changes have been saved, you will be taken back to the worksheet, where you can see the icon that represents that the promotion has been entered next to the employee. This can be seen next to Ellen Marie Fosse in Figure 7.23.

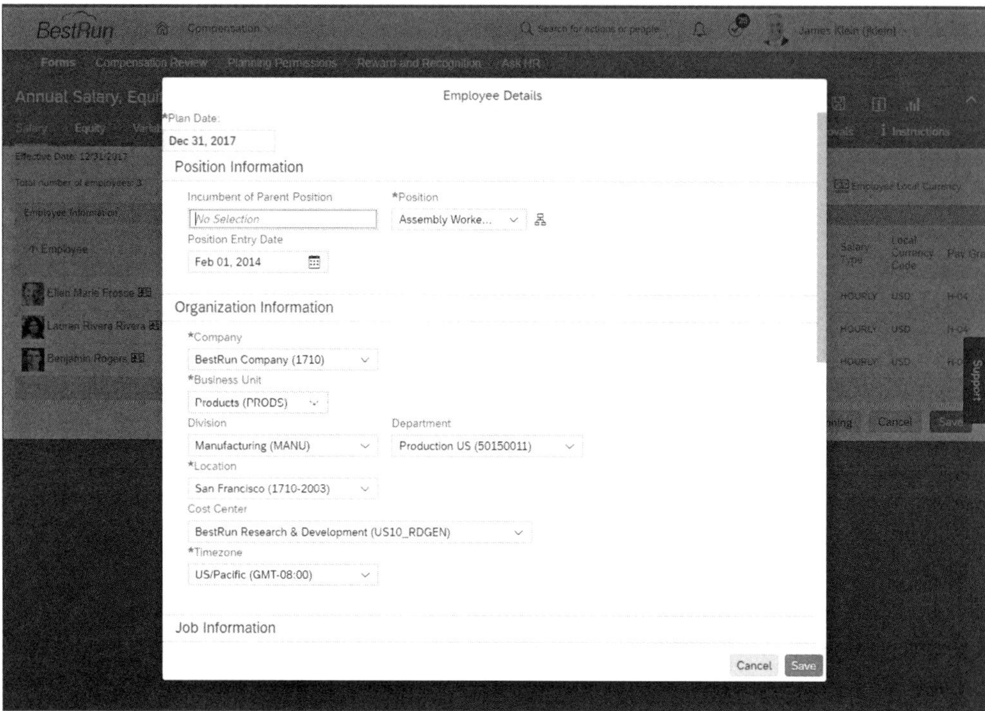

Figure 7.22 The Employee Details Screen

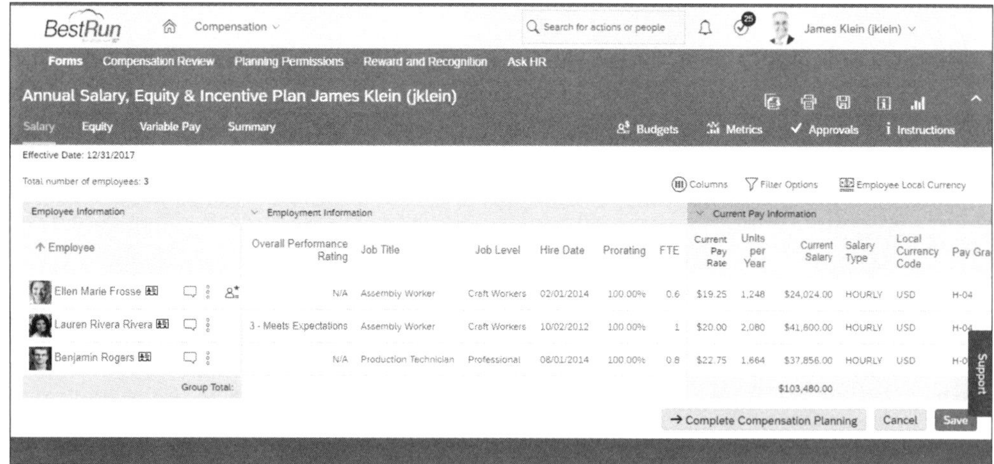

Figure 7.23 The Promotion Icon on the Worksheet

Further Resources

Further information can be found in the guide *Employee Central - Compensation Integration* under the SAP SuccessFactors Compensation product page on the SAP Help Portal.

7.5 Executive Review

The Executive Review functionality in the Compensation solution enables any active SAP SuccessFactors user to review (read) or adjust (write) compensation recommendations made for all employees in the organization.

The Executive Review functionality provides a different level of access to compensation planning data (i.e., it groups data from multiple users together), but otherwise works exactly the same way for both Compensation and Variable Pay. The user must be permissioned for this functionality and access to data for the appropriate employee population. At any given time, data generated within a single compensation plan template can be accessed by selecting the **Compensation Review** tab in the **Compensation** module (sometimes displayed as **Executive Review**), as shown in Figure 7.24.

After the compensation plan template is chosen, the user is presented with a page that exactly matches the design and layout of the compensation plan template. This page shouldn't be mistaken for the compensation form for a planner. Executive Review neither relies on a compensation form's workflow state nor behaves like a form. If compensation data is modified in Executive Review, you can send an email notification to the planners or reviewers of the affected underlying compensation form. Planners, HR managers, and administrators can filter data for employees they can edit or view.

The real advantage of using Executive Review is the ability to filter data. This can provide for a detailed analysis and update of compensation data by the administrators, HR professionals, and managers in your organization. Data visible on the **Executive Review** screen can also be exported in CSV format.

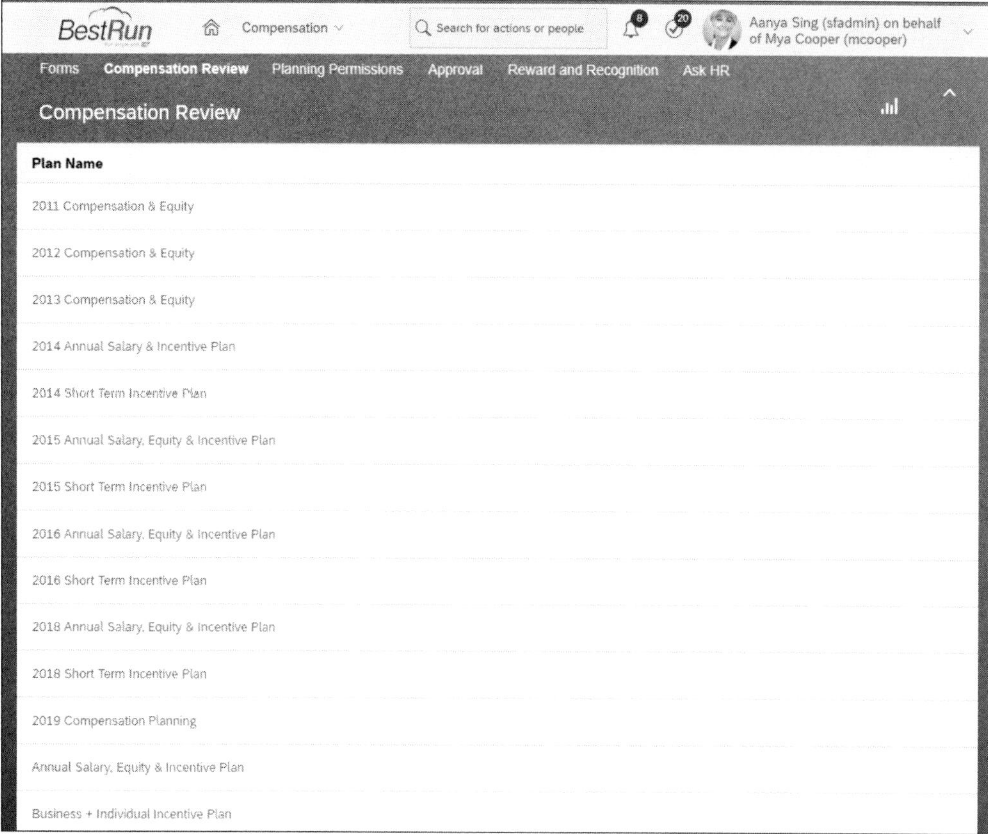

Figure 7.24 User Access to Executive Review

7.6 Reward Statements

Leading industry practices call for providing each employee with a personal compensation statement highlighting the employee's compensation results at the end of the compensation planning cycle. The Compensation solution facilitates this process by providing the capability to create a personal compensation statement template, as shown in Figure 7.25. You can modify the template with your organization's text, logo, multiple sections, and standard fields on the compensation plan template.

After all compensation forms have been reviewed and marked completed, only then can a personal compensation statement be generated for each employee. The personal compensation statement for an employee is available on the People Profile.

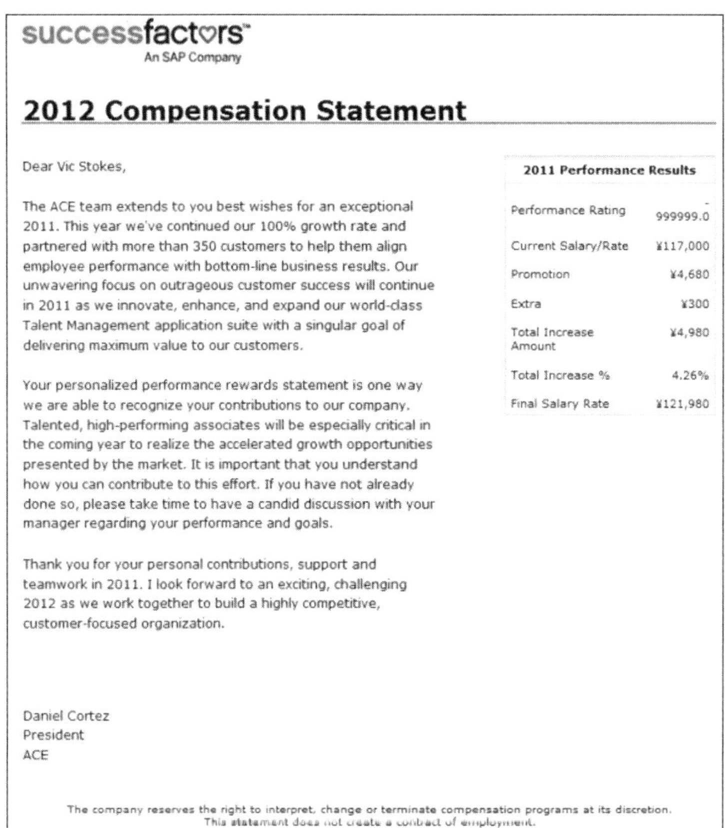

successfactors
An SAP Company

2012 Compensation Statement

Dear Vic Stokes,

The ACE team extends to you best wishes for an exceptional 2011. This year we've continued our 100% growth rate and partnered with more than 350 customers to help them align employee performance with bottom-line business results. Our unwavering focus on outrageous customer success will continue in 2011 as we innovate, enhance, and expand our world-class Talent Management application suite with a singular goal of delivering maximum value to our customers.

Your personalized performance rewards statement is one way we are able to recognize your contributions to our company. Talented, high-performing associates will be especially critical in the coming year to realize the accelerated growth opportunities presented by the market. It is important that you understand how you can contribute to this effort. If you have not already done so, please take time to have a candid discussion with your manager regarding your performance and goals.

Thank you for your personal contributions, support and teamwork in 2011. I look forward to an exciting, challenging 2012 as we work together to build a highly competitive, customer-focused organization.

Daniel Cortez
President
ACE

2011 Performance Results	
Performance Rating	999999.0
Current Salary/Rate	¥117,000
Promotion	¥4,680
Extra	¥300
Total Increase Amount	¥4,980
Total Increase %	4.26%
Final Salary Rate	¥121,980

The company reserves the right to interpret, change or terminate compensation programs at its discretion.
This statement does not create a contract of employment.

Figure 7.25 Personal Compensation Statement Template

7.7 Publishing to Employee Central

When you use Employee Central as your system of record for employee data, then you want any compensation planning results to write back to the employee's compensation information. Naturally, this is provided as a standard feature.

Eligibility rules created in **Configure Business Rules** are used to determine which employees are eligible for compensation planning in Compensation and Variable Pay.

Note

Planning results created from data received from a pay component group in Employee Central can only be written back as pay components when publishing to Employee Central.

If you are using Variable Pay, then you need to import employee history data before you can start the process. This is done in the Admin Center in **Compensation Home** by following these steps:

1. Select the variable pay plan.
2. Click **Plan Setup.**
3. Click on the **Manage Users** dropdown.
4. Select **Import Employee History from Employee Central**.

If the option in the last step is not available, then you need to check the configuration of your variable pay plan template.

Once compensation planning has been completed, you are ready to publish the results back to Employee Central. This is done the in the Admin Center in **Compensation Home** by following these steps:

1. Select the plan for which you wish to publish the results back to Employee Central.
2. Click **Complete Compensation Cycle**.
3. Click on the **Publish Data** dropdown.
4. Select **Publish in Employee Central**.
5. If you want to check the status of form, then click **Check Forms Status**.
6. Click **Submit**.

An administrator can use the Job Monitor to track the status of the publishing of the data. The job type is **Publish EC Data for Template**. Once the job is run, the data will be written to **Compensation Information** in Employee Central.

Further Resources

Further information can be found in the guides *Employee Central - Compensation Integration* and *Employee Central - Variable Pay Integration* under the SAP SuccessFactors Compensation product page on the SAP Help Portal.

7.8 Spot Awards

The Spot Award program provides you with another way of planning the spot award of bonuses as part of your compensation planning program but outside of your set compensation planning period. Spot awards are typically awarded to a limited group of employees and so the use of worksheets is impractical, and since this type of awards is still subject to budgets, guidelines, eligibilities, and workflow approvals, then a framework is needed to support compensation planners in providing spot awards.

> **Note**
>
> If you use Employee Central, this functionality is intended to replace the Spot Award functionality provided in Employee Central.

Spot Award programs enable you to award spot awards to select employees. You can setup multiple Spot Award programs. Setting up a Spot Award program follows a workflow and uses a guided wizard to take you through each step of the workflow. The steps for setting up a Spot Award program are:

1. Create the program.
2. Define the program settings. Set the following various attributes of the program (see Figure 7.26):
   - Program name
   - Functional currency
   - Currency conversion table
   - Start date
   - End date
   - Whether the program is active
   - Whether there is a budget associated with this program
   - Whether nominators can override the recommended award amount
   - Any messages to be displayed to nominators that are overriding the guideline amount
   - Whether eligibility is via a business rule or dynamic group
   - Whether the program should be integrated with Employee Central
   - When the program is integrated with Employee Central, which pay component to use for the spot award

3. Define/import the budget for the program.
4. Define award categories and levels. You can define up to 20 categories and levels; categories can be anything that your organization deems as important for employees to be measured against, such as skills or behaviors.
5. Define the guidelines by uploading the guideline amounts that compensation planners can use, based on the categories and levels defined in the previous step of the wizard.
6. Define eligibility (i.e., define the business rule or dynamic group that defines who is eligible for the program). Which option is available depends on the settings made in the second step of the wizard.

Figure 7.26 shows the **Settings** page of the Spot Award program wizard.

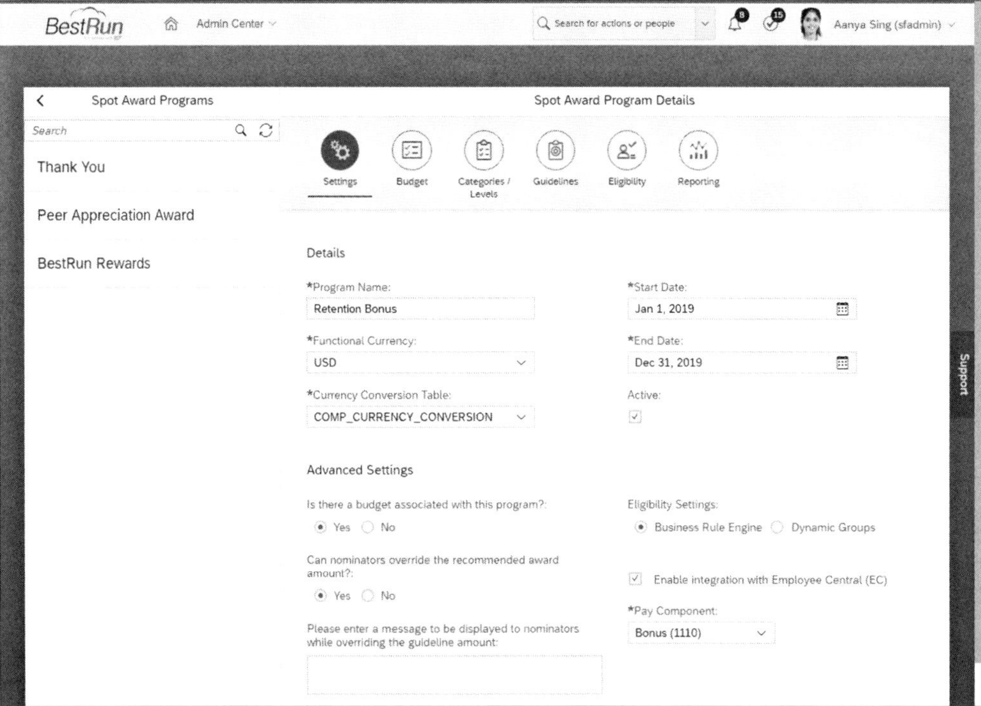

Figure 7.26 Spot Award Program Details

Spot Award programs can have workflows assigned to them, so that spot awards can be approved or declined.

Spot awards are awarded through multiple methods. The main methods are via the following:

- Home page: Select the **Recognize and Reward Someone** tile. Select an employee in the **My Team** tile and select **Reward and Recognition** in the **Take Action** menu.
- Quickcard: Select **Reward and Recognition.**
- People Profile: Select **Reward and Recognition** in the **Actions** menu on the employee's profile.

Depending on the option you select, the first one or two steps will differ. For example, if you launch the process by select the **Recognize and Reward Someone** tile, you need to first select a program and then select the eligible employee(s) you want to award a spot award to before you are taken to the screen to select the award category. If you select **Reward and Recognition** in the **Actions** menu on the employee's profile, then you are taken straight to a screen to select the Spot Award program and the award category.

Once the process of selecting a Spot Award program and employee has begun, you have to select the award category, the award category level, and the award amount (you can go ahead with the guideline amount or change it); enter a reason for the reward; and then review and submit the award for approval (see in Figure 7.27).

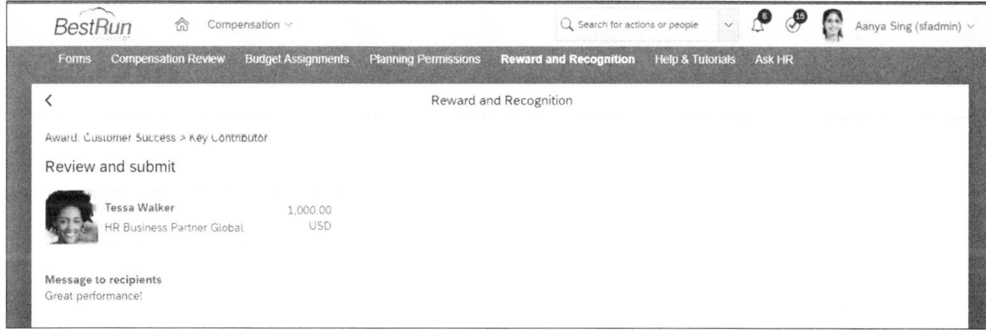

Figure 7.27 Reward and Recognition of an Employee

Should the Spot Award program be integrated with Employee Central, then after the spot award is approved, it will be automatically added to the employee's Compensation Information portlet using the pay component defined during the setup of the Spot Award program.

Further Resources

Further information can be found in the guide *Reward and Recognition: Spot Awards* under the SAP SuccessFactors Compensation product page on the SAP Help Portal.

7.9 Reporting

The two standard options for compensation reporting are **Rollup** and **Aggregate Export**; these are available as part of the **Actions – All Plans** menu. Let's take a quick look at each:

- **Compensation aggregate export**
  This is an export of all employee and planning data available within a specific compensation plan template. The extract includes all standard and custom fields (if marked as reportable) defined on the compensation plan template.
- **Compensation rollup**
  This option allows for the generation of the compensation planning and budget information report based on a planner's hierarchy for the selected compensation plan template. Figure 7.28 shows a rollup summary.

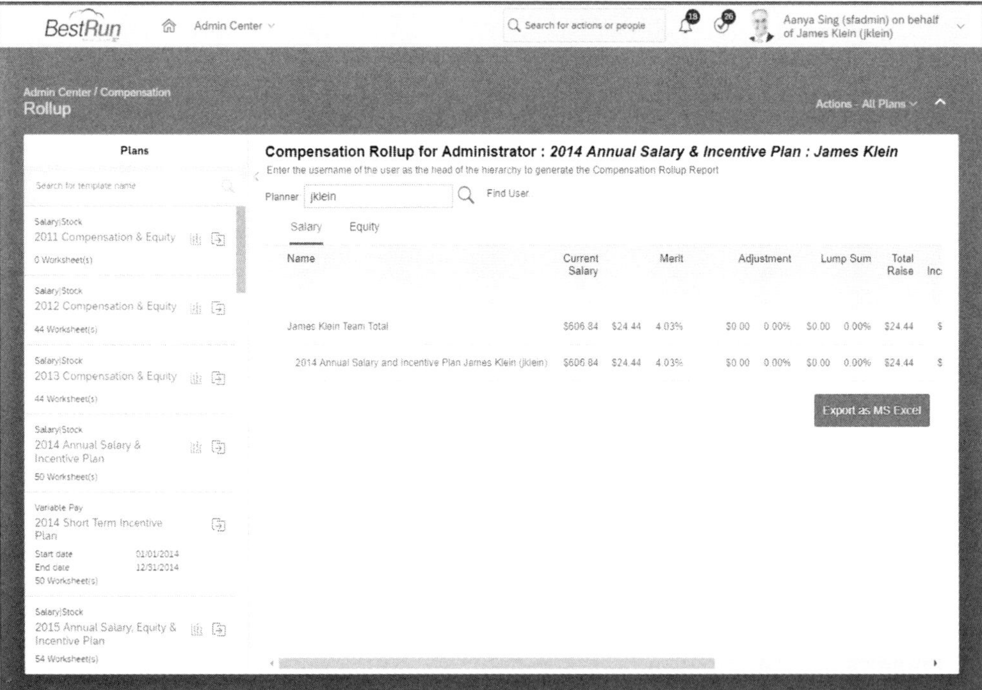

Figure 7.28 Compensation Rollup Generation Menu

7.10 Implementation Tips

There are a number of tips that can help you make the most out of your Compensation or Variable Pay implementation. We'll look at a few now:

- **Data**
  Data is a critical aspect of compensation planning. If salary and compensation data is not accurate, then your entire compensation planning process will produce results that can inadvertently impact your payroll.
- **Design**
  Most organizations have exceptions to their processes. To have the most effective compensation planning process, it is important to design for 90 percent of use cases and not for the exceptions. Typically, the exceptions can make a straightforward process become convoluted and cumbersome, which can damage adoption and success of the compensation program.
- **Employee lifecycle changes**
  It is important to understand employee lifecycle event changes and how they impact compensation. For example, a promotion can mean a change in the data of an employee mid-process, or a leave of absence could make an employee ineligible. You also have to consider how new employees are considered and whether they might become eligible through a rule in the system when they should not be eligible for the process so soon into their new job.
- **Workflows**
  Workflows should be designed to be streamlined and, wherever possible, few approvers should be included. Because the process involves salary data, it can be tempting for organizations to include multiple senior-level individuals as approvers in the process. However, this slows down the approval process and doesn't drive accountability to the compensation planners.

7.11 Summary

The Compensation and Variable Pay solutions provide a robust platform to meet the complex needs of an organization's compensation design and truly enforce a pay-for-performance culture. The solution offerings in Compensation provide the organization the agility needed to effectively manage a successful compensation cycle by streamlining the planning process. Integration capabilities with SAP ERP HCM and Employee Central provide the benefit of not having to manage multiple data points.

In this chapter, you learned what is required to set up yearly compensation and variable pay forms, and how to design your compensation worksheets. You also learned how to execute a compensation review and complete the compensation process.

In the next chapter, we'll look at the SAP SuccessFactors Recruiting solution and how it can support recruiting management, applicant tracking, and recruiting marketing activities.

Chapter 8
Recruiting

Recruiting in today's competitive environment encompasses three phases that are all critically important to ensuring that you hire the right candidates to drive business results. SAP SuccessFactors Recruiting provides all the tools to attract, engage, and select the best talent for your organization.

Legacy applicant tracking systems (ATS) have focused almost exclusively on selecting candidates. While many tools are now available on the market to help companies find and engage candidates, most aren't connected to the application and selection processes and tools. But, in today's competitive hiring environment, finding the best candidates isn't enough. You need to get them engaged and moving through your hiring process quickly so you do not risk losing them to a different opportunity.

The SAP SuccessFactors Recruiting module brings together Recruiting Marketing and Recruiting Management to combine the best features of an ATS, application processing and candidate management features, and high-powered tools to attract and engage candidates in one solution. This complete recruiting solution sits inside the SAP SuccessFactors HCM Suite, enabling customers to connect it to their other modules, such as SAP SuccessFactors Workforce Analytics, SAP SuccessFactors Workforce Planning, SAP SuccessFactors Succession & Development, SAP SuccessFactors Learning, SAP SuccessFactors Performance & Goals, SAP SuccessFactors Compensation, and other collaboration solutions. As shown in Figure 8.1, Recruiting is an integral piece of a complete HCM solution that drives business execution results and is the first step for customers to optimize their workforces—finding the right people for the right jobs.

Recruiting not only manages the transactional components of a traditional ATS from a requisition and application perspective, but also goes beyond that, providing tools to ensure that customers can attract and engage the best candidates in their recruiting process.

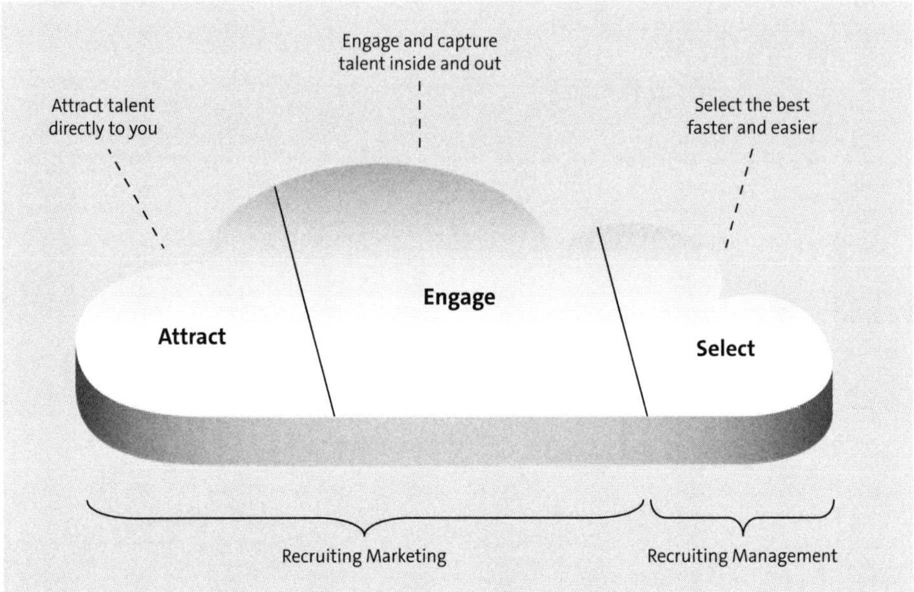

Figure 8.1 Recruiting Landscape

In this chapter, we'll walk through key features and functionality available in Recruiting. We'll explore creating and approving requisitions, job posting and sourcing, and candidate management topics. We'll also take a look at data privacy, managing offers, and hiring, onboarding, and referring employees. We'll finish with a look at recruiting analytics and implementation tips.

Before we dive in, let's begin with a look at the basics of Recruiting.

8.1 Recruiting Basics

The recruiting process with the Recruiting module is driven by collaboration. It allows different players in the process—recruiters, hiring managers, coordinators, and others—to actively participate in managing an open position, reviewing and assessing candidates, and eventually selecting the right candidate for hire.

The system is intuitive and easy to use; any player in the process can log in and understand what to do and where to do it with very little training. For recruiters who spend all day in the system, Recruiting saves time and frustration by reducing the number of mouse clicks to complete an action, from maintaining a requisition to moving candidates through the talent pipeline and eventually processing the successful candidate for hire. Recruiting provides one of the most comprehensive metrics engine in the industry. It provides metrics such as cost per hire; time to hire; and candidate quality by source, location, and other criteria, Recruiting provides the raw data customers need to evaluate the effectiveness of their recruiting processes and tools.

As with the rest of the SAP SuccessFactors HCM Suite, Recruiting is highly configurable. It offers more than 30 standard fields available for use on the requisition and application and supports unlimited custom fields. The customer's branding and messaging is supported by SAP SuccessFactors' best practices and platform.

In this section, we'll establish the foundations of Recruiting, starting with key roles and templates.

8.1.1 Recruiting Roles

Roles associated with the recruiting process are identified by each customer, based on who needs to approve requisitions and view candidates. These process roles are then associated with the standard Recruiting roles, which define the following:

- Field, button, and feature permissions on the requisition
- Field, button, and feature permissions on the candidate application
- Which role creates the approval workflow for the requisition and reviews the requisition

Within the Recruiting module, seven roles can be permissioned. These roles are separate from roles created in role-based permissions (RBPs) and are defined and permissioned directly in the requisition template configuration. Roles correspond to operator fields on the requisition (for example, the **Recruiter** in the example provided in Figure 8.2). The following recruiting roles are available:

- Originator
- Recruiter
- Hiring manager
- Sourcer
- Coordinator
- Second recruiter
- Vice president of staffing
- Approver

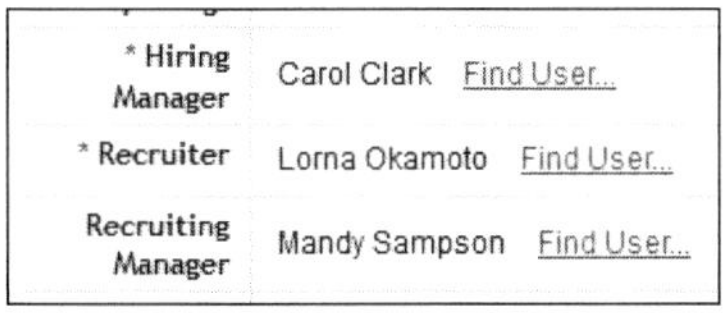

* Hiring Manager	Carol Clark Find User...
* Recruiter	Lorna Okamoto Find User...
Recruiting Manager	Mandy Sampson Find User...

Figure 8.2 Requisition Operator Roles

Operator user selection can be limited by using recruiting groups. For example, recruiter groups can have the list of all recruiters in the company or region. That way, selection of users can be limited for stricter controls. In a different scenario, if no group is associated to an operator, then you can select any user in the system, which provides a great amount of flexibility in who can participate in the recruiting process.

The originator determines the user for each role when the requisition is created. In addition to these roles, additional approvers of the requisition assume the role of **V**. Additional signers are determined by the route map or by manually indicating additional signers for that specific job opening. We'll take a look at each in this section.

8.1.2 Recruiting Templates

There are three main components of configurable templates within Recruiting: the job requisition data model (JRDM), the candidate data model (CDM), and the Candidate Profile template (CPT). For customers who use offer approval, there is also an Offer Details template that is configured.

Job Requisition Data Model

A requisition defines the requirements of the position being filled. Requisitions are created from a template that is configured during implementation; Figure 8.3 shows the **Create Requisition** step of the wizard.

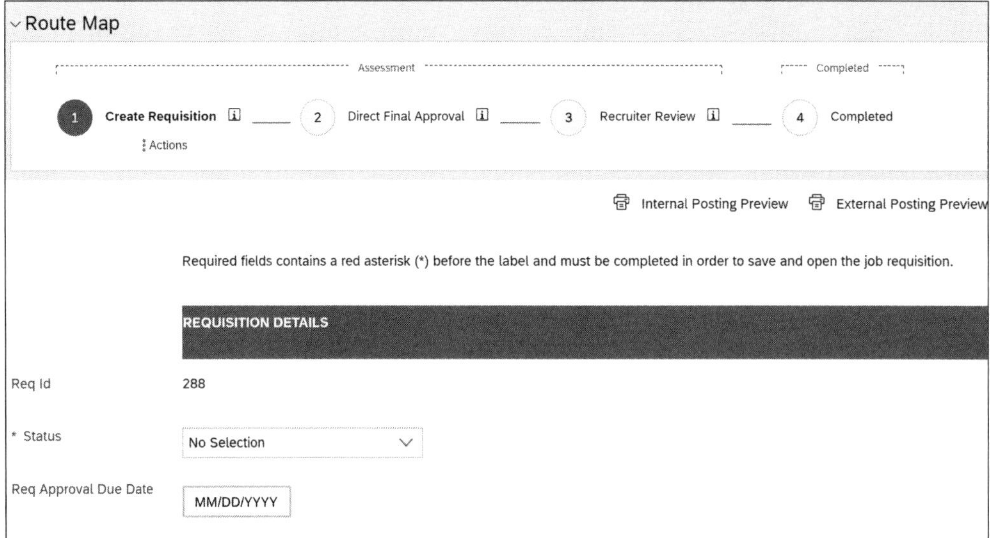

Figure 8.3 Job Requisition Form

As noted previously, the template is called the JRDM and specifies the fields on the requisition and who has permissions to read and write to each field. Requisitions are created manually by operators in the recruiting process, such as a hiring manager or recruiter. Integration now supports open positions in SAP ERP Human Capital Management (SAP ERP HCM), triggering the creation of a requisition in Recruiting Management. Requisitions are tied to a route map (or workflow) for approval before they are open and can be posted to the career site. The JRDM is completely configurable to meet customer requirements using either the standard fields for requisitions or any number of custom fields that may be required.

Candidate Data Model

The CDM is a Recruiting application. It defines information about a candidate who is applying for a position and contains identifying information, such as name and contact data; job-specific requirements the candidate possesses; and other demographic data the customer needs to capture, such as equal employment opportunity (EEO) status. The application template (as shown in Figure 8.4) is also completely configurable and can utilize the standard application fields or any custom fields required to support the customer's needs. The fields that are added in the application template can be mandatory or optional, depending on the customer's requirements.

Required fields contains a red asterisk (*) before the label and must be completed in order to submit your application.

* First Name	Test
Middle Name	
* Last Name	A
Email Address	TEST@TEST.COM
* Cell/Mobile Phone	305111111
Home Phone	305111112
* Address Line 1	123
Address Line 2	Address Line 2
* City	Miami
State/Region/Province	No Selection ▼
Zip	33076
* Country of Residence	1766 ▼
How did you hear about this position?	No Selection ▼
If Employee Referral, Provide Name	
	EMPLOYMENT INFORMATION
Have you ever been employed here before?	No ▼
* Please indicate your notice period	No Selection ▼

Figure 8.4 Candidate Application

Candidate applications can have country-specific questions. The fields can have advanced conditions, which can be shown based on the country. For example, a field such as "Are you eligible to work in the US?" will be only shown for US-based jobs, and a field such as "Are you eligible to work in Canada?" will be shown for Canada-based jobs.

Candidate Profile Template

The CPT is the candidate's online resume, as shown in Figure 8.5. It leverages Employee Profile functionality and can be designed to capture static information about a candidate, such as education, work experience, and references. The CPT can be synced to the Employee Profile for internal candidates, so that this information is entered only once. Once the candidate is hired as an employee, the candidate profile is synced to the employee profile, so that there is only one system of record and information is entered only once.

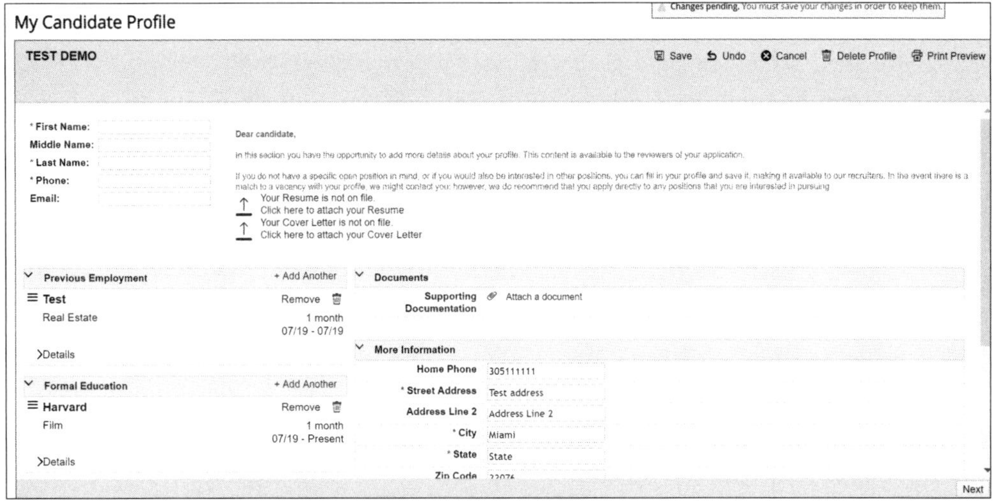

Figure 8.5 Candidate Profile

In addition to this, multiple candidate profiles can be merged based on predefined criteria such as address, phone number, and so on. This reduces duplication in data records, in addition to ensuring accurate reporting.

Offer Details Template

The Offer Details template is a collection of the salary, start date, and other elements the company wants to use while negotiating employment with the candidate. Offer details are entered by a recruiter or other authorized user, an ad hoc list of approvers is defined, and the offer is sent for approval. Approvers can approve or reject with comments.

It can pull data from fields on the requisition or application, or data can be entered directly onto the template. The approvers can be added ad hoc or leverage a predefined workflow that is configured into the template. This supports defining recruiting roles, recruiting groups, or specified users. During the process of offer approval, the users can add comments and attach a resume, which the approver can see.

8.1.3 Applicant Tracking

Recruiting Marketing assists in finding, engaging, and tracking talent for open positions.

The Recruiting dashboard and YouCalc metrics give an overview of the total number of total applications at any given time. The YouCalc metrics widget gives a quick snapshot of requisition data, as shown in Figure 8.6. Here, you can see information such as total number of applications, number of forwarded candidates, number of external active requisitions, number of internal requisitions, and the average number of days the requisitions have been open.

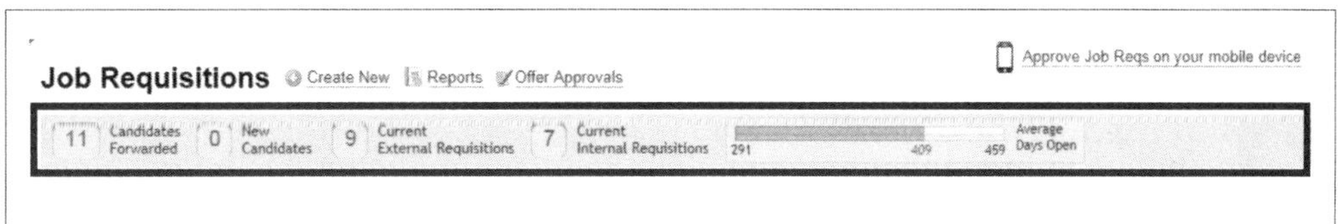

Figure 8.6 YouCalc Metrics

The Recruiting dashboard, a key part of the marketing aspect of Recruiting, displays metrics for elements such as the following:

- Budget savings
- How much time it takes to fill a position
- Best source for candidates

Recruiting also features smart job publishing for distributing jobs, search engine optimization (SEO) to drive more traffic, and a talent community to capture passive candidates.

8.1.4 Career Site Builder/Marketing Analytics

The Career Site Builder allows anyone to build a responsive career site. All standard marketing features in Recruiting are included with a Career Site Builder implementation. Customers can customize career sites by adjusting colors, images, and site layout. Users can also adjust the site's header and footer size, and other site layout component, like the distance between site components. With these adjustments, users can create sites with a custom look.

Recruiting Marketing advanced analytics combines data from Recruiting Management and Recruiting Marketing to create full line-of-site data from a candidate's first visit to their eventual hire. Recruiting Marketing advanced analytics is a reporting application for reporting trends in analytics data. Recruiting Marketing advanced analytics has more sophisticated reporting than the Recruiting dashboard, including the following reports:

- Candidate quality
- Candidate quantity
- Cost per hire
- Time to fill
- Source behavior

8.1.5 Recruiting Posting Options

The Recruiting Posting module (formerly known as multiposting) allows customers to access any number of job board marketplaces. It also allows companies to cross-post jobs, internships, job boards, and alumni associations to more than 2,000 schools and universities. Using recruiting posting makes it easier to manage job offers, even after publication. The recruiting posting home page allows you to see the latest job postings, along with an analysis of job board usage.

Now that we've laid a foundation to discuss Recruiting, let's take a look at the recruiting process.

8.2 Requisition Creation and Approval

The recruiting process in Recruiting begins with creating a requisition and sending it through the approval workflow, or route map. This gives each operator in the approval workflow an opportunity to review the position requirements, make additions or correct data, and send it back if there is an issue that needs to be addressed. After the requisition is approved, it can be posted to the internal and external career portals, job boards, or agency portal. We'll take a look at the key processes in this section.

8.2.1 Requisition Creation

Requisitions can be created in few ways: an open vacancy in SAP ERP HCM or an open position in SAP SuccessFactors triggers the requisition, or a recruiting operator manually creates a requisition. For manually created requisitions, any user who has been granted permissions to create the requisition form can start the requisition process. The user who creates a requisition, like the one shown in Figure 8.7, is known as the originator and has permissions on the requisition that have been granted in the requisition configuration for the originator role. The originator role completes the operators who need to approve the requisition and any other fields for which they have permissions.

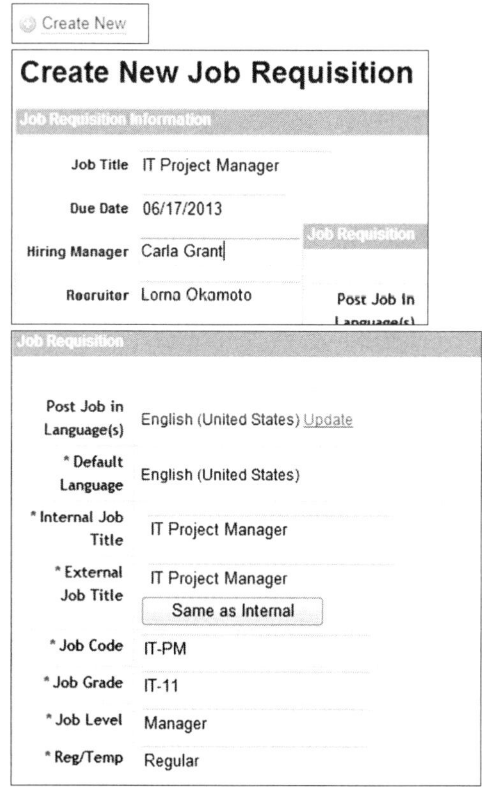

Figure 8.7 Creating a New Requisition

Requisitions created via the integration with SAP ERP HCM appear as preapproved requisitions in the Recruiting dashboard. Fields of data may be updated or completed as needed, and the requisition is sent through the route map for approval. Some fields in requisition form can be prefilled based on the position, so that there is less data entry for the originator.

8.2.2 Integration with Position Management

Requisition creation becomes very easy when Recruiting Management is integrated with Position Management. The customer needs to have Position Management as a prerequisite for the integration to Recruiting Management.

Requisitions can be created from Position Org Chart, as shown in Figure 8.8. These requisitions can have prefilled noneditable or editable fields (such as salary) in the job requisition to ensure tighter controls.

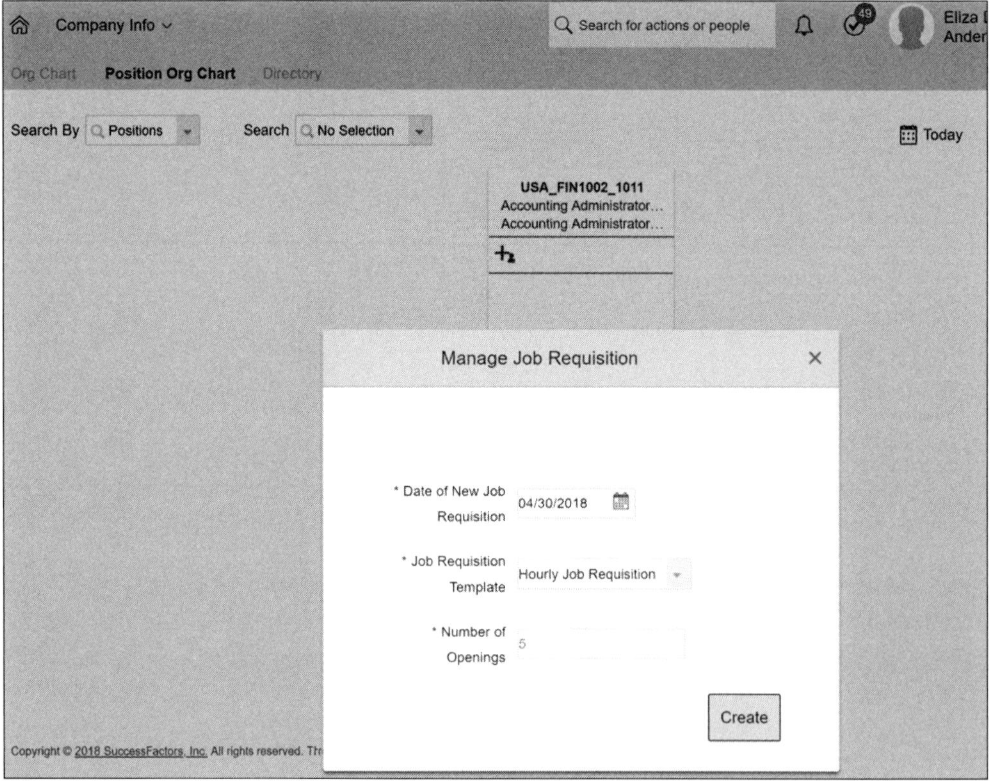

Figure 8.8 Creating Requisition from Position Management

The Rules Engine can be used to derive the accurate job requisition template based on the type of requisition (for example, exempt/nonexempt, hourly/salary, etc.).

For more detail on Position Management, see Chapter 4, Section 4.1.4.

8.2.3 Requisition Approval Workflow

Each job requisition template can be associated with one approval workflow, called a route map. A route map electronically moves a requisition from one user to the next until all appropriate approvals have been received (see Figure 8.9).

Figure 8.9 Requisition Route Map

While the route map defines which users touch the requisition, the permissions assigned to each role in the route map define what the users can see and do to the data in the requisition. Steps in the route map can be linear or iterative. Iterative steps involve two or more parties and allow the requisition to be sent back and forth between the two parties until it's ready to move forward. After the requisition is approved, it can be posted, and candidates can view it on the career portal. We'll cover this step next.

8.3 Job Posting and Sourcing

Open requisitions can be posted so candidates can search for them and apply. Job posting is where the power of Recruiting's marketing capabilities come into play and illustrate SAP SuccessFactors' dedication to candidate engagement. SAP SuccessFactors is committed to delivering data-driven and user-centric best practices that optimize site conversion rates and maximize the user's experience.

The power of Recruiting Marketing is making job postings available to the brightest and best talent possible. A common problem facing talent acquisition professionals is that their jobs are not easy to find. Recruiting Marketing leverages proven marketing techniques such as SEO, social media integration, and customized landing pages, while applying them to talent sourcing in new ways to drive applicant flow. Talent communities capture passive candidates who may have been previously lost to recruiters. SAP SuccessFactors implemented what was originally known as Recruiting Marketing internally in early 2012, and within 10 months of implementation, visitors to its career site increased from 10,000 to more than 80,000, resulting in more than 150 hires.

Easily accessible sourcing analytics provide new visibility to marketing strategies and their effectiveness at any given time. Dashboards on recruiting marketing sources provide real-time data on where candidates are coming from, enabling customers to evaluate and adjust recruiting marketing strategies and dollars in an agile manner. These advanced analytics support tracking candidates from sourcing to hire to retire.

SAP SuccessFactors treats every job as a campaign to attract candidates to your sites based on their interests and skill sets. Customized landing pages attract candidates based on their particular interests and drive them to the main career site within Recruiting. Talent communities are candidate-centric, automated recruiting pools that grow over time. They connect talent with the company's brand, store contacts in a centralized place, and track visitors to a customer's site who begin the application process but don't complete it. Talent communities open communication channels with candidates who would not otherwise exist.

Jobs are posted through the **Job Postings** page and, from there, are picked up and distributed to the predetermined channels based on the criteria established during implementation.

As shown in Figure 8.10, approved requisitions are available for posting in various places within Recruiting:

- **Internal Posting** (internal career site)
- **External Posting** (external career sites)
- **Job board postings** via eQuest
- **Agency Listings** (SAP SuccessFactors' agency portal)

Jobs posted to the intranet appear on the **Careers** tab within the SAP SuccessFactors HCM platform and are available to all employees. Corporate postings are those made to the microsite created for external candidates. Customers have one default microsite but can create additional sites as requirements dictate. This flexibility enables sites to focus on certain populations or target candidates. However, the decision to create additional microsites should be made in the context of the Recruiting Management strategy employed by each customer. Microsites are most powerful for companies that choose to implement Recruiting Management before Recruiting Marketing or opt not to implement Recruiting Marketing at all.

Jobs can be posted for a specific period of time by providing a **Posting Start Date** and a **Posting End Date**. If a job should be posted indefinitely, no **Posting End Date** is provided, and it stays posted until the posting is removed by the recruiter.

Figure 8.10 Job Postings in Recruiting

Job board postings are an add-on service provided by SAP SuccessFactors' partner eQuest. The job boards available depend on a customer's separate contract and subscription with eQuest. This aggregator allows recruiters to post jobs to multiple places via one interface. Specific fields must be configured on the requisition template to support the fields eQuest requires to post.

SAP SuccessFactors supports working with agencies using its agency portal. There is one agency portal that is shared by all customers, and each customer sets up individual agency accounts for those agencies they want to post jobs for, as shown in Figure 8.11. The agency portal functionality has increased and allows agency users to track the progress of the candidates they submit to requisitions. There are also email triggers that can be set up to communicate with agency users.

After agencies have been set up in the Admin Center and granted access to the agency portal (see Figure 8.12), recruiters can post jobs to the portal and agency users can submit candidates for open positions. Agency candidates are easily identifiable from the Candidate Workbench, as well as within the Candidate Snapshot (see Section 8.5).

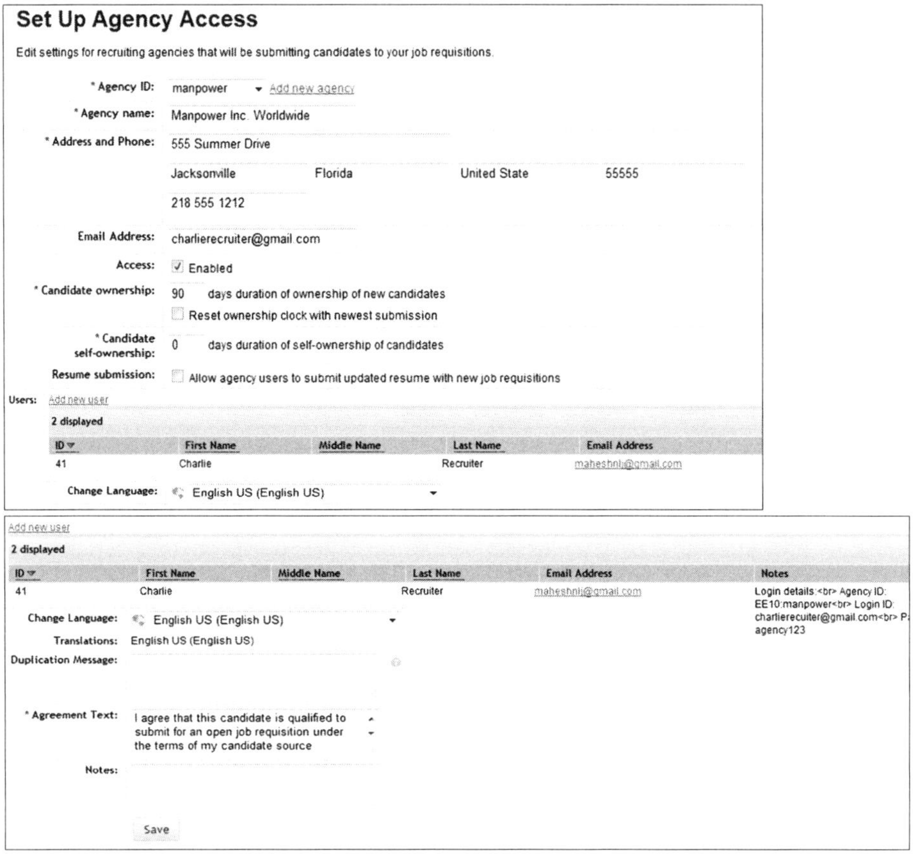

Set Up Agency Access
Edit settings for recruiting agencies that will be submitting candidates to your job requisitions.
* Agency ID: manpower Add new agency
* Agency name: Manpower Inc. Worldwide
* Address and Phone: 555 Summer Drive
Jacksonville Florida United State 55555
218 555 1212
Email Address: charlierecruiter@gmail.com
Access: Enabled
* Candidate ownership: 90 days duration of ownership of new candidates
Reset ownership clock with newest submission
* Candidate self-ownership: 0 days duration of self-ownership of candidates
Resume submission: Allow agency users to submit updated resume with new job requisitions
Users: Add new user
2 displayed
ID First Name Middle Name Last Name Email Address
41 Charlie Recruiter maheshnl@gmail.com
Change Language: English US (English US)
Add new user
2 displayed
ID First Name Middle Name Last Name Email Address Notes
41 Charlie Recruiter maheshnl@gmail.com
Login details:
 Agency ID: EE10:manpower
 Login ID: charlierecuiter@gmail.com
 P
agency123
Change Language: English US (English US)
Translations: English US (English US)
Duplication Message:
* Agreement Text: I agree that this candidate is qualified to submit for an open job requisition under the terms of my candidate source
Notes:
Save

Figure 8.11 Setting Up Agency Access in the Admin Center

SuccessFactors
Agency
Access
Agency ID:
Email:
Password:
Forgot your password?
Sign In

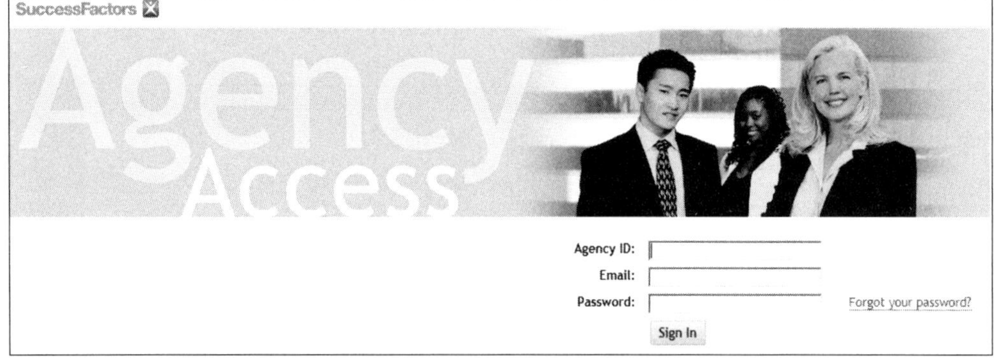

Figure 8.12 The SAP SuccessFactors Agency Portal

8.4 Candidate Experience

Candidates interact with the system in several ways. They can search for open positions and set up a Candidate Profile, apply for jobs, manage job applications already submitted, and set up job alerts to be notified of future positions that become available.

The Candidate Profile and CDM are two major elements of the candidate's job search experience, and they work together to provide recruiters and hiring managers a complete picture of the candidate. This picture is used to evaluate the candidate against the job requirements, leading to the selection of a qualified candidate. This section looks at how the two elements of the candidate experience—the Candidate Profile and CDM—work together to provide recruiters and hiring managers with a complete picture of a candidate's background and qualifications for a position. We'll also take a look at the Data Privacy Consent Statement (DPCS), which allows candidates to understand how their data is used.

8.4.1 Career Sites

As we saw in Section 8.3, jobs are posted in two places within Recruiting: an internal careers page (where internal employees go to find open positions for which to apply through SAP SuccessFactors) and microsites (where external candidates can view jobs and set up an account via one or more external career sites).

External sites like the one in Figure 8.13 are generated in the Admin Center, and a customer can have multiple microsites within its Recruiting system.

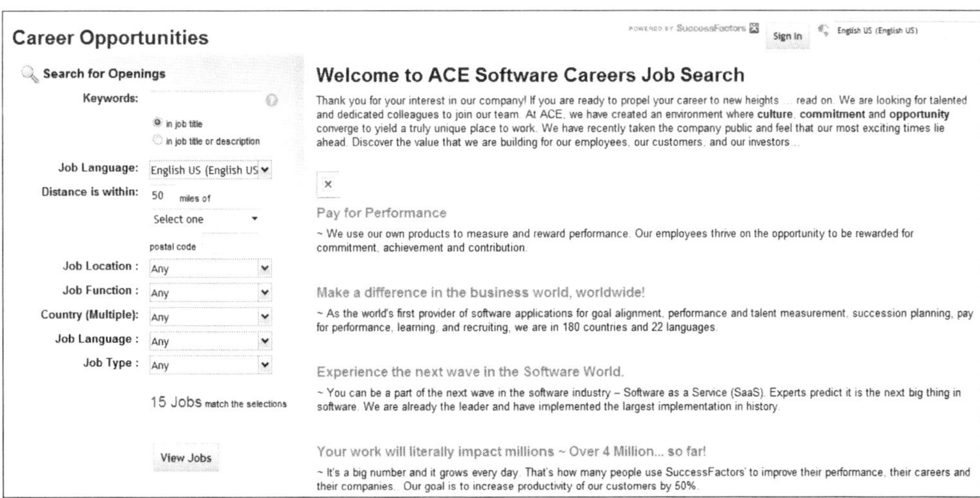

Figure 8.13 External Career Site

Each site has its own URL and can be used for marketing jobs to specific audiences. This is irrespective of other channels that funnel jobs in Recruiting.

Search Criteria

From the **Career** page, candidates can use search criteria to find positions that interest them. By clicking the **View Jobs** button, they can display more detail on each position before drilling into job descriptions to view the requirements of each position, as shown in Figure 8.14. Customers can define welcome messages in the right two-thirds of the **Career** page. This is also done in the Admin Center, and it supports graphics, hyperlinks, and deep links to other URLs.

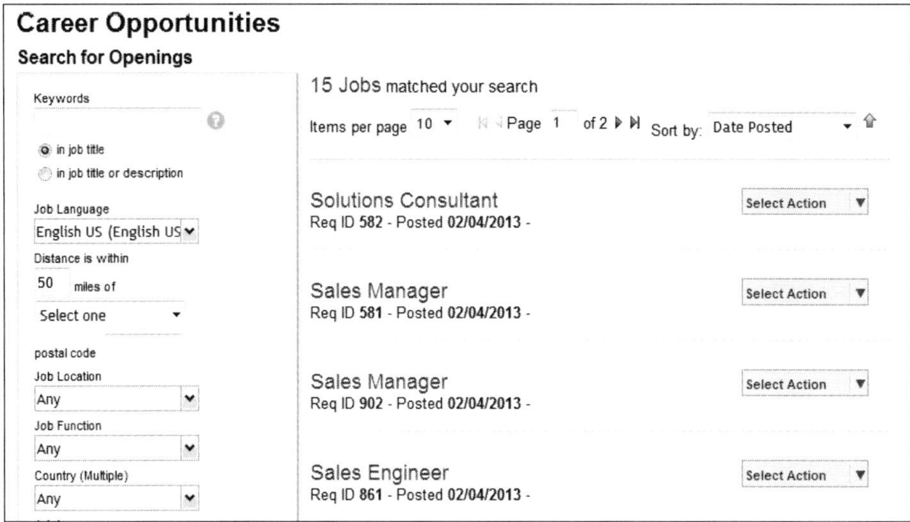

Figure 8.14 View Job Search Results

Search criteria are defined by the customer during implementation. There are standard search criteria that can be activated, such as keyword search and radial search. And customers may define unique search criteria that use data from the requisition to help candidates find positions of interest.

Candidates can create an account to set up a Candidate Profile and apply for jobs. External candidates are identified by their email address, which is also their user ID.

Candidate Home Page

After candidates log on to the career site, they are taken to a **Home** page, like the one shown in Figure 8.15. This provides additional space for the company to communicate with candidates and gives candidates an easy way to jump to actions they want to perform, such as searching for a job or maintaining their profile. Whether to use a **Home** page is a configuration decision, and the **Home** page can be turned on or off, depending on the customer's requirements.

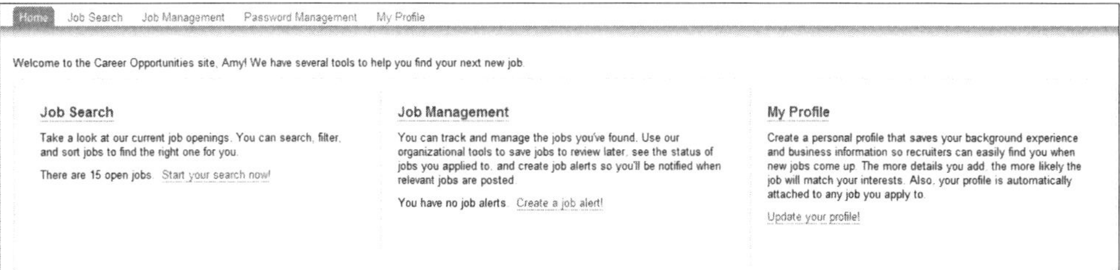

Figure 8.15 Career Page Home Page

8.4.2 Candidate Profile

The Candidate Profile serves as a candidate's online resume. It leverages Employee Profile functionality to capture static candidate information, such as name and contact information, work history, education, languages spoken, and geographic mobility, among others, as shown in Figure 8.16. It serves to capture all of the information about a candidate that isn't job specific and applies to any position to which the candidate applies. Candidates enter this data just once in a central location that is visible to and searchable by recruiters. The Candidate Profile exists for all potential candidates, including all existing employees with access to SAP SuccessFactors and external candidates who create an account.

Data collected on the Candidate Profile is searchable by recruiters who may be sourcing positions and others who have been permissioned to conduct candidate searches. To ensure consistency for internal employees between the Employee Profile and Candidate Profile, the system supports mapping of the data elements configured on each profile template. Fields that reside on both the Employee Profile and Candidate Profile can be synced so that internal employees need to maintain information in only one place. The trend is moving toward capturing more information on the Candidate Profile, rather than the application (or CDM), so candidates have one place to update information that remains fairly constant from one position to another.

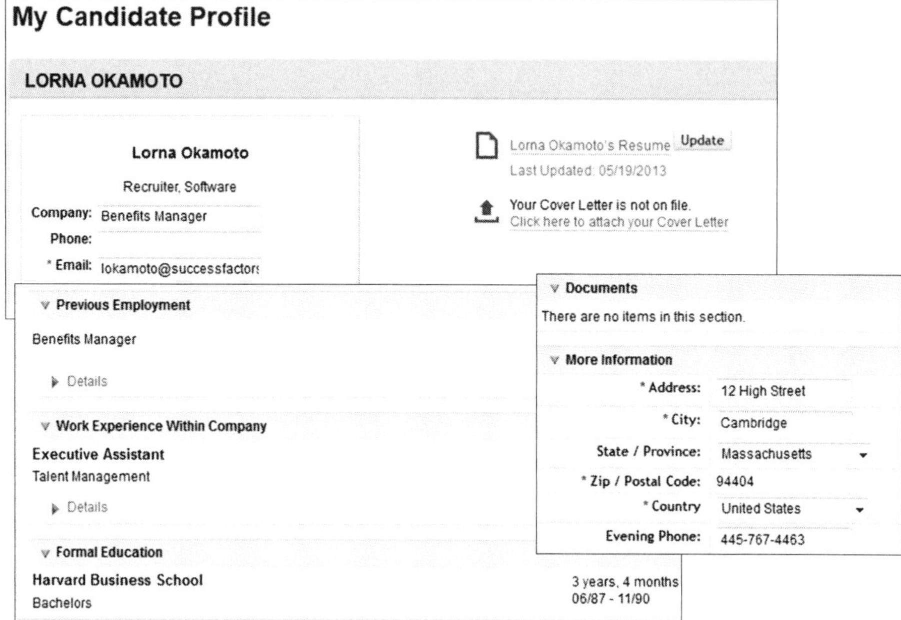

Figure 8.16 Candidate Profile

There is only one CPT that is used for both internal and external candidates. This is critical to keep in mind during design, because both types of candidates need to use the same template but often have varying data needs. Recruiting supports configuration for internal and external audiences to assist with this situation.

It's possible to have fields configured on the CPT that are visible only to internal candidates; likewise, fields that apply and are visible only to external candidates can also be configured. For internal candidates, background elements on the Candidate Profile that are duplicates of Employee Profile background elements can be mapped so that data is synced between the two. This alleviates the internal candidate from having to maintain the same data in two places in the system.

8.4.3 Candidate Data Model

The CDM shown in Figure 8.17 defines the data that the applicant submits to apply for a job. The CDM captures job-specific information, such as special qualifications and skills that are applicable to the position for which the candidate is applying.

The CDM and Candidate Profile can be configured so that data entered into one is mapped to the other. So, for example, if the candidate opens the application and completes the Candidate Profile first, information such as name, address, email, and phone number is populated on the application. Any documents such as resume and cover letter uploaded to the Candidate Profile are also available on the CDM. Updates to documents made on the CDM are updated on the Candidate Profile, as well.

Application Form

* First Name:	Lorna
Middle Name:	
* Last Name:	Okamoto
National ID:	
Date of Birth:	MM/DD/YYYY
Daytime Phone:	
Evening Phone:	445-767-4463
Fax Number	
Street Address:	12 High Street
City:	Cambridge
State:	Massachusetts
Zip / Postal Code:	94404
Country:	No Selection
Cover Letter:	Your Cover Letter is not on file. Click here to attach your Cover Letter
* Resume:	Lorna Okamoto's Resume Update Last Updated: 05/19/2013

Work Examples / Other Attachments:	Attach a document
* Have you ever been convicted of a crime (for other than a traffic violation)?	No Selection
If yes, please briefly describe the nature of the offense, the date of the charge, the county and state, and the status of the case	
* Do you have relatives employed by ACE Corp?	No Selection
If yes, what department	
If yes, what is the relationship	

Figure 8.17 The Candidate Data Model

The CDM also controls what individuals in the recruiting process see when viewing candidates who have applied to positions. For example, the hiring manager may be permissioned to see all fields on the CDM, except self-identification fields such as gender and veteran status, while the recruiter can see all fields.

Country-specific field configuration is also supported if a customer has a need to display certain fields only to candidates in a certain country. For example, a customer that sources jobs in the United States often collects EEO data from candidates. Of course, they would not want these fields to be displayed to a candidate applying for a job in Canada or the United Kingdom, because they aren't applicable. Country-specific configuration can be applied to these fields so that they appear only for positions based in the United States.

Together, the Candidate Profile and CDM present the complete picture of the candidate to the recruiter and others evaluating them for a position. This complete picture is presented in the Candidate Snapshot (see Figure 8.18) and gives the recruiter the full view of a candidate's experience, qualifications, and interests. From the Candidate Snapshot, recruiters can view the resume, cover letter, Candidate Profile, Candidate Profile elements, and any screening details from questions added to the requisition. Every type of candidate is identified by the banner across the top as internal candidate, external candidate, or agency candidate.

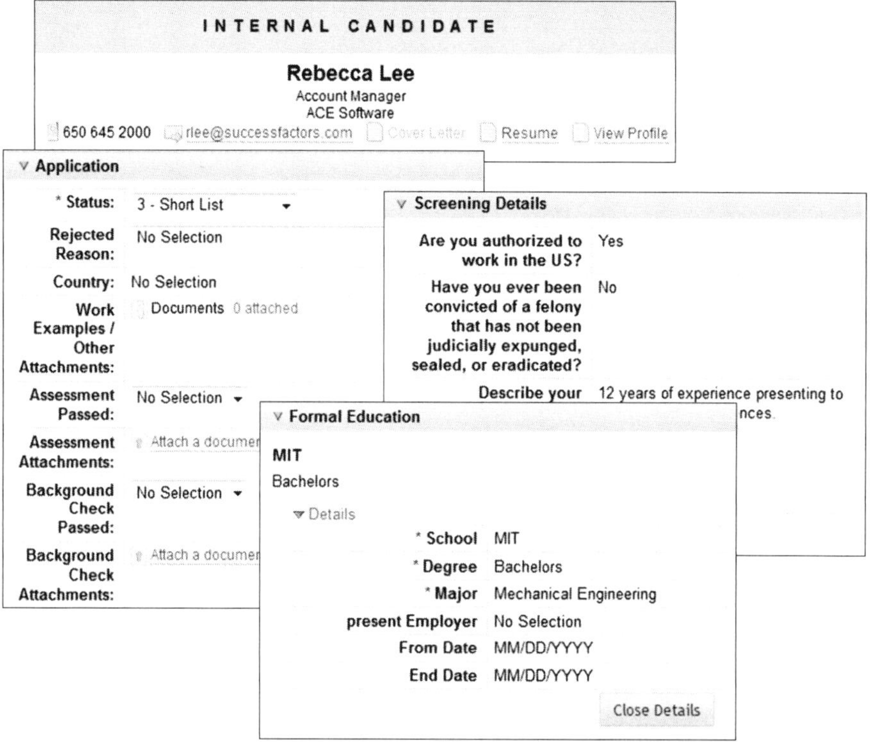

Figure 8.18 The Candidate Snapshot

By default, the system is configured so that a candidate may choose to complete the Candidate Profile before or after submitting an application. However, there is a setting that mandates that the Candidate Profile be completed prior to submitting the application. This recommended setting requires candidates to provide as much background information as possible for recruiters and hiring managers to use when evaluating them for the position. The required fields on the application may be very few, so without completing the Candidate Profile before applying for a job, candidates wouldn't otherwise be providing a well-rounded representation of their skills and experience. The CPT view provided to recruiters in the **Candidate Detail** view is a "snapshot" of the CPT at the time the candidate submits an application. If the candidate has not yet completed the Candidate Profile, much data about the candidate's education, experience, and other qualifications isn't available in this view.

The advantage of setting up this configuration is that customers can ensure that candidates have completed all required fields on the Candidate Profile before submitting an application. Any subsequent applications follow the same process of taking the candidate to the Candidate Profile to update any necessary information or provide an updated resume before continuing with the application submission.

8.4.4 Data Privacy Consent Statement

When a DPCS is set up, then the candidate gets a notification detailing how the company handles their personal data. They can either accept or reject the notification. The candidates must accept the statement in order to go forward with the application process.

Country-level data privacy statements can be configured easily by customers. Data privacy statements can be configured in different languages as well.

Customers can track and report on candidates' DPCS acceptance to demonstrate that candidates have willingly submitted their data to their database. This tracking and reporting also helps customers understand how candidate data is used and handled.

Candidate data can be anonymized based on number of days of inactivity. The definition of inactivity depends on the country and the company. For customers in the European Union, they can define the number of days of inactivity, and if the candidate exceeds that number of days without any system activity, the candidate is marked for anonymization or purge, depending on the Data Retention Management (DRM) configured. System activity is defined by any kind of activity on a candidate's profile, application, or candidate statuses. The candidates can be purged daily, depending on the setup.

8.5 Candidate Selection Management

After jobs are posted and candidates begin applying, the recruiter has numerous tools available for evaluating candidates and making sure the best quality candidates are identified and ushered through the hiring process quickly. The two main tools are the Candidate Workbench and Interview Central, along with interview scheduling. We'll discuss each in this section.

8.5.1 Candidate Workbench

The Candidate Workbench is the place recruiters spend most of their time. It gives them access to the applications and profiles of candidates who have applied to each position and shows how candidates rate against the requirements established in the requisition (see Figure 8.19). From here, recruiters begin dispositioning candidates—or moving them through the talent pipeline—in multiple ways:

- Selecting one or more candidates and using the **Action** column to perform any number of actions on a candidate, such as changing their status or emailing them
- Updating the **Status** field within the Candidate Snapshot
- Using the **Move Candidate** button to update the candidate status in the Candidate Snapshot
- Dragging and dropping a candidate into the appropriate status

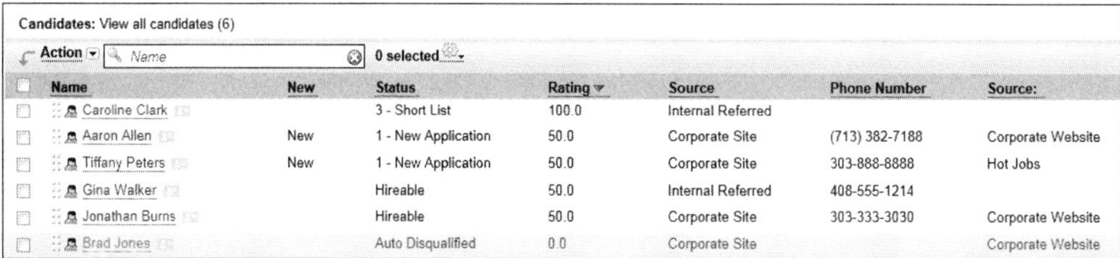

Figure 8.19 The Candidate Workbench

The **Talent Pipeline** contains all of the statuses in the hiring process, as well as some system default statuses (see Figure 8.20). It organizes the candidates as they are evaluated against job requirements and moved through the process. It is divided into three sections:

- **Default statuses**

  The **Forwarded** and **Invited to Apply** statuses are tied to specific functionalities in the system, whereby a user can forward a candidate to a job through a candidate search and then invite the candidate to apply via an email link to the job posting, if their qualifications match up to the those of the position. These statuses can't be edited or disabled.

- **In-progress statuses**
  This section of the pipeline contains all new applications and is configured to represent all of the stages of a customer's hiring process, such as resume review, interview, background check, offer, and hire. In-progress statuses should encompass all stages of a customer's hiring process for candidates who remain under consideration until they are disqualified for any reason.
- **Disqualified statuses**
  These statuses capture the reasons that candidates are not selected to move through the process, including the system status of **Auto-Disqualified**, which is tied to a candidate answering required questions on the requisition incorrectly.

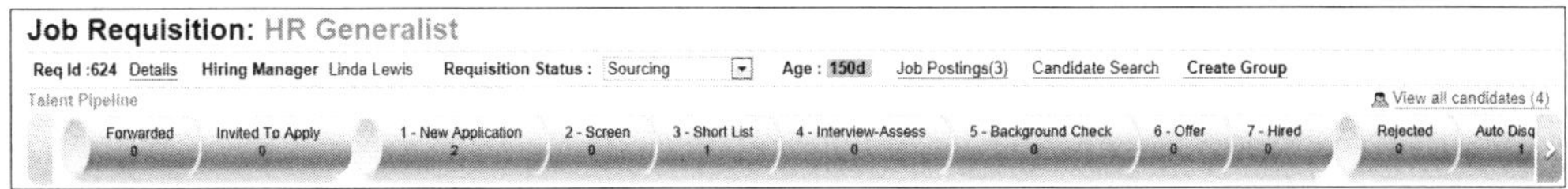

Figure 8.20 The Talent Pipeline

Statuses in the talent pipeline are completely configurable by the customer, with the exception of the system statuses **Forwarded**, **Invite to Apply**, and **Auto-Disqualified**. The customer can create any number of statuses required for assessing candidates for hire or dispositioning them to a disqualified status that is reportable. While the number of statuses dictates the length of the pipeline visually, the system scrolls through the pipeline using the left and right arrows on each end of the pipeline, making navigation quick and easy.

Several of the actions recruiters can make against candidates, such as scheduling interviews or generating offer approvals and letters, are controlled by a Features Permissions functionality that is configured within the requisition template. This means that customers can decide when they want recruiters to have access to the Set Up Interviewers portlet or the Offer functionality, as an example. These decisions are made during implementation and are configured directly into the requisition. Customers can also decide which roles can perform certain actions. So, if they want recruiting coordinators to set up interviews but not generate offers, they can use feature permissions.

8.5.2 Interview Central

Interview Central is where the interview team can evaluate candidates. Recruiting is based on a competency evaluation and leverages the competency library within the SAP SuccessFactors platform. Customers can define a competency library containing interview-related competencies that are added to the requisition and are then available to rate candidates against in Interview Central.

Setting Up Interviews

Setting up interviews is a feature permissions functionality that can be configured against one or more in-progress statuses in the talent pipeline. When a candidate is moved into one of these statuses, such as **Interviewing**, the **Set up Interviewers** portlet, shown in Figure 8.21, is available within the Candidate Snapshot. Recruiters can define the interview team and set dates and times for each interviewer to evaluate the candidate. The recruiter also has the option of emailing this information to the interview team and including the candidate's resume and cover letter.

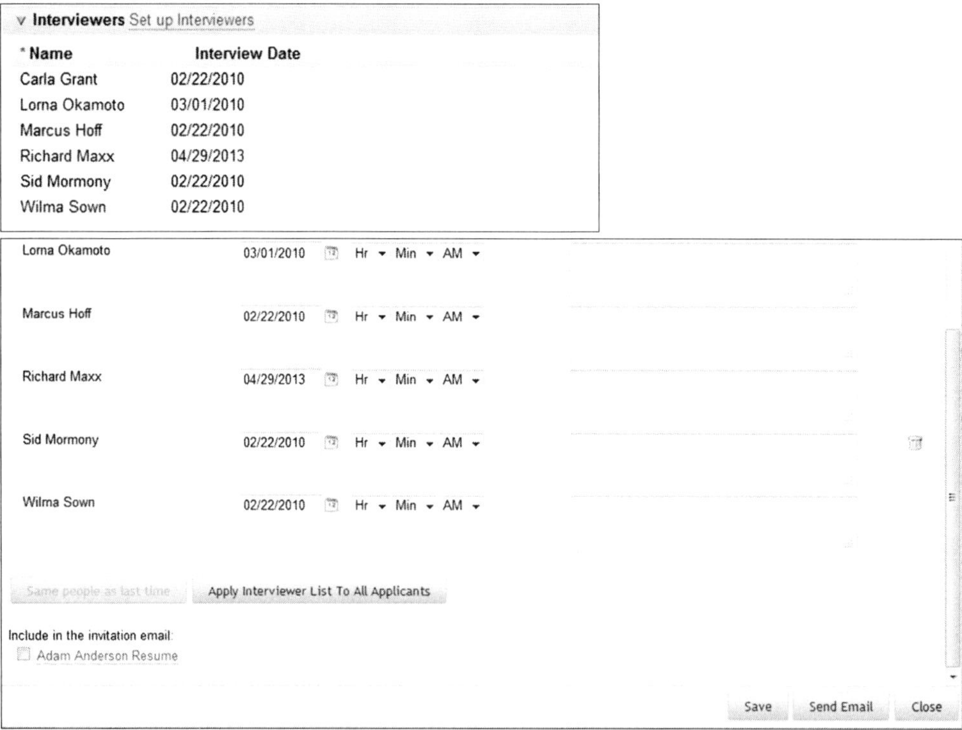

Figure 8.21 Set Up Interviewers

Note that this option does not put a calendar entry on the interviewers' calendar. To do this, the recruiter needs to use the **Create Meeting** button to use email to send a meeting invitation via that avenue.

One of the newest features of Recruiting is Outlook integration with an online interview scheduling interface. This has two facets: online scheduling of interviewers and allowing candidates to book themselves into interview blocks via the candidate portal. First, recruiting operators need to set up the interview blocks with the interviewers who are available in each time block.

Interview scheduling supports integration with the Microsoft Office Outlook Calendar. When Outlook integration is enabled, interview schedules, invites, and meetings appear directly on the user's Outlook Calendar.

With Outlook integration, recruiting users no longer need to manually update the SAP SuccessFactors calendar. The availability in SAP SuccessFactors calendar directly comes from the user's Outlook Calendar. This makes it easier to schedule interviews.

Evaluating Candidates

Interview Central is where competencies added to the requisition come into play. It provides tools for interviewers to provide feedback and rate candidates against those requisition competencies. They can access all candidates they are scheduled to interview, by job. From the main screen, shown in Figure 8.22, they can see who has been evaluated, who has yet to be evaluated, and how all candidates stack against each other.

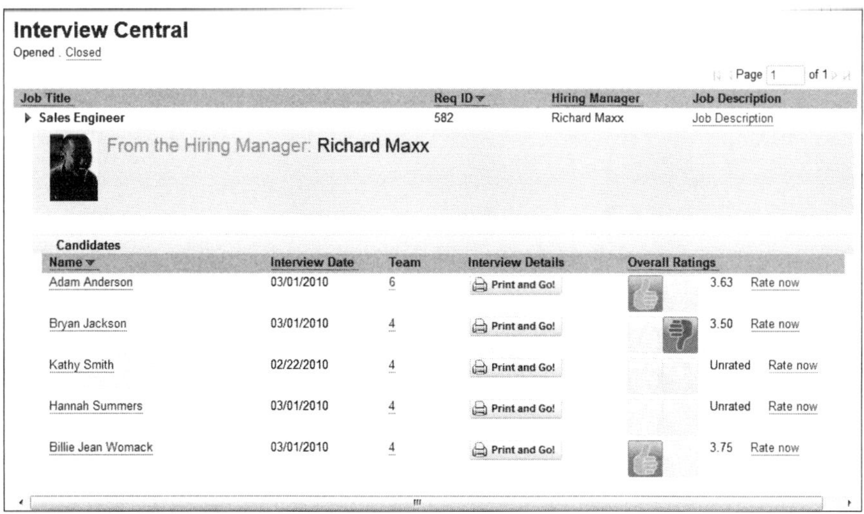

Figure 8.22 Interview Central Main Screen

Notes from the hiring manager about the particular job, if provided on the requisition, are displayed to all interviewers, and they can choose to use the **Print and Go** feature to print a hard copy of the candidate's resume, cover letter, and the job description, with competencies to be rated.

Evaluating candidates is as easy as selecting the **Rate Now** link to see all candidates evaluated for that job. Interview Central utilizes the Stack Ranker functionality to give a visual of all candidates against each other. This also makes rating quick and easy, and can be done for all competencies and all candidates at the same time. As ratings are given, an overall score is generated based on the rating scale defined for the requisition.

Interviewers can provide comments on each competency and overall comments on their rating. They can also upload a document if they take notes electronically. These notes are available to recruiters managing the position. Finally, interviewers provide an overall rating of **Thumbs Up** or **Thumbs Down** on each candidate, for a dashboard-like view of how the candidates rate against each other (see Figure 8.23).

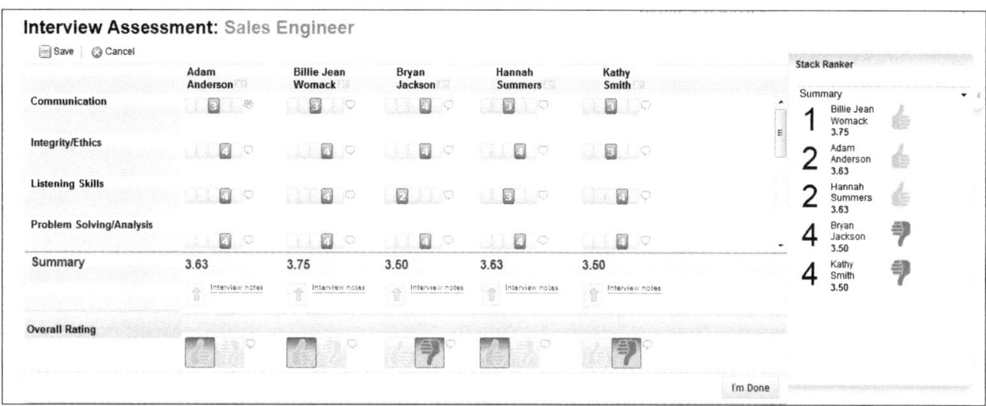

Figure 8.23 Interview Assessment Stack Ranker

8.5.3 Interview Scheduling

Interview scheduling is one of the new additions to the Interview Central feature within Recruiting. Candidates can enter their availability directly into the system so that the users can schedule interviews with them, or let the candidates themselves self-schedule an interview. The interface for scheduling interviews is shown in Figure 8.24.

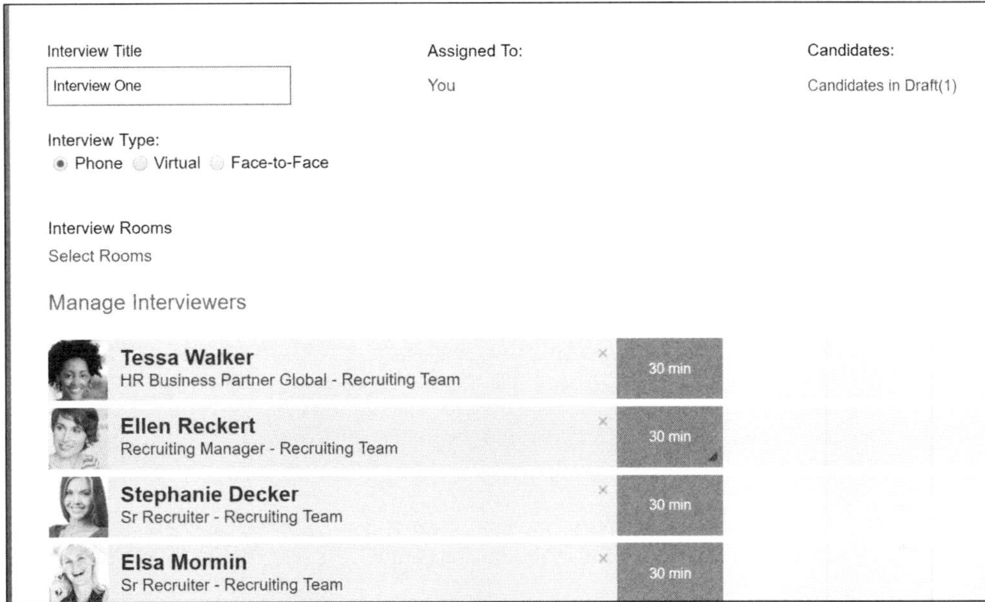

Figure 8.24 Scheduling Candidate Interviews

This feature allows recruiters to set availability for interviews, organize interviews with other interviewers, and email candidates about available interview time. There are notifications that can be set up which are sent automatically, as soon as the interview is booked, cancelled, or rescheduled.

8.6 Offer Management

Offer Management in Recruiting offers two alternatives for customers. Offer letters can be generated from the system and sent to candidates, or the offer can be formally approved in the system before the offer letter is created.

Recruiting enables customers to create and maintain multiple offer letter templates to meet a variety of requirements. Recruiting administrators can create or edit offer letter templates at any time in the Admin Center (see Figure 8.25). Tokens are available to embed in each template, so that information can be dynamically populated into each offer letter.

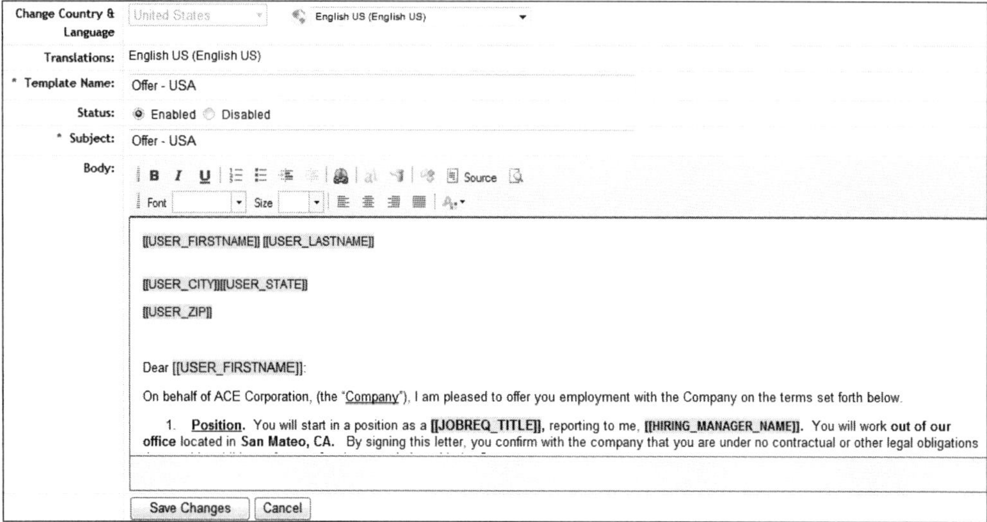

Figure 8.25 Offer Letter Template in the Admin Center

Let's take a closer look at the offer and approval process.

8.6.1 Offer Letter

Offer letters are tied to statuses in the talent pipeline. Offer letters can be made available in one status or several statuses, depending on the customer requirements. Recruiters have the option of generating PDF versions of the offer letter or sending them as text embedded in an email. This is illustrated in Figure 8.26. The offer letter and verbal offer are captured in the audit trail for each candidate.

8.6.2 Offer Approval

For customers who have a more formal approval process for offers, the system supports defining an **Offer Details** template, like the one shown in Figure 8.27, which we introduced in Section 8.1.2.

This template captures the particulars of each specific offer, such as job title, salary offered, vacation, and bonus details, among others. Information can be mapped from the requisition, application, and Candidate Profile, so this is already on the offer details at creation. Recruiters can then enter any additional data related to the offer for each candidate.

Offer Letter: Larry K. Lindsley for Sales Engineer

Email as PDF attachment | Email as text | Print | Verbal Offer

Dear Larry :

On behalf of ACE Corporation, (the "Company"), I am pleased to offer you employment with the Company on the terms set forth below.

1. **Position.** You will start in a position as a **Sales Engineer,** reporting to me, **Richard Maxx.** You will work **out of our office** located in **San Mateo, CA.** By signing this letter, you confirm with the company that you are under no contractual or other legal obligations that would prohibit you from performing your duties with the Company.

2. **Compensation.** You will be paid wages of **$[[SALARY_BASE]]** on an annual basis, less payroll deductions and all required withholdings. You will be paid your salary in accordance with the Company's regular payroll policy. The Company may modify compensation from time to time as it deems necessary.

3. **Benefits.** You will also be entitled to receive the standard employee benefits made available by the Company to its employees of your same level to the full extent of your eligibility including, medical, dental and vision insurance, ten (10) days Paid Time Off ("PTO") and two (2) floating holidays annually. During your employment, you shall be permitted, to the extent eligible, to participate in the Company's Flexible Spending Account plan and 401(k) plan or any other similar benefit plan of the Company that is available to employees generally. Participation in any such plans shall be consistent with your rate of compensation to the extent that compensation is a determinative factor with respect to coverage under any such plan. Details about these benefits plans are available for your review. Company may modify compensation and benefits from time to time as it deems necessary.

4. **Compliance with Company's Policies and Procedures.** As a Company employee, you will be expected to abide by the Company's policies and procedures and acknowledge in writing that you have read and abide by the Company's Employee Handbook. Your acceptance of this offer and commencement of employment with the Company is contingent upon the execution of the Company's Proprietary Information and Inventions Agreement, a copy of which is enclosed for your review and execution prior to or on your Start Date.

Figure 8.26 Send Offer Letter as PDF or Text, or Make Verbal Offer

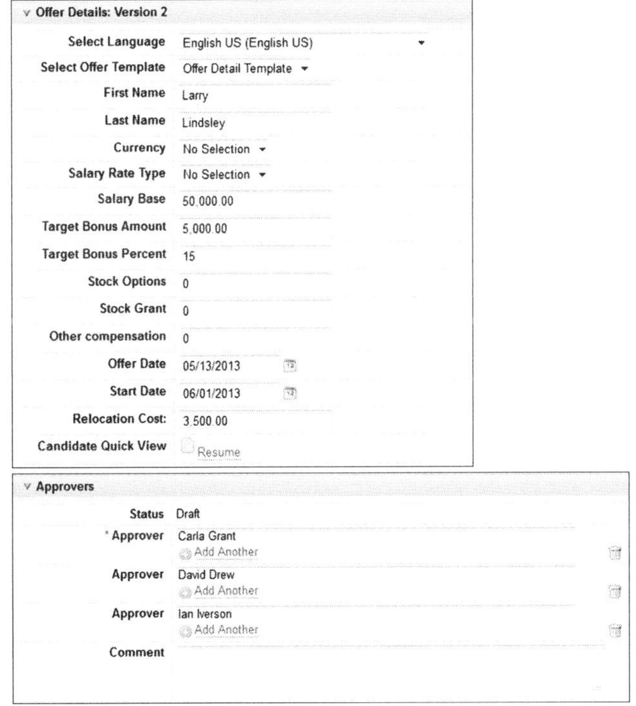

Offer Details: Version 2

Select Language	English US (English US)
Select Offer Template	Offer Detail Template
First Name	Larry
Last Name	Lindsley
Currency	No Selection
Salary Rate Type	No Selection
Salary Base	50,000.00
Target Bonus Amount	5,000.00
Target Bonus Percent	15
Stock Options	0
Stock Grant	0
Other compensation	0
Offer Date	05/13/2013
Start Date	06/01/2013
Relocation Cost:	3,500.00
Candidate Quick View	Resume

Approvers

Status	Draft
* Approver	Carla Grant Add Another
Approver	David Drew Add Another
Approver	Ian Iverson Add Another
Comment	

Figure 8.27 Offer Approval Details Template

The approval chain for an offer detail may be completely ad hoc or predefined in the Offer Details template. This predefined workflow can support recruiting roles, recruiting groups, or defined users. This workflow can be modified to add additional ad hoc approvers, as well. Ad hoc approvers can be anyone from the user database. The approval process is defined by the users in the order they are added as approvers. After one user approves the offer, it is available for the next approver, until all approvers have approved the offer. Each approver has the option to decline the offer and add comments for the recruiter about what needs attention before the offer is approved.

After the offer detail is approved, the offer letter may be generated and sent to the candidate in the formats we discussed in the previous section.

8.6.3 Online Offer Acceptance with E-Signature

Online offer acceptance is also now available, as shown in Figure 8.28. This method sends candidates a link to view and accept their offers electronically, rather than printing an offer letter, signing it, and trying to return it to the recruiter. The offer letter process also supports documenting a verbal offer that may occur. And, with the most recent release of SAP SuccessFactors, customers can now integrate with DocuSign for e-signature of offer letters. This requires a separate agreement with DocuSign. With both online acceptance and e-signature, results are tracked and available from within the Offer portlet in the **Candidate Details**.

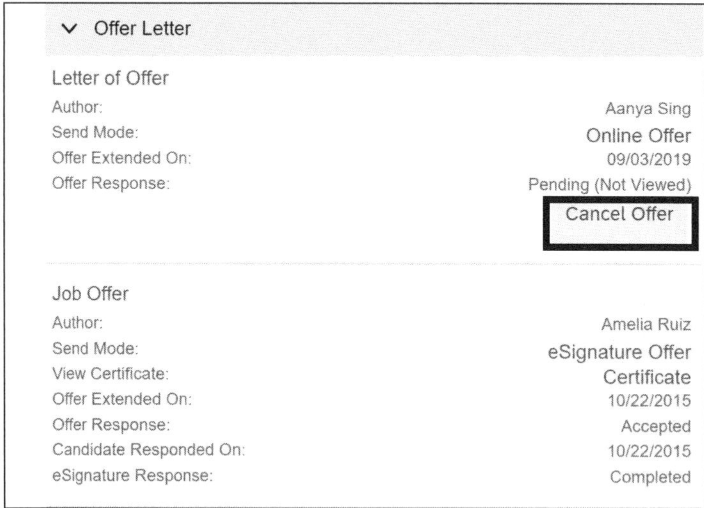

Figure 8.28 Online Offer

8.7 Hiring and Onboarding

After a candidate is identified and an offer is made, Recruiting offers several options for transferring the candidate to Employee Central or core HR and getting them onboarded as employees.

8.7.1 Integration with Employee Central

If a customer is running Employee Central as their human resource information system (HRIS), Recruiting has standard functionality to transfer candidates to Employee Central after they are moved into a status with the type of **Hirable**. This status is unique to Employee Central and tells the system to send them over to the Employee Central module as a pending hire.

A configured template defines the data from the recruiting process that should be transferred over to Employee Central in order to complete the hiring process. Data such as job title, job grade, level, salary, and others can be sent directly from Recruiting to prepopulate the foundation objects in Employee Central to ease the hiring process.

SAP provides new hire integration for clients using both SAP ERP HCM and Recruiting via an integration pack that allows you to transfer applicant data from Recruiting into SAP ERP HCM using SAP Process Integration.

To facilitate this integration, SAP ERP HCM and Recruiting must include certain prescribed configurations. Configuration for both Recruiting and SAP ERP HCM, plus additional details on the add-on, can be found in Chapter 16.

8.7.2 Integration with Onboarding

The SAP SuccessFactors Onboarding module is a prerequisite for this integration. Onboarding fields and recruiting fields are mapped using a mapping tool that allows data to flow flawlessly. Once Onboarding is configured, customers can select **INITIATE Onboarding** from the status pipeline. The applicants should be placed in one of the application statuses configured to initiate onboarding. Customers can initiate onboarding for a single application from the **Take Action** menu on the application portlet. Setting up Onboarding integration in the Admin Center allows fields to be mapped from recruiting to onboarding. For example, application fields such as first name, last name, and address details, along with requisition fields like organizational structure, job title, work location, and so forth, can all be mapped to Onboarding.

Recruiting offers onboarding services through the Onboarding module, which we'll discuss in Chapter 9.

8.8 Employee Referral

Employee referral functionality enables customers to increase employee engagement in the recruiting process by providing them with an avenue to participate in building the potential talent pool within the company. This leverages LinkedIn and Facebook profiles to allow employees to match their friends and professional contacts to jobs. Existing employees can do the following:

- Match jobs to contacts
- Refer a contact to a recruiter
- Track the progress of their referrals
- Determine what referral bonuses they have earned

8.9 Implementation Tips

We'll now walk through a few tips for your Recruiting implementation. It's beneficial to keep the following points in mind:

- **Provisioning setup**
  Baseline configuration is crucial for any configuration. Some options are required to enable functionalities and can significantly affect module performance. It is important to stay away from retiring features.
- **Admin Center settings**
  For appropriate access to settings, it is important to grant the right roles and permissions to the user.
- **Candidate Profile**
  The Candidate Profile is the candidate's online resume; therefore it is important to ensure that as much data as possible is collected, and that this data can be synced back to Employee Profile if the candidate is hired.
- **Job requisition**
  Opening a job requisition and sending it through an approval workflow is a prelude to hiring the right candidate. A typical requisition includes a job title; external job title (in case the internal job title is very company specific and the external job

title is more generic, to attract the right candidates); organizational details such as department, location, division, and so on; and some screening questions and competencies. These competencies can be used to objectively rate candidates during the interview process.

Most requisitions follow an approval process flow. It's important to streamline the fields in the requisition form and grant the right permissions for visibility and stricter controls.

- **Application**
  Application forms include candidate-specific details. Candidate applications may contain country-specific questions, such as "Are you eligible to work in this country?" Permissions in the application control what the candidate sees during and after applying for a job, based on the job post country, and what a recruiting user sees when viewing candidates who have applied for a job. By using country-specific questions, accurate candidate data and eligibility can be determined.
- **Offer**
  Here, *offer* refers to both the offer approval process and actual offer letter. Offer approval may have a preset offer approval route map, which is a summary of offer details, along with application fields like first name, last name, resume, and requisition fields, such as job title and so forth, along with base salary and bonus percentage, if any.

  The ideal offer template uses as many tokens as possible from the job requisition template and application template, which will ensure less data entry and stricter controls.
- **Interview Central and interview scheduling**
  Once the candidate goes through the candidate status pipeline, the Recruiting user can add list of users as interviewers. After adding the users, the interviewer and the candidate may get an email notification, depending on the setup. The candidate is placed in the **Interview Central** tab, where the interviewer can go to view the resume or job requisition specifics. Interview scheduling helps in scheduling interviews based on availability of the interviewers and candidates, and the system can send email notifications once finalized. The interview assessment form pulls competencies from the job requisition and allows the interviewer to provide an objective numeric rating and overall thumbs up or thumbs down. In order to make the best use of the feature, it is always best to associate job requisition to specific competencies.

- **Data Privacy Consent Statement**
  The DPCS allows you to notify candidates about how the company intends to use their data. The candidate must accept this if they want to continue with the application process. If the statement is created in the Admin Center, candidates must accept this statement before entering their data.
- **Data Retention Management**
  DRM allows users to configure the removal of the candidate date from the system. The versions of DRM and DPCS should always match. Once a customer is migrated to DPCS 2.0, they should also migrate to DRM 2.0. Implementation of the deprecated DRM 1.0 version is not recommended for new customers. DRM 1.0 removed records entirely from the customers' instance and the database. In DRM 2.0, candidate records are anonymized rather than purged; the data is retained for reporting purposes, which is why DRM 2.0 is a recommended option.

8.10 Summary

With Recruiting, customers have all of the transactional components of traditional applicant tracking systems, combined with powerful tools to market their jobs to attract and engage the best possible candidates. The players in the recruiting process are actively involved in creating open positions and reviewing candidates, including approving critical recruiting documents and providing candidate feedback on their mobile devices. Recruiting's intuitive features allow users to log in, understand what to do with very little training, and get up to speed, using the system immediately. This enables companies to accelerate their recruiting processes while ensuring that only the most qualified candidates are selected for hire.

In this chapter, we've looked at the foundation for and components of Recruiting. We've explored creating and approving requisitions, as well as job postings and sourcing. In addition, we've looked at the candidate experience, the selection process for those candidates, and managing offers to candidates. We've also discussed the hiring and onboarding processes that are offered in the Recruiting solution.

Now you should understand how the Recruiting solution can provide value for your recruiting, candidate, and application tracking processes. In the next chapter, we'll examine Onboarding, which supports the onboarding of new employees into your organization, as well as crossboarding and offboarding.

Chapter 9
Onboarding

Onboarding new employees into any organization can be a complex process with a significant impact on time to productivity and first-year employee retention. Being able to quickly educate, integrate, and prepare new starters for their new roles can significantly reduce costs and improve engagement, retention, and time to contribution.

Companies not only work hard to attract, engage, and select the best candidate for their critical jobs; they also spend a tremendous amount of money. Research in the employee engagement and onboarding space overwhelmingly shows that many new hires decide to leave their new jobs within the first few months, which means the pressure is on to make the most of that recruiting investment to help get new hires engaged and contributing to the organization as quickly as possible. While most customers purchase SAP SuccessFactors Onboarding to eliminate the voluminous paperwork involved in hiring new employees, there are several other business drivers that could bc involved, including:

- Getting new employees to be productive more quickly
- Increasing employee engagement
- Improving employee retention
- Assimilating new hires faster and more efficiently

Statistics show it can take up to six months for new hires to reach the break-even point, where they start contributing to the performance of the company. If you lose a new hire within those first six months, you've lost every bit of investment made in that new hire up to that point and you're in the hole. Enter Onboarding, a state-of-the-art solution that offers organizations a platform on which to build robust onboarding programs that can eliminate all that paper, introduce your new employees to the organization and their team, begin the goal-setting process, and get the ball rolling on that all-important training.

Onboarding not only provides feature-rich functionality that supports the onboarding of new employees into your organization; it also supports the building of effective offboarding programs for terminated employees and can facilitate the crossboarding of internal employee movements that may require additional paperwork or other orientation or training.

In this chapter, we will discuss some basic concepts around Onboarding programs and then dive into the meat of this critical module, including the onboarding process (posthire verification tasks, new employee tasks, and orientation tasks), crossboarding, offboarding, integration with SAP SuccessFactors Recruiting and SAP SuccessFactors Employee Central, and some implementation tips.

Note

At the time of writing (fall 2019), Onboarding 2.0 is not generally available, and so will not be covered in this chapter. It's expected to be released in Q4 of 2019.

Let's start with discussing the basic Onboarding concepts.

9.1 Onboarding Basics

Onboarding recognizes that companies that excel at onboarding can see quite significant improvements in first-year retention and employees meeting first-year performance metrics. As a result, it is geared to help customers excel at this often-neglected business process. Studies show that companies that do onboarding well can see more than 90 percent retention in first-year employees, and more than 60 percent of those employees meeting first-year milestones. Conversely, companies that struggle with onboarding see numbers as low as 30 percent in first-year retention and less than 20 percent meeting first-year goals.

SAP SuccessFactors views onboarding new employees like mountain climbing. The new hire is expected to scale the mountain to reach the top and succeed, but do they have the right equipment and training? Onboarding is focused on equipping new hires with what they need to reach the top of the mountain. From the moment they log in, they can immediately start connecting with the people and information they need to be successful on their first day and beyond. With a personalized experience, new hires connect with their mentors, teammates, and other peers, and gain access to critical content and resources. The Onboarding experience adapts with a new hire to help them assimilate and develop.

It leverages the SAP SuccessFactors platform, as well as existing functionality found in solutions such as Employee Central and SAP Jam, and is therefore easy to use and intuitive for individuals to quickly begin onboarding activities. It significantly reduces the time and effort required by managers and human resource (HR) professionals to manually manage the onboarding process and ensure that forms are completed correctly. Onboarding also provides a complete set of new hire activities specifically designed to help them assimilate as quickly as possible.

In addition, it acts as a starting point for other HR and talent processes, such as Goal Management, Performance Management, and SAP SuccessFactors Learning. And with the ability to provide access even before the new employee has started with your company, new hires can hit the ground running and begin making a meaningful contribution as soon as they arrive on their first day.

The Onboarding platform is designed upon the three principles of "guide, connect, and develop." Let's take a brief look at these principles and how they create the foundation of the system to support any organization's onboarding program:

- **Guide**
  Onboarding guides both new employees and hiring managers through easy-to-follow steps using a series of wizards. You want your new employee to have the best possible experience as they surf waves of paperwork, government forms, benefit elections, and payroll information as their first real introduction to their new company. Likewise, onboarding may be something hiring managers do once per month, or maybe once per year. Some hiring managers excel at it, and others need more support. Making the onboarding experience as easy for the hiring manager as it is for the new employee increases the overall effectiveness of the process.
- **Connect**
  SAP SuccessFactors recognizes that it's important to connect the new employee with the company and that the more connected they are, the faster they are on the road to productivity. Even before their first day on the job, Onboarding provides a social platform for new hires to meet and interact with their new team members, manager, and company. Extending features of the SAP SuccessFactors platform such as SAP Jam and Employee Profile, you can personally welcome each new hire to the company, provide critical information, and reduce the fear of the unknown they would otherwise face on day one. Provide a point of contact by assigning a "new hire buddy" on whom they can rely for the questions they may be afraid to ask. Robust collaboration options within Onboarding not only gives the new hire the opportunity to meet their new team; it gives the new employee the opportu-

nity to introduce themselves. By beginning to complete their profile, recording their name, and providing a short bio, new hires can tell their new team who they are and what their background is.

- **Develop**
  Then, Onboarding helps develop the new hires right from the beginning by empowering them with integrated talent management. Of course, Onboarding is a natural fit for Recruiting, but it also fits with goal setting, development, performance, and learning. From the first day, new hires and their managers can discuss what is expected in their new role and set the first performance goals captured on the new hire goal plan. Thirty-, sixty-, or ninety-day reviews are easily supported in Performance Management, and Learning knows exactly who employees are and what role they fill in order to assign training to the learning plan automatically.

9.2 Onboarding Process

The Onboarding process is actually composed of three subprocesses (or steps):

1. Post-hire verification
2. New employee paperwork
3. Orientation

In each step, as illustrated in Figure 9.1, information is reviewed and gathered from various participants in the process, such as a hiring manager, the employee, and/or HR.

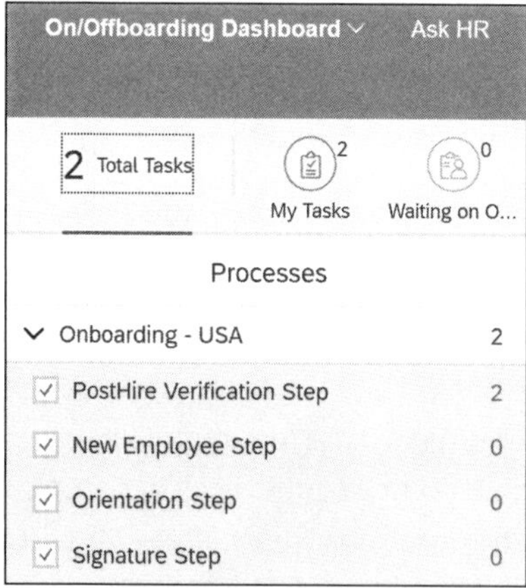

Figure 9.1 Post-Hire Verification, New Employee, and Orientation Steps in the Onboarding Dashboard

Gathered data is passed through the system so that it can be used to hire the employee in the organization's human resource information system (HRIS). In this section, we discuss each step in the Onboarding process, beginning with post-hire verification.

9.2.1 Post-Hire Verification

When a candidate is selected for hire, data from Recruiting is passed over into Onboarding in the **PostHire Verification Step** (see Figure 9.2). Here, either a hiring manager or an HR business partner reviews certain elements about the candidate and the job data before moving the process along. Typical information in this step includes:

- Candidate name
- Candidate email (which is important because completing this step initiates an email to the candidate)
- Business unit, division, department of the job
- Location of the job
- Salary offered
- Benefits packages offered
- Any other data the customer deems critical

This step usually involves very little data entry; it's more about verifying what has been passed from Recruiting and entering the candidate's email address.

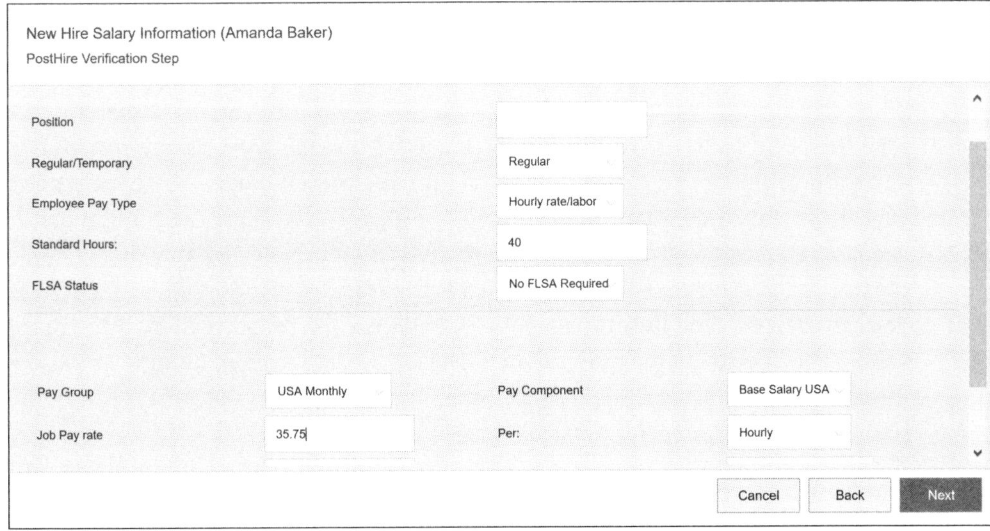

Figure 9.2 New Hire Salary Information

Sometimes customers will have users in this step provide additional data that wasn't captured in Recruiting. Ideally, this step is very short and can be completed quickly. Once all screens have been stepped through, and data validated and/or entered, the process moves to the new employee step, so candidates can complete their paperwork. An email is triggered to the candidate with instructions on how to log in and complete this next step.

9.2.2 New Employee Step

Once the post-hire verification step is complete, the Onboarding process moves to the candidate being hired to complete the paperwork that goes with being hired for a new job. Surveys of HR professionals show that that as much as 80 percent of onboarding paperwork is completed by the new employee in person on their first day on the job, either alone at their new desk, or in a conference room in a new hire orientation session. But all of this paperwork can be daunting and even overwhelming. And it cuts into valuable time that the new employee could spend in training, meeting with their manager, or getting connected with their peers—not to mention the burden on HR of collecting, tracking, and storing all of those paper forms.

The **New Employee Step** automates the distribution and completion of all of that paperwork, as illustrated in Figure 9.3, while gathering electronic signatures and tracking completion of every step in the process. Giving new employees the freedom to complete this paperwork over time, in the privacy of their home, can help them deal with often overwhelming amounts of information and source documentation that is required to complete this critical piece of a new job. And best of all, this frees them up on their first day to focus on real value-added activities.

When a new employee accesses the Onboarding system for the first time, they are presented with a user-friendly interface that walks them through various panels that either convey information or request data from the new employee. You can create an engaging experience for these new employees by presenting a welcome message from their manager, introducing their new team members by allowing them to view the Org Chart with pictures, and introducing their new hire buddy, if one is assigned. You can even enable a "home page tour" experience that can walk them through the system and how to get the most out of it. The home page tour guides new employees through features of the Onboarding system and helps them understand how it can support them during their onboarding process.

This is a great way to begin engaging the new employee and helps them feel at home in the organization. They are also presented with information they have previously provided during the recruiting process and are asked to provide additional information. With a few simple steps, they are guided through a short wizard to provide this information, complete critical forms, and receive the information they'll need, such as company policies and procedures and critical benefits information, for example.

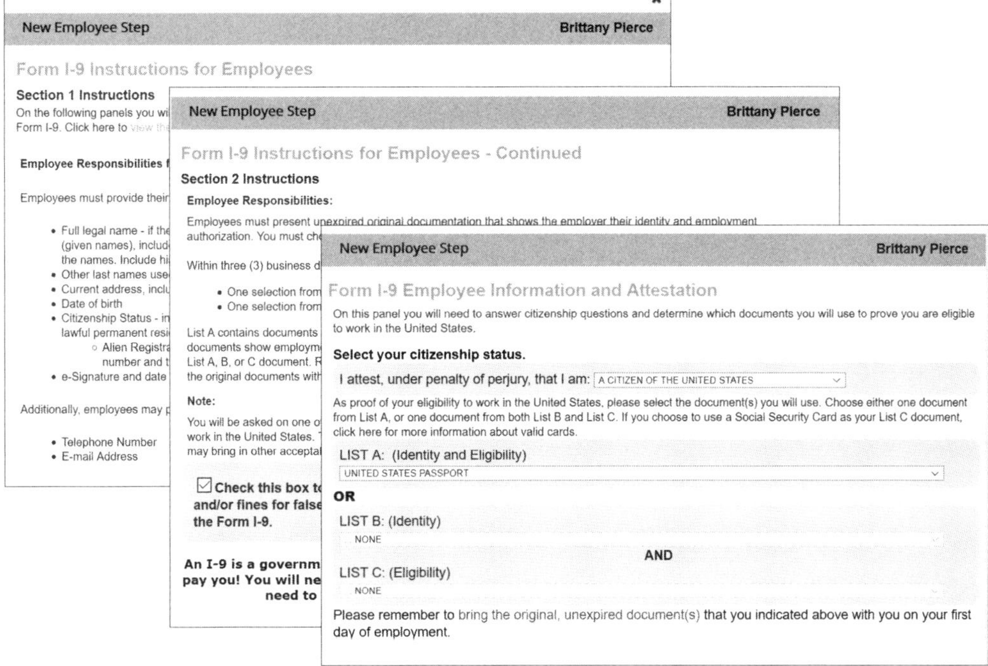

Figure 9.3 New Employee Step

As new employees step through panels that request information, that data is gathered and will be used to populate forms that are signed at the end of the process. One of the largest benefits of the Onboarding system is gathering information to populate critical government tax forms. The system provides standard tax forms for the following countries:

- United States
- Canada
- Australia
- India
- United Kingdom

Additionally, with the configurability of the system, you can create panels to complete tax and other government forms for other countries as needed. Figure 9.4 illustrates panels that collect information used to populate government forms. These forms are presented to new employees, completed and ready for signature, at the end of the new employee step.

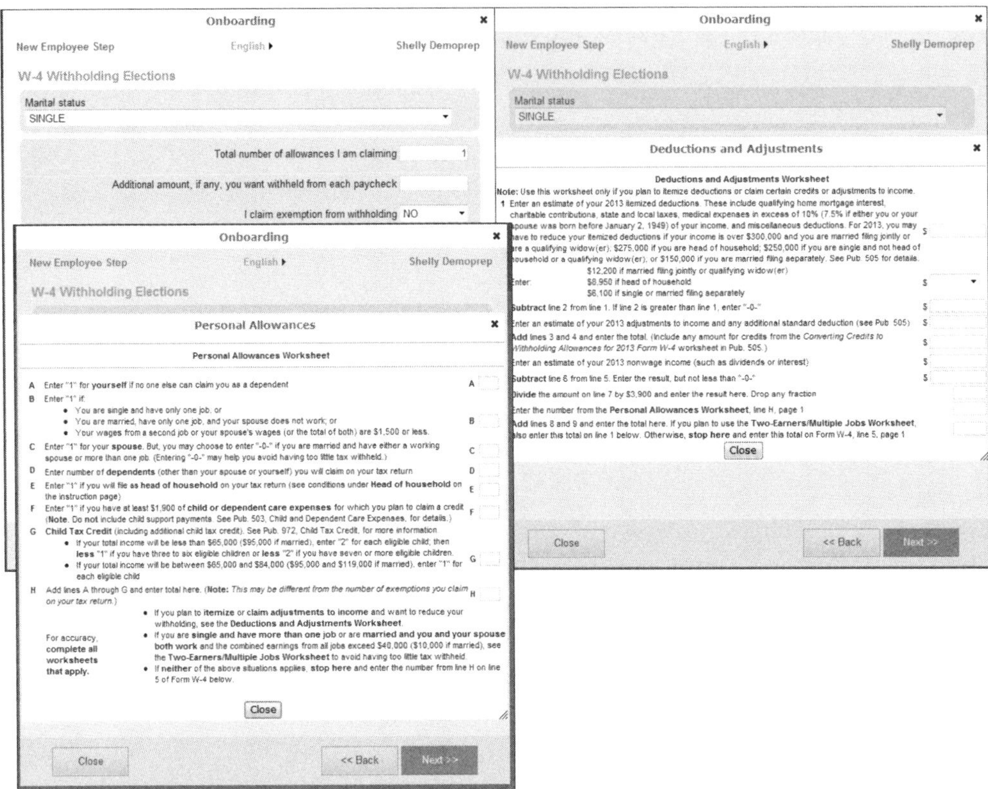

Figure 9.4 Onboarding Panels for Data Collection

New employees continue through numerous panels to complete all necessary paperwork and forms. Additional information, such as direct deposit information, can be collected and passed to necessary parties. Often customers will solicit emergency contacts as well as direct deposit information that will be passed to Employee Central with the hiring action. Once all paperwork is completed, the forms are presented for review and signature. Employees can electronically sign by entering their **Password** and a **Pin Code**, as shown in Figure 9.5. Additionally, SAP Signature Management by DocuSign is available, so that electronic signatures can be captured on all necessary forms.

Throughout the process, managers and HR can keep tabs on how each new hire is progressing through the process and can provide assistance as needed. All of the forms are presented for electronic signature at the end of the process and are stored in the Document Center, or can be downloaded locally or printed as the need arises.

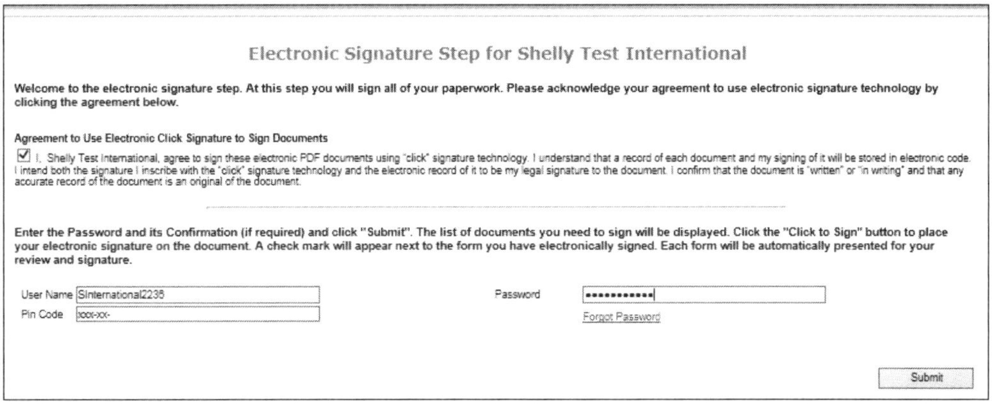

Electronic Signature Step for Shelly Test International

Welcome to the electronic signature step. At this step you will sign all of your paperwork. Please acknowledge your agreement to use electronic signature technology by clicking the agreement below.

Agreement to Use Electronic Click Signature to Sign Documents

☑ I, Shelly Test International, agree to sign these electronic PDF documents using "click" signature technology. I understand that a record of each document and my signing of it will be stored in electronic code. I intend both the signature I inscribe with the "click" signature technology and the electronic record of it to be my legal signature to the document. I confirm that the document is "written" or "in writing" and that any accurate record of the document is an original of the document.

Enter the Password and its Confirmation (if required) and click "Submit". The list of documents you need to sign will be displayed. Click the "Click to Sign" button to place your electronic signature on the document. A check mark will appear next to the form you have electronically signed. Each form will be automatically presented for your review and signature.

User Name SInternational2238
Pin Code xxx-xx-
Password ••••••••••••
Forgot Password
Submit

Figure 9.5 Electronic Signature Screen

9.2.3 Orientation

When new employees complete their portion of the process, the final step is an HR orientation that typically takes places on the first day of employment. Instead of sitting new employees down with a stack of paper and a pen as soon as the arrive for a few hours of paperwork, this orientation step can take just a few minutes. In this step, usually managed by HR, the focus is on validating identification information and ensuring that all data required to complete the hire in Employee Central has been provided and is accurate. Typical activities conducted in the **Orientation** step include:

- Viewing the new employee's government issued identification to verify identity
- Collecting or viewing any documents that the new employee is requested to provide, for example a diploma or a police check report (in Canada)
- Processing e-Verify and I-9 verification (in the United States)
- Finalizing the process with an electronic signature

This can be completed in a matter of minutes, and the new employee can continue with their first day on the job doing things that are value-added, rather than spending hours filling out paperwork that needs to be handled by HR. This is a win-win situation for the new employee and HR. At the end of the orientation step, the HR representative will electronically sign off on the process. It's not uncommon for the new employee to need to sign a document or two as well, and with the electronic signature with PIN embedded into the Onboarding platform, this can all be done paperless.

9.3 Crossboarding

Transitions don't just occur when an employee joins or leaves an organization. They also occur when an employee moves from one part of the organization to another, to a different geographic region, or even to a new role within the organization. The process for transitioning existing employees internally is known as crossboarding, and Onboarding supports these types of employee movements, which may require completion of new or different paperwork. Let's discuss some considerations that might drive defining a crossboarding process and touch on how Onboarding can support this critical process.

There are three types of transfers that require crossboarding:

- **Transfer from one business unit to another**
  In large organizations, it's common for employees to change jobs that take them from one line of business to another. These changes can be accompanied by different job duties and requirements that may necessitate completing paperwork, but most often with new training and development requirements. If the organization is regulated by a government agency, the critical nature of these requirements, and ensuring they have been met, may be quite strong with severe consequences if they are not completed properly.
- **Transfer to a new country**
  When an employee moves to a new geographic location, there can be nearly as much paperwork, possibly more, than onboarding a new employee. And with changes such as a new manager, HR team, and colleagues, there are also changes in language and country customs. This crossboarding process can be very similar to an onboarding process conducted in the particular country. You must ensure all the necessary paperwork is included—new policies and procedures and any relocation information that may be needed. Connect the employee to a network in their new location as early as possible, so they can be a part of the transition and the team rapport and networking can begin before the employee arrives. Provide additional resources as needed.

- **Transition to a new role in the organization**
  Transitioning to a new role with increased responsibilities can bring new challenges in a different way than starting with a new company. Customers don't always think about defining a process for helping employees transition to positions with significantly new responsibilities. But this should not be overlooked. Employees moving to a leadership or management role for the first time will need support in order to be successful. They will often need training on things such as giving feedback, settling disputes, and often specific HR or compliance training.

When an internal candidate is selected for a role in Recruiting, data is transferred to crossboarding (just as with onboarding) and the employee will be prompted to provide additional information, complete new forms, and complete other tasks that are defined in the crossboarding process. Once complete, the data is then transferred to Employee Central so the job change can be completed.

9.4 Offboarding

Onboarding also supports development of an offboarding process to help transition employees out of the company. As with onboarding, most companies have a very manual offboarding process that is followed haphazardly, with large pieces missing. This can result in critical data not being captured. And just as an effective onboarding experience creates a good experience for new employees, a good offboarding experience can leave an exciting employee with a good feeling and create a great advocate for your company in the market.

Departing employees have power because they leave with their years of industry experience, company knowledge, and intellectual property earned through their service with the organization. They can also freely share their opinions of the company with whomever they choose once they leave. They can be your best advocate or your worst detractor. To ensure they are advocates, companies need to understand that offboarding is much more than turning in a badge and a computer. Offboarding is the chance to create a positive voice in the market place. We live in the digital age, where social networks run rampant and individuals are connected through numerous communication channels. While you can never guarantee former employees won't post scathing comments about the organization, you can significantly decrease that likelihood with a strategic of boarding process. What might this include?

The first key step is to show departing employees that they are valued. Employees leave for various reasons, but unless they are terminated for cause, they represent a valuable member of the team who has made contributions to the success of the organization. Simply remembering this will help ensure they are treated with respect and care as they depart for other opportunities. You never know whether they will become a customer or competitor, or possibly even a return employee. Leaving a good impression with them will help ensure they are champions of the organization long after they are gone.

The second step is to have a process. This seems so obvious, but it is surprising how few companies have an established offboarding process that they follow consistently. Departing employees need information on benefits continuation and options for job retraining; they need to turn in equipment and security badges, their system access needs to be terminated, and they need to receive their last paycheck. All of these details, and others, make the difference between a positive and negative offboarding experience. With Onboarding you can define an offboarding process to support transitioning employees out of the organization. Let's review a brief checklist of things that should be covered in an offboarding process and, more importantly, that can be built into the Onboarding solution:

- Define a knowledge transfer plan.
- Issue a final paycheck and other financial remuneration due.
- Provide information on health coverage/continuation (such as Consolidated Omnibus Budget Reconciliation Act [COBRA] coverage, as shown in Figure 9.6).

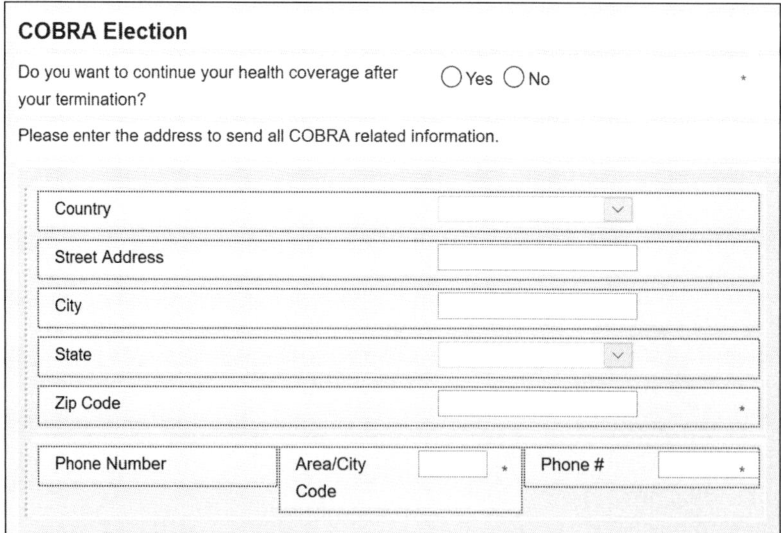

COBRA Election

Do you want to continue your health coverage after your termination? ○ Yes ○ No *

Please enter the address to send all COBRA related information.

Country

Street Address

City

State

Zip Code *

Phone Number | Area/City Code * | Phone # *

Figure 9.6 The COBRA Election Form

- Return physical equipment.
- Transition intellectual property.
- Execute noncompetition and nondisclosure agreements, as applicable.
- Conduct an exit interview.

The offboarding process should begin immediately once an employee resigns or is terminated. Just as onboarding has three steps, offboarding can also have several steps that need to be completed, depending on how you design the system during implementation. These steps might look like this:

- **Initiation Step**
  In the **Initiation Step**, you review and enter data about the employee who is terminating, such as their name, employee ID, email address, and organizational information. You can specify whether they have equipment to return and even schedule the exit interview with their manager or HR.
- **Employee Step**
  In the **Employee Step**, the employee can view the equipment they need to return and when their exit interview is scheduled. They can also view information on continuing benefits (in the United States they can elect COBRA coverage) and download any other documents or information you need to distribute to them.
- **Exit Interview**
  Finally, the **Exit Interview** step will confirm all equipment was returned and provide a checklist to ensure the employee has received all information they need, and you can even include some survey questions and gather their feedback.

The important thing to remember is that the process can be built to meet any organization's needs, to ensure their offboarding process is executed well and provides the departing employee with the best experience possible. Now let's look at how Onboarding integrates with Recruiting and Employee Central.

9.5 Integration with Recruiting and Employee Central

As we have seen in this chapter, Onboarding features integration with a number of solutions in the SAP SuccessFactors HCM Suite. It features employee data used across the suite and integrates with SAP Jam for groups, Learning for the learning plan, and Goal Management for new hire goal plans. Two of the most important integrations are with Recruiting on the front end of Onboarding and Employee Central on the backend to hire the new employee. The integration with Recruiting initiates the

Onboarding process from the Candidate Workbench, pulling information from the requisition and candidate profile. Onboarding also integrates with Employee Central to create users and complete the hiring process.

Let's first discuss how Onboarding integrates with Recruiting.

9.5.1 Integration with Recruiting

As companies source candidates to their jobs, they are collecting a lot of valuable data about their prospective new employees along the way. Recruiting also contains data about the job being filled, and to create a smooth transition from Recruiting to Onboarding, we want to make as much of this data from Recruiting available in Onboarding. Setting up the Onboarding and Recruiting integration requires initial configuration of templates and field mapping between the two modules to facilitate information passing from one system to the other. Onboarding is accessible to users in Recruiting via a feature permission configured in the requisition template. Feature permissions define operator access to certain special functionalities, such as Offer Approval, Offer Letter, and Onboarding. This permission setting will make the **Initiate OnBoarding** action accessible in the specified status(es) within the talent pipeline, as you can see in Figure 9.7, and must be granted separately for each status. For example, if you want two recruiters to be able to initiate the Onboarding process from the **Offer Accepted** status, as well as the **Conditional Offer Accepted** status, the requisition template would require two feature permission sets.

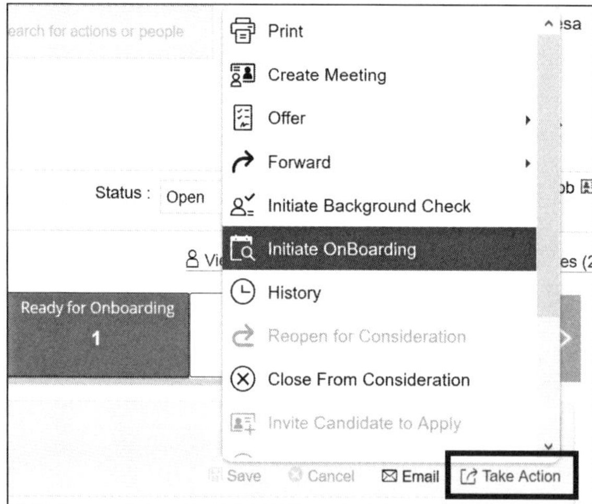

Figure 9.7 Initiate Onboarding

In addition to the feature permission(s) required on the requisition, there are role-based permissions (RBPs) that will also need to be updated to allow certain roles to access the Onboarding tab from the home menu. You will need to permission the appropriate admin users to access the **Setup Onboarding Integration** feature in the Admin Center under **Manage Recruiting** ❶. Individual users will also need to have the permission to initiate onboarding (**Onboarding Initiate Permission**) ❷. These permissions are shown in Figure 9.8.

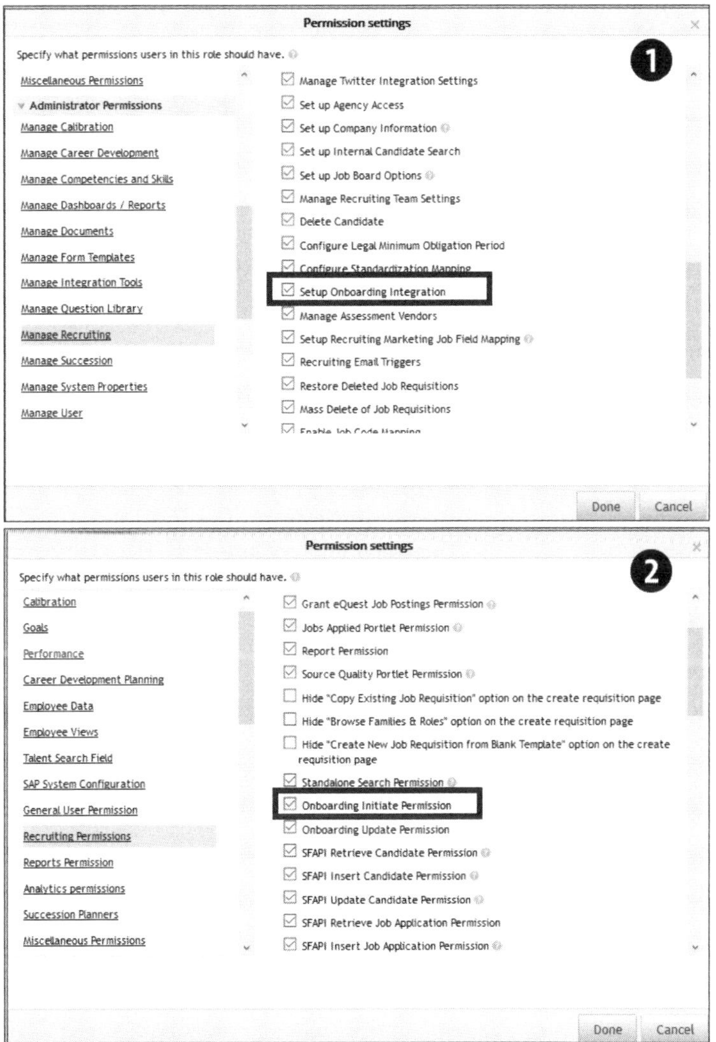

Figure 9.8 RBPs for Onboarding

There are several settings and mappings that must be done to complete integration with Recruiting, which we'll take a look at in the following sections.

Settings

The Onboarding integration settings allow for the enabling Onboarding for all requisition templates or specific templates, if you have multiple templates in use. From within **Setup Onboarding Integration** on the **Settings** tab, shown in Figure 9.9, enable Onboarding according to your needs. Onboarding may only be limited to requisitions based on one field or criteria, and this needs to be kept in mind when configuring the integration. By way of example, if a customer uses Recruiting globally but is utilizing Onboarding only in the United States to start, they would set up the criteria so that Onboarding options are only available on requisitions for jobs in the United States.

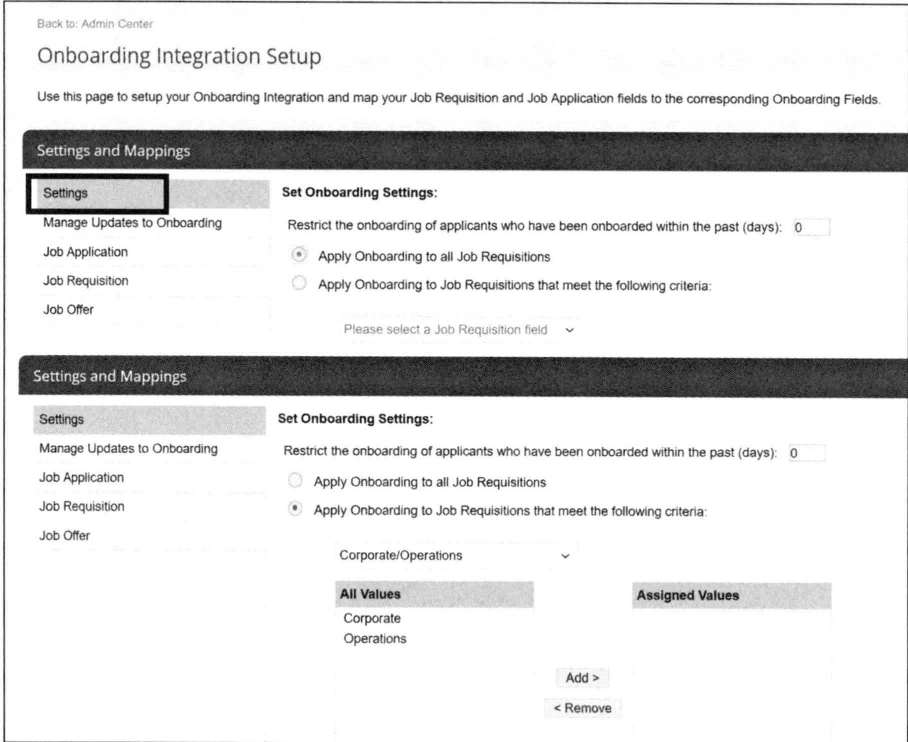

Figure 9.9 Onboarding Settings in Admin Center

You can also restrict Onboarding for applicants who have already been onboarded in the past number of days. This setting specifies a number of days after which a candidate could be eligible to be onboarded again. This would apply if, for some reason, a new hire started onboarding but it was not completed for some reason. This setting could be restrictive, so you should take care when deciding how many days to set and also test all business scenarios thoroughly.

On the **Manage Updates to Onboarding** tab, the settings determine if data updates can be sent from Recruiting to Onboarding once it has already been initiated. An example would be if Onboarding has begun but there is a change to a new employee's start date or if the position has somehow changed. You can also choose to have the system reassign activities in Onboarding if the hiring manager is changed in Recruiting. This could feasibly happen if there is an unexpected reorganization, or if the current hiring manager terminates or is promoted.

When deciding how to make these settings, it's advisable to discuss where data changes should be managed in relation to the overall talent acquisition process. There may be no need to make changes to the data within Recruiting, and then one would just choose to update the information in Onboarding and keep the process moving.

Mapping Data

Part of what makes Onboarding a win for the business and the new hire is the ability to have data in Onboarding that was captured in Recruiting during the requisition approval, application, and candidate evaluation process. There are several elements that need to be mapped from Recruiting to Onboarding:

- Field mapping from requisition templates
- Mapping picklists
- Mapping the corporate structure

There are a few standard fields in Recruiting that are passed to Onboarding by default:

- **JobReqId**
- **ApplicationId**
- **CandidateId**
- **InternalHire** (true/false)
- **EmployeeLogin** (for internal hires)

The other standard and custom fields can be mapped as needed. Data can be mapped from three templates in Recruiting:

- Job Requisition template
- Job Application template
- Job Offer Details template

You can see an example of the field mapping in Figure 9.10. If you utilize multiple templates in Recruiting, you should repeat the field mapping for each template for which Onboarding integration is being configured. If you already have Recruiting in place when implementing Onboarding, it may be necessary to reconfigure some Recruiting fields to put them on the entities (templates) available for mapping to Onboarding. This should be taken into account in the overall implementation plan and timeline.

Note

It's not possible to map fields from the Candidate Profile or any other Recruiting entities. This should be taken into consideration when implementing Recruiting, so that you ensure that all data you want to pass to Onboarding is captured on a template that can be mapped to Onboarding.

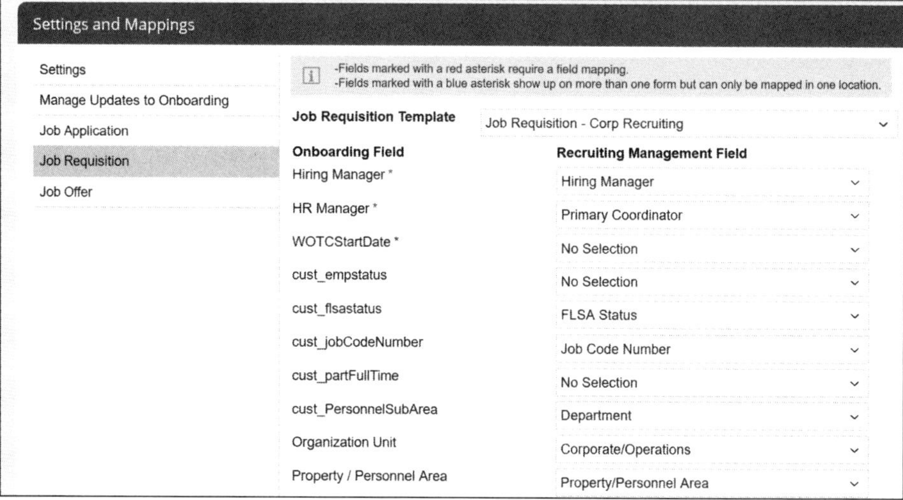

Figure 9.10 Mapping Fields from Recruiting Templates

When you are talking about Recruiting integration with Onboarding, what you refer to as a template in Recruiting is called an "entity" in Onboarding. From the **Setup Onboarding Integration** screen, choose the appropriate Recruiting entity and select the appropriate template. All the fields made available in the Onboarding Data Dictionary will appear here, and you may do the mapping between the Onboarding field and the corresponding Recruiting field. This field mapping exercise is very similar to mapping fields between Recruiting Management and Recruiting Marketing, as well as mapping fields to support resume parsing in **Configure Standardization Mapping**.

Note

When mapping fields between Recruiting and Onboarding, fields marked with a red asterisk are required to be mapped. Fields marked with a blue asterisk represent fields that are present on more than one like template (e.g., **Requisition**).

There will likely be some fields that don't have a corresponding mapping.

Mapping Dropdown Lists

In addition to mapping fields that will pass data from Recruiting into Onboarding, it's necessary to also map the dropdown lists. Here, you'll need to understand the types of lists of values fields and how each is used. As this is a critical component of the integration of data, we'll take a closer look at these types of fields:

- **Data lists**
  Data lists are used in dropdown fields on panels within Onboarding. There are up to four different list types, including:
  - **Lists**: All data lists in this list type are stored in the same table (like corporate structure). This list type supports multiple properties and localization. The user can create and maintain these lists.
  - **Global DB**: This type will display countries and other global database lists.
  - **Provisioning**: All provisioning lists are shown in this list type.
  - **Table Mapped**: Will display table-mapped data lists such as countries and states. In addition, it will display custom tables as custom data lists.
- **Provisioning lists**
  Provisioning lists allow you to create and manage the standard dropdown list values within Onboarding. Examples of these include gender and marital status.
- **Picklists**
  Picklists are the preferred method of handling fields with dropdown lists in Onboarding, to facilitate the mapping of data from Recruiting. Picklists should be used instead of the data lists and provisioning lists whenever possible, since picklists are a standard SAP SuccessFactors system feature. Picklists are created and maintained in the Admin Center, as covered in Chapter 17. Here you can export existing picklists, make modifications, and reimport and also create new picklists. This is where all picklists used throughout SAP SuccessFactors are managed so you will have access to all picklists, not just those used in Recruiting and Onboarding.

Refer to Chapter 17, Section 17.9, for more detailed information on managing SAP SuccessFactors picklists.

Mapping the Corporate Structure

As we've mentioned, one of the values of the integration between Recruiting and Onboarding is carrying over data maintained or captured in Recruiting and passing it to Onboarding so it doesn't have to be reentered. The corporate structure in Recruiting contains critical information about the job, such as organizational data, location, salary grade, and other data. We map the corporate structure to Onboarding so that this data is passed with the new hire and can drive specific paperwork or forms to be completed, ensure adherence to location-specific policies, or even allow managers in certain parts of the organization to drive the onboard process.

If the corporate structure is mapped, the data on the requisition is carried to Onboarding, along with the new hire's personal data. If you do not map the corporate structure, when Onboarding is initiated for a new hire, Onboarding takes the first value listed to populate the level 1 information. For example, if the first value listed is the Division of Finance, then every new hire onboarded will placed in that division in Onboarding. While this can be changed in the post-hire verification step, this is an unnecessary update that can be avoided by simply setting up the integration correctly.

There is much more to say about the integration between Recruiting and Onboarding. The purpose here is to provide a high-level understanding of what this integration looks like and cover some of the key aspects of setting up the integration. Now let's discuss how Onboarding integrates with Employee Central.

9.5.2 Integration with Employee Central

Onboarding to Employee Central integration allows customers to convert candidates into employees, with or without an integration with Recruiting. In most scenarios, the integration will be Recruiting to Onboarding to Employee Central, where data is captured in Recruiting and mapped to Onboarding to support that process. Additional information is gathered during Onboarding, such as national identification and date of birth information; the new hire data is then passed onto Employee Central. Candidate data is wholly extracted from either Recruiting or Onboarding and sent to Employee Central. It is not possible to pull some data from Recruiting and some from Onboarding for the same candidate. If you want any Onboarding data sent to Employee Central, then you must pass any recruiting related data into Onboarding to pass through to Employee Central.

The goal with the integration among these modules is to exploit the data already residing in the system and reduce the amount of data users need to enter in order to complete their Onboarding experience. Not only does this create the best possible user experience; it also increases data integrity by eliminating the need to duplicate data entry introducing the likelihood of mistakes. For example, you will want to pass the job-related information that began in Recruiting on the requisition into Onboarding and then back into Employee Central. This information may include title, salary and pay grade information, benefits, organizational data, and location. It's critical that this data is correct when it is processed in Employee Central, as it can impact an employee's organizational data as well as their compensation.

Let's discuss the key tasks to complete for integration with Employee Central.

Setting Up Message Notifications

In order to enable the Onboarding to Employee Central integration, you first must establish SAP SuccessFactors message notifications. There are three notification messages available to enable in the Onboarding super admin:

- **CandidateCreate** message to SAP SuccessFactors once the new hire is created.
- **PostPHV** message to SAP SuccessFactors once the posthire verification is completed.
- **PaperWorkDone** message to SAP SuccessFactors after the new employee step is completed by the new hire.

Once the notifications are enabled, make sure the Onboarding fields are available for mapping. If Onboarding is integrated with Recruiting, this likely was already done, as discussed previously. However, if you do not have Recruiting in your landscape, you will need to perform this activity. It's recommended to verify the field mapping before you begin the integration effort in earnest. Fields may need to be updated in the Data Dictionary within Onboarding and then mapped in SAP SuccessFactors HCM Suite in the Admin Center.

There are some fields that will not map from Onboarding to Employee Central:

- Any I-9 fields that begin with I9
- W-4 fields that begin with W4

These fields should not be mapped from Onboarding to Employee Central and should not be included in the **Fields Attached to the Tag List**. Note that Employee Central cannot accept W4 fields for tax information in the United States.

Note

For customers using Recruiting and Employee Central, the field type must be the same among the three modules in the field definition. For example, if the field being mapped from Recruiting to Onboarding is a string field in Recruiting, it must also be a string field in Onboarding, and likewise in Employee Central. Also, the field value must match exactly, including case.

New Hire Processing

Once the integration has been enabled and any repeating fields have been configured, you need to set up the transformation of data between Onboarding and Employee Central. This can be done in one of two ways:

- Configure an XML transformation template and upload in Provisioning
- Set up the data transformation in the Admin Center

The first option is to configure an XML transformation template and upload it via Provisioning (see Figure 9.11). If this option is chosen, you must include a mapping attribute for each field for which you wish to send data from Onboarding to Employee Central.

```
<?xml version="1.0" encoding="UTF-8" standalone="yes"?><objectMappingsType mappingXML-createdBy="UI"><entity-details-mapping>
    <!-- Personal Info -->
    <mapping-attribute><source multi-valued="false" entity-type="ApplicationInfo" refid="FirstName"/>
        <target variant="" refid="personalInfo.first-name"/>
        <processes><process>onboarding</process></processes>
    </mapping-attribute>
    <mapping-attribute><source multi-valued="false" entity-type="ApplicationInfo" refid="LastName"/>
        <target variant="" refid="personalInfo.last-name"/>
        <processes><process>onboarding</process></processes>
    </mapping-attribute>
    <mapping-attribute><source multi-valued="false" entity-type="ApplicationInfo" refid="MiddleName"/>
        <target variant="" refid="personalInfo.middle-name"/>
        <processes><process>onboarding</process></processes>
    </mapping-attribute>
    <mapping-attribute><source multi-valued="false" entity-type="ApplicationInfo" refid="Suffix"/>
        <target variant="" refid="personalInfo.suffix"/>
        <processes><process>onboarding</process></processes>
    </mapping-attribute>
    <mapping-attribute><source multi-valued="false" entity-type="ApplicationInfo" refid="EMail"/>
        <target variant="P" refid="emailInfo.email-address"/>
        <processes><process>onboarding</process></processes>
    </mapping-attribute>
    <mapping-attribute><source multi-valued="false" entity-type="ApplicationInfo" refid="DateOfBirth"/>
        <target variant="" refid="personInfo.date-of-birth"/>
        <processes><process>onboarding</process></processes>
    </mapping-attribute>
```

Figure 9.11 Configure an XML Transformation Template

The second option to configure the transformation template is the recommended one and is completed in the SAP SuccessFactors mapping tool. This is basically an XML front-end interface that makes changes in the XML file based on the values entered.

To complete the mapping, first find the appropriate Onboarding field and enter the following information:

- **Category**: Select from the list.
- **Field Mapping**: Based on the category, select the corresponding Employee Central field.
- **Variant**: Based on the field being mapped, select the correct variant. Not all fields will have a variant. Fields such as email or address will have a variant where you select business or home/personal variant.
- **Process**: Select the correct Onboarding **Process** for this mapping.

Do this for all fields that need to be mapped. You can see an example of this mapping tool in Figure 9.12.

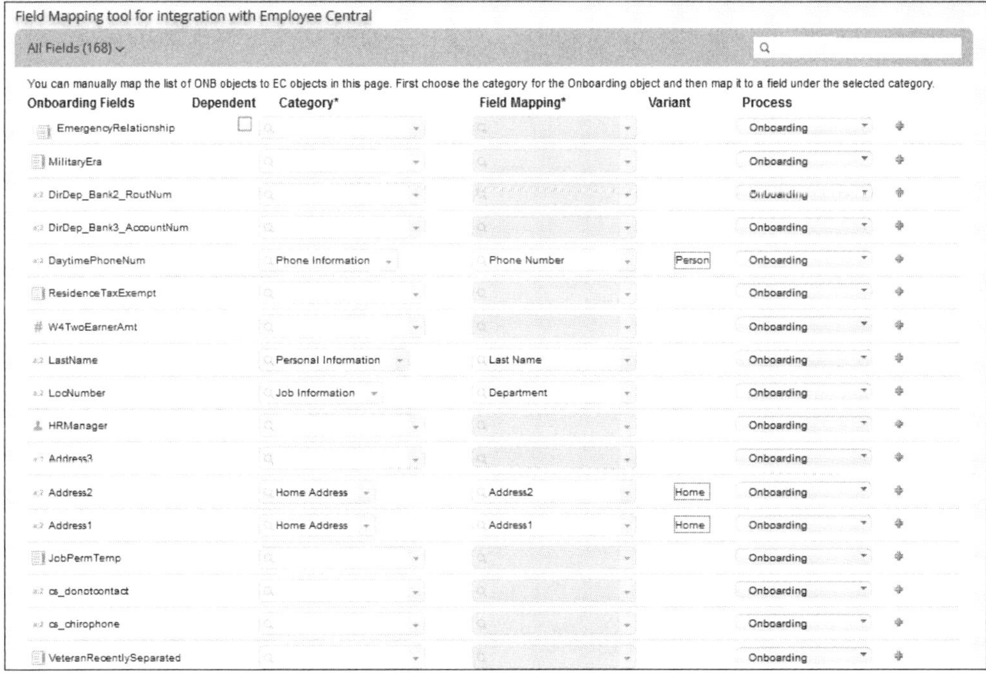

Figure 9.12 Field Mapping Tool

Once the data is mapped between Onboarding and Employee Central and new employee data is sent over to Employee Central, the new employee will appear in the pending hires queue for processing the hire. Administrators will pick up each employee in the queue and step through all the screen to hire an employee, except most fields will already be complete from the field data mapping.

Note

If propagation rules are configured in Employee Central, these rules will overwrite data that is coming into Employee Central from Onboarding.

We've just briefly touched on how Onboarding integrates with both Recruiting and Onboarding. There is so much more to say about how these three critical modules play together and pass data among themselves.

9.6 Implementation Tips

When you are implementing Onboarding, it may be helpful to keep these few tips in mind:

- **Customization**
  Capture and review all onboarding activities across the organization, including all business units and geographies; best practice is to design a common global process to the lowest common denominator and then customize as needed for business operations and country-specific differences.
- **Documentation**
  Gather all the paperwork, forms, policies and procedures new hires are currently completing; revise any internal policy or procedure documents prior to including them in Onboarding so they represent the most current version.

  Review all documentation and assess what, if anything, can be removed; likewise, identify what documentation is not currently captured that should be.
- **Roles**
  What are the roles that will be involved in your new Onboarding process and what will they do? Will there be any training required for any players in the process? If so, what will that include and when will it be delivered? How will this be sustained ongoing?

How much collaboration with extended team members will you include in your process? Will you utilize the "Buddy" and "Recommended People" components within Onboarding? If so, what are the expected responsibilities of these roles, and how will you communicate them to those who fill these roles?

- **Timing**
  When do you want new hires to begin their Onboarding experience, will this be before their first day on the job or just start on day one? The answer will impact the timing of certain activities within Onboarding.

  Also, how long will your Onboarding process last? What posthire activities and expectations are there for your new employees, and how will Onboarding support these?

- **Integration with other modules**
  Will your Onboarding process simply capture paperwork, or do you want to introduce integration with other processes, such as goal setting and training? If the latter, how and when will you integrate those modules within the Onboarding process?

- **Panel design**
  When you design panels within Onboarding, keep in mind the experience of the end user, as well as system performance. While it may seem better to include numerous fields on a panel and keep the clicks down, its actually recommended to create more panels with fewer fields on them. Best practice is to include no more than six to eight input fields on a single panel. When you are adding picklists, include no more than four per panel to ensure performance isn't negatively impacted.

- **Advanced conditions**
  Advanced conditions can be set up to determine under what conditions a form will be displayed for a new hire. Examples might be union forms or various country forms. PDF forms are part of form groups. These not only store related forms, but they can also have conditions that will apply to all forms within a particular group. Administrators can create new form groups, edit or delete existing groups, and assign forms to groups. Your group list can be printed or exported to Excel. Once a PDF form has been assigned to a group, an administrator can view or edit the form attributes. It is recommended that you have a forms group for all the corporate forms that are uploaded into Onboarding.

9.7 Summary

Onboarding is a value-adding and time-saving solution to enable quick and efficient onboarding of new employees, designed to also improve time to productivity, employee engagement, and employee retention. It removes the manual effort required by managers and HR professionals during the onboarding process and allows employees to become oriented with their new colleagues and working environment before they even set foot in the office. With robust crossboarding and offboarding processes to deploy, you can also provide your internal employees transitioning within the organization, and those employees leaving, with great experiences.

The integration with Recruiting and Employee Central creates a very powerful triangle of functionality and data that supports three very key processes within HR.

We've looked at the features and functionality that support this and discussed the integration that exists. You should now have an overview of what the solution offers and what the process is for onboarding an employee with the solution.

In the next chapter, we'll take a look at the Learning solution.

Chapter 10
Learning

SAP SuccessFactors Learning is a robust, state-of-the-art learning management system that can accommodate any organization's learning process and requirements. Its intuitive interface is easy to navigate and highly configurable to provide employees, managers, and administrators with the best learning experience possible.

SAP SuccessFactors Learning manages the entire learning lifecycle. Users may be auto-assigned to compliance-based learning, be given the option to manage their own learning through catalog searches and recommendations, and track their progress with learning history details and other end-user reporting. Managers can access the learning plan of each employee in their direct, in-direct, or dotted-line reporting hierarchy to manage their team's learning, as well as their own. The learning department will also have access to the administrator interface to complete tasks such as maintaining catalogs, auto-assigning learning using assignment profiles, managing online and scheduled training, and running reports.

This learning management system (LMS) is highly configurable—and the majority of the configuration occurs in the interface itself. In this way, customer administrators are heavily involved in the implementation; they learn how to "configure" the solution as the project progresses and take ownership of the system configuration almost from the beginning of the project. The functionality delivered by Learning is enough to fill a book on its own, so this chapter will provide a high-level overview of the features of Learning—from the various interfaces, to training delivery options, to managing online learning and curriculums and beyond—explaining how users of all types can interact with the system.

Before we dig into the features of Learning, we want to introduce a few foundational concepts that you should understand.

10.1 Learning Basics

There are many ideas of what an LMS should be. Some see it as a means for delivering and tracking online course content. Others may focus on the scheduling aspects of instructor-led training or tracking on-the-job training (OJT). Beyond the various delivery types, there are equally as many approaches to learning management, whether it is compliance-based structured assignment versus more open forms of self-directed learning. With so many options, the scope of an LMS can be hard to pin down. This chapter will provide an overview of the primary components of the system.

In Learning, *assignment profiles* provide the key mechanism for learning management. There are two steps to building an assignment profile:

- Defining the audience
- Determining what is assigned to the audience

To define the audience, it is important to have consistent and complete user data coming through the SAP SuccessFactors platform or your core HR system. For example, learning audiences based on your organizational structure require that organization data is uniformly applied to each user. The same is true for position-based or location-based user data. Any variation of values being applied inconsistently has the potential to render the audience incomplete.

Once audiences are defined, the assignment profile is then structured to determine what is assigned. Some of your choices are:

- **Items**
  This is the list of courses that are assigned to members of the assignment profile audience. Items may be required or optional, depending on their assignment type. We will discuss more about items in Section 10.3.
- **Curricula**
  This is the list of certification-based activities (normally with retraining intervals) assigned to members of the assignment profile. See the curricula information in Section 10.4.
- **Programs**
  This is the list of structured learning programs assigned to members of the assignment profile. See the program information in Section 10.4.
- **Catalogs**
  Members of the assignment profile may be assigned to one or more catalogs. This

determines the list of items, curricula, programs, and other learning activities that appear to users in a catalog search.

- **User roles**
  This defines the permissions assigned to a user and utlimately what they are able to do in the user interface. You may want to restrict some permissions to specified users (for example, you may not want consultants to search the catalog, but only see their assigned courses). User roles combined with assignment profiles provide the means for managing these permissions.
- **Recommended items/programs**
  This provides an alternative to directly assigning items and programs. For self-directed learning, recommendations provide a method for suggesting courses and highlighting them for groups of users.

Assignment profiles provide the automated mechanism for managing learning and form the basis of what a learner views in the system. Ad hoc assignments of items, curricula, and programs can also be performed by administrators with access to the administration interface. Let's now turn our attention to the primary interfaces of Learning.

10.2 Multiple Interfaces

LMSs require participation from a variety of roles in support of the learning process. We can define them within two distinctive categories; administrative roles and user roles. In the SAP SuccessFactors platform, you will use role-based permissions (RBPs) to grant access to the Learning administration interface (using the **Manage Learning – Administrator** permission) and the Learning user interface (using the **Learning – User** permission).

Learning administrators use the administration interface to work behind the scenes of the LMS. Many tasks can be managed from this interface. We have already discussed the assignment profiles that administrators build for managing learning. The administrator interface is also used for creating learning objects, monitoring learner activities, defining catalogs, and many other tasks. These tasks require a specific interface that includes all menus and features that allow administrators to build up the learning system.

The user interfaces provide the environment for learners, managers, and instructors to interact with the learning system. Learners require the ability to see their assigned learning, search the catalog for optional courses, and view their learning history. Managers may then gain access to view the learning activities and progress of employees within their hierarchy. Instructors assigned to learning events can also use a specified instructor interface to manage their class enrollments, track attendance, and even launch virtual training room sessions.

It's important to note that Learning can support both internal and external users. For the purposes of this book, we'll focus on internal user interactions from within the SAP SuccessFactors platform. We'll now move on to an exploration of each interface type in further detail.

10.2.1 User Interface

There are a few prerequisites that must be in place before a user is able to navigate from the SAP SuccessFactors platform to Learning as a learner:

- An active user record must exist in the SAP SuccessFactors platform with the Learning user permission assigned.
- An active user record must exist in Learning.
- The user records in SAP SuccessFactors platform and Learning must have matching user IDs.
- The user record in Learning must have an assigned user role.

Users can then access the system from their SAP SuccessFactors HCM Suite home page, as they can with the other SAP SuccessFactors modules. The **Take Courses** tile on the home page displays learning activities on a user's learning plan in the order that they are due. Users may also navigate to the Learning home page by clicking on the **Home** menu and selecting **Learning** from the dropdown list.

What a user can access in the Learning module is dictated by which learning activities, catalogs, and permissions have been assigned to them. *User roles* define the permission to grant varying levels of access to different kinds of users. For example, a company may have contractors that require access to complete some learning, but they should not have the same level of system access as employees (for example, access to search and select courses frorm the catalog). You can define user roles for employees and contractors to differentiate the levels of access and then assign them to users accordingly.

Learning activities may be assigned in one of the following ways:

- Automated assignment using an assignment profile
- Manual assignments by learning administrators through the administrator interface
- Manual assignments by their supervisor
- Self assigned from the catalog

Once the correct permissions, assignments, and catalog access are in place and users navigate to Learning, they land at the **My Learning** tab (see Figure 10.1). During your implementation of Learning, you will design the layout and select the relevant tiles for this home page. The combination of this selection and permissions in the user roles will determine what a user sees on this home page. For the purpose of this chapter, we will highlight the most commonly used tiles:

- **My Learning Assignments**
  The **My Learning Assignments** tile displays learning activities assigned to the learner by administrators, managers, an automatic assignment, or self-assignment from the catalog.
- **Find Learning**
  Catalog searches can be accessed from the **Find Learning** tile.
- **Recommendations/Featured**
  Learning clients will often use the **Recommendations** or **Featured** tiles to highlight courses they want to promote.
- **My Curricula**
  The **My Curricula** tile provides a view for learners to manage their assigned curricula.
- **History**
  Completed learning items and certificates of completion can be accessed from the **History** tile.
- **Links**
  The **Links** tile provides quick access to other parts of the system.

Learning administrators may also choose to design custom tiles for the **My Learning** home page that could include embedded welcome videos, links to support materials, or any other information relevent to their training audience.

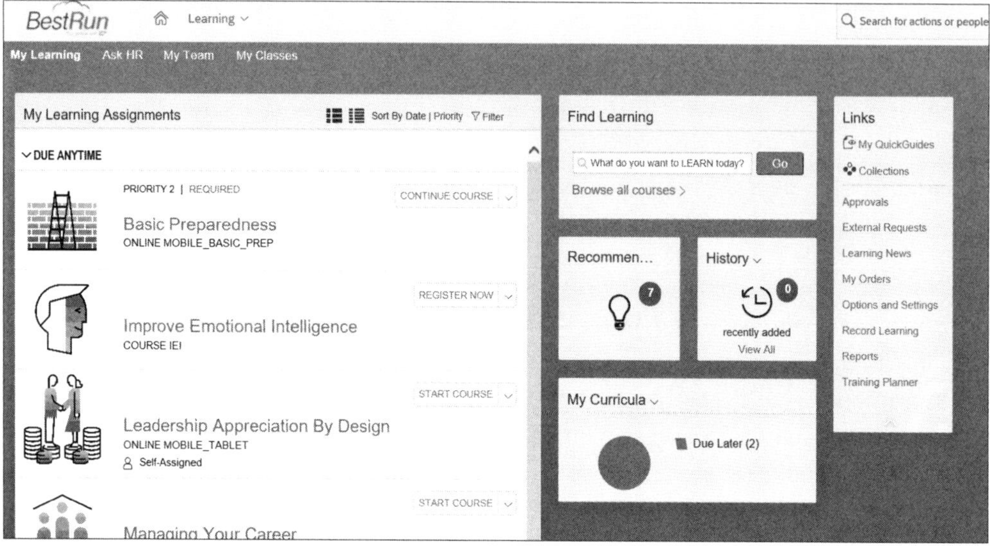

Figure 10.1 My Learning Default Tab

10.2.2 Manager Interface

There are additional prerequisites that must be in place before a user is able to navigate from the SAP SuccessFactors platform to Learning as a supervisor:

- The user ID for the record must appear in the **Supervisor** field for at least one other user record in Learning. Anyone who has direct reports in SAP SuccessFactors is recognized as a supervisor in Learning and automatically has access to their employees' records.
- The user record in Learning must have an assigned user role that includes supervisor permissions.

Once these prerequisites are in place and the manager navigates to Learning in the main SAP SuccessFactors menu, they land at the default tab **My Learning**, where they can see their own learning. The manager can then click on the **My Team** tab to review the learning activities of employees in their hierarchy. Figure 10.2 illustrates the bird's-eye view that managers get of their teams' learning status from the **My Team** tab.

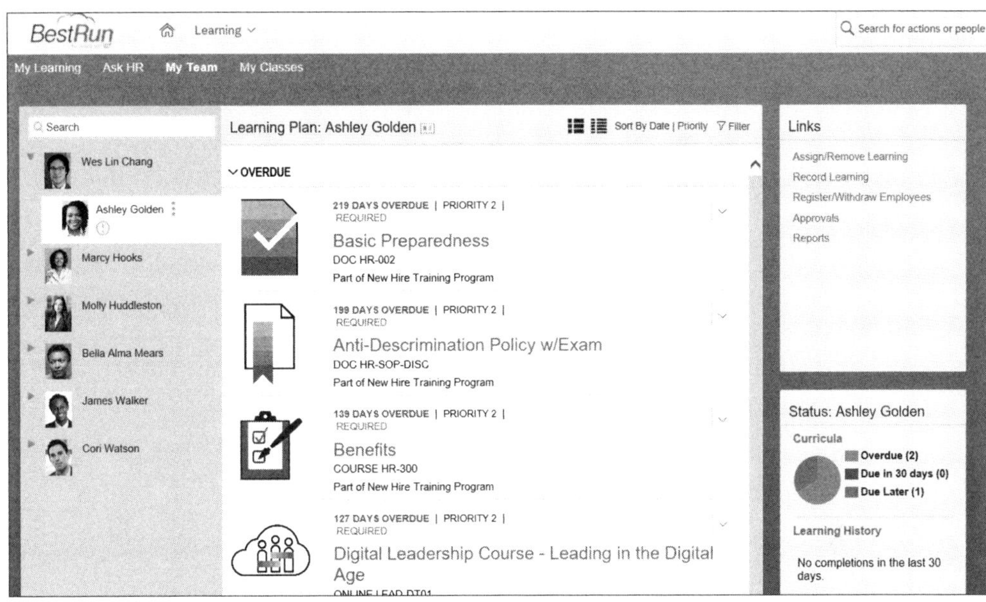

Figure 10.2 My Team Tab

You are not able to configure the layout and selection of tiles on this **My Team** page in the same way you were able to for the **My Learning** page. The supervisor permissions in the assigned user role defines the available links and actions available on this screen. The **Links** tile on the top-right corner of the screen contains actions that supervisors can perform. These permissions may grant supervisors the ability to manage learning for their employees, including:

- Viewing assigned learning, the curriculum status, and overdue learning for all team members
- Assigning or removing the learning activities of their teams
- Registering or withdrawing team members in scheduled offerings
- Recording learning events/completions for their teams
- Running reports that contain records for their own learning, direct and indirect team members (multiple levels of reporting), as also include alternate (dottted line) team members
- Delegating responsibilities to other users
- Assigning alternate supervisors for their teams

10.2.3 Instructor Interface

There are additional prerequisites that must be in place before a user is able to navigate from the SAP SuccessFactors platform to Learning as an instructor:

- An active instructor record must exist in Learning.
- The user and instructor records in Learning must have matching user IDs.
- The instructor record in Learning must have an assigned instructor role.

Once these prerequisites are in place, instructors will see a **My Classes** tab (see Figure 10.3) providing access to their classes and attendee enrollment status. The instructor roles that you create will define the actions available through this instructor interface, which may include:

- Accessing scheduled offering details, which includes the ability to launch virtual sessions
- Adding walk-ins
- Initiating evaluations
- Printing rosters
- Recording attendance
- Recording learning completions
- Recording learning completions for ad hoc classes
- Viewing scheduled offering documents

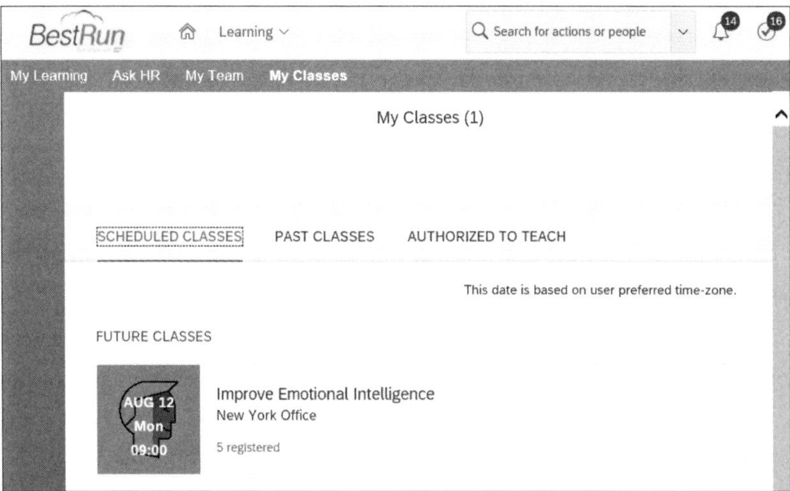

Figure 10.3 My Classes Tab

If these permissions are insufficient for actions that your instructors perform, you may decide to create an administrator account, rather than using the instructor interface.

10.2.4 Administrator Interface

There are a few prerequisites that must be in place before a user is able to navigate from the SAP SuccessFactors platform to Learning as an administrator:

- An active user record must exist in the SAP SuccessFactors platform with the **Manage Learning – Administrator** permission assigned.
- An active user record must exist in Learning.
- The user records in SAP SuccessFactors platform and Learning must have matching user IDs.
- An active administrator record must exist in Learning.
- The user and administrator records in Learning must have matching user IDs.
- The administrator record in Learning must have at least one assigned administrator role.

Once these prerequisites are in place and the administrator navigates to **Admin Center** in the main SAP SuccessFactors menu, and then searches for the **Learning Administration** tool, they land at their home page for **Learning Administration** (see Figure 10.4). Many permission workflows are available for assignment to administrators. It is also possible to define a domain security structure to control data access for each administrator. The combination of workflow permissions in the assigned administrator role(s) define the menus displayed the administrator interface. This section of the chapter will review a sample of the vast administrator capabilities in the system.

Learning Administration Home Page

The **Learning Administration** site is organized with menus across the top navigation bar and **Quick Links** in the middle of the screen. Clicking on the yellow star button expands a left panel for quick navigation to **Recents** (the most recent records) and **Bookmarks** (a method for bookmarking records you regularly use). Figure 10.4 illustrates this home page with the left panel expanded.

There are nine menus are available along the top of the administrator interface: **Home**, **Users**, **Performance**, **Learning**, **Content**, **Commerce**, and **System Admin** are located along the top left section of the screen, and **References** and **Reports** are located at the far right.

Figure 10.4 Learning Administration Home

Home Menu Quick Links

As shown in Figure 10.5, administrators can set up their own custom **Home** page with *quick links* by clicking on the pencil icon next to the **Quick Links** title. Administrators utilize quick links often for their common tasks, and it's quite helpful to modify these based on an administrator's role and the tasks that they routinely perform in the system.

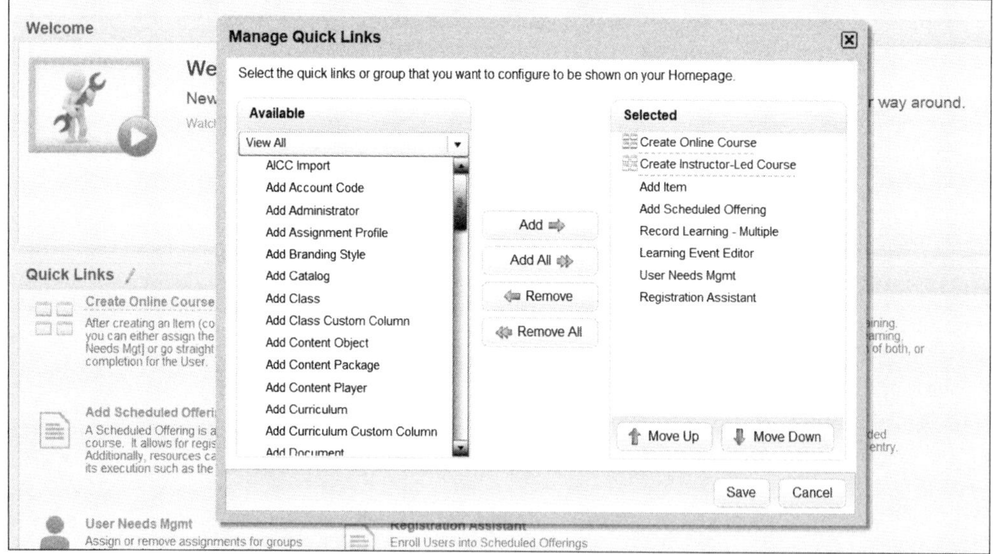

Figure 10.5 Manage Quick Links

Users Menu

The **Users** menu contains all of the actions an administrator can perform related to user records and related information. Each menu item has searchable fields for easy retrieval of records. This **Users** menu (see Figure 10.6) includes functions to manage user data, build assignment profiles for automated learning assignment, manage other user data like job codes, organizations, and groups, and manage account requests. The **Tools** menu shown in Figure 10.7 expands to include mass record management tools such as record learning, edit learning records, merge users, and user needs management.

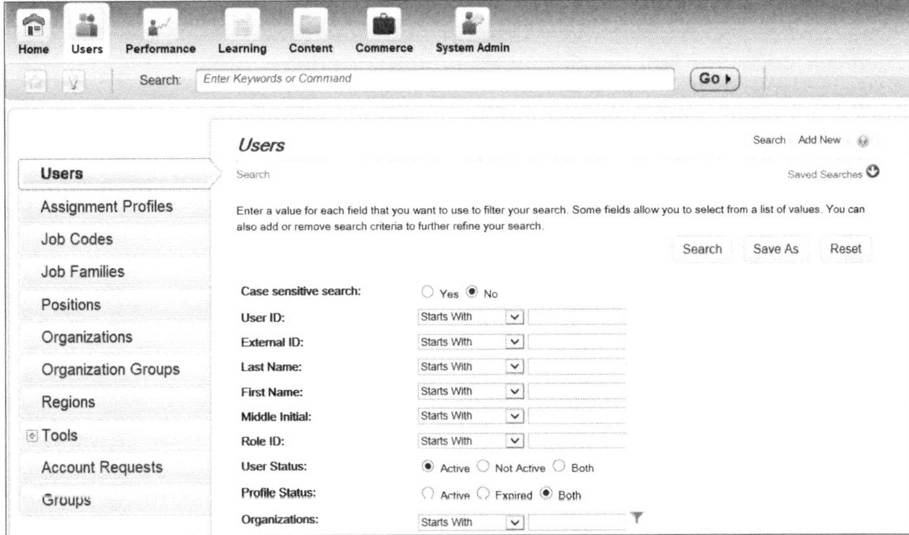

Figure 10.6 Users Menu

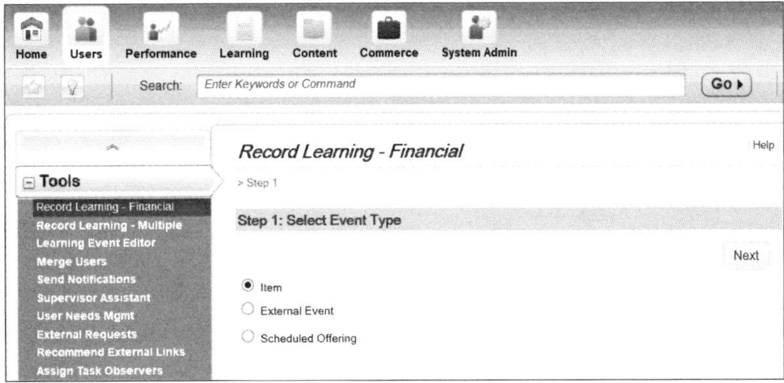

Figure 10.7 Users Menu with Tools Expanded

Performance Menu

This menu is a legacy system functionality related to performance. This is superseded by SAP SuccessFactors Performance & Goals.

Learning Menu

The **Learning** menu actions control the creation and modification of learning activities that reside in the system (see Figure 10.8). Here, administrators maintain items (the smallest assignable unit), group items into curricula or programs, create new catalogs, and add scheduled offerings to the calendar, just to name a few. You can also create or modify instructors and build tasks for OJT (see Section 10.3.3).

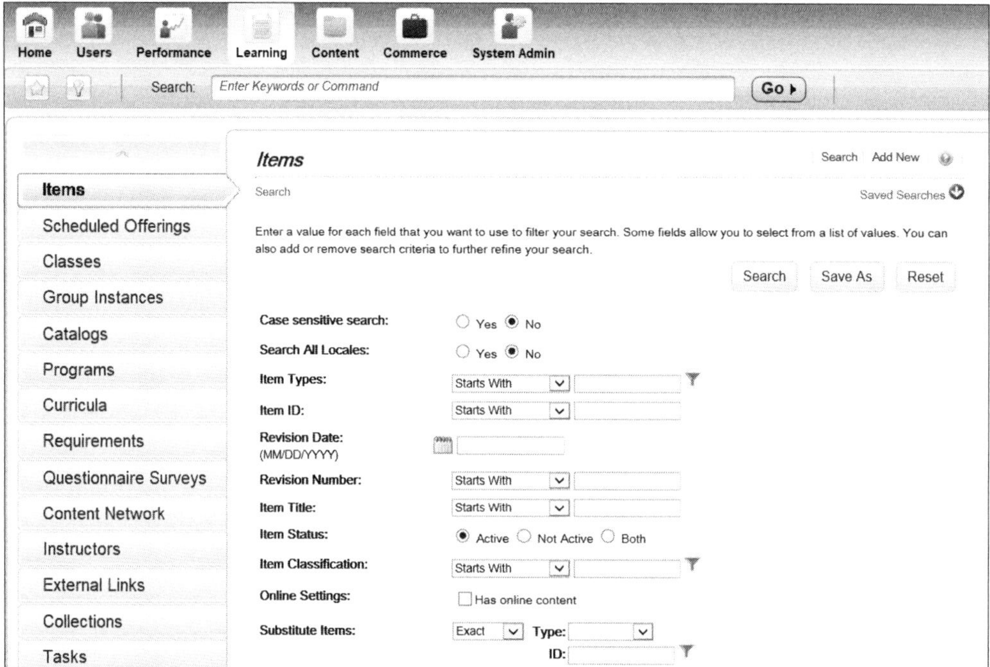

Figure 10.8 Learning Menu

Expanding the **Tools** option under the **Learning** menu (see Figure 10.9) controls actions related to scheduled offerings such as closing and cancelling, editing required dates, and using the **Registration Assistant**, which allows an administrator to register, withdraw, or hold seats for users. We will take a closer look at the scheduling features of Learning in Section 10.3.1.

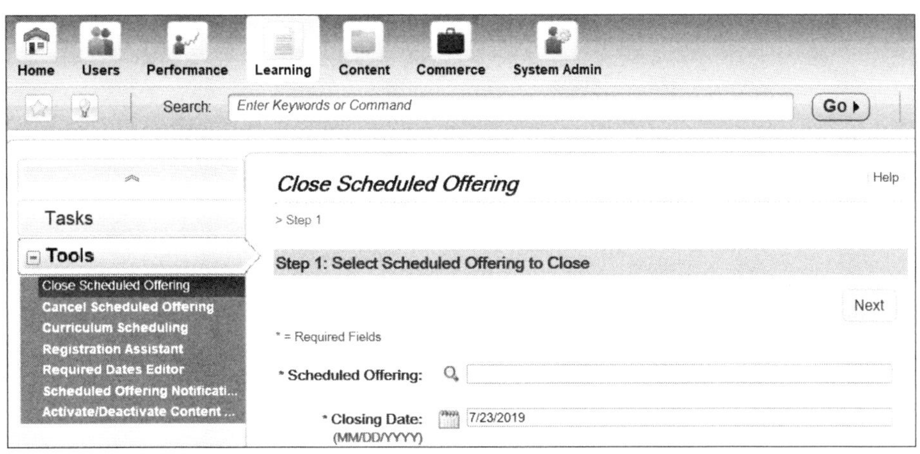

Figure 10.9 Learning Menu with Tools Expanded

Content Menu

As the name implies, the **Content** menu organizes all of the functions related to online content (see Figure 10.10).

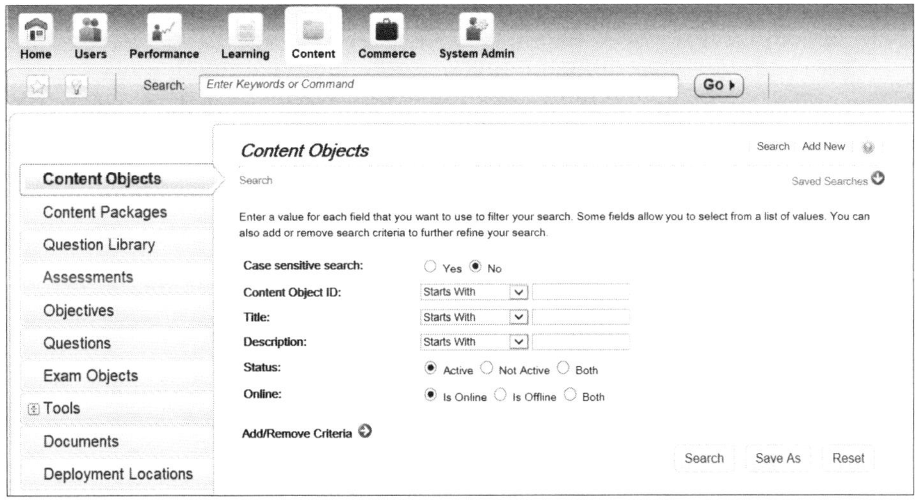

Figure 10.10 Content Menu

An important note about Learning and online content is that the system points to content that is stored elsewhere. One storage option includes a content server (iContent) that is included with your Learning license. Online content can be in the form of a web-based training course on iContent, a policy document from your internal file-share systems, third-party online content managed from an external site, or an online exam that is created from the internal **Assessments** tool (see Section 10.5.2). For more information about the online content management features of Learning, see Section 10.3.2.

The **Import Content** option available from the expanded **Tools** menu (see Figure 10.11) controls actions related to adding new content, adding content to an existing item, replacing content for an existing item, or enabling mobile or offline content for an existing item.

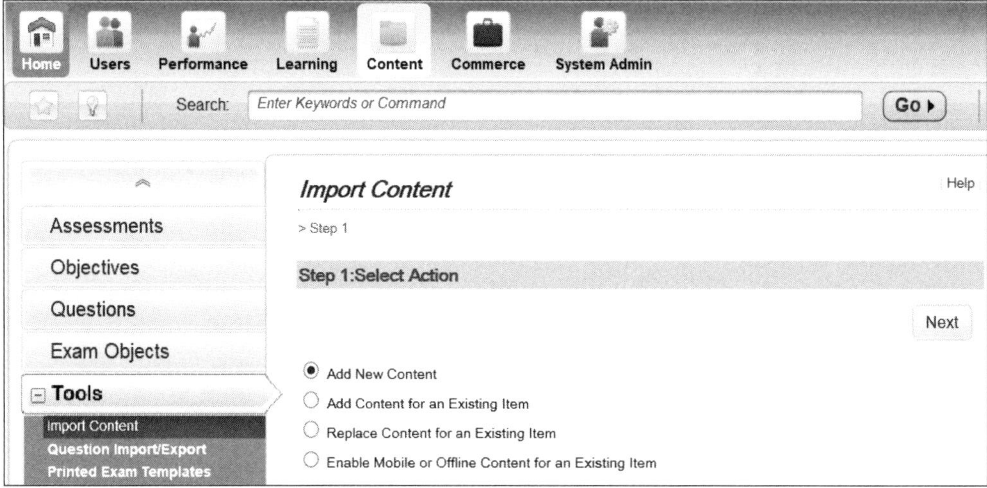

Figure 10.11 Content Menu with Tools Expanded

Commerce Menu

The **Commerce** menu is where you would set up all financial transaction information to enable Learning commerce. This includes options to create purchase orders, coupons, and subscriptions.

System Administration Menu

The **System Admin** menu is where all system administration functions and configuration occur (see Figure 10.12). This menu should be granted only to "true" system administrators who understand the power of these features and oversee the LMS as a whole. Configuration occurs in the system by setting up connectors, creating automatic processes, configuring custom columns, and configuring background jobs.

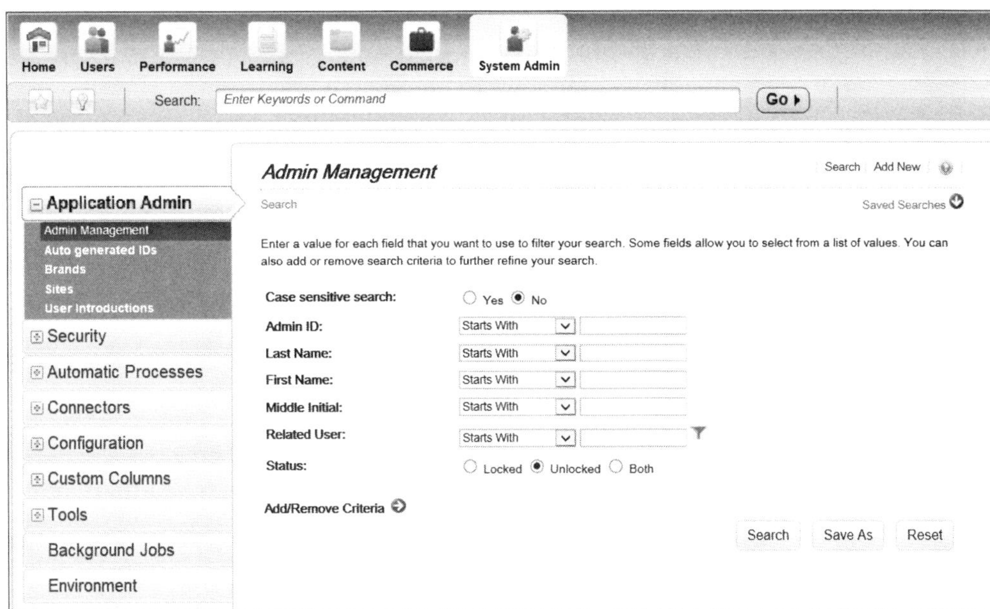

Figure 10.12 System Admin Menu

Security is also a main feature of this menu. This is where domains and domain restrictions are managed. Roles are also created here. Administrators create multiple roles and then assign these roles to users or groups of users. Some common examples of administrator roles are content admins with permissions restricted to content features of the system, training admins with permissions restricted to the scheduling features, and report admins with limited permissions to run system reports.

References Menu

The **References** menu is used primarily during the initial configuration of your Learning module. This may include reference values for your items, such as item types, item completion status, item delivery methods, and item sources, just to name a few. References are also used for creating physical resources used in scheduling (see Section 10.3.1) and setting workflow settings such as approval processes.

Reports Menu

The **Reports** menu (see Figure 10.13) houses all of the learning reports. When you first implement the system, the reports page will contain all standard default reports that are included with your license. This includes reports for learning history, assignment status, user details, scheduled course information, and many more. Administrators use this reports menu to generate admin-based reports, and this includes the ability to filter reports based on specific users, items, and other learning data. Users will use the **Reports** link from the user interface (see the **Links** tile from Figure 10.1) to run reports, and they would be limited to reports on their own learning records, or managers can run reports for their hierarchy.

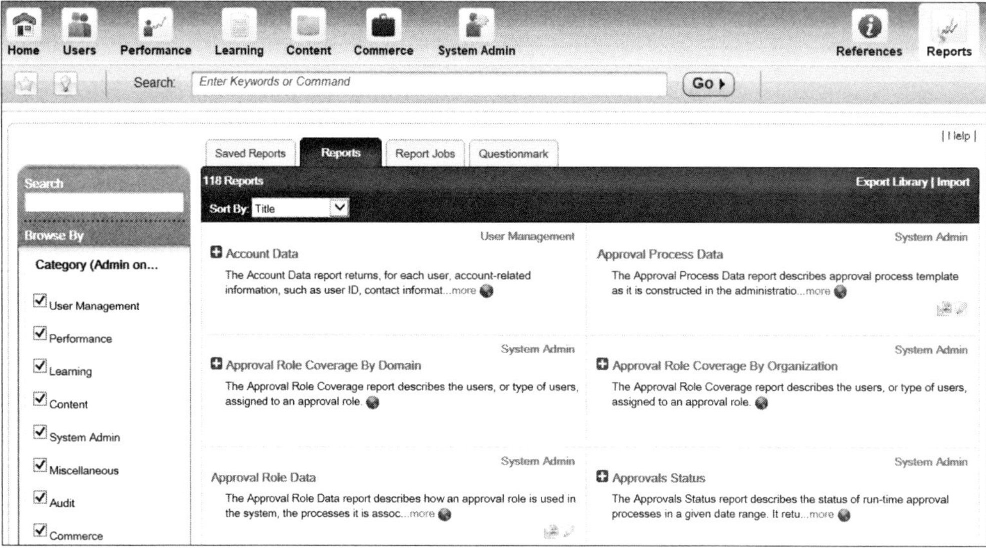

Figure 10.13 Reports Menu

Now that you have an understanding of the different user roles and interactions available through the various interfaces, let's turn our attention to the concept of *items* and how they are used for learning delivery.

10.3 Item Management

An *item* in Learning represents the smallest assignable unit. The components assembled within an item will automatically classify it as one of the following:

- **Instructor-led training**
  The item is comprised of one or many segments of time. These segments are used as the basis for scheduling the course over one or many days. See Section 10.3.1 for more details.

- **Online**
  The item is comprised of one or many content objects or assessments. Online learning is self-paced, so no scheduling elements are required. See Section 10.3.2 for more details.
- **Blended**
  This item is composed of both segments of time and online content. Students assigned to a blended course will complete a combination of online learning and scheduled events.
- **Other**
  This item has neither segments nor online content. A common use of this classification is OJT. See Section 10.3.3 for more details.

We will now look deeper into the structure and setup of instructor-led training.

10.3.1 Instructor-Led Training

Instructor-led training is a form of training conducted by an instructor or facilitator at a specified date, time, and location (normally in a classroom, either physical or virtual). LMSs support this method of training by providing the following functionality:

- Physical Resource Management: Scheduling instructors, booking classrooms, managing inventory of classroom equipment and materials
- Schedule Management: Defining the number of hours or days required to conduct training
- Registration Management: Enrollment, waitlists, cancellation, approval workflow
- Record keeping: Attendance tracking, recording grades and completions

We will now explore the features of Learning that support these instructor-led training functions.

Physical Resource Management

In Learning, you have the ability to manage instructor records, facilities, locations, equipment, and material. While it is not required to have these records in place to use instructor-led learning, these resources can provide useful information for learners, especially if you plan to enable self-registration.

To create an instructor record, it must have at a minimum an ID and an instructor role assigned. If you intend to use the instructor interface (see Section 10.2.3), the instructor record must be aligned with a user record to provide the means for logging into SAP SuccessFactors. There is also plenty of additional data that you can maintain in the instructor record. The most notable data includes:

- **Biography**: This is user-facing information that provides background information about the instructor.
- **Email Address**: The system uses this address for instructor notifications and calendar invitations.
- **Authorized to Teach**: Administrators can maintain a list of courses the instructor is able to teach. You may choose to lock down the system to limit scheduling only to authorized instructors.
- **Costs**: You have the option to add base costs, item cost, and additional costs for each instructor record. Costs may also be tracked for the other physical resources such as facilities, locations, and equipment. There are standard reports available to calculate the total cost of your learning events based on each resource added to your events.
- **VLS Settings**: This is the virtual learning server settings for each instructor and provides the ability to connect an instructor's Webex, Adobe Connect, or Skype account for the purpose of launching virtual training sessions.

There are other physical resources you may add to your Learning system for providing more information about instructor-led training sessions:

- Facilities: Facilities records identify the location of the building where training will take place.
- Locations: Location records identify the room location within the facility.
- Equipment: You may choose to track inventory and availability of equipment needed for your training. This could include laptops, projectors, flipcharts, or other equipment related to the topic of the course.
- Materials: Learning provides the ability to track inventory of your training manuals and other materials.

Schedule Management

When setting up instructor-led training, you need to ensure that the instructor and learners know when and where to show up for the session(s). They will also want to know when to expect the session to end. As a Learning administrator, you will have the ability to define the number of days and hours within each day to schedule for the course. In Learning, this is called a *segment*. A course must have at least one segment for the system to classify it as instructor-led. When a Learning administrator takes the action of scheduling the course, the segments determine the number of days and duration for each day. It is also during this process where administrators have the option to add physical resources (described in Section 10.2.4). After creating the scheduled offering, Learning administrators have full control over the layout of the days, start times, and end times.

You may choose to allow learners or managers the ability to register into scheduled offerings from the user interface (see Figure 10.14), or you may lock down this task to Learning administrators only within the administrator interface. This control is available for each course you create in the system.

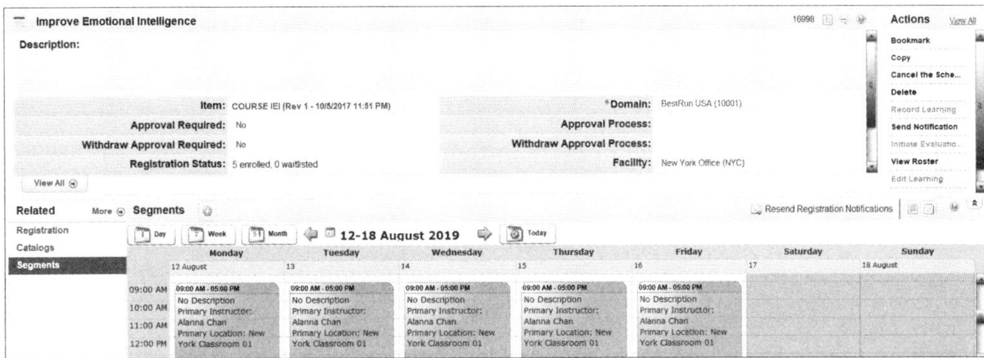

Figure 10.14 Scheduled Offering—Segments Menu

Registration Management

Enabling *self-registration* and *supervisor registration* for a course, and adding scheduled offerings to a catalog, provides the ability for learners and supervisors to enroll, request approval, join the waitlist, or cancel from a scheduled offering (see Figure 10.15). Learners and supervisors search the catalog, find scheduled courses available to them, and then make a selection to *register*. If the course requires approval, they are notified of the approval process and the registration remains in a **Pending** state until the approval process is complete. If the course is full, the individual is notified and may be given the option to go on a waitlist. They are later notified if a seat becomes available. If neither condition applies, then the learner is registered into an enrolled status. Learning administrators may also manage registrations to provide oversight and class management (see Figure 10.16).

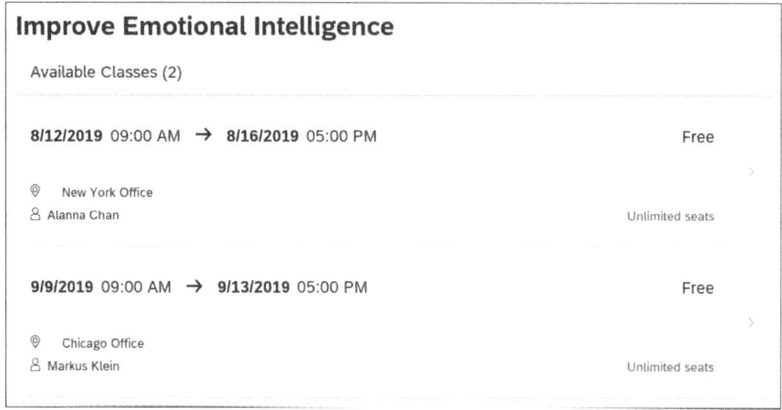

Figure 10.15 User Registration Screen

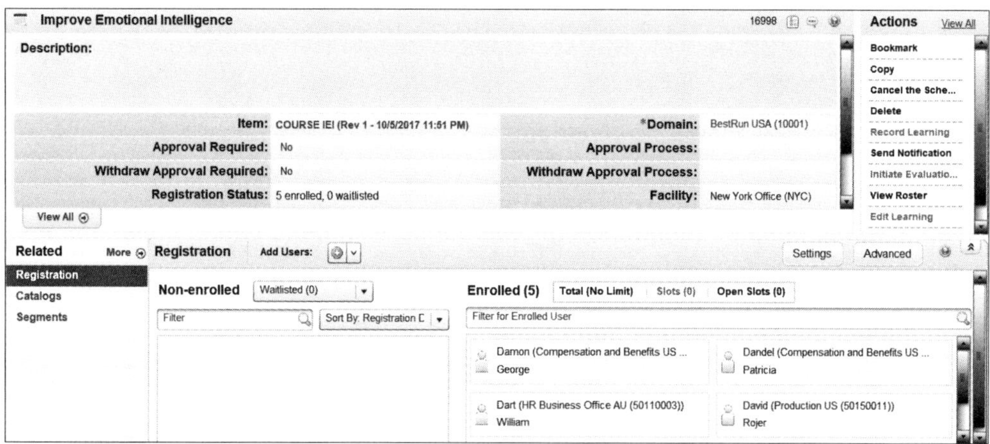

Figure 10.16 Scheduled Offering—Registration Menu

Record Keeping

While the sessions are in progress, instructors have the option to track attendance. There are a few ways to access attendance tracking:

- Instructor interface: The instructor role defines whether attendance tracking is available from this interface.
- Administrator interface: Scheduled offering records provide another location for tracking attendance.

When the course is completed, it is important for either an instructor or administrator to mark completion. This completion must have a date and time, and may also include a grade and comments. Once the record learning option is complete, the learner views this record from the **My Learning** user interface in the **History** tile with the option, if enabled, to print a certificate (see Figure 10.17).

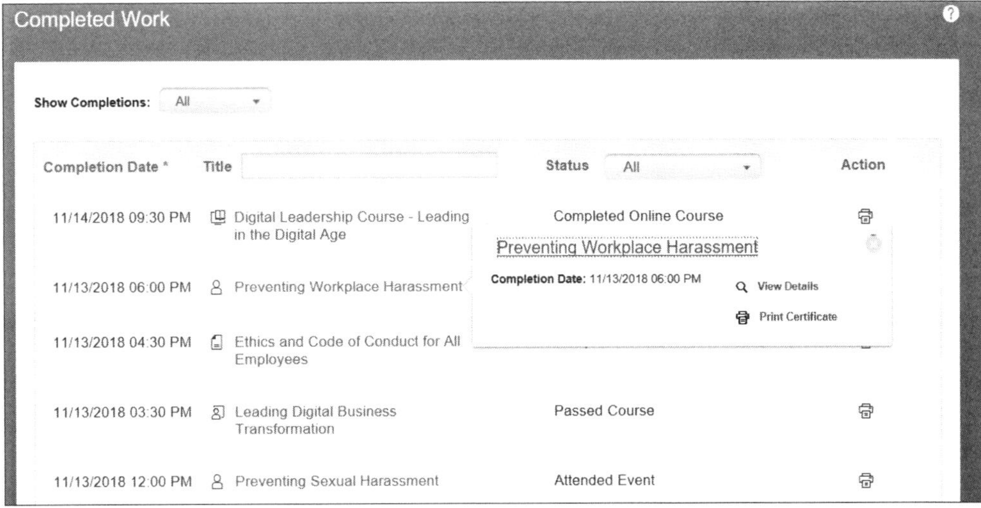

Figure 10.17 Learning History Details

This section has covered Physical Resource Management, Schedule Management, Registration Management, and record-keeping features of Learning to support instructor-led training. Let's now look at online learning.

10.3.2 Online Learning and Content Management

Online learning provides a self-paced method for meeting learning objectives. LMSs support this method of training by providing the following functionality:

- Content development: Creation of custom online content.
- Content management: Storing online content, creating links to preexisting content, integration with third-party content.
- Automated record keeping: Recording grades and completions as a result of learner interaction.

We will now explore the features of Learning that support these online learning functions.

Content Development

The Learning module on its own does not have a content development tool. The system is content agnostic and tracks any Aviation Industry Computer-Based Training Committee (AICC) or Shareable Content Object Reference Model (SCORM) published content. SAP sells another product, *SAP Enable Now*, which is used to create e-learning content that you may integrate with your Learning module. Otherwise, will you produce content in a stand-alone content development tool such as Adobe Captivate, Adobe Presenter, or Articulate Storyline (just to name a few), and you will decide via which of the following formats to publish your e-learning content:

- **AICC**
  This is the most basic format of e-learning content that automatically tracks completion, bookmarking, and duration of the e-learning session.
- **SCORM 1.2**
  This is the next level up of e-learning formats. It has a cross-domain limitation, so is best to store SCORM published content on the iContent server.
- **SCORM 2004 (2nd and 4th edition)**
  This is the most recent version of SCORM, which includes the ability to define adaptive sequencing rules.

Another option for developing online content is to reuse your existing files (for example, PDF policy documents, PowerPoint presentations, video or other media files) and enable tracking using the built-in *AICC wrapper*. This feature allows an administrator to "wrap" a file and requires users to read and acknowledge that they either accept or reject it. The AICC format of this wrapper provides tracking of content completion as well as the total duration of the content session. The details of this tracking are then available in the Learning **History**.

You may also elect to purchase third-party content to integrate with your Learning system. Many third-party content vendors provide simplified integration through the *Open Content Network*, and the interaction is seamless to the learners. Currently, the list of vendors available through the Open Content Network are:

- Open Sesame
- LinkedIn Learning

- Open HPI
- Coursera
- Harvard Managed Mentor
- Udacity
- Learning Hub
- EdX

Additional third-party providers can also be added to this configuration.

Once you have your content created, identified, or purchased, you will then direct your attention to managing your online content.

Content Management

The purchase of the Learning module includes 25GB of web server space through a product titled *iContent*. During your initial implementation of Learning, your implementation consultant will set up iContent as a *deployment location*. You will have the option to set up additional deployment locations to your other content servers if you wish, but iContent is recommended specifically for SCORM content as it provides storage on the same domain as your LMS.

The *Import Content tool* in the **Content** menu provides the mechanism for performing one of the following steps:

- **Add New Content**
- **Add Content for an Existing Item**
- **Replace Content or an Existing Item**
- **Enabled Mobile or Offline Content for an Existing Item**

This import tool provides a number of steps based on the action you have selected. As a result of completing the steps, *content objects* and *content packages* are added to your Learning system and content is uploaded to your content servers.

Content objects compose a singular content record that contains the launch parameters of the online content. Figure 10.18 provides an example of the launch parameters for a wrapped policy document. The launch type is set to **AICC**, the **Use AICC Wrapper** box is checked, the **Filename** provides the path to where the document is stored, and **Enable Mobile Access** is checked.

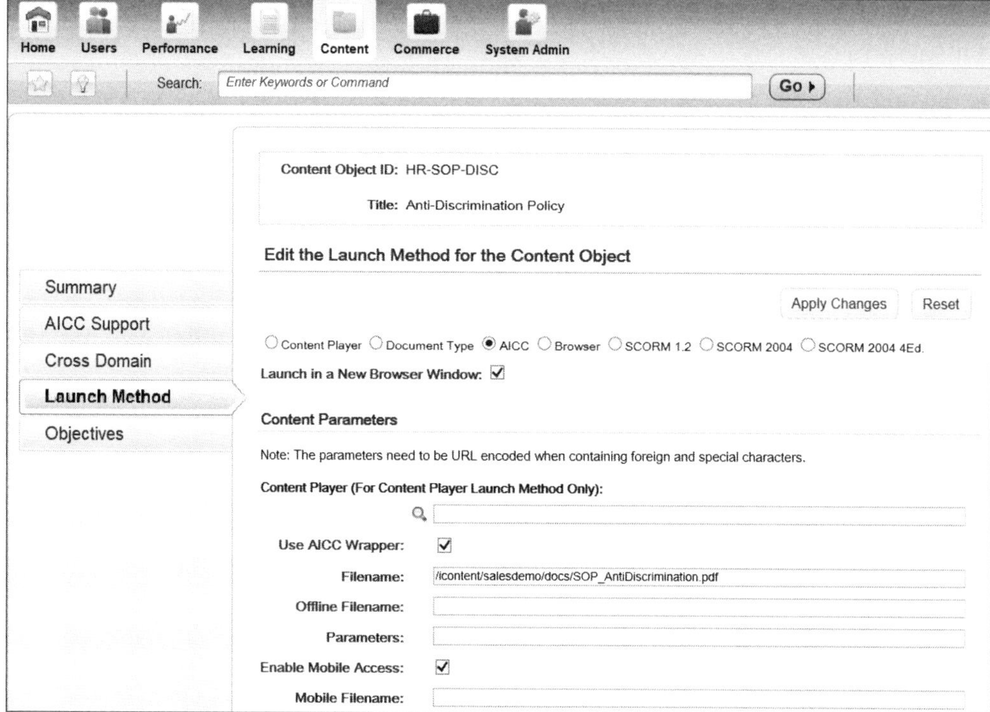

Figure 10.18 Content Object—Launch Method

Content packages allow for the bundling of multiple content objects to add them to an item in one step. Whether you are working with content objects or content packages, you must add content to an item to allow for assignment and tracking of online content. Let's now look at how content objects and items are assembled to enable automated record keeping of online learning from your Learning system.

Automated Record Keeping

For online learning, the item record is used for assembling the content (one or many). In Figure 10.19, we have the item titled **Anti-Discrimination Policy w/Exam**, which contains the policy content object from Figure 10.18 and an exam (see Section 10.5.2 for more information on assessments) in the **Online Content** menu. The order and title of each content object is defined when the administrator adds content using the green **+** icon. By clicking on the **Settings** button, the learning administrator determines if learning is recorded when all content is complete, and then sets the completion status for a successful completion of the content, and failure status (optional) for unsuccessful completion.

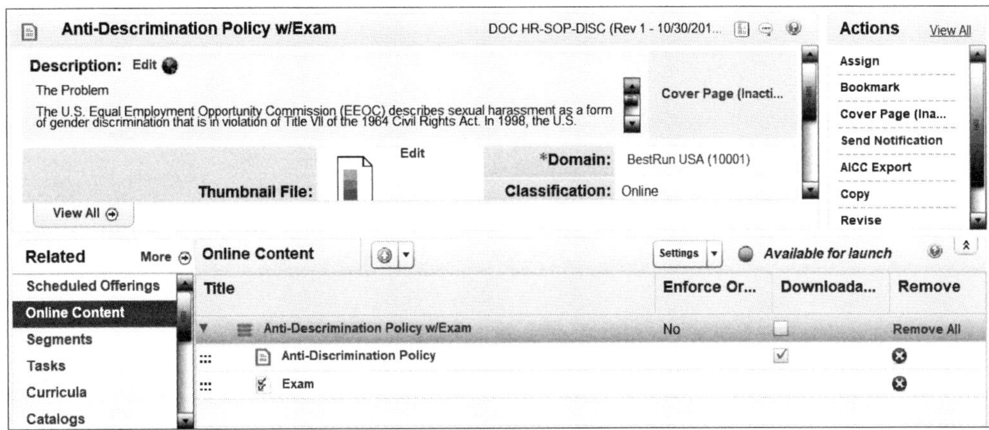

Figure 10.19 Item—Online Content

Now that you have an understanding of the two primary course classifications of instructor-led training and online content delivery in Learning, we will turn our attention to OJT management.

10.3.3 On-the-Job Training

Learning includes the features and functionality to create task checklists for observational learning. OJT requires two primary actors—the learner and an observer:

- **Learner actions**
  When OJTs appear on a user's learning plan, the learner must select an observer, prepare for the observation, and then arrange to meet with the observer to demonstrate skills based on a task checklist.
- **Observer actions**
  The observer launches the task checklist (see Figure 10.20), confirms successful completion of each task (options include the ability to add comments and track duration of each task), and marks the overall completion of the checklist.

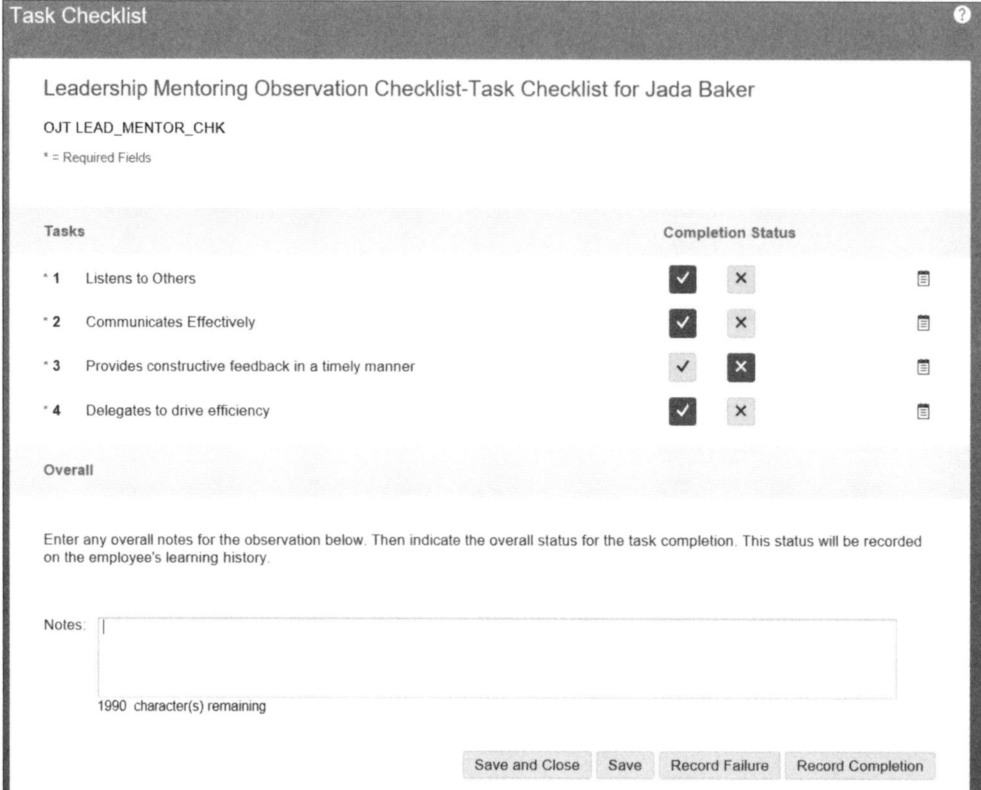

Figure 10.20 Task Checklist

We have covered the primary types of items you'll manage as the smallest assignable unit. It is possible to combine multiple items together using curricula and programs. Let's look at these concepts now.

10.4 Curriculum and Program Management

Curricula and programs provide the means for assembling multiple items into one larger assignable unit. You will use curricula when courses must be retaken on a retraining interval (for example, courses that need to be completed on a yearly basis). Items, requirements, and subcurricula are elements that can be assembled within a curriculum. Figure 10.21 illustrates how curricula appear to the learner once they are assigned. Each item within a curriculum appears individually on the **My Learning**

Assignments tile with a link to the associated curriculum. You can see the item title ❶ and curriculum title ❷.

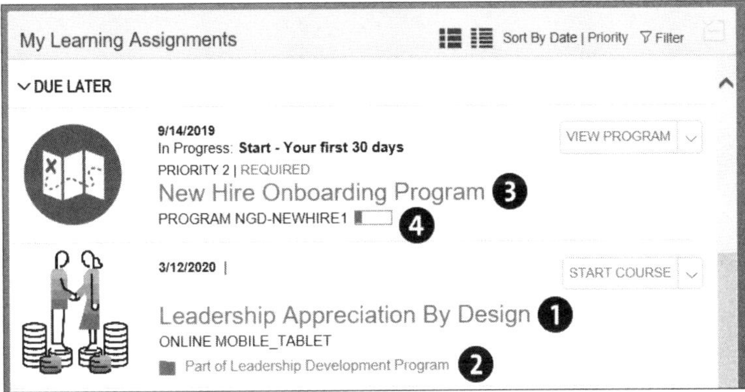

Figure 10.21 My Learning Assignments—Curriculum

Programs, on the other hand, should be used when learning activities must be completed within a set order and no retraining is required. For example, a new hire onboarding program may have a series of learning activities that you want the learners to complete in the first 30 days of hire and then other events between the first 30 to 60 days of hire. There are many types of learning activities available to assemble within a program, and they include items, external courses, and self-marking activities such as links, text, or HTML instructions. Programs contrast from curricula in many ways, primarily how they appear on the **My Learning Assignments** tile. Figure 10.21 also illustrates how a program ❸ appears as one item in the assignments with a progress bar ❹ to indicate how far the learner has advanced through the program activities. The detail of learning activities will only appear after the learner has clicked on the **VIEW PROGRAM** button.

The choice between curricula and programs is based on a variety of factors, which can include:

- **Duration and revisions**
  Curricula are ongoing, and any changes made to the structure of the curricula will impact learners who are assigned. Programs have a completion, and any changes made to a program after completion will not impact the learner.
- **Prerequisites**
  Curricula will honor prerequisites between items. Programs ignore item prerequisite settings, and the order of activities is dictated by the program agenda.

- **Completion history**
  The individual items within a curricula will appear on the learning history, but the curriculum will not. Programs appear in the learning history as one completion record.
- **Order of assignments**
  The order of completion for items within a curriculum is primarily dictated by the due date, with the option to re-sort by a suggested order. The order of completion for activities within a program is dictated by the program agenda.

Whether you are planning to assign individual items, or items assembled within curricula or programs, it is wise to evaluate the effectiveness of your training through various levels of assessments. We'll now turn our attention to the evaluation and assessment tools available within the Learning module.

10.5 Evaluation and Assessment

SAP SuccessFactors supports the Kirkpatrick model of evaluation; the first three levels within the Learning module, and the fourth level through Learning analytics, which is an additional module that you may purchase. Table 10.1 lists the four levels of evaluation, a description, and the feature that supports each level.

Kirkpatrick Level	Description	Feature
Reaction	Evaluates user satisfaction with the course	Survey—item evaluations (see Section 10.5.1)
Learning	Evaluates knowledge gained as a result of the course	Assessments (see Section 10.5.2)
Behavior	Evaluates the application of learning as a result of the course	Survey—follow-up evaluations (see Section 10.5.1)
Results	Evaluates impact of training on business outcomes	Learning analytics (this topic is not covered in this book)

Table 10.1 Comparison of Kirkpatrick Levels to SAP SuccessFactors Features

We'll now dig a little deeper into the two main evaluation tools within the Learning module.

10.5.1 Surveys

There two types of surveys available in Learning:

- **Item evaluations**
  Item evaluations are immediately assigned to the learner upon completion of the course. Configuration for each completion status will determine if this evaluation is assigned based on successful or unsuccessful completions. The learner is the only person who receives this evaluation, and it can be mandatory or optional. Questions within this evaluation should address learner satisfaction of the course.
- **Follow-up evaluations**
  This is an evaluation that the learner and/or supervisor completes at a set duration after the course is completed. The same completion and optional settings are available for this evaluation type. Questions within this evaluation should address the learner's change of behavior as a result of completing the course.

It is important to note that a learning survey cannot be assigned independently. It must be assembled as part of an item and is only assigned when item completion is achieved. Figure 10.22 illustrates how the **Item Evaluation** and **Follow-up Evaluation** is added to an item.

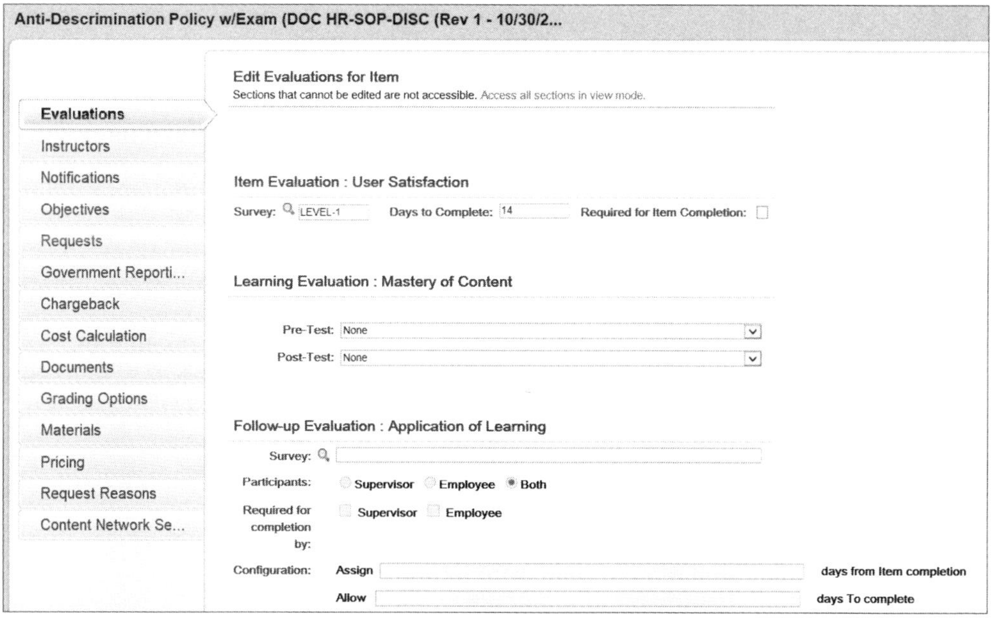

Figure 10.22 Item Evaluations

For the second level of Kirkpatrick evaluation, you will use assessments.

10.5.2 Assessments

The first step when creating an assessment is to select the type. There are two options (see Figure 10.23): **Add New Quiz** and **Add New Exam**.

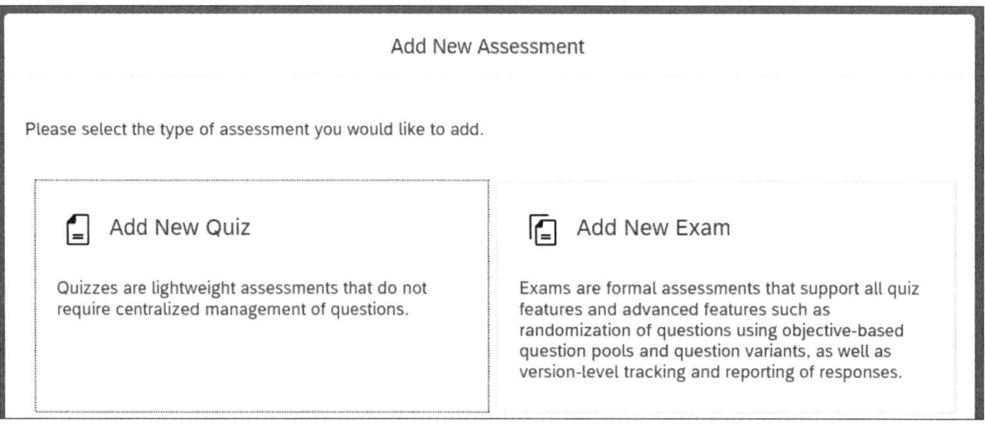

Figure 10.23 Add New Assessment

Both options give you the ability to design an assessment with a variety of question types (multiple choice, multiple select, true/false, fill-in-the-blank, and ordering), and options to offer the questions and answers in a random order. The main difference with exams is the ability to create an objective-based pool of questions. The number of questions within a quiz is based on the number of questions created, while the number of questions within an exam is based on random selection of a defined number pulled from the pool of questions.

Similar to learning surveys, assessments cannot be assigned independently. They must be assembled as part of an item and is only assigned as part of the online content. Refer to Figure 10.19 to see how the assessment is added as online content within an item.

This concludes the overview of the interface and learning activities available within Learning. We will now turn our attention to implementation best practices and advice for a successful launch of your system.

10.6 Implementation Tips

When planning for a Learning implementation, you will want to compile a list of all course and define if it is instructor-led, online, or OJT. It is also helpful to map out the compliance requirements of your training into a *training matrix*. Things to consider in the creation of your training matrix include:

- **Different training audiences**
  You will likely have training compliance requirements for different types of employees in your organization—for example, training for all employees, training for office employees versus field employees, and training based on specific jobs or departments. This information may be readily available through recent audits, or you may need to meet with many stakeholders to get a full understanding of training requirements for specific job roles or departments.
- **Existing catalog**
  The existing catalog can include courses, curricula, or programs that you are currently managing. You may also have third-party content that will need to be integrated into your new LMS. Take inventory of all existing content, determine if it is still relevant, and align the courses with the audiences you've identified.
- **Initial and retraining intervals**
  To complete the training matrix, you'll need to know the initial and retraining timeframes for each course aligned with the different audiences. For example, when a course is required, it could be initially due within 30 days, and retraining is required on a yearly basis.

The creation of this matrix helps gain a better understanding of learning activities that you need to populate into your Learning system. It will also help to know the user data needed to define the unique learning audiences for learning assignments or catalog access. Data planning is a critical step in the planning of your LMS. Not only will it be used for assignment, but it will improve the quality of data available in learning reports.

10.7 Summary

Learning's two main interfaces—the user interface and administrative interface—and robust functionality provide employees, managers, and administrators with a plethora of tools to manage learning needs for organizational, team, and individual development. It's a best-in-class system that is capable of meeting nearly any business requirement. The user interface puts learning needs and requirements at the fingertips of the individual learners and gives their managers the necessary tools to monitor and participate in their teams' learning activities. Instructors have the ability to track their classes from the user side as well. Each user-based interaction is a critical piece of the overall SAP SuccessFactors HCM Suite talent management picture.

Learning administrators have a completely flexible system that can be mostly configured directly from the Learning administrator interface. As an active part of implementation, learning administrators learn by doing, from the beginning, how to maintain the system configuration to meet growing and changing requirements within the company.

In addition to the multiple interfaces, we also covered the different types of learning activities that you can build into Learning. Online learning provides an independent learning activity that is completed once learners meet the requirements of the content. Instructor-led training is a facilitated activity that needs to be scheduled at a specified date, time, and location (may be physical or virtual locations). OJT facilitates learning-related observations through a task checklist. These activities can then be combined using a program or curricula. The built-in survey and assessment tools provide the means for measuring the effectiveness of your learning activites.

In this chapter, we've touched on what Learning can offer an organization from a very high level. We've discussed implementation tips to get you started on a successful go live of your system. You should now have a general understanding of how Learning can work for you and your organization.

We'll now turn our attention to SAP SuccessFactors Succession & Development in the next chapter.

Chapter 11
Succession and Development

Managing succession plans and employee career development is critical to maintaining organizational sustainability and mitigating against unwanted losses. Personal development provides engagement across the workforce and increases competency, productivity, and leadership in critical positions.

Managing succession plans is a crucial exercise, and being able to develop high-performing and high-potential employees into future leaders and holders of your most critical positions is of utmost importance. Hiring and onboarding are costly exercises, and key talent can be difficult, if not impossible, to replace, particularly at the senior and boardroom levels. Studies have shown that employees value nontangible benefits, such as development and career advancement, more than financial benefits, which means employee retention can be directly impacted by ensuring that you offer employees the possibility to develop their careers within your organization.

In this chapter, we'll take a look at the SAP SuccessFactors offering for these processes: SAP SuccessFactors Succession & Development. We'll begin with the basics, before moving on to key data components, features, and implementation tips.

11.1 Succession and Development Basics

Succession & Development is a comprehensive and easy-to-use solution that offers all of the core features and functionality of a best-practice succession management and career development planning (CDP) solution. It allows the management of key positions, successors, career plans, and development plans and enables a talent manager or HR professional to view bench strengths, nominated and assigned successors, and key talent data, such as performance, potential, and risks. In addition, it features classic features such as the nine-box grid, organizational chart, talent search, and reports.

The development planning functionality provides management of development activities that integrate with the SAP SuccessFactors Learning module and leads to the development of competencies. It also gives employees a platform to manage their careers and make choices about where they want to go in your organization.

In short, Succession & Development features the type of functionality that you would expect in a comprehensive succession planning and CDP solution. The solution is split into two core modules that are accessed from the module navigation menu:

- The Succession module focuses on the succession planning process. We will run through how the Succession module supports succession planning in Section 11.2, and then we'll look at the process of nominating successors in Section 11.3.
- The Development module, which is also known as CDP, provides development planning, career planning, and learning activities management. In Section 11.4, we'll explore how these support the growth of an employee's competencies and career within your organization and how they can be used to develop successors into the leaders of tomorrow.

The succession management process typically kicks off after the annual performance appraisal process has been completed, either in SAP SuccessFactors Performance & Goals (see Chapter 6) or an external performance management system. If the succession management process begins before the annual performance process has completed, then Succession & Development offers the opportunity to maintain performance ratings ad hoc. Quite often, employees are reviewed and calibrated before the process begins so that they can be assigned to talent pools. These talent pools are used to supply talent to the succession plans of key positions and keep track of high-performing or high-potential employees. During the process of assigning successors, you can evaluate and rate the potential and possible risks of employees.

After successors have been assigned to succession plans, their development plan can be updated to reflect the competency gaps identified during assignment. Learning activities can be assigned to the development plan to obtain the required competency. (If Learning is used, then learning activities can be integrated from the solution; otherwise they are entered manually.) Employees should maintain their career plans on a periodic basis to help inform managers and talent professionals of how they want to move within the organization, because this will have an impact on the decision to make them a successor.

Management of key positions is an ongoing activity and isn't generally confined to just the core of the succession planning process. Generally, most key positions are identified during implementation and set as such, but sometimes new requirements or organizational changes may necessitate the assignment of new key positions or removal of key statuses of existing positions.

11.2 Succession Planning Data

Succession planning is focused on the data available to make key decisions regarding which positions need to have successors, which talent is available and how talent can be identified, and how talent can be assigned as successors to the right key positions.

Let's look at some key functionality that is provided to support the succession planning process.

Note

Succession data can be reviewed in a talent review meetings. These can be prepared using the Presentations module that we discussed in Chapter 3, Section 3.15.

Data can be calibrated in a Presentations session or in the Calibration module (see Chapter 6, Section 6.4).

11.2.1 Organizational Charts

Succession is focused on leveraging one or more Org Charts to support visualization of succession plans across areas of the organization. These charts provide greater breadth of visibility of succession plans, risks, and coverage over teams. We'll take a look at two key charts in this section.

Succession Org Chart

The main focus of the Succession module is the *Succession Org Chart*. This chart, which is shown in Figure 11.1, provides the foundation of organizational-based succession planning and allows an overview of succession plans across different departments within the enterprise.

The Succession Org Chart displays the logged-in user and all of the user's direct reports. Each of the direct reports of each direct report can also be viewed, and so forth. In addition, there are several options to search within, display, and sort the Org Chart, as well as to display the Org Chart and the contents of each box.

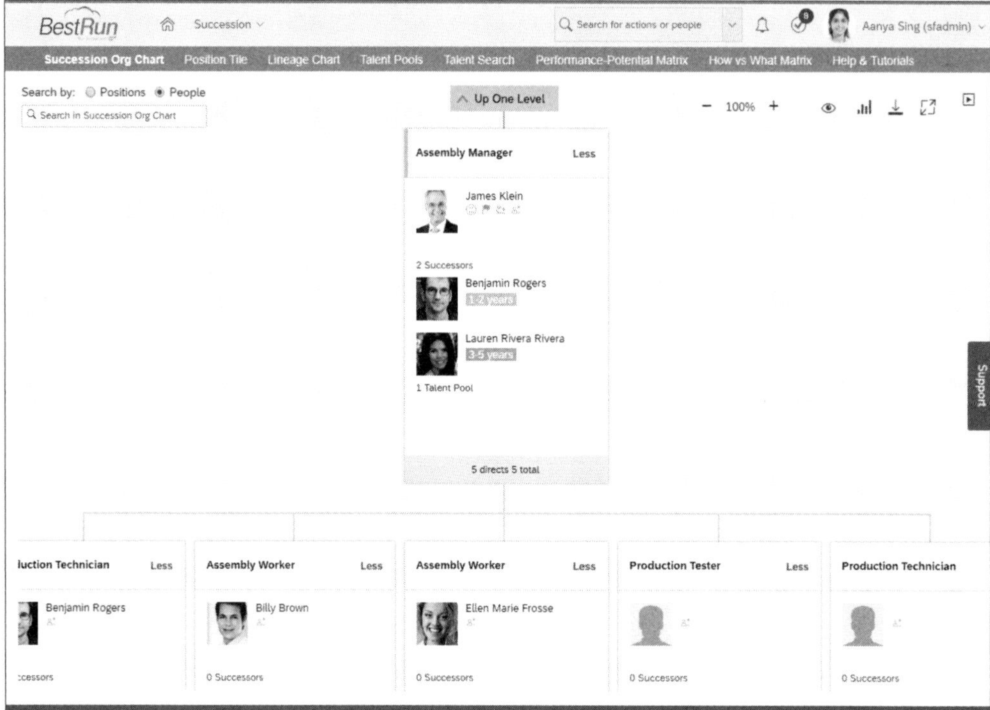

Figure 11.1 Succession Org Chart

Most of the data within the position boxes can be switched on or off, such as photo, risk of loss, impact of loss, newness to company, bench strength, and so forth. You can also choose to highlight key positions.

Each box represents a position and has a lot of information and options. Clicking on a position shows its quickcard with the following information:

- **Name** and **Code**: Name of the position and its code.
- **Bench Strength**: Bench strength is a subjective evaluation of the succession plan and the cascaded succession plans (chain of succession).
- **Key Position**: Whether the position is considered key in the organization.
- **Incumbents**: The holder(s) of the position.
- **Successors**: Any successors assigned to the position.
- **Talent Pools**: Any talent pools that the position is part of or are linked to the position.

Clicking on an employee will show you their talent card. Figure 11.2 shows the quickcard of a position and the talent card of an employee.

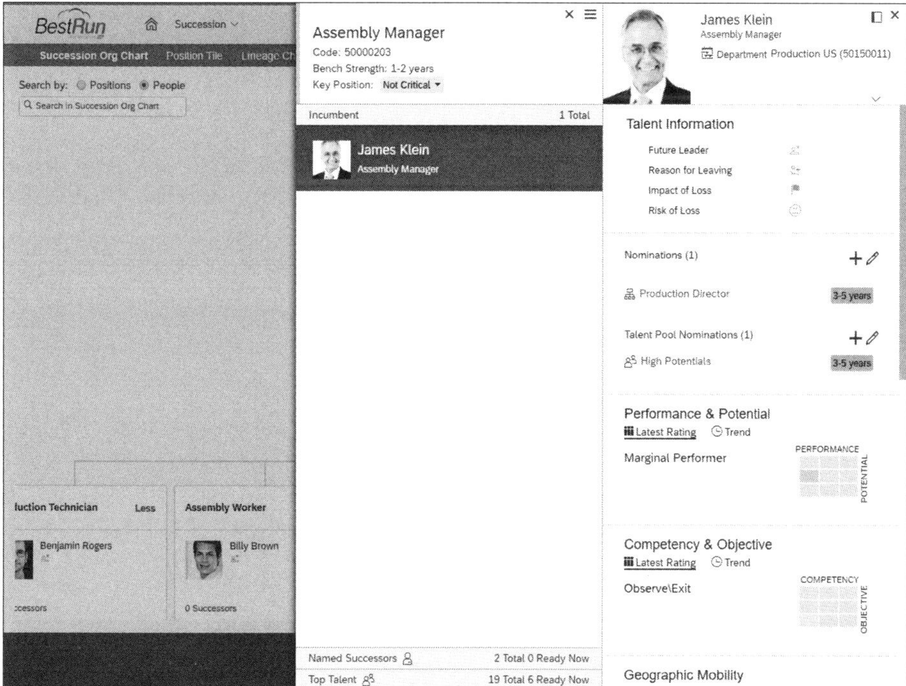

Figure 11.2 Position Quickcard and Talent Card

As we discussed in Chapter 3, Section 3.13, the *talent card* provides a set of talent-related data. A talent card can be configured in the Admin Center for Succession. Typically, the talent card would contain such data as talent information, nominations, performance and potential, competency and objectives, geographical mobility, and much more.

Using the **Add** button in the **Nominations** box, you can assign an individual as a successor for a position or talent pool. It is also possible to edit existing nominations here.

The position box action dropdown menu (located in the top-right corner of a position box) provides a number of options that include editing, deleting, and hiding the position; finding successors; viewing the position in the Lineage Chart; viewing the nomination history; and creating a job requisition in SAP SuccessFactors Recruiting. By using the dropdown next to **Key Position:**, you can set a position as a *key position*.

However, the most interesting feature of the Succession Org Chart is the information available within the position boxes.

The wealth of information that can be either shown in or hidden from the boxes as required provides the opportunity to get an overview of the status of succession across your team and, if required, their reports below. For example, it can be very easy to see the overall risk of loss for each of your team members or get the total coverage of successors and bench strength.

As with the holder of the position, each nominated successor can have their talent card viewed by clicking on them. You can open multiple talent cards and so make a side-by-side comparison of multiple employees/successors.

Lineage Chart

Succession also offers the Lineage Chart, which shows the chain of successors. It shows the employee's successors and that employee's successors in turn. Click where the number of successors is listed to expand your view to the next level of successors, and so forth, as shown in Figure 11.3. This provides a quick overview of how well covered a position is and the positions of the nominated successors—something measured with bench strength.

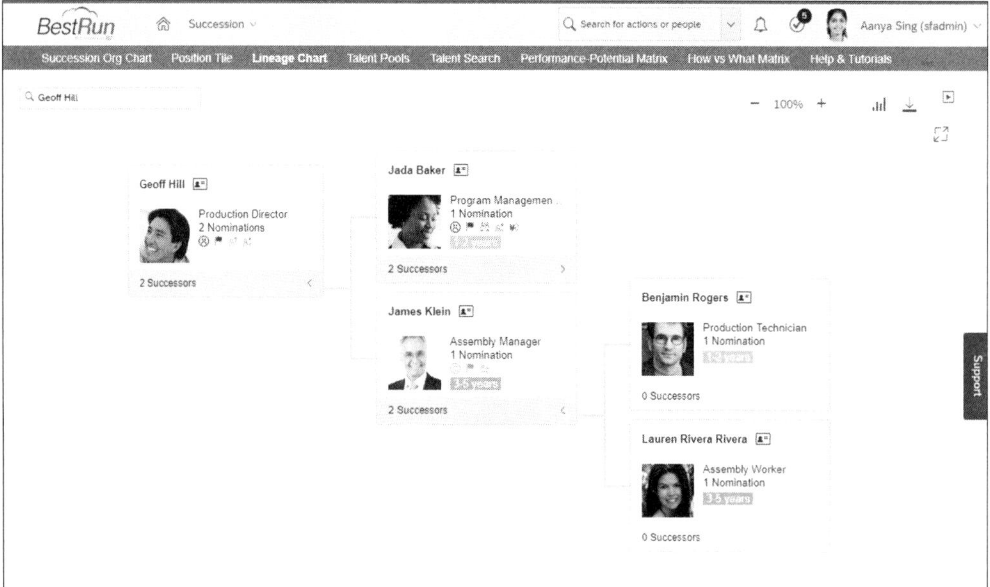

Figure 11.3 Lineage Chart

Now that we've covered the Org Charts that are used in Succession, let's look at the different matrices that can be used for reviewing and identifying the talent that will be used to nominate successors.

11.2.2 Matrices

The performance-versus-potential nine-box grid is commonly used within a best-practice succession planning process. Succession & Development features not only the *Performance-Potential Matrix*, but also the *How vs. What Matrix* grid, as we'll see in the following sections. Both matrices can be used to source talent for succession plans and feature a host of filter options for the search that can encompass large areas of the organization. They are also both separately configurable in the Admin Center, including components such as labels, ratings, and icons. They are both accessed from the options at the top of the page of the Succession module.

For filter options, both matrices allow you to report by your team or the team of a direct report for up to three levels below; by the succession management and Matrix Report permissions; or by a group. Groups are custom made based on specific characteristics, such as job code, department, division, location, and so on. The matrices allow you to view data based on any department, division, or location for any date range.

Performance-Potential Matrix

The Performance-Potential Matrix is used to help identify the high-performing, high-potential individuals who are the most likely to progress through the ranks of your organization. It plots individuals into a grid based on their performance and potential ratings so that it's easy and quick to identify not only which individuals are the top talent within your organization, but also which individuals are in need of support to improve their performance. Essentially, this helps provide an overview of how development activities can be focused to ensure that individuals are performing to the level required by your organization.

Figure 11.4 shows the **Performance-Potential Matrix** with a number of employees plotted within each square, called a quadrant. Each quadrant on the matrix has a name (for example, **Rising Star** or **Marginal Performer**) and lists the number of employees; percentage of the total employees in that quadrant; and employees themselves, with icons for their key talent ratings (for example, **Risk of Loss**, **Future Leader**, etc.). Clicking on an employee will open up the talent card.

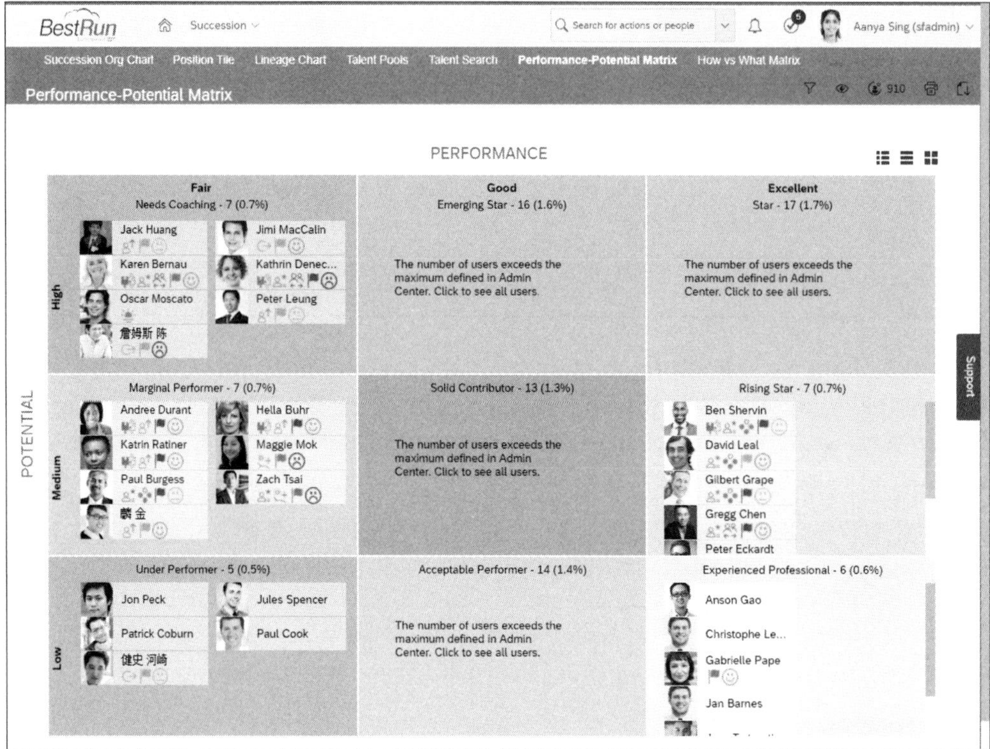

Figure 11.4 Performance-Potential Matrix

The matrix can also have icons displayed or turned off. An option exists to view all employees who are unrated or are too new to rate. You can also print or export the matrix to a PDF or Microsoft Excel file to be used in talent review meetings or calibration sessions.

After employees have been reviewed, you can nominate an employee for a succession plan or a talent pool (see Section 11.2.6) by selecting the employee's talent card and taking the necessary action (see Section 11.3).

How vs. What Matrix

A unique feature in the Succession & Development solution is the **How vs. What Matrix**, shown in Figure 11.5. This grid plots employees based on their competencies ("how") and their objective ratings ("what"), so that individuals who are higher achievers and regularly meet their objectives with distinction can be easily identified.

Although the outcome of using this matrix is the same as the Performance-Potential Matrix, it provides a different method of achieving it through objectives, rather than solely job performance and future potential.

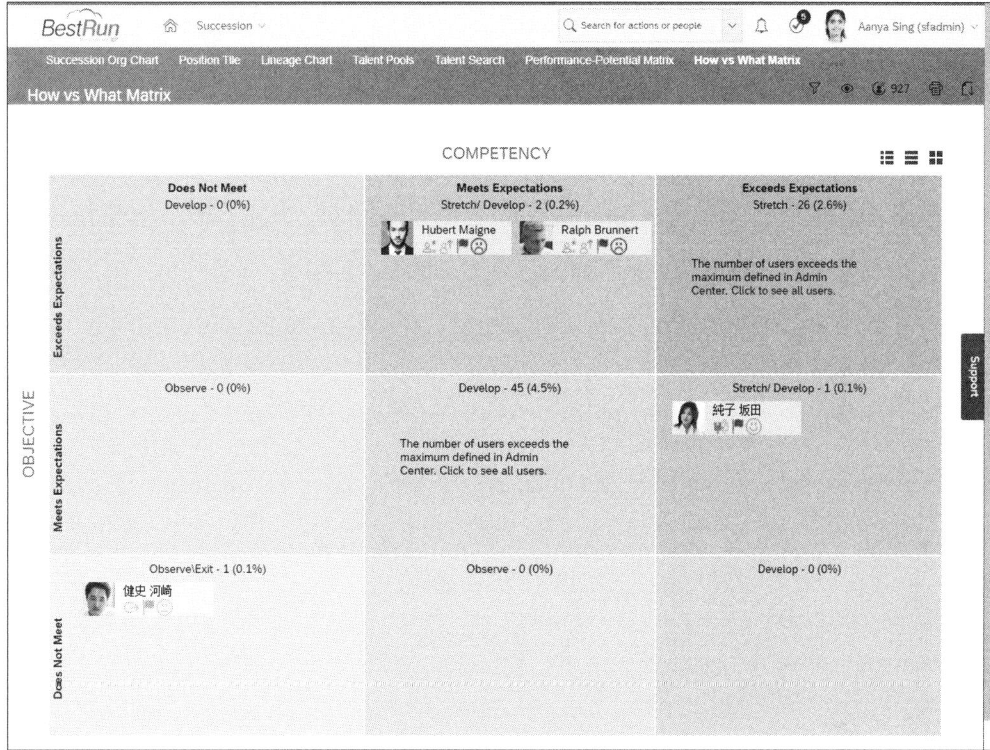

Figure 11.5 How vs. What Matrix

11.2.3 Portlets in the People Profile

There are various blocks on the People Profile available for succession planning. We covered most of these in Chapter 3, Section 3.11.1, when we talked about the different blocks on the People Profile. However, we'll point them out here briefly for reference.

The **Nomination Portlet** displays nominations for succession plans for talent pools. By selecting the **Add Nomination** link in the top-right corner, the user can make additional nominations for succession plans and talent pools.

The **Talent Information** block contains the **Risk of Loss**, **Impact of Loss**, **Reason for Leaving**, **New to Position**, and **Future Leader** attributes. This block is visible only to the manager or HR specialists, and not to the employee. You can maintain each of these attributes here by clicking the **Edit** link.

The **Successor Portlet** block shows all of the succession plans that the individual is nominated to. Nominations can be added or deleted from here, and details of each nomination displayed.

11.2.4 Talent Search

Talent search provides a powerful interface for finding, filtering, and matching employees for key positions and talent pools. It provides managers and HR with the ability to search for individuals by numerous criteria, such as job role, background criteria, and competencies. Search criteria can be saved so that it can be reused again, or even created specifically to be used by certain teams or departments within your organization.

Note

When you are searching for talent, you may have to use a number of different searches with different criteria to find the right candidates. Make sure to use all of the search criteria to ensure the best possible results.

Let's walk through your searching options and results.

Searching

You access the talent search by selecting **Talent Search** from the options at the top of the page of the Succession module. After navigating to the talent search you are immediately presented with the search criteria, which allows you to enter any search term and execute the search. You can either use a free text keyword search or you can select search terms based on the following sections:

- **Basic Information**: Any field in the UDF
- **Advanced Information**: Any background element
- **Ratings & Competencies**: One of the following People Profile blocks:
  - **Overall Competency**
  - **Overall Objective**
  - **Potential** (manager view only)
  - **Performance** (manager view only)

Under **Ratings & Competencies**, you can also select one or more competencies to search by. You can select multiple search criteria in each section. Figure 11.6 shows an example of the possible search criteria that can be selected in **Talent Search**.

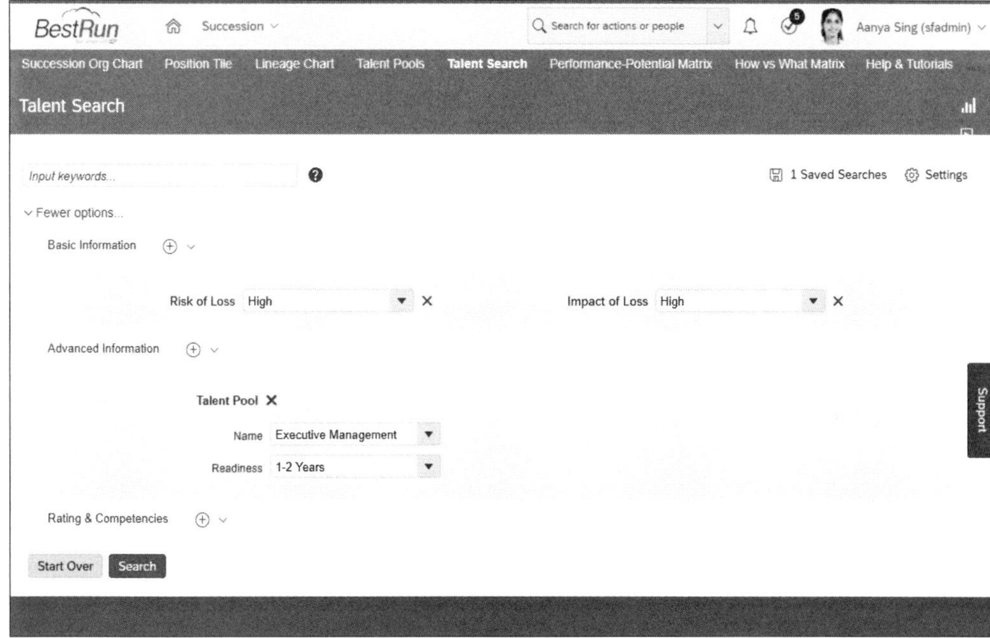

Figure 11.6 Talent Search

After you've entered search criteria, you can execute the search using the **Search** button.

Results

After a search has been executed, the results are displayed on a new screen. Each record in the results displays the name, photo, business card icon, and percentage of match, as shown in Figure 11.7. The search criteria can be saved and it is also possible to update the criteria of the search.

By selecting one or more results records, you are presented with four options:

- **Add to pool**: Add the employee(s) to a talent pool
- **Export**: Export the records to CSV
- **Compare**: Compare the employee(s)
- **Nominate**: Nominate the employee(s) as a successor

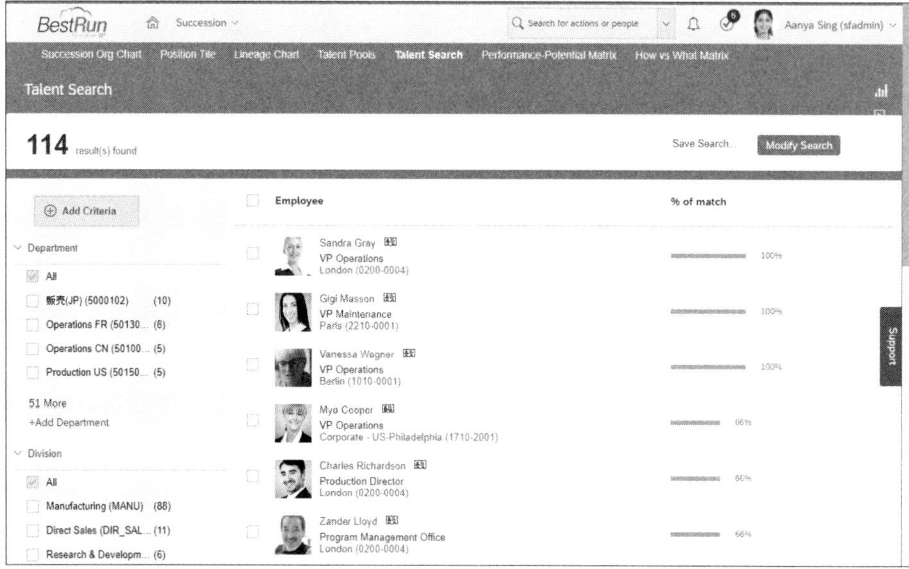

Figure 11.7 Talent Search Results

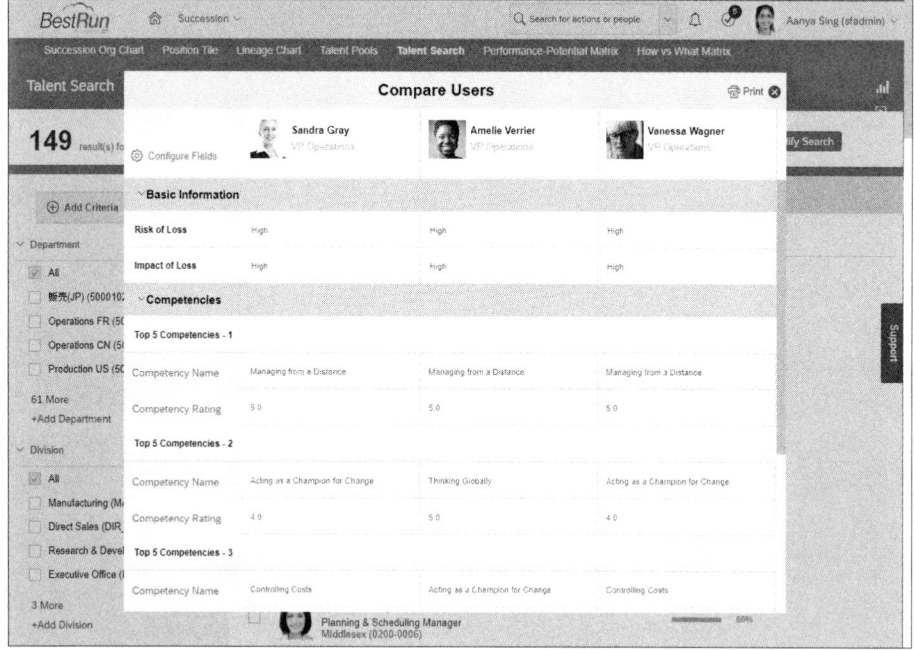

Figure 11.8 Compare Successors Feature

The most interesting feature of these is the **Compare** option. This option allows individuals selected in the search results to be compared for a variety of different attributes. By comparing multiple individuals, you ensure that the best possible candidates can be chosen. Figure 11.8 compares three employees. You can configure which fields you want to view by clicking on the **Configure Fields** option and also print the comparison.

After candidates have been identified, they can be nominated to talent pools or succession plans.

11.2.5 Position Tile View

The **Position Tile** view is an alternative to the Succession Org Chart that provides a tile-based list view of positions for succession planning. You access it by selecting **Position Tile** from the options at the top of the page of the Succession module.

The **Position Tile** view provides a more visual method of performing succession planning by showing all positions and successors, rather than using a hierarchy, as shown in Figure 11.9. This can be useful for succession planners of the entire organization, specific groups of positions, or teams.

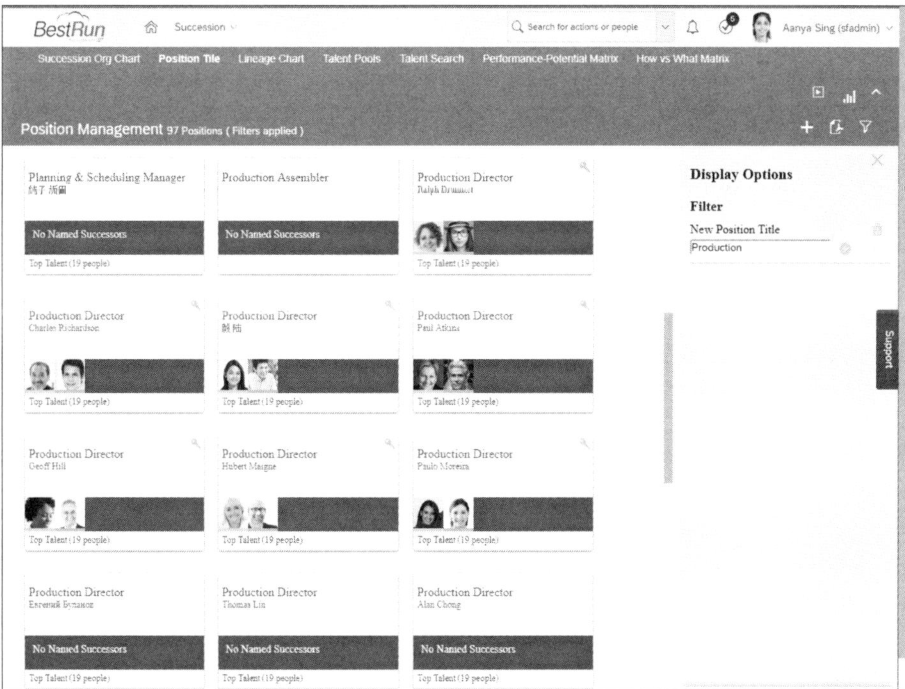

Figure 11.9 Position Tile View

Clicking a position shows an overview of the position where any assigned successors are displayed and their succession details (e.g., readiness) displayed. These details can also be edited. Successors can also be added and removed, and the talent card of any assigned successors can be viewed. Figure 11.10 shows the position overview.

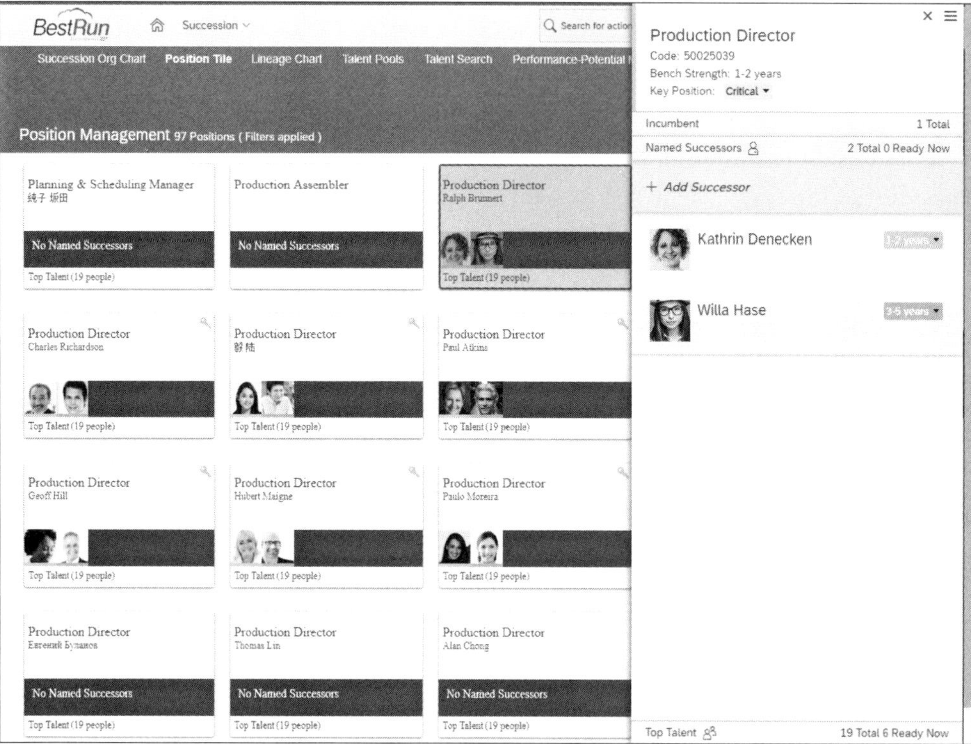

Figure 11.10 Position Overview

11.2.6 Talent Pools

Talent pools provide a way of classifying and aggregating individuals to groups so that they can be sourced for succession plans, talent searches, and development plans. This enables organizations to scale their succession planning effort and begin identifying, tracking, and preparing candidates for future roles, even though they may not be nominated as a successor to a position yet.

Talent pools are accessed by selecting **Talent Pools** from the options at the top of the page of the Succession module. The **Talent Pools** screen shows all of the talent pools that have been created, with an overview of the individuals assigned to each talent pool. You can create new talent pools or view existing talent pools. Figure 11.11 shows the **Talent Pools** screen.

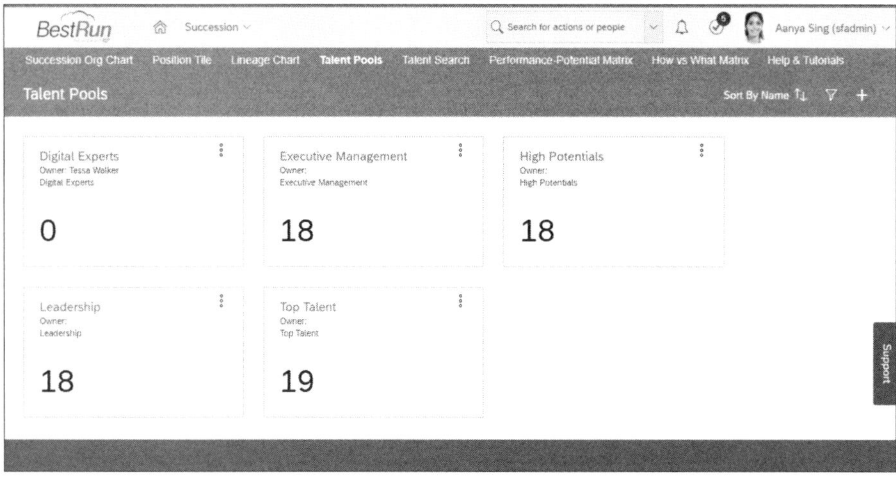

Figure 11.11 Talent Pools Application

You can also open a talent pool from the **Nomination Portlet** in the People Profile and from the Succession Org Chart from the talent card of any employee who is a member of that talent pool. In Figure 11.12, you can see the **Executive Management** talent pool.

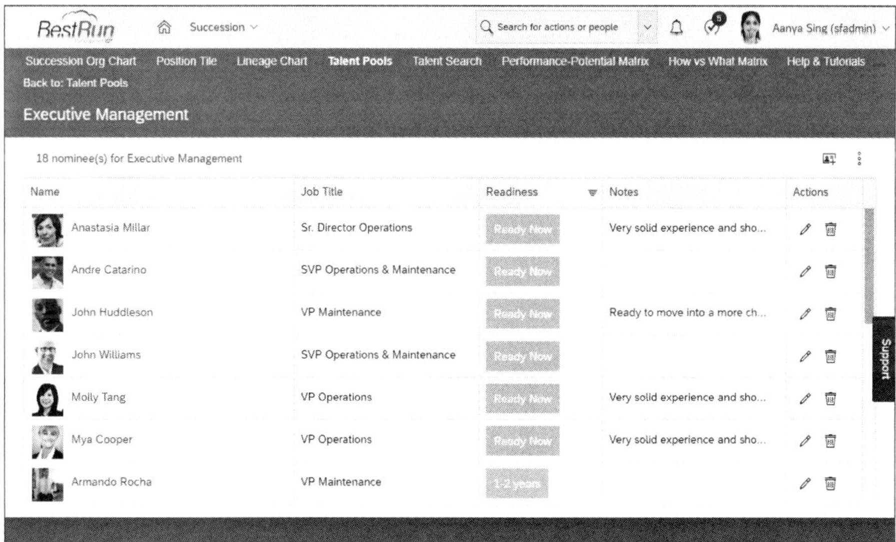

Figure 11.12 Executive Management Talent Pool

On this screen, the **Add Talent Pool Nominee** button can be used to add employees to the talent pool. When adding an employee, the readiness is selected and optionally a description can be entered. The menu button allows you to view the talent pool configuration and make any changes.

11.2.7 Position Management

Succession & Development can support various types of succession planning when it comes to positions, including role-person (sometimes called incumbent-based), legacy positions (essentially job codes), and Position Management.

Position Management considers positions as a separate entity from a job code and an employee. Position Management is part of the Metadata Framework (MDF) and is also used by Employee Central. Because succession planning is focused on positions and you may not use these objects or Employee Central in your SAP SuccessFactors system, it's necessary to have these objects within the MDF.

If the MDF is not used for positions, it is still possible to use position data. Positions can be created by synchronizing employee data using the **Sync Position Model with Employee Data** option under **Position Management** in the Admin Center. This creates both the positions and the reporting relationships between the positions. Position data can be imported in the Admin Center using the **Import and Export Data** option. The import file must include the position code, employee's ID, reporting position, and job code for vacant positions. Positions can also be marked as a key position within the import file.

We'll walk through creating and maintaining positions in the following sections.

Creating Positions

SAP SuccessFactors offers various ways of creating position objects if they don't exist, including the following:

- **Using the Succession Org Chart**
  Within the Succession Org Chart, you can create new positions by selecting the **Add Direct Report** option in the **Actions** dropdown menu on the position box of the parent position.
- **Importing position data**
  In the Admin Center, you can import position data by using the MDF data import/export option **Import and Export Data** under **Employee Files**.

- **Using the Admin Center**
  In the Admin Center, the option **Manage Positions** under **Employee Files** is used to both create and manage position objects.

Maintaining Positions

Positions can also be maintained through the Succession Org Chart and the MDF. Within the Succession Org Chart, the **Show and Edit Position** option in the actions dropdown of a position box allows the user to maintain information about that position (shown in Figure 11.13), while the **Delete Position** option from the same menu deletes that position. The MDF can also be used to edit position objects, as described previously.

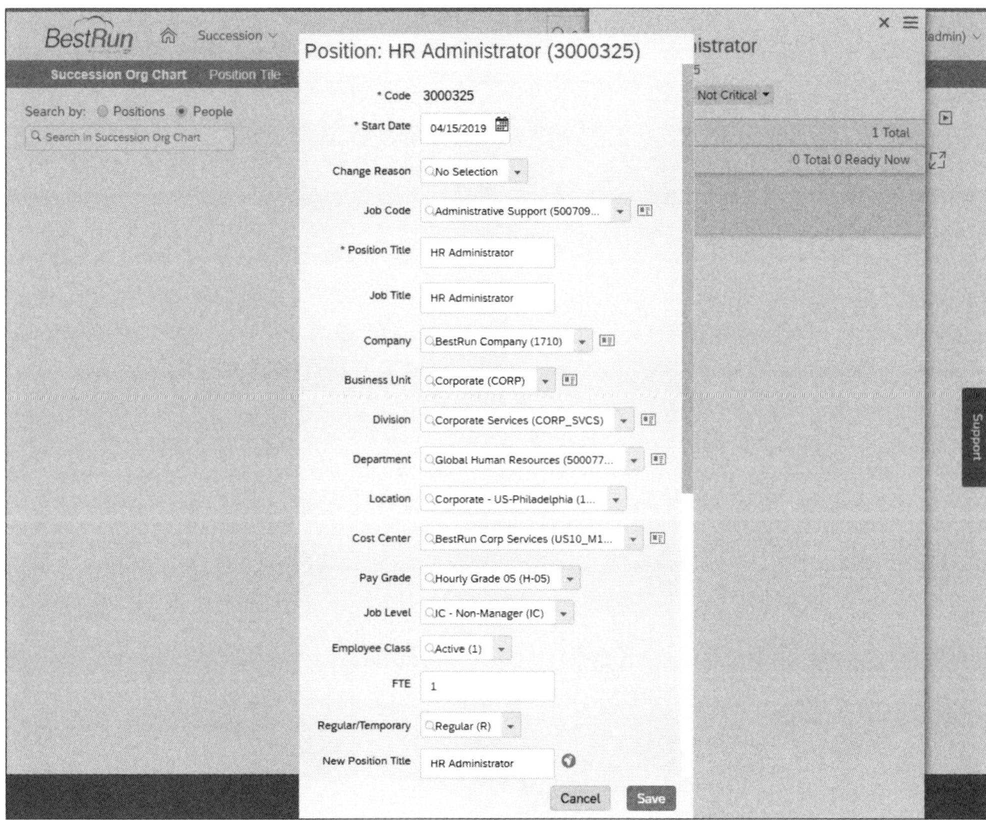

Figure 11.13 Edit Position Window in the Succession Org Chart

Further Resources

More details about Position Management can be found in the guide *Employee Central Position Management* at the SAP Help Portal under the SAP SuccessFactors Employee Central product page.

11.2.8 Reporting and Analytics

There are a number of tools in Succession that can be used for reporting, such as talent search (which we covered in Section 11.2.4) and nomination history (which we'll discuss in Section 11.3). In addition to these tools, ad hoc reporting can be used to report on Succession data, and the built-in insights (see Figure 11.14) provide real-time analytics at your fingertips.

Figure 11.14 Succession Insights

The ad hoc reporting feature in SAP SuccessFactors allows you to combine specific succession data with demographic or other organizational data to produce your own meaningful reports. From here, users can create their own ad hoc reports based on criteria chosen from a list of more than 250 different fields for each of the succession planning domains:

- Succession (incumbent-based nominations)
- Inclusive succession (position-based nominations)

- Succession history (incumbent-based nominations)
- Succession history (position-based nominations)

A number of succession analytics are available in SAP SuccessFactors Workforce Analytics (see Chapter 12).

11.3 Nominating Successors

After you've identified the supply of talent, you can begin the process of nominating successors. In Succession & Development, nominating successors is form based; you must configure and assign a template in the Admin Center before nominating can begin.

In the Succession module, functionality is provided to seek and nominate individuals *for* a specific position (i.e., from the position perspective) or nominate a specific individual *to* a position (i.e., from the employee perspective). Managers are responsible for nominating successors for positions within their teams, and they can also nominate their direct reports as successors for other positions.

Successors can be nominated to positions in a number of different ways:

- Succession Org Chart
- Lineage Chart
- Position Tile view
- People Profile

In the Succession Org Chart, Lineage Chart, and Position Tile view, an individual can be nominated as a successor to the position by clicking **Add Successor** in the **Named Successors** box on the position card. In the People Profile, you can nominate an individual to a position by selecting the **Add Nomination** button in the **Nomination Portlet**.

The process of nominating a successor doesn't differ greatly between the position perspective or from the employee perspective. However, adding a successor using the Succession Org Chart, Lineage Chart, or Position Tile view gives the optimal experience.

When assigning successors to positions in the Succession Org Chart, the system will automatically show a list of recommended successors to add. This can be seen in Figure 11.15.

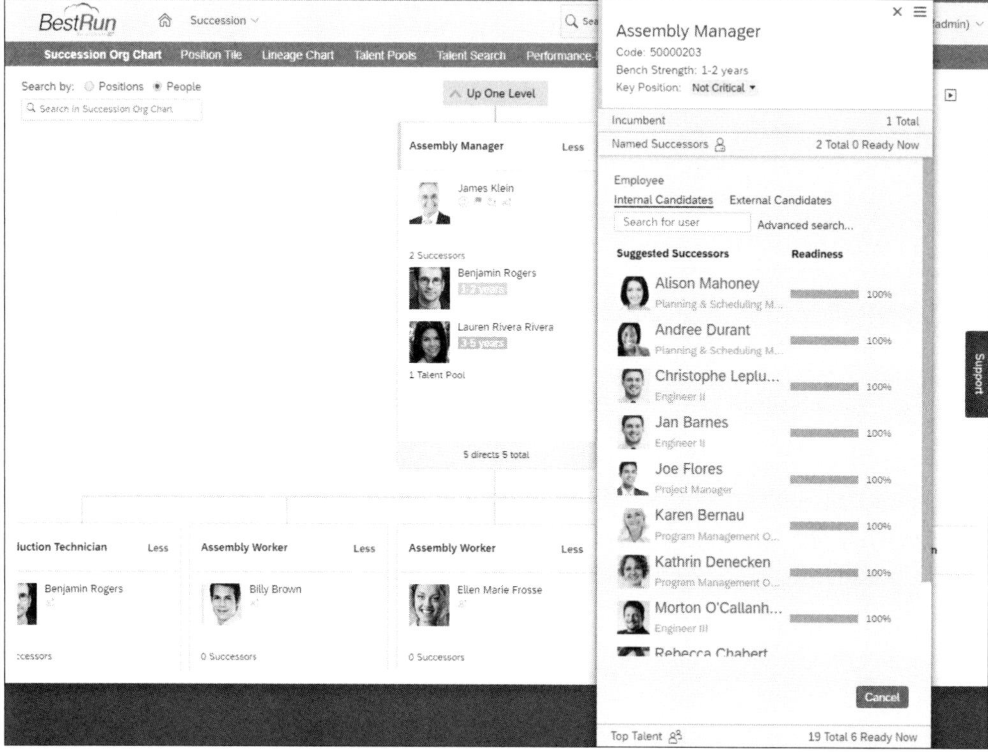

Figure 11.15 Assigning a Successor in the Succession Org Chart

During the nomination process, you can identify a position either by searching or browsing through job families. You can select **Readiness**, assign a ranking, and enter any notes as part of the successor assignment.

A useful feature of Succession & Development is your ability to nominate an external candidate as a successor. This can be a job candidate from Recruiting or a defined individual, such as a candidate that has been headhunted outside of the standard recruitment process. External candidates are nominated during successor assignment via the Succession Org Chart position card by selecting **External Candidates** and either searching for a candidate or adding a new candidate.

Nomination history can be viewed for a position by selecting **Nomination History** in the action dropdown menu of a position box in the **Succession Org Chart**. Figure 11.16 shows the nomination history for the **Assembly Manager** position.

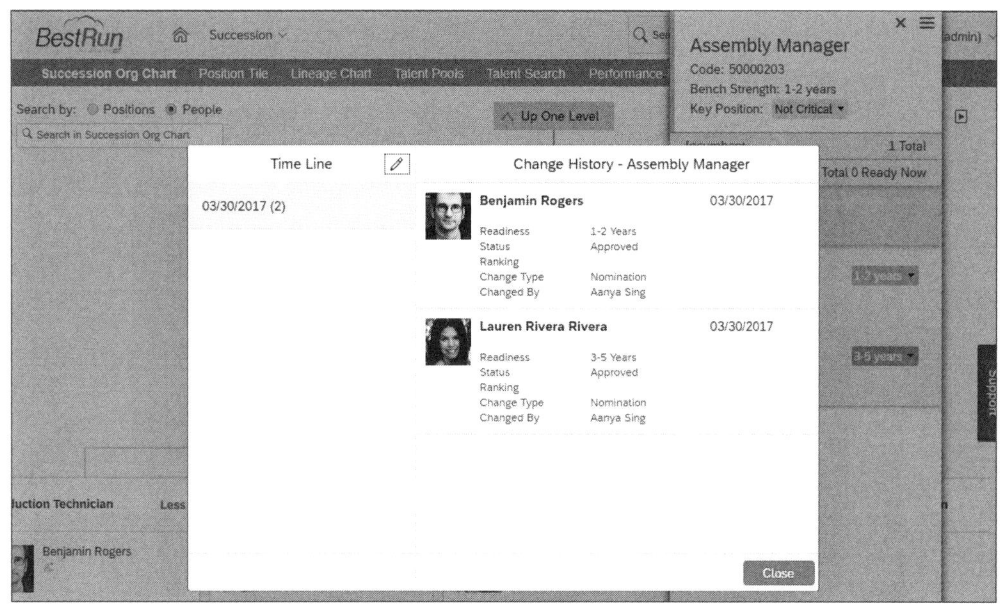

Figure 11.16 Nomination History

11.4 Ongoing Development

The CDP module, usually known simply as Development, provides the ability to create development plans, link them to career plans, and plan learning activities to support them. This makes the Development module an actionable and powerful tool for companies to close the talent gap and utilize and retain talent with high merit for succession planning and overall personnel development activities.

Development plans are similar to goal plans found in the Performance & Goals solution—both technically and functionally—although the key difference is that goal plans are job-based and typically a year in length, while development plans are career-based and usually span a multiyear period (e.g., five years).

Development activities are accessed by selecting **Development** in the navigation menu. There are four parts to the Development module:

- Development plan
- Career worksheet
- Career path
- Mentoring

Now let's take a look at how each of these supports Development activities.

11.4.1 Development Plan

After successors have been assigned to succession plans, a suitable development plan is required to ensure the development and readiness of the successors. The development plans are accessible by the individuals, as well as their managers.

Development plans comprise *development goals*, which are oriented toward developing skills and competencies in the chosen direction for career progression. Unlike goal plans in Performance & Goals, these plans can span multiple years. The Development module comes with a comprehensive and integrated design that enables organizations to accomplish this very important aspect of ensuring that they have the right talent in the right position.

Figure 11.17 illustrates a development plan and its various goals.

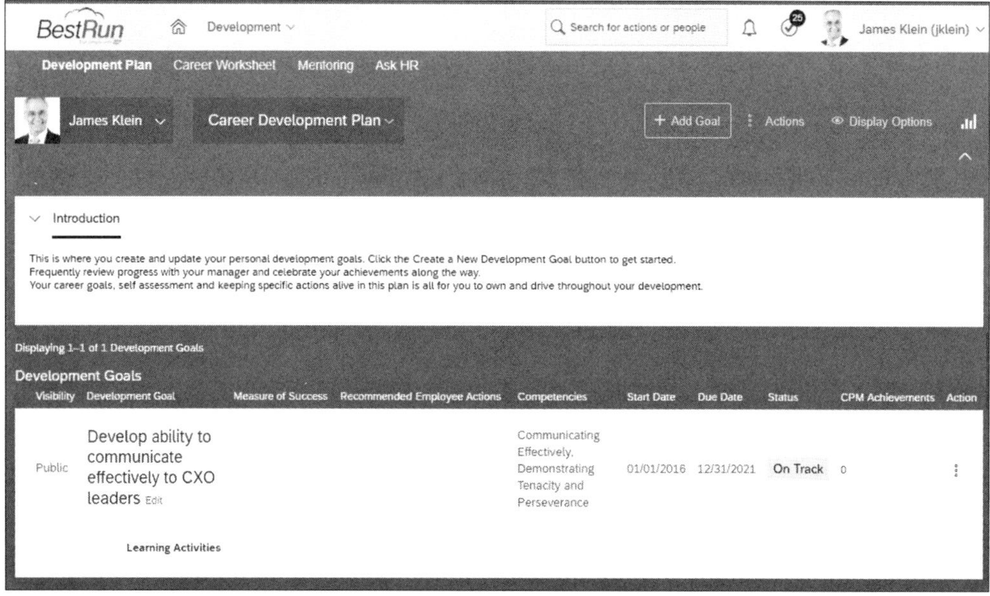

Figure 11.17 Example of a Development Plan

Like the goal plan in Performance & Goals (covered in detail in Chapter 6), the development plan can be created from a template and configured according to the needs of the organization. Various information of a development goal can be displayed or hidden by selecting it in the **Display Options** section. This includes **Alerts**, **Visibility**, **Measure of Success**, **Competencies**, **Start Date**, **Due Date**, **Status**, and **Learning Activities**.

Note

The development plan does not integrate with the goals or goal plan in Performance & Goals, since these two sets of goals and plans have different purposes. However, achievements from Continuous Performance Management can be added as development goals on the development plan.

Within each development plan, it's also possible for a manager to select their own development plan or the development plan of any of their direct or matrix reports.

Development goals are added to a development plan by clicking the **Add Goal** button and selecting the **Create a New Development Goal** option. This opens the **Add Development Goal** window (see Figure 11.18), where details of the new development goal can be defined.

Several different attributes can be chosen for a development goal, but only the **Goal** description and **Competencies** fields are compulsory:

- **Visibility**
  Defines whether the development goal is publicly visible or visible only to the individual and the corresponding manager
- **Development Goal**
  Freeform text box to describe the development goal
- **Measure of Success**
  Freeform text box to describe the measure of success for the development goal
- **Start Date**
  The start date of the development goal
- **Due Date**
  The date by which the development goal should be completed
- **Status**
  The status of the development goal, which can be set and changed throughout its lifecycle to one of the different predefined statuses
- **Competencies**
  The one or more competencies from the competency library that is/are gained after the development goal is completed
- **Purpose**
  Whether the development goal is for a current role, future role, or general skill set

The **Development Goal** and **Measure of Success** fields feature both a spell checker and the Legal Scan feature. The values for **Status** are defined in the development plan template.

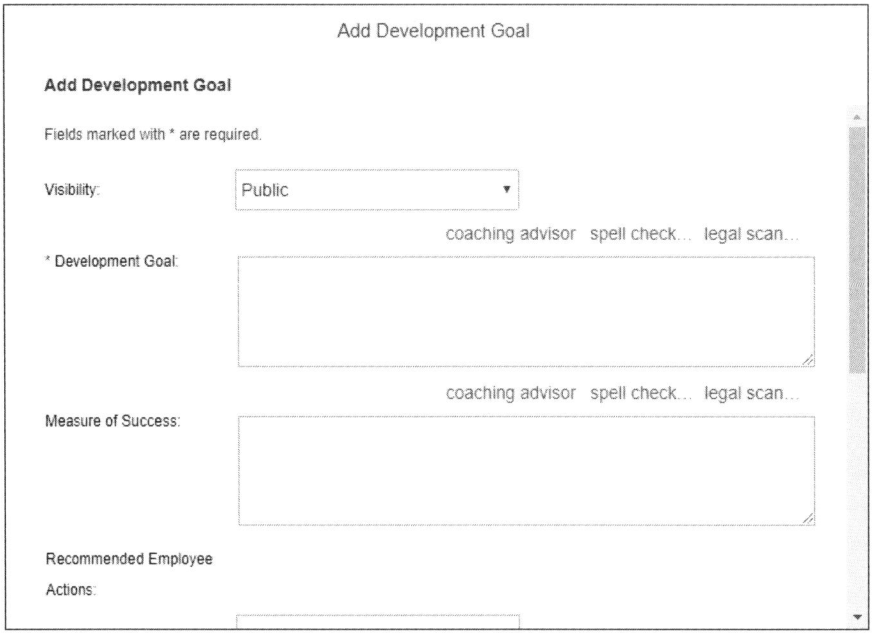

Figure 11.18 Add Development Goal Window

You can also copy development goals from another development goal template by clicking the **Add Goal** button and selecting the **Copy From Other Development Goal Plan** option.

After you've created a development goal, you can assign one or more learning activities to it via the **Add New Learning Activity** button found on the development goal. Learning activities can be selected from the learning catalog, or custom learning activities can be created. This provides organizations with the possibility to assign learning to aid the development of the required competencies of a position for which the individual is a successor, or just to increase their productivity within their existing role.

Development goals can be edited, removed, or added as required. Editing a development goal—including changing its status—can be done freely at any time. This enables development goals to be altered as an employee develops or changes roles, and supports tracking of the current status. The audit history of a development goal can be displayed by selecting **View Development Goal Detail** in the **Actions** menu of the development goal.

Managers and employees can view the development goals in People Profile in the **Development Objectives** block (shown in Figure 11.19), which increases visibility and actionable analytics to the career development processes. Development goals can also be added here.

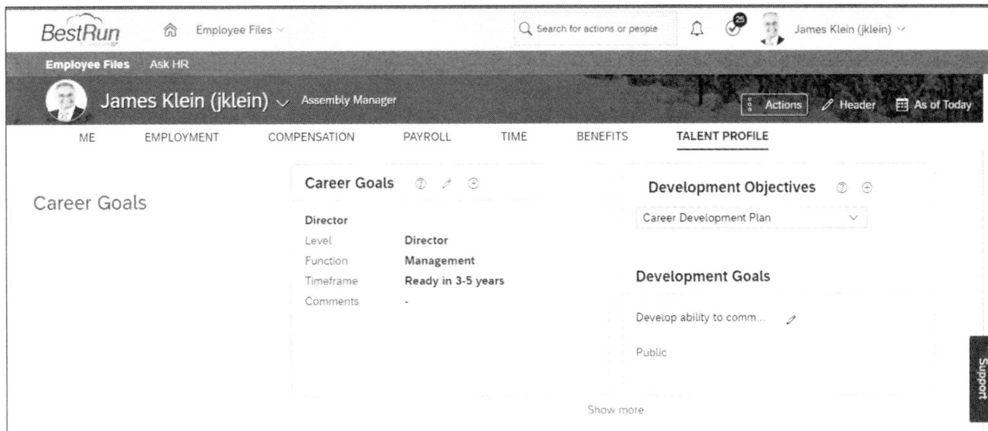

Figure 11.19 Development Objectives Block

To maximize returns from a development plan, it's imperative that you also align it with the individual's career plan. We'll explore the career worksheet and how it enables organizations to integrate the development plan with the career path of its talent next.

11.4.2 Career Worksheet

The *career worksheet* is the main focus of the CDP module and serves as an actionable view of an employee's career path, current and future roles, and existing and required competencies. Because it's linked to the development plan, it's a powerful tool to align your talent's development goals with the planned career progression for current and/or future goals. You can assess the readiness of your talent for a particular role that they have been nominated for using the career worksheet (see Figure 11.20). If no career worksheet exists, the user can perform a self-assessment of their current job role.

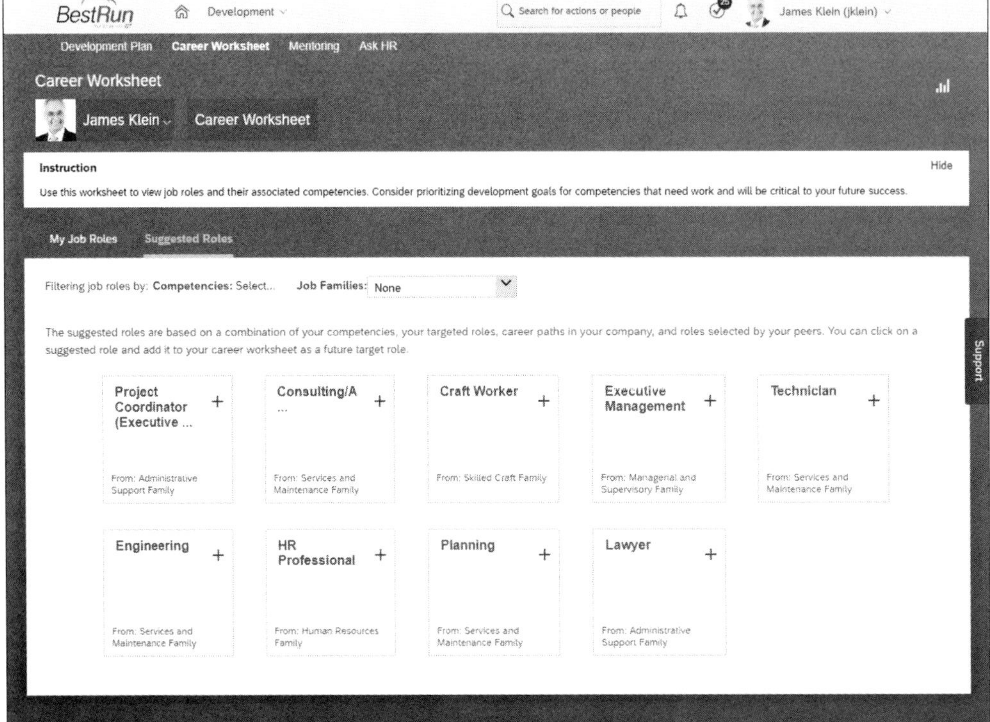

Figure 11.20 Career Worksheet

The career worksheet allows an individual or the individual's manager to map out the individual's career by adding potential jobs, viewing competency gaps, and adding development goals aligned with the competencies required to ensure the readiness of the future role. This is based on the assumption that a prior activity has been performed to add competencies for various job roles for your organization. New competencies added to a job role are immediately available for consumption in the Development module.

The **My Job Roles** tab on the **Career Worksheet** page, as shown in Figure 11.21, displays the job roles that the individual is considering. You can switch between the job roles being considered and current job roles using the options at the top of this area (**Job Roles I'm Considering** and **My Current Roles**). For each job role that is being considered, a readiness percentage is displayed alongside a color-coded measurement. Additional job roles to be considered can be added by searching for them in the search box. You can also browse job roles or display suggested roles, both by selecting the relevant hyperlink options under the search box.

The box immediately below the **My Job Roles** tab shows the competencies for the current selected job role (see Figure 11.21). The competencies for each job role can be switched by selecting the job role in the **My Job Roles** tab. Competencies are listed by groupings. The first group is the competencies of the job role that require development activities (e.g., those wherein the employee has not yet met the competency requirement). The second group is those competencies for which the employee has met the requirements.

Each competency is displayed with the individual's current and expected rating. You can view details of each competency as a pop-up by hovering the mouse over the **Competency Description** icon to the right of the competency name. You can add development goals for each competency by selecting the **Add Development Goal** icon above the words **Development Goals** to the right of the competency rating. The development goals added here also get reflected in the development plan.

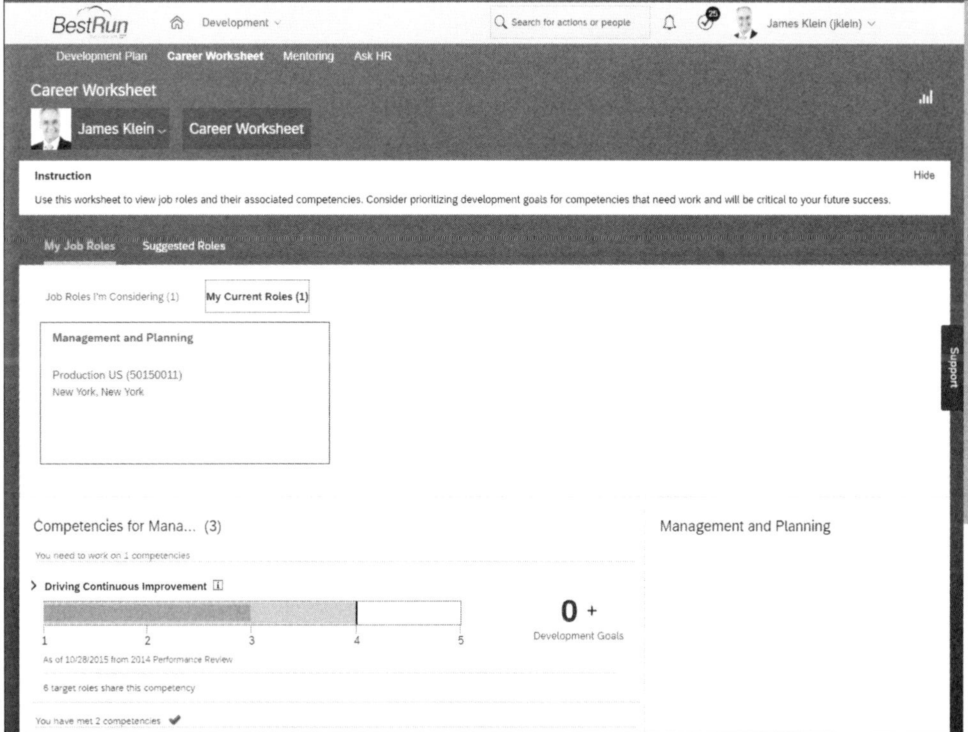

Figure 11.21 Job Role Details

11.4.3 Career Path

One of the useful features of the Development module is the ability to view the career path of the job role, shown in Figure 11.22, which you display by selecting the **Career Path** option at the top of the screen.

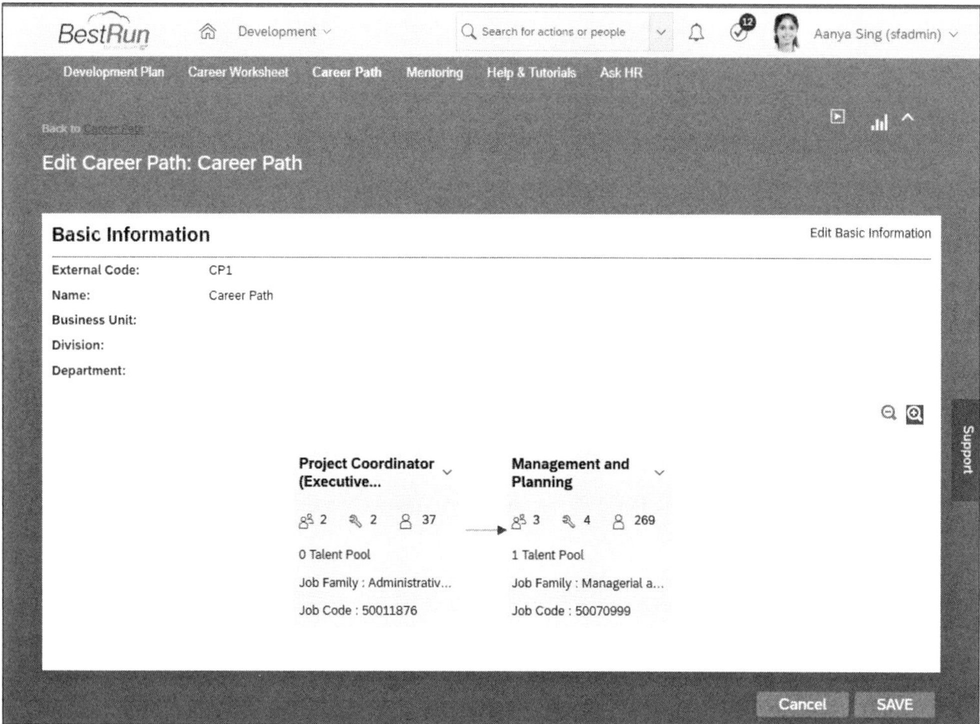

Figure 11.22 Career Path

Here you can create your own career paths by building out the roles that you want to work toward to develop your career. You can create as many career paths as you wish. A career path is created by clicking **Create New Career Path**. Here, you can add a role and then add roles that lead to that role or lead from that role. You can also perform maintenance on the career path.

11.4.4 Mentoring

When you run mentoring programs, the Development module gives you the ability to manage these programs in SAP SuccessFactors. Mentoring programs are created in the Admin Center and accessed by employees through the **Mentoring** page.

Mentoring programs are created and managed in the Admin Center in **Manage Mentoring Programs**, which can be seen in Figure 11.23. Here you can create, maintain, and launch mentoring programs. Mentors and mentees can be assigned to each mentoring program.

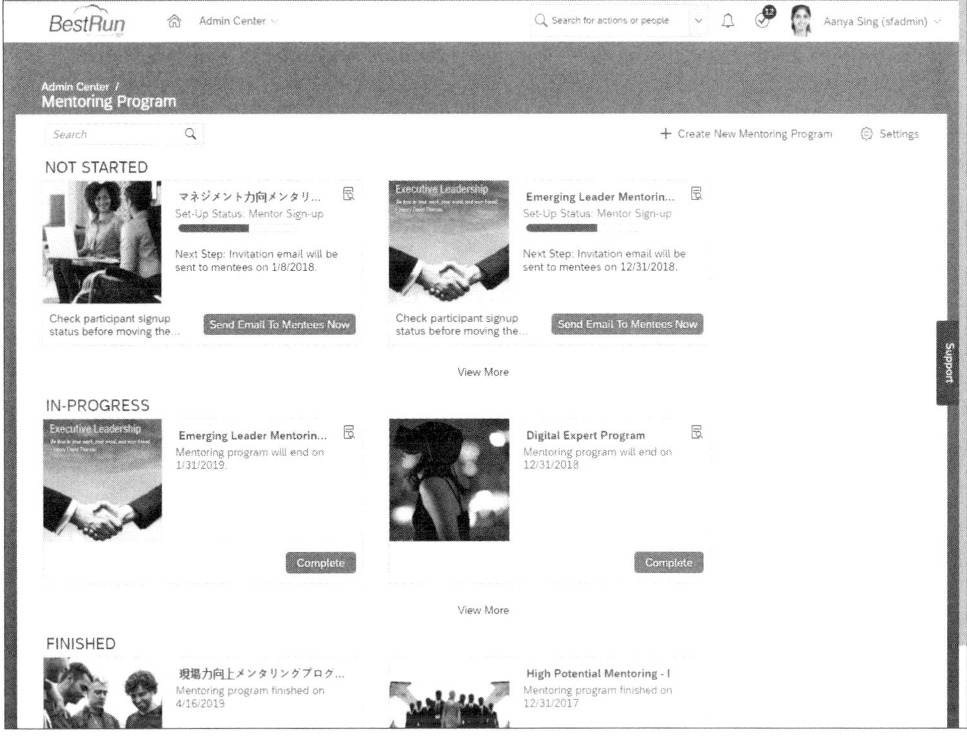

Figure 11.23 The Manage Mentoring Programs Page

You can create three different types of mentoring programs:

- **Supervised**
  Admin invites mentors and mentees to the program and mentee sign-up begins once mentor sign-up ends. These programs are time limited.
- **Unsupervised**
  Admin invites mentors and mentees to the program and mentees send requests directly to mentors. These programs are time limited.
- **Open enrollment**
  Anybody can join the program and mentees send requests directly to mentors. There is no time limit to the program.

New mentoring programs are created by selecting **Create New Mentoring Program** in **Manage Mentoring Programs**. When creating new mentoring programs, you have various options throughout the creation wizard. The wizard takes you through four main steps of creating a mentoring program:

1. **Mentoring program details**
   In this step (shown in Figure 11.24), you define the name and description, set limits (mentee per mentor and mentor per mentee), set whether to allow participants to end mentoring relationships, and define the following dates for supervised and unsupervised mentoring programs:
   - Start and end of the mentoring program
   - Start dates of mentor and mentee sign-up period
   - Start date of mentor/mentee matching
2. **Mentors**
   In this step, you select mentors. You can search by name or by group.
3. **Mentees**
   In this step, you select mentees. You can search by name or by group.
4. **Sign-up form**
   In this step, you define the questions to go onto the mentor and mentee sign-up pages. You can also configure the email notification that will be sent to mentors and mentees prior to the sign-up date.

You'll end up at the **Summary** page, where you review the details of the mentoring program and launch it.

The questions on the sign-up forms allow you to use a picklist or a free text for your question response. You can then define a question for the mentor and/or the mentee.

Once a mentoring program has been created, the system is set up to automatically send out the emails to the mentors and mentees on the sign-up dates. You can also manually send them out earlier if you want.

When a mentor or mentee receives an email, they can login and navigate to the **Mentoring** page. There are three pages available:

- **My Mentoring Programs**: Programs that you are a mentor or mentee in
- **Invitations**: Invitations to join a mentoring program (seen in Figure 11.25)
- **Open Enrollment**: Mentoring programs that are open for enrollment for anyone

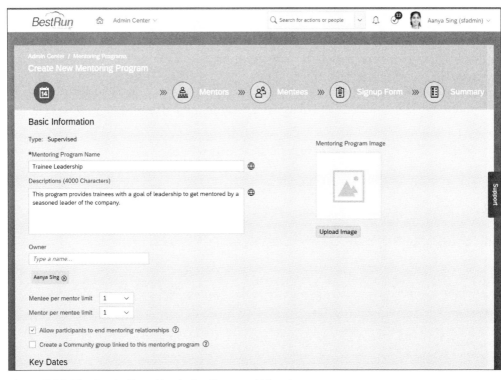

Figure 11.24 The Create New Mentoring Program Wizard

Figure 11.25 Mentoring Program Invitiations

When an employee has invitations to join a mentoring program, they click the **Sign Up As Mentor** or **Sign Up As Mentee** button. They will then see details of the program and can proceed to the second step to answer the questions that were set when the program was setup. They can then select to see recommend matches or manually search for a mentor/mentee, before making a selection.

Once the sign-up process is completed, then the program administrator can review the mentor and mentee matches, accept suitable matches, and manually match mentors and mentees. After this, the program can be started.

When a program is running, mentors and mentees can record their activities. Figure 11.26 shows a running program with an activity set.

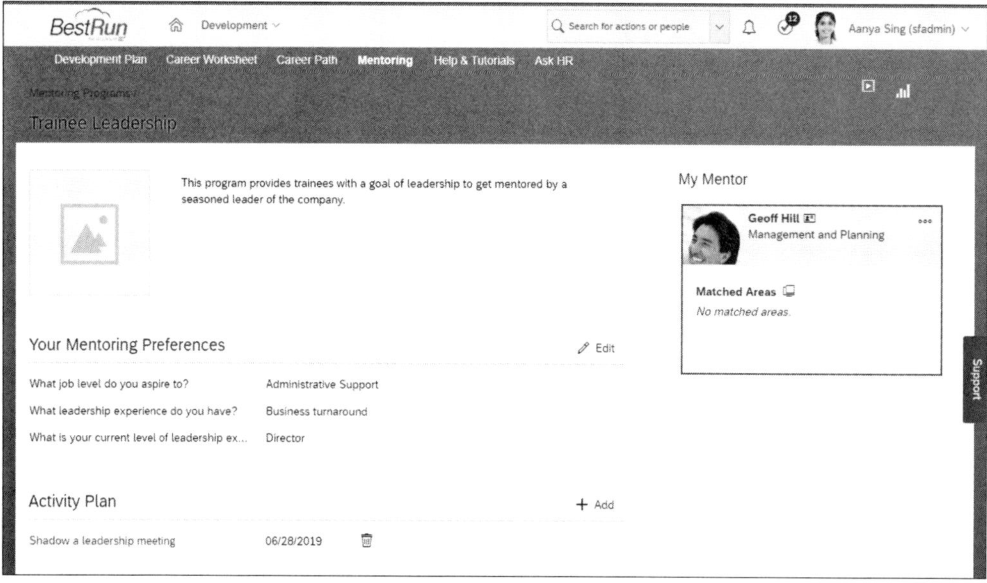

Figure 11.26 An Active Mentoring Program

When your program ends, you can end it in **Manage Mentoring Programs**.

11.5 Implementation Tips

Succession planning and CDP both have significant impacts on your long-term workforce planning. Here are a few tips that will help you get the best out of your implementation of Succession & Development:

- **Process**
  Succession planning and CDP are 90 percent process and 10 percent technology.

The technology provides a great platform to manage your processes in a systematic and aligned methodology and brings capabilities you don't have otherwise, but the focal point of your succession planning program should be your processes. The system should follow your process.

Define the factors, criteria, and characteristics that successors need to have, how you identify key positions, definitions (e.g., how does someone qualify as having a "risk of loss" or what is the criteria to become part of a talent pool), and what is needed to build development plans for successors.

- **Succession Org Chart**
  The Succession Org Chart is your focal point for succession planning. It gives you access to the succession plans across the company and coupled with the Lineage Chart can give you a full chain of succession. It also enables you to find and nominate successors. Typically, it will be your entry point for succession planning.
- **Information**
  Information is critical in a process like this, so you should make sure that People Profile data is well grouped together so it can be accessed quickly. Make use of icons in the Succession Org Chart, position card, and talent card.

  You should also design your talent card to focus on the key data needed to make decisions during the process.

11.6 Summary

Succession & Development is a twofold solution for managing organizational sustainability through succession planning and CDP. Its core functionality enables full management of the succession planning process and of employee career paths. It also enables employees to make choices about their own careers and actively develop their own skills and competencies.

In this chapter, we've learned how the Succession module supports the full succession planning process through the Succession Org Chart, matrices, talent search, and talent pools, as well as by leveraging Position Management. We also covered the reporting possibilities that exist in the solution.

We explored the Development module and how it supports competency growth and career planning for all employees, as well as those planned for critical or leadership positions. We looked at how all of this integrates with other solutions within the SAP SuccessFactors HCM Suite.

In the next chapter, we take a look at the Workforce Analytics module and discover a world of data, analytics, and metrics that can significantly enhance your HR decision-making.

Chapter 12
Workforce Analytics

SAP SuccessFactors Workforce Analytics is a purpose-built application that offers human resources (HR) and managers across the company a robust set of metrics and analytical models that are used to influence talent management decisions. Unique to the application is a set of metrics packs that ensure a "single version of the truth" and confidence in the data.

12

Using data for talent management decisions is one of the most exciting and important opportunities for the modern HR function. Yet, many organizations struggle to translate raw data on their workforce into fact-based insights that leaders can consistently use. SAP SuccessFactors Workforce Analytics provides visibility into workforce issues, risks, and opportunities, and links HR initiatives to organizational strategy through standardized HR metrics, key performance indicators, predictive analytics, and interactive dashboards.

The role of HR can commonly be thought of as managing an organization's human capital assets toward any of four principal outcomes: generating revenue, minimizing expenses, mitigating risks, and executing strategic plans. The function pursues these goals in an era of increasing global complexity, workforce agility, and dependence on technology as a means to create competitive advantage. Data and analytics have become a critical element in how HR measures progress towards its objectives.

In this chapter, we'll provide you with an understanding of the multitude of analytic capabilities delivered by Workforce Analytics, including standardized metrics packs and data governance, the benchmarking program, and reporting functionality and advanced analytical tools. The chapter concludes with a description of the implementation methodology.

12.1 Workforce Analytics Basics

Before diving into a review of Workforce Analytics, it is important to understand what workforce analytics is, and is not.

Essentially, analytics is a methodology for creating insights on how investments in human capital contribute to the success of those four outcomes. By applying statistical methods to integrated HR, talent management, financial, and operational data, HR analytics could be used to measure investments in, for example, reskilling that will deliver the right competencies to support a new revenue model, using data-driven insights to modify the training offering as sales results emerge. The effectiveness of workforce analytics could therefore be measured as whether it adds business value through better decision-making.

This is quite different from HR reporting, which is concerned with the efficient delivery of transactional data, often real-time, and for which the measure of success is the speed, not necessarily the business value, of this information.

For more than 15 years, Workforce Analytics has been the benchmark for purpose-built analytics applications in HR, making it a key differentiator in the SAP SuccessFactors product suite. By empowering companies to integrate, validate, and visualize the billions of transactional records commonly stored in today's talent management systems, HR users and their peers across the company can obtain a more holistic picture of their workforce, as well as identify areas of opportunity to drive actions resulting in either cost savings or increased revenues.

The Workforce Analytics solution clears the hurdles commonly experienced in launching and sustaining a workforce analytics program by guiding you in what to measure and how to verify the accuracy of your data. It also provides methods for utilizing the analysis, visualizing results, and recommending actions. The process of telling stories with data enables HR to combine quantitative information with qualitative knowledge, thus improving the ability of HR practitioners to deliver insights in a compelling manner. Additionally, companies that utilize Workforce Analytics can leverage a standardized metrics catalog to compare individual results against various categories of benchmarks, such as industry, geographic region, organization size, or revenue.

In this section, we'll introduce the fundamental pieces of Workforce Analytics, including how it transforms raw data into insights, the concept of metrics packs, and key data processes.

12.1.1 Workforce Analytics on SQL versus SAP HANA

Prior to 2017, Workforce Analytics was implemented solely on Microsoft SQL server. A second option was then introduced: Workforce Analytics on SAP HANA, specifically for customers using SAP SuccessFactors Employee Central for core HR.

The key advantages of deploying Workforce Analytics on SAP HANA are daily data updates, support for weekly and daily time models in Query Workspace/Investigate, and full support for development in a test environment. Other differences with Workforce Analytics on SAP HANA include:

- **Prerequisites**
  This deployment option is only available to Employee Central customers and data can only be sourced from SAP SuccessFactors systems. In contrast, Workforce Analytics on SQL can extract data from any core human resource information system (HRIS) (SAP ERP, PeopleSoft, Oracle, and so on) and the data universe is potentially unlimited—customers have included data from third-party systems, homegrown tools, spreadsheets, and even pieces of paper.
- **Metrics packs**
  The scope of the customer implementation is limited to the following metrics packs, all of which must be sourced from SAP SuccessFactors systems (no third-party data is permitted, in contrast to the SQL version, as noted previously):
  - Core Workforce and Mobility
  - Performance Management
  - Goals Management
  - Succession Management
  - Recruiting Management
  - Compensation Management
- **Implementation partners**
  In contrast to Workforce Analytics on SQL, for which only SAP SuccessFactors can manage the data extract, transform, load (ETL) process, partners with certified consultants are able to use a multitenant configuration tool to deploy Workforce Analytics on SAP HANA from end to end (including the data ETL portion).

The following features are available in Workforce Analytics on SAP HANA:

- Measure template pages
- Query Workspace/Investigate
- Online Report Designer
- Report Distributor
- Tree security
- Drill-to-Detail

- Export to Excel
- Daily incremental data synchronization
- Support for separate test and production instances
- Benchmarks (for measures)
- Custom calculations, members, and sets
- Analytics tile and insights panel
- Connector to SAP Analytics Cloud

The following features are not yet fully supported in Workforce Analytics on SAP HANA:

- Analytics Workspace
- Strategic workforce planning
- Benchmarks (for dimensions)

Note

At the time of writing (fall 2019), SAP SuccessFactors is making a significant investment in upgrading the capabilities of the Workforce Analytics product, combining the data engine, metrics packs, and HR content with powerful visualization tools offered by SAP Analytics Cloud. The next generation of capabilities for analytics may include expanded benchmarking datasets, more flexible templates for workforce planning, and smart investigation tools. The official roadmap will specific how these concepts will be delivered in future releases of what is being termed "People Analytics – Advanced".

12.1.2 Metrics Packs for Workforce Analytics

In this section, we'll examine the foundation of the Workforce Analytics solution. All Workforce Analytics implementations begin with the base metrics pack, known as Core Workforce and Mobility, which is used as a foundation to extend into more specific functional areas (for example, SAP SuccessFactors Learning, SAP SuccessFactors Performance & Goals, SAP SuccessFactors Recruiting, and so on) through additional metrics packs.

The concept for, and standards contained within, the metrics packs were established by Infohrm, a company acquired by SuccessFactors in 2010 (SuccessFactors subsequently being purchased by SAP). Based on more than 30 years of global consulting experience in the fields of workforce analytics and planning, Infohrm was an influential presence in the development of "content"—metrics, formulas, definitions, and interpretations—specifically for analytics software.

Metrics packs serve a valuable purpose, often overlooked in the race to finish technology implementations on time. Rather than starting with a blank sheet of paper, customers can take advantage of hundreds of time-tested metrics, each with their own reasoning and logic. Of course, customers can add their own metrics, or change the formulas, but many defer to the published metrics, asking, "Why do we need to be different to every other organization?"

Let's take a closer look at metrics packs, their implementation, and their methodology in the following sections.

Metrics Packs Benefits

Despite the availability of systems that continuously collect and store workforce data, many HR functions struggle to derive reliable insights that can be applied to talent management decisions. The following are several of the most common reasons for why this is the case; if any of these resonate with you, consider evaluating the Workforce Analytics product for your organization:

- **Data accessibility**
  While HRIT certainly has access to talent management data, experience has shown that gaining consistent access to non-HR systems (finance, operations) has proven difficult, even when a strong business case (such as wishing to measure retail store manager performance or understand workforce capacity) exists. Having pre-built templates for financial data that indicate how the data will be transformed and published may help gain access to that information.
- **Data quality**
  Talent data is one of the most difficult datasets to manage. Data entry is often subjective and suffers from regional variations (for example, *ethnic minority* would be defined differently in Australia than Canada). Even calculating headcount can be problematic, when taking into account temporary labor, interns, or staff on leave. Consequently, business leaders question HR's data validity and credibility, due in part to the lack of standardization around HR metrics.
- **Data preparation**
  One of the most time-consuming aspects of transforming raw HR data into consumable analytics is the work needed to prepare that dataset—joining, cleaning, and normalizing massive amounts of data, all while mapping every employee

record to multiple organizational structures. The data ETL processes that underpin the metrics packs are designed to simplify these activities, reducing the burden placed on HR to manage data and redirecting their time away from data production to data consumption.

- **Incomplete logic**
  Lack of access is compounded when seeking to make informed decisions based on all available insights. Business intelligence (BI) tools are built for finance and IT departments and may not contain sufficient data or logic appropriate for analyzing employee issues.
- **Analytical capability and capacity**
  While conventional wisdom suggests that HR practitioners are not as analytical as their counterparts in other functions, the lack of capacity—time available to investigate workforce trends with data—is increasingly a challenge in complex, fast-paced organizations.

Workforce Analytics is designed to address each of these challenges, and metrics packs play a key role in minimizing the effects of these issues.

Implementing Core Workforce and Mobility

The first phase of any Workforce Analytics implementation begins with the Core Workforce and Mobility metrics pack. Depending on implementation providers and methodologies, this may take anywhere from two to four months.

This metrics pack consists of a specific set of data sourced from an HRIS and includes more than 130 input and calculated/derived metrics for headcount, staffing rates, terminations, movements, and hires. In addition, the pack typically includes at least 20 analysis options (also referred to as dimensions, analysis options, or dimension hierarchies), which are used to "slice and dice" the core workforce and mobility metrics. Examples include age, gender, diversity, job family, pay band, and many dimensions typically housed in the HRIS. The final component of the Core Workforce and Mobility implementation includes organizational structures of which the four most common are cost center, supervisor/reports to, location, and organizational unit. We will delve deeper into both analysis options and organizational structures at the end of this section.

Let's begin by deconstructing the base metrics pack, which forms the foundation of Workforce Analytics. The Core Workforce and Mobility metrics pack supports the necessary data items required to generate measures and reporting structures for a comprehensive analytics solution.

Note

The Core Workforce and Mobility metrics pack should not be confused with "all data in an HRIS." It primarily consists of measures in the Workforce Profile and workforce mobility categories and includes a limited number of measures in the Workforce Productivity, Workforce Compensation and Benefits, and Staffing Function categories. If clients choose to purchase additional metrics packs, such as the Payroll and Benefits metrics pack or the Financial metrics pack, these categories become more comprehensive.

The standard metrics included in the Core Workforce and Mobility metrics pack are bucketed into operational measure categories and associated subcategories:

- **Workforce Profile**
  Describe the organization's workforce using a range of enterprise and personal characteristics such as organizational structure, age, employment status, occupational group, tenure, gender, and diversity. These measures provide insight into workforce demographics and their implications on workforce skill and experience levels. Headcount measures include start- and end-of-period headcount, average headcount, and full-time equivalent (FTE).
- **Workforce Productivity**
  Provide macro indicators are helpful when calculating the cost of human capital outcomes, such as terminations. This section combines a range of input and output/outcome measures that can be considered together in an examination of organizational effectiveness.
- **Workforce Mobility**
  Monitor and compare the flow of the workforce into and out of the organization. These include measures of employee recruitment, transfer/promotion, and separations. Subcategories include recruitment, movement, and termination.

Note

Customers will often ask, "Which is the most common metric used in workforce analytics?" Generally, the answer is Termination Rate. Why? As a risk-averse function, HR will monitor turnover to avoid losing critical talent to precipitate aggregate shortages in headcount. Terminations are highly visible, easy to define (an employee either stays or leaves) and calculate the cost of, and typically are of high volume, making statistical analysis more powerful.

- **Workforce Compensation and Benefits**
  Monitor and compare the remuneration to reward and motivate employees. For example, the Average Annual Salary metric is included in the subcategory called compensation.
- **Staffing Function**
  Provide an overview of the effectiveness of the staffing function from the perspective of new hire terminations. For example, the Quick Quits metric turnover rate <30/90 days is included in the subcategory called staffing effectiveness.

> **Note**
> The FTE, external hires, termination, and retirement measures included within the Core Workforce and Mobility metrics pack are all requirements for the SAP SuccessFactors Workforce Planning solution. The Workforce Planning solution allows organizations to create forecasts using either headcount or FTE metrics, and leverages the underlying analytics engine to include projected retirements, terminations, and hires into the forecast. We will discuss Workforce Planning in more detail in Chapter 13.

Additional Metrics Packs

Beyond the Core Workforce and Mobility metrics pack, Workforce Analytics customers using the SQL version can take advantage of several other packs in order to analyze information in conjunction with the core workforce data:

- Absence Management
- Compensation Planning
- Employee Central/ADP GlobalView
- Employee Relations
- Fieldglass Contingent Labor
- Finance Management
- Goal Management
- Health and Safety
- HR Delivery
- Learning
- Leave Accrual
- Payroll and Benefits
- Performance Management
- Recruiting Management
- Recruiting Marketing
- Span of Control
- Succession Management
- Survey
- Talent Flow Analytics

Organizations can also implement custom metrics packs based on domains or systems not listed here.

After the Core Workforce and Mobility metrics pack is implemented, you can begin to map in additional metrics packs from other data sources (e.g., Absence Management, Learning, Succession Management, etc.). Note that with the SQL version of Workforce Analytics, you can use virtually any data source, including homegrown systems and Excel worksheets, as the source of data for any metrics pack. The preferred, and most common, method is to extract raw data from a source system because this mitigates the risk of importing incorrect data often held in Excel or other similar data files.

Note

Customers may prefer to send data from an existing data warehouse; however, this is not recommended because of the following reasons:

- Not every piece of data required for Workforce Analytics will be included in the warehouse
- The data will have already undergone a transformation process, with logic applied, for which Workforce Analytics will need to account

Depending on the complexity of the metrics pack, the typical length of time to implement ranges between three and six weeks. By integrating data from your core HRIS with other systems, you can yield more powerful insights and analyses than a singular view would allow.

For example, the integration of learning data with sales data can allow you to analyze the effect of specific training courses on sales output. Essentially acting as a data warehouse, Workforce Analytics provides you with a tool to move beyond operational reporting and counting of things (for example, how many employees took a specific training course) to become a more strategic partner to the business (for example, sales went up by 30 percent for employees who took the training course).

To provide another example, one of the most popular metrics packs is Performance Management, which is helpful for assessing performance against expectations and understanding whether investments in talent are building up workforce capabilities. For example, the Performance Management metrics pack includes the following metrics:

- Staffing Rate—High Performers
- Employee Downgrade Rate
- Performance Appraisal Participation Rate (see Figure 12.1)

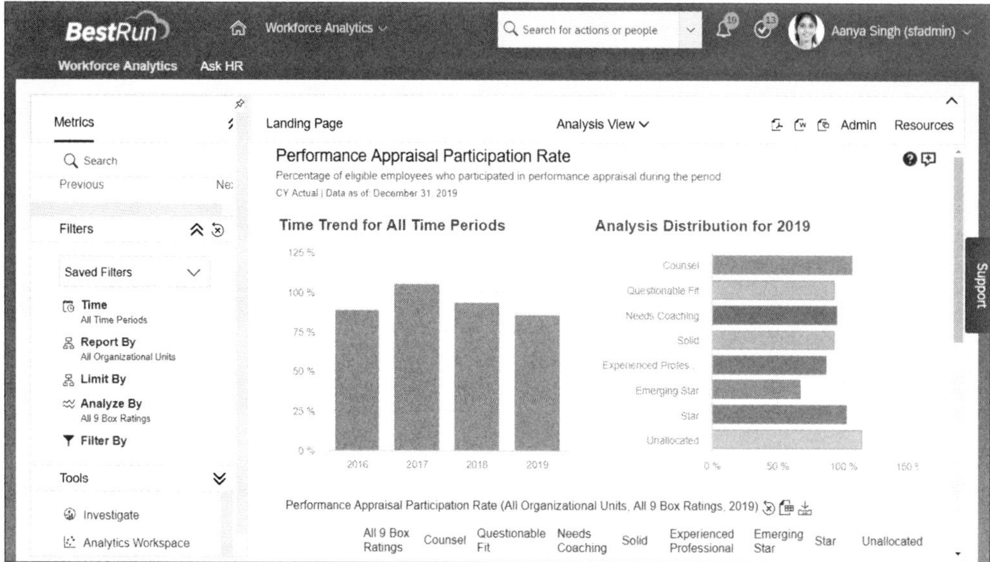

Figure 12.1 Performance Appraisal Participation Rate in Workforce Analytics

When you cross these metrics with your core workforce data, you can begin to answer questions like the following:

- What percentage of our involuntary termination rate is due to poor performance?
- What is the retention rate for high performing employees?
- What rate of employees improve their performance from one assessment period to the next?
- What rate of employees' performance decreases from one period to the next?
- What is the distribution of performance across the organization broken down across key employment segments?
- What is the percent increase in employee performance as the result of every one percent increase in pay?

Note

Let's consider an example. One of SAP SuccessFactors' retail customers, who was previously limited in the metrics they had access to, created a one-page "talent index" for review at business strategy meetings. The objective was to inform managers of key trends in workforce development without overwhelming recipients with too much data.

The index prefaced the metrics with four questions:

- Are our most solid performers staying with the company (high performer turnover rate)?
- Are we growing capacity for high performance in our workforce (high performer growth rate)?
- Are we able to turn-around performers needing improvement (associate turnaround)?
- Are new people doing well (new hire performance)?

Metric Methodology

Now that we've explained the concept of metrics packs, let's take a deeper look at the metric methodology. If we were to ask you what the starting point is for workforce analytics, of course, your answer would be data. However, the tricky part is advancing from mere data points to full-fledged analytics.

The metric methodology is the same for all metrics packs, so we'll use the Core Workforce and Mobility metrics pack to illustrate the process. The first step is to define the metrics sourcing logic, which are the data fields sourced from the HRIS (e.g., Employee Central for Workforce Analytics on SAP HANA or any HRIS for Workforce Analytics on SQL). Data from the core HRIS is mapped to standardized formulas by the SAP SuccessFactors data transformation engine to generate what are called base input measures (e.g., FTE) and dimension hierarchies (e.g., gender). These base input measures are filtered through the dimension hierarchies to generate a rich set of derived input measures (e.g., # of FTE—Female).

The derived input measures are combined in formulas to generate result measures (e.g., male to female staffing ratio) commonly used in analysis and reporting and are displayed in the form of rates, ratios, percentages, averages, and so on. In other words, the derived input measures and the base input measures are the numerators and denominators making up each rate or ratio, respectively. See Figure 12.2 for an example of the metrics methodology using the Performance Management metrics pack.

All measures (base input, derived input, or result) and dimension hierarchies represented by the dotted box are available to support a customer's analytics agenda.

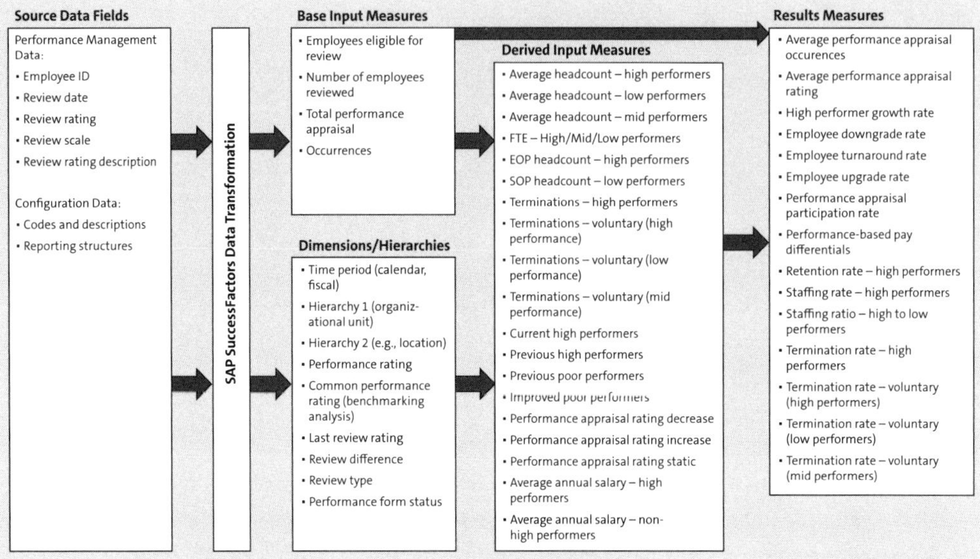

Figure 12.2 Performance Management Metrics Pack Graphic

Now that we've examined how metrics packs facilitate the transformation of raw data into calculated measures, the next section will cover key concepts in how customers' data is acquired and validated.

12.1.3 Data Acquisition and Governance

In this section, we'll look at how SAP SuccessFactors acquires and manages inbound data from Workforce Analytics customers. The focus will be on the Workforce Analytics on SQL option, which requires customers to deliver data to SAP SuccessFactors; in contrast, with Workforce Analytics on SAP HANA, SAP SuccessFactors or partners manage the transfer of data between SAP SuccessFactors modules.

> **Note**
>
> In 2018, SAP SuccessFactors introduced a new approach to implementing Workforce Analytics that emphasizes fast, agile sprints and creating a "leading practice" instance that customers use to visualize their data far earlier in the implementation timeline than under the prior approach. Given the broad nature of the audience for this book, the information that follows is presented as a set of key concepts rather than a definitive implementation process, which may differ by partner.

Acquiring Data

To populate Workforce Analytics, data must be acquired from the customers' source systems (HRIS, talent management, finance, etc.). This data is extracted from the customer's system(s) in the form of text file dumps and sent to SAP SuccessFactors for processing. Typically, with Workforce Analytics on SQL, the process takes place each month. With Workforce Analytics on SAP HANA, daily feeds are the norm.

SAP SuccessFactors needs a way of identifying an individual employee within the company. Typically, this takes the form of a unique employee identifier, and most companies will have a way of determining this within their existing HRIS systems. SAP SuccessFactors will use this unique identifier to link all data records together and to verify that all the steps it performs to process the data from the extract are correct. While an employee ID is essential for identifying and joining data, SAP SuccessFactors doesn't request other personal information such as an employee's social security number, home address, or telephone number.

Let's walk through the steps required to extract and transfer raw data from the customer's HR and talent management systems to the Workforce Analytics servers:

1. **Submitting data**

   The most common method of submitting data extracts to SAP SuccessFactors is where customers initiate a data deposit process by placing their data on to a SAP SuccessFactors-controlled File Transfer Protocol (FTP) server. SAP SuccessFactors also supports a data retrieval service, whereby appointed SAP SuccessFactors staff log onto a customer-controlled server and retrieve data files placed there.

   SAP SuccessFactors strongly recommends that customers consider a data deposit approach in preference to a data retrieval approach. The reason for this is that, to reduce the turnaround times involved in processing cyclic data extracts provided by customers, SAP SuccessFactors has automated many of the steps involved in processing data ready for publication to a customer's Workforce Analytics solution. One of these steps includes the process to automatically download and decrypt data placed on the SAP SuccessFactors FTP server. If this process detects that a full set of data files has been received from the customer, it will automatically commence the first of the automated processes for processing that data. These services run 24 hours a day and 7 days a week.

   If customers do not place their data on the SAP SuccessFactors FTP server but instead require that SAP SuccessFactors staff manually collect data from a customer-controlled server, it will lead to longer processing turnaround times.

2. **Specifications document**
   This document is used as the blueprint to process customers' data and will be presented to the customer for review and feedback. Several iterations of the review/feedback process may be required to finalize the document. When all the sections have been satisfactorily completed, the document is presented to the customer for acceptance and written sign-off. The accepted version will then be used to start processing (staging) the data. The document is maintained under version control and will continue to be updated to incorporate new measures or modifications to the processing rules.
3. **Extract scripts**
   SAP SuccessFactors tries to make the process of extracting data as simple as possible. The extract programs (scripts) that are provided produce a simple text file for each table, where each record in the table corresponds to a row in the file, and the columns are separated by tabs (i.e., tab delimited). The purpose of providing extract scripts is to minimize the resource and time commitments required of organizations participating in SAP SuccessFactors. For each identified table SAP SuccessFactors aims to provide a customized script to facilitate the extraction of the data. The scripts provide a simple mechanism for extracting the data for the required database table columns to an ASCII file. Where a customer prefers to create their own extract programs, SAP SuccessFactors provides guidance on the tables and columns to extract and the output format required.
4. **Data encryption**
   Data security and privacy is foremost in SAP SuccessFactors practices. To this end, it is recommended that all extracted data is encrypted or, at a minimum, zipped and password protected prior to delivery. The most common encryption package used by customers is PGP (Pretty Good Privacy). With this method, SAP SuccessFactors provide the member with a public encryption key. Other encryption options can be considered if required.
5. **Data transfer**
   For the actual transfer of data from the customer to SAP SuccessFactors, the most commonly used vehicle is a customer-specific FTP site hosted on SAP SuccessFactors' servers. Each FTP site is accessible only by that member and by designated staff in SAP SuccessFactors. Access to the FTP site requires individual usernames and passwords for each organization. Some organizations prefer to use their established VPN sites and give SAP SuccessFactors access to specific areas to collect the data. The recommended transfer mechanism is FTP over a secure connection (sometimes referred to as *secure FTP*).

Validating the Data

During the process of data transformation (from customers' raw, transactional data to the calculated metrics offered by Workforce Analytics), SAP SuccessFactors must verify that their interpretation of the data aligns with that of the customer. Essentially, this means that before SAP SuccessFactors can go live with the Workforce Analytics application, the customer must be comfortable that the calculations are correct. For example, does the customer's own headcount number match the end-of-period headcount input in Workforce Analytics?

There are three main goals of the verification process:

- Provide as accurate a Workforce Analytics application as possible (a "single version of the truth")
- Uncover data processing issues not discovered in the data specifications phase
- Understand why SAP SuccessFactors' results may reasonably differ from customer's internal reports

After processing data from the customer's HRIS system (using the Core Workforce and Mobility metrics pack), SAP SuccessFactors will generate discrepancy reports. The data elements that are most critical to verification—those that represent employment actions and movements—are initially verified. By lining up the SAP SuccessFactors employee ID reports with the customer's internal employee ID reports (from the submitted verification reports), SAP SuccessFactors can determine exactly which employees "fall out" or are not counted correctly.

For example, SAP SuccessFactors can identify the employees that the customer shows as part of headcount but SAP SuccessFactors does not, and the employees that SAP SuccessFactors identify in headcount but the customer does not. To support the Workforce Analytics application verification process, customers also provide summary or verification reports that SAP SuccessFactors will use to check the results of its processes prior to publication.

These reports, generated from a customer's HRIS system, will list the figures that a customer believes are correct for end-of-period headcount, hires, terminations, and analysis options like age, gender, ethnic background, tenure, and so forth. Again, as for the data extracts, these reports will contain a unique employee identifier and coded information about an employee that supports the analysis options.

Publishing the Data

Once written sign-off is received from the customer, stating acceptance and completion of verification activities, SAP SuccessFactors will commence the beta-site publication.

SAP SuccessFactors has established a separate verification site that will only be reviewed by key project team members. The first time a site is published to this separate environment, it is considered a *beta* site. Moving forward, as the customer conducts regular data refreshes, this environment is referred to as the *preview* site; this version permits SAP SuccessFactors and the customer's project team to review, for example, newly published measures or organization structures for accuracy before they are available to a wide user audience. SAP SuccessFactors will never publish data directly to the production site; it will always publish first to the preview site and move to production upon the customer's approval.

In the next section, we'll discuss the benchmarking program in depth.

12.2 Benchmarking

External benchmarks are extremely useful for organizations to utilize as a reference point to gauge performance against competitors. Additionally, you can leverage benchmarks as an input in the target-setting process or to understand whether your organization is following or deviating from macroeconomic trends over time. Many customers find the benchmarking program to be a key value-add from their Workforce Analytics investment.

In this section, we'll examine the benchmarking program methodology, the categories and subcategories for viewing benchmarks, and how to access benchmarks in Workforce Analytics.

12.2.1 Benchmarking Methodology

Every customer using Workforce Analytics contractually agrees to share their data for benchmarking purposes. Unlike other popular benchmarking programs (for example, Saratoga or Watson Wyatt), SAP SuccessFactors does not use a survey methodology to collect data for benchmarking purposes. Instead, SAP SuccessFactors accesses customers' raw data to calculate the benchmarks using standard formulas and definitions. This ensures that all data is being viewed in an apples-to-apples comparison and increases the quality of the benchmark figures.

Another quality assurance check embedded in the benchmarking program is the minimum sample size criteria. For a benchmark to be calculated, there must be a minimum of eight organizations providing the data elements necessary to generate a benchmark result. This rule also acts as a safeguard for organizational anonymity.

Because benchmarks are always reported in aggregates, the minimum sample size also provides confidence that no single organization's individual results are identifiable. The benchmarks are typically published once a year, usually during the first quarter after year-end data has become available.

Now, we'll look at the various categories of benchmarks available for analysis purposes.

12.2.2 Benchmarking Categories

The total benchmark database is called the SAP SuccessFactors North American Companies; for organizations based in North America, this is your best bet for finding an acceptable sample size for the metrics you're interested in benchmarking.

However, sometimes it's helpful to look at specific slices of the database, such as by industry, organization size, or revenue. The benchmarking program provides customers with seven main categories of benchmarks to choose from, in addition to the total North American Companies results.

Figure 12.3 shows the main categories available to customers for benchmarking purposes.

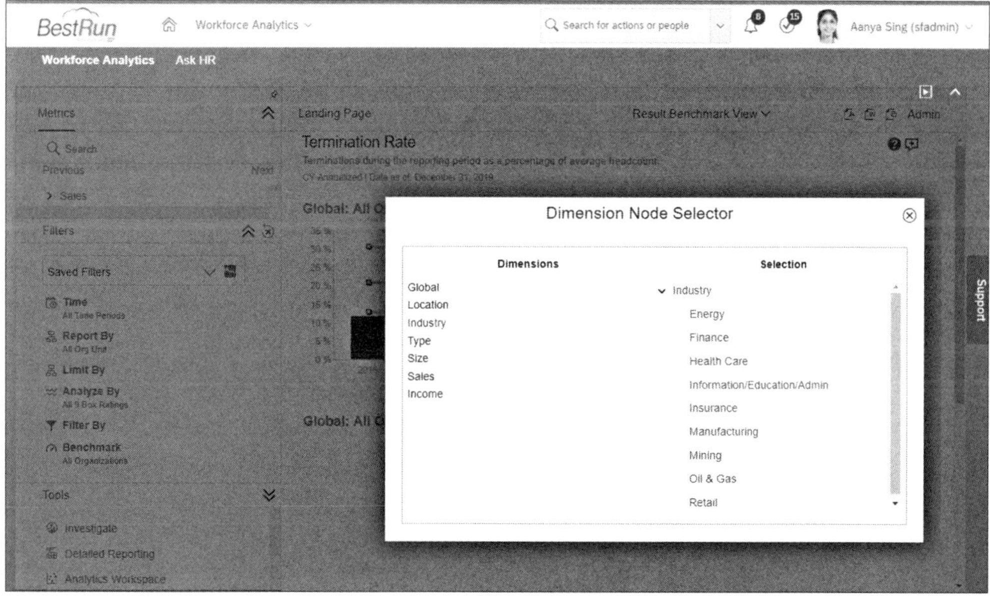

Figure 12.3 Workforce Analytics Benchmarking Categories

When you select one of the benchmark categories, a list of subcategories appears for you to choose from to further refine your selection. Note that as you restrict your selection, the sample size criteria may not be met, and therefore no benchmark result is displayed.

Now we'll look at how to navigate through the Workforce Analytics application to apply benchmarks to specific metrics.

12.2.3 Applying Benchmarks

Benchmarks are embedded within the Workforce Analytics technology and, therefore, cannot be turned "off" on your specific instance. There are a few different methods for accessing the benchmarks, the easiest of which is to navigate to a specific measure page where the benchmark result for that measure is displayed as a component of the standard page layout. For example, if you were interested in seeing the benchmark for voluntary termination rate, you would see the standard page layout, as depicted in Figure 12.4.

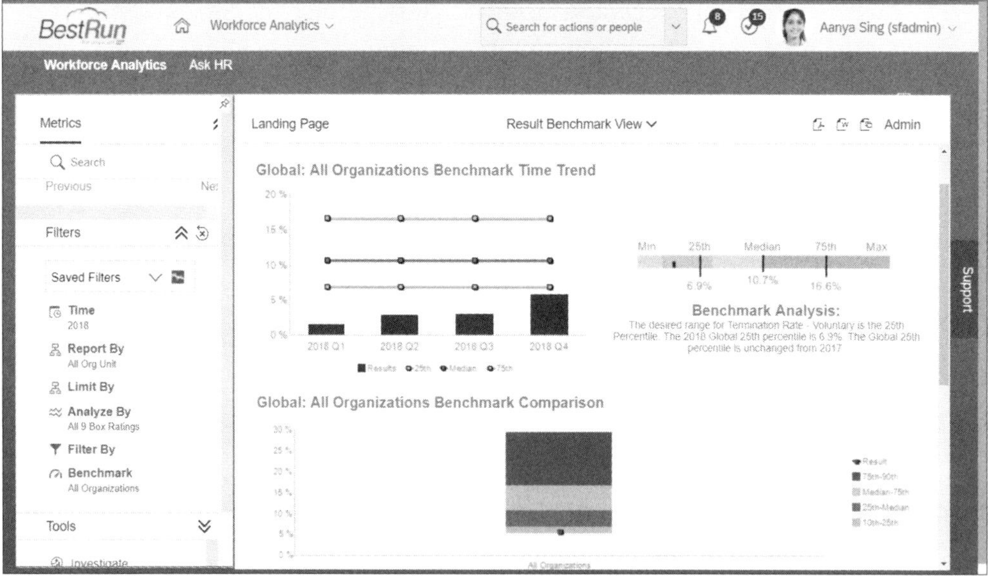

Figure 12.4 Benchmarks in the Metrics Page

As you can see, each measure page shows a gauge image for the benchmark result, including breakdowns for the 25th, 50th, and 75th percentiles. The title below the spectrum denotes the benchmark group you're viewing—in this case, the default **All Organizations**. Note that customers can choose to set their default benchmark group to any of the categories or subcategories available.

The benchmark spectrum also utilizes the stoplight methodology (i.e., red/yellow/green color coding) to indicate where desirable and undesirable results fall within the provided ranges. Users can view their organizations' results by either reading the digital result in the bottom of the gauge or hovering on the needle.

If you want to see how your organization's result compares to a different benchmark group, you can easily make this selection in the **Filters** pane.

You can see that the current selection is **All Organizations**, but let's say you want to view benchmarks for the Healthcare industry instead. After clicking **Benchmark**, a new window pops up that allows you to select the industry category in the **Dimension Node Selector** window, and then a list of subcategories appears in the selection window (see Figure 12.5). After you click **Energy**, the window closes, and the benchmark image, title, and percentile ranges change to reflect this selection.

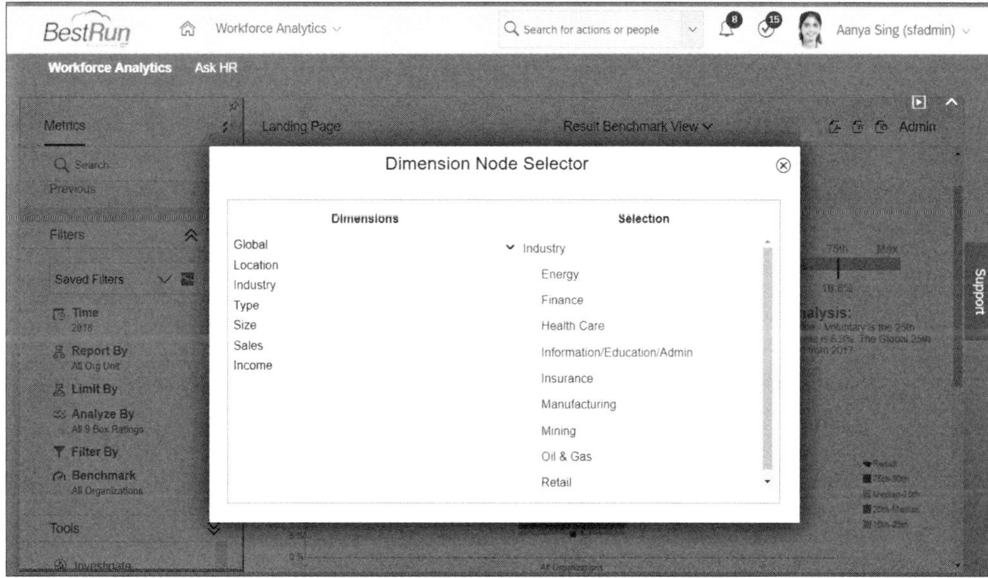

Figure 12.5 Energy Benchmark Selection on a Measure Page

In the next section, we will take a look at different views a user can employ to analyze their workforce analytics data.

12.3 Reporting and Analytics

According to Peter Howes, founder and CEO of Infohrm, "Aggregate data is, at best, useless and, at worst, dangerous." In this section, we'll unpack how Workforce Analytics avoids this issue by enabling users to dive into the data and identify segment-level concerns or opportunities.

For many Workforce Analytics customers, simply being able to publish an accurate measure of headcount is a major breakthrough in their human capital reporting. Beyond core facts such as the number of employees, terminations, and diverse staff, customers using the application can correlate metrics, forecast future results, and explore the data to identify segments—high-performers, staff with low engagement, female employees, and so forth—for which new investments may yield above-average returns.

As data analysts, we often use the phrases "slicing and dicing" or "drilling through the data" to describe the process of dissecting the total organizational result to identify patterns, trends, and insights. Often, this can be a challenging task that requires a high level of manual effort because data is usually available only in an aggregate form. Workforce Analytics includes numerous analysis options for easy slicing and dicing of data results, many of which are presented in the metrics pages, discussed as follows.

12.3.1 Metrics Pages

As discussed in Section 12.1, the foundation of Workforce Analytics is the metrics packs which simplify the process, for customers, of normalizing their raw data into measures backed by time-tested industry standards. In the application itself, the foundation extends to the metrics pages, with prebuilt content and visuals that allow for easy navigation.

Note

An SAP SuccessFactors customer for Workforce Analytics describes the metrics pages as a "choose your own adventure," as the data can be explored via numerous paths and filters.

The metrics pages offer users—HR analysts business partners, generalists, and managers—simple, guided navigation from aggregate results to segments of specific interest.

By segmenting the workforce, we can break down the all-organizational result and see which employee populations or business functions are driving the total result for the organization.

Let's take a look at the example in Figure 12.6, which shows the voluntary termination rate by organizational tenure. In this example, we can see that, at nearly 40 percent, the **1-<2** year tenure band has considerably higher voluntary turnover than other tenure groups. This may indicate a low tenure turnover problem, which could warrant further investigation and, ultimately, targeted interventions.

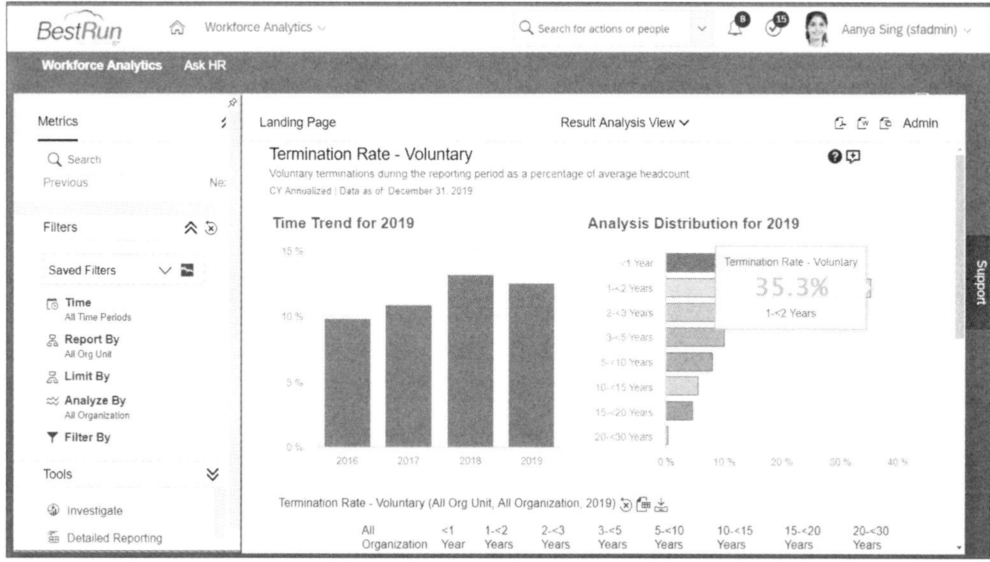

Figure 12.6 Voluntary Termination Rate by Organizational Tenure

In the following sections, we'll illustrate a sample analytics process, using different filters to investigate the metrics.

Organizational Structures

The next logical step in the analytics process is to determine where in the organization the low tenure turnover problem is occurring. To do this, we need to drill through the organizational structure to identify locations where voluntary turnover rates are highest for the 1 to <2 year tenure band. Organizational structures represent a hierarchical relationship, of which the four most common in Workforce Analytics are business units, cost centers, reporting relationships, and geographic locations.

The most common organizational structure used in human capital analytics is the business unit hierarchy.

In Figure 12.7, we can clearly see that the **Healthcare** business unit has significantly higher low-tenure (**1-<2 Years**) voluntary termination rates (**78.1%**) than the rest of the organization.

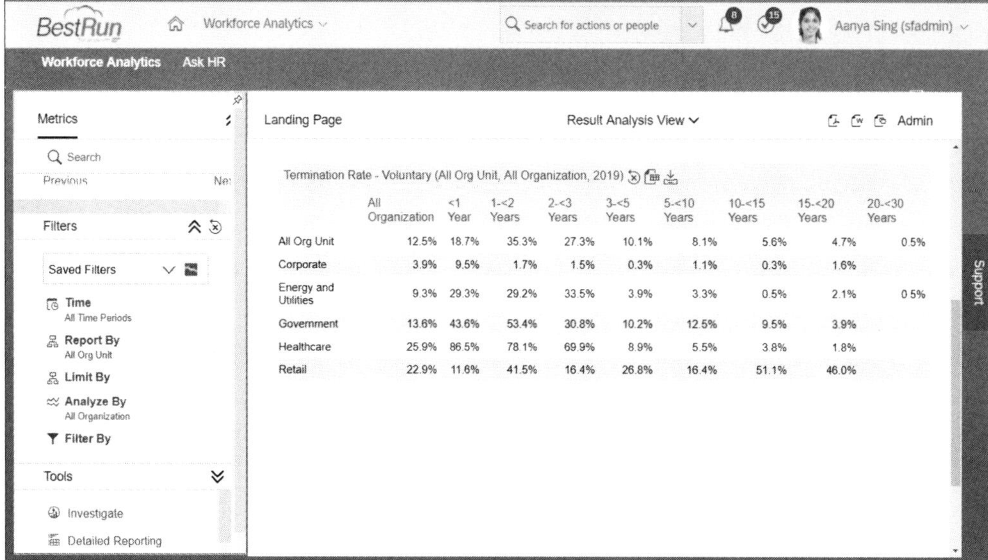

	All Organization	<1 Year	1-<2 Years	2-<3 Years	3-<5 Years	5-<10 Years	10-<15 Years	15-<20 Years	20-<30 Years
All Org Unit	12.5%	18.7%	35.3%	27.3%	10.1%	8.1%	5.6%	4.7%	0.5%
Corporate	3.9%	9.5%	1.7%	1.5%	0.3%	1.1%	0.3%	1.6%	
Energy and Utilities	9.3%	29.3%	29.2%	33.5%	3.9%	3.3%	0.5%	2.1%	0.5%
Government	13.6%	43.6%	53.4%	30.8%	10.2%	12.5%	9.5%	3.9%	
Healthcare	25.9%	86.5%	78.1%	69.9%	8.9%	5.5%	3.8%	1.8%	
Retail	22.9%	11.6%	41.5%	16.4%	26.8%	16.4%	51.1%	46.0%	

Figure 12.7 1 to <2 Year Tenure Voluntary Turnover by Organizational Unit

Analysis Options

Now that we've identified a business unit with a low tenure turnover issue, we can continue to slice and dice our results to understand which populations within the **Healthcare** business unit are of particular concern. This can be done by applying additional analysis options, such as job family, gender, ethnic group, or age group.

In Figure 12.8, we've analyzed low-tenure voluntary turnover within the **Healthcare** business unit by those employees in critical job roles, and you can see that 68.3 percent of employees with between 1 and 2 years of tenure in critical job roles have exited the organization in 2019. This illustrates the power of the Workforce Analytics application in spotting major issues at a segment-level that would have otherwise been masked by the all-organizational results.

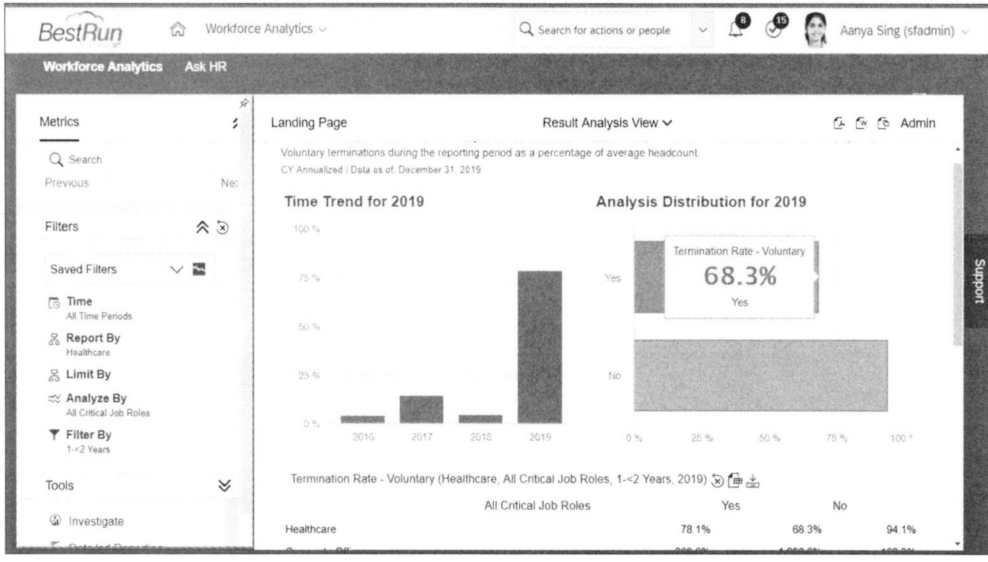

Figure 12.8 Low-Tenure Voluntary Turnover by Critical Job Role (Healthcare Division)

Filtering

Sometimes, it can be useful to apply a second level of analysis when you are trying to pinpoint the hot spot in your data, and this is done using the **Filter By** option (also located in the **Analytics** pane and shown in Figure 12.8). This feature effectively allows you to go one level deeper into your analysis by limiting the data to one specific node of an analysis option. For example, we sliced the 1 to <2 year tenure voluntary turnover in the **Healthcare** business unit by critical job roles.

Now that we've identified a low-tenure turnover issue in the **Healthcare** business unit for employees in critical job roles, we may want to view the employee-level details that make up this population.

Drill-to-Detail

A common question asked by leaders when viewing human capital metrics for the first time is "Which employees are included in this result?" The Drill-to-Detail functionality answers that question.

Drill-to-Detail enables users to verify which employees are included within a particular result. This customer-driven enhancement is a tool for validating the quality of the data to gain credibility with the business.

The Drill-to-Detail functionality is embedded within the Workforce Analytics application and allows users to click any hyperlinked result (for example, percentage or raw count). Doing so, the tool generates the details of the individual records represented in the result in a transactional list-based view. Customers can limit what is returned in the Drill-to-Detail view, but in theory, they can choose to show any of the fields that are included in the data file that is sent as part of the data refresh cycle. Figure 12.9 shows the employee-level detail when we used the **Drill-to-Detail** hyperlink to identify which employees in critical job roles left the organization in 2019.

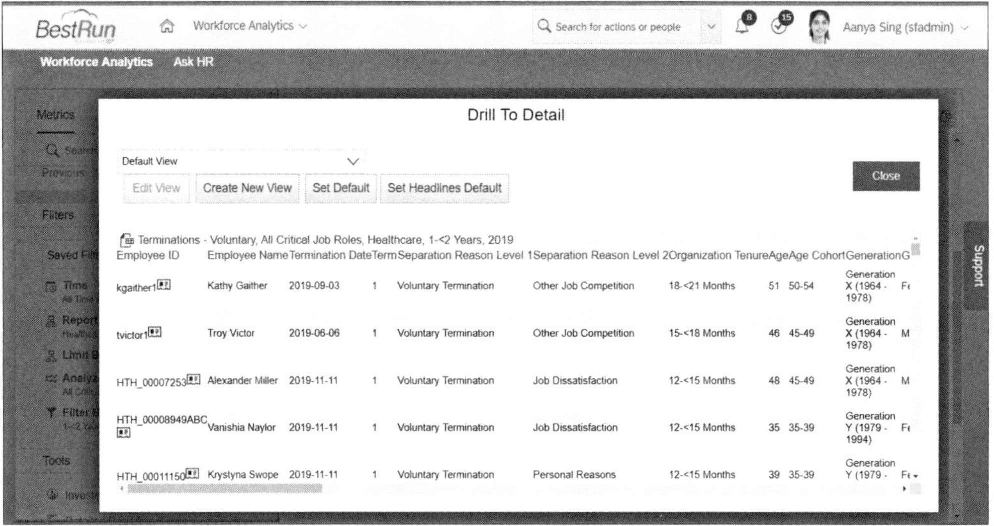

Figure 12.9 Drill-to-Detail Result

Also, note that clicking the **Excel** icon in the upper-left corner of the table allows a user to export the table for further analysis or distribution. One tip is that, if you're accessing Workforce Analytics through single sign-on (SSO) and your organization also utilizes SAP SuccessFactors Employee Profile, you can click the quickcard icon next to any Employee ID to see that individual's profile.

12.3.2 Report Designer

One of the key components of any analytics software is a reporting strategy designed to get key information into decision makers' hands on a regular basis. The Workforce Analytics application speeds up this process by making the creation of reports, and the subsequent distribution, much easier to manage than typical reporting tools. Additionally, customers find that the reporting process is significantly more efficient because the data is automatically refreshed in every report each month (with Workforce Analytics on SQL; Workforce Analytics on SAP HANA customers refresh data more frequently). Users can build one master report and send it pre-sliced to each different business unit every month with minimal effort. The reduced manual effort through this approach can save a significant amount of money in your organization, as well as free up your analytics team to do more strategic analysis. Let's now review the key functionality within the Report Designer.

Accessing Report Designer and Existing Reports

To access the Report Designer tool, a user role must have access granted through the role-based permission (RBP) framework. Similar to other power user tools, the primary users of Report Designer is the analytics team. To access the Report Designer, click the Report Designer button found on the **Tools** menu in the **Analytics** pane. A new page refreshes, displaying the Report Designer library. All users can create as many reports and folders as they wish; however, report "owners" can restrict other users from modifying your existing reports.

In the Report Designer, you are prompted to select a report from the folders or create a new report. The **Analytics** pane is replaced with a **Manage Reports** section, which is where you find the **New report** button, as shown in Figure 12.10.

The **Manage Reports** section in the **Analytics** pane houses the main reporting functions. Beginning with the **File** dropdown menu, you can choose to link reports to the reporting menu, edit ownership of reports, delete reports (either permanently, or put them in the recycle bin if you want to access certain pages again in the future), and edit headers and footers. Next, you can choose to either add a blank page to your report or copy a page from any existing report. The **Folders** dropdown allows you to manage your folders by creating new folders, naming them, or deleting existing folders.

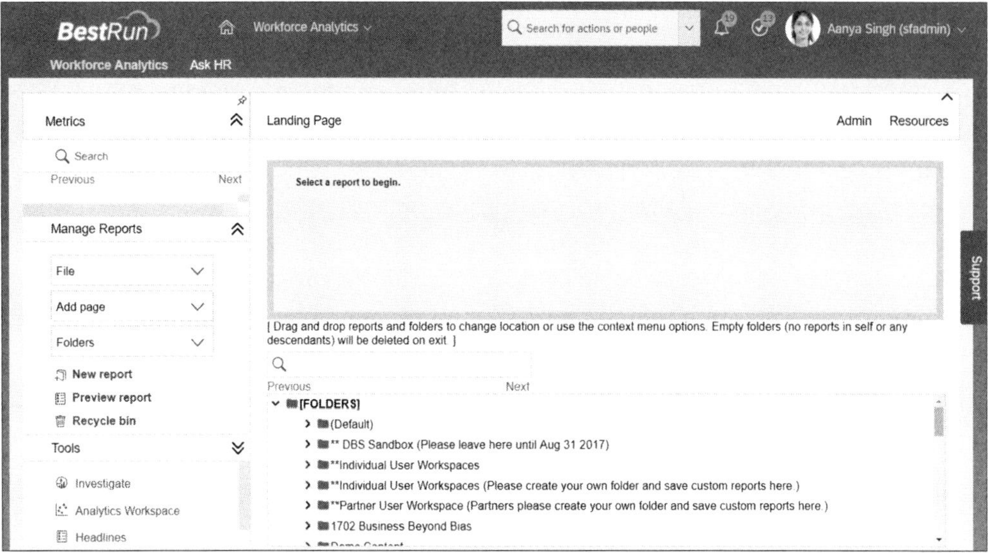

Figure 12.10 Accessing the Report Designer

The final button we'll cover in the **Manage Reports** pane is the **Preview report** button, which allows you to view a report on the main site as an end user would experience. This functionality temporarily moves the report out of design mode and allows the report builder to check that the report features are working as expected.

When you click an existing report in a folder, the gray box above the folders populates with key information about the selected report, such as the report owner's name, the number of pages in the report, the last date/time the report was modified and by whom, and whether the report is currently linked to the **Reporting** menu. In this view, you can also modify any existing pages in the report you've selected, add new pages to the report, or reorder the pages in the report.

Report Designer Components

Users have complete flexibility in the Report Designer to create a multitude of data visualizations, known as components. Components are the building blocks of a report page and can be charts, tables, text, images, or composite queries. All components can be edited to fit a user's preferences, including the font, size, color scheme, and so on. Each of the components has a different purpose that can be used on Report Designer pages, ranging from basic tables to complex queries utilizing formulas and conditional formatting. If you can imagine it, you can build it in the Report Designer.

When you add a blank page or copy of an existing page to the report you're building, a new menu appears in the **Analytics** pane with one tab to add components and a second tab to edit components. Accessing the choices for components is simple because they are all arranged by type in the **Add Component** window, as shown in Figure 12.11.

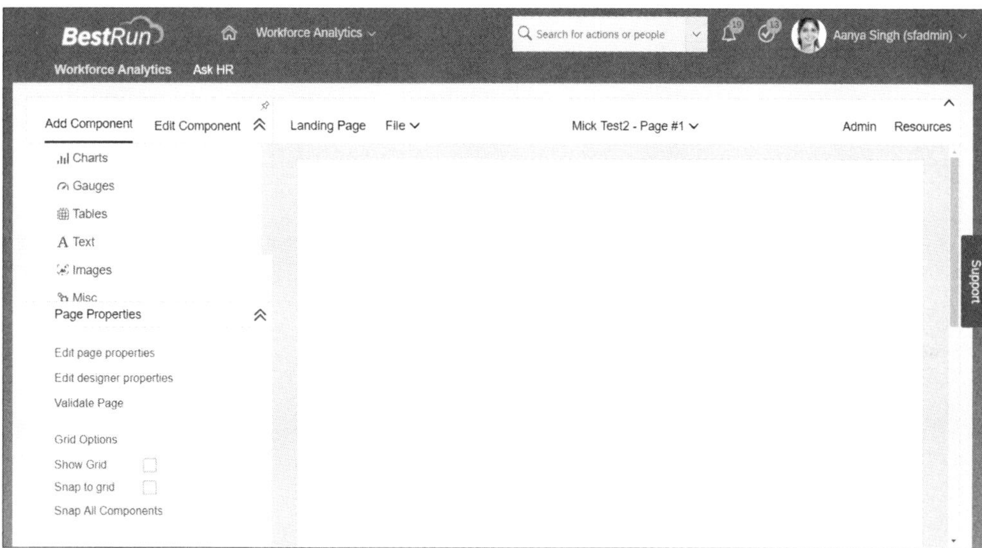

Figure 12.11 Report Designer Add Component

You'll also notice that there is a new pane below the **Add Component** pane called **Page Properties**. This is where you can modify the page margins, switch to landscape view, validate that the components on the page are working properly, and enable a grid view to ensure that components are properly aligned.

To edit a component, you must first drag and drop one of the component options onto the page. After you do so, a default image shows up in the component box with demo data to illustrate the type of component you've chosen (for example, table vs. chart). After you drop the new component onto your page canvas, the **Add Component** menu is replaced by the **Edit Component** menu.

Now you have several options for editing your component, all of which can also be accessed by right-clicking on the component as a shortcut. The **Edit Component** menu, shown in Figure 12.12, allows users to do all normal editing activities, such as changing the chart type (for example, pie vs. bar chart), changing the color scheme, adding data labels or a legend, and adding a chart/table title. You can create a custom color palette utilizing your corporate colors, which you can later incorporate into charts, reports, and so on.

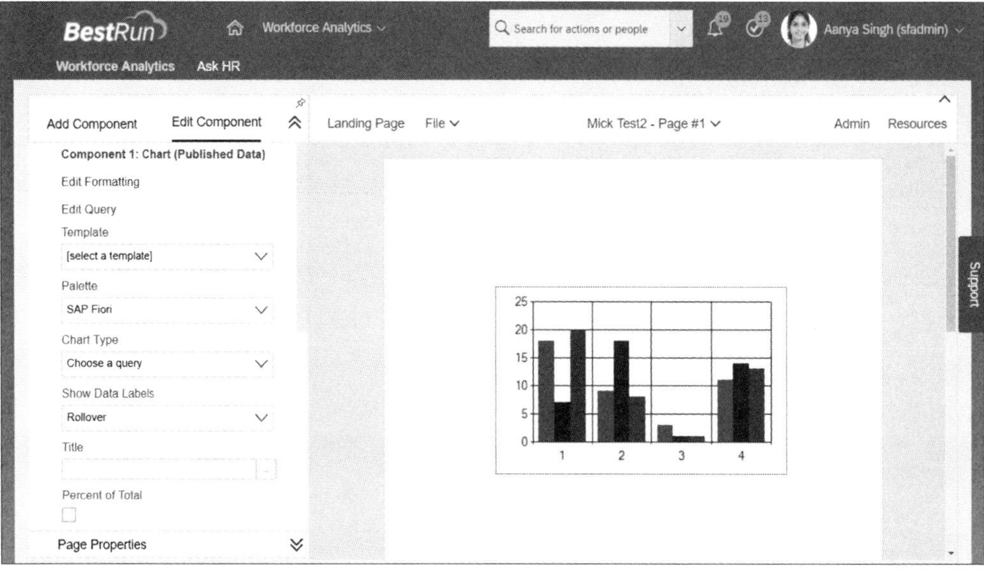

Figure 12.12 Report Designer Edit Component

In addition, you'll notice a **[Click for Full Editor]** link (not shown). Clicking this link opens a new edit window that includes an option to link your component to an existing query in **Query Workspace**. This is a great time saver because you don't need to rebuild all queries from scratch for reporting purposes. Also, in the full edit window, you have the option to preview your component to avoid repeatedly clicking in and out of the editor to make changes. Finally, the copy-and-paste right-click feature works nicely in Report Designer, which can save time editing and formatting components.

Report Distributor

Half the battle of establishing a regular reporting process is automating the report schedule. To eliminate this challenge, the Workforce Analytics solution has an embedded Report Distributor tool that allows clients to set up "bundles" to be delivered on a regular basis.

The analytics team can determine what information the end user should receive and how often. For example, you may want the chief financial officer (CFO) to receive a report via email already drilled down to the finance organization. This feature, which can be found on the **Tools** menu, is a key piece of delivering analytics in a scalable manner across the organization.

Reports can be distributed via FTP or email or run offline. Word, PowerPoint, and Excel file formats are supported. Workforce Analytics reports can also be included in the Report Center, the central hub of reporting across all SAP SuccessFactors products.

12.3.3 Investigate

Investigate is the next generation of Query Workspace and is intended to accelerate how HR analysts create custom views of their metrics. Investigate suggests recommended metrics, analysis dimensions, and visualizations (line graphs, bar charts, and so on). In addition, search capabilities allow analysts to quickly find metrics, and the introduction of Collections is a simplified method for sharing and exporting insights for use with colleagues.

Once a customer has enabled Investigate, it becomes the default framework for querying and investigating data in the Workforce Analytics application. However, should users wish to revert back to Query Workspace, they can do so by clicking **Switch To Classic View** when creating a new investigation.

Let's now review the most important functionality that comes with Investigate.

Accessing and Navigating Investigate

To access Investigate in the Workforce Analytics application, click on the **Investigate** link under **Tools**. Users are then prompted to open an existing investigation (the names of which are presented in the center of the screen) or start an investigation from scratch.

To locate an existing investigation, users can sort the list or use the **Search** functionality and type in a word or phrase.

If you choose to select an existing investigation, you can rename it, move it (to a different folder, if multiple folders are available), and share it (send the investigation to a fellow user).

Creating a New Investigation

As shown in Figure 12.13, when you click **New**, you are presented with two options:

- **Open Query From Query Workspace**: Users can select an existing query from the legacy tools for exploration with Investigate.
- **Start New Investigation**: Users can begin a new exploration.

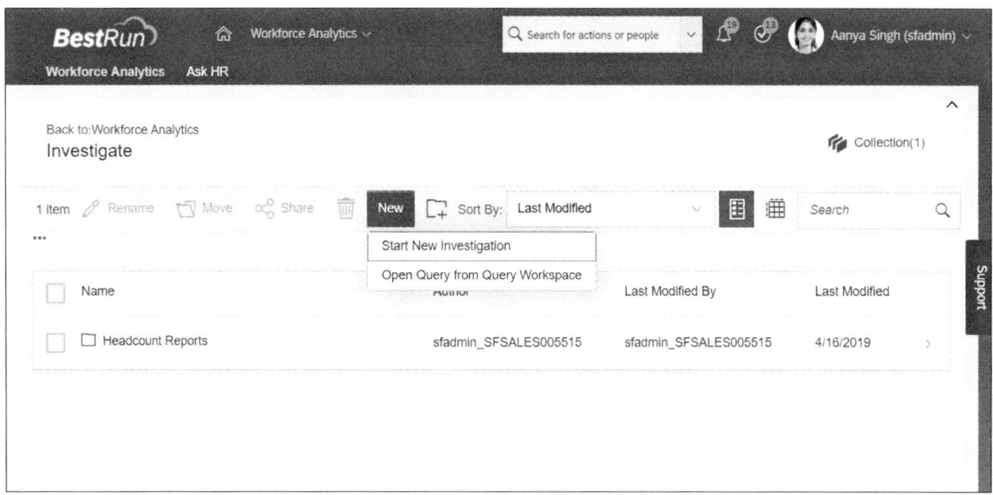

Figure 12.13 Accessing Investigate

Choosing **Start New Investigation** brings you to a blank canvas. You'll notice that there are two navigation options on the right-hand side. The **Data** tab contains a menu of metrics, dimensions, organizational structure options and time models. The **Analyze** tab can be accessed after starting an investigation; this is where you can select options for forecasting future results and for selecting different visualizations.

To begin, you can either select a metric from the **Data** tab or search for a measure. In this example, typing "retire" into the **Search** box returns all metrics that contain that word in their name. Selecting **Staffing Rate—Approaching Retirement Eligibility** populates the canvas with trended results over the last four years. The result for 2019 is 13.2 percent, indicating that only a small proportion of the total workforce is within five years of retirement eligibility. This is also shown in a table beneath the graphic.

> **Note**
>
> An SAP SuccessFactors customer for Workforce Analytics used the phrase "talent cliff" to illustrate the serious risk posed by the impending retirement of a significant portion of their workforce.

As with the metrics pages, we want to slice this result to identify specific areas of concern. Using the **Data** tab on the right, you can scroll down and select **Job Family** to see if there are any major differences in retirement risk by types of jobs. We find that, in Figure 12.14 for 2019, 29.5 percent of **Account Managers (Sales)** are approaching retirement eligibility, which would be a major concern for any organization for which experienced sales leaders are crucial to driving revenue.

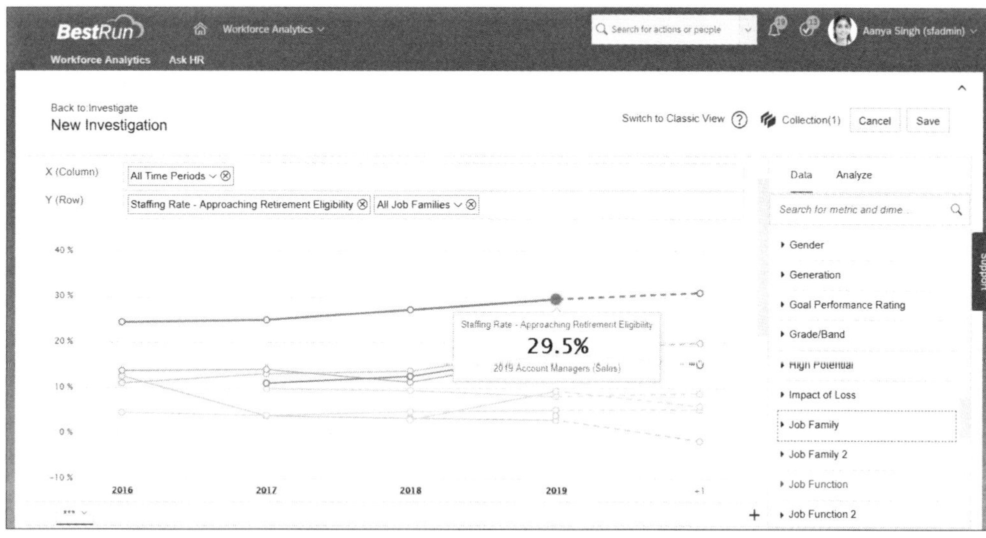

Figure 12.14 Investigating Staffing Rate—Approaching Retirement Eligibility

As with the graphical view, the table beneath it automatically updates with the new data (**Staffing Rate—Retirement Eligibility**, by **Job Family**) and clicking on any cell will show the **Drill To Detail** and employee-level information.

To add more context to these results, switching to the **Analyze** tab allows the user to forecast, via linear regression, up to five periods (years, quarters, months, etc.) into the future. Selecting **Trendlines** (to show the progression of results over time) and **Annualized** (to round-up partial-year data) are options here. Under **Views**, the application automatically suggests alternate visuals (e.g., switching from a line graph to horizontal bar chart) to improve ease of interpretation. Additional suggestions for graphics are available in the **Chart Library** and **Chart Styling** buttons in the horizontal menu bar.

At the bottom of the screen, users can rename the query and add more tabs, thus creating a story with multiple views. For example, while the first tab examines retirement eligibility by job family, the second tab might show retirement data related to grade or critical positions.

To save the investigation, users can add the query to a **Collection**, which can later be shared with other users (by typing in their name or email address), exported, or viewed quickly.

In the next section, we'll cover the more advanced analytical tools available in the Workforce Analytics application.

12.3.4 Analytics Workspace

As your analytics program begins to mature, some analyses might require more powerful statistical analysis tools. The Analytics Workspace feature of the Workforce Analytics solution includes several additional data analysis tools that can be extremely useful for identifying, refining, and visualizing your key findings. the Analytics Workspace is controlled through role-based security and is located on the **Tools** menu in the **Analytics** pane. Note that all queries built in Analytics Workspace can be included in reports built in the Report Designer. The following tools are accessible in Analytics Workspace:

- **Scatterplots**
  A scatterplot is a data visualization tool that quantifies a relationship between two measures, or one measure over two time periods, while also analyzing the strength of that relationship through correlation and regression. To access the Scatterplot tool, you must first click the **Analytics Workspace** tab in the **Tools** menu and then click the **Scatterplot** graphic. A new page displays a sample scatterplot and, similarly, to other tools within the Workforce Analytics solution, a user can choose to open an existing query or build a new scatterplot from scratch. When using the Scatterplot tool, you can view only two measures from the same data cube in one query, meaning that measures from different data sources cannot be analyzed together.

- **Data highlighting**

  Data highlighting is an effective tool for searching through the large amounts of data in Workforce Analytics. Essentially, this analytical tool allows you to define the parameters of your search, and it returns the results that meet your criteria in a list-based table. The results in the table are drillable, meaning that you can quickly navigate to the measure page for the result you're interested in investigating further.

  The data-highlighting functionality is particularly useful when there is a specific issue you're trying to home in on within your data (for example, business units with voluntary turnover rates greater than 20 percent). Additionally, you can add expressions using and/or logic that enables more complex searches and thus more refined results.

- **Significance testing**

  While Workforce Analytics does not require sophisticated statistics to be effective, sometimes there is a need to perform more advanced statistical tests to ensure that the data results are significant. For those well versed in statistics, there is an ability called significance testing in the Analytics Workspace that allows users to perform chi-squared and z-tests. The chi-squared test is used to determine the probability that results are due to chance or whether your results are significant according to the significance level you define (usually 5 percent). After you have the chi-squared test results, you can choose to perform a z-test to determine whether the results are statistically equivalent for two groups.

- **Predictive Models**

  While the Predictive Models tool sits within the Analytics Workspace of the Workforce Analytics solution, the output is typically leveraged for strategic workforce planning purposes. Essentially, the Predictive Models analytical tool allows organizations to model the relationship of two variables across time, both from a historical perspective and to predict future trends. For example, if you want to determine the impact of sales roles on profitability, the tool shows the historical performance of these metrics against each other, in addition to leveraging an underlying algorithm to predict future performance. This becomes useful during the action planning phase of strategic workforce planning, to determine which strategies should be implemented to drive specific organizational outcomes.

  In addition, the Workforce Planning solution allows custom demand models to be built in the Predictive Models tool and then uploaded into demand forecasts for more sophisticated analyses. Demand forecasting is covered in more depth in Chapter 13.

- **Career Trajectory**
  The newest tool to be added to the suite of tools in Analytics Workspace is Career Trajectory, which maps the path, progression, or line of development for individual employees or groups of employees (e.g., organizational unit or location). The upward mobility or succession of employees can then be set against the desired career path to determine whether they are within the career target zone (where the organization expects people to be at that tenure level). The goal of this analytical tool is to give greater focus for managing career trajectories as part of the succession management and employee development process.

All tools within the Workforce Analytics solution have associated product documentation and can be found in the **Help & Resources** section located in the top-right corner of any screen.

12.4 Implementation Tips

Unlike most other SAP SuccessFactors modules, analytics may be a new concept for the customer. As such, it is important to prepare for an implementation with both strategic goals ("How will analytics improve our talent management practices?") and technical considerations ("What resources do we need to create a successful implementation?"). Tips for both are presented in this section.

Let's begin with the following tips on analytics strategy for implementation:

- **Create a clear vision/mission for what analytics means to your HR function**
  While simplistic in nature, having a clear set of expectations about how the Workforce Analytics application will impact decision makers is often overlooked in the rush to deploy the technology. A well-crafted mission statement increases the visibility and focus of the analytics program, provides clarity on individual expectations of internal stakeholders/champions/HR staff, and ensures that resources are allocated to analytics endeavors that have the strongest link to business outcomes.
- **Build the right organizational model to support utilization**
  In contrast to other domains—such as recruiting—where a staff already exists, many customers deploy Workforce Analytics without a well-defined user group. Many organizations initially conceive of analytics as being a broad-based capability that should be a small part of HR staff member responsibilities. This is realistic but risks poor utilization as HR teams focus on other activities. Infusing analytics into the day-to-day operations of HR is crucial for building awareness of data.

- **Distribute data and insights with greatest relevance to consumers**
  While the termination rate metrics is undoubtedly the most popular measure within Workforce Analytics, it is crucial for the success of analytics to share insights that are relevant to the end consumer. For example, operations leaders may not understand the impact of termination rates unless translated into meaningful insights, such as the impact on operational efficiency or customer service. Likewise, finance professionals may care more about the cost of turnover than the implications for headcount gaps.

Additionally, the following tips are useful for a technology strategy for implementation:

- **Know exactly what is being configured**
  Workforce Analytics is very different to a reporting tool. The latter offers real-time, employee-level transactional reporting with very limited data governance procedures (whatever data is in the system is available for reporting). In contrast, Workforce Analytics transforms billions of raw datapoints into a set of metrics and actionable workforce insights. But not every piece of data in a core HRIS will be used for analytics—it is important to understand the concept of metrics packs to become familiar with what metrics come "out of the box."
- **Identify resources with a mix of skills for each stage of implementation and go-live**
  While Workforce Analytics does not consume the same level of resources as an on-premise analytics deployment, certain roles and skill sets are essential during the implementation process. For example, at the outset, the roles of executive sponsor and HR expert are important to set expectations for how Workforce Analytics will deliver value. As the implementation commences, stakeholders include HRIT (to provide guidance on systems and data availability) and HR analysts (confirming how data is defined). Moving toward go-live, important resources might include HR business partners (a common user group) and reporting staff (to create dashboards).
- **Review metrics definitions**
  The success of the go-live is often predicated on users validating that the metrics definitions are correct, at least in their opinions. Many customers use SAP SuccessFactors as the gold standard for how human capital metrics are defined and are reluctant to persist with their own definitions. Others make a strong case for keeping their own definitions/formulas. In either case, customers should be clear on which definitions are to be used and ensure that, post-go-live, their consumers understand how those decisions were reached.

12.5 Summary

You should now have a thorough understanding of the Workforce Analytics solution and how this innovative technology, combined with best practices, helps organizations achieve quantifiable business results. By providing customers with a standardized metrics catalog across the various HR domains and business functions, coupled with powerful and intuitive data analysis tools such as Investigate or Analytics Workspace, organizations can begin to uncover the insights in their data that translate into cost savings or increases in revenue.

The metrics pack overview we covered in the beginning of this chapter aids organizations in adhering to the standard definitions and tried-and-true formulas, which in turn allows organizations to communicate metrics in a common language across the business. Further, the benchmarking program allows clients to make comparisons to external data and is a key differentiator from competitors in the analytics solution marketplace. The Report Designer capability brings all of these data elements together by allowing users to easily create scorecards, dashboards, and standard reports across the business in a scalable and repeatable manner. Investigate, the newest tool in the Workforce Analytics portfolio, is a significant upgrade over Query Workspace and provides the user both with flexibility for creating unique queries as well as predictive forecasting. Finally, the Analytics Workspace offers users several tools for more robust statistical analysis.

The Workforce Analytics solution continues to make fact-based decision-making a part of HR's day-to-day business operations, which is the ultimate goal of analytics in talent management.

In the next chapter, we'll cover the SAP SuccessFactors methodology for strategic workforce planning. In conjunction with the theory behind workforce planning, we'll provide an in-depth review of the Workforce Planning solution in terms of how organizations approach long-range workforce planning.

Chapter 13
Workforce Planning

Despite a growing global labor force (in most, if not all countries), higher rates of intra- and inter-border mobility, and better tools to identify high quality talent, there is little doubt that the speed of technology change makes legacy skills obsolete faster and the shortage of skilled workers makes strategic workforce planning more important than ever.

Strategic workforce planning is a process for forecasting the future demand and supply of labor across time horizons, extending anywhere from two to ten years. Yet, to business leaders more accustomed to just-in-time, rapid-fire decision making, long-term workforce planning can be viewed as archaic, static, or disconnected from the reality of how organizations' design and execute strategy. This viewpoint discounts the fundamental purpose of strategic workforce planning—safeguarding the organization from future workforce risks by assessing, today, the feasibility of those threats. Without such activities, organizations rely primarily on "gut feelings" to make long-term strategic workforce decisions, and more often than not, the resulting plan isn't an accurate representation of the future landscape and doesn't leverage the wealth of historical workforce data that resides in the organization's human capital management (HCM) system.

Additional benefits of strategic workforce planning include:

- Financial
  - Lower turnover costs, through more precise human resources (HR) interventions (focused development or retention plans, and so on)
  - Reduced hiring/temporary labor costs, by more accurately forecasting future staffing needs and building internal pipelines
- Operational
  - Improved assessments of human capital risks (aging workforce, shortage of external supply, and so on) threatening growth plans

- Greater visibility for managers of their team's performance and career development
- **Human capital**
  - Better identification of skills and competencies required for successful operations over the next one, three, five, and seven years
  - Speedier hiring of staff to fill critical jobs
  - Increased number of "ready now" succession candidates

SAP SuccessFactors Workforce Planning provides a platform and proven process to aid organizations in proactively planning for the types of business challenges associated with critical talent shortages and surpluses. In effect, the solution facilitates the process of matching workforce supply with workforce demand to determine where talent gaps exist and provides the ability to forecast and model changes to the workforce across the business. The application also highlights risks, capability and skill gaps, cost modeling, and best-practice strategies to successfully execute strategy and plan action for the long term.

The application is an extension of the SAP SuccessFactors Workforce Analytics module and is fed underlying data from the Workforce Analytics engine. In addition, the Workforce Analytics module plays a key role in the ongoing monitoring and reporting of critical areas of the business, which is the final step in the strategic workforce planning process.

In this chapter, we'll cover the basic methodology and theory behind strategic workforce planning, as well as the key functionality within the Workforce Planning solution. This includes an in-depth review of the key activities in strategic workforce planning, such as demand and supply forecasting and gap analysis, risk identification and action planning, and what-if financial modeling.

13.1 Workforce Planning Basics

Let's begin by defining strategic workforce planning as presented in the Workforce Planning solution. Essentially, strategic workforce planning is a process to ensure that your organization has the right people in the right place with the right skills at the right time, and all for the right price. In theory, if you are doing all of these things properly, you can execute your business strategy successfully and proactively mitigate risks along the way.

Note

Let's consider an example. One customer's data analysis revealed an aging workforce problem within the engineering and technician job families. Using Workforce Planning, the company created both enterprise and business unit-specific workforce plans for 17 job functions, resulting in heightened awareness of workforce risks. Senior leaders were subsequently tasked with measuring progress toward hiring and retention goals based on the long-term workforce plan.

A common challenge today is that "workforce planning" can encompass all manner of activities, including:

- Scheduling of staff against available shifts
- Determining availability for future projects
- Assessing competency gaps that fuel individual development planning
- Succession planning
- Headcount budgeting

However, at its core, the strategic workforce planning process forecasts changes to workforce supply and demand across, typically, a three- to five-year timeframe and how those talent flows may impact the execution of business strategy. On a related note, it's important to understand what strategic workforce planning is *not*: it's not short-term resource planning to fill open headcount, and it's not succession planning for named resources.

In general, organizations tend to be better at considering the right place and time when planning for future demand, but they place less emphasis on the right skills and the right price. With strategic workforce planning, you start to ask questions such as the following:

- Do we know what skills we'll need in the future?
- Do we have sufficient quantities of those skills?
- If so, with which business units or job roles are the skills most commonly found?
- If not, can we build or borrow critical skills, or do we need to buy them from the external labor market?

To answer questions like these, organizations need a proven process to guide strategic talent management decisions, with a broad objective of transitioning from "firefighting" hiring to being more proactive about hiring, retaining, and moving employees.

The first step in understanding how Workforce Planning achieves this goal is to review the metrics packs and the data extract, transform, load (ETL) processes that underpin the application.

13.1.1 Metrics Packs for Workforce Planning

As discussed at length in Chapter 12 on Workforce Analytics, metrics packs are used to transform raw data into standardized metrics based on time-tested logic and formulas. Each metrics pack contains a related set of measures and reporting dimensions that do the following:

- Define a standard set of metrics specific to a range of topics (performance, recruiting, and so on)
- Define a standard set of dimensions/hierarchies (for example, full-time versus part-time workers) to support further analysis of the metrics
- Map metrics to the data needed to populate them
- Include common business logic that can be customized by clients

The Core Workforce and Mobility metrics pack, Workforce Planning version, supports the necessary data items required to enable the generation of measures and reporting structures needed for strategic workforce planning, including a full-time equivalent (FTE) measure set that allows organizations to forecast using either headcount or FTE metrics. Otherwise, the Core Workforce and Mobility metrics pack for Workforce Planning operates in a similar manner as that for Workforce Analytics.

13.1.2 Data Acquisition and Governance

In this section, we'll look at how SAP SuccessFactors acquires and manages inbound data specifically for strategic workforce planning. In short, the process for building the data asset that powers the Workforce Planning application is almost identical to that which powers Workforce Analytics. As such, a detailed review of the data acquisition process can be found in Chapter 12, Section 12.1.3.

For customers embarking on strategic workforce planning for the first time, or upgrading from spreadsheets to the Workforce Planning solution, an oft-asked question is "What data do we need to conduct long-term workforce planning?"

Data elements can be generally divided into the following categories:

- Core: Requirements which are largely essential for standard strategic workforce planning processes
- Supplemental: Requirements which are important, but not essential, to standard processes

As we will see later in Section 13.3, the employee ID is combined with demographic data (age), employment history (hire date, any separations/retirements), and organizational information (structures, job families, employment status, and so on) to produce a standard workforce planning process. Supplemental data might include FTEs, capabilities, and workforce costs. Table 13.1 provides examples of the different types of data that could be included in Workforce Planning.

Data Element	Core	Supplemental
Common employee ID	Yes	
FTE calculation/standard hours (for FTE forecasting)		Yes
Hire date	Yes	
Birth date	Yes	
Separation/retirement date	Yes	
Organizational structure (unit, location, cost center, etc.)	Yes	
Employment status (full/part time)	Yes	
Non-employee data (contractors, consultants, etc.)		Yes
Job family/role	Yes	
Demographics (gender, ethnicity)		Yes
Capabilities/competencies for selected job families/roles		Yes
1+ year of historical data	Yes	
Financial data (salaries, turnover costs, etc.)		Yes
Standard definitions of workforce planning metrics	Yes	

Table 13.1 Core and Supplemental Data Useful for Workforce Planning

In workforce planning, strategic measures typically comprise a mix of labor-force mobility (internal and external), retirement eligibility and take-up rates, and models of financial impact. Of particular importance is calculating the projected number of voluntary terminations over the forecast period (three years, five years, and so on). This can be accomplished by taking the voluntary turnover for each job family and organizational unit and overlaying the data with tenure and age trends (to account for retirement eligibility-driven terminations).

Naturally, there is the potential for significant variation in termination projections as the data becomes less reliable at lower levels of the organization. However, such discrepancies will normally be accounted for in the enterprise-wide plan.

In the next section, we'll discuss how to prepare for a strategic workforce planning process using the SAP SuccessFactors solution.

13.2 Preparing for Workforce Planning

Customers can access Workforce Planning by clicking the **Workforce Planning** link from the SAP SuccessFactors homepage, as shown in Figure 13.1.

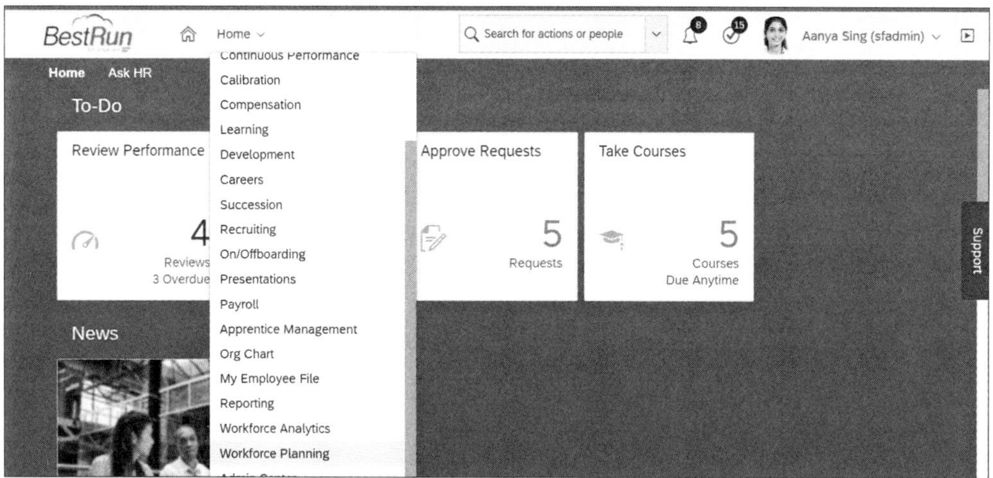

Figure 13.1 Accessing Workforce Planning

The Workforce Planning module follows a five-step strategic workforce planning methodology:

1. Strategic analysis

2. Forecasting
3. Risk analysis
4. Strategy, impact, and cost modeling
5. Actions and accountability

The five-step process flow can be seen on the Workforce Planning home page screen, as shown in Figure 13.2. Note that, in the past few years, SAP SuccessFactors has updated the methodology to include a "pre-step" that is known as the Workforce Planning Foundation (not shown) at the base of the staircase. While this isn't an actual step in the technology process, it was added to act as a blueprint to ensure that customers have the critical data elements (for example, job family framework) and support mechanisms (for example, staff resources) in place before kicking off the strategic workforce planning process.

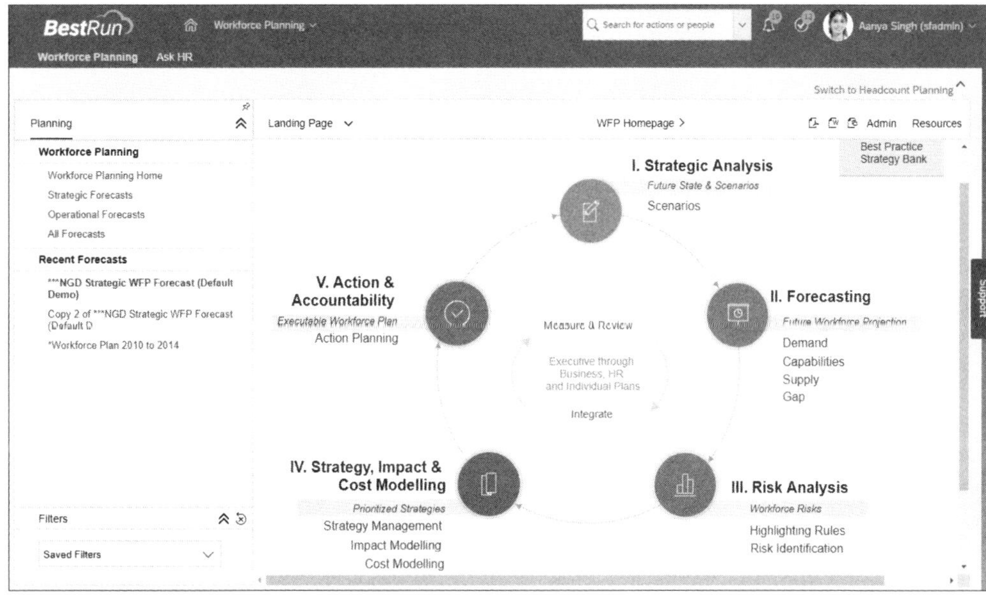

Figure 13.2 The Home Screen of Workforce Planning

The Workforce Planning solution acts as a wizard, taking users through each of the steps to consolidate the qualitative and quantitative data in one forecast for a complete yet simplified analysis. Because strategic workforce planning is very much a qualitative process, much of the information is collected in workshop- or interview-style settings and then input into the tool. In addition, the **Help** button located at the top of every screen is populated with valuable information about tips and tricks for navigating the tool and populating the various tabs throughout the planning process.

Let's walk through each of the phases, beginning with how to create a forecast in Workforce Planning.

13.2.1 Forecast List

The first entry point in Workforce Planning is the *forecast list*, which can be accessed on the **Workforce Planning** home page (refer to Figure 13.2). Within the **Planning** tab, there are a few options:

- **Workforce Planning Home**
- **Strategic Forecasts**
- **Operational Forecasts**
- **All Forecasts**

For the purposes of this example, we'll look at how to access an existing strategic forecast or build a new one from scratch. When you click the **Strategic Forecasts** link, a new page refreshes that shows all previously built strategic forecasts, as shown in the center of Figure 13.3.

From here, you can edit or copy an existing forecast by clicking the **Edit** dropdown, or you can build a new forecast from scratch by clicking the **New** dropdown. The forecast details for the selected forecast are shown on the right-hand side of the screen, in the **Summary** window. Directly below the **Summary** window is another box called **Explore Forecast**, which contains quick links to the various phases of the five-step methodology. Also, each forecast within the list is color coded, with green denoting a completely built forecast, yellow indicating that the forecast is in the process of being built, and gray indicating incomplete forecasts.

Users can build as many forecasts as they like, but keep in mind that all users can see all forecasts. However, administrators of the Workforce Planning solution can determine what level of access users of the system will have—either full access for building forecasts (power users) or a more limited workforce planning role that allows users only to modify the demand or supply numbers of existing forecasts.

In the next section, we'll walk through the steps of building a new strategic forecast.

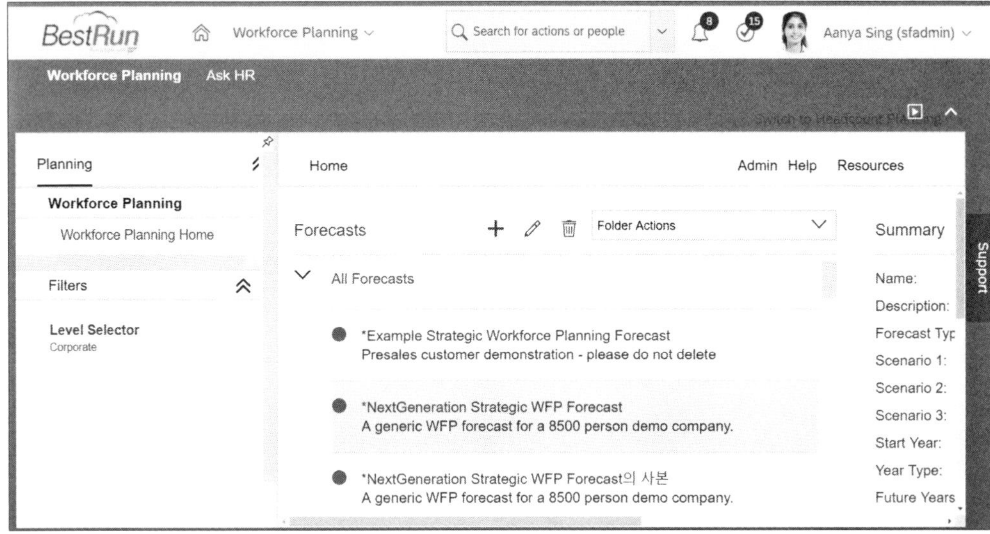

Figure 13.3 Strategic Forecasts Available in Workforce Planning

13

13.2.2 Creating a Strategic Forecast

Within the Workforce Planning solution, strategic plans are called *forecasts* and fall into three types of forecasts:

- Strategic forecast (two or more years into the future)
- Operational forecast (six months to 48 months into the future)
- Amalgamated strategic forecast (combine separate strategic forecasts into one)

After a forecast type is selected, a new window opens with six main tabs, which are outlined in the process flow at the top of the screen, as shown in Figure 13.4. These six steps to build a strategic forecast include defining all data elements that will be analyzed, as well as the future scenarios that we'll plan against:

1. **Forecast Basics**
2. **Set Scenarios**
3. **Set Dimensions**
4. **Set Retirements**
5. **Set Structure**
6. **Build**

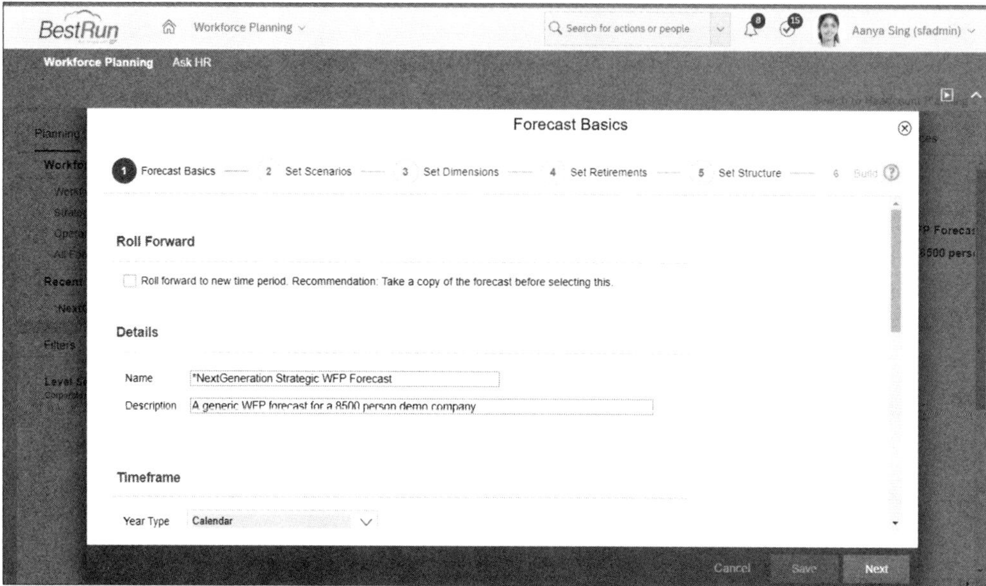

Figure 13.4 Creating a Strategic Forecast

Let's take a look at an example of how to build a strategic forecast for a company expanding its retail operations.

Forecast Basics

The first step of creating a strategic forecast is to provide the basic information for the forecast, which you can do by clicking the **New** button and selecting **New Strategic Forecast**. Doing so causes a new window to appear with the title **Forecast Basics**, and you're prompted to enter the details and factors of your forecast. Essentially, the information in the following sections and fields is the backbone of your workforce plan:

- **Details**
  Name and description of your forecast
- **Timeframe**
  Year type (calendar or fiscal), start year, and future years you'll be forecasting against
- **Business Factors**
  Headcount or FTE, termination rate, hire rate, movements-in rate, movements-out rate, and vacancies

Let's take a closer look at the **Business Factors** section. This is where you choose which underlying measures the tool will leverage from the Workforce Analytics solution. This information is used mainly to populate the **Supply** tab with predictions on headcount, terminations, hires, movements, and vacancies based on historical data. For instance, users can choose to forecast against end-of-period (EOP) headcount or FTE, depending on how headcount is reported in their organization. This section of Workforce Planning must be configured to show the measures that you want to make available for users to choose from.

Additionally, different termination measures can be configured to choose from in the **Termination Rate** dropdown. Typically, forecasts leverage the voluntary termination rate (minus retirements) measure as the standard. The reason this is the most common slice of termination rate for strategic workforce planning purposes is that retirements are broken out, which allows users to define the retirement logic in the **Set Retirements** tab (covered later in this section).

The additional measures that can be enabled for the forecast are movements in, movements out, external hires, and vacancies. The external hire rate is generally included; however, best practice states that movement data (e.g., promotions and transfers) should be incorporated in the forecast only if there is a clearly defined career path program for the specific job roles you're planning against.

Lastly, the **Vacancies** field can be enabled only if a client has configured the Workforce Analytics solution to include vacancy rates.

The final piece to consider when filling out the **Business Factors** section of the forecast is the source year for each data element. Next to each measure, there is a dropdown list called **Source Year**, which shows all the previous years of historical data that are captured in the Workforce Analytics solution. Using the external hire rate as an example, if you select 2018 as the source year, the tool leverages the 2018 external hire rate as a baseline to predict the number of hires for the next five years. However, if 2018 was an unusual year in terms of hires, you might decide to use 2017 as a baseline instead because it was a more "normal" year to represent the organization's hiring patterns.

After you've entered these details into business factors, the screen should look like Figure 13.5.

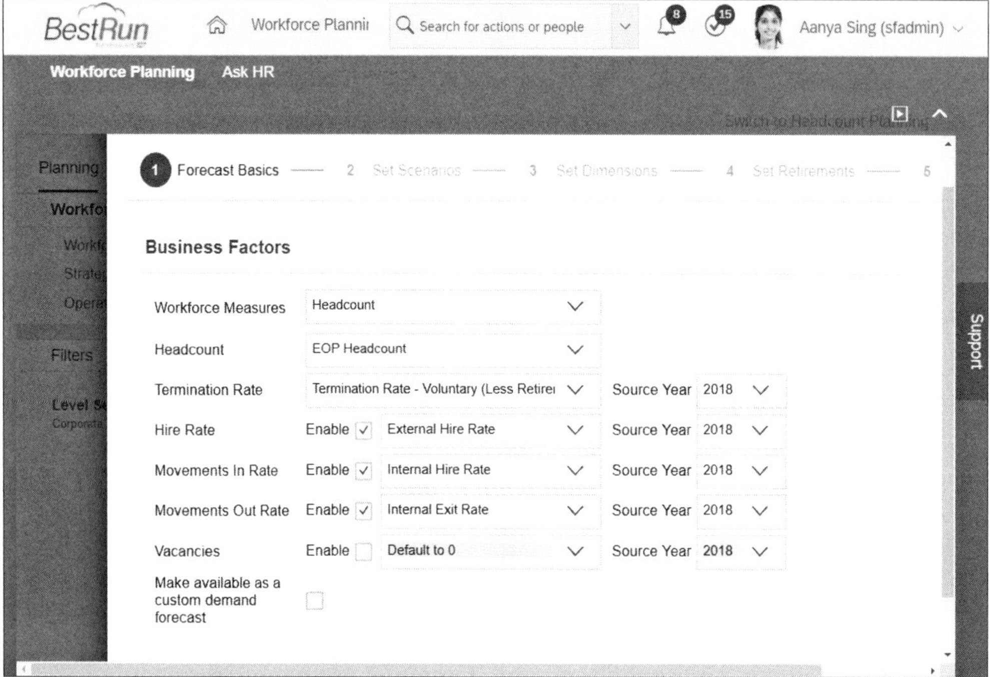

Figure 13.5 Completed Business Factors

Let's move on to the next tab: **Set Scenarios**.

Set Scenarios

Defining plausible future states, known as scenarios, is a key step in the strategic workforce planning process, and it typically takes place in a workshop setting with key business leaders and workforce planners. At this stage of the process, the key stakeholder group comes together to discuss the strategy of their areas of the business in relation to the overall company strategy for the forecast period. The objective is to identify a set of unknowns that could potentially affect demand for the critical talent necessary to execute strategy. Simply stated, scenarios are an articulation of what you predict will significantly impact the business during the forecast period.

We develop robust scenarios for the following reasons:

- To understand the drivers of demand to estimate the future demand for labor
- To help identify critical job roles

- To get risks/issues out in the open, including workforce capacity and capability
- To understand the organizational strategy in conjunction with the drivers of change, with a focus on the talent impact

During scenario planning, the focus is mainly on external business factors that are outside of the organization's control (e.g., regulations, politics, socioeconomic factors, etc.). In addition, because the goal is to limit the number of scenarios to a maximum of three, scenarios should be plausible, rather than possible. The final step of scenario planning is to obtain sign-off on the scenarios that will be included for forecast purposes. Let's review a common set of two scenarios: one for high growth and a second for low growth. As shown in Figure 13.6, the **Set Scenarios** tab has **Scenario 1** entered as the default.

If you click **Scenario 1**, a new window opens where you can enter the details and comments that are critical to capture from the scenario planning session. In this window, you can rename the scenario and give a short optional description, so let's change the name to "High Growth." You can add any information that will be helpful to consider during the demand forecasting process into the accompanying text box. Lastly, you can add assumptions common to all scenarios, which are defined as factors that are likely to happen regardless of either scenario's playing out.

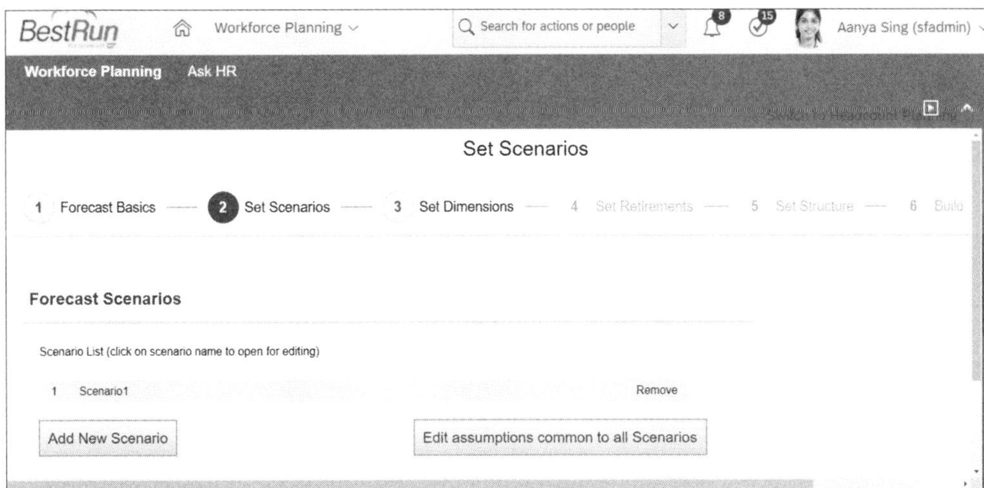

Figure 13.6 The Set Scenarios of Creating a Strategic Forecast

After your forecast is built, all scenarios can be accessed on the **Strategic Analysis** tab in the tool. We can now move on to the next tab: **Set Dimensions**.

Set Dimensions

The third step of building a forecast is to set *dimensions*. In this step, you can add multiple dimensions, which is how you define the critical population that you'll be forecasting against. This is where you determine what those critical jobs roles are and how you're going to analyze them. The most commonly used dimensions for strategic workforce planning are job family, grade, and critical job role.

> **Note**
>
> Organizations differ in which employee populations should be included in strategic workforce planning. Typically, SAP SuccessFactors has encouraged firms to focus on critical job roles, which might comprise 15–25 percent of the workforce; however, it is not common for organizations to conduct strategic workforce planning for a majority of their employees.

For this example, let's say that you're planning for job roles in specific job families, and you want to analyze those that have been marked as critical. When you click the **Add Dimension** button, a list of available dimensions that have been configured for Workforce Planning populates in a dropdown list, and you add **Job Family**. The dimension populates with the various nodes that have been defined. Users can select or deselect specific nodes to be included in the forecast by highlighting them or choose to include all nodes. In this specific example, we'll select all nodes within the **Job Family** dimension.

> **Note**
>
> Let's consider an example. In one instance, an SAP SuccessFactors customer used Workforce Planning to measure historical turnover and predict future attrition by "high-risk disciplines," including business units with a high average workforce age, those with positions that historically have been hard to fill, or those that suffer from excessive internal churn.

You still need to add a second dimension for **Critical Roles**, which you can do by clicking the **Add Dimension** button.

All dimensions have an **[Add Node]** link at the bottom of the node list. This is for users to create a placeholder for anticipated future nodes that don't exist yet. For example, under **Job Family**, you may not have an existing job family today for a job that you know will be critical in the future, but you can create a place to capture that in your forecast here in the **Set Dimensions** tab.

Finally, the order of the dimensions is important because this is how they appear on your demand spreadsheet. Simply click the red left or right arrows to move certain dimensions up or down in the order list.

One final tip in the **Set Dimensions** tab is that if you scroll to the bottom of the window, you see the option to choose whether to leverage a *capability framework*. By checking the **Use a Capability Framework?** checkbox, you have the ability to forecast by capabilities (also known as skills, competencies, and so on), as well as build a rating scale to rate the current and future skill levels of employees in critical job roles. If you build your forecast without selecting this checkbox, you'll be unable to enter capability demands in the forecasting section of the tool.

The Workforce Planning solution comes with an embedded capability framework, which can be selected as the default in the **Select a Framework** dropdown. However, most clients opt to enter an organization-specific capability framework into the tool instead.

Next, you're prompted to choose an importance scale, which can be either a 5- or 10-point scale. Typically, the five-point scale will suffice, although both options are available. We'll cover how to enter a custom capability framework and assign values to the rating scales in Section 13.3.3.

We can now move on to the next step, which is to set the retirement profile.

Set Retirements

The set retirements step allows you to define the *retirement profile(s)* that can be applied to your critical job roles in the **Set Retirements** tab. There are two options for defining the retirement profile: **Fixed Retirement Age** or **Mathematical Approximation**.

The **Fixed Retirement Age** option allows a fixed value to be defined for the retirement age. For example, if you know based on historical data that employees in job role X typically retire by age 68, you can set this age as the cutoff.

The second option, **Mathematical Approximation**, shows the curved line progression of retirements by defining the start and end age of the retirement wave. Users can either show this in a **Straight line** or **Exponential curve**, with **Exponential curve** being the typical selection. From here, you can select the **Start age** from the dropdown menu and define the **End age**, as well. The last option is to enable the **Use cutoff age** checkbox, which says that all employees will retire by age X. As you change your retirement model criteria, the chart at the bottom of the window updates with a graphical representation of your selection showing the rate at which you can expect employees to retire.

For this example, we chose to enable the **Mathematical Approximation** model with the **Exponential curve**, with a **Start age** of 65 and an **End age** of 75, as shown in Figure 13.7.

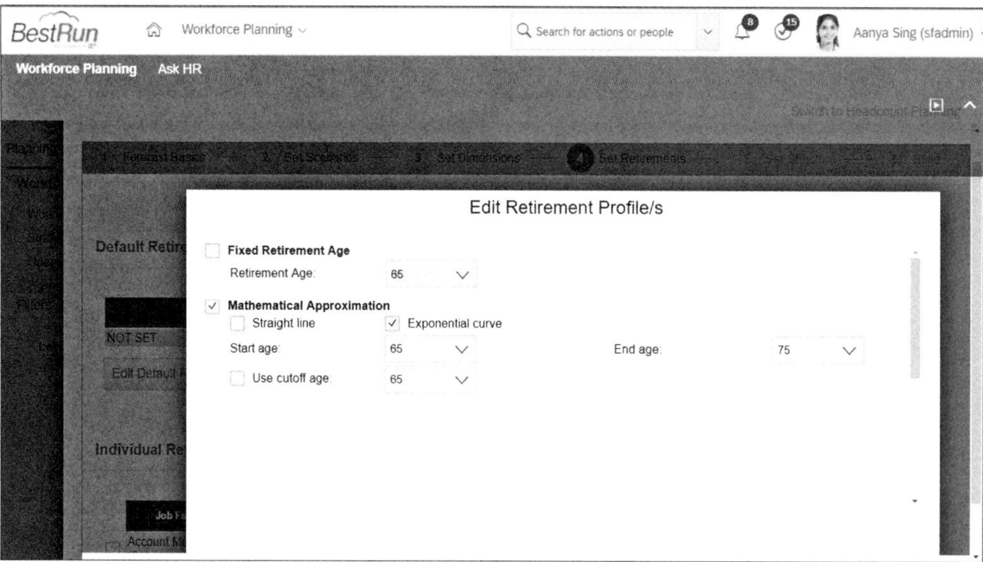

Figure 13.7 Edit the Retirement Profile Screen

In addition to defining the general retirement model, you can set individual retirement profiles for specific job roles in your forecast, which overrides the default retirement model for only the job roles that you assign (see Figure 13.8). This becomes very useful when you're forecasting for a job such as an airplane pilot, wherein there are regulations specifying the specific age when pilots must retire.

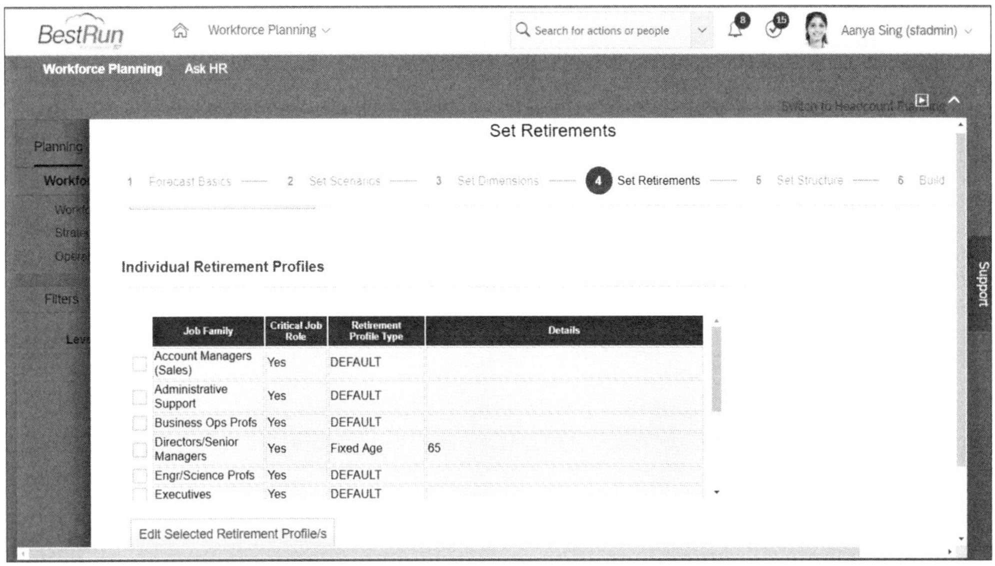

Figure 13.8 Setting Individual Retirement Profile

Let's move on to the next tab: **Set Structure**.

Set Structure

In the **Set Structure** tab, you can define the organizational structure for your forecast. As discussed in Chapter 12, customers can have multiple organizational hierarchies such as organizational units, cost centers, supervisors, or location structures. The most common structures for long-term planning tend to be organizational units or locations (cost structures are typically used with headcount cost planning and supervisor structures are typically used for succession planning).

When you click the **Structure** dropdown arrow, all available structures are displayed, but only one can be selected. The most common hierarchy is the organizational unit structure.

As an example, let's say you only want to run a workforce planning process for the five of the most important business units in the retail division. First, click the plus (**+**) button to expand the top node of the organizational structure called **All Organizational Units.** From here, expand the **Retail** level, and select **Retail** and the selected business units beneath it, as shown in Figure 13.9. Also, all existing hierarchies show a link node called **Add Level**, which is used to create a node for a business unit, cost center, location, and so on that doesn't exist today but that you predict will exist in the future.

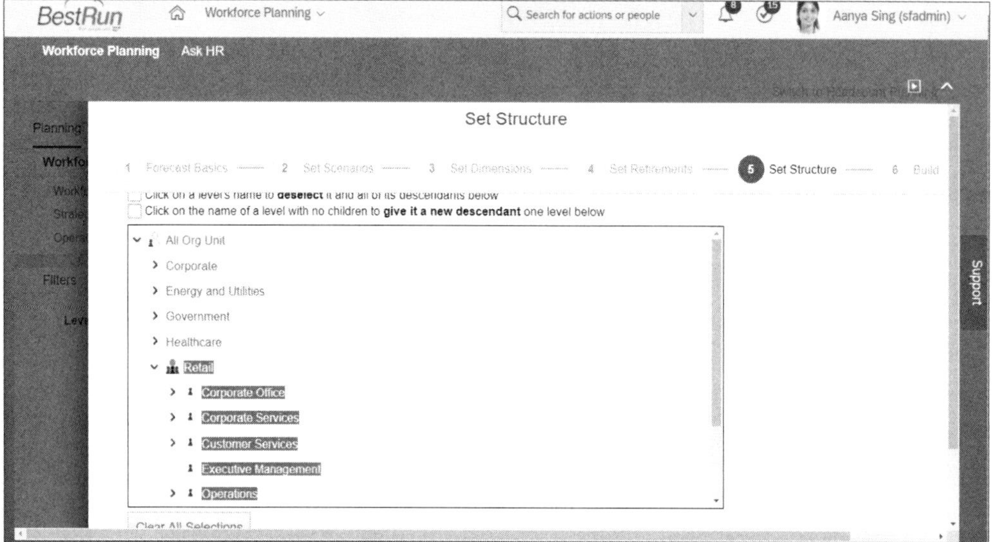

Figure 13.9 Setting the Structure

At the bottom of the **Set Structure** tab, you'll see the **Summation Level Editing Enabled** checkbox, which allows users to edit the total level (top level) of the forecast. While all forecast data entered at the business unit or department level automatically rolls up to the top-level node selected, sometimes it's necessary to edit at the total level, as well.

Let's move on to the final tab.

Build Forecast

The final step of building the forecast is to verify your forecast selections and create the forecast using the **Build Forecast** button. Until the build is complete, your forecast has a yellow dot next to it in the **Strategic Forecasts** list. After the forecast build is complete, you receive an email notification, and the dot turns green in the **Strategic Forecasts** list.

On the right-hand side of the **Forecasts** screen, you can see an overall summary of what you've selected, as shown in Figure 13.10. To summarize, you're looking at two different scenarios (high growth vs. low growth), and you're starting in the 2018 calendar year and forecasting out for 2019, 2021, and 2013. Finally, you're analyzing job family by critical roles for the retail business unit and incorporating the 2018 voluntary termination rate (minus retirements).

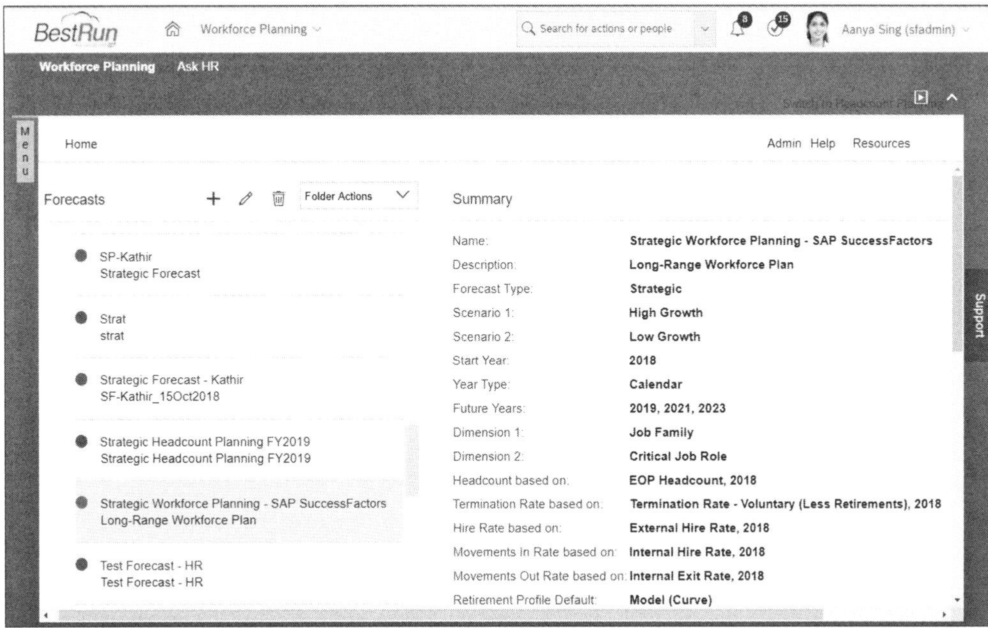

Figure 13.10 Summary View

Now that the forecast has been built, we'll cover the forecasting step in the strategic workforce planning process.

13.3 Forecasting

Forecasting is the process of evaluating scenarios to identify any gaps between your existing talent pool and the optimal organizational mix of people and skills that will be needed in the future. In strategic workforce planning, forecasting is generally broken down into two separate steps: *demand forecasting* (includes both capability and capacity forecasting) and *supply forecasting*.

This section will demonstrate how to conduct a strategic workforce planning process, starting with the deployment of our scenarios.

13.3.1 Scenarios

Because setting scenarios is entirely text-based, Workforce Planning allows users to enter qualitative descriptions of the scenarios. This plays a key role in helping your demand forecasters understand the business goals for the next few years, so the level of granularity is important here. The more detail you can give in each scenario, the easier the job of the demand forecaster is when they are determining how many people with what skills they are going to need to be successful in the future.

When setting up our forecast, we created a number of scenarios that we will use for our workforce plan. For example, we created two scenarios: high growth and low growth.

In Figure 13.11 you can now see these scenarios, which can be edited to add more detail; for example, users can add economic data, strategic priorities, and organiza tional knowledge.

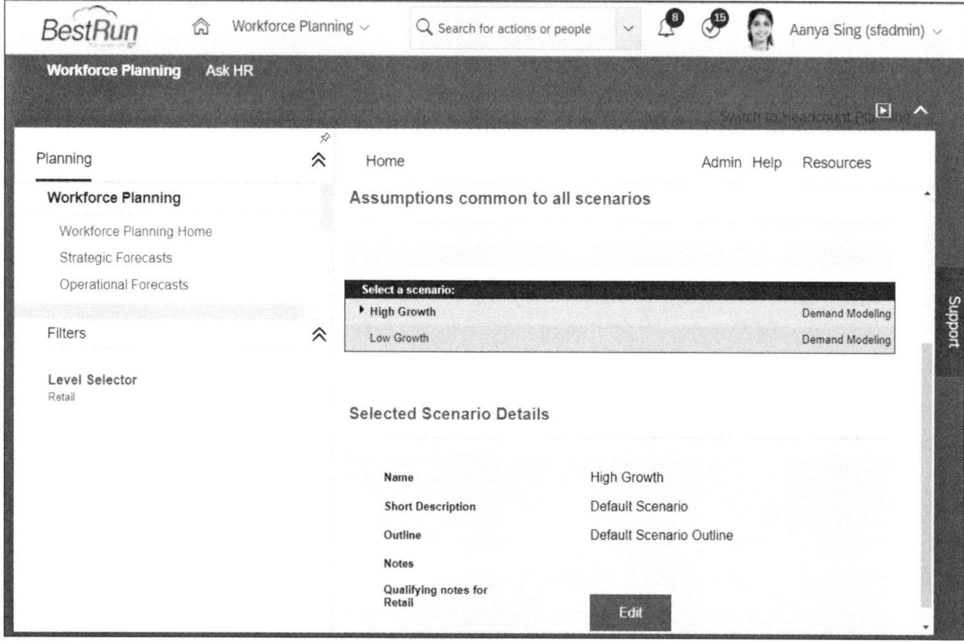

Figure 13.11 Scenarios in Strategic Workforce Planning

13.3.2 Demand Forecasting

Forecasting demand is the process of determining the number of people you'll need in each of the critical job roles that have been identified under each scenario. Critical job roles are defined as those that do the following:

- Conduct the core business of the organization
- May become part of the core business under either scenario
- Have had a high number of vacancies in the past 12 months
- Have been historically difficult to fill
- Require a long training time to develop the skills for the role
- Have the largest number of staff

From a demand standpoint, directors/managers who have expert knowledge of the business are asked to forecast how many people they will need in each critical job role over the next one, three, and five years to meet the demand of each scenario.

In addition, many organizations forecast demand in terms of not only the number of people needed, but also the specific capabilities that will be necessary to execute the organizational strategy. In *capability forecasting*, you're looking to differentiate between skills needed today and those that will be needed in the future.

Typically, the process of determining demand is done in a demand workshop setting or through a series of demand interviews. Lastly, the demand forecasting should be zero-based to estimate demand as if you're starting from scratch. However, it's helpful to understand the current headcount of each critical job role, to give forecasters a frame of reference in terms of the amount of growth or downsizing that needs to occur.

After you've collected your demand numbers by critical job role, you can enter the forecast into the Workforce Planning solution via the **Demand** link under the **Forecasting** heading. When you enter the **Demand** screen, you first see a graphical representation of your demand forecast. Because we haven't yet inputted any demand numbers, the tool automatically assumes a steady-state forecast. This means simply that the demand for each job family over the five-year forecast period remains the same as the starting headcount in 2018 (the beginning year of our forecast). Figure 13.12 shows the steady-state demand forecast for the **Retail** business unit.

You can also display the demand forecast as a table. In the table view, you can modify the demand numbers for each critical job family, scenario, and year of the forecast. The demand page view can be customized to show the data elements or cuts that are of specific interest (e.g., only one scenario, only the first two years, etc.). Similarly, if you want to focus on only one department at a time, you can do so by clicking the **Level Selector** in the **Filters** pane and selecting a specific node.

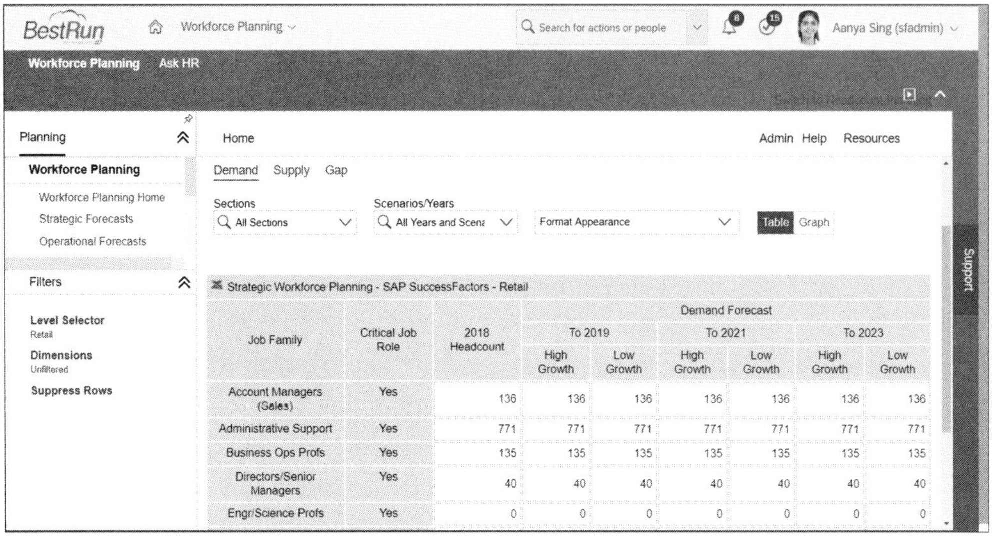

Figure 13.12 Steady-State Demand

Let's say you want to forecast demand for **Customer Services** and select this node only. Users can export this demand forecast to Excel by clicking the **Excel** icon in the top-left corner of the spreadsheet. By providing this customized view to customer services managers, they can more easily forecast demand for their critical job families (as opposed to seeing the entire retail business unit). After the headcount demand is finalized by managers for the customer services department, you can upload the revised demand forecast into Workforce Planning by clicking the **Upload (Import from Excel)** link, eliminating much of the manual data entry.

If a demand forecaster's preference is to modify the demand numbers directly in the Workforce Planning solution, you can simply click a cell and manually override the existing entry in a new window called **Edit Values**, as shown in Figure 13.13.

Forecasters repeat the process for each critical job family, under each scenario, for each year until the forecast is complete. Often, it's helpful to enter comments in the **Edit Values** window so that others can quickly understand a forecaster's logic for the demand estimates.

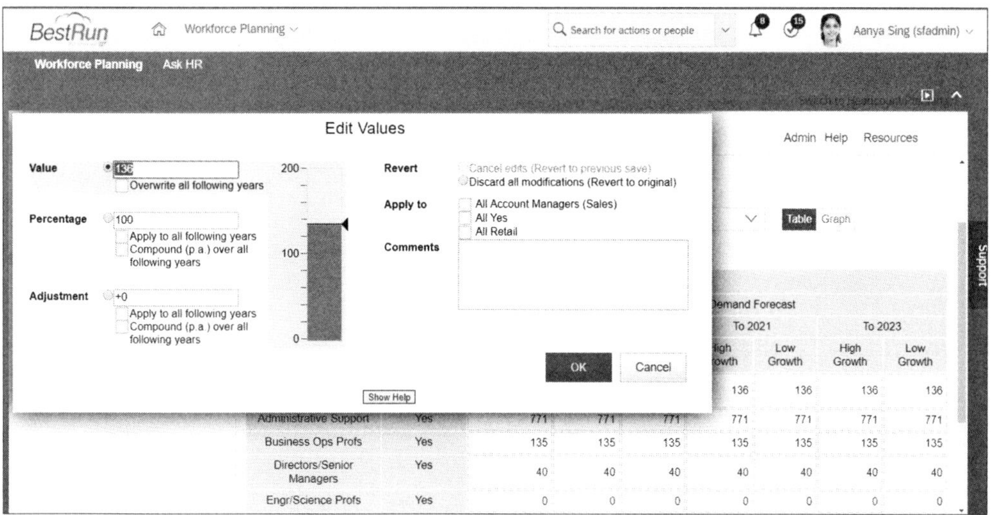

Figure 13.13 Edit Values

Let's move to the next link in the **Forecasting** tab called **Capabilities**. This tab is available only if you've enabled the capability framework when building your forecast.

13.3.3 Capabilities

When you click the **Capability** link, a new screen refreshes that shows each critical job family with no capabilities attached. The goal here is populate the most important capabilities for each job role we are forecasting against. Users can enter the names of specific capabilities, the importance of each, the current rating (for example, **Not Acceptable**) and the desired rating. You can also enter comments about the importance and ratings you've assigned.

Figure 13.14 shows the completed capabilities table for the several job families. Multiple capabilities can be added to each job family and, similar to other tabs in Workforce Planning, the capability spreadsheet can be exported to Excel. Users can also toggle between a table and graph view.

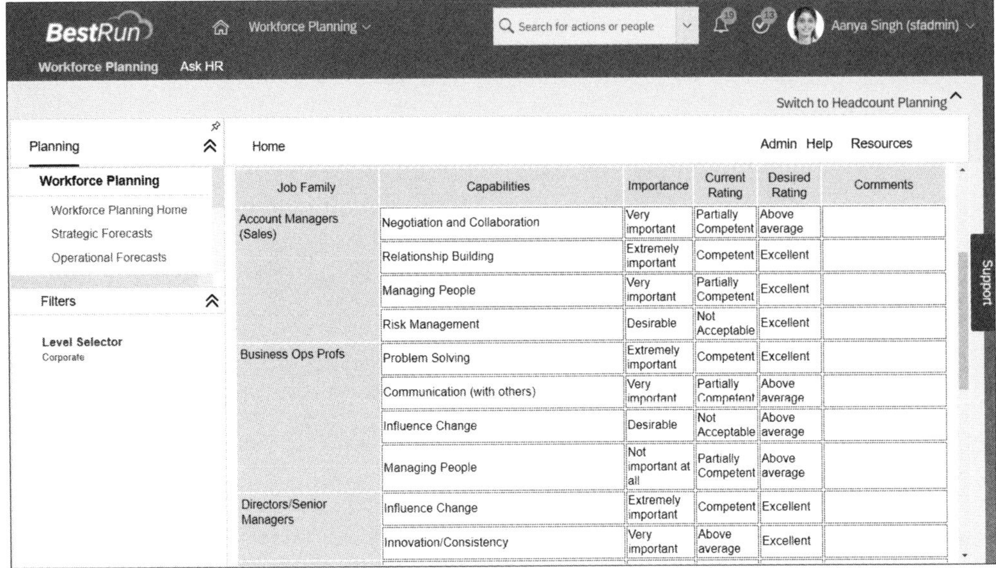

Figure 13.14 Completed Capability View

Now that we've walked through how to forecast capabilities, let's discuss supply forecasting, which you can access by clicking the **Supply** link.

13.3.4 Supply Forecasting

Supply forecasting is where you leverage the measures taken from the underlying analytics engine, meaning that the tool is applying historical rates to forecast estimates for terminations, hires, movements, and vacancies (depending on what you enabled while building the forecast). Similar to the **Demand** tab, when you click **Supply,** the first screen shows a graphical representation of supply for each critical job family over the forecast period. By clicking the **Table/Graph** toggle button, you can view the supply figures in a table, which is the preferred format for forecasting supply.

In the table view, we're starting with the 2018 headcount for each critical job family, and the tool is using the 2018 voluntary termination rate (minus retirements) as a baseline for supply into 2019, 2012, and 2022. This measure truly is a baseline, meaning that you can edit the historical supply estimates to more accurately model out expected future patterns. Exactly as you did in **Demand**, you can click any one of the cells in the supply table to modify the value.

To the right of the current headcount, terminations, retirements, and external hires are incorporated to give a more granular understanding of what the forecast will look like from a supply perspective across the next five years, as shown in Figure 13.15.

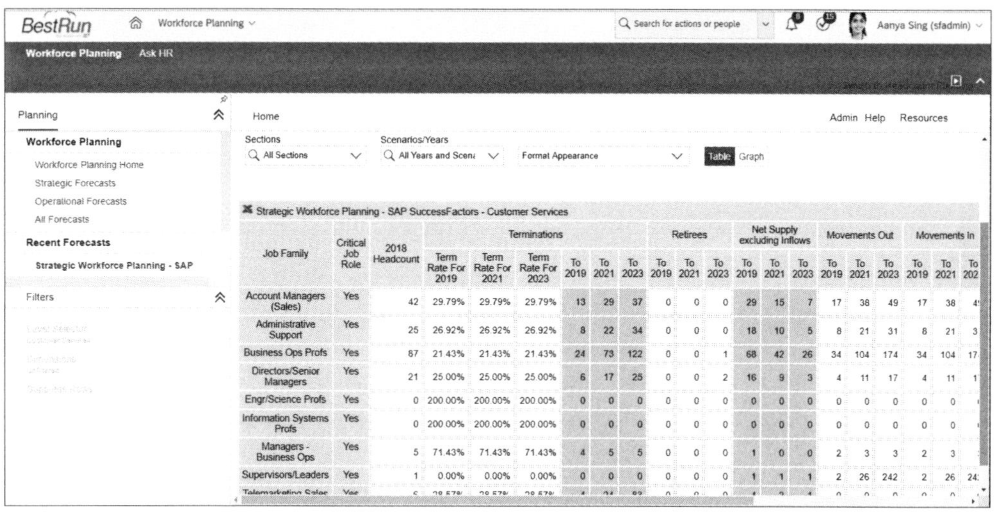

Figure 13.15 Supply Table

As with demand, you can view the supply forecast in a graph, and there are a few different charting options. One particularly useful view is the **Net Supply Excluding Inflows** view, which essentially shows you where you'll be at the end of the forecast period if you do nothing differently. In other words, the supply curve is only showing outflows (terminations and retirements), without factoring in any new hires (internal or external) to backfill positions.

Now that the necessary changes have been made to the supply forecast, let's move to the final forecasting step: analyzing the gap.

13.3.5 Gap Analysis

Gap analysis is a simple calculation of demand minus supply, and it helps you identify the key workforce risks for both capacity (numbers) and capabilities. In the **Gap** tab, you're pairing together supply and demand and breaking it down by scenario. Once this is calculated, you can see the overall net supply, as well as the magnitude of the gap per scenario, as either a shortage or a surplus.

13

The **Gap** tab shows a graphical view on the initial screen. You can toggle to the **Table** view to see a more granular view of both demand and supply in one table, and you can customize the columns shown in the table. Figure 13.16 shows the **Gap** table for the **Customer Services** department, which identifies shortages across all critical job families, regardless of scenario.

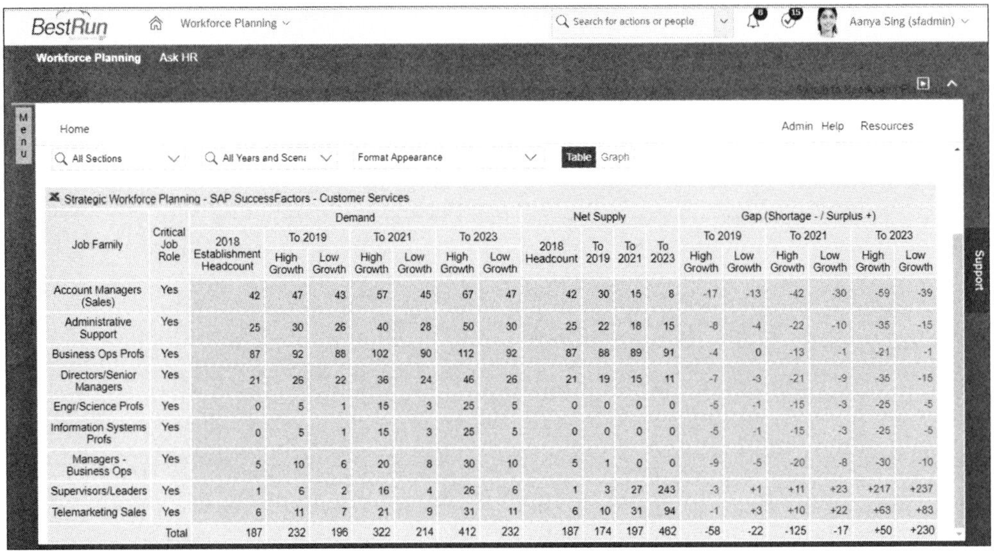

Strategic Workforce Planning - SAP SuccessFactors - Customer Services

Job Family	Critical Job Role	Demand							Net Supply				Gap (Shortage - / Surplus +)					
		2018 Establishment Headcount	To 2019		To 2021		To 2023		2018 Headcount	To 2019	To 2021	To 2023	To 2019		To 2021		To 2023	
			High Growth	Low Growth	High Growth	Low Growth	High Growth	Low Growth					High Growth	Low Growth	High Growth	Low Growth	High Growth	Low Growth
Account Managers (Sales)	Yes	42	47	43	57	45	67	47	42	30	15	8	-17	-13	-42	-30	-59	-39
Administrative Support	Yes	25	30	26	40	28	50	30	25	22	18	15	-8	-4	-22	-10	-35	-15
Business Ops Profs	Yes	87	92	88	102	90	112	92	87	88	89	91	-4	0	-13	-1	-21	-1
Directors/Senior Managers	Yes	21	26	22	36	24	46	26	21	19	15	11	-7	-3	-21	-9	-35	-15
Engr/Science Profs	Yes	0	5	1	15	3	25	5	0	0	0	0	-5	-1	-15	-3	-25	-5
Information Systems Profs	Yes	0	5	1	15	3	25	5	0	0	0	0	-5	-1	-15	-3	-25	-5
Managers - Business Ops	Yes	5	10	6	20	8	30	10	5	1	0	0	-9	-5	-20	-8	-30	-10
Supervisors/Leaders	Yes	1	6	2	16	4	26	6	1	3	27	243	-3	+1	+11	+23	+217	+237
Telemarketing Sales	Yes	6	11	7	21	9	31	11	6	10	31	94	-1	+3	+10	+22	+63	+83
	Total	187	232	196	322	214	412	232	187	174	197	462	-58	-22	-125	-17	+50	+230

Figure 13.16 Gap Table

After receiving sign-off on both the demand and supply forecasts for each department within the Retail business unit, it's time for the *risk, strategy, and action* phase, which you can access by selecting the **Risk, Strategy, and Action** tab.

Essentially, after you've identified the gaps, you need to analyze where the largest shortages and surpluses are occurring and what might be causing them. Typically, there are three main drivers of gaps:

- Growth
- Resignations
- Retirements

By looking at the various data elements on the gap spreadsheet, such as terminations or retirements, you can identify which of these three drivers are causing the gaps. Next, you must prioritize the gaps in terms of significance and impact. You'll also want to consider how the gaps differ by scenario and what impact changes in capabilities have on gaps. Ultimately, you're trying to determine the risks that are most likely to occur and have the largest impact on your ability to execute your strategy.

13.3.6 Highlighting Rules

The next screen is **Highlighting Rules**, which leverages the data highlighting tool embedded within the Analytics Workspace in the Workforce Analytics solution (see Chapter 12, Section 12.3.4). The first step is to define the rules that you want the tool to search for in the data. A few common rules are listed here as defaults (e.g., high turnover, significant gaps, and large numbers of forecasted retirements).

Next to the list of rules is a summary window that shows the criteria of the selected rule. To view the criteria of each rule, simply click the rule description until that row turns green, and the summary window refreshes with the selected rule's details. You can add multiple rules, or edit the parameters of the default rules.

13.3.7 Risk Identification

The next link is **Risk Identification**, which also comes prepopulated with common risks associated with the rules that you defined in the **Highlighting Rules** section. The risks are listed at the top of the screen, with the selected risk highlighted in green and a table below showing where in the forecast (by business unit, department, or job family) each specific risk is an issue (denoted by a green cell). You can also add new risks by clicking the **New Risk** button. Essentially, in this step, the tool has listed specific risks that map to the rules you've previously defined.

For example, you might have a shortage of critical job roles due to high projected termination rates, as shown in Figure 13.17. If you scroll down, you can easily see where in the forecast this particular risk is an issue because it's highlighted in green.

Data highlighting is an easy method of sifting through all of the data in your forecast to quickly highlight the areas with the greatest risks. In this case, you can see that account managers in the **Corporate Services** department are at risk for a shortage due to increasing demand, as well as high termination rates.

You can also see that each risk is color coded in the **Priority** column. However, the priority level always defaults to low (gray color). You can change the priority level based on your organization's circumstances. Depending on the risk level assigned, a red, yellow, or gray color is assigned to the risk. A few quick tips are that risks are listed in order of priority (red to gray), and any cell in the table can be manually overridden and coded according to the specifications a user defines.

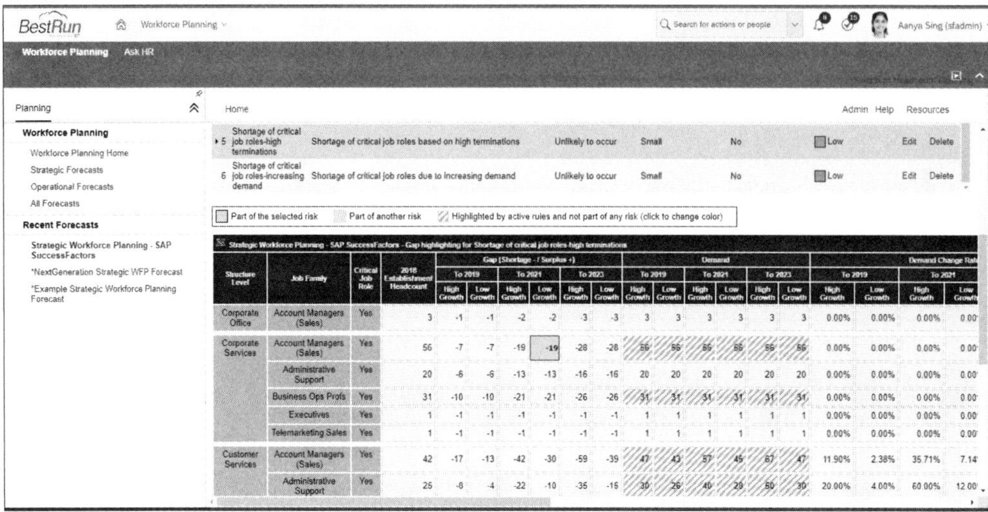

Figure 13.17 Risk Identification

13.3.8 Strategy Management

The next step in the process is to determine which strategies will be most impactful in terms of mitigating the identified risks. Strategic workforce planning focuses on making decisions that will have the most impact, which means you'll make decisions about what you will and will not do to address workforce risks related to the following:

- Critical job roles
- Significant capability gaps
- Significant staff surplus/deficit
- Significant turnover in key roles
- Workforce trends, such as an aging workforce

When you click the **Strategy Management** link, a new screen refreshes with your risk list, as well as suggested tactics for the selected risk. Tactics are pulled directly from the SAP SuccessFactors strategy bank—as shown in Figure 13.18—which is embedded in the application and contains more than 30 years of best-practice strategies. You can view the full strategy bank by clicking the **Add or Remove Tactics** button; a new window opens, where specific tactics can be checked or unchecked, depending on whether you want to include them.

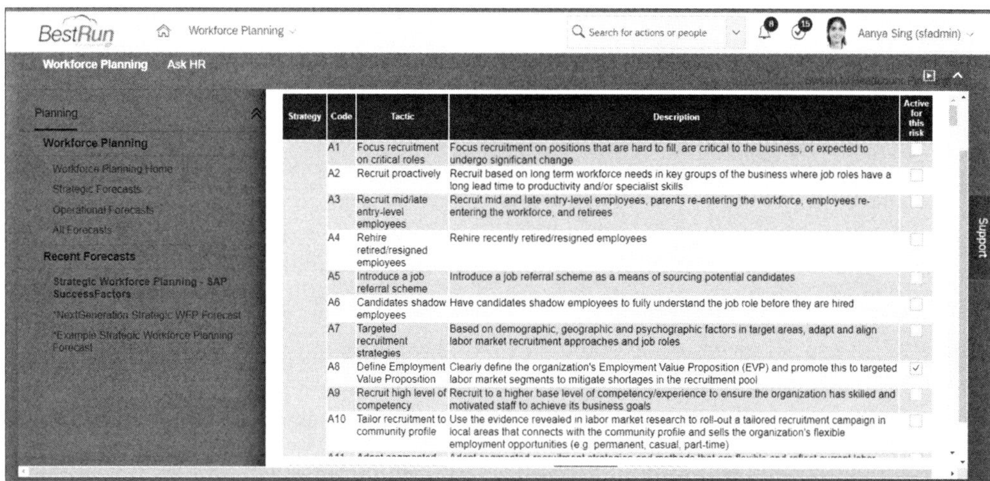

Figure 13.18 The Strategy Bank

To the right of each tactic is the **Tactic Characteristics for Risk** window, which allows users to rate each tactic on both impact and feasibility. Similarly to risk identification, the color associated with each tactic changes based on how the tactic is rated. Figure 13.19 shows the **Strategy Management** screen.

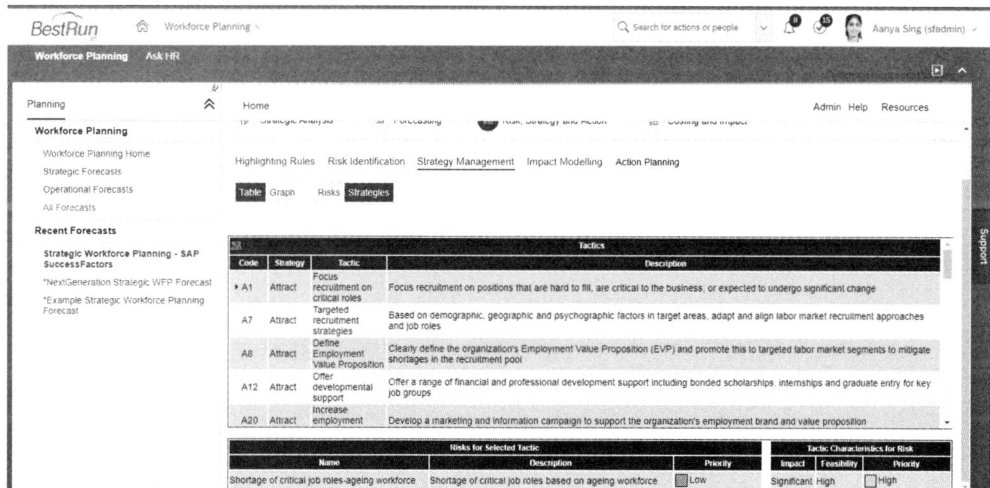

Figure 13.19 Strategy Management

In the next section, we'll cover how to model the impact of strategies to mitigate the risks already identified in the forecast.

13.3.9 Impact Modeling

Impact modeling can be a powerful tool for identifying which strategies are going to be the most impactful and cost-effective to implement. Typically, customers create different models by strategy type and can then compare the models side by side to determine which strategy should move forward to the action planning phase.

When you access the **Impact Modeling** link, a blank screen refreshes, alerting you that you haven't yet assigned any risks to the model, and therefore, it's blank. You can choose from a generated list of risks which risks you'd like to assign to the model.

For our model, let's select tactics that apply to a buy sourcing strategy (e.g., **Raise Industry and Job Profiles, Proactive Candidate Networking**, and so on).

Now the page displays a table view of where the selected risks and gaps are occurring within the forecast. You can save and title your model.

The application asks whether you want to copy the selected risks and tactics from the current model or start with a clean slate. Similar to demand and supply forecasting, the **Impact Modeling** section allows users to change the numbers across the forecast depending on a specific strategy's outcome. For example, initiating a new hiring process would allow the user to increase the hiring rate in employee populations affected by the new policy.

Doing so will automatically reduce the size of the workforce gap for each population. Users can later compare, side by side, different strategies and their potential impact on the gaps or surpluses identified in the workforce plan.

Now you can build an action plan and assign activities to individuals in the next section.

13.3.10 Action Planning

The final step in most strategic workforce planning processes is determining what interventions to take to close the gaps or reduce any surpluses. Action planning is where users can assign responsibility to either individuals or teams to ensure that the selected initiatives are completed in a timely fashion. In effect, this is a great tool to drive accountability and ultimately brings workforce planning from an "exercise" to an "executable strategy." In addition, based on the strategy, you can start to frame the workforce planning discussion in terms of business realities.

The action plan should include an outline of how the strategy will be executed, targets for achievement, the required resources, and timelines and key milestones. Figure 13.20 shows the **Action Planning** screen in the Workforce Planning solution.

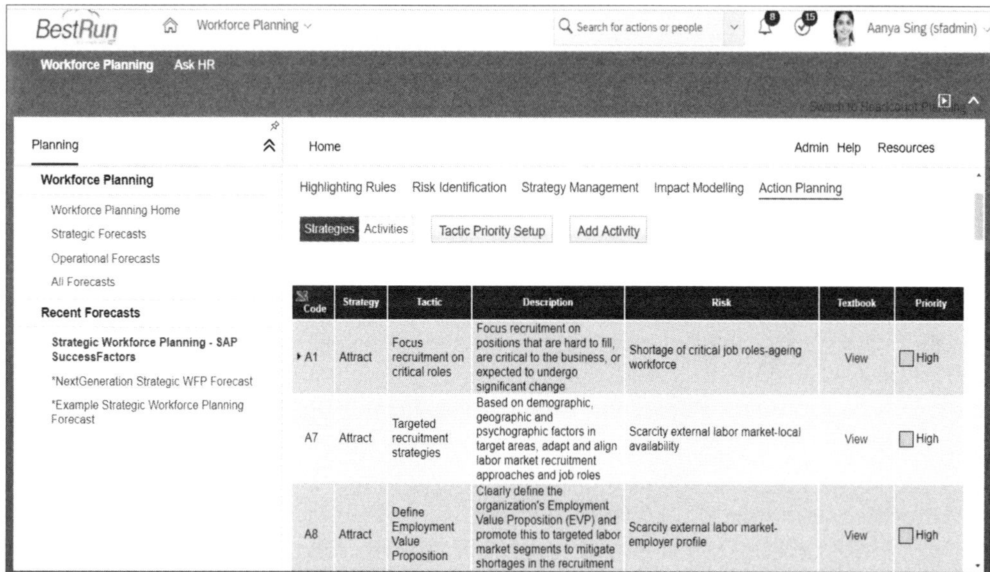

Figure 13.20 Action Planning in the Application

There are several different buttons at the top of the **Action Planning** screen. If you click **Tactic Priority Setup**, a new window opens that allows users to modify the strategies included from the strategy bank, the tactic priority rating scale, the tactic feasibility rating scale, the associated color coding, and where the tactic falls on a three-by-three tactic matrix. For example, you might identify a tactic that has a high feasibility of being implemented and will have a significant impact if prioritized. Alternatively, you might identify a tactic that has a low feasibility of being implemented and will have a low impact, so it would not be a priority.

You can add activities using the **Add Activity** button, where you enter the name of the person who will be held accountable, the timeline for implementation, and any additional resources needed.

After activities have been assigned, you can toggle between the **Strategies/Activities** tabs to see different views. Until an activity has been added, the activity view is unavailable.

Note

At the conclusion of the quantitative forecasting process, an SAP SuccessFactors customer created 89 potential action items to use as interventions. Business leaders convened a Workforce Planning summit to determine which strategies were to be implemented, subject to line-of-business budget constraints.

While the action planning step is the final phase of the strategic workforce planning process, some organizations opt to integrate financial data for modeling purposes before determining which strategies to implement.

13.3.11 What-If Financial Modeling

The final tab of the Workforce Planning solution is **Costing and Impact** (also known as what-if financial modeling). This section provides context around the financial ramifications of the decisions that you're making today, helps optimize the composition of the workforce from a financial perspective, and allows organizations to prove that strategic workforce planning is a necessary business process and not just an HR exercise.

This part of the application is extremely flexible; users can add their own financial data or, if using the Finance Management metrics pack in the Workforce Analytics solution, can also configure the financial metrics to flow through to the What-If tool.

When you first click into the What-If tool, you're provided with an overall financial dashboard that outlines your company's financial profile (assuming the Finance Management metrics pack is configured) and includes views such as overall total cost of workforce, total operating revenue, and profit per FTE. There is also a chart displaying the cost to fill the gap broken down by the two scenarios across the forecast period. From a financial perspective, all figures take into account measures such as salary growth, composition of the workforce, different costs of training, recruitment, and cost of turnover. The ability to model the numbers to generate different outcomes is what makes the tool truly "What-If?"

The **Financial Dashboard** in Figure 13.21 provides a number of visualizations from a financial perspective. There are also other dashboards that can be viewed, including the following:

- **Comparison View**
- **Gap Analysis Dashboard**
- **Market Comparisons and Productivity**
- **Efficiency Analysis**

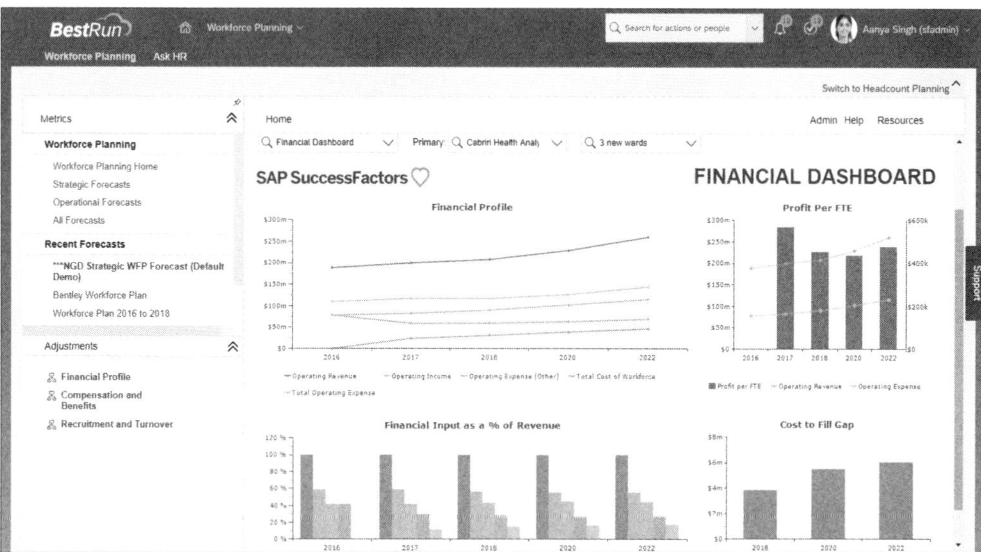

Figure 13.21 Costing and Impact Screen

Specific to workforce costs, users can create a range of models, including compensation and benefits (users enter data related to average annual salary, salary growth, and benefits costs), workforce mixes (for example, temporary versus permanent vs. contractors), or bonus structures to see the impact on your financial profile, and other expenses, such as cost to fill, turnover costs, and training expenses.

This concludes the strategic workforce planning process in Workforce Planning. Now we'll touch on recommendations for implementing Workforce Planning.

13.4 Implementation Tips

Strategic workforce planning is a combination of qualitative knowledge (creating scenarios, designing interventions, etc.) and quantitative assessments (supply versus demand, cost modeling, etc.). Thus preparing for implementation requires that organizations consider opportunities and risks from both perspectives.

Let's first discuss qualitative considerations for strategic workforce planning implementations (these questions are excerpted from the Workforce Planning Foundation step referenced in Section 13.2):

- **What workforce factors are driving the need for strategic workforce planning?**
  Answering this question is important not only for determining the focus (aging employees, shortage of talent in critical roles) of your workforce planning process, but also for communicating the business impact of failing to address the issues. Similarly, organizations should capture and share the urgency with which workforce planning needs to be conducted, to drive attention and action.
- **How conducive is the organizational culture to supporting a strategic workforce planning process?**
  Rarely considered—but extremely important—is tailoring the process to the organization's culture, especially in situations whether the culture is one of just-in-time hiring and fast decisions on talent investments. For example, an annual, in-depth strategic workforce planning process may need to be sensitive to monthly hiring plans, providing shorter-term gap-closing recommendations rather than waiting until next year to implement the plan.
- **What is the organization's workforce planning capability and experience of the planning team?**
  As discussed earlier, an effective strategic workforce planning process requires input from multiple stakeholders—business leaders to help build scenarios, HR business partners to assess demand for headcount, and talent management centers of excellence to implement the interventions. If strategic workforce planning is a new, or immature, process, extra effort will be required to socialize the process with formal and informal stakeholders. To build the right planning team, organizations may need to "draft in" staff from outside the HR function to provide cross-functional perspectives on aligning talent and operational goals for workforce planning. One of the most common derailers to successful workforce planning is the lack of human resources to run and execute the process.

- **What is the scope of strategic workforce planning?**
  Too often, organizations suffer from scope-creep when discussing the goals of strategic workforce planning; rather than centering on future forecasts for supply and demand of staff in critical job roles, the conversation morphs into how to plan for a myriad of talent issues—absence, skills, projects, costs, diversity, and so on. While not inconsequential, these "side plots" can cause significant delays to the execution of a workforce planning process and should be addressed in other HR activities.
- **What defines success of strategic workforce planning?**
  Starting with the end in mind, organizations should enter the implementation phase with a clear understanding of how they will measure, and communicate, the outcomes for which workforce planning will be responsible. These metrics may be tactical in nature—such as fewer shortages in a specific job role or more strategic when measuring overall employee productivity.

There are also the following quantitative considerations for strategic workforce planning implementations:

- **Accepting that your data will never be perfect**
  Most organizations possess more robust data than they think. By accessing your core workforce data (demographics, hires, terms, retirements), you can start a basic workforce plan. It is important to remember that workforce planning data will almost never be 100 percent correct; we are forecasting headcount numbers up to 10 years into the future, making it critical that we take action to avoid future risks rather than create a performance prediction.
- **Deciding the right metrics to include in your workforce plan**
  As noted previously, a basic workforce plan might exclude supplemental data on contractors or capabilities. For the metrics you do select, give careful consideration to which historical information you want to include and what data best reflects the currently workforce supply—headcounts terminations, retirements, and so forth. It is better to start small and with high confidence in your assumptions than to overreach and try to measure everything.

13.5 Summary

Now that we have covered the main features and functionality of the Workforce Planning solution, you have a thorough understanding of how organizations use this comprehensive solution to create strategic plans to ensure that you have the right people in the right place at the right time for the right cost. Strategic workforce planning is a combination of quantitative forecasting and qualitative inputs that determine what interventions to make, so even with the most sophisticated technology, the quality of the workforce plan will depend heavily on driving business leaders toward action.

In the next chapter, we'll turn to a new SAP acquisition: Qualtrics.

Chapter 14
Qualtrics

Employee experience is one of the most important facets of a human resources (HR) strategy and has become the modern buzzword of HR. Qualtrics provides customers with the ability to gather feedback from employees and track trends over a period of time, and this data can be used to continuously develop the experience for your employees.

Experience Management (XM) has been recognized as a crucial theme to get ahead of the competition by creating more loyal and engaged customers and employees, who really love the organization and their products. To achieve this, it's not enough to analyze "hard facts"—it's important to understand the sentiments and emotions customers or employees feel when interacting with the organization. Qualtrics is one of the leading providers of XM solutions helping their customers collect, understand, and act upon this data. Recognizing the power of combining the operational data their business solutions hold with experience data to explain why things happen, SAP acquired Qualtrics in January 2019.

In this chapter, we'll take a tour of the features and functionality offered by Qualtrics for employee XM, exploring what employee XM is, the various survey types available, and the survey process, using engagement surveys as an example. We'll conclude with a look at implementation tips.

14.1 Experience Management Basics

As with our previous topics, we'll first lay the foundation of XM and Qualtrics before we dive into the functionality. Employee XM is best understood in the context of XM in general and customer experience in particular, as this is where the concept was first applied and grew from. So, in this section we introduce XM before the background of the so-called "Experience Economy", and then explain how the concepts apply to employee experience (EX) and how the two are connected.

14.1.1 The Experience Economy

The "Experience Economy" used to be a buzzword primarily in the world of branded consumer goods and services. However, organizations across all industries as well as the public and charity sectors are now increasingly realizing that the experience they create is crucial for their success.

Measuring this experience can be tricky. After all, it is each individual customer's perception that counts. You may have certificates confirming that your online shop is as user-friendly as it gets, but if the perceptions of your customers are that they have a poor experience, that's the only thing that counts. So, to understand customer experience, you need to ask them directly or collect their feedback in some other way.

This is where XM starts: collecting information about customers to understand their experience with your organization, product, or service. But it's only the first step. Add intelligent analytics and actions based on these results to actually improve experience to get a full XM process. The same end-to-end view is important when it comes to IT: an XM solution is much more than just a survey tool. Modern XM solutions add further data sources to the mix (for example, by collecting feedback and sentiments from social media and other sources). More importantly, they also include:

- Powerful analytics supported by machine learning to understand drivers of a positive or negative experience and of the intended behavior
- Tools for the visualization and distribution of insights
- Intelligent tools to suggest, plan and monitor actions
- A framework to manage the information and users involved efficiently and in line with data privacy rules
- Smooth integrations with other IT solutions like customer relationship management (CRM) or finance

However, XM goes beyond just technical solutions and requires a well-thought-out strategy. An end-to-end EX strategy looks beyond HR tools and applications and at aspects of an employee's day-to-day work, such as the policies you have in place, employee benefits, the tools and systems used in everyday work, and much more. Using the data gathered in XM solutions such as Qualtrics, you can measure the effectiveness of this strategy and understand if your implementation is improving the EX. Additionally, XM solutions can help you continuously shape and optimize your EX strategy using the feedback given and trends identified in the solution.

14.1.2 Employee Experience with Qualtrics

So, how is this all related to EX? There are three answers to this:

- While XM has been used for customer facing activities first, pretty much the same principles apply to the management of EX.
- As HR is considering employees to be their customers, they should take a leaf out of their marketing colleagues' book and care about experience.
- Companies using XM for customers *and* employees consistently report that a positive EX drives a positive customer experience.

Despite this strong connection using the same generic tool for customer experience as well as EX, is not best practice: the relationship an organization has with its customers is different from the one it has with employees, and this has to be reflected in the way experience is managed.

That's why Qualtrics, as one of the leading global XM vendors, has developed four different XM solutions following their original "research core" solution used in academic research:

- Customer XM
- Brand XM
- Product XM
- Employee XM

In this chapter, we are focusing on the Employee XM solution. But before doing so, let's answer the question: "Why is Qualtrics EX relevant for organizations interested in implementing or improving SAP SuccessFactors as a human capital management (HCM) solution?"

For most organizations, the objectives of a digital HR transformation with SAP SuccessFactors include improving one or more of the following:

- Employee retention
- Employee engagement
- Employer brand
- Talent attraction
- Employee productivity
- EX

With Qualtrics EX, customers are able to understand the EX at the starting point, identify the gap, shape their transformation program to close this experience gap, and monitor progress along the way, as illustrated in Figure 14.1.

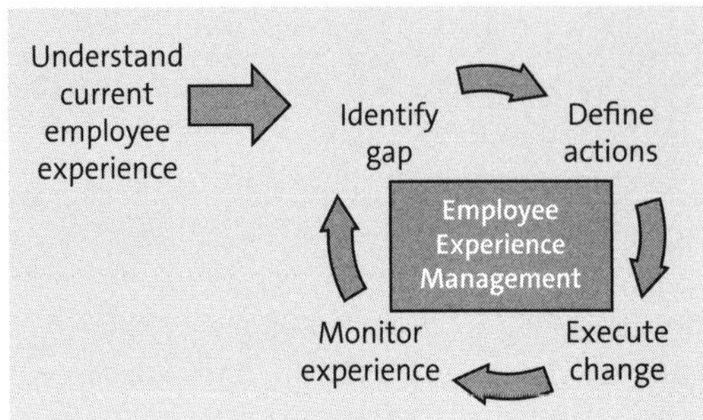

Figure 14.1 Employee XM Cycle

So, with Qualtrics EX, organizations can achieve better results in their SAP SuccessFactors-based digital HR transformation. However, this isn't a one-way road. Experience data (X-data) is most powerful when combined with operational HR data (O-data).

Using Qualtrics alone can only answer questions such as the following:

- How many employees expect to leave the organization in the next two years?
- How are employees perceiving their work-life balance?

On the other hand, using SAP SuccessFactors alone answers questions such as the following:

- What was our staff turnover last year?
- How many people use a flexible working model?

Combining X-data from Qualtrics with O-data from SAP SuccessFactors answers the interesting questions such as the following:

- How do leavers perceive work life balance?
- Does perceived work life balance improve when employees switch to a flexible working model?
- Which groups by age, gender, department, or hierarchy level feel they have the best or worst work-life balance?

So, using SAP SuccessFactors and Qualtrics together provides powerful insights for HR and the executive team, as well as line managers tailored to their teams. These insights allow for targeted actions to improve EX and therefore, ultimately, also customer experience and business performance. When used in conjunction with the wider EX strategy, Qualtrics can help drive improvements in the EX not only with SAP SuccessFactors, but across the board.

14.2 Survey Types

Qualtrics offers different types of "projects," or surveys, to serve different purposes. In this section, we introduce the basic types of surveys briefly starting with the simple, traditional "engagement survey," which we'll also use in the next section to explain the main features of Qualtrics EX.

14.2.1 Engagement Surveys

On the surface, Qualtrics engagement surveys follow the traditional way of an annual engagement survey represented by a questionnaire. In fact, there is much more behind it, as we will see in Section 14.3.

The characteristics of an engagement survey are:

- It is sent as a one-off to a large number of employees.
- It is usually repeated on an annual basis or even less often. Questions usually vary slightly between occurrences.
- Due to its low frequency, it's usually a long survey (>20 questions often in block, like the five questions shown in Figure 14.2).
- All participants receive the same survey (variations may occur dynamically, as Section 14.3.1 will show) at the same point in time.
- It takes a snapshot across the workforce—often compared with a historic result from previous years.
- In a modern organization, results are not only discussed in HR, but shared with other stakeholders tailored to their roles, including employees' line managers and the board.

The format of this survey can be used for all kinds of other one-off or annual surveys, not just for measuring engagement from health and safety reviews to diversity and inclusion surveys to canteen satisfaction feedback.

How strongly do you agree or disagree with each of the following statements?

	Strongly agree	Somewhat agree	Neither agree nor disagree	Somewhat disagree	Strongly disagree
I have a good understanding of this company's strategy and objectives	◉	○	○	○	○
I agree with this company's current objectives	○	○	◉	○	○
I clearly understand how my role contributes to the company's current objectives	○	◉	○	○	○
This company provides me with the tools to effectively do my job	◉	○	○	○	○
I am comfortable communicating with my superiors at this company, even when I'm communicating bad news	◉	○	○	○	○

Figure 14.2 Typical Question in Engagement Survey

14.2.2 Pulse Surveys

A pulse survey is similar to an engagement survey at first glance, but its purpose is to monitor certain aspects more closely, often with quarterly or monthly surveys and usually with shorter questionnaires.

The purpose could just be to monitor key data collected in an annual engagement survey at shorter intervals to measure success of actions. However, it's also often used to ask a set of bespoke questions during a time of fast change, like a merger or acquisition situation or a major restructuring exercise. In these cases, pulse surveys are perfect for monitoring how the workforce perceives the change and take timely action, if needed.

Note

To avoid survey fatigue from too frequent pulses, send the survey to a random subset of the workforce only every time (e.g., 40 percent). In a workforce of several thousand people, the big picture will still be pretty accurate, while individual employees don't have to bear the full number of surveys. When doing this, make sure you communicate accordingly, so individuals do not feel left out.

14.2.3 Lifecycle Surveys

Quite often, employers require feedback related to certain events. This could be an onboarding process, a seminar, or the termination of employment.

Rather than asking questions about these events in the next engagement survey, lifecycle surveys ask for feedback only from the employees affected, when the memory is still fresh. The trigger events are often called "moments that matter," indicating that an employer identifies important events in the employee lifecycle and requests feedback as and when they happen. Qualtrics lifecycle surveys recognize these triggers and send the questionnaire to the right employees at the right time.

14.2.4 Digital Listening

It can be argued that the "moments that matter" described previously do only matter to the employer, who defines them. This leads logically to the concept of allowing employees to provide feedback whenever they want.

For this purpose, an "always-on" feedback form is required—easily accessible, ideally through mobile. Digital listening is a new feature being rolled out by Qualtrics. It's a milestone in supporting a listening culture and really tapping into the wisdom of the whole workforce to drive improvements.

14.2.5 360-Degree Feedback

The 360-degree feedback survey is also called the "multi-rater" and basically does what you'd expect: it collects feedback for each individual in scope by a group of people—typically peers, superiors, and direct reports.

The questionnaire is technically the same as in the engagement survey, but the questions are tailored to this specific purpose. The results can do the following:

- Provide individuals with valuable feedback for their own development
- Help HR or coaches to develop individuals
- Give line managers a different view on the capabilities of their teams

For SAP SuccessFactors customers it may be interesting to compare the Qualtrics 360-degree feedback with the corresponding 360 Multi-Rater assessment in the SAP SuccessFactors Performance & Goals module (see Chapter 6, Section 6.3.3). Table 14.1 provides an overview of both tools' relative advantages.

SAP Success Factors 360 Multi-Rater Assessment	Qualtrics 360-Degree Feedback
Included in the Performance & Goals subscription fee	High flexibility in questionnaire design and survey flow
Fully integrated in SAP SuccessFactors for user interface and HR data without extra effort	More modern look and feel
Questionnaire content can be dynamic based on competency assignment—something that cannot be completely replicated by complex survey flows	Better report output

Table 14.1 Comparing SAP SuccessFactors 360 with Qualtrics 360 Feedback

Depending on requirements, each of these could be the best option for one organization. If features don't make for a clear decision, then it may come down to cost, which is zero for the SAP SuccessFactors option, if the Performance & Goals module is being used anyway.

14.3 Survey Processes

This section introduces the main elements of the Qualtrics solution using engagement surveys as an example and then point out key differences in lifecycle and 360-degree feedback surveys. We'll explore the key steps of the survey process: building, managing participants, running, and analyzing.

14.3.1 The Survey Builder

The Survey Builder defines the actual questionnaire, with questions, flow, look and feel, and a number of options. Let's walk through some key features.

Questionnaire

The questionnaire is composed from a number of questions, as well as passive elements like instruction texts that can be divided into blocks and pages. The flexibility provided here is huge, starting with a number of question types and layouts, including the side-by-side layout illustrated in Figure 14.3, where you can ask two different questions on each topic. Other options include the following:

- Random sequence of all or some questions
- Randomly hiding a number of questions
- Conditional skipping of questions

	How important is this infrastructure for your job			How satisfied are you with this infrastructure		
	Not important	Somewhat important	Very important	Not satisfied	Somehwat satisfied	Fully satisfied
IT	○	○	●	●	○	○
Desk	○	●	○	○	●	○
Mobile Phone	○	○	●	○	○	●
Car	●	○	○	○	○	●

Figure 14.3 Side-by-Side Questions

Survey Flow

The survey flow can be changed very flexibly based on a variety of conditions, most notably based on answers to previous questions or O-data fields. It even allows to communicate with data outside the survey using web services.

Look and Feel

For the look and feel, a number of design and theme templates are available and can be amended, but custom Cascading Style Sheets (CSS) can also be applied.

The usability can also be driven by small decisions, like using a back button, and obviously by the question design in the questionnaire itself mentioned previously.

> **Note**
>
> As many participants will fill in the survey on mobile, it's important to keep it mobile friendly. Qualtrics supports this with an iQ score that measures mobile friendliness, among other things, as a mobile view in the browser for the preview mode. However, you should also test surveys on actual mobile phones using the makes most common in your workforce.

14.3.2 Participant Data

Obviously, Qualtrics needs data of the survey participants, if individuals are to be invited with their personalized survey link. Apart from name and email address, participant data comprises organizational data and further fields (called "metadata"). Metadata can be used to decide the survey flow, but more importantly to add structure and additional information for analytics and dashboards.

Directory

Participants can be loaded to the survey directly or from a directory, which is usually updated on a regular basis. These updates are usually done via simple file upload (manual or with Secure File Transfer Protocol [SFTP] automation) or with more sophisticated application programming interface (API) based interfaces, but participants can also be added manually.

Hierarchies

For analytics purposes and to provide each line manager with a dashboard for their own reports, an org structure is required. Qualtrics uses three types of org hierarchies:

- Level-based, where levels can be team, department, division, and so forth (see Figure 14.4)
- Parent-child, representing the typical reporting structure between individuals
- An ad hoc structure, which can be created manually as needed

The first two options can be created based on import data and are easily aligned with the typical structures in SAP SuccessFactors.

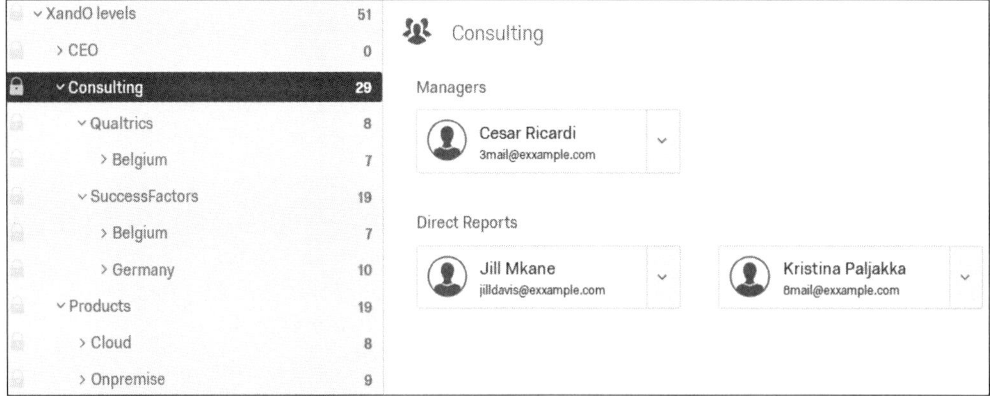

Figure 14.4 Level-Based Org Hierarchy

14.3.3 Running the Survey

Once the survey is built and the participants are in the system, the survey can be launched and managed. Launch happens via email with personalized links and further messages can be sent as reminders or to invite line managers to view dashboards once they are ready.

Just like the survey itself, all messages can be translated into several languages.

Note

Qualtrics standard texts or template content are already available in several languages. When you amend that or use custom content, you also need to take care of translations. A particular risk is posed by last-minute changes to questions, when it is easy to forget translations. This can lead to discrepancies that make it impossible to compare results filled in in different languages.

Ideally, participants are always invited through a personalized link. This makes sure that all required data for the employee is available and accurate (e.g., org assignment, role, age range) and the system can stop individuals from submitting the same survey twice.

However, personalized reasons may not be possible due to privacy concerns. In that case, the system can use anonymous links. This means it is unknown who fills in a survey. Some data (e.g., org assignment) can be added by the participant, but that may not be accurate.

Note

Qualtrics has other measures in place to protect data privacy. When data is analyzed and shared, a minimum threshold of participants can be set, so a line manager can never use filters to see results from less than, say, four individuals. If there are concerns about privacy, explain this feature before going for anonymous links.

Another reason for using anonymous links might be that email addresses are not available for all participants, so links have to be provided on shared pages like the intranet or SAP SuccessFactors home page. Users starting their survey through these links also can't be recognized, but if privacy concerns are not an issue, that can be solved by requiring some authentication.

14.3.4 Analysis and Actions

This is where organizations finally get value out of the process. The analytics tools and dashboards provide important insights, allowing management to take action, which we'll discuss in this section.

Stats iQ

Stats iQ provides a number of statistical tools, including regression analysis, which will be appreciated by specialists, but also come with good guidance for those not familiar with statistical methods. These tools allow users to identify dependencies between answers and drivers of key performance indicators (KPIs).

Figure 14.5 shows an example where answers to a question are highly correlated to gender. In this example, female participants are much less likely to recommend the employer than male or diverse participants. This insight is an important first indicator that requires further digging to find out why the organization seems to provide a poor EX for women.

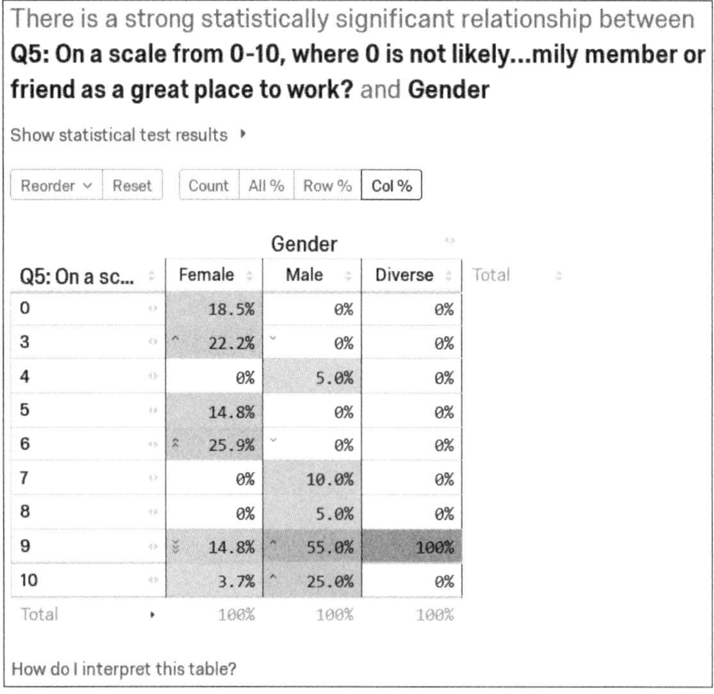

	Gender			
Q5: On a sc...	Female	Male	Diverse	Total
0	18.5%	0%	0%	
3	22.2%	0%	0%	
4	0%	5.0%	0%	
5	14.8%	0%	0%	
6	25.9%	0%	0%	
7	0%	10.0%	0%	
8	0%	5.0%	0%	
9	14.8%	55.0%	100%	
10	3.7%	25.0%	0%	
Total	100%	100%	100%	

Figure 14.5 Spotting Dependencies between Survey Results and Operational Data

You can use Stats iQ to find the interesting correlations and insights, and then use role-based dashboards to share these insights with stakeholder groups like line managers.

Text iQ

Traditionally, analytics experts didn't like free text, as it was impossible to report on it properly. This paradigm is now fading quickly, as machine learning enables solutions to put some structure into free text data. Instead of manually working through the content of 10,000 comment boxes, you can let the system do the heavy lifting and just look at the big picture.

With Text iQ, organizations can not only discover the most important themes in free text feedback from their employees, but also pick up the sentiment that comes with it. After all, knowing that most employees talk about compensation does not allow any conclusions, if you don't know, whether they have a positive or negative feeling about it. In the example of Figure 14.6, Text iQ identified three main topics, all with a primarily positive sentiment.

14

Figure 14.6 Text iQ Result Overview

This is a real game changer, as predefined questions and answer patterns often mean that organizations only gain the insights they are already expecting, while unexpected facts remain hidden, because the right questions to unearth them are not asked. Being able to ask open, free-text questions *and* analyze them is much more likely to deliver surprising results that allow businesses to respond to challenges or opportunities early.

As the use of machine learning in this context is still quite new, we can expect a lot of progress in the months and years to come.

Note

At this stage, the sentiment analysis is not correct in all cases, as the system does still misunderstand natural language in many cases. However, as we are interested in the big picture rather than individual results, it doesn't really matter if 10 percent of the sentiments are wrong one way or the other.

Role-Based Dashboards

One of Qualtrics' biggest assets are the dashboards. At the end of the day, Employee XM is not about collecting data or about creating insights for a small team of specialists. It's about providing a positive experience for employees through the various aspects of their everyday work. Spreading these newfound insights across the organization and acting on them to improve the EX provides significant value for enhancing the productivity and engagement of the workforce.

Traditional EX management models often involve a third-party vendor collecting data and then spending significant time analyzing it before presenting results to their customer's HR team in the form of frozen (non-interactive) spreadsheets or presentations. Due to the length of the process, it is possible that recommendations are no longer relevant or are out of context. Therefore, by that time, line managers have potentially lost interest, executives may have other priorities, and employees are asking themselves, "Whatever had happened to that survey I have filled in ages ago? That was a waste of time."

For a successful program, you need to engage employees and line managers in a meaningful way. For employees, that means sharing some overall results and demonstrating that actions are taken. For line managers, that means providing insight that is relevant for managing their team and guidance to take appropriate actions.

The good news is that all this is easily feasible with Qualtrics. Dashboards can be built easily by a trained admin person on the customer's EX team and made available to line managers with all the insights as soon as the survey is closed.

Figure 14.7 shows a typical dashboard that could be provided for line managers, containing the following sections:

❶ The top KPI, in this case the overall promoter score (likelihood of employees recommending the employer to family and friends). In this case, a mediocre result that needs improving.

❷ Some statistics on the composition of the team reported on.

❸ A diagram with results to all questions, where the questions with the best and worst results are featured.

❹ A column indicating which impact the answer to each question has on the top KPI. Ideally, you would like the questions with the strongest impact to be those with the best results on the top. However, in this example, one of the worst-rated questions (the last one visible in the image) has the strongest impact. While this is unpleasant, the insight is extremely valuable, because this is where action needs to be taken: the aspects with the biggest potential for improvement and the strongest impact on our top KPI.

❺ The action planning column. Simply by clicking on the link, the line manager can create an action in his action plan.

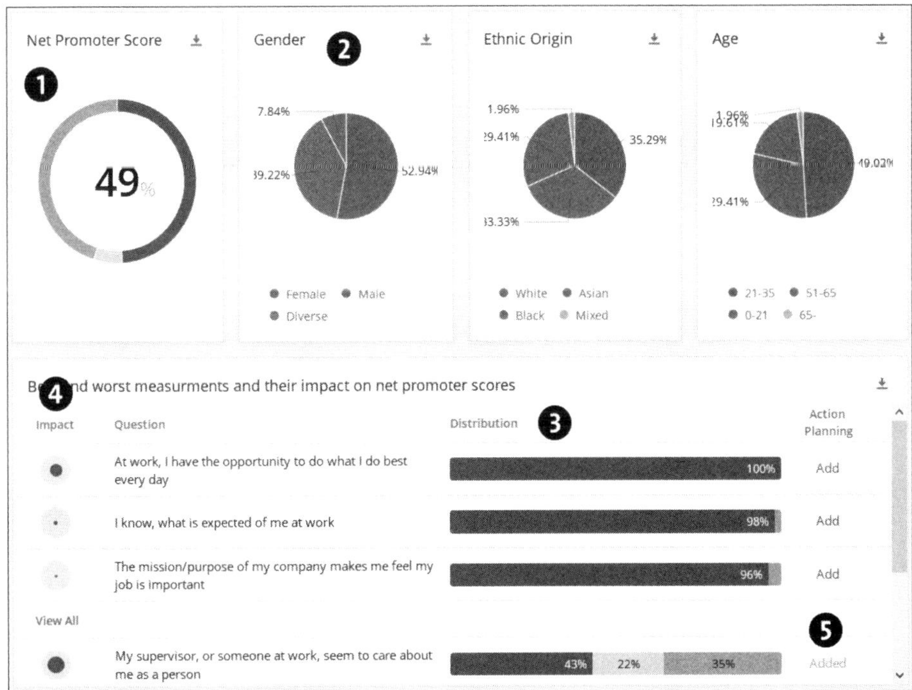

Figure 14.7 Dashboard with Impact Analysis

Note

Many people argue that employees don't like filling in surveys too often. While this is true, employees do like being taken seriously and having an impact. So, if they are involved in the communication and see that their feedback triggers actions, they are usually happy to provide feedback.

There is a simple recipe to avoid frustration: before submitting your survey, go through the questions and ask yourself, "As an organization, are we prepared to take action if the answers to this question require it?" If the answer is "no," remove the question. If you can't change the color of the office, don't ask employees which color they'd like.

Figure 14.8 shows a section of a dashboard featuring details for some aspects of the survey on a mobile device.

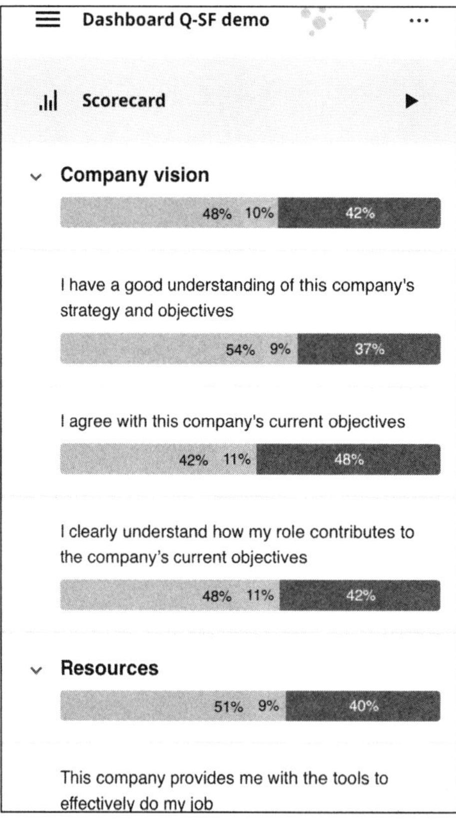

Figure 14.8 Dashboard on Mobile Phone

Among other points, it says that only about half of the people in this team understand how their role contributes to company objectives or believe that they have the right tools to do their job effectively. What's most interesting about this example is that it is displayed on a mobile app. So, busy line managers can make use of transit time or discuss results with their HR business partner in the breakroom. To make people engage with the experience insights, they must be as easily accessible as possible.

These insights also have to be interactive, so dashboard users are not just passive consumers of information, but can look at things from different angles relevant for them. In Qualtrics, line managers can filter by location, gender, high potential flag, or any other field captured during the process or loaded from SAP SuccessFactors. Most importantly, even while applying filters, Qualtrics always makes sure that the minimum threshold of participants included in the result is maintained, so the user cannot isolate individual participants' answers.

Action Planning

Taking action is the most important element of the most important part of the employee XM process. While some action planning happens on corporate level, others are best owned by line managers, who usually need some guidance. We have already seen in Figure 14.7 how a dashboard can point users to the aspects, where actions add the most value. Figure 14.9 shows a part of an action plan with one task created for the topic of **Resources**.

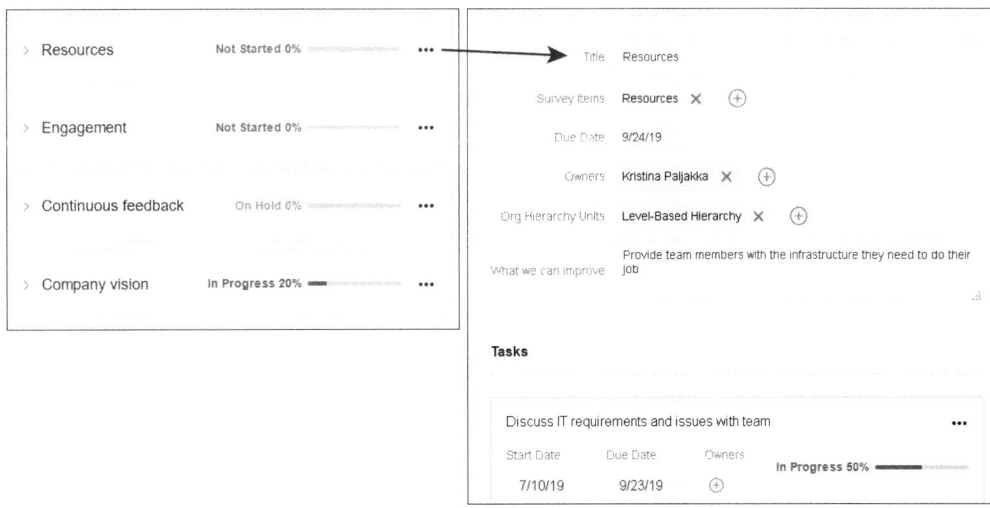

Figure 14.9 Action Planning

The solution can also provide further guidance by suggesting actions based on the results and Qualtrics benchmark data or bespoke configuration. Prescriptive Insights and Guided Action Planning are two of Qualtrics' latest innovations to actively support line managers.

The action plan page of the dashboard then allows one to manage and monitor the execution of actions further. In the next survey (or the next pulse of the same survey, if a pulse survey is used) the dashboard would usually be set up to include a comparison with the last survey to measure progress in the outcome.

14.3.5 Special Elements for Lifecycle Surveys

Most of the features discussed so far apply to lifecycle surveys as well. The main difference is that participants are not picked at a single point in time, but the system picks participants from the directory, as and when they meet certain criteria, such as "hired one month ago" to trigger an onboarding survey.

The scattered distribution of responses over time also has an impact on when and how you distribute insights to avoid loss of anonymity.

14.3.6 Special Elements for 360 Feedback

The 360 Feedback or Multi-Rater survey follows a very similar process to the engagement survey, but the big difference are the participants. Unlike other survey types, we have a subject or evaluee on the one side and evaluators on the other side, where the evaluators fill in a questionnaire about the subject. Typical examples for evaluators can be peers, superiors, direct reports, or the subjects themselves (for the self-evaluation). Figure 14.10 shows some evaluators for one subject and their relationships with the subject.

A solid integration with SAP SuccessFactors or another HR system pays off here, as it can create all these relationships automatically. In addition to that, subjects can have the right to nominate their own evaluators from anywhere or out of a defined group with or without line manager approval. There is a lot of flexibility in this, as is in the design of the questionnaire and the survey flow, and these are also the advantages of the Qualtrics 360-degree feedback over SAP SuccessFactors 360 Multi-Rater assessment.

The second significant difference between 360 feedback and the engagement survey is that it doesn't use dashboards but specifically designed reports, which have a good look and feel, but aren't quite as flexible and user-friendly as the dashboards.

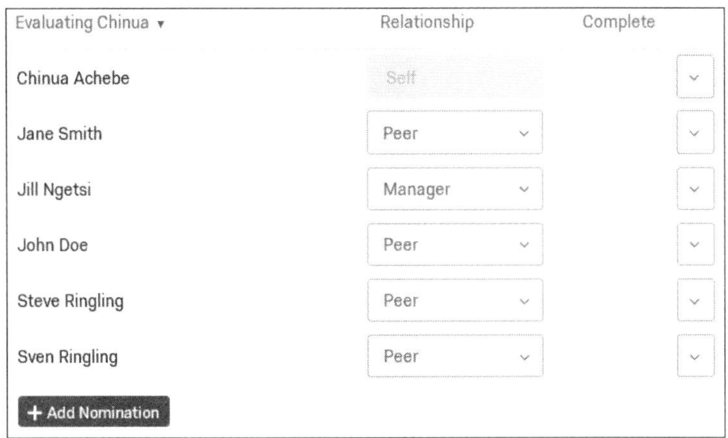

Figure 14.10 Evaluators for One Employee

14.4 Implementation Tips

There are a few key tips to keep in mind for your implementation, as follows:

- **Define your EX strategy**
  Qualtrics alone will not create a positive EX, but it can help you understand what you need to do to get there and help you constantly improve. Creating an EX strategy will help you identify where you want to be. Using this, you can then determine how you will use Qualtrics to gather the data you need to get you from where you are to where you need to be; you can also use Qualtrics to continuously shape your strategy as you go along your EX journey.
- **Libraries**
  Qualtrics includes a library, where the following elements, including translations, can be stored and reused:
  - Whole surveys, blocks, and questions
  - Message texts
  - Graphics
  - Any files
- **Templates**
  Qualtrics already offers a number of predefined templates, like onboarding and exit feedback and solutions for particular scenarios, including but not limited to the following:

  - Training feedback
  - Corporate responsibility
  - Work-life balance
  - Personal professional growth and development
  - Benefits optimization

  In addition to this, some partners also offer their own templates.

> **Note**
>
> Using predefined content can reduce cost and time to value, but it's important that the information collected is relevant and actionable for the organization.

- **Integration options**

  Integrations with third-party solutions can be done using file-based automation (e.g., via an SFTP connection or application programming interface (API) technology). While API-based integrations are more elegant and offer more options, file-based solutions are often sufficient and can be set up quickly with very little additional cost.

  At the time of writing (fall 2019), Qualtrics and SAP do not offer a productized/out-of-the box integration between Qualtrics and SAP SuccessFactors. SAP plans to provide an integration in due course.

- **Project planning**

  While general project planning principles apply here as well, there are some things worth pointing out compared to typical SAP SuccessFactors projects:

  - The implementation project is considered to run from technical kickoff to availability of dashboards for line managers. The actual publishing and running survey is therefore not at the end of the project.
  - You may discuss dashboards during the initial build phase, but as the actual results are determined, what you want to present, dashboard build, is usually finalized after the survey has closed.
  - Standard implementations leave most of the actual survey configuration to the customer after initial handholding. However, you can ask for more support from the implementation partner.

  A typical engagement survey with simple integrations and dashboards can take 12 weeks to build and run, as illustrated in Figure 14.11. Factors that can stretch the project plan are complex integrations, legacy data conversion for historic comparisons, and lack of decision-making regarding the survey content.

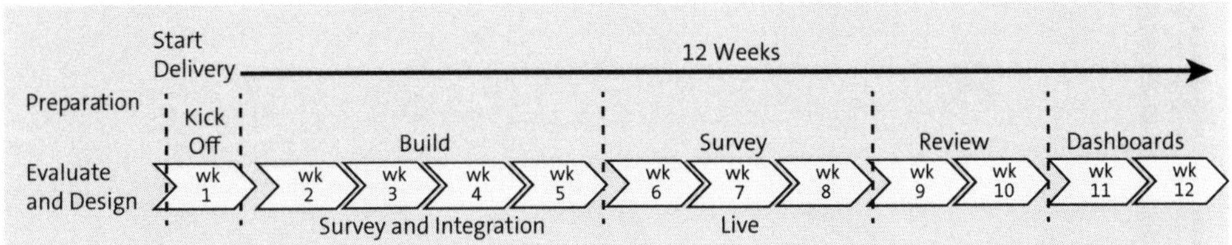

Figure 14.11 Typical Project Timeline for Engagement Survey

14.5 Summary

Qualtrics is a leading tool for managing employee engagement. Organizations who have only used survey tools or third-party services without live, interactive result visualization will see a huge benefit in switching to Qualtrics.

Given that improving EX is often one of the reasons to implement SAP SuccessFactors, the insights and action planning provided by Qualtrics can help to close the gap and make it much easier to achieve this objective. Some people may see Qualtrics EX as the crown jewel to be added at the very end of a cloud HR transformation journey. This view doesn't unlock the full value. Used from day one, Qualtrics EX can help any HR transformation start with the right plan and adjust it as the journey progresses. It also drives engagement by allowing employees and line managers to take an active part in the journey, rather than just being passengers.

From the old paper-based questionnaire of the twentieth century, employee XM has come a long way, from being batch driven, slow, and inflexible, to being agile and interactive. Open listening, Text iQ, and guided action planning are the latest steps in this direction. As machine learning capabilities are improving and further data sources, starting with portals like Glassdoor, are added, this trend is going to continue and will make world-class EX tools a must-have in the quest to attract, retain, and engage top talent.

In the next chapter, we'll take a look at the mobile offerings available for various modules with SAP SuccessFactors Mobile.

Chapter 15
SAP SuccessFactors Mobile

SAP SuccessFactors Mobile is focused on putting the most critical human resource (HR) and talent management functions in the hands of users whenever and wherever they need them. It takes the virtual teaming concept to the next level by enabling users anytime access from anywhere.

SAP SuccessFactors has taken the ease of its human capital management (HCM) suite of applications and delivered the most critical processes to the mobile device through its mobile app. This enables employees and managers to stay connected and manage their HR activities or data both at the desk and away from it. It enables field workers to be part of HR processes and provides a platform for training and education without needing to be at a computer.

SAP SuccessFactors Mobile has added a significant amount of functionality in the past five years. In addition to features such as the Org Chart, performance form approvals, requisition approvals, and to-dos, the app now supports employee and manager self-services, time entry and vacation booking, benefits management, continuous performance management, an extensive range of learning functionality (including offline learning), issuing spot awards, going through onboarding, and much more. In addition, the user interface (UI) has been revamped to provide a much greater experience. A full list of features can be found in the *Mobile Feature Matrix* guide on the SAP Help Portal under SAP SuccessFactors Mobile.

In this chapter, we'll cover the basic capabilities of the mobile app, starting with basics of the mobile app, such as accessing the app, security, and administration management of the app, general platform features, and then going through each available module of the SAP SuccessFactors HCM Suite.

Note

Not all SAP SuccessFactors modules are supported by the mobile app. We only cover the modules with mobile functionality in this chapter.

We'll now take a brief look at some of the features and tools available in the mobile app.

15.1 Mobile Basics

The mobile app provides much of the functionality of SAP SuccessFactors, and SAP SuccessFactors continue to build out the functionality available in the mobile app. It enables employees on the go to manage their HR activities between mobile device and their computer. For example, a vacation request can be raised by an employee on their mobile and this can be approved in SAP SuccessFactors or on the mobile app. Likewise, a promotion can be made in SAP SuccessFactors and the approval request can be reviewed and action on the mobile app. This extends the user experience of SAP SuccessFactors to provide employees to manage their HR activities wherever they are.

Mobile differs from the rest of the SAP SuccessFactors HCM Suite in that releases are monthly instead of quarterly. However, no release typically occurs in January. SAP only provides support for the current and the previous two versions of the app.

Further Resources

The minimum supports devices, operating system, and browsers for the mobile app can be found in the guide *HCM Suite End User System Requirements* found on the SAP Help Portal under the SAP SuccessFactors HCM Suite product page.

There are several different aspects of the mobile app that you can control as an administrator. There is also the activity of downloading and activating the app. We'll cover these aspects in this section, starting with basic setup of the app.

15.1.1 Setup

The mobile app itself is already configured and ready to go. However, there are some parts of the app that you can setup in the Admin Center in **Enable Mobile Features** (seen in Figure 15.1). Here you can configure various aspects of the app, including:

- Enable or disable features
- Manage mobile users
- Configure email notification templates
- Manage permission roles

When configuring email notification templates and permission roles, you use the standard screens for configuring these for all applications in the system.

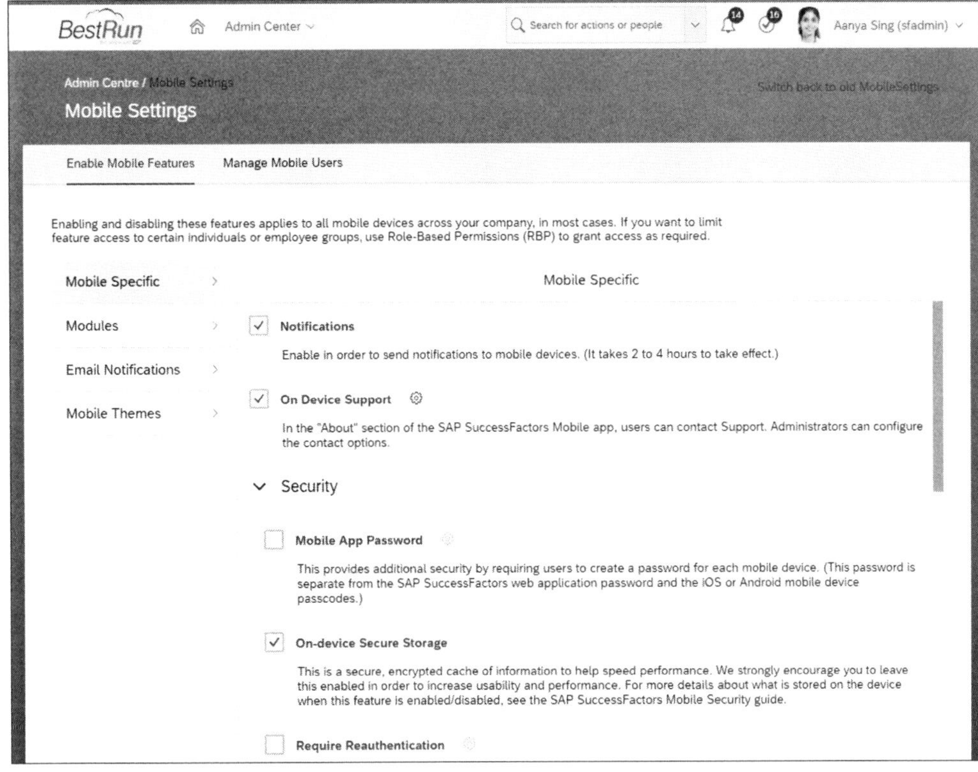

Figure 15.1 Mobile Settings Transaction in the Admin Center

The following are some of the mobile features that you can configure:

- Enable notifications to be sent to mobile devices
- Enable in-app support
- Force users to create a password for each mobile device they use
- Enable on-device storage of a secure, encrypted cache of information to help speed up app performance
- Force periodic reauthentication
- Allow third-party PDF viewers to be used to view PDF files on Android devices
- Restrict activation to managed devices
- Disable the need for the profile password to be used on managed devices

In addition to these settings, you can also enable or disable the following modules:

- Employee Central Service Center
- Performance Management
- Continuous Performance Management
- Goal Management
- Recruiting
- Onboarding
- Learning
- Development
- Presentations
- 360 Multi-Rater
- SAP Jam

For some modules, you can enable or disable module-specific features, such as:

- **Platform**
  - Org Chart
- **Employee Central**
  - Time Off
  - Time Sheet
  - Global Benefits
- **Employee Central Payroll**
  - Pay Summary
  - Display Payroll Information
- **Compensation**
  - Reward and Recognition
- **Learning**
  - QuickGuide
- **Workforce Analytics**
  - Analytics Headlines
  - Metric Tiles
- **Intelligent Services**
  - Intelligent Services Summary Content

You can also manage mobile users. You are able to see each user's devices and deactivate any device; you can search for users using the **Search** box. You can also export a list of all mobile app users.

Deactivation of a user removes the application from the device, prevents future use of the application on the device, and removes all application-specific information that is stored on the device.

After you've enabled any specific features you want, you need to look at who and how you permission the app. Let's look at this now.

15.1.2 Security and Permissions

SAP SuccessFactors Mobile enables team management and collaboration on the go within a secure environment. Administrators control who has access to the mobile app, and with the user authentication, it can be accessed only from an active user account. Further, access to each component of the mobile app is permissioned in the Admin Center by system administrators. For example, a company can permission all employees to the Org Chart and People Search, and only managers to the To-Dos. Permissions for mobile now match permissions for the web version of SAP SuccessFactors, and administrators have a consolidated view of all mobile permissions. These increased permissions mean the mobile app is now more of a platform for data that is already available to users via a browser.

The Profile Switcher feature now enables multiple users to log in and out from the app without activating and deactivating the application. Now a single user can access multiple SAP SuccessFactors instances from the same device and the same app. This is great for users who are involved in testing because they can now log in and out of the test instance and production instances from the same mobile device.

Aside from permissions and usability, security from a data perspective is simple: data accessed via the mobile app remains secure because all data can be erased from the device if it is lost or stolen.

15.1.3 Data Protection

The Data Privacy Consent Statement (DPCS) that is configured in the Admin Center is used in the mobile app.

When a user is deactivated, the data stored locally and on the mobile server is deleted. If the process is not completed for any reason, some data may remain on the mobile server, but this data is never visible in the mobile app. Users can be deactivated through the Admin Center, or are automatically deactivated when the user leaves the company or are locked out for failing the password policy or for too many failed attempts.

Data that is deleted or purged in SAP SuccessFactors will be deleted in the mobile app when it is next opened by the user.

15.1.4 Password Protection

Administrators have a variety of password options, which are configured in the Admin Center (as we mentioned in Section 15.1.1). Such options available include:

- Choose whether users activate the app with their SAP SuccessFactors user credentials or whether they set a password for the device
- Enable fingerprint login
- Prevent a password being the same as one of the previously used five passwords
- Set the number of failed unlock attempts before the app is locked
- Set the minimum length of the password
- Set the password expiry period or whether passwords should not expire
- Set the minimum unique characters that must be in a password

If a mobile device password is set during activation, then the mobile app will prompt for the password when it is launched or when it is re-accessed from a background process.

Each time the password policy is changed then users are required to change their password.

15.1.5 Mobile Device Management

The mobile app supports the use of Mobile Device Management (MDM) platforms to allow organizations to control access to the app via corporate-controlled devices and personal devices used under a bring your own device (BYOD) policy. The mobile app uses the AppConfig Community standards set to enable MDM.

Further Resources

You can find more information about AppConfig at *http://s-prs.co/v485804*.

At the time of writing (fall 2019), the mobile app supports the following MDM applications for iOS and Android platforms:

- IBM MaaS360
- Microsoft Intune
- MobileIron
- SAP Mobile Secure
- VMware AirWatch

For Android devices, the mobile app uses the MDM capabilities that are provide through Android Enterprise (previously called Android for Work). Only Android devices that support Android Enterprise can be managed with MDM.

The mobile app is only available through the Apple App Store, Google Play Store, and the Amazon China Appstore. Because of this, the MDM application used needs to support the App Catalog function. SAP SuccessFactors do not provide iOS *.ipa* or Android *.apk* files for customers to provide the app internally.

15.1.6 Accessing the App

Once you've downloaded the SAP SuccessFactors mobile app from the Apple App Store, Google Play Store, or the Amazon China Appstore, there are four ways to activate it:

- **Search-based activation**
  Users search for their company using the company ID or SAP SuccessFactors URL
- **Email-based activation**
  Users receive an email with an activation link
- **MDM-based activation**
  Users are activated via the corporate MDM platform
- **QR code activation**
  Users activate the app using a QR code in the web application, which is shown in Figure 15.2

Once activated, the app is ready for users to use.

When a user first enters the mobile app, they are shown a screen that displays certain functions, depending on their permissions. For example, managers might see the people search, to-dos, and their Continuous Performance Management activities while employees might see the people search, their performance reviews, and any vacation they have booked.

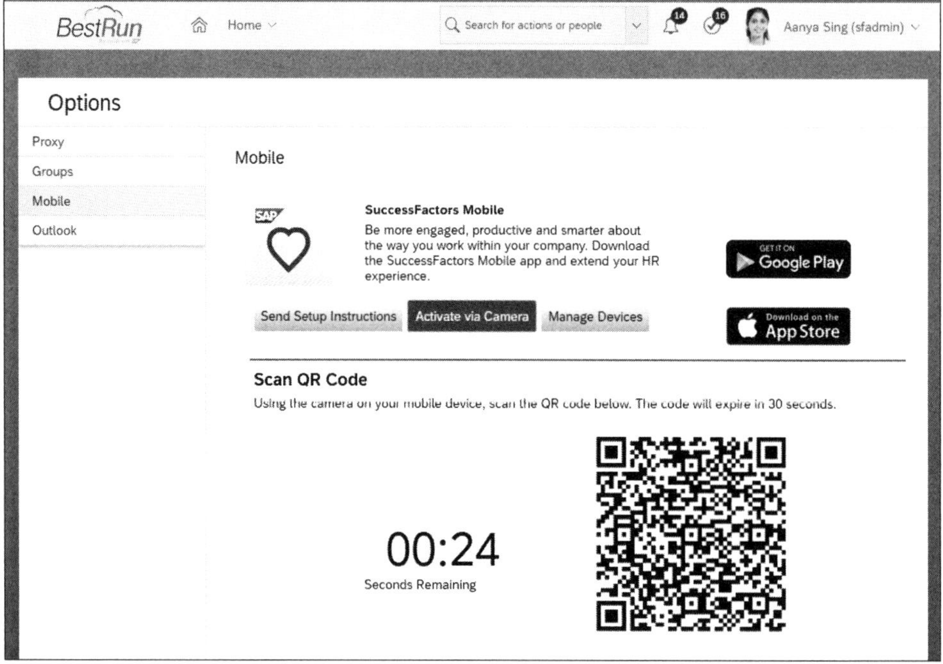

Figure 15.2 Activating the Mobile App Using a QR Code

When a user clicks the menu icon (three horizontal lines above each other), they can see all of the functions they can access. They can also see the **Settings** option and **Sign Out** option.

Further Resources

More information on setting up and deploying the SAP SuccessFactors mobile app can be found in the guides *Mobile Deployment Guide* and *Mobile Security Guide* on the SAP Help Portal under the SAP SuccessFactors Mobile page.

15.2 Platform

The basic features and functionality from the SAP SuccessFactors HCM Suite platform are available in the mobile app. This means every customer has access to features such as:

- People search: Search for employees and view them in the Org Chart
- To-dos and approvals: See the to-do notifications that the user has and action or approve notifications
- Org Chart: Access the Org Chart for your company
- People Profile: View the profile of an employee that is selected in the Org Chart or in a feed in SAP Jam (either in the main feed or in a group feed)

While all of these features will be familiar to managers, HR users, and executives—and most of them to employees—in SAP SuccessFactors, they do operate a bit differently in the mobile app. This isn't to say they are inferior; on the contrary, they are streamlined for mobile use and serve the appropriate information for those who need on-the-go access to HR data.

15.2.1 People Search

Users can search for employees using the people search (shown in Figure 15.3). The **People Search** is located on the home screen. The search uses autocomplete to display employees that match what is entered in real-time. Selecting an employee will show the employee in the **Org Chart**. From there, the user can navigate to the employee's People Profile. 15

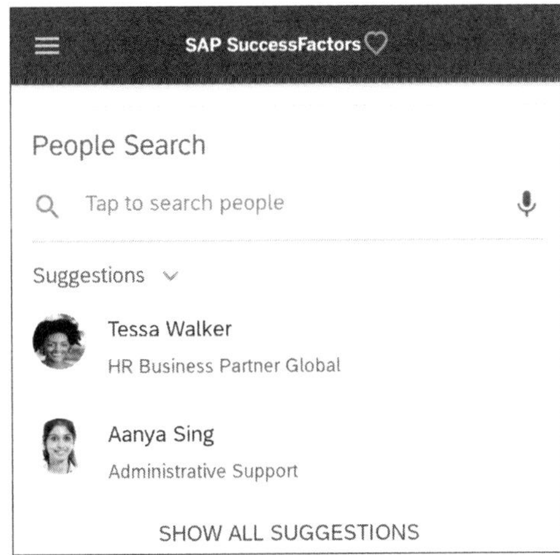

Figure 15.3 Home Page Showing the People Search

15.2.2 To-Dos

A user's to-dos are seen in the **To-Do** section on the home screen (shown in Figure 15.4), which shows when a user opens the app or when they select **Home** in the menu. A selection of the user's to-dos are shown here, and the user can view all requests by clicking **SHOW ALL REQUESTS**. The user can select a request and see all of the details of the request, as well as choose to approve the request, withdraw the request, or send the request back. This is consistent with the approval options for a workflow request in SAP SuccessFactors. If the user has permission, they can also add a comment.

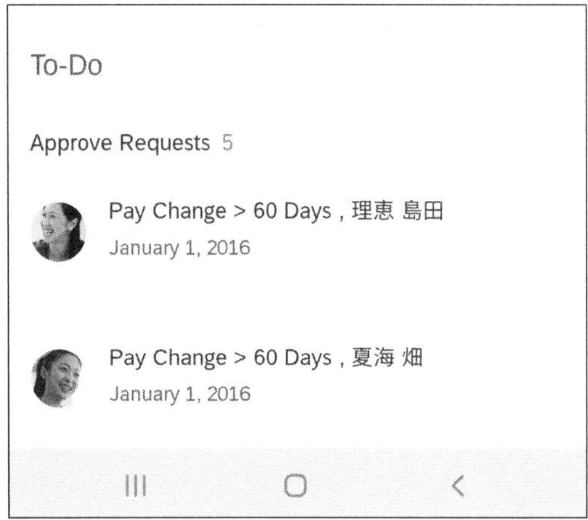

Figure 15.4 Home Page Showing the To-Dos

15.2.3 Org Chart

The Org Chart, shown in Figure 15.5, is accessed by selecting **Org Chart** in the menu. The mobile Org Chart has a different look and feels from the SAP SuccessFactors system, and the navigation is optimized for mobile access. When a user accesses the Org Chart, they will see themselves in the center of the chart. From here, the user can navigate through the chart by dragging an employee to the center of the chart or by selecting an employee.

By dragging an employee to the center of the chart, the user can see the employee's reports below them and the employee's manager above them. The user can drag the employee down, and their manager will become the center of the chart. By dragging the employee up, the report below them becomes the center of the chart. The user can scroll through an employee's peers by selecting any employee on that level and dragging them left or right. The same can be done for peers. Any employee in the Org Chart that is selected becomes the center of the Org Chart. If you select the employee in the center of the Org Chart, then you will be taken to their People Profile, which we'll discuss in the next section. You can also see the employees in the Org Chart in a list by selecting the list button in the top-right of the screen.

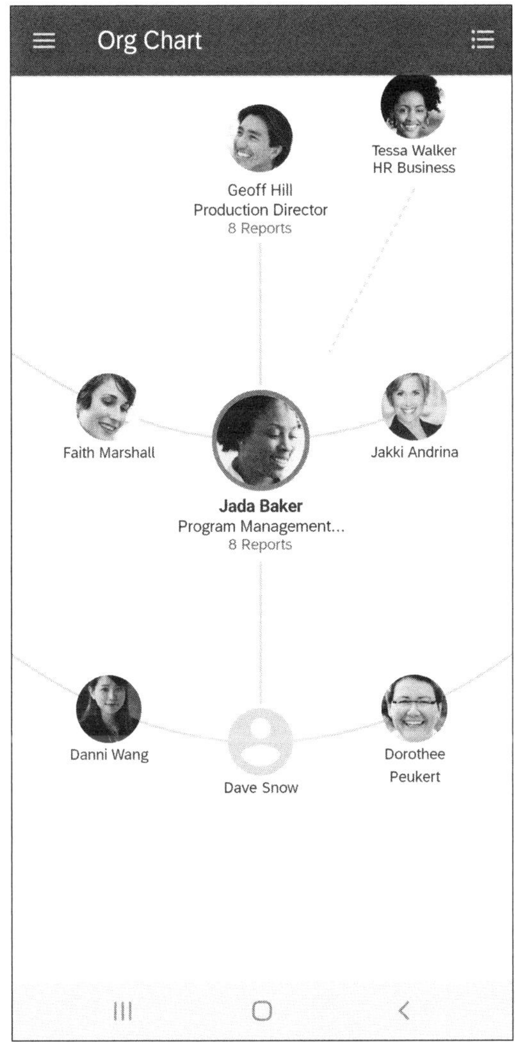

Figure 15.5 The Org Chart

15.2.4 People Profile

Whenever an employee is selected, the user is taken to their **People Profile** (seen in Figure 15.6). The header shows the employee's photo, name, job, number or reports and team size, and their background pictures. Some of these features will be familiar if the user viewed the People Profile of the same employee in SAP SuccessFactors. Below this information, the phone number, email, location, time zone, and the local time of the employee are displayed. You can launch a text message or email address from here.

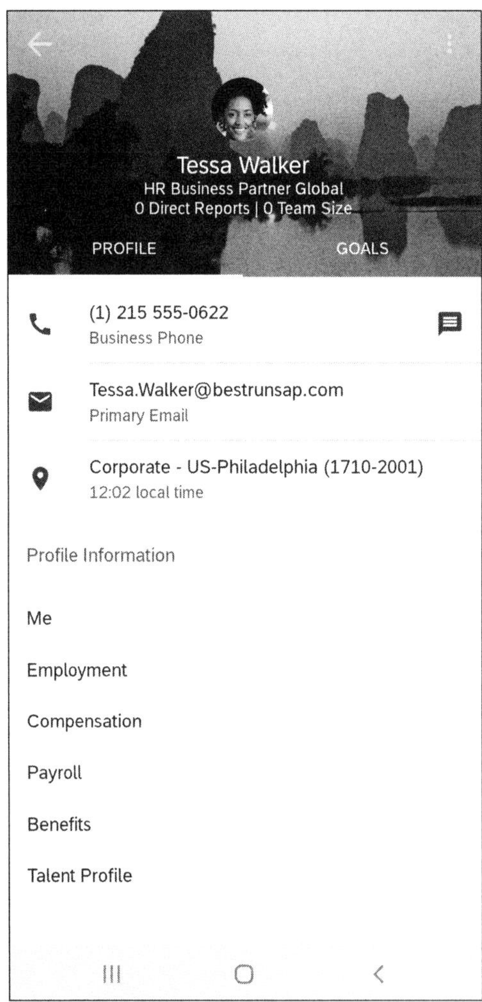

Figure 15.6 People Profile

Under this are all of the available selections to view further blocks of data. Depending on what other applications in the SAP SuccessFactors HCM Suite you are using, you may see various different options. The Talent Profile is always available to view, but if you use Employee Central you'll see the same blocks available in Employee Central, including custom blocks. Figure 15.7 shows an employee's **Job Information** from Employee Central in the People Profile.

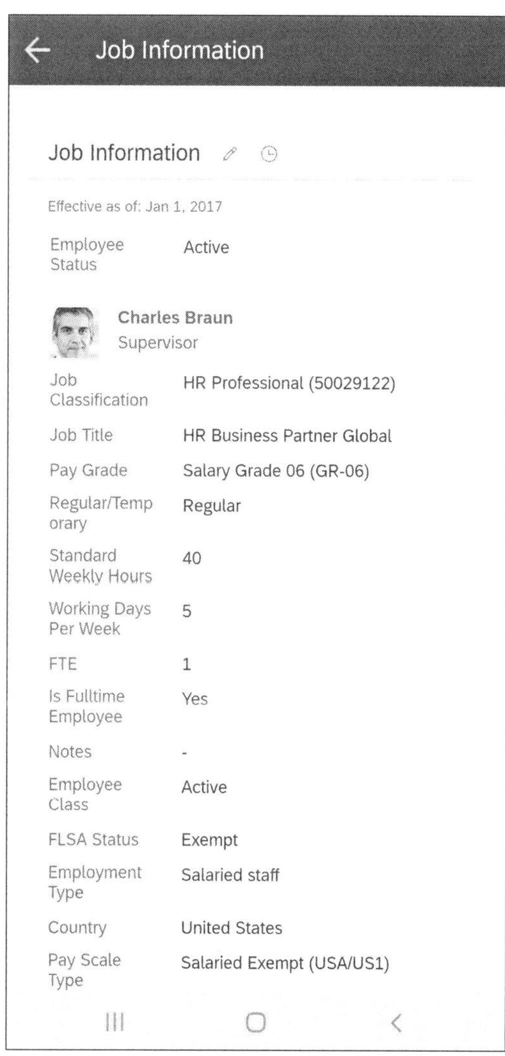

Figure 15.7 An Employee's Job Information in the People Profile

15.3 Employee Central

The mobile app provides plenty of features for Employee Central customers. In addition to the platform features, organizations using Employee Central can provide their employees with self-service activities. Whether the user is a manager, HR professional, executive, or employee, they are able to perform the necessary HR tasks and activities on the mobile app as they can in SAP SuccessFactors.

Aside from approving workflows, users can also maintain their data in the People Profile, view the People Profile of other employees, enter time, book a vacation, view benefits information, and make benefits claims. We'll take a look at this functionality now.

15.3.1 Self-Services

Employees and managers can see the same data in the mobile app as they can in SAP SuccessFactors. Self-services capabilities for employees and managers are accessed through the People Profile, just as with SAP SuccessFactors. And like with SAP SuccessFactors, self-service data changes are made in a similar manner. Employees can edit their data using the **Edit** icon (pen icon) in a block, while managers can launch actions using the **Actions** menu (three vertical dots icon) in the top-right of the People Profile screen or by using the **Edit** icon in a block.

Managers are able to perform the following actions in the mobile app that are available in SAP SuccessFactors (depending on what is enabled and permissioned in SAP SuccessFactors):

- **Change Job and Compensation Info** (shown in Figure 15.8)
- **One-Time Payments**
- **Employment Details**
- **Terminate**
- **One Time Deduction**
- **Manage Recurring Deductions**
- **Manage Alternative Cost Distribution**
- **Reward and Recognition**

A manager can also save the employee to their contacts, which is not possible in SAP SuccessFactors.

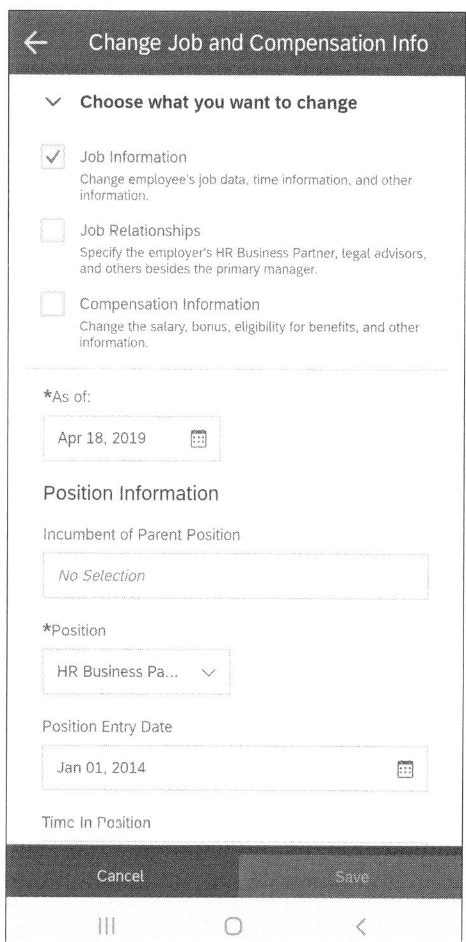

Figure 15.8 Making a Job and Compensation Info Change

Just like in SAP SuccessFactors, any changes subject to workflows will trigger a workflow.

15.3.2 Time Sheet

Users who have to record their working time in SAP SuccessFactors can do this on the mobile app. Users can record time for multiple time types and against a cost center in their time sheet (as shown in Figure 15.9), as well as record on-call time and allowances as part of the time sheet. They can also amend time sheets.

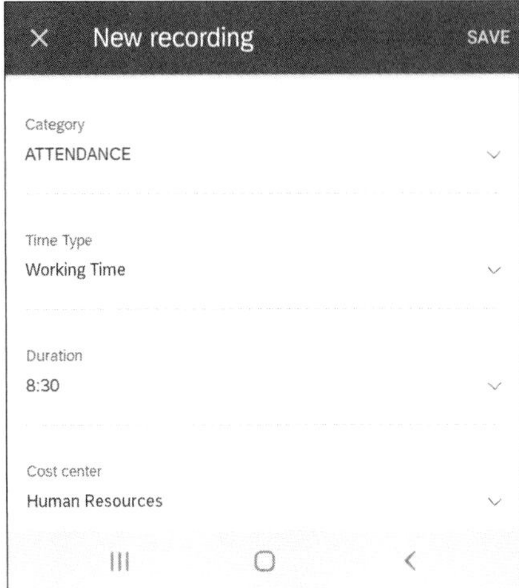

Figure 15.9 Recording Time in the Time Sheet

Users can review their time sheets for each week in the **Week List**.

15.3.3 Time Off

Users can manage their time-off requests and check balances right from their mobile devices. The mobile app allows users to view their time-off balances (at any point in time), submit time-off requests for any of their available time types, view upcoming absences, and view absences and public holidays in the **Absence Calendar** (shown in Figure 15.10).

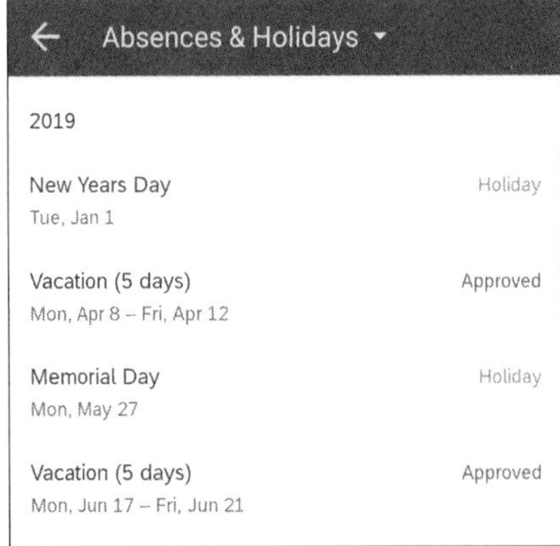

Figure 15.10 Upcoming Absences

15.3.4 Benefits

Some of the benefits information and actions available in SAP SuccessFactors are also available in the mobile app. In the mobile app, users can view their active enrollments and enroll for open benefits enrollments, as well as make claims against eligible benefits and view benefits claims history. In Figure 15.11, a user is viewing one of their benefits and can click the **Add** icon to make a claim against that benefit.

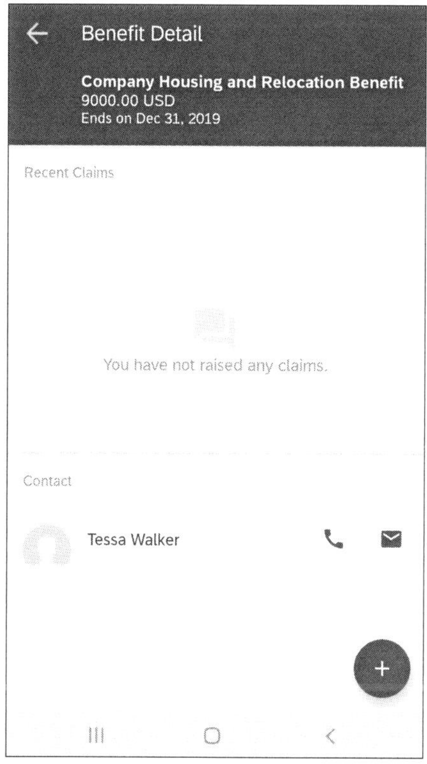

Figure 15.11 Viewing a Benefit

For each claim that is made, the user can attach a photo for the claim submission documentation, as well as view the contact information for the administrator of the benefit.

Further Resources

At the time of writing (fall 2019), the mobile app does not support custom fields or benefits with multiple proofs enabled. For custom fields, the behavior of the mobile app depends whether you are using it on an Android, iPhone, or iPad device. For more details, refer to the guide *Using Global Benefits in Employee Central* found on the SAP Help Portal under the SAP SuccessFactors Employee Central product page.

15.4 Employee Central Payroll

Customers that use Employee Central Payroll can give employees access to their pay slips, tax documents, and other documents and forms in the mobile app as they can in Employee Central Payroll. Users can access their pay slip history and view each pay slip (as shown in Figure 15.12) through the **Payroll** option in the menu or through the **Payroll** option on the People Profile. Managers can view the payroll details of their reports through the People Profile.

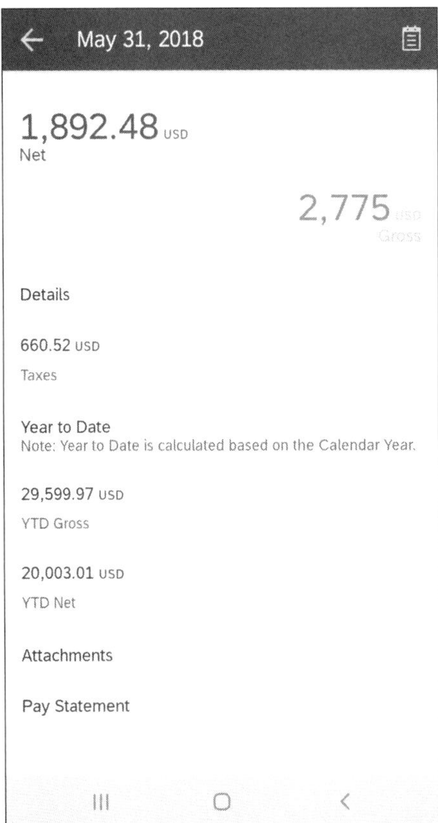

Figure 15.12 Viewing Pay Information

15.5 Employee Central Service Center

The Ask HR feature that can be used in Employee Central is also available on the mobile app via the **Ask HR** menu option. Users can create, view (as shown in Figure 15.13), edit, submit, reply to, and manage Ask HR tickets. Users can also search for and filter their Ask HR tickets (using criteria service category, status, or priority). The mobile app also enables users to call or email their HR service center.

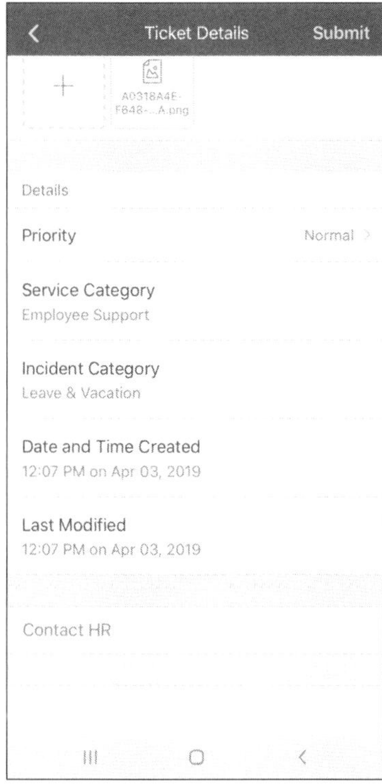

Figure 15.13 Viewing Details of a Ticket

At the time of writing (fall 2019), the mobile app does not support the knowledge base search.

15.6 Performance and Goals

SAP SuccessFactors Performance & Goals—as one of the strongest modules in the SAP SuccessFactors HCM Suite—has a raft of features in the SAP SuccessFactors mobile app. Customers can perform their performance management processes—whether "classic" performance management or continuous performance management—and also support goal management and 360 reviews on the mobile app.

We'll take a look at each of these now.

15.6.1 Performance Management

Performance Management on mobile supports most features available in the web version, including performance forms, route maps, routing actions, user roles, rating options, and rating scale options. Some form sections and some options such as attachments, notes, and team overview are not supported.

Figure 15.14 shows the **Mid-Year Review** feature as it appears in the mobile app.

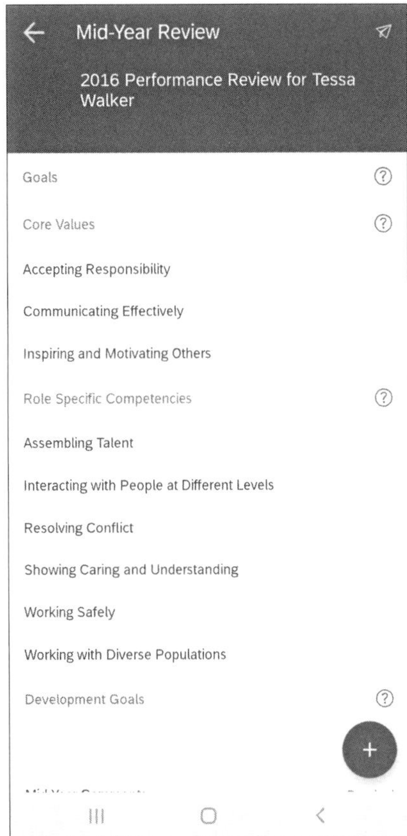

Figure 15.14 Mid-Year Performance Review

Further Resources

For more details on the functionality available, refer to the guide *Performance Management v12 Acceleration* found on the SAP Help Portal under the SAP SuccessFactors Performance & Goals product page.

15.6.2 Continuous Performance Management

As part of Continuous Performance Management, users of the mobile app can request feedback, respond to requests for feedback, and give feedback. When responding to a request for feedback, the functionality to give the feedback is the same as when a user voluntarily gives feedback.

Further Resources

For more details on the functionality available, refer to the guide *Continuous Performance Management* found on the SAP Help Portal under the SAP SuccessFactors Performance & Goals product page.

15.6.3 Goal Management

SAP SuccessFactors Mobile supports a number of features from Goal Management, including:

- View all active goal plans
- Add, edit, and delete goals (adding a goal can be seen in Figure 15.15)
- View all personal goals description and details
- View and update status-related fields (percentage complete, state/status, target/actual)
- View and update goal name field

Employees can perform all of the actions listed previously, based on the permissions provided in SAP SuccessFactors. Managers also have the ability to perform these actions for their team.

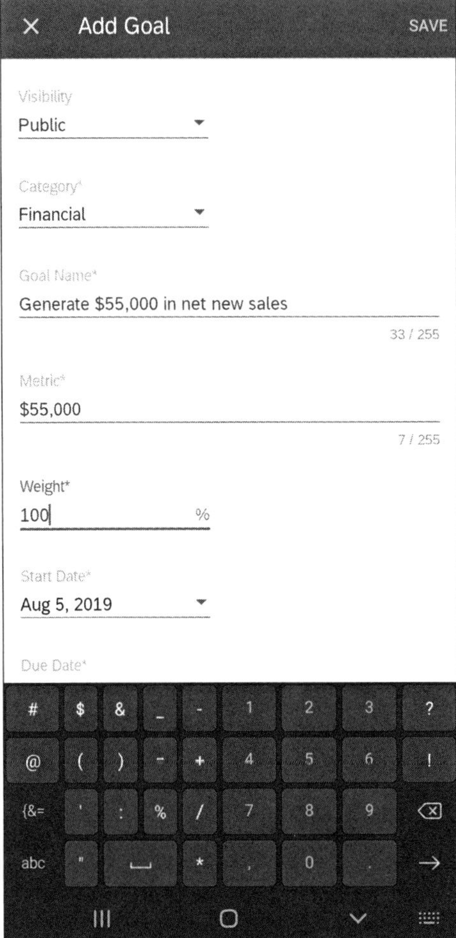

Figure 15.15 Adding a Goal

There are a number of features that are currently not supported, with some that are slated to be supported in the future.

Further Resources

For more details on the functionality available, refer to the guide *Goal Management* found on the SAP Help Portal under the SAP SuccessFactors Performance & Goals product page.

15.6.4 360 Reviews

360 reviews can be performed on the mobile app. A selection of features are currently supported, with some features partially supported in plain text only. These include:

- Raters provide feedback for an employee
- Custom 360 form sections
- Performance goal/objective sections:
  - **View Performance Goal** (name and metric field only)
  - **Performance Goal Rating**
  - **Performance Goal Rating Scale Description**
  - **Performance Goal Comments** (plain text comments only)
  - **Section Introduction** (plain text only)
  - **Performance Goal** section comment (plain text comments only)
  - **Add Performance Goal**
  - **Edit Performance Goal**
  - **Delete Performance Goal**
- Development goal/objective sections:
  - **View Development Goal** (name and metric field only)
  - **Development Goal Rating**
  - **Development Goal Rating Scale Description**
  - **Development Goal Comments** (plain text comments only)
  - **Section Introduction** (plain text only)
  - **Development Goal** section comment (plain text comments only)
  - **Add Development Goal**
  - **Edit Development Goal**
  - **Delete Development Goal**
- Competency sections:
  - **View Competency** (name, weight, and description)
  - **Competency Rating**
  - **Competency Rating Scale Description**
  - **Competency Comments** (plain text comments only)

- **Section Introduction** (plain text only)
- **Competency** section comment (plain text comments only)

- Summary sections:
  - **Calculated Rating**
  - **Adjusted Calculated Rating**
  - **Introduction** (plain text only)
  - **Comment** (plain text comments only)
- Evaluation stage
- All roles
- Rating option 0
- Circle icon rating scale
- Rating scales 1–3, 1–5, 1–7, circle icon, and custom scales

There are a number of features not supported or are planned to be supported in the future.

Further Resources

For more details on the functionality available, refer to the guide *360 Reviews* found on the SAP Help Portal under the SAP SuccessFactors Performance & Goals product page.

15.7 Compensation

The Spot Award feature of Compensation—which we discussed in Chapter 7, Section 7.8—is available in the mobile app. It is accessed through the self-services functionality that we discussed in Section 15.3.1. The functionality for awarding an employee is identical in the mobile app as in SAP SuccessFactors. Figure 15.16 shows the award level step of issuing a reward.

As of the time of writing (fall 2019), this is the extent of the Compensation functionality available in the mobile app.

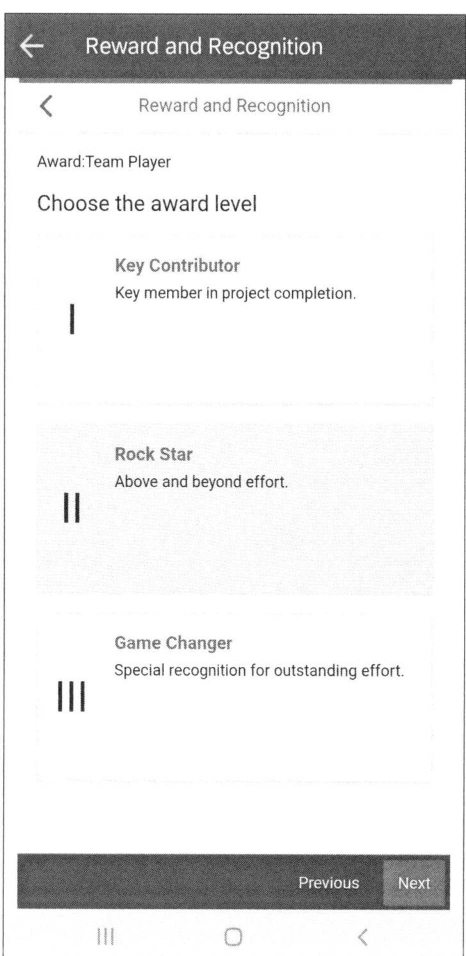

Figure 15.16 Awarding a Level to a Reward

15.8 Learning

Mobile Learning frees employees to take their learning on the go. Work travel and remote work arrangements are greatly enhanced from the ability to access learning from a mobile device. This is why the Learning module is an integral component of the SAP SuccessFactors mobile app. The SAP SuccessFactors product team continues to add functionality in this area.

Employees can use the mobile app to manage their learning assignments and recommendations, search and launch mobile-enabled learning content, and manage course information and instructor-led training registrations simply and easily from their mobile device. Let's look at each of these topics in greater detail.

15.8.1 Assignments and Recommendations

The importance of mobile learning is clear from the design of the mobile app. Both **Learning Assignments** and **Learning Recommendations** appear prominently on the main **To-Do** screen, providing one-click access to learning activities (see Figure 15.17).

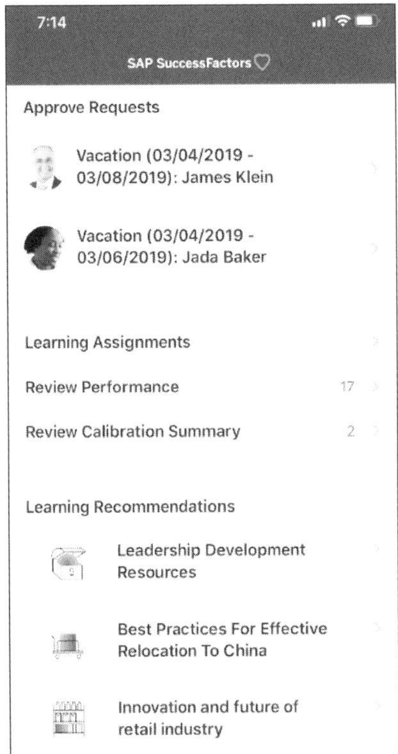

Figure 15.17 Mobile To-Do Screen

Clicking on **Learning Assignments** navigates the mobile user to a list similar to the **Learning Assignments** tile you were introduced to in Chapter 10, Section 10.2.1. Each assignment appears in the order it is due. From this list, mobile users have the ability to launch an on-the-job training task checklist, identify if online content is mobile-enabled, view available offerings for instructor-led training, and view program details.

Learning Recommendations uses the power of system-generated, peer-initiated, or machine-learning-enabled recommendations to highlight learning content that may be of interest to mobile users. From the list of recommendations, the mobile user can view details and launch content.

Since much has already been mentioned about mobile content, we will now dig further into this topic.

15.8.2 Mobile-Enabled Content

If you'll recall in Chapter 10, we mentioned briefly that online content can be mobile-enabled. This provides the opportunity to offer a version of content that is specifically designed with mobile in mind. For learning designers, they'll need to consider the limited screen space, a lack of hover and mouse control, and mobile media formats. It is for this reason that SAP SuccessFactors has created a companion app called the *Learn Test app*. Learning developers can load their mobile designed content into the Learn Test app to see how it behaves and renders on different device screen sizes. Once content is tested and loaded into Learning, mobile users can launch online content from the convenience of their mobile device. For iOS devices, there is the additional capability to download content directly to the mobile device to complete learning while out of network range. When the user returns to network access, the online content progress is updated.

The benefits of launching self-paced online training anytime, anywhere are clear. Time spent away from the office or outside of network range is optimized through this learning delivery. Scheduled training may also be managed through the mobile app. Let's take a look at that now.

15.8.3 Course Information

Whether the mobile user is working through their learning assignments, or searching the catalog for interesting courses, they will be able to view available offerings for instructor-led training, register for an offering, and check approvals. If there are prerequisites for any course, instructor-led or online, the prerequisites are listed in the course information. Once training is complete and recorded in the system, the learning history is available from the mobile app to provide access to completions and view or download course certificates.

Further Resources

This just scratches the surface of all the mobile learning features available from the SAP SuccessFactors mobile app. For more information on this topic, check out *SAP SuccessFactors Learning: The Comprehensive Guide* by Joelle Smith, Alan Yang, and Alex Churin (SAP PRESS, 2018).

15.9 Recruiting

In today's environment, recruiting is a 24/7 process. Candidates view open positions, apply for jobs, and monitor their progression through the process at any time of day or night. Likewise, recruiters often deal with hiring managers and approvers who are traveling or based in different time zones all over the globe. The Recruiting features of the mobile app keep the most crucial elements of the recruiting process accessible across the globe at any time.

Requisitions can be approved via the mobile app. The app supports iterative route map steps. Configuration on the requisition identifies those fields that should appear on the mobile app. Operators can also view list of job applications organized by job requisitions or status pipeline. Depending on permissions, they can edit job requisitions or make modifications in the interview ratings.

With Interview Central access on the mobile device, SAP SuccessFactors enables the fastest interview feedback possible. Interviewers can provide candidate ratings by competency, an overall rating, and comments along the way. The side-by-side feature of Interview Central lets interviewers rate candidates against each other in an easy interface. As shown in Figure 15.18, requisition approval and interview feedback are easily performed on the mobile device, keeping the recruiting process moving forward. The mobile app also supports multistage applications.

After a candidate is selected for hire, approving the official offer becomes a time-sensitive task. Mobile offer approvals again put the right information in the hands of the right people to provide recruiters, hiring managers, and candidates with the fastest, smoothest hiring process possible.

Text message notifications can be also configured with the use of SAP Mobile Service, which requires an additional contract with SAP. With the SMS feature, messages and notifications can be sent out to candidates for upcoming interviews. Customers can also configure personalize the wording of SMS trigger instructions and provide options for opting out of text messages.

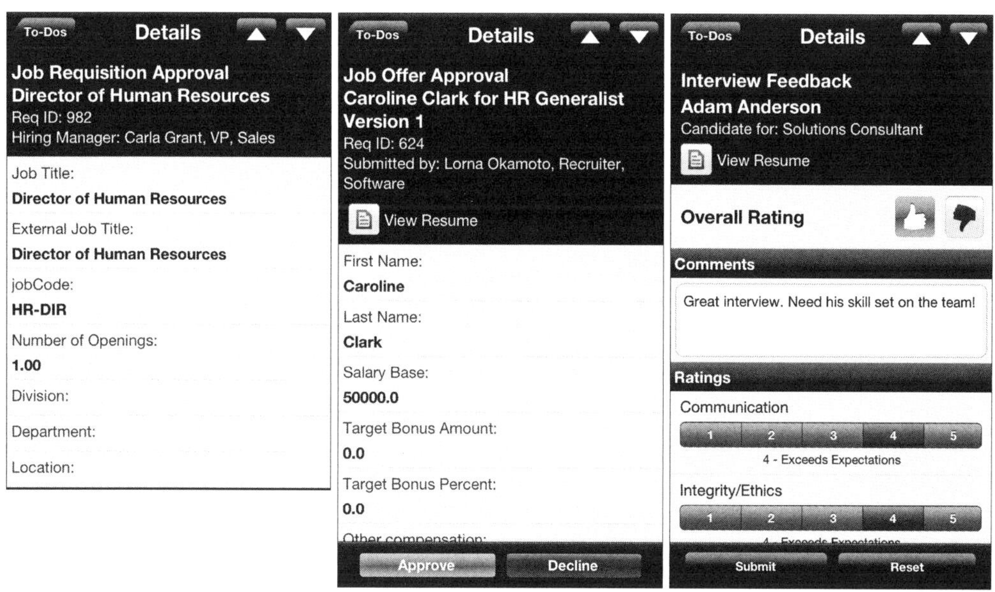

Figure 15.18 Mobile Recruiting

15.10 Onboarding

Onboarding mobile is extremely user friendly. It provides an easy platform for not only hiring managers to provide information to new hires before the first day, but also for connecting the new hires to their potential team and giving an overview about their first day.

The mobile feature for new hires is called Mobile First Day Experience. This provides them with a countdown to their first day on the job and answers the "who," "what," and "where" questions that accompany a new job. The interactive manager and buddy "mobile quickcard" answers any "who" questions on day one by connecting new hires with their new manager and their "buddy." Meeting timelines and agendas and a link to the Mobile Profile help answer the "what" questions and alleviate many questions from the new hire on how they will spend their first days of employment. Finally, the "where" questions are answered via information on office location(s) that comes with a mobile map app integration.

The mobile feature in Onboarding also features First Day Countdown, which is configured during the onboarding process. This is a fun way to connect with the new hire and provide a countdown toward the number of days to joining the company.

The new employee can download the mobile app before the start day. The Onboarding mobile app is the same SAP SuccessFactors application and expires after 30 days after start date. Using the same application gives the flexibility to the employee to continue using the app even after onboarding (for example, Learning, Performance & Goals, etc.).

15.11 Succession and Development

The mobile app offers users the ability to manage the goals on their development plan. Users can add, edit, or delete goals on any of their development plans.

Managers can view the development plans of their direct reports. Figure 15.19 shows the **Development Objectives** view in the mobile app.

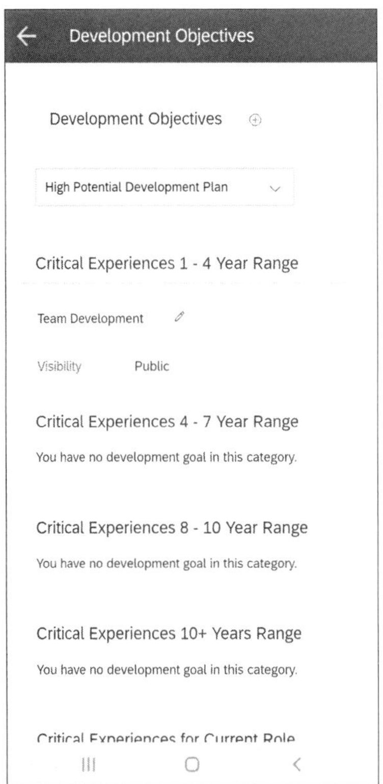

Figure 15.19 Viewing Development Objectives from the Development Plan

15.12 Workforce Analytics

Workforce Analytics does not yet have many features available for the mobile app. Key functionality currently includes the Headlines feature and metrics, which we'll briefly touch on in this section:

- **Headlines**
  The Workforce Analytics Headlines feature was created specifically with a mobile-first design approach, allowing HR managers and executives the ability get direct transparency into how data trends are affecting their teams. They can get a clear picture of their workforce's performance in order to identify problem areas that need to be addressed, without the clutter of irrelevant data.

  Headlines also includes an Alerts feature, which delivers alerts without the often complex or obscure language that comes with analytics. This way, HR managers can easily understand what is being conveyed in a visually engaging way, and they can drill down for further insight as needed.
- **Metrics tile**
  Every metric published in the Workforce Analytics solution can be viewed on mobile devices. In addition, metrics that are displayed on a user's SAP SuccessFactors home page—in the form of tiles—may also be viewed in the SAP SuccessFactors native mobile app.

  Metrics and insights are delivered to HR professionals, managers, leaders, and executives on the mobile device and on the desktop, when and where they need the information.

15.13 SAP Jam

Although SAP Jam has its own mobile app, the mobile app provides some SAP Jam functionality to enable users to view their feed, access groups, and view SAP Jam notifications.

The three options available in the mobile app menu are:

- **Feed**: View the company feed
- **Groups**: View your groups
- **Notifications**: View any notifications you have

These features will be familiar to SAP Jam users, although they are optimized and streamlined for focused use in the mobile app. The **Follows Feed** shows all of the activities that are seen in SAP Jam, which can be seen in Figure 15.20.

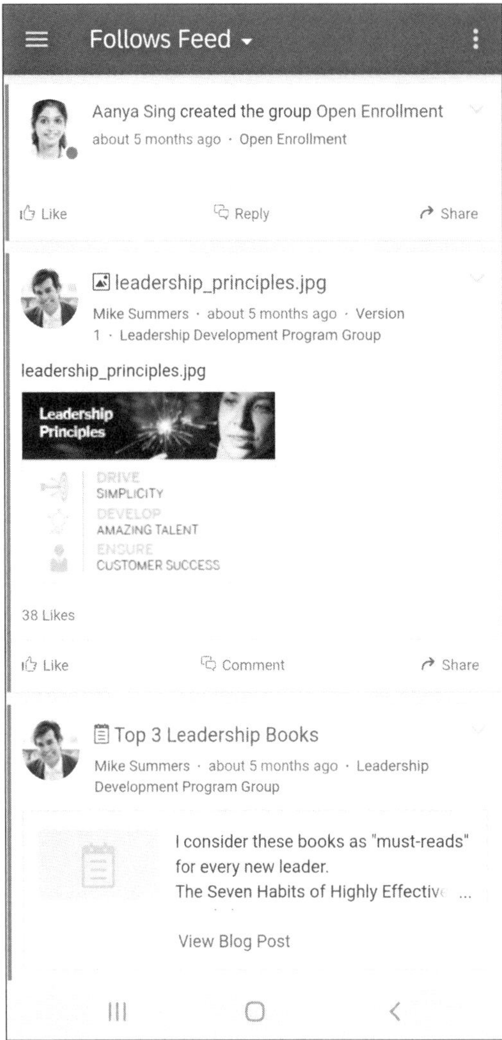

Figure 15.20 The Company Feed

Group Details—as shown in Figure 15.21—give users the core functionality needed to use SAP Jam groups, including:

- Group overview
- Group feed
- Content
- Questions
- Ideas
- Discussion forums
- List of members

The **Jam Notifications** feature is like-for-like with the notifications functionality in SAP Jam. Figure 15.22 shows the notifications in the mobile app.

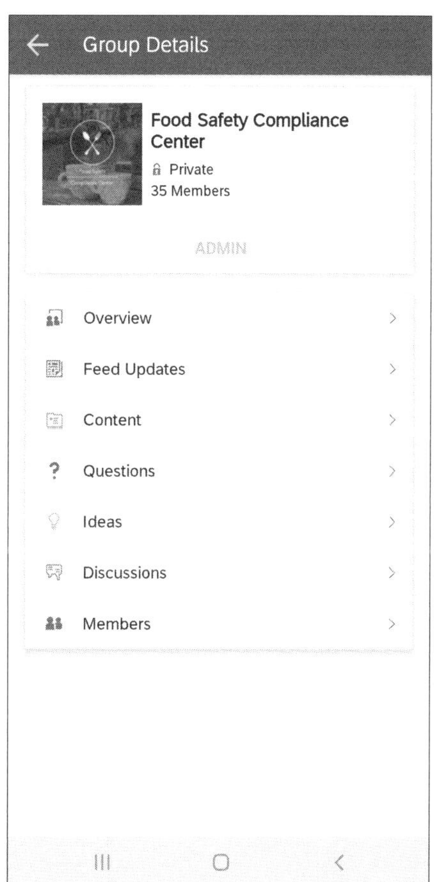

Figure 15.21 The Group Details Screen for a SAP Jam Group

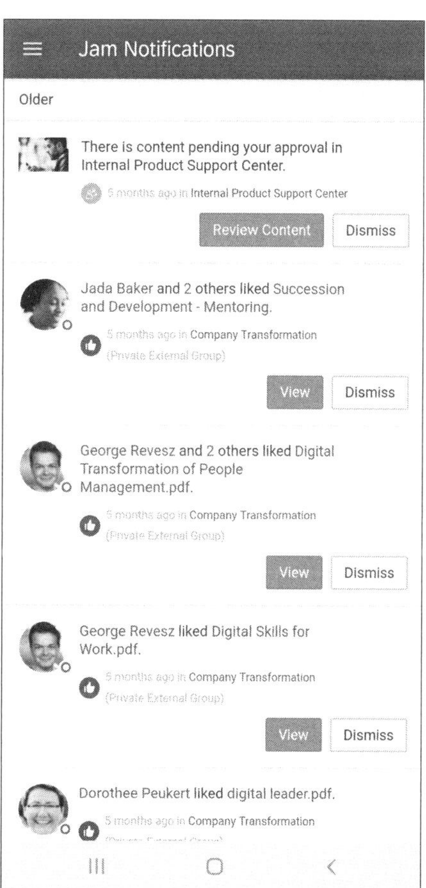

Figure 15.22 Notifications in the Mobile App

15.14 Summary

With the collaborative features of the mobile app, users are empowered to stay connected to their teams and actively participate in critical business processes, regardless of where they may be working on any given day. It delivers the tools they need to find and communicate with each other, stay current with learning needs and activities, stay on top of a variety of approvals, and participate in collaborative teams or projects managed via SAP Jam. Managers can keep critical performance-related processes and tasks moving right from their mobile devices by signing performance reviews, monitoring goal progress, scheduling meetings with their teams, and approving critical recruiting forms to ensure that the best talent is evaluated for their open positions. Employees can maintain data, view their payslip, make benefits claims, enter time, and request vacation.

In the next chapter, we'll look at integration and the various technologies and packaged integrations provided by SAP.

Chapter 16
Integration with SAP and Third-Party Systems

The SAP SuccessFactors HCM Suite has been integrated with other systems hundreds of times, using varying approaches and technologies. Since acquiring SAP SuccessFactors, SAP has worked on providing packaged integration content for a variety of different integration scenarios.

Integration is a mission-critical activity that is needed for almost any enterprise system implementation, and the SAP SuccessFactors HCM Suite is no exception. Thousands of customers have integrated SAP SuccessFactors with multiple different systems using a variety of middleware applications. In recent years, integration has become significantly easier and rarely is integration not successful when using experienced integration consultants. The difficulty of integration really depends on the complexity of the target system.

In order to support integration to other systems (including other SAP on-premise and cloud systems), SAP has provided a number of packaged integrations. For SAP SuccessFactors Employee Central customers, SAP bundles in their SAP Cloud Platform Integration middleware. Along with application programming interfaces (APIs) and other accelerators, SAP provides customers with the tools needed to build integrations between SAP SuccessFactors and other systems more rapidly.

SAP recognizes that many of their SAP ERP Human Capital Management (SAP ERP HCM) customers retain SAP ERP for multiple business processes and that some customers wish to retain SAP ERP HCM for core HR. Therefore, SAP has been building standard integration content for customers for its different delivery models. Many of these leverage SAP and non-SAP technology. SAP is focusing its efforts on providing data integration, process integration, and user experience integration that support a variety of different HR, payroll, and talent management processes.

Because SAP ERP HCM and the SAP SuccessFactors HCM Suite both store data, it's necessary to create integration so that data can flow between the systems and reside in one central system of record. The process of integration requires technology and mapping of the relevant fields in one system with those in the other and rules for data transformation and validation. Different process steps and triggers can also be part of an integration process, although this will depend on the extent to which integration is required. Whichever ways integrations are designed, a certain level of complexity is required—and SAP intends to reduce this complexity with standard content.

In this chapter, we'll evaluate the different technologies available to customers who want to integrate SAP SuccessFactors solutions with other solutions, plus the standard integration content available from SAP and the different APIs found in the SAP SuccessFactors system. We'll also look at some of the additional documentation available from SAP.

Further Resources

You can read more about integration between SAP SuccessFactors and SAP ERP in the book *Integrating SuccessFactors with SAP* by Venki Krishnamoorthy, Donna Leong-Cohen, Prashanth Padmanabhan, and Chinni Reddygari (SAP PRESS, 2015).

16.1 Integration Strategy

SAP has a deep, detailed, and evolving integration strategy. Although we will look at the key points of this strategy in this section, we will not cover all elements of it. SAP has designed and adopted a cloud integration framework to do the following:

- Identify and prescribe cloud deployment models for all products
- Support each cloud deployment model with packaged integrations
- Deliver fixed-price professional services packages and best practices for implementation
- Publish APIs to enable custom integrations
- Provide integration middleware technology in the cloud and on-premise

As part of this strategy, SAP has developed, productized, and released various packaged content to integrate the SAP SuccessFactors HCM Suite with SAP ERP HCM (for core HR, talent management, and analytics), SAP ERP (for other processes, such as payroll), SAP SuccessFactors Employee Central Payroll, and third-party solutions (such as time and attendance, and benefits). Integrations exist for all of the deployment models previously introduced.

16.1.1 Integration Pillars

The integration strategy looks to address three types of integration challenges through three strategic pillars:

- Data integration
- Process integration
- User experience integration

Data integration creates a basic data foundation within the SAP SuccessFactors HCM Suite so that core HR and talent management processes can be performed. This type of integration has been delivered for all deployment models. Two examples are the employee master data integration for Employee Central and SAP SuccessFactors Workforce Analytics extractors.

Process integration is event-driven, bidirectional data integration designed for specific HR processes that span both SAP SuccessFactors and SAP ERP HCM. These include the pay-for-performance (compensation management), attract-to-hire (recruiting), and define-to-hire (recruiting) processes. With this type of integration, data can be transferred to SAP SuccessFactors, and data produced in the SAP SuccessFactors HCM Suite is transferred to SAP, where it can be used in SAP-dependent parts of processes or stored in the system of record. SAP delivers and maintains this type of integration on an ongoing basis.

User experience integration is centered on creating a unified, single point of access for end users, irrespective of whether the processes being performed are within the SAP Enterprise Portal or the SAP SuccessFactors HCM Suite. This includes single sign-on (SSO) and integration of SAP SuccessFactors processes into employee self-services (ESS) and manager self-services (MSS) menus. The intention is that end users can move between Web Dynpro applications and SAP SuccessFactors solutions within the SAP Enterprise Portal or SAP Business Client without even noticing that they have changed applications. SAP delivered an SSO cookbook resource to configure SSO between SAP Enterprise Portal and SAP SuccessFactors HCM Suite, which we will look at in Section 16.7.1.

16.1.2 Integrations for Deployment Scenarios

SAP has delivered a number of integration scenarios that align with the three pillars of its integration strategy, as well as the deployment models that we discussed in Chapter 1, Section 1.3. These packages vary for each deployment model.

SAP continues to maintain the packaged integrations it has released, and SAP also delivers new integrations periodically. These packaged integrations provide a set of programs, tools, and methodologies to help leverage SAP ERP and SAP SuccessFactors processes seamlessly and with both minimal risk and low total cost of ownership (TCO). These integrations are robust; however, as they are packaged, they may require additional effort to extend the standard integration if custom fields or logic are required beyond the predefined standard.

Let's look at the strategy for each of the deployment scenarios now.

Talent Hybrid

SAP provides a number of packaged integrations for the talent hybrid deployment model, which we will cover in more detail in Section 16.4. SAP's aim is to provide packaged integrations to cover each of the integration pillars: data, process, and user experience. They enable changes to data in the SAP SuccessFactors HCM Suite to be written back to the SAP ERP HCM system at the point the data is needed for further processing. For example, the compensation process integration delivered by SAP is designed to write data to SAP only when it needs to become part of the payroll process.

It's important to note that all data transfers between SAP ERP HCM and SAP SuccessFactors are always initiated from SAP ERP HCM or from the middleware. No data is "pushed" from SAP SuccessFactors; rather, it is always "pushed" from SAP ERP HCM or the middleware.

Core Hybrid

Integration for the core hybrid deployment model has three focuses: integration with SAP ERP, data replication to Employee Central Payroll, and integration to third-party solutions. All integrations are from Employee Central, and the talent hybrid integrations are not needed in this scenario. The integrations are largely related to being able to support other SAP ERP processes (like payroll or time and attendance), SAP cloud processes (e.g., SAP Fieldglass or SAP Concur), or third-party processes (such as benefits management or user identity management).

Full Cloud HCM

Integration for the full cloud HCM deployment model is the same as for core hybrid, except that it does not include integration to SAP ERP. All integrations are from Employee Central, and the talent hybrid integrations are not needed in this scenario, since there is no SAP ERP HCM system. The integrations are largely related to being able to support other processes or cloud applications.

Side-by-Side

Side-by-side integration covers bidirectional integration to ensure that Employee Central and SAP ERP HCM are synchronized. This leverages the cloud hybrid integrations, as well as some side-by-side specific integrations, to transfer data between SAP ERP HCM and Employee Central.

Cloud hybrid, talent hybrid, and side-by-side specific integrations may be needed in the side-by-side deployment model, depending on the business scenario.

16.2 Integration Technologies

Several technologies are available to integrate the SAP SuccessFactors HCM Suite with other systems that offer different features, ease of setup, cost, maintenance effort, and flexibility. Previous integrations have used a variety of platforms; many of these are still available for customers, even if they are not covered by SAP's packaged integrations.

Some of the technologies available for integrating SAP SuccessFactors with other systems include the following:

- Flat-file transfer
- SAP Process Integration
- SAP Cloud Platform Integration
- SAP Data Services
- API Center
- Integration Center
- Intelligent Services
- SAP SuccessFactors APIs, custom-built APIs, or other middleware

Note

It should be noted that previously Dell Boomi AtomSphere (commonly referred to as Boomi) was included in the subscription of Employee Central, but at the time of writing (fall 2019), it is not offered to new customers but is available upon request.

Although the majority of existing integrations use flat-file or custom-built APIs, SAP wants to enable customers to use packaged content that leverages either SAP Process Integration or SAP Cloud Platform Integration for talent hybrid and SAP Cloud Platform Integration for core hybrid, full cloud HCM, and side-by-side. Table 16.1 summarizes the technologies available for standard packaged content from SAP.

Technology	Talent Hybrid	Cloud Hybrid/Full Cloud HCM/Side-by-Side
Flat-file transfer	X (partial)	
SAP Process Integration	X	
SAP Cloud Platform Integration	X	X
SAP Data Services		
APIs or other middleware	X	X

Table 16.1 Technology Options for Each Deployment Model

Figure 16.1 shows an example of the architecture of middleware technology in an SAP ERP HCM and SAP SuccessFactors scenario.

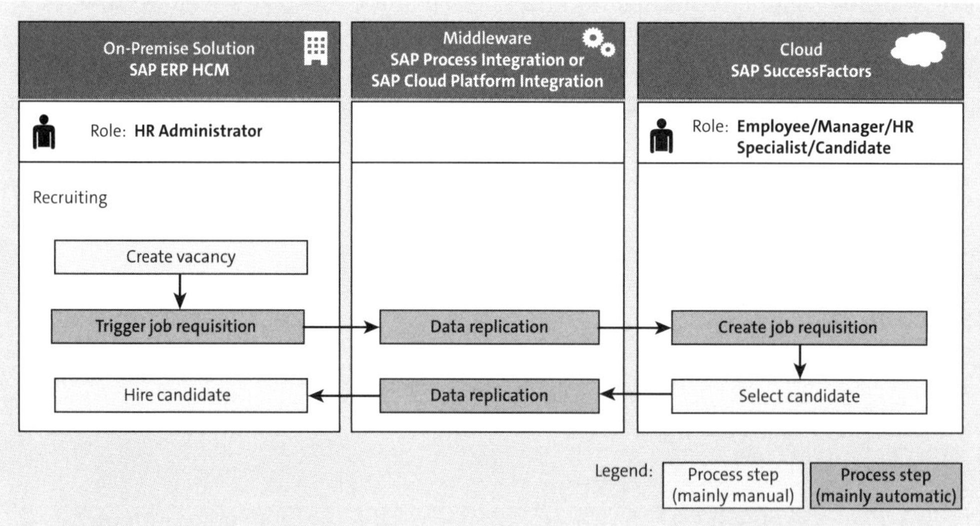

Figure 16.1 Diagram of Middleware Integration

We'll now run through these technology options in a bit more detail.

16.2.1 Flat-File Integration

Flat-file integration has been around for a number of years and is still a quick and reliable way to transfer data between two systems, albeit with a lack of standards and security compared to other mechanisms. Flat-file transfer usually involves extracting a file of data—often a comma-separated values (CSV) or text (TXT) file—from a system and then uploading it to another system. A *File Transfer Protocol* (FTP) or *Secure File Transfer Protocol* (SFTP) server is often used to transfer the file between the systems. Although this method is fairly simple to create and maintain, it does have some disadvantages that might be undesirable to some customers, such as a lack of security or encryption, standards or validation for data, and transformation and mapping capabilities. However, some tools are available that can validate or transform data in flat files. CSV files used to send data to SAP SuccessFactors support *Pretty Good Privacy* (PGP) software to encrypt the file. SAP SuccessFactors supports only SFTP.

Within SAP SuccessFactors, a flat file of data can be imported from the SAP SuccessFactors SFTP using one of the many options in the Admin Center or, on a regular basis, using a job set up by your implementation partner in the **Manage Scheduled Jobs** page within provisioning. Flat-file transfer can also be used to perform ad hoc or one-time data imports for generic objects, employee data, Employee Central foundation data, translations, and more.

The talent hybrid integration (covered in Section 16.4) can leverage flat-file technology to transfer basic organizational and employee data between SAP ERP HCM and SAP SuccessFactors for use in talent management processes. In SAP ERP HCM, a report provided in the integration add-on can be used to export a flat file of data to be uploaded to SAP SuccessFactors.

16.2.2 SAP Process Integration

SAP Process Integration is SAP's reliable/high-performance service-oriented architecture (SOA) middleware product for integrating and transferring message-based data between SAP systems and between other internal or external systems. It is a subcomponent of SAP Process Orchestration. Approximately 35 percent of SAP ERP HCM customers currently use a version of SAP Process Integration to integrate SAP systems.

Note

SAP Process Integration was called SAP Exchange Infrastructure until version 7.0 and was part of SAP Process Orchestration from version 7.30.

SAP Process Integration allows multiple different systems to connect to each other and exchange messages via the central SAP Process Integration engine component. Various adapters allow connectivity to a variety of systems and handle messages to ensure they are processed correctly by the Integration Engine. Business logic and transformations can be applied to messages to ensure compatibility of data between systems. Figure 16.2 depicts a typical message flow within the SAP Process Integration system.

Although SAP provides a large number of adapters, customers and integration partners can also build their own adapters to fill gaps within the SAP-delivered adapters or to connect to a brand-new system, such as the SAP SuccessFactors HCM Suite. The SAP SuccessFactors adapter—launched in early 2014—simplifies the process to build custom interfaces between SAP SuccessFactors and SAP ERP HCM.

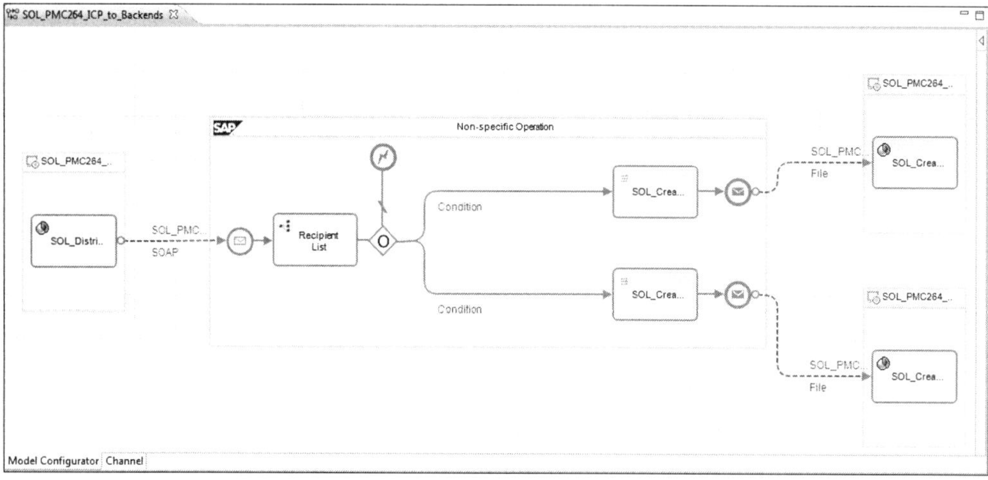

Figure 16.2 Message Flow in SAP Process Integration

The license for SAP Process Integration is included in the SAP licenses that every SAP customer should have. This means there are no licensing implications for using SAP Process Integration as an integration middleware.

Further Resources

You can read more about SAP Process Integration in the book *SAP Process Orchestration: The Comprehensive Guide* by John Bilay and Roberto Viana Blanco (2nd edition, SAP PRESS, 2017).

16.2.3 SAP Cloud Platform Integration

SAP's go-forward integration platform is SAP Cloud Platform Integration, which provides the same level of middleware integration among multiple systems, as is found in SAP Process Integration and other leading middleware platforms. SAP Cloud Platform Integration is an *integration-as-a-service* (IaaS) platform with an easy-to-use and intuitive user interface (UI).

SAP Cloud Platform Integration is specifically designed to integrate SAP's range of cloud solutions (such as SAP Concur, SAP Fieldglass, and, of course, the SAP SuccessFactors HCM Suite) with other cloud applications and on-premise systems. However, the platform does support integration of numerous external systems using web services or flat-file integration.

For customers who are not using or do not plan to use SAP Process Integration for SAP SuccessFactors integration, SAP Cloud Platform Integration is a good alternative. Like the SAP SuccessFactors HCM Suite, it benefits from many of the same advantages as an SaaS application, such as leveraging a subscription model, offering multitenancy, and being hosted and supported remotely. It also offers the same functionality expected from any enterprise-level middleware integration platform. Modeling of integration content is done in web-based UI, as shown in Figure 16.3.

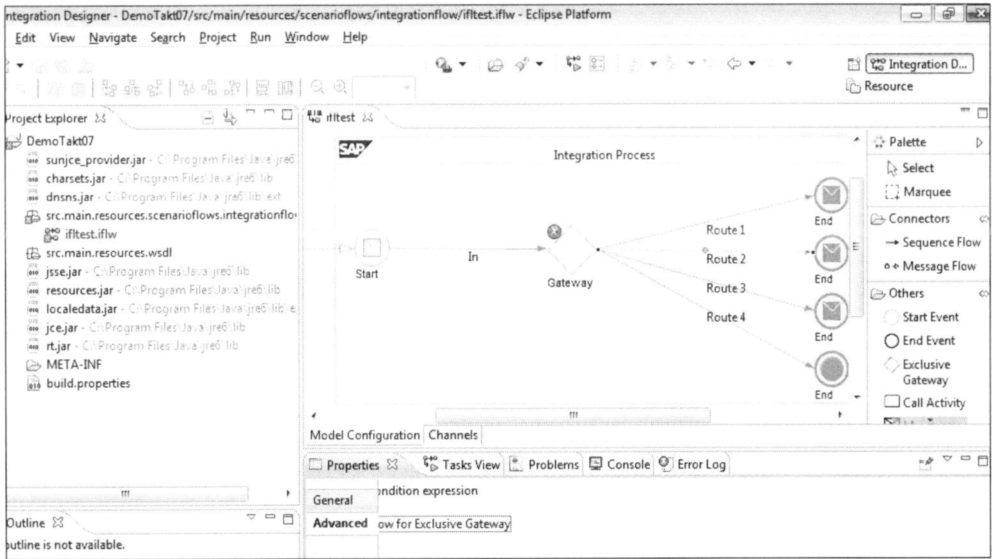

Figure 16.3 Modeling in SAP Cloud Platform Integration

The integration packages that SAP provides for integrating Employee Central with other systems and SAP provides for the talent hybrid model leverage SAP Cloud Platform Integration (the talent hybrid integrations are also available on SAP Process Integration). Integration content built in SAP Cloud Platform Integration is backward-compatible with SAP Process Integration, meaning that content created by other customers or partners on SAP Cloud Platform Integration can be provided to customers using SAP Process Integration. However, it's worth noting that content created in SAP Process Integration can't be used in SAP Cloud Platform Integration.

SAP Cloud Platform Integration also contains standard integration content and templates for integrating Employee Central with SAP ERP HCM, Employee Central Payroll, and third-party systems. SAP Cloud Platform Integration is included in the subscription for Employee Central.

Like for SAP Process Integration, an SAP SuccessFactors adapter is available for SAP Cloud Platform Integration as well, to simplify the building of custom interfaces.

Packaged integrations available on SAP Cloud Platform Integration can be viewed in the online integration catalog located on the SAP API Business Hub website.

Further Resources

You can read more about SAP Cloud Platform Integration in the book *SAP Cloud Platform Integration: The Comprehensive Guide* by John Mutumba Bilay, Peter Gutsche, Mandy Krimmel, and Volker Stiehl (2nd edition, SAP PRESS, 2018).

16.2.4 SAP Data Services

SAP Data Services is a solution that offers data integration, data quality, data profiling, and text data processing. It is used primarily with analytics-based scenarios that require transferring data from SAP ERP to SAP Business Warehouse (SAP BW), SAP HANA, SAP Rapid Marts, SAP IQ, and non-SAP data stores.

SAP Data Services is an *extract, transform, load* (ETL) solution, so its primary purpose is to extract data, transform the data, and load the data to and from any application for use in data integration or data warehouse projects. It provides a development workbench, metadata repository, data connectivity layer, runtime environment, and management console.

SAP Data Services can be used to integrate the SAP SuccessFactors HCM Suite with SAP BW. More details can be found in Section 16.7.4 and Section 16.7.5.

16.2.5 Single Sign-On

For user experience integration, SSO technology enables multiple technologies to be integrated from a security and logon perspective, so that the user can seamlessly switch between applications. Although the switch from one technology to another might not be seamless visually, from an access perspective, the user is not aware that they have been authenticated against another system using the credentials from their first point of access.

Many systems use a variety of industry-standard security mechanisms to provide SSO and protect against unauthorized access. The use of HTTPS as a secure protocol is widespread and provides additional security to data that is transmitted over internal or external networks. Technology such as OAuth, Security Assertion Markup Language 2.0 (SAML2) assertion, and Secure Sockets Layer (SSL) are used both between internal systems and with web-based applications.

There are also several access and identity management applications that can be used to manage access to SAP SuccessFactors using SSO, such as Okta or Microsoft Azure Active Directory. SAP Cloud Platform Identity Authentication is available for SAP SuccessFactors customers to use for SSO, password policy, and other services.

Further Resources

For more details on integration SAP SuccessFactors using SSO, refer to the guides *SuccessFactors SAML2 Single Sign-On* and *Setting Up SuccessFactors with SAP Cloud Platform Identity Authentication Service* found on the SAP Help Portal under the SAP SuccessFactors HCM Suite product page.

16.2.6 API Center

The API Center is the one-stop shop for all API related features in the SAP SuccessFactors HCM Suite. It is accessed in the Admin Center. The API Center home page—shown in Figure 16.4—displays a tile for each of the functions that can be accessed in the API Center.

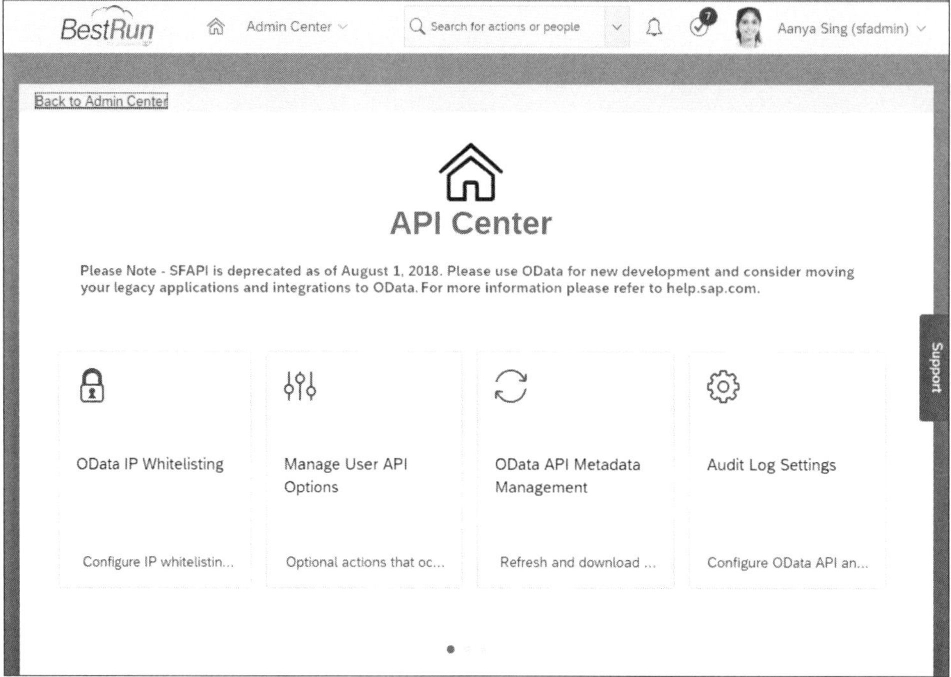

Figure 16.4 The API Center Home Page

The API Center gives you access to the following features, depending on your permissions:

- OData IP whitelisting
- Manage user API options
- OData API metadata management
- Audit log settings
- OData API audit log
- OData API Data Dictionary
- OAuth configuration for OData
- OData API version control
- Legacy SFAPI audit log
- Legacy SFAPI Data Dictionary
- Legacy SFAPI metering details
- Legacy SFAPI IP whitelisting

> **Further Resources**
>
> More details can be found in the *SAP SuccessFactors HCM Suite OData API: Developer Guide* on SAP Help Portal under the SAP SuccessFactors HCM Suite product page.

16.2.7 Integration Center

The Integration Center provides nontechnical users with the ability to quickly build, monitor, and maintain pattern-based flat-file and API integrations from within SAP SuccessFactors. It is not intended to be a full-blown development tool to support every level of complexity. The Integration Center supports both outbound and inbound integrations. Figure 16.5 shows the **My Integrations** screen in the Integration Center, where the user can see all of the integrations that they have created.

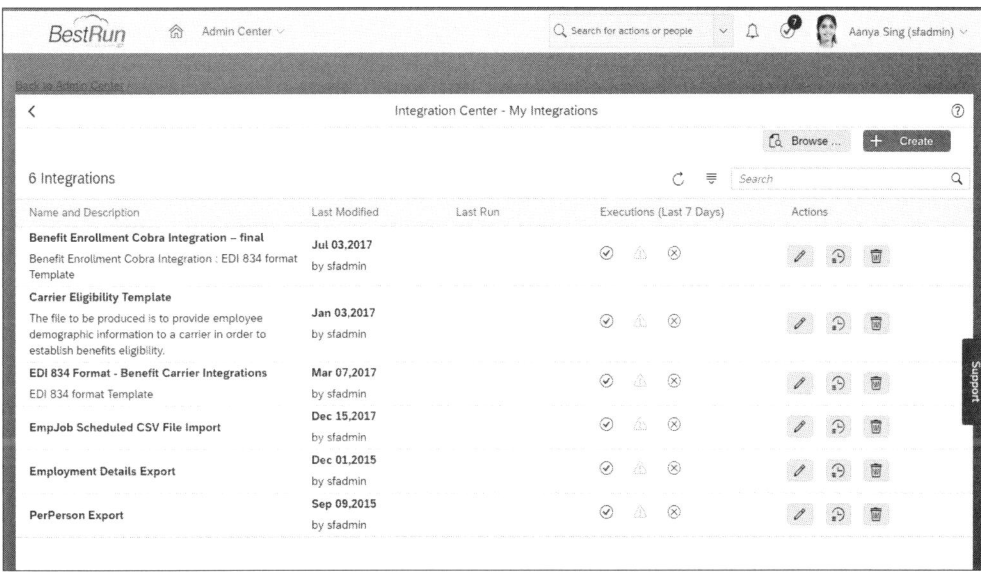

Figure 16.5 The My Integrations Screen of Integration Center

For outbound integrations, the following types of integrations are supported:

- **Web service-based**
  - Simple Object Access Protocol (SOAP)
  - Representational State Transfer (REST)

- **Data file exchange**
  - Comma separated value (*.csv*)
  - Text (*.txt*)
  - Extensible Markup Language (*.xml*)
  - Electronic data interchange (*.edi*)

For inbound integrations, the Integration Center can receive comma separated value (*.csv*) files.

Predelivered templates are available as a starting point and provide integration to commonly used systems such as the following:

- Benefit providers
- Time management solutions
- Payroll systems
- SAP ERP systems
- Other SAP applications, such as SAP Fieldglass

The Integration Center features the *Integration Catalog*, an online repository of preconfigured integrations available to SAP SuccessFactors customers. The integrations are broken down by product and functional area. Most of the integrations in the catalog relating to SAP SuccessFactors are for Employee Central. They include integrations between SAP products, as well as key functional needs such as external payroll vendors.

Creating integrations take a wizard-based approach where the user can select from various options and use the UI to configure the integration they are creating. For example, the user is able to configure the following attributes for their integration in the Integration Center UI:

- **Name** and **Description**
- **Output File Type**
- **Data Source** and **Destination**
- **Starting Point for Data Selection**
- **File Delimiter Type**
- **Header Type**
- **Footer Type**

- **Use Double Quotes**
- Fields to use in the integration, including **Ordering**, **Sorting**, and **Filtering**
- **Scheduling**

After the integration has been built, it is possible to perform a preview of the integration to see if the output matches what is expected.

After your integration has been completed and is scheduled to run, it can be monitored in the **Monitor Integrations** part of the Integration Center.

Further Resources

For more information, refer to the guide *Integration Center* on the SAP Help Portal under the SAP SuccessFactors HCM Suite product page.

16.2.8 Intelligent Services

Intelligent Services is a real-time, event-driven, message-based integration framework for propagating data and triggering features across the SAP SuccessFactors HCM Suite and with external applications. You can use Intelligent Services to trigger events that seamlessly propagate data across the SAP SuccessFactors HCM Suite in real time, and to trigger integrations with external applications. Additionally, Intelligent Services can consolidate all transactions pertinent to an event and guide employees through specific processes, which may involve both SAP SuccessFactors and external systems.

SAP SuccessFactors provides a number of standard-delivered events to use, but you can configure these events in the Intelligent Services Center. Events can also be monitored in the Intelligent Services Center.

A good example of a solution that the Intelligent Services works well for might be a long-term leave of absence, where an employee needs to have their calendar blocked, meetings in their calendar reorganized, an out-of-office notification enabled in their email service/application, their payroll data changed for the duration of the absence, and so forth. Intelligent Services can start these processes in external systems based on an event that is triggered inside SAP SuccessFactors.

Intelligent Services works by enabling a *publisher* (e.g., Employee Central) to raise an *event* (e.g., a manager change or new hire) that is sent to one or more *subscribers* (e.g., another SAP SuccessFactors application, an integration middleware, or a third-party application). Events can have specific subscribers defined, so not just any application can subscribe to an event. The Standard Event Framework publishes events to the SAP SuccessFactors system and outside of the system. The OData API is used in some events to fetch additional information about the event. Some events publish only to other internal SAP SuccessFactors subscribers, or to external third-party applications, or to both.

Further Resources

For more information, refer to the guides on the SAP Help Portal under the SAP SuccessFactors HCM Suite product page:

- *Intelligent Services Overview*
- *Setting Up Intelligent Services*
- *Intelligent Services Center*

16.2.9 Other Integration Technologies

Even with all of these technologies, there is still room for a number of other platforms. Customers may already be using another middleware platform, such as MuleSoft Mule or IBM WebSphere Cast Iron Cloud Integration, and they may want to continue leveraging that platform or to build custom APIs. The SAP SuccessFactors platform is open and technology agnostic, so customers can use various integration technologies to integrate SAP ERP HCM with SAP SuccessFactors solutions. This provides a great deal of flexibility and allows customers to retain existing technology and infrastructure that is being used for other solutions.

The SAP SuccessFactors OData API provide a high level of integration capabilities for SAP SuccessFactors. The API enables any web services-based middleware to query, read, and modify data in SAP SuccessFactors. SAP SuccessFactors are constantly enhancing the OData API to add new features and data access capabilities. See Section 16.6 for more details.

16.3 Employee Central and Cloud Hybrid Integrations

For SAP SuccessFactors Employee Central, a host of packaged integrations are delivered. Integrations are available on SAP Cloud Platform Integration, which is bundled with the Employee Central subscription.

These packaged integrations allow Employee Central to replicate data to and/or from other systems, such as SAP ERP or a third-party payroll or time and attendance providers. Figure 16.6 shows the current integrations for Employee Central.

Let's look at some of these integrations in a bit more detail.

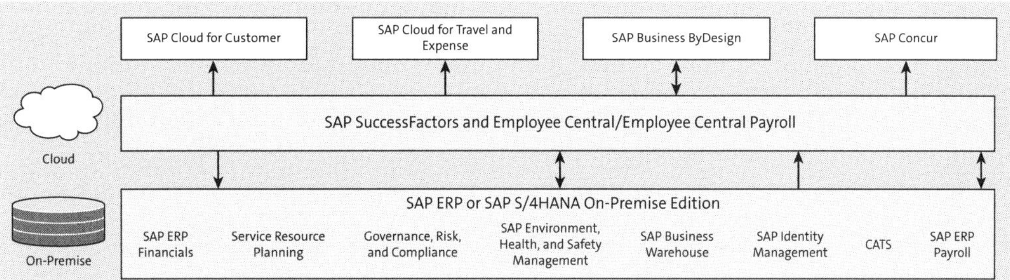

Figure 16.6 Current Employee Central Integrations

Further Resources

You can read more about SAP SuccessFactors Employee Central integrations in the book *SAP SuccessFactors Employee Central: The Comprehensive Guide* by Luke Marson, Murali Mazhavanchery, and Rebecca Murray (2nd edition, SAP PRESS, 2018).

16

16.3.1 SAP ERP and SAP S/4HANA

Several integrations exist for transferring data between Employee Central and SAP ERP or SAP S/4HANA. This is largely because many SAP ERP customers want to run their core HR processes in Employee Central instead of SAP ERP HCM but still retain other processes in SAP ERP. The most common integration scenario is where customers continue to run SAP ERP Payroll after moving their core HR to Employee Central. For SAP S/4HANA, the designated HCM module is the SAP SuccessFactors HCM Suite.

Note

The backend of the SAP ERP and SAP S/4HANA systems are the same in terms of customizing, so the aspects of and configuration steps for the integration are very similar—and in some case the same—in both systems.

SAP Notes can be found on SAP ONE Support Launchpad under the following components (see Appendix A):

- PA-SFI-EC for Employee Central integration
- LOD-EC-INT-EE for SAP ERP to Employee Central integration
- LOD-EC-INT-ORG for Employee Central to SAP ERP organizational integration
- LOD-EC-GCP-ANA for Employee Central reporting and analytics
- LOD-EC-GCP-PY for Employee Central Payroll and integration
- LOD-EC-GCP-PY-GLO for Employee Central Payroll and integration—globalization

Note

By default, many of the fields in Employee Central have a greater field length than SAP ERP and—in some cases—the middleware. It is important to consider this during the Employee Central design because many of the fields in Employee Central must have their field lengths reduced in order to integrate with SAP ERP.

Employee Master Data

HR master data—the data stored in personnel administration (PA) infotypes—is replicated from Employee Central to SAP ERP using a standard integration. This is often referred to as the mini-master. It enables a core set of employee data to be replicated to SAP ERP to support a number of processes. The integration includes the following data:

- Biographical information
- Personal information
- Address information
- Email address
- Job information
- Compensation information (recurring and nonrecurring)
- Cost distribution
- Direct deposit
- National ID information

This integration is served by component PA_SE_IN 100 in SAP ERP and integration package *SAP SuccessFactors Employee Central to ERP Employee and Organizational*

Data in the middleware. For PA_SE_IN 100, service package 3 is required, but the latest service package is always recommended.

Further Resources

The latest requirements for all systems involved in the integration can be found in the guide *Replicating Employee Master Data and Organizational Assignments from Employee Central to SAP ERP HCM (as of Q2 2017)* found on the SAP Help Portal under the SAP SuccessFactors Employee Central Integration to SAP Business Suite product page.

The integration works by the middleware calling SAP SuccessFactors Employee Central Compound Employee APIs (see Section 16.6) and retrieving data. This data is then converted as necessary and sent to SAP ERP, where it is processed by inbound web service interface and written to SAP ERP HCM infotypes. Records are created, edited, or delimited as required based on the data sent and the infotype framework in SAP ERP.

The Employee Key Mapping table (PAOCFEC_EEKEYMAP) is used to keep the systems synchronized. The table maps the USERID, person ID external, employment ID, job information ID, and internal ID of the employee's employment record from Employee Central with the personnel number and company code in SAP ERP. This enables the system to identify the exact employee that data is being replicated for, or whether the replication is for a new employee (in which case it fills the table with the new employee's details). When using the Infoporter to migrate data from SAP ERP HCM to Employee Central during implementation, the Employee Key Mapping table is filled automatically by the Infoporter as the data is extracted.

The add-on is customized in the Implementation Guide (IMG) via menu path **Personnel Management • Integration with SuccessFactors Employee Central • Business Integration Builder**. The key customizing activities are importing metadata, performing value mapping (e.g., picklists to F4 help values), and performing field mappings.

Many fields, such as marital status or gender, have different mappings in Employee Central, and special consideration should be taken during implementation to ensure correct values and mappings. Additionally, mapping tables exist for some mapping values, such as address type.

Dates is replicated to infotype 0041 for date events such as global assignments and payroll periods.

Two business add-ins (BAdIs) are provided to modify the logic and behavior of replicated fields. The first is to determine the Employee Central field to use for personnel number, and the second is to exclude infotype records from deletion for specific subtypes. Both of these are configured in the IMG.

Additionally, various mapping tables are provided to map values between Employee Central and SAP ERP. These include the following:

- Employee Central object codes to SAP ERP global data types (GDT)
- Employee Central object codes to SAP ERP code value lists
- Employee Central codes to SAP ERP code value lists for country-dependent fields
- Employee Central date types to SAP ERP date types
- Employee Central company object codes to SAP ERP company keys
- Employee Central cost center object codes to SAP ERP cost center keys
- Employee Central location codes to SAP ERP place of work keys
- Employee Central pay component and country combinations to SAP ERP infotype 0008 or infotype 0014

Other IMG settings are available that allow currencies to be assigned to wage types (so that currencies with more than two decimal places can be used without rounding to two decimal places), restrict which infotypes are replicated for certain countries, and filter which infotypes are replicated for which countries.

The integration supports replicating custom-specific fields and objects.

Further Resources

For more information on the details of the integration, configuration and customizing steps, field mappings, BAdIs, and more, refer to the guide *Replicating Employee Master Data and Organizational Assignments from Employee Central to SAP ERP HCM (as of Q2 2017)* found on the SAP Help Portal under the SAP SuccessFactors Employee Central Integration to SAP Business Suite product page.

Employee Organizational Data

For employees' organizational data, several types of information can be replicated from Employee Central to SAP ERP:

- Organizational objects
- Reporting relationships
- Employee's business unit, division, department, and job assignment
- Employee cost center assignment

This integration is served by the same SAP ERP and middleware components that are used for employee master data replication. The integration also works in a similar manner, although naturally some of the process flows differ due to the nature of the data that is being replicated.

For replication of business unit, division, and department objects, as well as their assignment to employees, the ID of the object in Employee Central is mapped to an organizational unit ID in table SFIOM_KMAP_OSI (organizational structure item key mapping) in SAP ERP. This can also be done manually. Alternatively, BAdI EX_SFIOM_KEY_MAP_ENH_ORG_STRUC (enhancements for key mapping of organizational structure items) in enhancement spot ES_SFIOM_PROCESSING can be used to define the logic to be used for determining mapping of these objects. Upon first replication, if no new organizational units need to be created, the mapping table should be maintained with all mappings.

The employee cost center assignment in Employee Central is stored against the employee's position in SAP ERP. 16

Further Resources

For more information on the details of the integration, configuration and customizing steps, field mappings, BAdIs, and more, refer to the guides *Replicating Employee Master Data and Organizational Assignments from Employee Central to SAP ERP HCM (as of Q2 2017)* and *Replicating Organizational Objects from Employee Central to SAP ERP HCM (as of Q2 2017)* found on the SAP Help Portal under the SAP SuccessFactors Employee Central Integration to SAP Business Suite product page.

Cost Center Objects

SAP provides a standard integration to replicate cost centers from Financial Accounting and Controlling in SAP ERP to Employee Central. This integration is served by component ODTFINCC 600 in SAP ERP and integration package *ERP to SAP SuccessFactors Employee Central Cost Center* in the middleware.

In SAP ERP, the data can be transferred by either IDoc or flat-file (CSV). Report ODTF_REPL_CC is provided to replicate the cost centers from SAP ERP to Employee Central. This report can be scheduled to enable periodic replication of cost centers to Employee Central.

The logic used to define cost center IDs can be modified using a BAdI that is part of enhancement spot ODTF_CC_REPLICAT_IDOCS_MODIFY. Depending on whether IDoc or flat-file integration is used, the BAdI varies. For IDoc integration, the BAdI ODTF_CC_REPLICAT_IDOCS_MODIFY MODIFY_COST_CENTER_EXTRACTOR is used, and for flat-file integration, the BAdI ODTF_CO_REPL_IDOC_COST_C_CSV MODIFY_COST_CENTER_EXTACT_CSV is used.

Further Resources

For more information on the details of the integration, configuration and customizing steps, field mappings, BAdIs, and more, refer to the guide *Replicating Cost Centers from SAP ERP to Employee Central Using SAP Cloud Platform Integration as the Middleware* found on the SAP Help Portal under the SAP SuccessFactors Employee Central Integration to SAP Business Suite product page.

Side-by-Side

The side-by-side deployment model enables data transfer from SAP ERP HCM to Employee Central so that the data for all employees is stored in Employee Central. Employees whose system of record is SAP ERP HCM are considered "mastered" in that system.

The packaged integrations for Employee Central to SAP ERP are used to replicate data of employees to SAP ERP HCM who are mastered within Employee Central. For the replication of employees from SAP ERP HCM to Employee Central, the Infoporter solution is used.

Employee-manager relationships are stored in table ECPAO_EE_MGNR. Report ECPAO_MNGR_EXTRACTION is provided to generate employee-manager relationships using relationship 012 and stores them in this table. Employee-manager relationships for employees are stored in Employee Central. You must maintain them in SAP ERP HCM by creating a user profile in Transaction SU01 and assigning it to a manager position in Transaction PPOSE or Transaction PPOME.

Report ECPAO_EMPL_EXTRACTION (Employee Data Extraction) is used to extract data from SAP ERP HCM to send to Employee Central. Figure 16.7 shows the select screen for report ECPAO_EMPL_EXTRACTION.

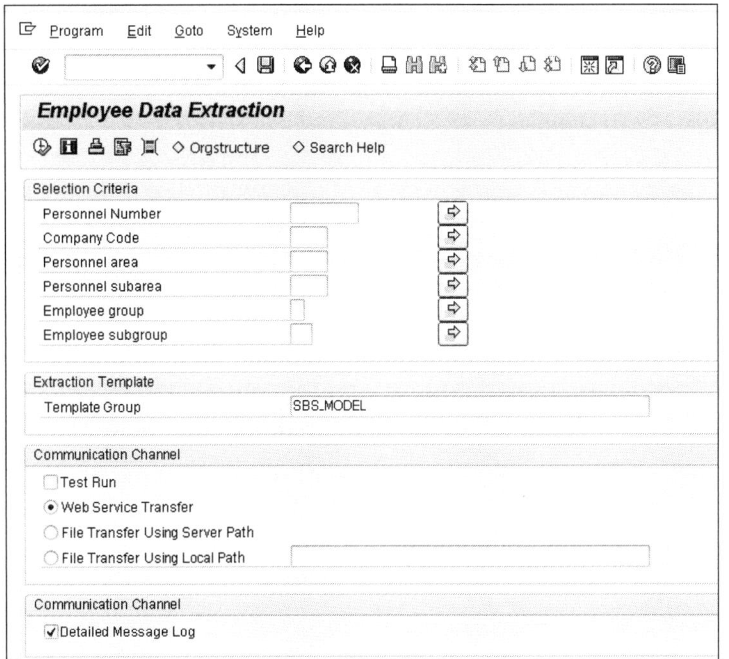

Figure 16.7 Employee Data Extraction Selection Screen

Note

The data synchronization reports RH_SFI_TRIGGER_EMPL_DATA_REPL and RH_SFI_SYNCHRONIZE_EMPL_DATA, as well as report RH_SFI_PREHIRE_EMPL_DATA, cannot be used when the side-by-side integration has been implemented.

Delta synchronizations are possible. Report RBDMIDOC creates change pointers whenever employee master data is changed. The change pointers are read by report ECPAO_EMPL_EXTRACTION, and the delta changes are then synchronized to Employee Central.

The mapping of SAP ERP HCM and Employee Central fields is performed in view cluster VC_ECPAO_MAP. There are three methods available to map fields:

- **Infotype mapping**
  Map each Employee Central field to an SAP ERP HCM infotype and field.
- **Preconfigured mapping**
  Use SAP's predefined mappings from tables `ECPAO_PREMAPPING` and `ECPAO_PREMAP_TT`.

- **BAdI mapping**
  Use BAdI EX_ECPAO_EMP_DATA_EXTRACT_OUT (Mapping of EC and SAP ERP Data for Employee Replication) to determine mappings between Employee Central fields and SAP ERP HCM infotype fields.

Optional BAdIs exist to overwrite the employee data extracted from SAP ERP HCM (EX_ECPAO_ERP_EMP_DATA_MODIFY) and define groups of employees to replicate to Employee Central (EX_ECPAO_EMP_VALIDITY_TAB). Additionally, BAdI EX_ECPAO_EMP_USYID_PRN_UNM_MAP (Mapping of User ID, Person ID, and User Name) can be implemented to map user ID, person ID, and user name of employees.

In addition to the data integration, a UI integration exists so that Employee Central can be used as the central hub for managers and employees. It enables a Web Dynpro application to be run inside Employee Central to perform actions on employees who are mastered in SAP ERP HCM.

Further Resources

For more information on the details of the integration, configuration and customizing steps, field mappings, BAdIs, and more, refer to the guides already mentioned in this section for the employee master data and employee organizational data integrations, as well as the guides:

- *Integrating SAP ERP HCM with Employee Central Using the Side-by-Side Deployment Option*
- *Replicating Employee Data from SAP ERP HCM to Employee Central Using SAP Cloud Platform Integration as the Middleware*
- *Replicating Organizational Data from SAP ERP HCM to Employee Central Using SAP Cloud Platform Integration as the Middleware*

These guides are found on the SAP Help Portal under the SAP SuccessFactors Employee Central Integration to SAP Business Suite product page.

Data Migration

For migration of employee master data and organizational objects from SAP ERP HCM to Employee Central, SAP provides the Infoporter. The Infoporter enables a repeatable migration process that uses the Business Integration Builder (BIB) framework that is used by the integration between Employee Central and SAP ERP. This enables customers to migrate data to Employee Central in a consistent format that will enable smooth replication back to SAP ERP. This reduces errors and also the effort to configure the data migration since the framework already has to be configured for the integration.

The Infoporter supports the migration of "placeholder" records in Employee Central so that you have the option to migrate dummy records to Employee Central before the cut-off date of the migration. This enables the records that are replicated to Employee Central to remain unchanged in SAP ERP once replication from Employee Central to SAP ERP begins.

The Infoporter functionality is also used in the side-by-side model to replicate data from SAP ERP HCM to Employee Central.

Further Resources

For more information on Infoporter refer to the guides on SAP Help Portal under the SAP SuccessFactors Employee Central Integration to SAP Business Suite product page:

- *Replicating Employee Data from SAP ERP HCM to Employee Central Using SAP Cloud Platform Integration as the Middleware*
- *Replicating Organizational Data from SAP ERP HCM to Employee Central Using SAP Cloud Platform Integration as the Middleware*

Notes on Object Differences

Not all SAP objects exist in Employee Central, and vice versa. For example, personnel area doesn't exist in Employee Central and, likewise, the org structure in Employee Central has objects that have no corresponding object in SAP. These must be considered when designing Employee Central and the integration. Additionally, value mappings could be needed to map business unit, division, and department objects from Employee Central with organizational units in SAP, as well as mapping of company code and cost center keys among other mappings. Further effort might be needed to program BAdIs to ensure that the relevant mapping and value transformation logic exists.

For more details, the handbooks provided by SAP and referenced in this section should be reviewed in detail.

16.3.2 Employee Central Payroll

Integration with Employee Central Payroll uses point-to-point (PTP) integration. This means that Employee Central and Employee Central Payroll communicate directly without the need of middleware. The integration itself follows the same principles as the employee master data integration that we discussed in Section 16.3.1. However, there are a number of configurations that need to be performed in Employee Central that are not needed for regular employee master data integration to SAP ERP.

Integration also exists between Employee Central Payroll and BSI TaxFactory SaaS for calculation of US employees' withholding taxes and, if required, BSI eFormsFactory for employees to maintain tax details.

Further Resources

For more details on BSI TaxFactory integration, refer to the *Integrating BSI SaaS Solutions with Employee Central Payroll* handbook.

For more information on the details of the integration, configuration and customizing steps, field mappings, BAdIs, and more, refer to the guide *Employee Central Payroll Using Point-to-Point Integration* found on the SAP Help Portal under the SAP SuccessFactors Employee Central Payroll product page.

16.3.3 Other SAP Systems

As expected, SAP provides packaged integration to integrate Employee Central with a number of other SAP systems, including:

- Cross Application Time Sheet (CATS)
- SAP Fieldglass
- SAP Ariba
- SAP Concur
- SAP Identity Management
- SAP governance, risk, and compliance solutions
- SAP Business ByDesign

16.3.4 Payroll Business Process Outsourcing

Integration is provided between Employee Central and three Payroll Business Process Outsourcing (Payroll BPO) providers:

- ADP GlobalView
- NGA euHReka
- NGA Payroll Exchange

Because these systems are built on SAP ERP Payroll, the integration and mash-ups are similar to those offered in the standard integration for SAP ERP. SSO also exists between Employee Central and these systems. Like with SAP ERP Payroll and Employee Central Payroll, Employee Central can display a pay slip directly from these systems.

SAP also provides a standard payroll integration template that can be used to integrate Employee Central with other payroll systems and Payroll BPO providers. This is covered in Section 16.3.8.

16.3.5 Time and Attendance

SAP provides integrations between Employee Central and both WorkForce Software EmpCenter and Kronos Workforce Central for time and attendance processes. Both are out-of-the-box integration packages and require no manual mapping for the United States; for other countries, additional configuration may be necessary. Both integrations also feature SSO, native UI integration, and data export to Employee Central Payroll, if required.

SAP also provides a standard time and attendance integration template that can be used to integrate Employee Central with other time and attendance systems. This is covered in Section 16.3.8.

Kronos Workforce Central

For Kronos Workforce Central integration, data is exported from the following Employee Central portlets:

- Personal information
- Phone information
- Email information
- Job information
- Employment information
- Recurring pay components

Further Resources

For more details, refer to the guide *Integrating SAP SuccessFactors Employee Central with Kronos Workforce Central (SAP Cloud Platform Integration)* on the SAP Help Portal under the SAP SuccessFactors Employee Central product page.

SSO can also be configured with Kronos Workforce Ready to enable a UI mash-up within Employee Central. This enables employees to maintain time and attendance data directly in Kronos Workforce Ready within an Employee Central portlet.

WorkForce Software EmpCenter

For WorkForce Software EmpCenter integration, data is exported from the same Employee Central portlets as the integration with Kronos Workforce Central, plus the following three portlets:

- Address information
- Job relationships
- Compensation information

SSO can be configured with the WorkForce Software EmpCenter application so that a UI mash-up can be accessed by employees directly in an Employee Central portlet.

Further Resources

For more details on the integration and UI mash-up, refer to the guide *Integrating SAP SuccessFactors Employee Central with WorkForce Software (SAP Cloud Platform Integration)* on the SAP Help Portal under the SAP SuccessFactors Employee Central product page.

16.3.6 Benefits

Benefits integration is provided for Aon Hewitt Core Benefits Administration, Benefitfocus, and Thomsons Darwin. All three are out-of-the-box integration packages and require no manual mapping. All integrations also feature data export to Employee Central Payroll, if required.

SAP also provides a standard benefits integration template that can be used to integrate Employee Central with other benefits administration systems. This is covered in Section 16.3.8.

Aon Hewitt Core Benefits Administration

For Aon Hewitt Core Benefits Administration integration, data is exported from the following Employee Central portlets:

- Person information
- Personal information
- Phone information
- Email information
- Address information
- Job information
- Employment information
- Compensation information
- Recurring pay components
- National ID card

Further Resources

For more details on the integration, refer to the guide *Integrating* SAP *SuccessFactors Employee Central with Aon Hewitt Core Benefits Administration* on the SAP Help Portal under the SAP SuccessFactors Employee Central product page.

Benefitfocus

For Benefitfocus integration, data is exported from the following Employee Central portlets:

- Person information
- Personal information
- Phone information
- Email information
- Address information
- Employment information
- Compensation information
- Recurring pay components
- National ID card
- Emergency contacts information

SSO can be configured with the Benefitfocus application, so that a UI mash-up can be accessed by employees directly in an Employee Central portlet.

Further Resources

For more details on the integration and UI mash-up, refer to the guide *Integrating SAP SuccessFactors Employee Central with Benefitfocus* on the SAP Help Portal under the SAP SuccessFactors Employee Central product page.

Thomsons Darwin

For Thomsons Darwin integration, data is exported from the following Employee Central portlets:

- Person information
- Personal information
- Phone information
- Email information
- Address information
- Employment information
- Job information
- Compensation information
- Recurring pay components
- National ID card

SSO can be configured with the Thomsons Darwin application, so that a link directly to the application can be accessed by employees directly in the Employee Central navigation menu.

Further Resources

For more details on the integration and UI mash-up, refer to the guide *Integrating SAP SuccessFactors Employee Central with Thomsons Online Benefits* on the SAP Help Portal under the SAP SuccessFactors Employee Central product page.

16.3.7 SAP Cloud Platform

SAP Cloud Platform enables extensions to be built for Employee Central. It features OData integration to enable transfer of Employee Central and Metadata Framework (MDF) data between Employee Central and the extension.

16.3.8 Standard Integration Templates

SAP provides three standard integration templates that can be used for integrating to the following systems:

- Payroll
- Time and Attendance
- Benefits

Each template uses the Employee Central Compound API and SAP Cloud Platform Integration to send a CSV file to the target system. Refer to Section 16.6.2 for details on the Employee Central Compound API.

Payroll

The standard payroll integration template is configured to export the following data from Employee Central:

- Person information
- Personal information
- Address information
- Phone information
- Email information
- Employment information
- Job information
- Compensation information
- Recurring pay components
- Non-recurring pay components

- Recurring deductions
- Non-recurring deductions
- Alternative cost distribution
- Dependents
- Direct deposit

Further Resources

For more details, refer to the guide *Standard Payroll Integration Template for* SAP *SuccessFactors Employee Central* on the SAP Help Portal under the SAP SuccessFactors Employee Central product page.

Time

The standard time integration template is configured to export the following data from Employee Central:

- Person information
- Personal information
- Address information
- Phone information
- Email information
- Employment information
- Compensation information
- Recurring pay components
- National ID card
- Manager
- Pay group foundation object

Further Resources

For more details, refer to the guide *Standard Time Integration Template for* SAP *SuccessFactors Employee Central* on the SAP Help Portal under the SAP SuccessFactors Employee Central product page.

Benefits

The standard benefits integration template is configured to export the following data from Employee Central:

- Person information
- Personal information
- Address information
- Phone information
- Email information
- Employment information
- Job information
- Compensation information
- Recurring pay components
- Non-recurring pay components

- Dependents
- National ID card
- Manager
- Pay group foundation object

Further Resources

For more details, refer to the guide *Standard Benefits Integration Template for* SAP *SuccessFactors Employee Central* on the SAP Help Portal under the SAP SuccessFactors Employee Central product page.

16.4 Talent Hybrid Integration Packages

SAP SuccessFactors delivers a packaged integration for the talent hybrid model. The packaged integration is called the *integration add-on for SAP ERP HCM and SAP SuccessFactors HCM Suite*, and it supports multiple integration scenarios across the SAP SuccessFactors talent modules. The packaged integration is delivered as an ABAP add-on for SAP ERP called SFIHCM. At the time of writing (fall 2019), the latest version is SFIHCM03 support package level 12 (SAPK-60012INSFIHCM03) and the add-on queries the SAP SuccessFactors OData API to extract or update information in SAP SuccessFactors. The integration is usually always triggered from the SAP ERP HCM system—with the exception of the qualification data integration—and in most cases any data that is transferred to SAP ERP HCM requires activation or processing in the system before it becomes active infotype data. How this works will become more clear and familiar as we walk through this section of the chapter.

16.4.1 Integration Scenarios

The integration add-on version mentioned above covers the following data and process integrations at the time of writing:

- **Basic employee and organizational data**
  - Employee data from SAP ERP HCM to SAP SuccessFactors
- **Evaluation data**
  - Data from SAP ERP HCM to Workforce Analytics
- **Recruiting process**
  - Vacant position data from SAP ERP HCM to Recruiting
  - New hire data from Recruiting to SAP ERP HCM

- **Onboarding process**
  - New hire data from SAP ERP HCM to Onboarding
  - Employee data from Onboarding to SAP ERP HCM
  - Onboarded employee data from Onboarding to SAP ERP HCM
- **Offboarding process**
  - Trigger offboarding in Onboarding from SAP ERP HCM
  - Offboarded employee data from Onboarding to SAP ERP HCM
- **Compensation processes**
  - Salary data from SAP ERP HCM to Compensation/Variable Pay
  - Employee history data from SAP ERP HCM to Variable Pay
  - Compensation planning results data from Compensation to SAP ERP HCM
  - Variable play planning results data from Variable Pay to SAP ERP HCM
  - Activation of planning results to update payroll infotypes in SAP ERP HCM
- **Qualifications process**
  - One-time upload of the Qualification Catalog and employee qualification history to SAP SuccessFactors Learning
  - Changes in employee qualifications and competencies from Learning to SAP ERP HCM

Figure 16.8 shows the different scenarios visually.

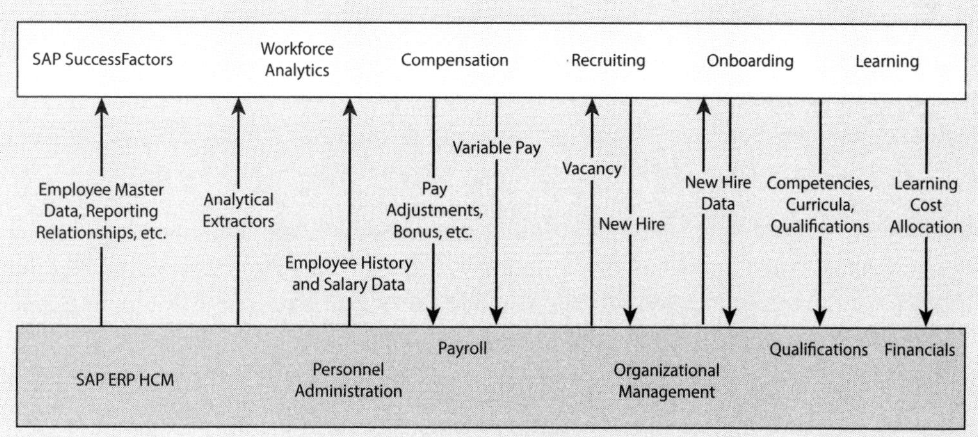

Figure 16.8 Talent Hybrid Integrations

The basic employee and organizational data and the evaluation data integration scenarios are available for both flat-file and middleware integration methods. The remaining integrations are available only via middleware platforms. These are SAP Process Integration or SAP Cloud Platform Integration.

Note

The employee data integration should always be triggered before all other integration scenarios. The only exception is evaluation data, where this is no dependency.

It is recommended to use the latest version of the integration add-on if you plan to install it for the first time. If you already use the integration add-on and plan to extend your use of it to other integrations then it is also advised to upgrade to the latest version. The latest version of the integration add-on contains all previous integration add-on versions, bug fixes, and new content introduced via support packages and SAP Notes.

In Table 16.2, you can see in which versions that new functionality was released. This can be useful to ascertain whether you need to upgrade your add-on version in cases where this can be difficult or not possible.

Version	Functionality Released
SFIHCM01	■ Basic employee and organizational data ■ Evaluation data integration
SFIHCM01 SP 02	Compensation integration
SFIHCM02	Recruiting integration (new hire data from Recruiting to SAP ERP HCM)
SFIHCM02 SP 02	Recruiting integration (vacant position data from SAP ERP HCM to Recruiting)
SFIHCM03	Qualification integration
SFIHCM03 SP 01	Variable Pay (employee history data from SAP ERP HCM to Variable Pay)
SFIHCM03 SP 02	■ Variable Pay (Variable Pay planning results data from Variable Pay to SAP ERP HCM) ■ Onboarding (new hire data from SAP ERP HCM to Onboarding)

Table 16.2 Integration Add-Ons Released Functionality

Version	Functionality Released
SFIHCM03 SP 04	Onboarding (employee data from Onboarding to SAP ERP HCM, onboarded employee data from Onboarding to SAP ERP HCM, and offboarding integration)

Table 16.2 Integration Add-Ons Released Functionality (Cont.)

Apart from the major functional releases noted in Table 16.2, there are various small functional released in addition to the bug fixes provided. In some cases, the support of both middleware platforms was introduced over two or more support packages.

Most of the process-based integrations (e.g., Compensation or Recruiting) use an ad hoc report in SAP SuccessFactors to extract the data needed in the SAP ERP HCM system. This is typically setup as part of the integration configuration.

The integration add-on can be downloaded from SAP ONE Support Launchpad and is available in eight languages: English, German, Spanish, French, Portuguese, Russian, Chinese, and Japanese. The latest version of the administrator and other product guides—including all technical prerequisites for the add-on—can be found on the SAP Help Portal under SFIHCM. SAP Notes and knowledge base articles (KBAs) can be found on SAP ONE Support Launchpad under components PA-SFI-TM and PA-SFI-TM-MW.

Because the integration add-on is delivered as an ABAP add-on, customers who are not familiar with this process should consult SAP Note 1708986 (Installation of SFIHCM01 600). HTTPS communication between each system and the middleware is mandatory.

The integration add-on is configured in the IMG. Depending on the process(es) you are configuring, different IMG customizing activities need to be configured. A set of basic settings need to be configured irrespective of which processes you are configuring. These include:

- Define customer-specific logic for authorizations and super users via the IMG or BAdI `HRSFI_B_AUTHORITY_CHECK` (Authorization Check for SAP SuccessFactors Integration).
- Define how the personnel numbers and SAP SuccessFactors user IDs are determined (e.g., if there are duplicates) via the IMG or via BAdI implementation `HRSFI_RCT_PERNR_USERID` of BAdI `HRSFI_B_PERNR_USERID` (Determination of SAP ERP Personnel Numbers and SAP SuccessFactors User IDs).
- When you use middleware, defining the credentials and package size via the IMG.

Now let's take a look at each of the talent hybrid integrations.

16.4.2 Employee Data

The Employee Data integration in the packaged integration provides one-way transfer of employee and organizational data from SAP ERP HCM to the SAP SuccessFactors HCM Suite to populate the user data file (UDF) for use in talent management processes. We covered the UDF in Chapter 3, Section 3.10. The add-on can use either flat-file or middleware technology to transfer the data. A series of ABAP programs, Web Dynpro applications, authorization roles, and BAdIs are included to process and extract data on a periodic basis and to monitor the process.

The add-on supports 49 standard UDF fields and can be extended to add more fields as required. Within these 49 fields are 34 predefined fields and 15 custom fields that can be freely defined. Nine of the fields are mandatory in SAP SuccessFactors and so must be extracted from SAP. The fields are listed in Table 16.3.

Field	Use	Required
Status	Employment status from PA0000-STAT2	X
User ID	Central person ID or person ID from PA0709	X
User Name	Employee's user ID or central person	X
First Name	First name from PA0002	X
Last Name	Last name from PA0002	X
Middle Name	Middle name from PA0002	
Gender	Gender from PA0002	
Email	Email address	X
Manager	Manager using relationship B012 or A002	X
Human Resource	HR administrator from PA0001	X
Department	Organizational unit or cost center from PA0001	
Job Code	Job from PA0001	

Table 16.3 Predefined Fields Used in the Extraction and Synchronization Reports

Field	Use	Required
Division	Company code from PA0001	
Location	Personnel area from PA0001	
Time Zone	Time zone of user	X
Hire Date	Initial hire date from feature entry	
Employee ID	Personnel number	
Title	Position or job from PA0001	
Business Phone	Business phone number from PA0032 or PA0105 SUBTY 0020	
FAX	Fax number from PA0105 SUBTY CELL	
Address 1	Description of personnel area from PA0001	
Address 2	Street of personnel area from PA0001	
City	City of personnel area from PA0001	
State	Region of personnel area from PA0001	
ZIP	ZIP code of personnel area from PA0001	
Country	Country key or country grouping of personnel subarea from PA0001	
Review Frequency	Performance appraisal frequency	
Last Review Date	Date of last performance appraisal	
Matrix Manager	Dotted-line manager using relationship A002	
Default Locale	Default locale of employee	
Custom Manager	Custom manager	
Second Manager	Second manager	
Proxy	Proxy user	
Login Method	Type of login (SSO or PWD)	

Table 16.3 Predefined Fields Used in the Extraction and Synchronization Reports (Cont.)

For each of the fields, a default field mapping selection exists. Customers can also define their own logic. The custom fields can be customized in the IMG or directly in the BAdI implementation HRSFI_B_EMPL_DATA_REPLICATION (Replication of Employee's Data).

The format to be used for the **First Name** and **Last Name** fields can be customized in the IMG. Additional API parameters can also be configured in the IMG or with BAdI HRSFI_B_SFSF_API_PARAMETER (Parameters for Checks of Employee Data Transfer).

Figure 16.9 shows the selection screen for the integration report.

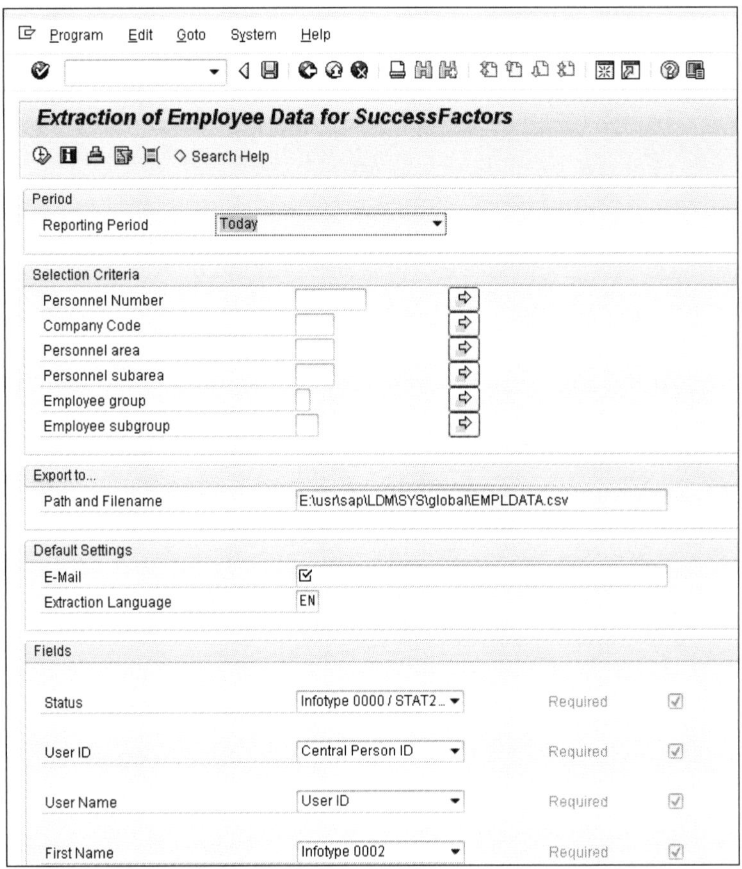

Figure 16.9 Extraction of Employee Data for SAP SuccessFactors Report

Additional parameters of the SFAPI can be set up in the IMG. This can also be done with BAdI HRSFI_B_SFSF_API_PARAMETER (Parameters for Checks of Employee Data Transfer).

Note

Although the integration add-on provides a report to extract the employee data (RH_SFI_TRIGGER_EMPL_DATA_REPL) and a report for synchronization of data (RH_SFI_SYNCHRONIZE_EMPL_DATA), we recommend that you use the synchronization report only.

Concurrent Employment

The add-on considers concurrent employment, but because SAP SuccessFactors currently handles concurrent employment differently than SAP ERP HCM, additional configuration is required before the extraction reports can be run. Concurrent employment is available in Employee Central, but at the time of writing (fall 2019), this has not been rolled out across the SAP SuccessFactors HCM Suite.

Each employee with multiple assignments (e.g., multiple personnel numbers [PERNRs]) must have their main assignments defined in infotype 0712 using subtype **SFSF**. This ensures that the main assignment and all related assignments are transferred to the SAP SuccessFactors HCM Suite. If no main assignment is maintained, the extraction report selects one of the assignments for data extraction, or if BAdI `HRSFI_B_LEADING_CONTRACT` (Determine the Leading Assignment for a Central Person) is defined, the logic of the active implementation is used.

Employee Data Extraction

Data transfer from SAP ERP HCM to SAP SuccessFactors is triggered using report RH_SFI_SYNCHRONIZE_EMPL_DATA. To transfer employees to SAP SuccessFactors prior to their being hired (e.g., to provide access to Onboarding or SAP Jam), use report RH_SFI_PREHIRE_EMPL_DATA.

Report RH_SFI_SYNCHRONIZE_EMPL_DATA can be scheduled to regularly transfer data from SAP ERP HCM to SAP SuccessFactors.

For flat-file transfer, the location of the CSV file and the regular scheduling of the report as a job need to be configured. If you are using middleware, the middleware integration platform needs to also be configured. The flat file can also be imported on an ad hoc basis using the **Import Employee Data** page under **Manager Users** in the Admin Center.

A variant is required to run the extraction report, which is created in the IMG. If multiple variants are used, they should always be run with the same frequency and in the same sequence.

Various fields are available within the report as selection criteria, including **Personnel Number**, **Employment Status**, **Company Code**, **Personnel Area**, **Personnel Subarea**, **Employee Group**, and **Employee Subgroup**. The type of transfer (middleware or file transfer), default email address, extraction language, and fields to transfer are configured as part of a variant but can also be changed after a variant has been selected. A default email address must be configured because this is a mandatory field in SAP SuccessFactors. The **Forced Synchronization** option forces a full data load. After the report is executed, either a flat file is generated, or, if middleware integration is selected, the data is transferred directly to SAP SuccessFactors. The log is also displayed to show any success, warning, or error messages. Figure 16.10 shows an example of the log.

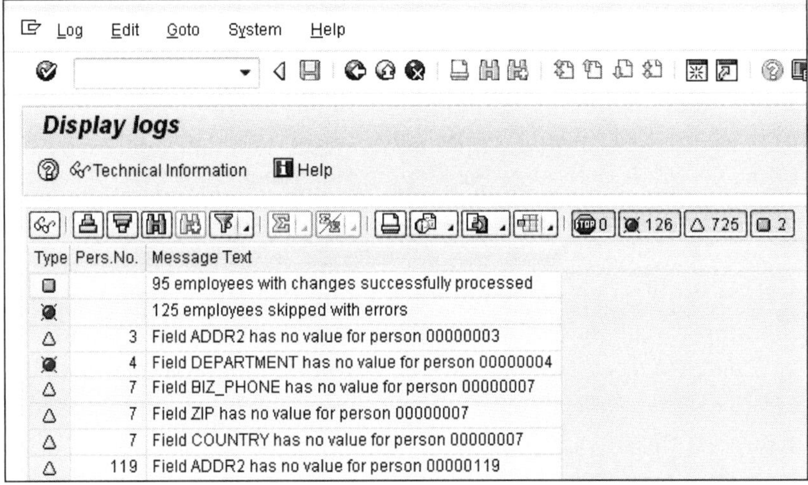

Figure 16.10 Display Logs Screen in the Employee Data Synchronization Report

After the report is executed, a log table is updated with all synchronized employees, with other tables being updated with the employees for which an error occurs. When the report is run the next time, a check is done against these tables to see if employees are new hires, have had data changed, or are terminated, and makes the appropriate data replication from SAP ERP HCM to SAP SuccessFactors.

Monitoring the Extraction Process

SAP supplies the Web Dynpro application HRSFI_MONITORING_EMPL (Success Factors—Transfer Monitoring) to monitor the transfer of employee data from SAP ERP HCM to SAP SuccessFactors that is triggered by report RH_SFI_SYNCHRONIZE_EMPL_DATA. The application can be seen in Figure 16.11, where the **Employee Data Transfer** area shows several backend messages.

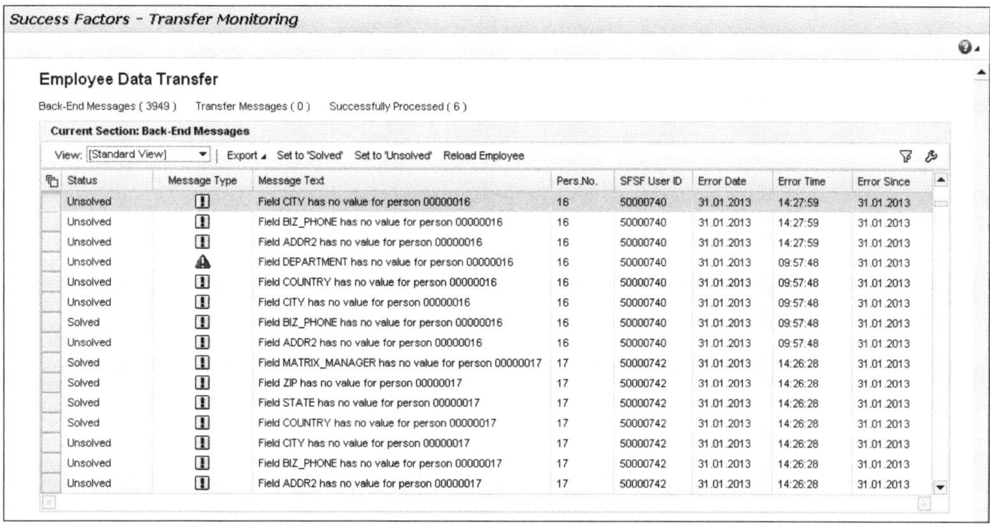

Figure 16.11 Employee Data Transfer in the Transfer Monitoring Application

The **Employee Data Transfer** list displays the messages that have been triggered during the data transfer process. The messages are displayed with a status, message type (error, warning, or success), employee number and SAP SuccessFactors user ID, extraction variant, and date and time. For the compensation transfer, the Compensation template ID and field set name are also displayed. Any fields can be hidden from display using the **Settings Dialog** option.

Messages can be viewed by type, as follows:

- Backend messages: Messages that were triggered in SAP ERP HCM
- Transfer messages: Messages that were triggered during transfer of data
- Successfully processed: List of employees with successful data transfer

Some actions can be taken to track and re-extract data for issues. The status can be switched to **Solved** and back to **Unsolved** using the **Set to 'Solved'** and **Set to 'Unsolved'** buttons. After issues with the employee data extract have been manually corrected in the backend and marked as **Solved**, they can be reextracted on an ad hoc basis. This is done by selecting a record and using the **Reload Employee** button; it uses the same variant as in the original processing.

Data Administration and Cleanup

The extraction of employee data can be stopped for one or more employees by using report RH_SFI_WITHDRAW_VARIANT.

After employees leave the company and the period of data retention has passed, report RPUDELPP can be used to delete the personnel IDs of those individuals in the synchronization logs. The BAdI implementation HRPAYXX_DELETE_PERNR (Personnel Number Deletion Reports) is used to define the logic for selecting the employee(s) to be deleted.

16.4.3 Evaluation Data

The integration add-on contains 30 extractors to transfer evaluation data from various infotypes to Workforce Analytics. It outputs a number of text (TXT) files for the SAP SuccessFactors SFTP to retrieve. These reports can be used as standard but configured to use customer-specific logic or fields in Transaction SE38. In total, 35 reports can be run to export a text file to be uploaded into Workforce Analytics.

The reports should be run as a batch job periodically to create the TXT files. Each report can be run individually and contains basic selection criteria to run the report for a group of employees or a group of objects.

A list of the reports and infotypes can be found in Table 16.4.

Report	Infotype
RH_SFI_HRP1000	1000 (Objects)
RH_SFI_HRP1001	1001 (Relationships)
RH_SFI_PA0000	0000 (Actions)
RH_SFI_PA0001	0001 (Organizational Assignments)
RH_SFI_PA0002	0002 (Personnel Data)
RH_SFI_PA0007	0007 (Planned Working Time)

Table 16.4 Extraction Reports for Evaluation Data

Report	Infotype
RH_SFI_PA0008	0008 (Basic Pay)
RH_SFI_PA0016	0016 (Contract Elements)
RH_SFI_PA0025	0025 (Appraisals)
RH_SFI_PA0041	0041 (Date Specifications)
RH_SFI_PA0077	0077 (Personnel Actions)
RH_SFI_PA0302	0302 (Additional Actions)
RH_SFI_T001	T001 (Company Codes)
RH_SFI_T001P	T001P (Personnel Subareas)
RH_SFI_T500P	T500P (Personnel Areas)
RH_SFI_T501T	T501T (Employee Group Names)
RH_SFI_T503T	T503T (Employee Subgroup Names)
RH_SFI_T505S	T505S (Ethnic Origin Texts)
RH_SFI_T510A	T510A (Pay Scales Types)
RH_SFI_T510G	T510G (Pay Scale Areas)
RH_SFI_T512T	T512T (Wage Type Texts)
RH_SFI_T513F	T513F (Appraisal Criteria Texts)
RH_SFI_T527O	T527O (Organizational Key Validation)
RH_SFI_T529T	T529T (Personnel Events Text)
RH_SFI_T529U	T529U (Status Values)
RH_SFI_T530T	T530T (Event Reasons Text)
RH_SFI_T542T	T542T (Employment Contracts)
RH_SFI_T545T	T545T (Corporation Texts)
RH_SFI_T548T	T548T (Date Types)
RH_SFI_T549T	T549T (Date Types)

Table 16.4 Extraction Reports for Evaluation Data (Cont.)

16

Report	Infotype
RH_SFI_T554T	T554T (Absence and Attendance Texts)
RH_SFI_T5U13	T5U13 (Jobs)
RH_SFI_T5UEE	T5UEE (EEO Occupational Categories)
RH_SFI_THOC	THOC (Public Holiday Calendar)
RH_SFI_THOL	THOL (Public Holidays)

Table 16.4 Extraction Reports for Evaluation Data (Cont.)

Authorization role SAP_HR_SFI_ANALYTICS is required for the analytics extraction.

16.4.4 Compensation Planning

Integration of compensation data—for both Compensation and Variable Pay processes—ensures that either or both of these processes can be performed in SAP SuccessFactors using employee salary and history data from SAP ERP HCM and that the compensation and variable play planning results can be transferred to SAP ERP HCM to be update the payroll infotypes.

The integration provides for either or both scenarios. You can integrate either or both of these scenarios:

- **Compensation**
  - Transfer of salary data from SAP ERP HCM to Compensation
  - Transfer of compensation planning results from Compensation to SAP ERP HCM
  - Activation of compensation planning results to update the payroll infotypes.
- **Variable Pay**
  - Transfer of employee history data from SAP ERP HCM to Variable Pay
  - Transfer of variable pay planning results from Variable Pay to SAP ERP HCM
  - Activation of variable pay planning results to update the payroll infotypes

The resulting planning result changes are written back to SAP ERP HCM from SAP SuccessFactors into a staging area prior to being manually released into the payroll infotypes so that they can be processed from the next payroll run. Figure 16.12 shows the process flow of the Compensation integration.

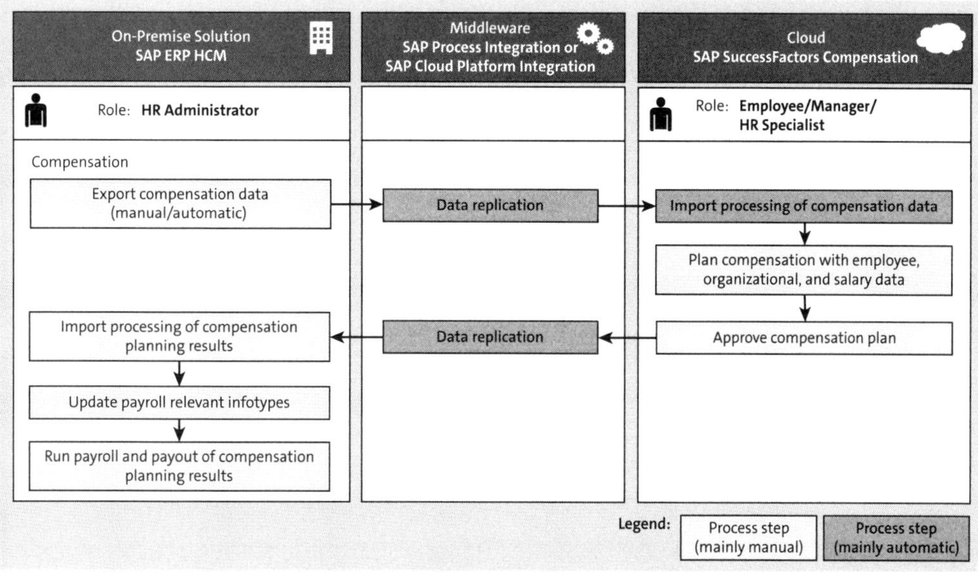

Figure 16.12 Process Flow of Compensation Integration

Figure 16.13 shows the process flow of the Variable Pay integration.

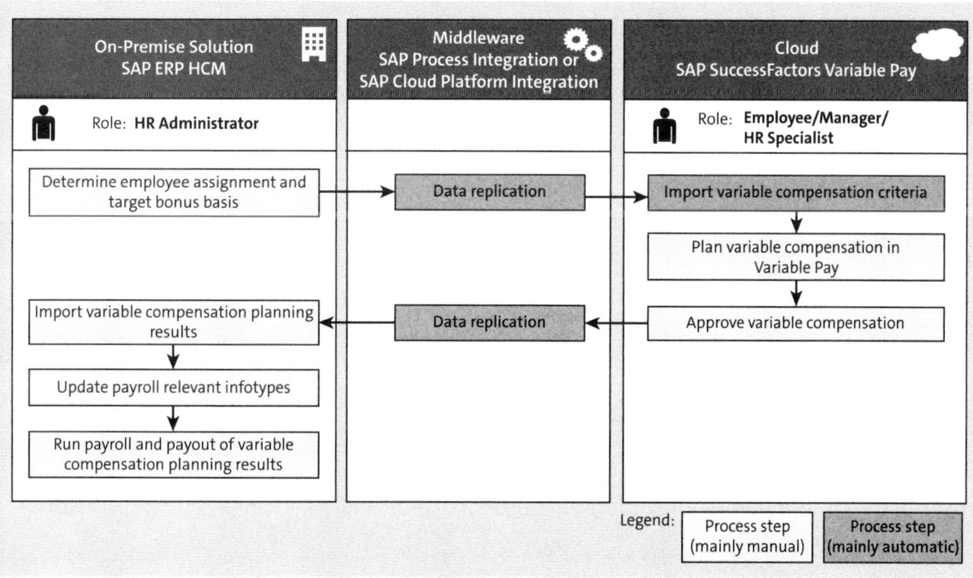

Figure 16.13 Process Flow of Variable Pay Integration

Both integrations use a set of customizing activities, although each integration also has some customizing activities specific to that integration. Both integrations have their own set of programs for running the integration and Web Dynpro applications for monitoring the integration. We'll cover these as we go through this section.

Setting Up the Integrations

In order to use the compensation integration, there are a number of customizing activities to perform in either **Integration Scenario for Compensation Data** or **Integration Scenario for Variable Pay**.

The sets of fields (called field sets) for the data export and import need to be configured in the IMG or via BAdI `HRSFI_B_COMP_FIELD_EXTRACTOR` (Extraction of Compensation Data). Some fields can also be set to have their values entered at the time of activation, rather than being predefined. These values can then be changed during the activation part of the process to suit customer-specific requirements.

BAdI `HRSFI_B_COMP_DATA_ACTIVATION` (Activation of Compensation Data Imported from SAP SuccessFactors) is used to determine how compensation data is imported into and activated in SAP ERP HCM and can also be configured in the IMG.

BAdI `HRSFI_B_VARPY_DATA_ACTIVATION` (Activation of Variable Pay Data Imported from SAP SuccessFactors) serves the same purpose for Variable Pay and can also be configured in the IMG.

BAdI `HRSFI_B_COMP_ACTIVATION_CUST` (Customizing Information Needed for Compensation Activation) can be used to determine additional data from SAP ERP HCM that is required to activate the imported compensation data but that cannot be imported from Compensation and can also be configured in the IMG. BAdI `HRSFI_B_VARPY_ACTIVATION_CUST` (Customizing Information Needed for Variable Pay Activation) serves the same purpose for Variable Pay and can also be configured in the IMG.

For Variable Pay, you also have to complete the following customizing activities in the IMG:

- Define the Variable Pay program that is used
- Import Variable Pay field metadata (also possible via report RH_SFI_SYNCH_VAR_PAY_METADATA or via Transaction SAP_HR_SFI_VARIABLE_PAY).
- Map Variable Pay fields to SAP ERP HCM fields (also possible in view cluster VC_SFI_VARPY_IMFS).
- Configure the eligibility rules to select only the employees that will be part of the Variable Pay compensation planning process.

Before the integration is run, the respective form(s) should already be created in Compensation or Variable Pay. For Compensation, the compensation form needs to be assigned to a compensation group ID in the appropriate IMG customizing activity. This compensation group ID is required as part of the synchronization report in SAP. An ad hoc report must be created in SAP SuccessFactors for the API to use to extract the data from SAP SuccessFactors that will be imported into SAP ERP HCM. Only fields from complete forms must be extracted.

Further Resources

If you need to integrate Compensation and SAP ERP HCM using multiple Compensation Group IDs then refer to the guide *How-To: Integrating Compensation Management Using Multiple Compensation Group IDs* found on the SAP Help Portal.

Transferring Salary Data to Compensation

Report RH_SFI_SYNCH_COMP_DATA is provided for transferring salary data to Compensation.

Figure 16.14 shows the selection screen for the report to transfer Compensation data to SAP SuccessFactors from SAP ERP HCM.

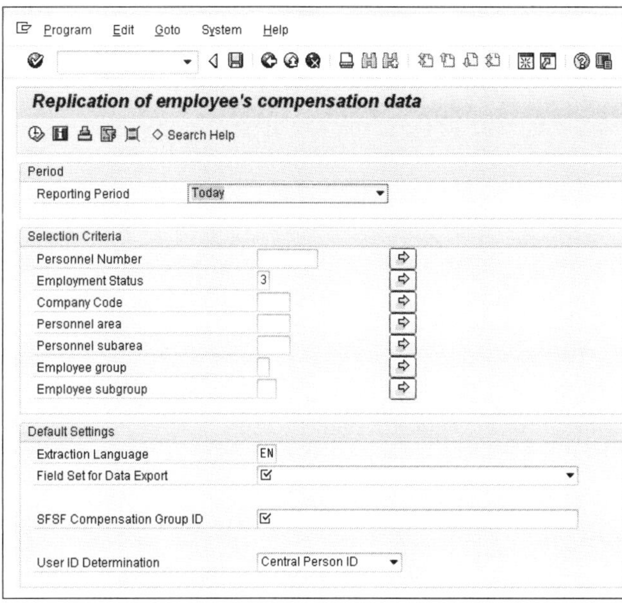

Figure 16.14 Replication of Employee's Compensation Data Report

The selection screen for report RH_SFI_SYNCH_COMP_DATA requires the reporting period to be selected, alongside the extraction language, set of fields to be used, compensation group ID from Compensation, and field to determine the employees' user IDs. The field to determine the user IDs of employees should be the same as that defined for the employee data extraction.

The same selection criteria fields that are available in the employee data synchronization report are also available in this report. After the report is executed, the data is transferred directly to SAP SuccessFactors, and the log is also displayed to show any success, warning, or error messages.

Transferring Employee History Data to Variable Pay

Report RH_SFI_SYNCH_VAR_PAY_DATA (also accessible via Transaction HRSFI_VARPAY_DATA) is provided for transferring employee history data to Variable Pay. The report transfers employee history data into the variable pay staging area in Variable Pay, where from here the data is consumed in the variable pay planning process. Figure 16.15 shows the report selection screen.

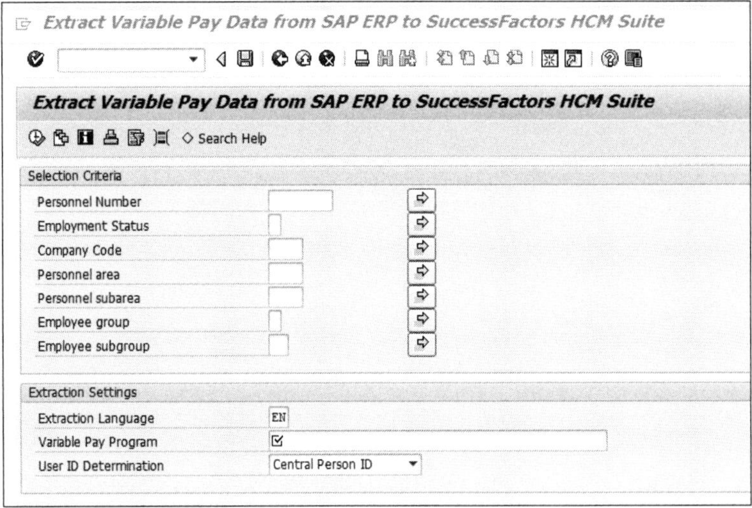

Figure 16.15 Replication of Variable Pay Data Report

Transferring Planning Results to SAP ERP HCM

After the compensation or variable pay planning process is completed in SAP SuccessFactors, the resulting planning data can be imported into SAP ERP HCM. This is done with one of the following reports:

- Compensation data: Report RH_SFI_IMPORT_COMP_DATA (accessible via Transaction HRSFI_COMP_DATA_IMP)
- Variable Pay data: Report RH_SFI_IMPORT_VARPY_DATA (accessible via Transaction HRSFI_VP_IMP_DATA)

The selection screens for reports RH_SFI_IMPORT_COMP_DATA and RH_SFI_IMPORT_VARPY_DATA are very similar to the selection screen for report RH_SFI_SYNCH_COMP_DATA (refer back to Figure 16.14). They have various attributes that need be provided, including the data selection period, the field set to be used, the name of the ad hoc report in SAP SuccessFactors, the form to use, and how to determine the employees' user IDs. After the report is executed, the data is imported into the staging tables in SAP ERP HCM, and the log is displayed to show any success, warning, or error messages.

The next stage of the integration process is activating the planning data in SAP ERP HCM so that it is available within the payroll infotypes. This is done with report RH_SFI_ACTIVATE_COMP_DATA for compensation planning data (accessible via Transaction HRSFI_COMP_DATA_ACT) and with report RH_SFI_ACTIVATE_VARPY_DATA for variable pay planning data (accessible via Transaction HRSFI_VP_ACT_DATA). The report selection screen requires the reporting period to be selected, alongside the field set to be used, the **Compensation Template ID**. Additionally, the same selection criteria fields that are available in the compensation data synchronization report are available in this report. You can run the report in test mode by selecting the **Test Only** checkbox.

After the report is executed, the data is imported from the staging tables into the basic pay and associated infotypes in SAP ERP HCM. The log is also displayed to show any success, warning, or error messages.

The final stage after you are finished with the integration process is to clean up the internal log tables and staging area used in the integration. These reports are:

- RH_SFI_CLEANUP_COMP_REPL: Transfer of salary data to SAP SuccessFactors (accessible via Transaction HRSFI_COMP_CLN_REPL)
- RH_SFI_CLEANUP_COMP_IMP: Compensation planning data imported into SAP ERP HCM (accessible via Transaction HRSFI_COMP_CLN_IMP)
- RH_SFI_CLEANUP_VAR_IMP: Variable Pay planning data imported into SAP ERP HCM (accessible via Transaction HRSFI_VP_CLN_IMP)

The compensation data integration process is now complete.

Monitoring the Data Transfer

A Web Dynpro application is provided for each process in order to monitor the data extraction from SAP SuccessFactors to SAP ERP HCM:

- Compensation: HRSFI_MONITORING_COMP
- Variable Pay: HRSFI_MONITORING_VARPAY

Figure 16.16 shows application HRSFI_MONITORING_EMPL.

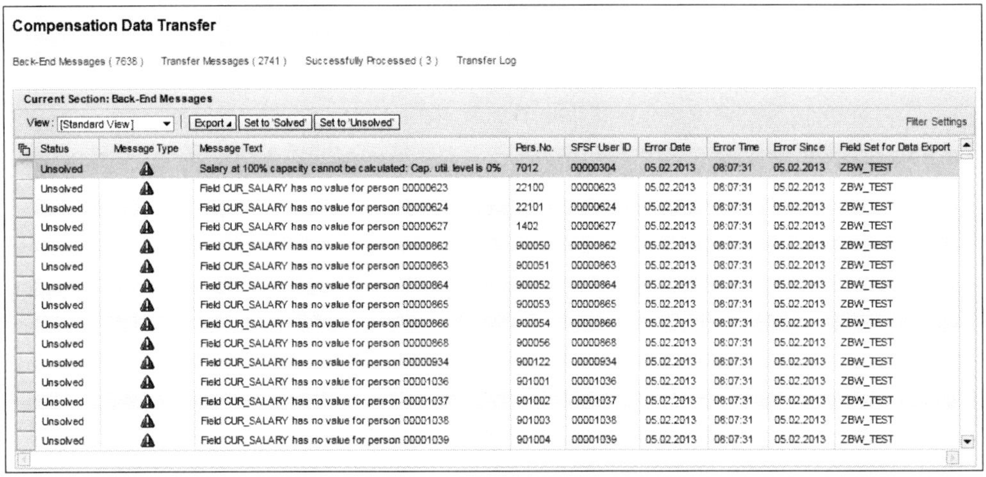

Compensation Data Transfer

Back-End Messages (7638)   Transfer Messages (2741)   Successfully Processed (3)   Transfer Log

Current Section: Back-End Messages

View: [Standard View] | Export | Set to 'Solved' | Set to 'Unsolved'   Filter Settings

Status	Message Type	Message Text	Pers.No.	SFSF User ID	Error Date	Error Time	Error Since	Field Set for Data Export
Unsolved	⚠	Salary at 100% capacity cannot be calculated: Cap. util. level is 0%	7012	00000304	05.02.2013	08:07:31	05.02.2013	ZBW_TEST
Unsolved	⚠	Field CUR_SALARY has no value for person 00000623	22100	00000623	05.02.2013	08:07:31	05.02.2013	ZBW_TEST
Unsolved	⚠	Field CUR_SALARY has no value for person 00000624	22101	00000624	05.02.2013	08:07:31	05.02.2013	ZBW_TEST
Unsolved	⚠	Field CUR_SALARY has no value for person 00000627	1402	00000627	05.02.2013	08:07:31	05.02.2013	ZBW_TEST
Unsolved	⚠	Field CUR_SALARY has no value for person 00000862	900050	00000862	05.02.2013	08:07:31	05.02.2013	ZBW_TEST
Unsolved	⚠	Field CUR_SALARY has no value for person 00000863	900051	00000863	05.02.2013	08:07:31	05.02.2013	ZBW_TEST
Unsolved	⚠	Field CUR_SALARY has no value for person 00000864	900052	00000864	05.02.2013	08:07:31	05.02.2013	ZBW_TEST
Unsolved	⚠	Field CUR_SALARY has no value for person 00000865	900053	00000865	05.02.2013	08:07:31	05.02.2013	ZBW_TEST
Unsolved	⚠	Field CUR_SALARY has no value for person 00000866	900054	00000866	05.02.2013	08:07:31	05.02.2013	ZBW_TEST
Unsolved	⚠	Field CUR_SALARY has no value for person 00000868	900056	00000868	05.02.2013	08:07:31	05.02.2013	ZBW_TEST
Unsolved	⚠	Field CUR_SALARY has no value for person 00000934	900122	00000934	05.02.2013	08:07:31	05.02.2013	ZBW_TEST
Unsolved	⚠	Field CUR_SALARY has no value for person 00001036	901001	00001036	05.02.2013	08:07:31	05.02.2013	ZBW_TEST
Unsolved	⚠	Field CUR_SALARY has no value for person 00001037	901002	00001037	05.02.2013	08:07:31	05.02.2013	ZBW_TEST
Unsolved	⚠	Field CUR_SALARY has no value for person 00001038	901003	00001038	05.02.2013	08:07:31	05.02.2013	ZBW_TEST
Unsolved	⚠	Field CUR_SALARY has no value for person 00001039	901004	00001039	05.02.2013	08:07:31	05.02.2013	ZBW_TEST

Figure 16.16 Compensation Data Transfer in the Transfer Monitoring Application

The HRSFI_MONITORING_COMP (Compensation Monitor—Import and Activation) application is similar to the employee data transfer monitoring application. The application is split up into two lists:

- The **Compensation Data Transfer** list displays an overview for each of the processes (**Transfer, Mapping, Test**, and **Activated**) in the importing and activation of data from Compensation to SAP ERP HCM. It uses a traffic light system of icons to show whether there were errors, warnings, or success messages for employees in each of the four processes. These can be seen in Figure 16.17. The list displays the personnel number, person ID, SAP SuccessFactors user ID, the Compensation template ID, set of fields used, SAP SuccessFactors ad hoc report, and a column for each of the four processes.
- The **All Employees** list displays messages that have been triggered during the data transfer process for each employee. It displays the status, message type, message text, personnel number, SAP SuccessFactors user ID, Compensation template ID,

field set, SAP SuccessFactors ad hoc report, and date and time. The status of each message can be switched to **Solved** and back to **Unsolved**.

As with the employee monitoring application, any fields in either list can be hidden from display using the **Settings Dialog** option.

Messages in both lists can be viewed by the following type:

- Transfer messages: Messages that were triggered during transfer of data to SAP ERP HCM
- Mapping messages: Messages that were triggered during transformation of data
- Messages on test activation: Messages that were triggered during the test run of the activation
- Messages on activation: Messages that were triggered during the activation

The main screen of the application is shown in Figure 16.17, which shows the status of each step of the Compensation integration process.

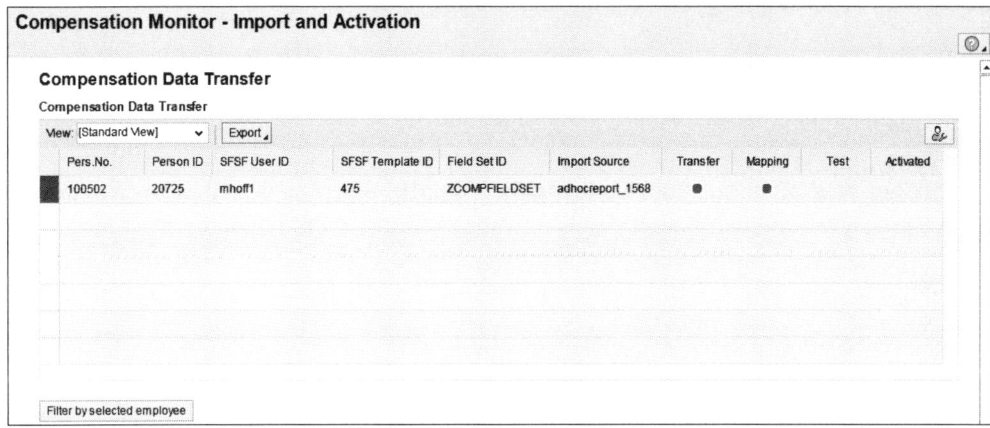

Figure 16.17 Compensation Monitor Web Dynpro Application

Web Dynpro application HRSFI_MONITORING_VARPAY operates in a similar way to HRSFI_MONITORING_COMP.

16.4.5 Recruiting

For the recruiting process, SAP provides integrations for the attract-to-hire and define-to-hire processes. These enable requisition requests to be created in Recruiting using organizational and position vacancy data from SAP ERP HCM and allow hiring or transfer actions to be started in SAP ERP HCM with data from Recruiting after a candidate has accepted an offer. Figure 16.18 shows the process flow of the integration.

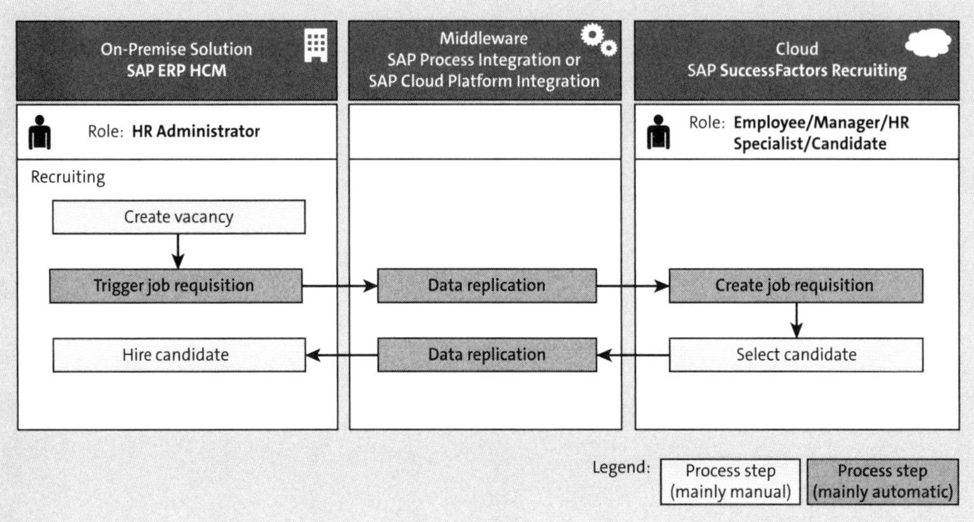

Figure 16.18 Process Flow of Recruiting Integration

This integration has various integration points between SAP ERP HCM and Recruiting. Data is transferred from one system to another at different stages of the recruiting process, and we will look into this shortly. The process for the recruiting integrations is as follows:

1. A vacancy record is created for a position.
2. A report in SAP ERP HCM is run to send vacant position information to Recruiting to create job requisitions.
3. Job requisitions are created in Recruiting with the value of the **State** field set to **Pre-Approved.** Infotype 1107 in SAP is updated with the requisition ID, along with fields such as **Requisition Template ID** and **Name**, and so forth.
4. The recruiting process is performed in Recruiting and an offer is made to a candidate. The status of the job application is changed to **SentToSAP** as part of the process.
5. A report in SAP ERP HCM is run to extract all JobApplication objects with status **SentToSAP** into a staging table in SAP ERP HCM.

6. For each JobApplication object that is sent to SAP ERP HCM, the status field in Recruiting is updated to **TransferedToSAP** if the transfer was successful or **TransferedToSAPError** if the transfer was unsuccessful.
7. Transaction HRSFI_RCT_HIRE is run in SAP ERP HCM to check the data transferred as part of the integration and launch a personnel action to hire, rehire, or transfer a candidate.
8. The status of the job application object in SAP SuccessFactors is set to **HiredAtSAP,** and the date is saved in the **Exported On** field.
9. The new employee's data is transferred to SAP SuccessFactors using the employee data integration.

A new infotype (1107) is introduced as part of the packaged integration to enable handling of vacant positions for job requisitions.

The flow of data between SAP ERP HCM and SAP SuccessFactors for the new hire process is illustrated in Figure 16.19.

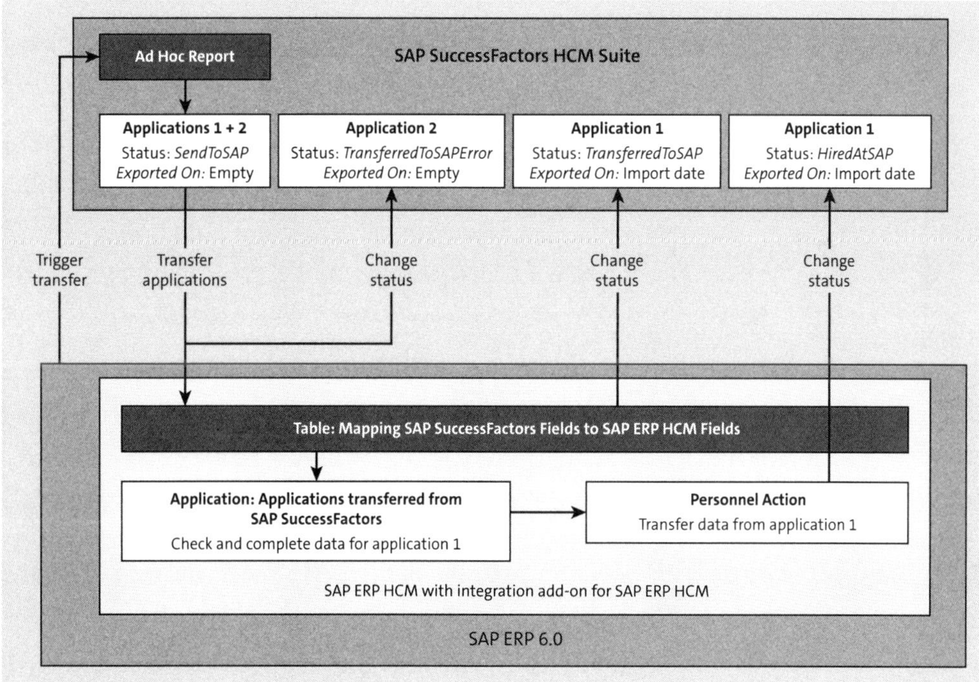

Figure 16.19 End-to-End Process Flow of the Recruiting Integrations

Setting Up the Integrations

Various settings must be made in the IMG in SAP ERP HCM and in Recruiting in order to use the integrations:

1. The first setting to be made is defining the integrations to be used in the IMG; you can use either or both of the recruiting scenarios.
2. If applicable, the BAdI used to determine which job requisition ID should be used for each group of positions (should more than one be used) must be defined. This is configured in the IMG or via BAdI `HRSFI_B_TEMPLATE_DETERMINATION` (Determination of Job Requisition Template from SAP SuccessFactors).
3. Whether to transfer position data for records in infotype 1007 (we'll cover more on this shortly) needs to be configured in the IMG. Report RH_SFI_MIGRATE_VACANCIES is available to migrate existing vacancies to Recruiting and create requisitions.

Once these steps are complete, most of the requisition integration is set up. Some further steps are required during the configuration of the new hire integration, when fields from both integrations need to be assigned to field sets.

The new hire integration steps begin with defining the settings for how the country grouping and personnel actions are determined. These are configured in the IMG or via BAdI `HRSFI_B_RECRUIT_MAPPING` (Determination of Further Data for Recruiting Scenario from SAP SuccessFactors), although no standard implementation exists within the system.

There are three Customizing activities available to configure the application HRSFI_RCT_HIRE in the IMG. With these, you can do the following:

- Define more columns for the **Transferred Job Applications** list
- Specify the headers and field labels
- Change the PDF overview for the job requisition

Within Recruiting, you need to make several configuration settings. It is a prerequisite that the JobApplication object has the field **sapError** available and that the **Hire** status category can be filtered. Four specific statuses must be made available in the **CandidateStatus** selection list that is used by the **Application Status** field. When the statuses are changed in Recruiting, they must also be changed in the IMG.

An ad hoc report needs to be created to transfer all JobApplication objects to SAP with the status **Send to SAP**, including the fields to be transferred. The ad hoc reports, fields, and metadata for this template and the Job Requisition template need to be imported into SAP ERP HCM to configure the remainder of the integration. This is done via report RH_SFI_SYNCH_METADATA (also accessible via Transaction HRSFI_SYNCH_METADATA). It can also be run directly in the IMG. When any of these objects change in SAP SuccessFactors, the report must be run to reimport the objects. This report can also be used to import compensation metadata from Compensation.

After the report is run, the imported ad hoc report needs to be mapped to field sets for both the **Job Requisition** and **New Hire** fields. This is performed in the IMG or in Transaction S_NWC_37000012.

Following this, fields from the field sets need to be mapped to SAP ERP HCM fields. Here, each Recruiting field can have its mapping mode defined (**Mapped via Table, Mapped via BAdI, or Not Individually Mapped**; e.g., display-only), whether the field is country-group dependent, and whether the field should be a required field. This is performed in the IMG or via BAdI `HRSFI_B_FIELD_MAPPING` (Mapping of SAP SuccessFactors Fields to SAP ERP Infotype Fields). It is important to note that not every field needs to be mapped via a BAdI.

Note

The Customizing performed in **Assign SuccessFactors HCM Suite Objects to Field Sets** and **Map SuccessFactors HCM Suite Fields and SAP ERP Fields to Each Other** is not transportable and must be completed in each of the target SAP ERP HCM systems.

16

Once all fields are mapped to field sets, a check should be run to ensure that all of the fields that are to be transferred to and from Recruiting exist and are set to **Required**. This is performed in the IMG or can be done directly with report RH_SFI_RECRUIT_REQ_FIELDS.

Multiple fields can be mapped to one or more fields in the IMG for job requisition integration and for new hire integration. These are also configurable via BAdI `HRSFI_B_CHANGE_MAPPING_RESULT` (Mapping of SAP SuccessFactors Fields to ERP Infotype Fields: Change of Mapping Result).

Transferring Vacant Position Data to Recruiting

You can transfer vacant positions to Recruiting to create job requisitions. The packaged integration comes with a new infotype, 1107. Positions with an active vacancy record in infotype 1007 are automatically copied into infotype 1107 so that they can be replicated to Recruiting. Customers who do not maintain infotype 1007 can turn off this functionality in the IMG so that these records are not transferred to Recruiting. Before the integration is actually run, Infotype 1107 must be maintained for one or more vacant positions that need to be replicated to Recruiting for the integration to function. If you decide to use infotype 1107, then you can use report RH_SFI_MIGRATE_VACANCIES (accessible via Transaction HRSFI_RCT_MIGR_VAC) to migrate existing vacancies to Recruiting and create requisitions.

Job requisition data for a position can be viewed in Transactions PPOCE, PPOME, or PPOSE, depending on whether you'd like to create, change, or display job the data, respectively. Within either of these transactions, the user can select a position and navigate to the **SFSF Job Requisition** tab to view the vacancy and requisition trigger information. If infotype 1007 is not used, a user can create and manage vacancy and requisition trigger information here, which update infotype 1107. Infotype 1107 has two subtypes that can be set in this tab: **Open Job Requisitions** (subtype 0001) and **Closed Job Requisitions** (subtype 0002). These affect whether a job requisition is created and/or remains active in Recruiting. This tab also displays information about the open job requisitions and any other job requisitions for the position. Only one open job requisition can exist for a position at any one time. Figure 16.20 shows the **SFSF Job Requisition** tab in Transaction PPOME.

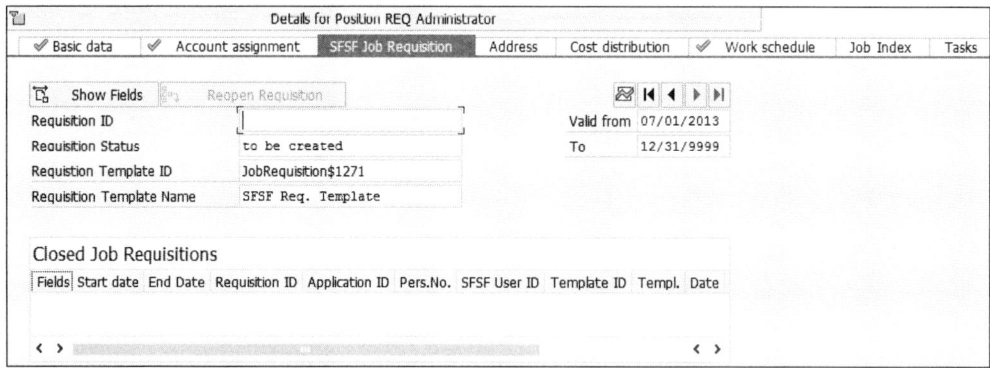

Figure 16.20 The SFSF Job Requisition Tab in Transaction PPOME

To create job requisitions in Recruiting for vacant positions, report RH_SFI_TRIGGER_JOB_REQUISITION is used; Transaction HRSFI_RCT_TRG_JOBREQ can also be used. This sends information about vacation positions to Recruiting and triggers the job requisition process.

Transferring Candidate Data to SAP ERP HCM

You must transfer candidates from Recruiting to SAP ERP HCM in order to hire them. There are two steps to the data integration process for this transfer: data import and further processing.

After a job offer has been accepted by a candidate in Recruiting, the status of the requisition needs to be changed to **SentToSAP** for the integration to import that candidate's data into SAP ERP HCM. Report RH_SFI_IMPORT_RECRUITING_DATA (also accessible via transaction HRSFI_RCT_DATA_IMP) is used to import the data from Recruiting, and this can be scheduled to run to regularly replicate the data.

In the report selection screen, select the ad hoc report to be run in SAP SuccessFactors. This also selects the field set defined for the ad hoc report during Customizing. After the report is executed, the data is transferred from SAP SuccessFactors into the staging table in SAP ERP HCM, and the log is also displayed to show any success, warning, or error messages. Figure 16.21 shows the selection screen for the report to import recruiting data to SAP ERP HCM.

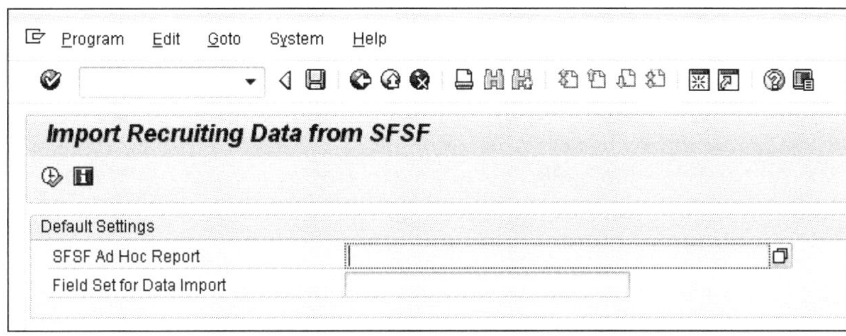

Figure 16.21 Selection Screen of RH_SFI_IMPORT_RECRUITING_DATA

The second step is the further processing of the data imported from Recruiting. This is performed in Transaction HRSFI_RCT_HIRE. The transaction displays a list of all job application data that has been transferred to the SAP ERP HCM staging area. The first three columns of the list display icons: the check status (green if a personnel action can be started, or red if one cannot), notes (either the **Create Note** or **Change Note** icons), and an icon if any messages were generated during the transfer. Selecting the **Message** icon shows the messages that were generated.

The subsequent nine columns display the applicant's first name and last name, start date, personnel number, action type, application ID from Recruiting, country grouping, status, and company code. Selecting any record provides information in the bottom panel of messages, notes, or details for the selected employee. The **Details** tab displays data about the applicant, application, data from SAP SuccessFactors, and last processor of the data/record.

Figure 16.22 shows the main screen for Transaction HRSFI_RCT_HIRE.

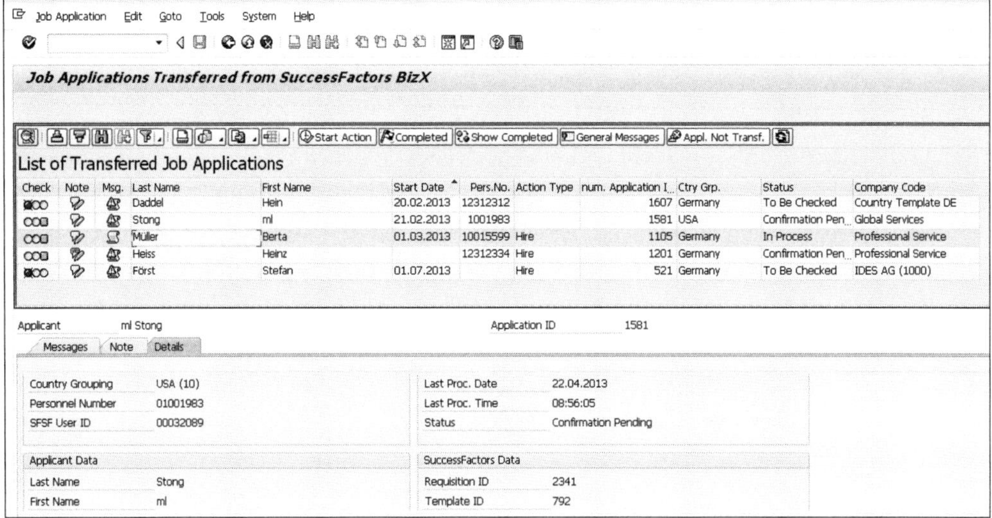

Figure 16.22 Transaction HRSFI_RCT_HIRE

Above the list are several options. In addition to the standard options for an ABAP List Viewer (ALV) list, such as sorting and exporting, there are several application-specific actions to enable the user to perform activities on selected job applications, such as trigger a personnel action, display a PDF of the job application information, and mark as completed. There are also options to only display job applications that are completed, have general messages (e.g., middleware connection issues), or were not transferred correctly to SAP ERP HCM.

The PDF produced when you click the **Data Overview (PDF)** button displays basic information about the application, the fields and data transferred from Recruiting to SAP ERP HCM, the SAP ERP HCM fields that data has been transferred to, and what data has been transferred to the SAP ERP HCM fields. Figure 16.23 shows an example of the first page of the PDF document.

Job Application Data

Name	Mark RECR4	Transfer Date	01/29/2013
Start Date	02/01/2013	Transfer Time	13:51:19
Requisition	1602	Status	New
Country Grp.	Germany (01)	Last Changed	GUNDELFINGER
Action	Hire (01)	Ad Hoc Rep. ID	AdhocReport_3482
Application	682	Ad Hoc Report	Hire Data SFI Final 2

SFSF Field	Content
Template ID	792
HiringManager_USERS_SYS_ID	RECR3
OFFER_DETAIL_LATEST_JOB_REQ_JO	2013-02-01
RCM_APPLICATION_ADDRESS	Colima Avenue NW
RCM_APPLICATION_CANDIDATE_ID	1041
	682
RCM_APPLICATION_CITY	San Diego
RCM_APPLICATION_COUNTRY_CODE	US
RCM_APPLICATION_DOB	
RCM_APPLICATION_EMAIL_ADDRESS	reiner_do@yahoo.de
RCM_APPLICATION_EXPORTED_ON	
RCM_APPLICATION_FIRSTNAME	Mark
RCM_APPLICATION_FORMER_EMPLOYE	N
RCM_APPLICATION_GENDER	
RCM_APPLICATION_HOME_PHONE	858-123456
RCM_APPLICATION_LASTNAME	RECR4
RCM_APPLICATION_MIDDLE_NAME	
RCM_APPLICATION_STATE	California
RCM_APPLICATION_ZIP	85413
RCM_APP_STATUS_STATUS_NAME	SendToSAP

Figure 16.23 PDF of Job Application Data in HRSFI_RCT_HIRE

The **Status** column indicates whether the record requires action, can be processed, or is being processed. When a record is set to **To Be Checked**, the record requires action before it can be set to **Start Action** and processed further. Usually, this is when there is a duplicate record identified (SAP ERP HCM uses the first name, last name, and date of birth to check whether an employee already exists in the system) or either the **Personnel Action** dropdown (the type of action that should be started) or the **Country Grouping** field in the **Process Data** section doesn't have a value or a correct value.

To correct a record, you need to select the red light in the **Check** column to open the **Check and Change Data** window, where the corrections can be made. Figure 16.24 displays the **Check and Change Data** window.

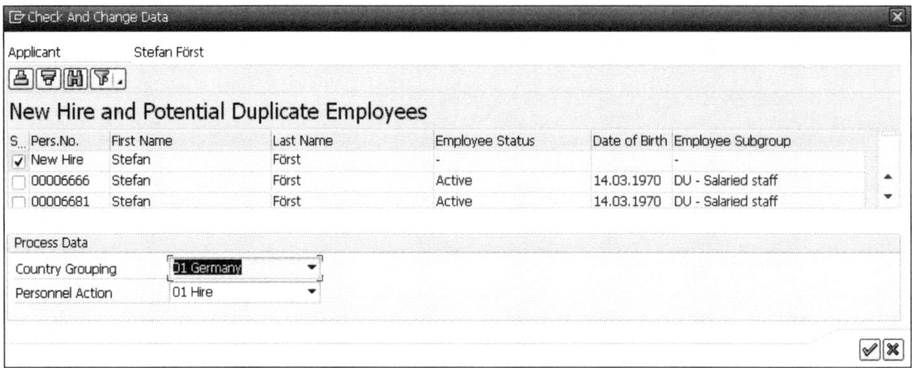

Figure 16.24 Check and Change Data Window in Transaction HRSFI_RCT_HIRE

After the record is corrected and the window closed, the record is set to **Start Action** in the **Status** column. You can start a personnel action by selecting a record with the status **Start Action** and selecting the **Start Action** button. Transaction PA40 (Personnel Actions) opens for the appropriate action and pre-fills the relevant data that has been sent over from Recruiting. By default, this is the start date, position ID, personnel area, employee group, and employee subgroup in the **Create Actions** screen (infotype 0001); first name and last name in the **Personnel Data** screen (infotype 0002); and address details in the **Create Addresses** screen (infotype 0006).

After the action is completed, the candidate is now hired into the SAP ERP HCM system, and personnel actions (Transaction PA40) are closed. The list of job applications in HRSFI_RCT_HIRE is once again displayed, and the record that has been processed in personnel actions is no longer displayed in the list. Use the **Show Completed** button to display the record, along with all other completed job applications. In Recruiting, the **Status** column of the job application changes to **HiredatSAP**.

You can manually close a job application by selecting the record and clicking the **Completed** button. This may be used if a personnel action needs to be manually performed (for example, if insufficient data is sent from Recruiting or if a personnel action has been performed already).

It is possible to retransfer one, multiple, or all job applications from Recruiting in the **Tools** menu using either the **Remap Data for Job Application** or the **Remap Data for All Job Applications** menu options. It's also possible to retransfer the status update for a job application marked as **Completed** to Recruiting if the original message was not sent (e.g., if the middleware was unavailable). This is done in the **Tools** menu using menu option **Resend Failed Confirmations to SFSF**.

A job application that is no longer required for processing can be removed from the list. This doesn't remove the job application in Recruiting, however. To perform the deletion, the user must have super user authorization. This also means that the user sees *all* job applications in the list. The deletion can be performed in the **Job Application** menu using the **Delete** menu option.

16.4.6 Onboarding and Offboarding

The packaged integration provides scenarios for both onboarding and offboarding integration between Onboarding and SAP ERP HCM. The integration works with or without Recruiting being used to trigger the onboarding or offboarding in Onboarding. This allows organizations to onboard employees in Onboarding, whether their data was first entered in SAP ERP HCM, came from Recruiting, or was first entered into Onboarding. It also allows organizations to hire employees in SAP ERP HCM when their data in Onboarding did not originate from SAP ERP HCM (i.e., it came from Recruiting or another recruiting system).

Figure 16.25 shows the process flow when the candidate flows to Onboarding from SAP ERP HCM.

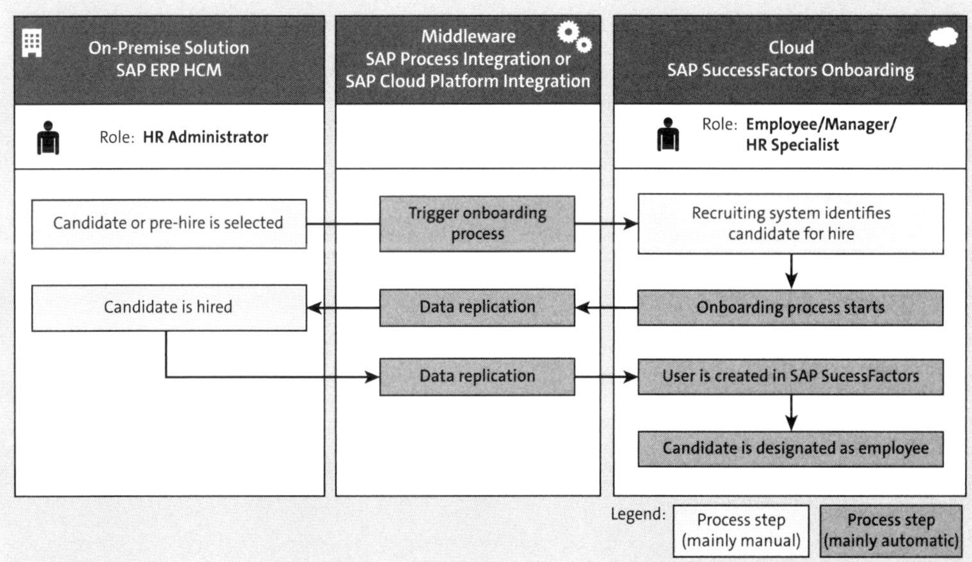

Figure 16.25 Process Flow of Onboarding Integration from SAP ERP HCM to Onboarding

Figure 16.26 shows the process flow when the candidate flows to Onboarding from Recruiting or another recruiting system.

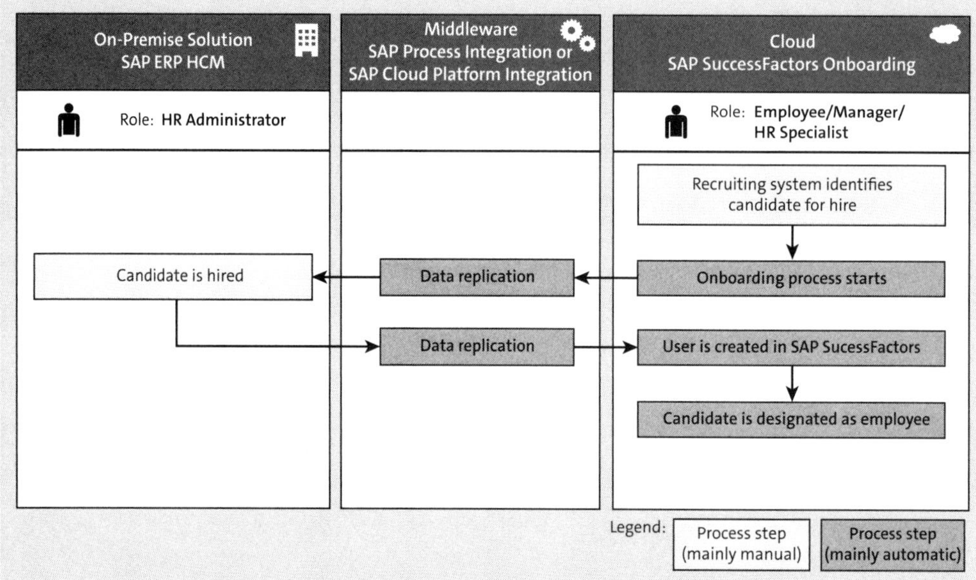

Figure 16.26 Process Flow of Onboarding Integration from a Recruiting System to Onboarding

Figure 16.27 shows the process flow when an employee from SAP ERP HCM is being offboarded in Onboarding.

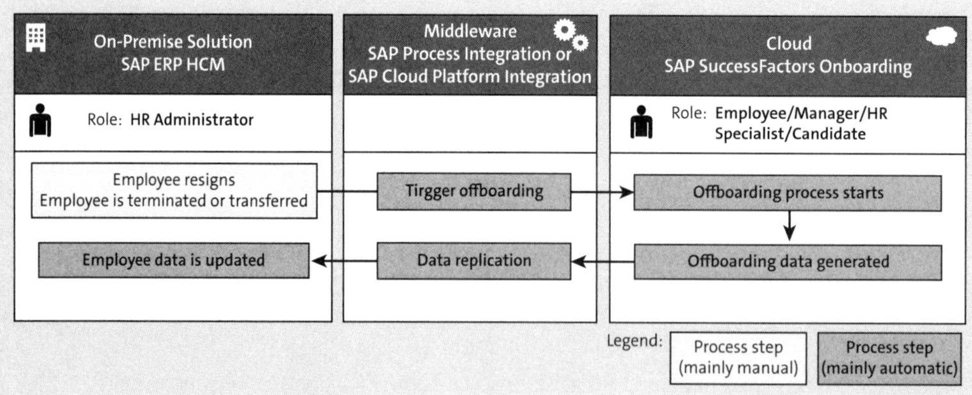

Figure 16.27 Process Flow of Offboarding Integration

Setting Up the Integrations

Like with the other integrations, there are a number of steps required to set up the integration. In SAP SuccessFactors, an ad hoc report needs to be created with the fields needed for the integration. In the IMG in SAP ERP HCM, there are several Customizing activities to configure:

- Define authorizations Import metadata from Onboarding
- Configure the Onboarding login Assign SAP SuccessFactors ad hoc report to field sets
- Map Onboarding fields from field sets with SAP ERP HCM fields
- Define fields that are displayed as additional columns in Transaction HRSFI_ONB_HIRE
- Specify headers and field labels for fields transferred from Onboarding to the SAP ERP HCM (also accessible via Transaction HRSFI_ONB_HIRE)

And like with the other integrations, there are a number of BAdIs provided to change the mappings and mapping results dynamically and to determine processing of further data.

Transferring Candidate Data to Onboarding

16

When hiring an employee in SAP ERP HCM that should go through onboarding in Onboarding, report RH_SFI_TRIGGER_ONBOARDING (also accessible via Transaction HRSFI_ONB_TRIGGER) is run to transfer the employee data to Onboarding. This report can be scheduled to run regularly.

Transferring Onboarded Employee Data to SAP ERP HCM

As with employee candidates in Recruiting, you must transfer onboarded employees from Onboarding to SAP ERP HCM in order to hire them. There are two steps to the data integration process for this transfer: data import and further processing.

After an employee has been onboarded in Onboarding, report RH_SFI_IMPORT_ONBOARDING_DATA is used to import the data (also accessible via Transaction HRSFI_ONB_DATA_IMP), and this report can be scheduled to run regularly. In the report selection screen, select the ad hoc report to be run in SAP SuccessFactors. This also selects the field set defined for the ad hoc report during Customizing. After the report is executed, the data is transferred from SAP SuccessFactors into the staging table in SAP ERP HCM, and the log is also displayed to show any success, warning, or error messages. Figure 16.28 shows the selection screen for the report to import onboarded employee data to SAP ERP HCM.

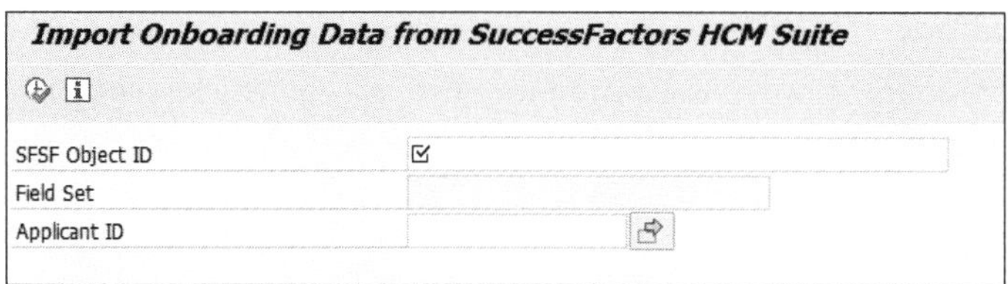

Figure 16.28 Report to Import Onboarding Data to SAP ERP HCM

By adding certain parameters to the report, it is also possible to have the employees who have been transferred to SAP ERP HCM hired automatically into the system without performing the second step that we will cover next. It is worth noting that there are the following constraints with automatically hiring employees with the integration:

- Only the initial hire is supported, for which the personnel action could be determined either from the incoming onboarding data or via BAdI
- You must use internal number generation for employee numbers
- Dynamic actions are not supported
- Time management infotypes (PA2***) are not supported and will not be created

Note

Report RH_SFI_IMPORT_ONBOARDING_DATA does not pick employees whose country grouping is 99. However, you can process those employees in Transaction HRSFI_ONB_HIRE as part of a mass hire.

The second step is the further processing of the imported Onboarding data. This is performed in Transaction HRSFI_ONB_HIRE, which is similar to the transaction used to process candidates imported from Recruiting that we discussed in the last section. The transaction displays a list of all onboarded employees that have been transferred to the SAP ERP HCM staging area. The first two columns of the list display icons: the check status (green if a personnel action can be started, or red if one cannot) and an icon if any messages were generated during the transfer. Selecting the **Message** icon shows the messages that were generated.

The subsequent 10 columns display the employee's application ID, personnel number, new hire ID generated in Onboarding, first name and last name, date of birth, start date, country grouping, action type, and status. Selecting any record provides information in the bottom panel of messages, notes, or details for the selected employee. The **Details** tab displays data about the employee, application, data from SAP SuccessFactors, and last processor of the data/record.

Figure 16.29 shows the main screen for Transaction HRSFI_ONB_HIRE.

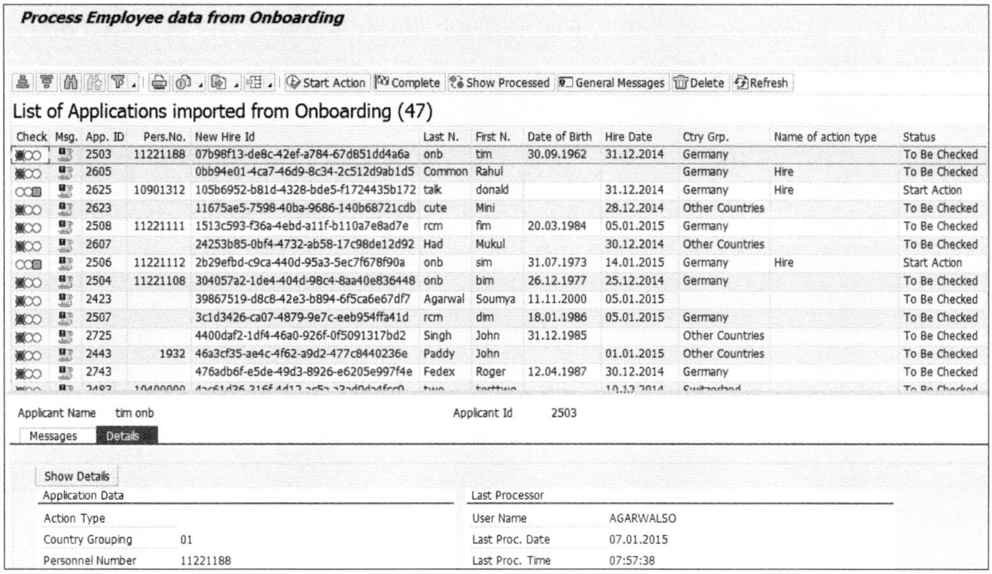

Figure 16.29 Transaction HRSFI_ONB_HIRE

Above the list are several options. In addition to the standard options for an ALV list, such as sorting and exporting, there are several application-specific actions to enable the user to perform activities on selected candidates, such as trigger a personnel action, mark as completed, or delete the record. There are also options to only display candidates that are completed or have general messages (e.g., middleware connection issues).

The **Status** column indicates whether the record requires action, can be processed, or is being processed. When a record is set to **To Be Checked**, the record requires action before it can be set to **Start Action** and processed further. Usually this is when there is a duplicate record identified (SAP ERP HCM uses the first name, last name, and date of birth to check whether an employee already exists in the system), or either the **Personnel Action** dropdown (the type of action that should be started) or the **Country Grouping** field in the **Process Data** section doesn't have a value or a correct value.

To correct a record, you need to select the red light in the **Check** column to open the **Check and Change Data** window, where the corrections can be made.

If you also use Recruiting and integrate applicant data to SAP ERP HCM, then click on the green light in the **Check** column to see if the employee has had data imported from Recruiting. If they have, then you can navigate directly to Transaction HRSFI_RCT_HIRE to process the employee.

You can start a personnel action by selecting a record with the status **Start Action** and selecting the **Start Action** button. Transaction PA40 (Personnel Actions) opens for the appropriate action and prefills the relevant data that has been sent over from Onboarding.

After the action is completed, the candidate is now hired into the SAP ERP HCM system and personnel actions (Transaction PA40) is closed. The list of employees in HRSFI_ONB_HIRE is once again displayed, and the record that has been processed in personnel actions is no longer displayed in the list. Use the **Show Processed** button to display the record, along with all other processed employees. If the user doesn't exist in SAP SuccessFactors, then the employee data integration will transfer the employee and organizational data to SAP SuccessFactors in the next scheduled run and the onboarded employee's record will be updated to show they have been hired as an employee.

Transferring Employee Data to Onboarding for Offboarding

When you are ready to offboard an employee in Onboarding, you can use report RH_SFI_TRIGGER_OFFBOARDING (also accessible via Transaction HRSFI_OFB_TRIGGER) to transfer the employee data from SAP ERP HCM to Onboarding so that the employee can go through the offboarding process.

The report identifies employees eligible for offboarding, sends employee data to Onboarding to run the onboarding process, and receives the HR data ID back from Onboarding to store in the staging tables.

Transaction HRSFI_OFB—which works similarly to the recruiting and onboarding programs that are used to process candidate and employee data—is used to check employees that have been transferred to Onboarding for offboarding. It can be used as a task list to identify which employees require additional data or need further action.

Transferring Offboarded Employee Data to SAP ERP HCM

Report RH_SFI_IMPORT_OFFBOARDING_DATA is used to transfer offboarded employee data from Onboarding to SAP ERP HCM (accessible via Transaction HRSFI_OFB_DATA_IMP). The report transfers the offboarded employee data into a staging data so that it can be processed. Transaction HRSFI_OFB is used to process the data that was transferred.

Transaction HRSFI_OFB works similarly to the recruiting and onboarding programs that are used to process candidate and employee data. It enables you to view the employees who have had data transferred from Onboarding but have not yet had their data processed. Like with the transfer of employee data to Onboarding for off-boarding, it can be used as a task list to identify which employees require additional data or need further action.

As with other uses of Transaction HRSFI_ONB and similarly to Transaction HRSFI_ONB_HIRE, the report enables you to process a PA40 action to process employee data.

16.4.7 Qualification Data

With the integration add-on, you manage your Qualification Catalog in either the SAP SuccessFactors competency framework or in the Learning curriculum catalog, instead of in SAP ERP HCM. The integration provides a one-time migration of the Qualification Catalog from SAP ERP HCM to SAP SuccessFactors, and then that becomes the system of record for qualification data; the qualification catalog in SAP ERP HCM should be set to read-only because the integration updates the qualification catalog with changes that occur in SAP SuccessFactors.

As part of this scenario, employee qualifications are then managed in SAP SuccessFactors and replicated back to the Qualification Profile in SAP ERP HCM. This integration scenario allows organizations to manage qualifications and qualification assignments in SAP SuccessFactors and retain a full and updated Qualification Catalog and updated employee Qualification Profiles in SAP ERP HCM.

This integration differs from other integrations in that it is triggered by the middleware rather than by a report in SAP ERP HCM. The one-time migration of qualification objects from SAP ERP HCM to SAP SuccessFactors is executed via a report in SAP ERP HCM.

If qualification data is managed as curricula in Learning, then changes to qualification data and employee qualifications can be transferred periodically to SAP ERP HCM. After the migration of employee qualification history to the SAP SuccessFactors competency framework, the competency data can be viewed on an employee's People Profile.

The process flow for the competency-based qualification integration can be seen in Figure 16.30.

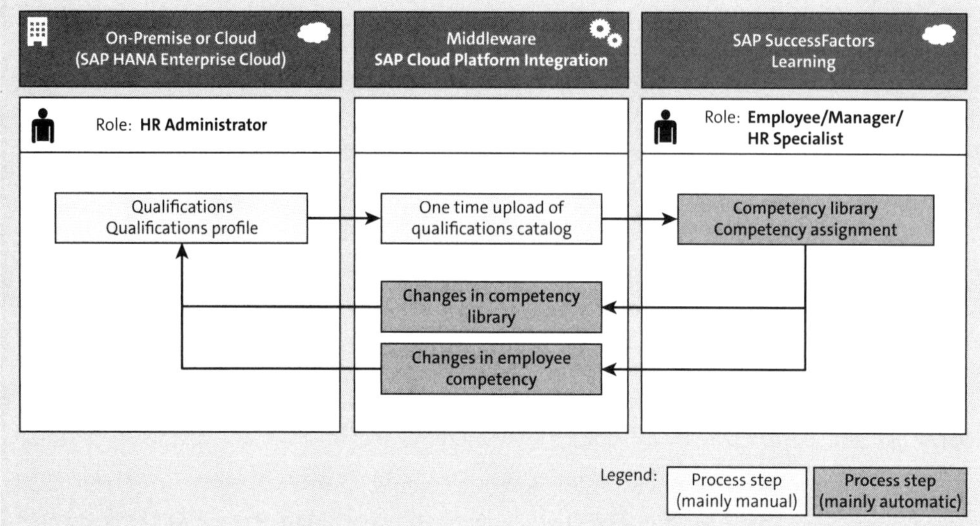

Figure 16.30 Process Flow of Competency-Based Qualification Integration

Likewise, the process flow for the curricula-based qualification integration can be seen in Figure 16.31.

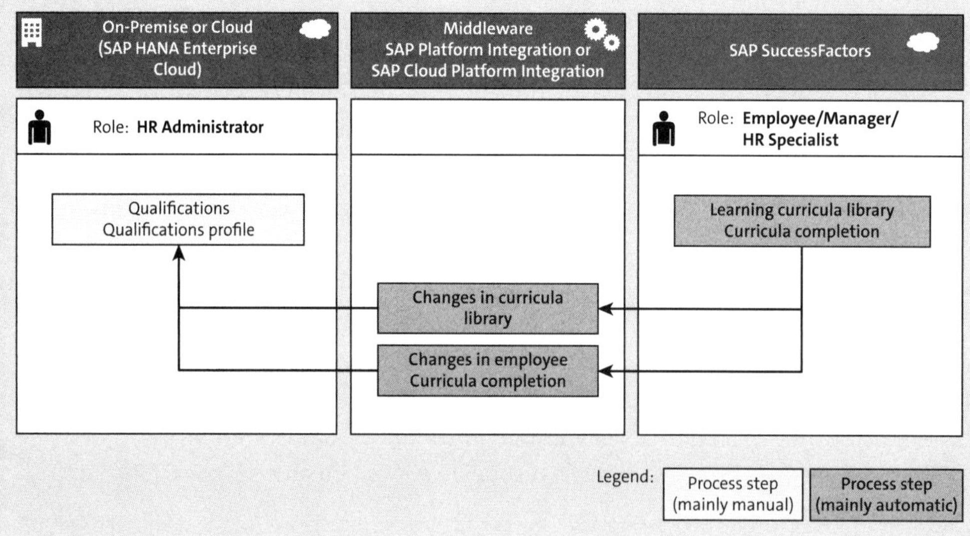

Figure 16.31 Process Flow of Curricula-Based Qualification Integration

Integration Details

The integration can handle either the use of competencies or curricula as methods of storing employee competencies in SAP SuccessFactors. Depending on which one is used, SAP SuccessFactors updates qualification data in SAP ERP HCM with either of the following:

- Changes to the competency library and employee competency ratings in SAP SuccessFactors HCM Suite
- Changes to curriculum types and employee curriculum statuses in Learning

The terminology between SAP ERP HCM and SAP SuccessFactors with regard to qualifications can be seen in Table 16.5.

SAP ERP HCM	SAP SuccessFactors	Learning
Qualification group	Competency library	Curriculum type
Qualification	Competency	Curriculum
Proficiency	Competency rating	Curriculum status

Table 16.5 Qualification Terminology across the Systems

The mapping of ratings from competencies in SAP SuccessFactors to qualification proficiencies in SAP ERP HCM needs to have specific mapping or logic defined during implementation of the integration. This is because there are differences in how SAP SuccessFactors collects and stores competency ratings compared to how this happens in SAP ERP HCM. In SAP SuccessFactors, it is possible to collect different ratings on the same competencies from different sources (e.g., from SAP SuccessFactors Performance Management or SAP SuccessFactors 360 review), while in SAP ERP HCM a qualification can only have one rating. During setup of the integration, you can define filters in the middleware to select which sources are used to determine the rating that will be mapped in SAP ERP HCM. Additionally, different rating scales can be used in each system, so these need to be mapped during setup of the integration and periodically if needed.

For Learning, the mapping is much simpler. Because only the curricula with the status of complete are replicated, the proficiency in SAP ERP HCM is simply mapped as "1". If the status of a curriculum changes from completed to incomplete, then the employee's qualification assignment in SAP ERP HCM is deleted.

Note

The integration supports only the legacy competencies in SAP SuccessFactors; it does not support MDF-based competencies. In addition, the integration supports only parts of competencies that interact directly with the employee. It does not cover skills, behaviors, teasers, or tuners.

The integration supports qualifications stored in SAP ERP HCM in either Personnel Administration (PA) or Organizational Management (OM)/Personnel Development (PD), and the integration automatically determines this by reading the PLOGI QUAL integration switch in SAP ERP HCM. No configuration is required in SAP SuccessFactors or in the integration add-on. If the PLOGI QUAL integration switch is changed from one value to the other during operation of the integration, then the integration should be re-implemented.

For the integration to function, table `T777SFI_GUID_MAP` is provided so that the GUID of the competency or the curriculum ID is mapped to the qualification ID in SAP ERP HCM. During the one-time export of the Qualification Catalog to SAP SuccessFactors, this table is populated by the integration.

Further Resources

You can find the field mapping for all aspects of the one-time data migration and integrations in the guide *Integration Add-On for SAP ERP HCM and SuccessFactors HCM Suite* at the SAP Help Portal.

There are some important notes to remember when considering or using the integration:

- Competencies or curricula that are deleted in SAP SuccessFactors must be manually deleted or delimited in SAP ERP HCM.
- When mapped to SAP ERP HCM qualification proficiencies, competency ratings may be rounded up or down.
- If items attached to the curricula catalog in SAP SuccessFactors are changed, the replicated status of the curriculum for related employees is invalid, and a full, forced synchronization must be triggered by an administrator.
- The integration does not affect the qualification hierarchy; it only transfers the individual competencies and proficiencies, and not relationships between competencies.

- Transfer of competencies or skills from SAP ERP HCM to Learning is not supported by the integration.
- In Learning, the curriculum object does not have its own validity dates; validity is derived from the items attached to the curriculum object. Since items only have an expiry date and do not have an explicit start date, the start date of the assignment is always the date on which the integration is executed. When multiple items are attached to a curriculum, each item can have an independent expiry date and the earliest expiry date is used as the expiry date for the curriculum.

Let's now take a look at setting up the integration.

Setting Up Competency-Based Qualification Integration

The OData APIs for qualifications data must be enabled in SAP Gateway. There are also a number of other Customizing activities that need to be configured:

- Determination of personnel numbers in SAP ERP from the user ID in SAP SuccessFactors
- The SFTP file path needs to be defined
- Mapping of existing qualification objects in SAP ERP need to competency objects in SAP SuccessFactors
- Mapping of competency ratings in SAP SuccessFactors to a rating scale of qualifications in SAP ERP

Setting Up Curricula-Based Qualification Integration

If PD qualifications are used, a default qualification group must be configured in the middleware for curricula that do not have a parent curricula type. This is because the curricula type is optional in Learning, but the equivalent qualification group object in SAP is mandatory.

In addition to the configuration of the middleware, the OData APIs for qualifications data must be enabled in SAP Gateway, as with setting up the competency-based qualification integration.

There are a number of other Customizing settings that need to be configured:

- Determination of personnel numbers in SAP ERP from the user ID in Learning
- If any existing qualification objects in SAP ERP need to be mapped to curricula objects in Learning

- Mapping of **Completed** and **Incompleted** statuses of curricula in Learning to a rating scale in SAP ERP

When you use PD in SAP ERP HCM and the integration needs to create a new qualification group, a rating scale must be assigned to the qualification group. Because this data is not stored in Learning, a default rating scale must be configured in the middleware for SAP ERP HCM to use when creating the qualification group.

Migrating Qualification Data from SAP ERP HCM to SAP SuccessFactors

The Qualification Catalog can be exported from SAP ERP HCM so that it can be imported into the SAP SuccessFactors competency framework. No capability exists for the Qualification Catalog to be imported into Learning.

The Qualification Catalog in SAP ERP HCM is exported as a flat file using report RH_SFI_EXPORT_QUALI. This report can also be run via Transaction HRSFI_QUAL_DATA_EXPT. As part of the export, report RH_SFI_EXPORT_QUALI updates table `T777SFI_GUID_MAP` with the mapping of the GUID that is used in SAP SuccessFactors with the object ID of the qualification. This mapping is needed for the integration back to SAP ERP HCM of competency data for existing qualification objects.

The exported file is imported into SAP SuccessFactors via the Admin Center or Provisioning. Figure 16.32 shows the selection screen of report RH_SFI_EXPORT_QUALI.

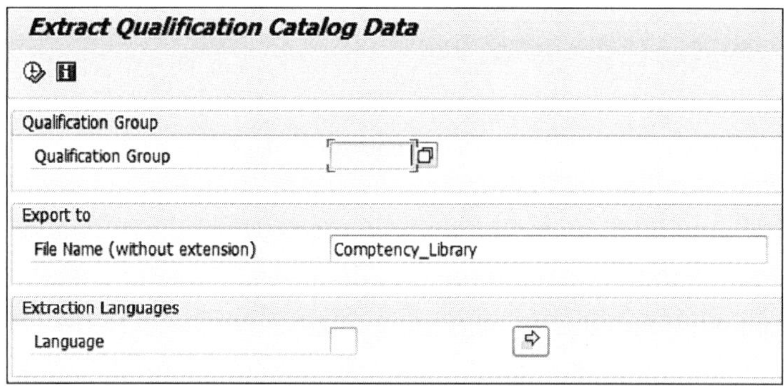

Figure 16.32 Selection Screen of Report RH_SFI_EXPORT_QUALI

Report RH_SFI_EXPORT_QUALI works whether you are using PA or PD qualifications in SAP ERP HCM. The field mapping used by the report is different depending on whether PA or PD is used in the system.

Transferring Competency-Based Qualification Data to SAP ERP HCM

When you make changes to a competency library or create a new competency library in SAP SuccessFactors, the integration process in the middleware transfers the competency data to SAP ERP HCM. This is done by a recurring export of the competency library from SAP SuccessFactors to an SFTP site. The middleware then reads the competency library data from the exported file on the SFTP site.

When a new competency library is created in SAP SuccessFactors, a new qualification group is created in SAP ERP HCM. When a new child competency is created in SAP SuccessFactors, a new child qualification of the qualification group is created in SAP ERP HCM.

Transferring Employee Competency Ratings to SAP ERP HCM

When you use the competency object in SAP SuccessFactors HCM Suite, the integration process in the middleware transfers the competency rating data for employees from the competency rating object in SAP SuccessFactors to SAP ERP HCM. This is done by a recurring export of the competency assignments from SAP SuccessFactors to an SFTP site. The middleware then reads the competency library data from the exported file on the SFTP site.

When a competency rating is created in SAP SuccessFactors, a new qualification is assigned in SAP ERP HCM. When a competency rating is changed in SAP SuccessFactors, the rating of the employee's assigned qualification is changed in SAP ERP HCM. The rating is determined using any value mapping configuration made during Customizing and the filtering configuration made in the middleware.

Transferring Curricula-Based Qualification Data to SAP ERP HCM

When you use the curriculum object in Learning, the integration process in the middleware transfers the changes to the curriculum from Learning to SAP ERP HCM.

Only curriculum that are active and with the status **Completed** are considered in the integration. The expiry date of a curriculum with multiple child item objects is taken from the object with the earliest expiry date. If no expiry date exists, the default end date of 31.12.9999 is used. The start date is always the date of the integration.

When a new curricula type is created in Learning, a new qualification group is created in SAP ERP HCM. When a new child curriculum is created in Learning, a new child qualification of the qualification group is created in SAP ERP HCM.

Transferring Employee Curricula Ratings to SAP ERP HCM

When you use the curriculum object in Learning for employee competencies, the integration process in the middleware transfers changes to the status of the curriculum object that is assigned to employees from Learning to SAP ERP HCM.

When a curriculum is created in Learning, a new qualification is assigned in SAP ERP HCM. When the status of a curriculum object is changed in Learning, the rating of the employee's assigned qualification is changed in SAP ERP HCM. The rating is determined using any value mapping configuration made during Customizing and the filtering configuration made in the middleware.

16.5 Other Packaged Integrations

SAP has released other types of packaged integration content to enable integration between SAP SuccessFactors and other providers, such as Box or third-party recruiting candidate assessments.

For the SAP SuccessFactors suite, there is integration with Box for document management and DocuSign for digital signatures.

For Learning, there is integration to the SAP ERP Financial Accounting and Controlling components to enable posting of learning costs to the finance ledger in SAP ERP or SAP S/4HANA. There is also the ability to migrate Skillsoft data to Learning, integrate Learning with virtual meeting room providers like WebEx and Adobe Connect, and to integrate various content providers.

Several packaged integrations are provided for Recruiting that enable integration with third-party systems. The list of integrations grows periodically and should be checked with SAP or in one of their customer or partner resources. Examples of available integrations include Recruiting and PeopleAnswers for candidate assessments or eQuest for job posting.

Further Resources

Further details can be found on the SAP Help Portal in the respective product pages for the SAP SuccessFactors HCM Suite, Recruiting, and Learning under the Integration header.

16.6 Application Programming Interfaces

SAP provides two APIs for replicating data in and out of SAP SuccessFactors using web services:

- OData API
- Employee Central Compound API

Additionally, the legacy SFAPI is still available for preexisting integrations, but it has been deprecated for new developments. In the future it is likely to be decommissioned after existing integrations have been migrated to the OData API.

Each API has different flexibility, depending on the intended use. They can both be managed in the API Center that we covered in Section 16.2.6.

Further Resources

Further details, including details handbooks, can be found on the SAP Help Portal under the SAP SuccessFactors HCM Suite product page.

We'll now take a brief look at the OData API and the Employee Central Compound API.

16.6.1 OData API

The OData API is built on the Open Data Protocol (OData) version 2.0, a standardized protocol for creating and consuming data. It replaced the original proprietary SAP SuccessFactors SFAPI. Although OData is a standardized protocol, SAP SuccessFactors still has the ability to disable some operations. This is the case for deleting a user entity, for example.

This API is used in packaged integrations and can be used to build customer integrations on the middleware of your choice.

Further Resources

At the time of writing (fall 2019), the OData API supports a range of API entities across all modules of the SAP SuccessFactors HCM Suite. The list of available entities is fairly broad, and it is recommended to review the guide *SAP SuccessFactors HCM Suite OData API: Reference Guide* found on the SAP Help Portal under the SAP SuccessFactors HCM Suite product page to learn about what entities are available for you to use.

The OData API supports multiple operations that can be triggered through an HTTP call, including web services-based middleware application. The OData API supports the following operations:

- Create, query, or update data
- Select, order, filter, skip, top, format, or expand queries
- Create, update, or delete links between entities

Further Resources

For more details, there are three guides available on the SAP Help Portal under the SAP SuccessFactors HCM Suite product page:

- *SAP SuccessFactors HCM Suite OData API: Developer Guide*
- *SAP SuccessFactors HCM Suite OData API: Reference Guide*
- *SAP SuccessFactors Employee Central OData API: Reference Guide*

Now let's take a look at the Employee Central Compound API.

16.6.2 Employee Central Compound Employee API

The Employee Central Compound Employee API is a SOAP web services-based API provided to extract employee data from Employee Central. The focus of the API is to replicate data from Employee Central to SAP ERP, payroll, and benefits systems and, as such, fields designed for these types of replication scenarios are supported by the API. Because not all fields are supported, we recommend that you check that the API supports the required fields prior to implementing an integration that leverages the API.

This API is used in Employee Central employee master data integration to replicate employee data and assignments into SAP ERP and Employee Central Payroll.

At the time of writing (fall 2019), the Employee Central Compound Employee API supports the following data entities:

- Person information
- Person relationships
- Personal information
- Address information
- Phone information
- Email information
- Dependents
- National ID card

- Job information
- Job relationships
- Employment information
- Compensation information
- Recurring pay components
- Non-recurring pay components
- Payment information
- Alternative cost distribution
- Recurring deductions
- Non-recurring deductions
- Global assignments
- Emergency contact information
- Work permit information
- Income tax declaration

The API uses an SQL `SELECT` statement to extract data and support the `WHERE` clause. It does not support the `Order By` clause, nor does it support updating or deleting data because the API is designed only to extract data. The `FROM` clause is always `FROM CompoundEmployee`. Listing 16.1 shows an example statement to extract person information and job information for employees whose company is SAP and whose data was modified after 01/01/2000.

```
SELECT person, job_information
FROM CompoundEmployee
WHERE company='SAP'
AND last_modified_on > to_datetime ('2000-01-01','YYYY-MM-DD')
```

Listing 16.1 Sample SQL Code

16

Further Resources

For more details, there are two guides available on the SAP Help Portal:

- *Implementing the Employee Central Compound Employee API*
- *Implementing the Employee Central Compound Employee API in Delta Transmission Mode*

16.7 Other Integration Content

In addition to the standard integrations that have been and will be released, SAP has also released various other types of content for integrating the SAP SuccessFactors HCM Suite with SAP ERP (or vice versa) and other systems not covered by the aforementioned integrations or deployment models. We'll walk through this content in the following sections.

16.7.1 Cookbooks and How-To Guides

SAP has released various "cookbooks" and how-to guides to help customers and partners enable system-related integration, such as user experience or connecting multiple SAP ERP systems to SAP SuccessFactors. These cookbooks are essentially how-to documents on enabling this connectivity. These types of documents are released when human intervention is required more than a standard software solution. They can be found on the SAP Help Portal. SAP has released the following cookbooks and how-to guides to date:

- *Cookbook: Integration of Multiple SAP ERP HCM Systems with SuccessFactors BizX Suite* discusses various scenarios and the impact of those scenarios when you are integrating multiple instances of SAP ERP HCM, with one instance of SAP SuccessFactors. It covers SAP ERP HCM as both the source system and the target system.
- *How-To: Integrating Compensation Management Using Multiple Compensation Group IDs* provides the steps required to enable integration between Compensation and SAP ERP HCM when multiple compensation group IDs are used in Compensation.
- *How-To: Enhancing the Employee Integration with Custom Fields Using SAP Process Integration* provides the steps required to extend the employee data integration extraction reports for customer-specific fields in SAP SuccessFactors. It doesn't cover the steps to add fields in SAP SuccessFactors—only the steps for SAP Process Integration and SAP ERP HCM.
- *Integration of SuccessFactors Business Execution into SAP Enterprise Portal via Single Sign-On* out of maintenance guide providing information on the prerequisites for setting up SSO integration between the SAP Enterprise Portal and SAP SuccessFactors, as well as the steps to do the following:
  - Configure SAML2.0 in the SAP Enterprise Portal
  - Collect required information from SAP SuccessFactors
  - Configure SSO in SAP SuccessFactors
  - Create links within the SAP Enterprise Portal

16.7.2 Other Guides

SAP also provides the following guides on the SAP Help Portal under the SAP SuccessFactors HCM Suite product page:

- *HCM Suite Boomi Development Standards Guide*
- *SuccessFactors HCM Suite Boomi Connector Reference Guide*
- *SAP SuccessFactors HCM Suite SFAPI: Developer Guide*

16.7.3 SAP SuccessFactors Adapters

SAP SuccessFactors adapters have been released for SAP Process Integration and SAP Cloud Platform Integration. These adapters provide connectivity and configuration capabilities so that custom integrations can be built on these platforms. The following adapters are available on both middleware platforms:

- SuccessFactors REST (sender and receiver adapter)
- SuccessFactors SOAP (sender and receiver adapter)
- SuccessFactors OData V2 (receiver adapter)
- SuccessFactors OData V4 (receiver adapter)

Each adapter supports a number of operations, while the OData adapters also support features such as pagination and navigation.

Further Resources

Further details can be found in the following guides on SAP Help Portal:

- SAP Process Integration: *Designing Cloud Integration Content for SAP Process Integration 7.5 SP0*
- SAP Cloud Platform Integration: *SAP Cloud Platform Integration*

16.7.4 SAP Data Services Agent

If you use the SAP Data Services Agent to connect cloud and on-premise systems and you want to use it to integration SAP SuccessFactors with other systems, then you can take advantage of the SAP SuccessFactors adapter that is provided as part of the SAP Data Services Agent.

Further Resources

For more information, see the guide *Configuring the SAP Data Services Agent* on the SAP Help Portal.

16.7.5 SAP Data Services Adapter

A standard SAP SuccessFactors adapter is provided in SAP Data Services 4.1 SP 01 to enable you to view, import, and use SAP SuccessFactors data in SAP Data Services data flows. Potentially, data can also be transferred bidirectionally into the SAP SuccessFactors HCM Suite.

Further Resources

For more information, see the guide *Supplement for Adapters* on the SAP Help Portal under the SAP Data Services product page.

16.8 Summary

SAP is continuously making progress on its journey to deliver robust packaged integration content and technical capabilities. It has already laid out a detailed foundation of how to reach its goal, which is to ensure that customers have relevant, specific, and maintainable integration content. SAP has set its strategy and chosen to leverage SAP integration technology to provide bidirectional middleware integration between the SAP SuccessFactors HCM Suite, SAP ERP, and third-party systems.

Shortly after completing the acquisition of SuccessFactors, SAP delivered the first part of its packaged integration content and followed these up with cookbooks to facilitate additional integration scenarios, such as SSO, for the SAP Enterprise Portal. SAP has continued to deliver additional integration content to provide process integration for multiple talent management processes. SAP has also built a set of integrations for Employee Central to enable it to integrate with SAP ERP and other systems so that organizations can run end-to-end HR processes in the cloud and on-premise.

Having read this chapter, you should now be familiar with SAP's strategy, the integration technology and content that SAP offers, and how to configure and use this content for core HR and talent processes.

In the next chapter, we're going to look at administering the SAP SuccessFactors system. We'll cover some of the common administration activities, as well as those that are essential to keeping your system functioning and usable.

Chapter 17
Administration

Congratulations on implementing SAP SuccessFactors! Now that you are live, you will need to maintain the system. Common activities can be performed easily in the system and thus allow for painless ongoing administration.

SAP SuccessFactors—like any system—requires administration after implementation and go-live. The system is designed so that a business stakeholder, such as an HR business partner, can manage and maintain the system. It requires no special technical skill or programming ability. As the system landscape becomes slightly more complicated with integrations to SAP ERP Human Capital Management (SAP ERP HCM) and other systems, some customers are sharing administration responsibility between IT and human resources (HR) functions. There has been concerted effort over the last few years to put more control of the system in the hands of the customer via the Admin Center.

In this chapter, we will review some of the many administrative components of the SAP SuccessFactors HCM Suite that you will enable you to administer, update, and support the system. We'll go through a quick overview of general system configuration and administration before looking at various administrative activities, such as role-based permissions (RBPs) and management of users. From there we'll identify the best method for administering necessary authentication and password policies to keep the system secure, and then move on to modifying email notifications and managing picklists. Then, we'll discuss the topic of data administration, including data protection and privacy topics such as data purging, consent agreements, and more. We'll continue with a discussion of managing instances, managing various types of access, and managing documents, before wrapping things up with a look at your reporting options.

17.1 System Configuration and Administration

SAP SuccessFactors HCM is a configurable system that is flexible and scalable. Much of the system is configured via the Admin Center, although the initial setup of the system and some limited configurations still takes place in the Provisioning "backend" (shown in Figure 17.1). Customers do not have access to Provisioning. Customers need to understand which elements of the system they can administer and which will need additional support if something needs to be activated or configured in Provisioning. As of the time of writing (fall 2019), most configurations are done in the Admin Center.

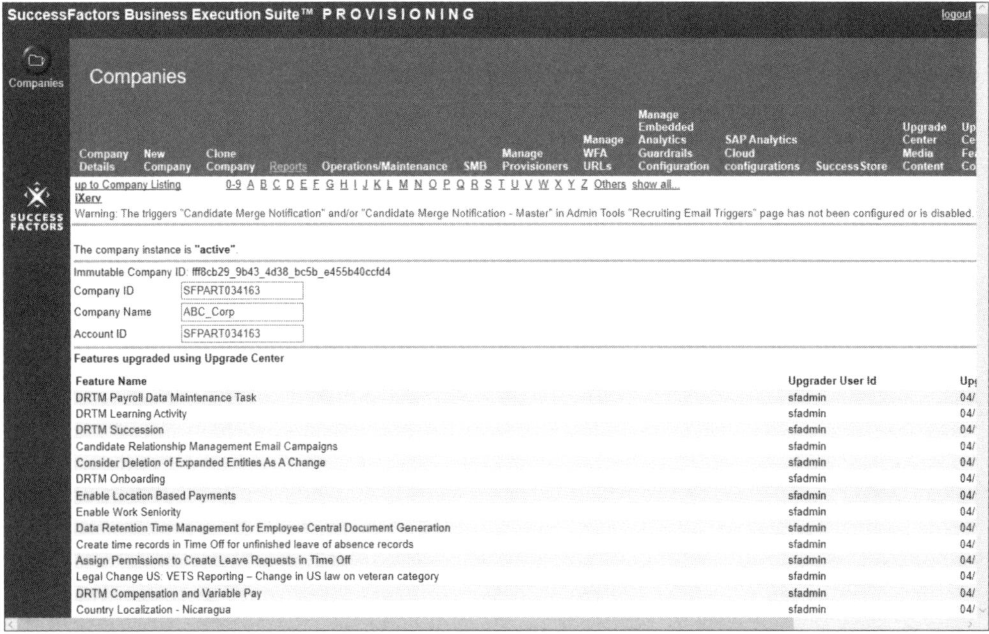

Figure 17.1 Company Settings Made in Provisioning

Some of the other features maintained in Provisioning include scheduled jobs that support data imports and exports and scheduled reports.

The Admin Center provides customers and consultants control over maintaining settings, data, custom objects, and the rules that govern their instance. The Admin Center is intuitive and organized into module-specific activities, such as Employee Central, Performance Management, Recruiting, Compensation, and others. Let's take a deeper look into this critical part of SAP SuccessFactors now.

17.2 Admin Center

Administrators within SAP SuccessFactors have access to a powerful administration center for performing all aspects of administration and management of the SAP SuccessFactors instance. The Admin Center—shown in Figure 17.2—provides administrators with a place to monitor the system through various tiles, access transactions to perform period checks or maintenance, and configure modules and their processes. It ranges from editing picklists to configuring email notification templates to setting a password policy—and more. The current version of the Admin Center is sometimes referred to as the "Next Gen Admin" by SAP.

The Admin Center is accessed by from the navigation menu. It can be made the default starting page in SAP SuccessFactors in the user options menu. Naturally, only users permissioned to access one or more transactions in the Admin Center get access to the page (and only get to see parts of the Admin Center page that they are permissioned to see).

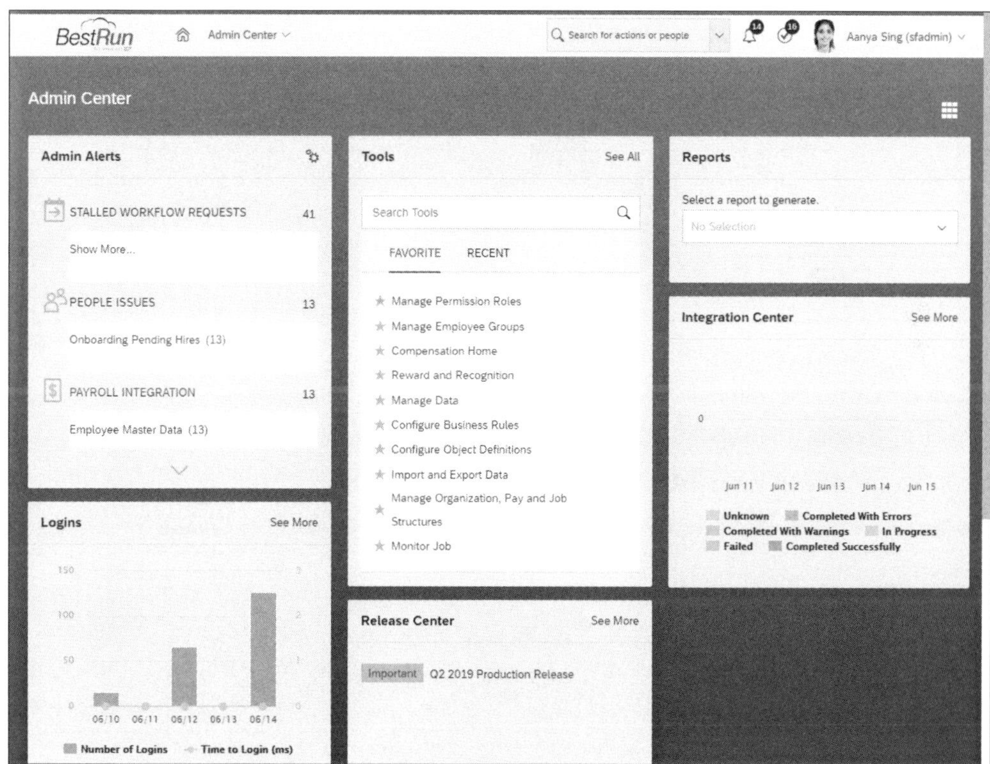

Figure 17.2 The Admin Center

Various tiles are provided in the Admin Center to help administrators monitor system activities and access transactions they need to perform administration tasks. These include:

- **Admin Alerts**
  Displays alerts for data for issues, such as:
  - HR data (e.g., invalid foundation objects on employee records)
  - Stalled workflow requests
  - People data (e.g., onboarding hire issues)
  - Payroll integration
- **Data Subject Information**
  Displays how many data privacy/General Data Protection Regulations (GDPR) reports are ready for download, processing, or have failed. You can also navigate to the **Data Subject Information** page from here (see Section 17.10).
- **Integration Center**
  Displays the status of integrations run in the Integration Center over the previous few days; additional detail can be accessed by clicking **See More**.
- **Intelligent Services Center (ISC)**
  Displays the top-three events published by the Intelligent Service Center.
- **Latest Check Tool Results**
  Displays the latest result of the check tool; additional detail can be accessed by clicking **See More**.
- **Logins**
  Displays a chart of the number of logins and time to login over the previous few days; additional detail can be accessed by clicking **See More**.
- **Looking for help?**
  Displays links to useful websites—like the SAP SuccessFactors Community and the SAP Help Portal—and search capabilities to find resources across the various SAP SuccessFactors websites.
- **Page Views**
  Displays a chart of the number of page views and the averaging loading time of pages; additional detail can be accessed by clicking **See More** (shown in Figure 17.3).
- **Reports**
  Quickly generate a report from a drop-down list of ad hoc reports.

- **Release Center**
  Lists details of the latest release; the Release Center can be accessed by clicking **See More**.
- **Schedule Jobs**
  Displays a chart of how many scheduled jobs were successful and how many failed.
- **Tools**
  Provides access to the vast range of transactions needed to maintain, configure, and monitor the system; also displays favorite and recently accessed transactions.

The tiles that are displayed in the Admin Center can be enabled or hidden by clicking the tile icon in the top-right corner of the Admin Center (nine small squares).

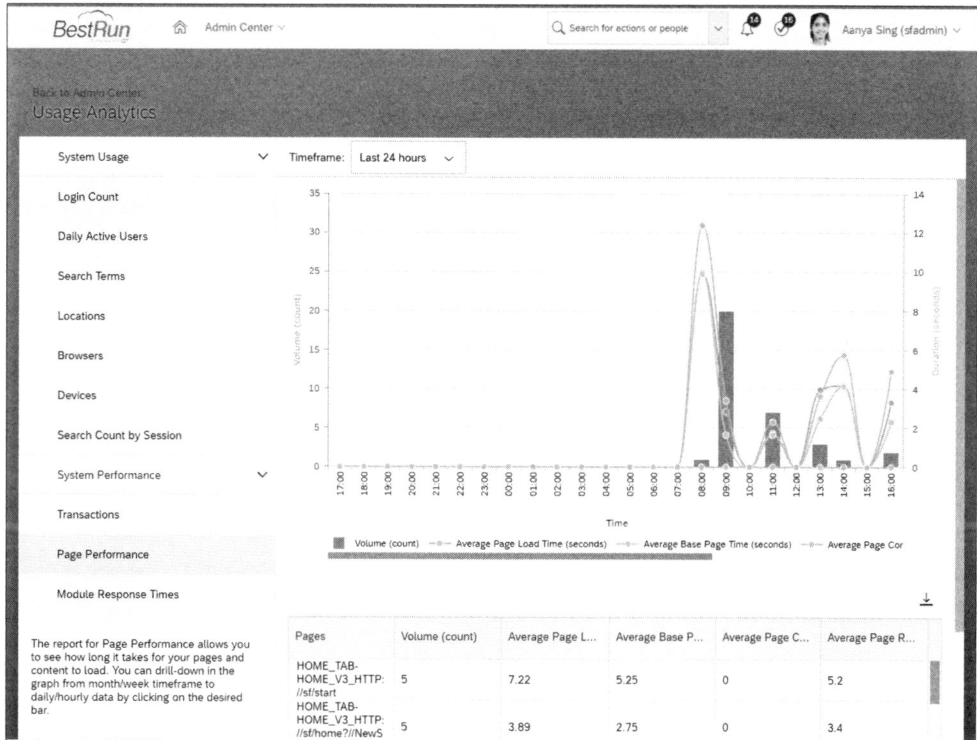

Figure 17.3 Usage Analytics Page

You can find any transaction in the Admin Center in a number of ways:

- Navigating through a list of all supporting transactions by clicking **See All** in the **Tools** tile (as shown in Figure 17.4)

- Using the search in the **Tools** tile
- Using the **Action Search** (this can be used from any part of SAP SuccessFactors)

You can mark regularly used transactions as a favorite so that they can be quickly accessed in the **Favorite** list in the **Tools** tile, illustrated in Figure 17.4.

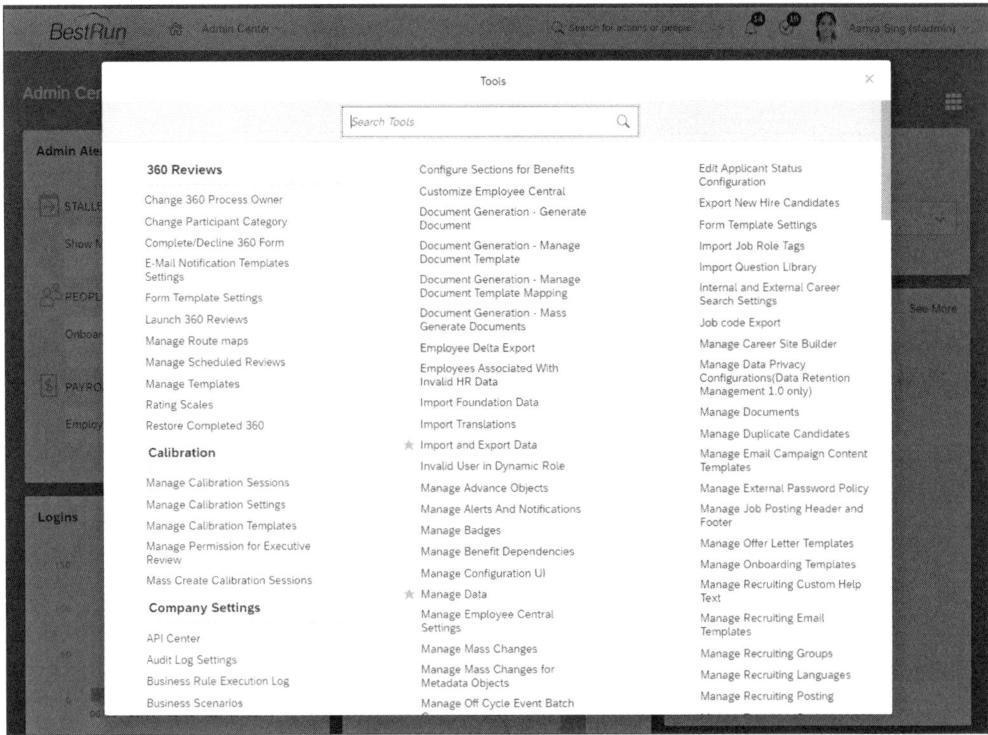

Figure 17.4 List of All Administration Transactions Available in the Admin Center

As with all parts of SAP SuccessFactors HCM Suite, the Admin Center features can be permissioned. Administrative roles can be created and managed in RBPs to segment access to the Admin Center. For instance, it is common for a recruiter to have a role that provides access to the Recruiting administrative features but restricts access to the rest of the Admin Center. In Figure 17.5, you can see how the Admin Center can differ for a user who has a small set of permissions versus the administrator's view that we saw in Figure 17.2.

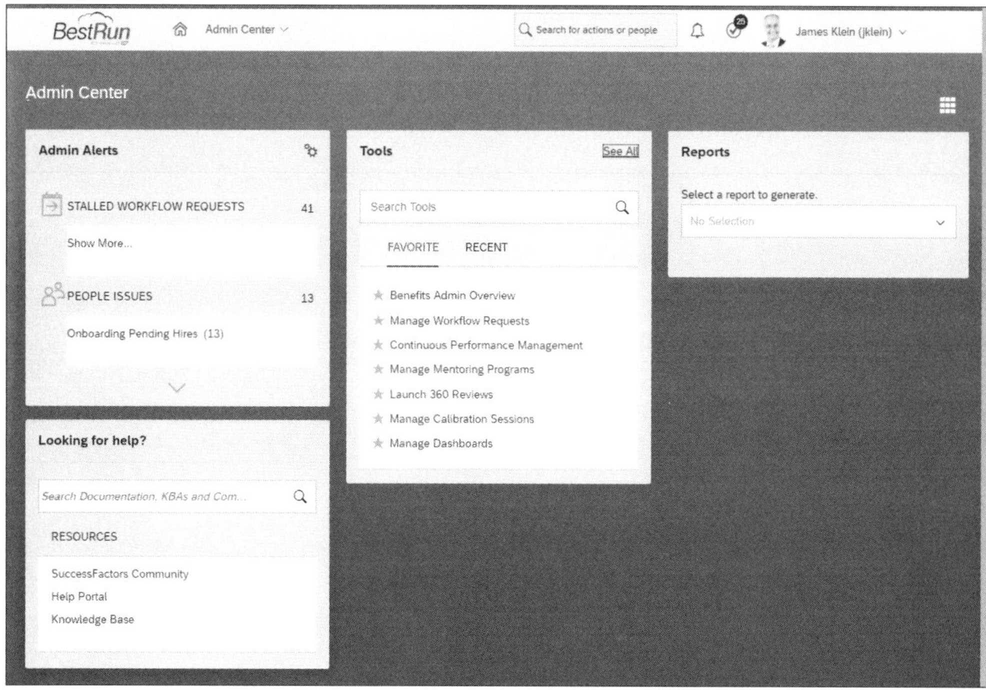

Figure 17.5 View of the Admin Center by a User with Limited Permissions

Now that we've looked at the basics of using the Admin Center for system administration and configuration, we can take the first look at performing an activity. One of the most important of these activities is user management.

17.3 Upgrade Center

The Upgrade Center allows customers to apply enhancements from quarterly release to their instances without having to log a customer support ticket or engaging an implementation partner. Most enhancements are available via the Upgrade Center, although in some occasions some enhancements need the support of an implementation partner. The Upgrade Center categorizes upgrades as follows:

- **Important Upgrades**
- **Recommended Upgrades**
- **Optional Upgrades**

Each upgrade has a detailed description of the upgraded feature, what to expect once the upgrade is applied, and other supporting information, as applicable. The Upgrade Center, shown in Figure 17.6, is accessed via the action search or by selecting **See More** in the **Release Center** tile in the **Admin Center** and then selecting **Upgrade Center**.

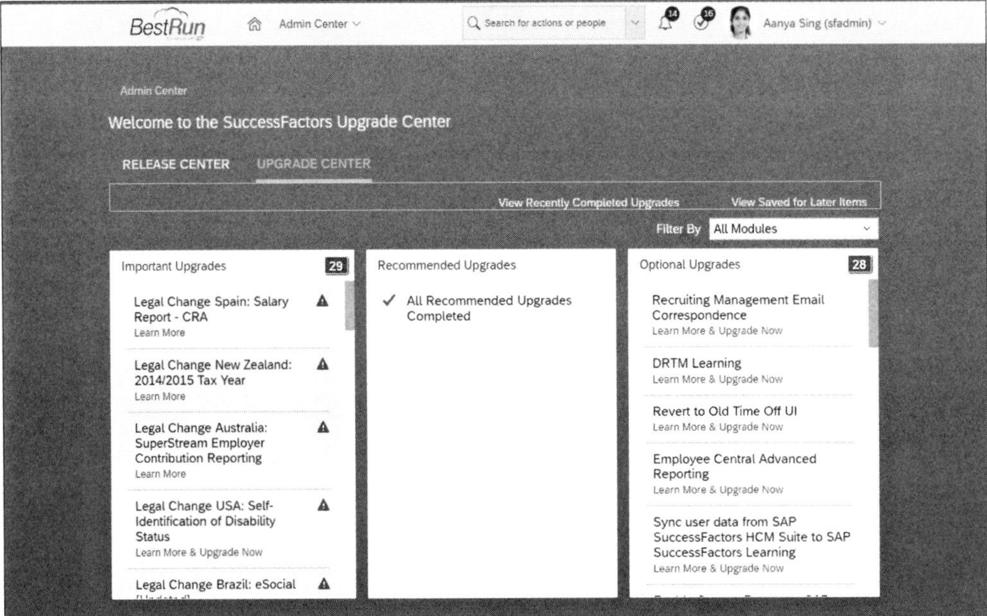

Figure 17.6 Upgrade Center

Within the Upgrade Center, the screen is split into three columns that represent each of the categories that we mentioned in the list above. The available updates for each category are displayed in each column, and they can be filtered by application.

Details of any update can be viewed by selecting the **Learn More & Upgrade Now** link found under the name of the update. For future-dated or upcoming changes, the link is called **Learn More**. Here, a description of the update is provided, along with important notes and any RBP requirements needed to run the upgrade. Figure 17.7 shows an update in the Upgrade Center.

To apply an update, select the **Upgrade Now** button at the bottom of the screen. You are then prompted to confirm that you want the update to be made. Once it is confirmed, the update is applied to the system. This needs to be done separately in the test and production systems.

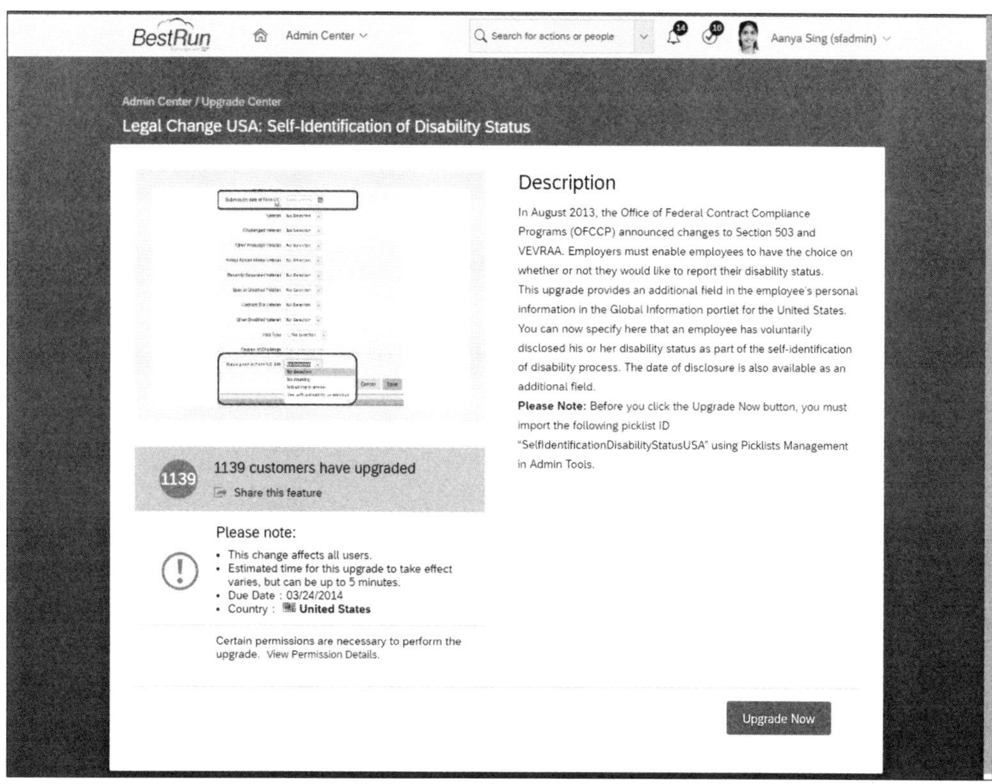

Figure 17.7 An Upgrade for Self-Identification of Disability Status in the United States

17.4 Release Center

The Release Center, shown in Figure 17.8, provides a description of each new feature in each release. You are shown the list of features from the latest release by default, but you can select a different release to view the features in that release.

You can view each feature that is part of a quarterly release by type (**Universal Features**, **Optional Features**, or **All**); you can also filter them by module. For each feature, you have the option to navigate to the SAP SuccessFactors Community or to the SAP Help Portal for additional information and documentation. You can also navigate to the Upgrade Center from the Release Center so that you can view further details of a feature and—if desired—enable that feature.

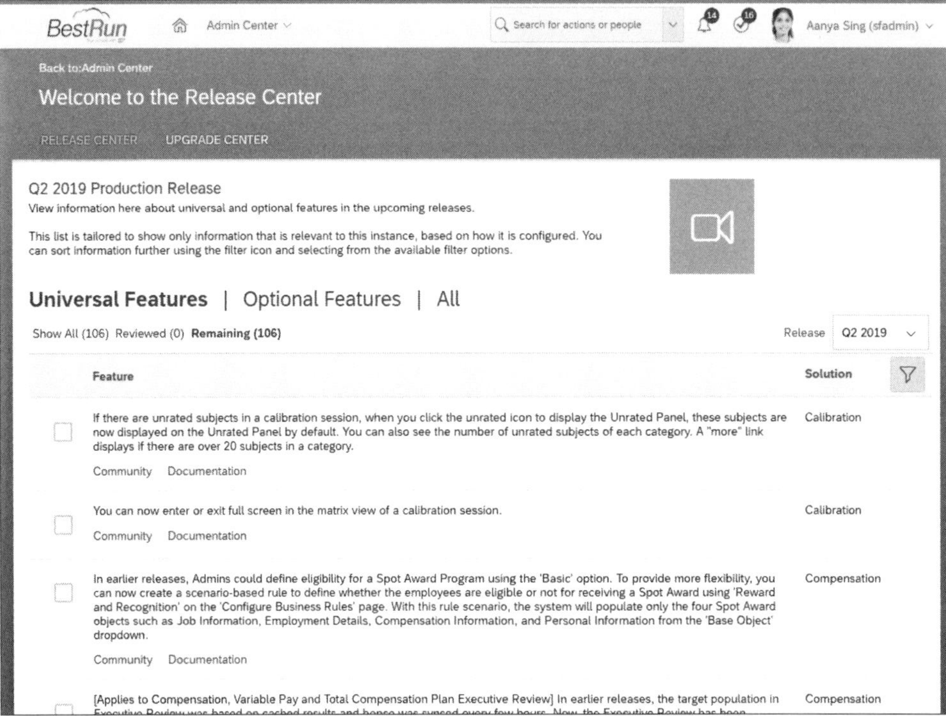

Figure 17.8 The Release Center

17.5 Role-Based Permissions

The RBP framework in SAP SuccessFactors is designed to provide robust control of access to features, processes, actions, administration, and data in the system. The RBP framework is focused on assigning roles to groups of users that are identified based on various available criteria. The target groups of users that the assigned roles will be effective on can be defined with the same granularity. Because a user can be assigned multiple roles, it makes administration of RBPs simpler. We will cover this in more detail in the following sections.

17.5.1 Configuration and Audits

The RBP framework is configured in the **Set User Permissions** menu in the **Manage Employees** section of the Admin Center. In addition, permissions can be checked for users in this menu. The following menu options are available:

- **Manage Permission Groups**: Create, edit, copy, delete, view summary of, and view change history of permission groups
- **Manage Permission Roles**: Create, edit, copy, delete, view summary of, and view change history of permission roles
- **Security Permission Reports**: View the Proxy Management report
- **View User Permission**: View permissions assigned to a user

We will cover some of these options as we look deeper into the RBP framework.

17.5.2 How the RBP Framework Works

The core authorization concepts of the RBP framework are built primarily upon three elements:

- *Permission roles:* Group of permissions
- *Granted users*: Users who are assigned a permission role
- *Target population*: Employee population on which the permissions in the permission role are applied

Practically, these work together as such: granted users are assigned a permission role that is effective on the target population.

We'll look at each of these three components of the RBP framework in the remainder of this section. However, we'll first take a look at *permission groups* because they are a key component of the RBP framework that supports these aforementioned concepts.

17.5.3 Permission Groups

Permission groups are simply groups of either granted users or target employees. In some instances—depending on the design—the same group can be used for both.

Permission Group Membership

Many different criteria are available to identify the members of each permission group. By default, these are the fields from the user data file (UDF), although Employee Central fields can be added to this list. The default list contains fields such as **Country, Department, Division, Hire Date, Job Code, Job Title, Location**, and **Username**.

Within a permission group, one or more *people pools* can be created. One or more criteria can be used within each people pool, and so combinations can be used to narrow down groups of employees. For example, a permission group criterion could be created with a **People Pool** to select employees with a **Job Code** of **Manager** and a **Location** of **Chicago**, and another **People Pool** to select employees with a **Location** of **Boston.** Figure 17.9 shows a **Permission Group** and how this example would look.

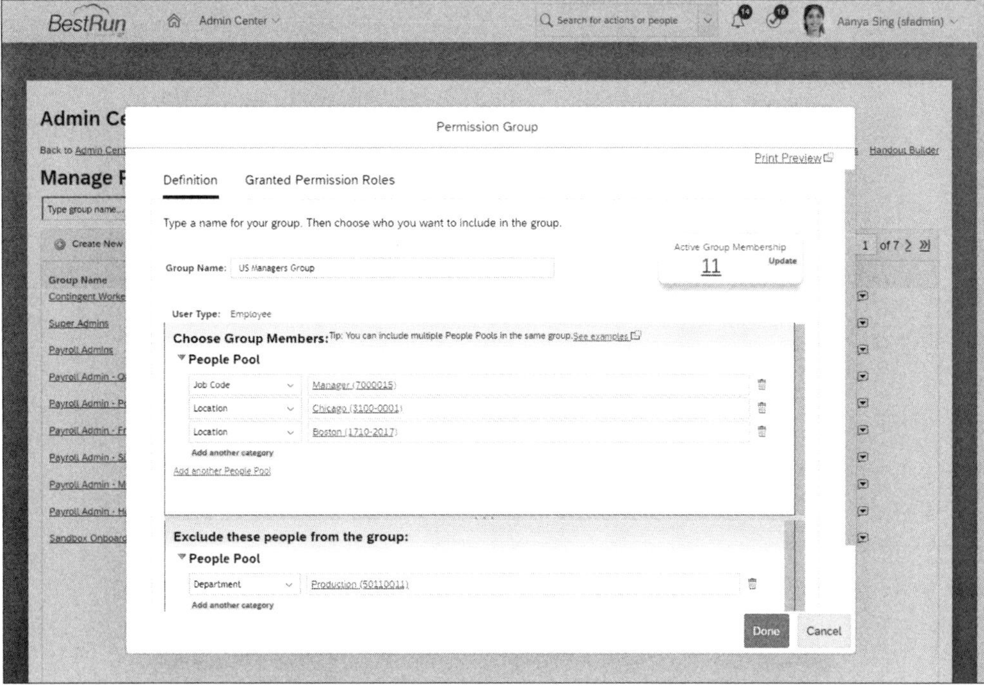

Figure 17.9 An Example of a Permission Group

In addition to identifying members to include in a permission group, the same criteria can be used to exclude members from a permission group. In Figure 17.9, the **Production** department has been excluded.

Creating Permission Groups

Permission groups are created in **Manage Permission Groups**. In the **Manage Permission Groups** screen, click the **Create New** button to create a new permission group. The **Permission Group** window opens, and it looks similar to Figure 17.9. The **Permission Group** window is split into two tabs: **Definition** and **Granted Permission Roles**.

The **Definition** tab is where the permission group name and people pools for included and excluded members can be defined, as mentioned previously. The **Active Group Membership** box displays the number of members in the permission group, which can be seen in the upper-right corner in Figure 17.9. Clicking the number shows a list of the members in the permission group. The **Update** button can be used to update this figure in real time.

The **Granted Permission Roles** tab displays which permission roles this permission group has been assigned to.

17.5.4 Granted Users

As mentioned in Section 17.5.2, granted users are a group of users who are assigned a permission role for the target population of employees. We'll cover this process in Section 17.5.6. Granted users are assigned directly to a permission role with one of the following options:

- **Permission Group**: Granted users are selected from a permission group.
- **Managers**: Granted users are all employees who have direct reports.
- **HR Managers**: Granted users are all employees assigned as an HR manager to one or more employees.
- **Matrix Managers**: Granted users are all employees assigned as a matrix manager to one or more employees.
- **Custom Managers**: Granted users are all employees assigned as a custom manager to one or more employees.
- **Second Managers**: Granted users are all employees assigned as a second manager to one or more employees.
- **Calibration Facilitators**: Granted users are those who facilitate calibration sessions in the Calibration module.
- **Home Managers**: Granted users are all employees who have direct reports and are out on global assignment elsewhere in the organization.
- **Home HR Managers**: Granted users are all employees who are assigned as an HR manager to one or more employees out on global assignment elsewhere in the organization.
- **Host Managers**: Granted users are all employees who have direct reports and are on global assignment in their team.

- **Host HR Managers**: Granted users are all employees who are assigned as an HR manager to one or more employees who are on global assignment in their area of responsibility.
- **Everyone (All Employees)**: All employees are selected as the granted users.

All options—except **Permission Group** and **Everyone (All Employees)**—can be filtered with one or more permission groups. Depending on the option selected, the available options for the target population vary. These options will be covered in the next section.

Note

The **Calibration Facilitators** role displays only if the calibration application is enabled. The four global assignment options display only if the global assignment functionality is enabled in Employee Central.

17.5.5 Target Population

The target population are those employees who can be accessed by the granted users. The options depend on which **Granted User** option is selected, and we'll walk through them in this section.

Permission Group or Everyone

If the option selected for the granted users is either **Permission Group** or **Everyone**, the target population options are as follows:

- **Everyone**: All employees are the target population.
- **Granted User's Department**: All employees in the granted user's department are the target population.
- **Granted User's Division**: All employees in the granted user's division are the target population.
- **Granted User's Location**: All employees in the granted user's location are the target population.
- **Granted User (Self)**: The granted user themselves is the target population.

Figure 17.10 shows the granting of granted users to a target population for a permission role using permission groups.

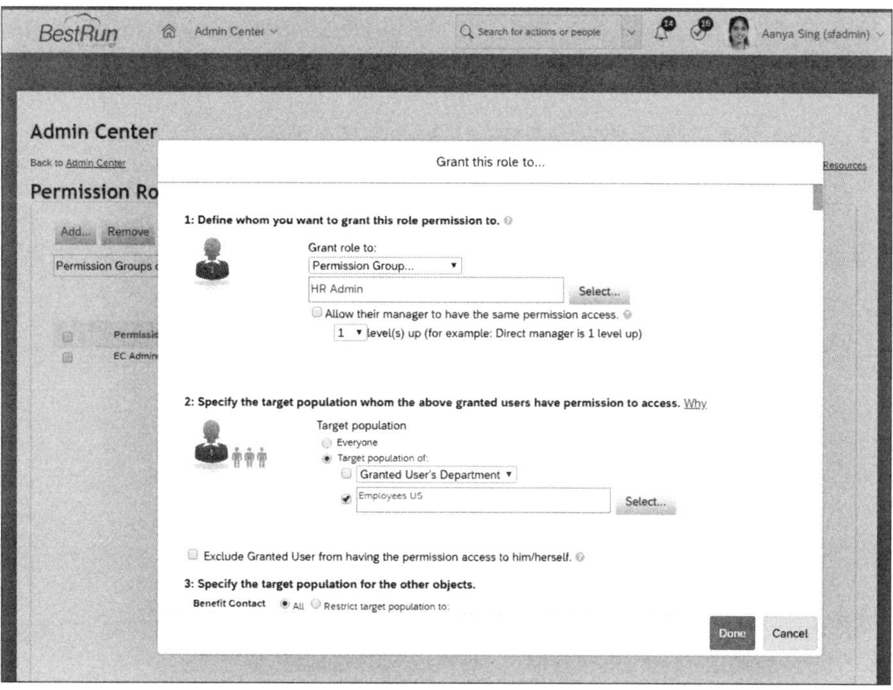

Figure 17.10 Granting Permission with Permission Groups

Managers

If the option selected for the granted users is any type of manager (e.g., manager, HR manager, home HR manager, and so on), the target population options are as follows:

- **Granted User's Direct Reports**: All of the granted user's direct reports are the target population.
- **Granted User's Direct Reports in a Specific Permission Group**: All of the granted user's direct reports in a specific permission group are the target population.

For all manager roles, with the exception of the global assignment manager roles, the number of levels of indirect reports can be selected. The options are one level down, two levels down, three levels down, or all levels down. The user can also have the permissions applied to themselves in this population with the option **Include access to Granted User (Self)**. Managers can be further filtered with one or more permission groups.

Figure 17.11 shows the granting of granted users to a target population for a permission role for managers. In this example, only managers in the permission group **HR Group** are granted the role for the manager's direct reports and one level of indirect reports.

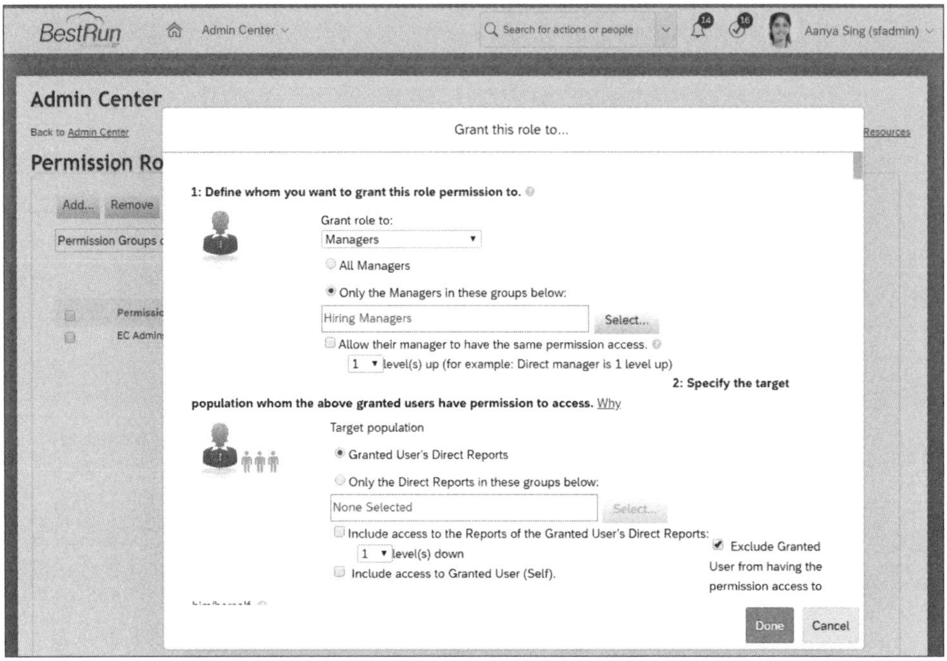

Figure 17.11 Granting Permission for Managers

Calibration Facilitator

When the **Calibration Facilitator** option is selected for the granted users, the target population is automatically set to **Granted Calibration Subjects**.

17.5.6 Permission Roles

Permission roles are simply the collection of permissions that are assigned to granted users. They are created in **Manage Permission Roles**. A role has two parts to its definition: the selected permissions and the granting of the role to granted users for a target population. A permission role can be granted multiple times to different granted users and target populations.

Permissions

Permissions are split into two categories: *user permissions* and *administrator permissions*. User permissions cover all of the permissions that allow a user to access functionality or create, edit, and/or delete data. Administrator permissions provide administrators the ability to access administrative functions and allow integration users to query and update data via application programming interfaces (APIs). Within each of these categories are a number of subcategories that cover application-specific or system-specific functionality and data fields, such as career development planning or succession planners. Permissions can have three types of settings, depending on what the effect is:

- Non-effective-dated fields: **View** and **Edit**
- Employee Central effective-dated fields: **View Current**, **View History**, **Edit/Insert**, **Correct**, and **Delete**
- Functionality/settings: On or off

> **Note**
>
> Module page permissions for Performance Management, Goal Management, Compensation, and Development are controlled at the form level.

Permissions for non-effective-dated data found in Employee Central and the Employee Profile are shown in Figure 17.12. You can control the settings by selecting the various checkboxes.

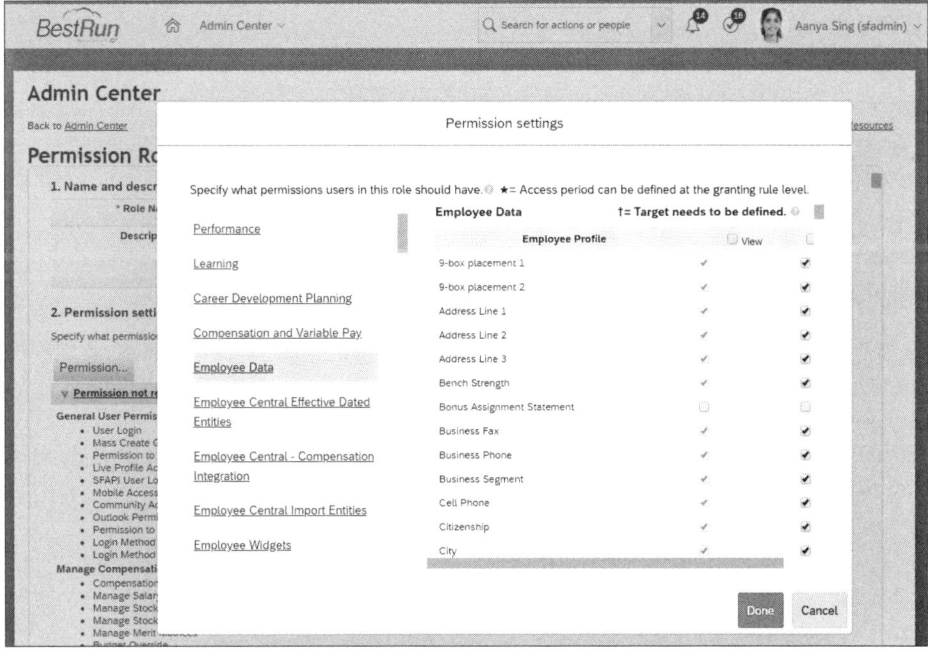

Figure 17.12 Employee Data Non-Effective-Dated Field Permissions

Figure 17.13 shows the Employee Central effective-dated fields permissions.

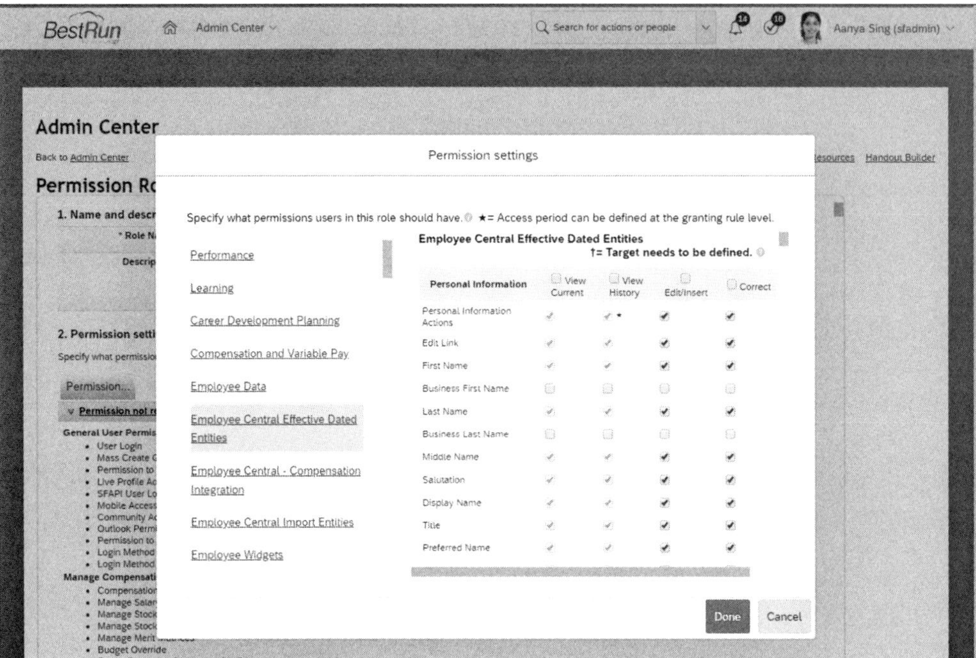

Figure 17.13 Employee Central Effective-Dated Field Permissions

More often than not, only HR or system administrators are given **Correct** or **Delete** permissions.

The permissions for enabling functionality or settings are, for the most part, a simple checkbox. Some of these permissions may require a target population to be defined, which is indicated with a † next to the permission.

Generic object permissions, usually categorized under **Miscellaneous Permissions**, work in a similar way. Typically, they have multiple options per object (such as **View** or **Edit**), which depend on whether the generic object is effective-dated or not. In addition, individual field-level overrides are possible for each generic object field (see Figure 17.14).

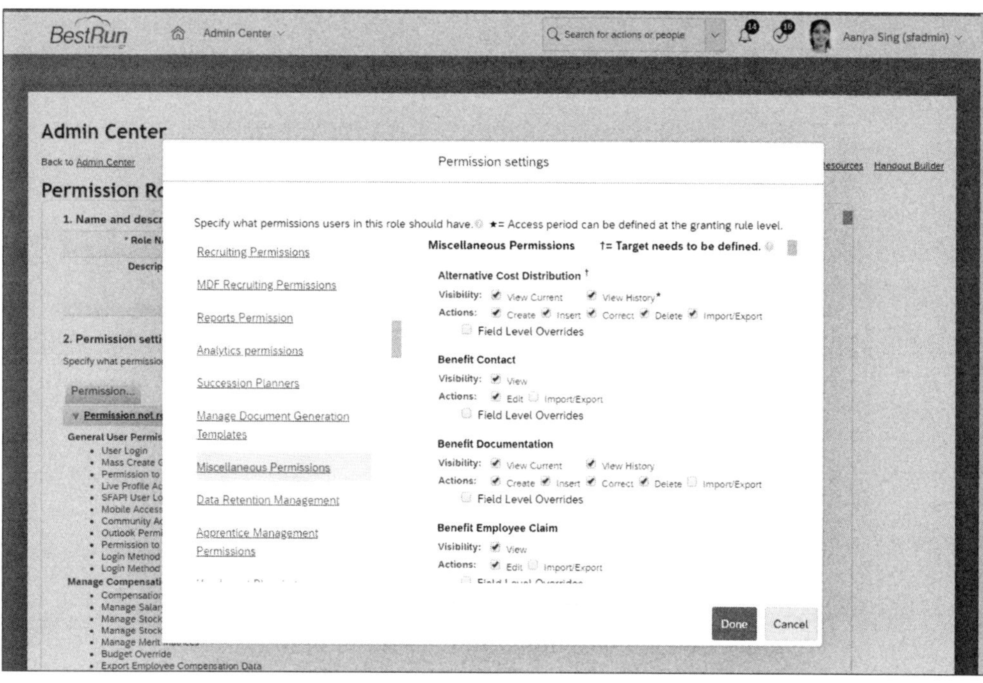

Figure 17.14 Generic Object/Miscellaneous Permissions

Assigning Permission Roles

You can assign permission roles—called *granting*—to granted users for target populations once a permission role is configured and can be modified as required. Without granting, a permission role remains inactive in the system. Figure 17.15 shows a summary of the granting of a permission role, as seen at the bottom of the screen when configuring a permission role.

A user can be granted multiple permission roles as part of one or more permission groups or managers. When this happens and a user is granted the same permission with different rights (e.g., **View** and **Edit** access for the same field), the user receives the most powerful permission.

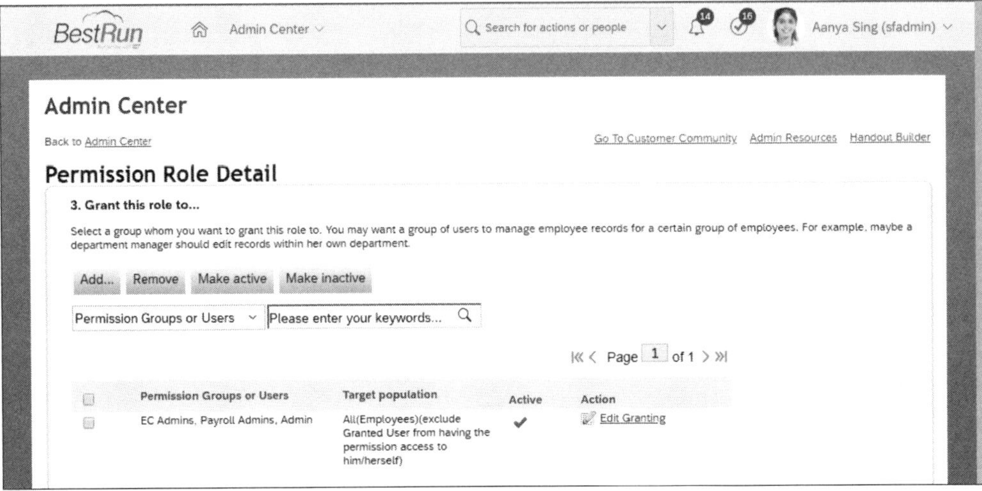

Figure 17.15 Summary of Granting of a Permission Role

Delegation

When using Employee Central, permission roles can be assigned to up to two delegates of a user. Delegates are defined in the user's **Job Relationships** block on the People Profile. The delegates will have access to the direct and indirect reports of the user and can perform tasks that have been permissioned to them.

17.5.7 Reporting and Audit

Four ad hoc reports are available in the system for reporting on RBPs:

- *RBP User to Role Report*: Displays users assigned to each permission role
- *RBP Permission to User Report*: Displays permissions assigned to each user
- *RBP User to Group Report*: Displays users assigned to each permission group
- *RBP Permission Roles Report*: Displays details about each permission role

These reports can be run in the Report Center by creating a new table report and selecting one of the four options provided to create a report.

In Figure 17.16, a preview of an RBP **User to Role report** ad hoc report that was generated by a user is displayed.

In addition to the ad hoc reports, an administrator can view the permissions assigned to any user in **View User Permission**. This displays each of the permissions and from which permission roles these have been assigned. Figure 17.17 shows the report.

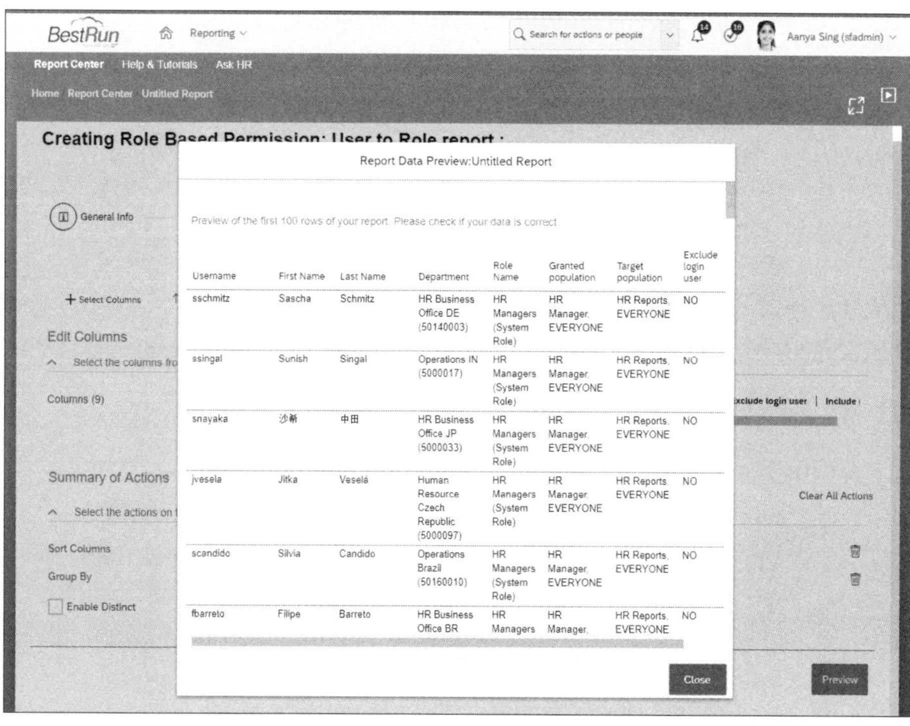

Figure 17.16 A Preview of the RBP User to Role Report

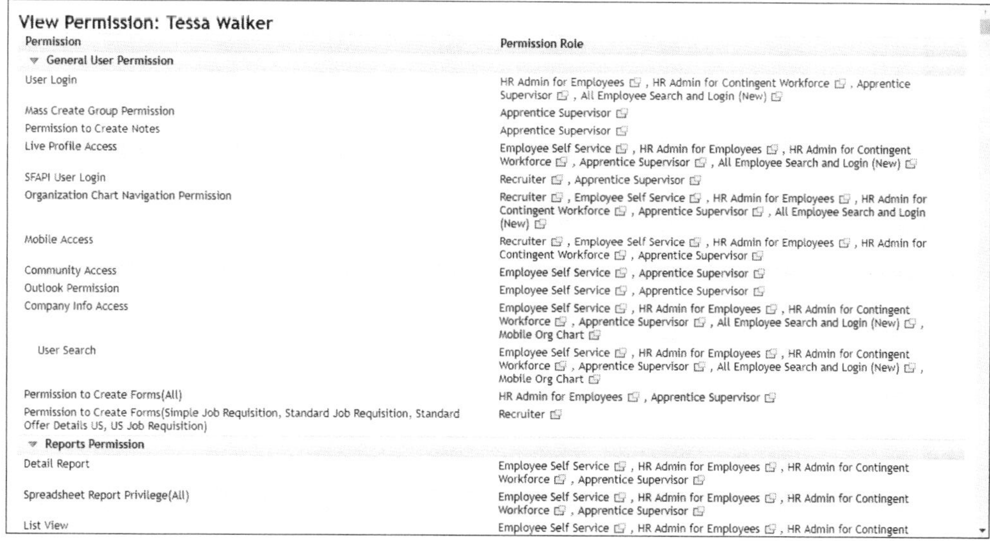

Figure 17.17 The View User Permission Window

17.5.8 Copying RBP Configuration between Instances

RBP configuration can be copied one from instance to another using the Instance Synchronization tool. We cover the Instance Synchronization tool in Section 17.11.1.

This Instance Synchronization tool allows synchronization of permission groups and permission roles between difference instances in your landscape and is used for cutting over to other instances (e.g., cutover to production) during an implementation or to keep a test system synchronized with a production system. An option to perform a dry run is available to test whether the process would work.

There are a couple of things to know about synchronizing permission groups:

- The user who created the permission group in the source instance must also be a user in the target instance for the synchronization to be successful.
- If a permission group already exists in the target instance then you are able to choose to overwrite it or not overwrite it; not overwriting the permission group will result in the permission group not being synchronized.

Likewise, there are a few things to know about synchronizing permission roles:

- Before you can synchronize a permission role, you must first synchronize all permission groups attached to the permission role.
- Any data configured in the permission role (e.g., fields, templates, etc.) must exist in the target instance.

Now we've looked at the RBP framework, we'll now look at managing users in the system.

17.6 User Management

The Admin Center provides several features to administer and maintain users in the system. From importing data, resetting user passwords, and unlocking accounts to managing the proxy feature, administrators have a wide range of control over the users and related data in the system. Some of these features may not be accessible if a customer has an integration with SAP ERP HCM for user data.

17.6.1 Updating User Data

When a customer uses Employee Central, employee and user data is maintained in that system. However, if you don't have Employee Central and you aren't replicating user data into the system, then you can use **Manage Users** to manage users in the system (such as add, edit, or make users inactive), as shown in Figure 17.18, or you can import user data. You have the option to export user data, which can be used to modify existing users.

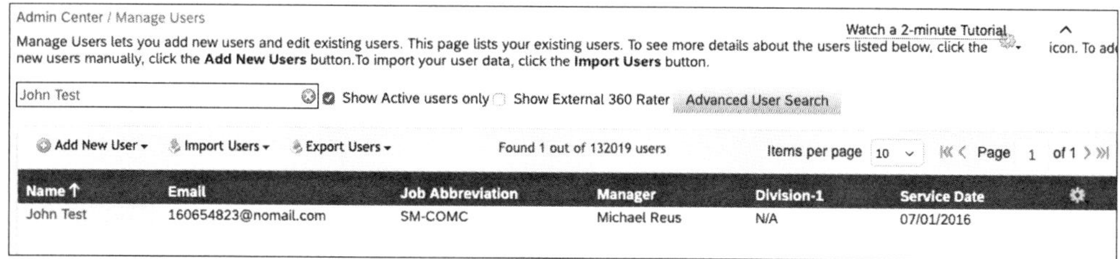

Figure 17.18 Manage Users

User data is imported using **Import Employee Data**. This allows an administrator to download templates and upload a CSV file containing all of the users, user names, roles, and hierarchy. Figure 17.19 shows the **Import Employee Data** screen and some of the useful options that administrators can use to populate users in the system. This transaction is also used to load Employee Central data.

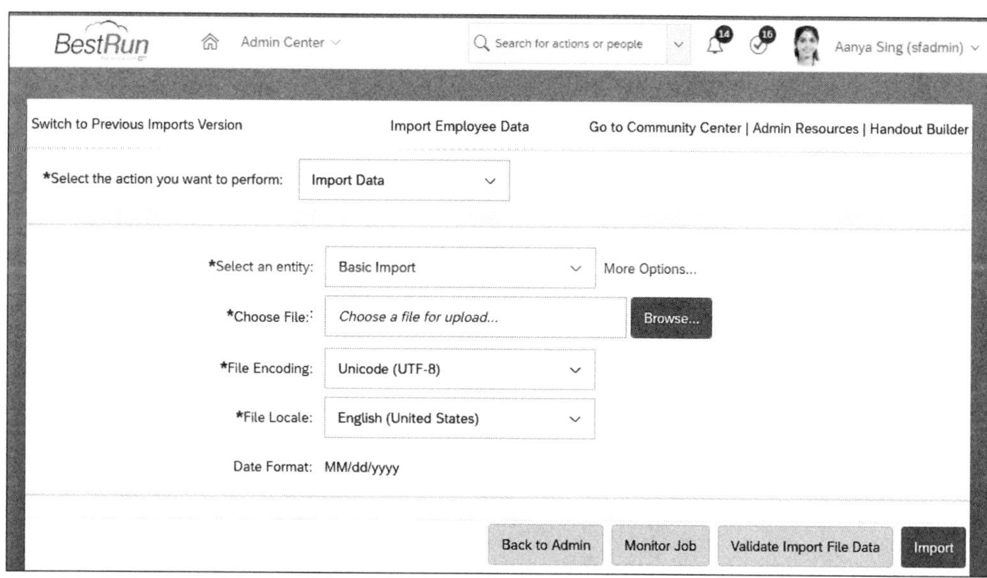

Figure 17.19 Import Employee Data

17.6.2 Proxy Management

Administrators can manage *proxy users*. Proxy users enable users to act as delegates for other users—for example, to access another user's data and functions. This can be useful when a user is on vacation or they are on extended absence.

This, of course, needs to be carefully maintained because the proxy user can view sensitive data that belongs to employees outside of their normal span of access. However, this functionality can be useful for troubleshooting issues for users or testing new features. You can select a setting that allows users to nominate their own proxies, but most companies keep this powerful feature centralized for control and privacy of performance and compensation-related data (see Figure 17.20).

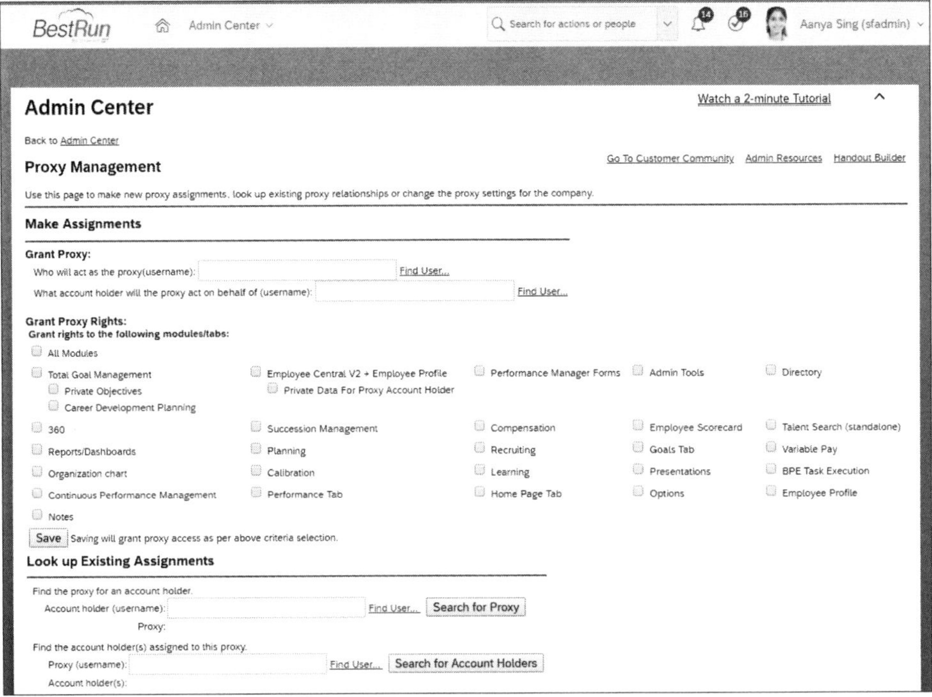

Figure 17.20 Proxy Management Screen

17.7 Password Management

Managing the password policy and administering user password management will become an inevitable part of your system administration activities. In this section, we'll take a look at managing your password policy and user passwords.

17.7.1 Password Policy Management

Your corporate password and login policies can be configured in **Password & Login Policy Settings**, illustrated in Figure 17.21.

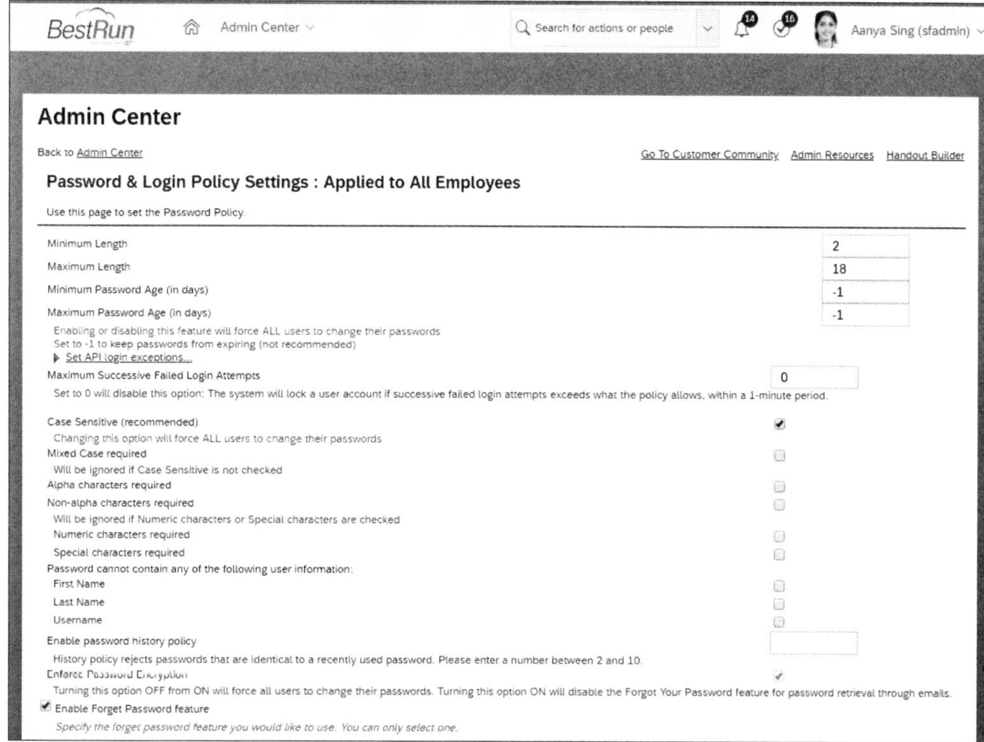

Figure 17.21 Password and Login Policy Setting Screen

Here, you can set minimum and maximum length and age of passwords, as well as enable case sensitivity and settings related to users' forgetting and resetting their own passwords.

17.7.2 Managing User Passwords

Administrators have a few options available to them to manage user accounts and passwords, based on the password policy setup (as we discussed in the previous section).

Administrators can unlock accounts of users who have attempted too many failed password attempts in **Reset User Account**. For customers that use single sign-on (SSO), this feature is not used.

Along the same lines with user administration, administrators need to be able to set new passwords, reset passwords, and set password rules for users. This is done in **Resetting User Passwords**, which is shown in Figure 17.22. All users, not just administrators, can set and reset passwords.

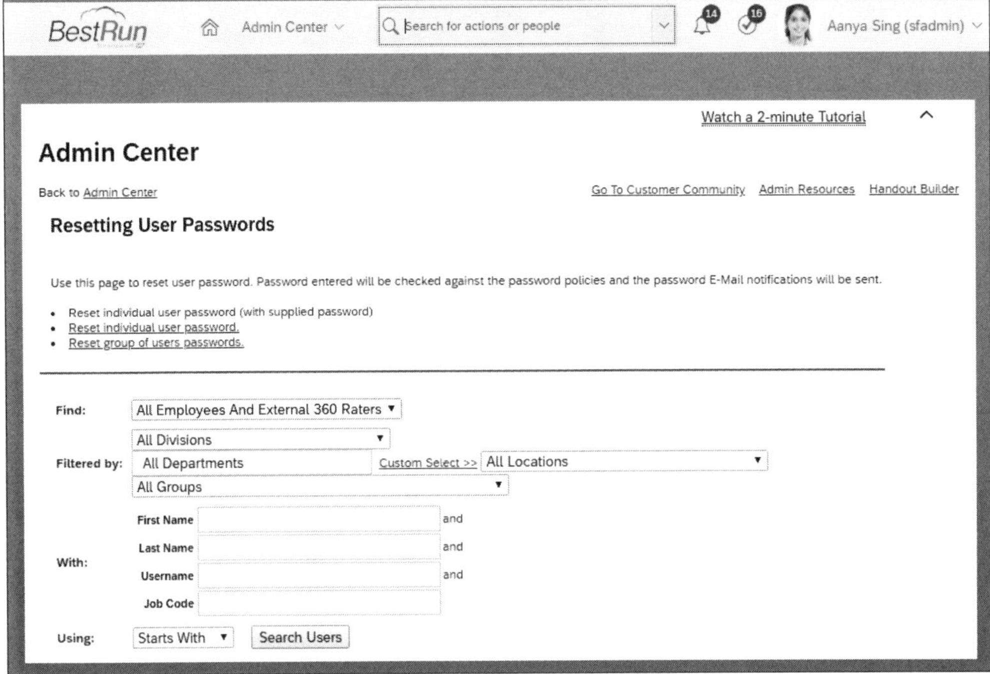

Figure 17.22 Reset User Passwords Screen

17.8 Email Notifications

Beyond general user management and maintenance, another important function that is used by all applications within SAP SuccessFactors is *email notifications*. Notifications are a powerful way to communicate system information to users. There are email templates provided with the application that can be enabled and disabled as appropriate with sample subject lines and text that can be modified by customers to suit their needs. These email notifications range from functions such as routing notifications that are sent each time a form is routed to a new user, when a goal has been created or deleted, to external recruiting candidates forgetting their password. Figure 17.23 shows a sample list of the system-wide **E-Mail Notification Templates** that can be activated and customized. There are also additional ad hoc email templates and triggers that can be defined within the Recruiting Management module, but those sit within the Recruiting administration area.

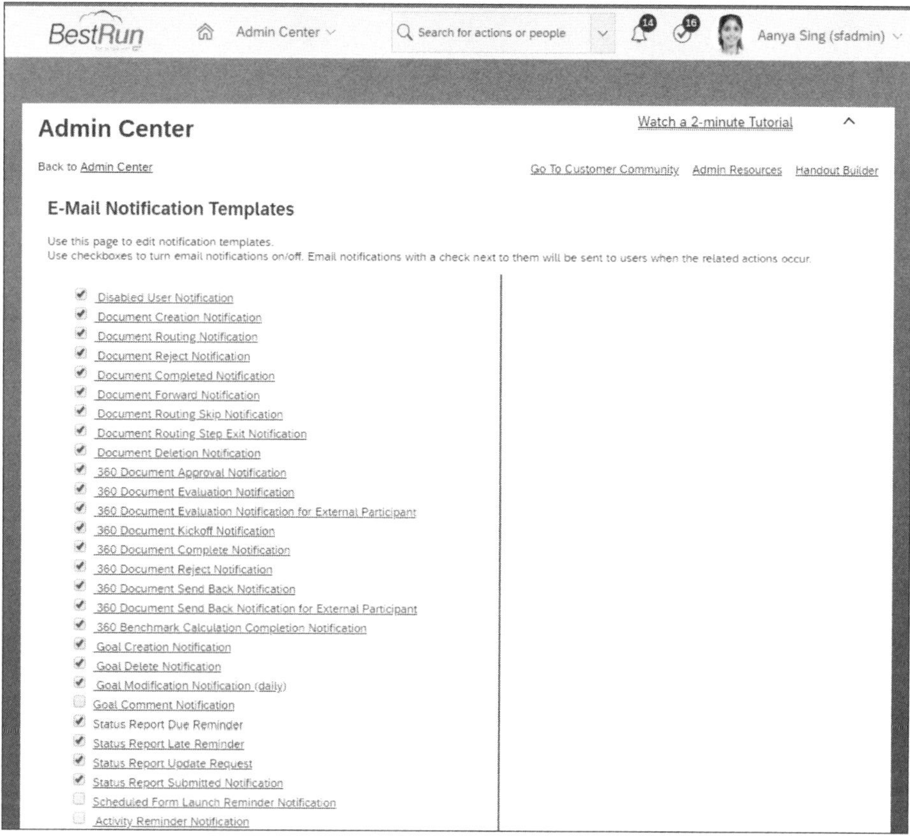

Figure 17.23 Email Notification Templates and the Option to Enable or Disable Them

After you activate email notifications, the actual notification can be customized to change the text on the screen or add a logo. Each application has its own notifications that can be customized. Figure 17.24 shows the notification customization.

Email notification templates use tags to enable context-specific data to be inserted into an email, such as the first name or job code of the subject of the workflow.

Further Resources

You can find an up-to-date list of available variable codes in the guide *Employee Central Workflows: Implementation and Administration* found on the SAP Help Portal under the SAP SuccessFactors Employee Central product page.

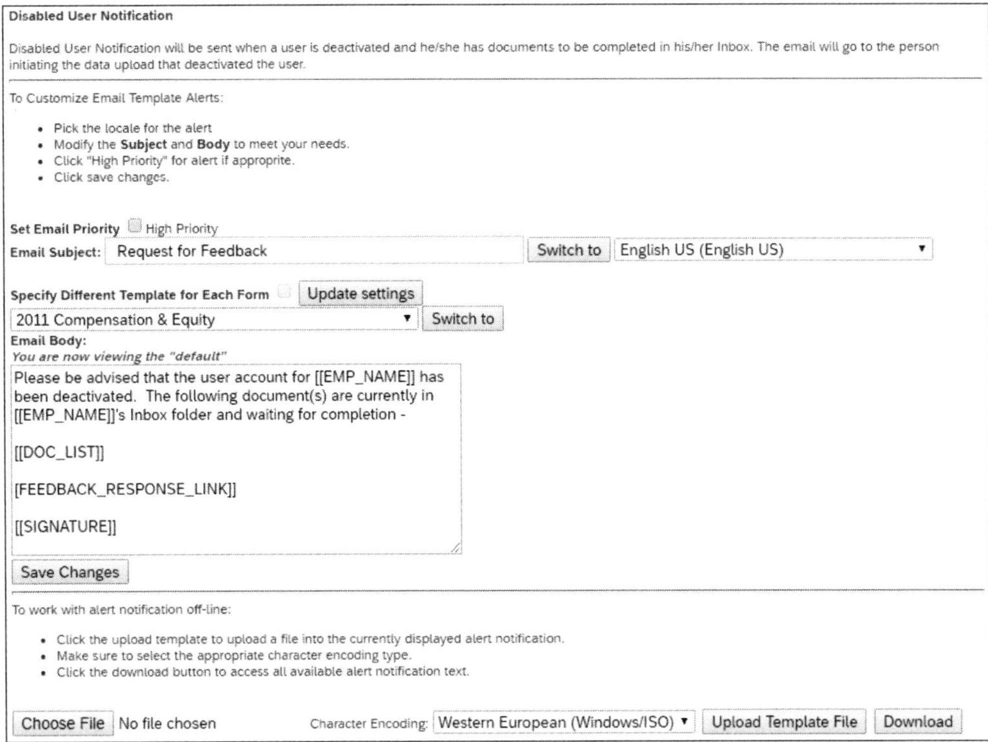

Figure 17.24 Notification Customization

In Employee Central, it is possible to customize workflow email notifications using the Document Generation feature. Document Generation groups can be created to assign to a step in a workflow configuration. Document Generation templates can be created and assigned to Document Generation groups. These are then used instead of the standard-delivered workflow templates.

We've seen how we can configure existing email notifications. In a similar vein, we'll now look at how we can configure and add picklists.

17.9 Picklist Management

SAP SuccessFactors uses picklists throughout the applications of the suite. Picklists enable users to only select a value from a predefined list, which enables data integrity for fields that use picklists. Picklist values are maintained in the Admin Center in the Picklist Center (shown in Figure 17.25). From here, administrators can create new picklists or update values in existing picklists. These updates may include adding, reordering, or deleting values from the list.

Note

At the time of writing (fall 2019), SAP SuccessFactors is in the process of migrating customers from legacy picklists to the picklists functionality that we will cover in this section. Because many customers have mix of both in their landscape or may be still running legacy picklists functionality, we will include some information on legacy picklists management in this section.

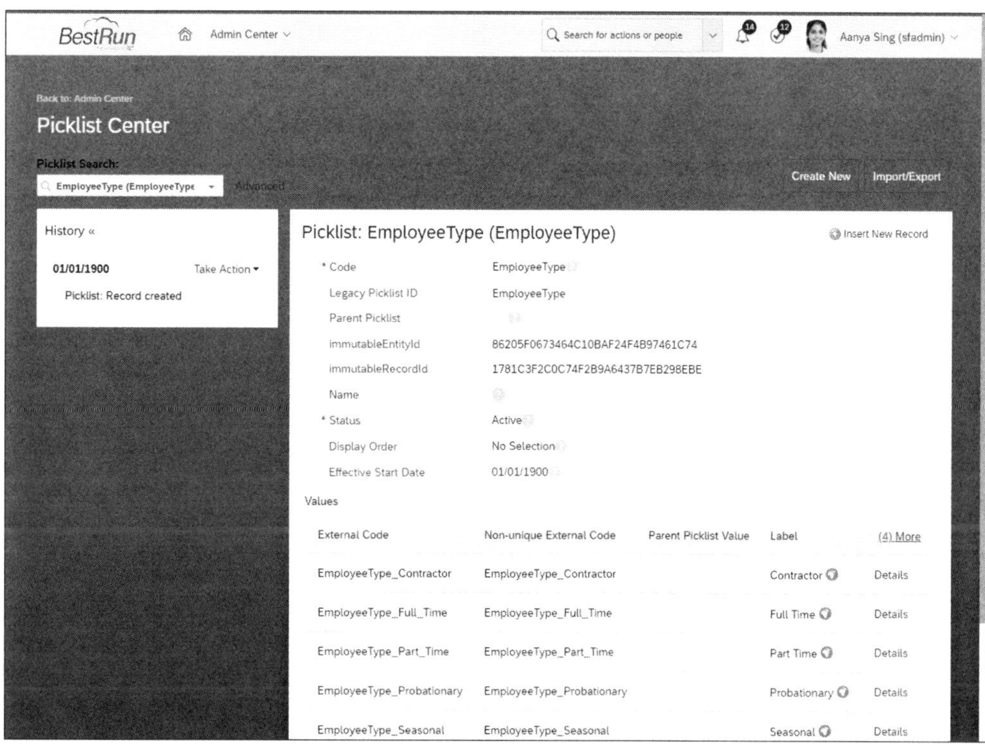

Figure 17.25 Picklist Center

To create a new picklist, it is necessary to enter a few key elements of data, such as the **Code**, **Parent Picklist** (if applicable), **Name**, **Status**, **Display Order**, and **Effective Start Date**. After this, you can enter the picklist values. For each value, you need to

17

maintain a unique **External Code**, **Label**, and **Status**. You can also maintain a nonunique external code, a parent picklist value (if applicable), a minimum value, and a maximum value.

It is also possible to export a picklist, edit it, and then upload it to the system.

When maintaining legacy picklists, you need to download the picklist CSV file, make the changes, and then upload the CSV file back into SAP SuccessFactors (see Figure 17.26). The following are some of the main fields that need to be modified:

- **PicklistID**
  Is the value or key that is used to map the picklists to fields in the configuration (data model, templates, etc.).
- **OptionID**
  Is the value or key that is used to map edits to a previously established value. This value is assigned by the system, and you should leave the field blank when creating new picklist values and not changes when editing existing picklists.
- **Status**
  Controls whether the picklist value is displayed in the list of values in the interface; there are three options:
  - **Active**: Means the value is available in the system
  - **Deleted**: Means the value is disabled from use in the system
  - **Obsoleted**: Means the value is disabled from the list of values but still available for reporting
- **en_US**
  Is the default language coding and is required for all picklist values. Other codes (such as **fr_FR** for French or **de_DE** for German) can be included for other languages, but each language code should be in its own column.

When you're working with picklists, it's important to select the correct options in the import/export screen. The best practice is to first export the picklist values and work with picklist or picklists that require updating. You can also use the template to create new picklist values. Note that you cannot create a new picklist and update an existing picklist in the same file. Updates to picklists are immediately rendered in the system.

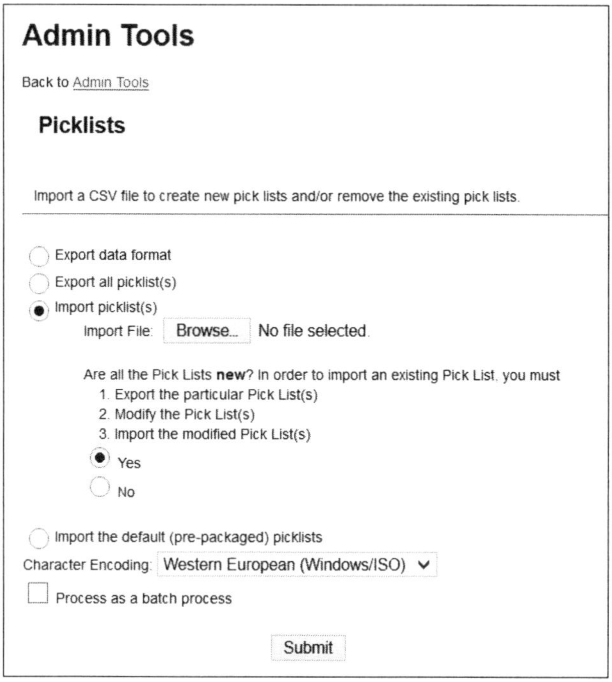

Figure 17.26 Picklist Import Options

Now, we're going to switch our attention to data privacy.

17.10 Data Protection and Privacy

SAP SuccessFactors takes data protection and privacy seriously, and therefore provides a set of functionalities that enables data to be purged, access to data blocked, and audits on data access to be run. This functionality enables customers using SAP SuccessFactors to be compliant with various data privacy and protection regulations, including GDPR of the European Union (EU).

There are five categories of data protection and privacy tools available:

- Data purging
- Data blocking
- Change audit
- Information report
- Consent agreements

Each of the five categories are available for all modules of the SAP SuccessFactors HCM Suite, except for data blocking (only available for Employee Central, Employee Central Payroll, and reporting) and consent agreements (only available for Performance & Goals, Learning, Recruiting, and Onboarding).

Further Resources

You can find more information on the data protection and privacy features in the guide *Setting Up and Using Data Protection and Privacy* found on the SAP Help Portal under the SAP SuccessFactors HCM Suite product page.

We'll now take a look at each of these capabilities.

17.10.1 Data Purging

This feature allows for purging of data that is obsolete or has to be purged for legal compliance reasons. Data can be purged as needed or be scheduled to be deleted once a certain period of time passes. This ensures that customers can stay compliant with local data protection and privacy legislation.

SAP SuccessFactors offers the possibility to:

- Run a full purge of inactive users and their data, based on a common retention time.
- Run a partial purge of specific data, for either active and inactive users, based on a retention time configured for that type of data.
- Run a purge of all audit data for all users, both active and inactive, based on a different retention time for each type of audit data.
- Create a list of users who should not be purged (i.e., they are part of a litigation hold or other action that requires preservation of a user's data that would normally be outside of the retention period).

Different data purge rules can be set up to define the retention period per country for each type of data. An example of this can be seen in Figure 17.27.

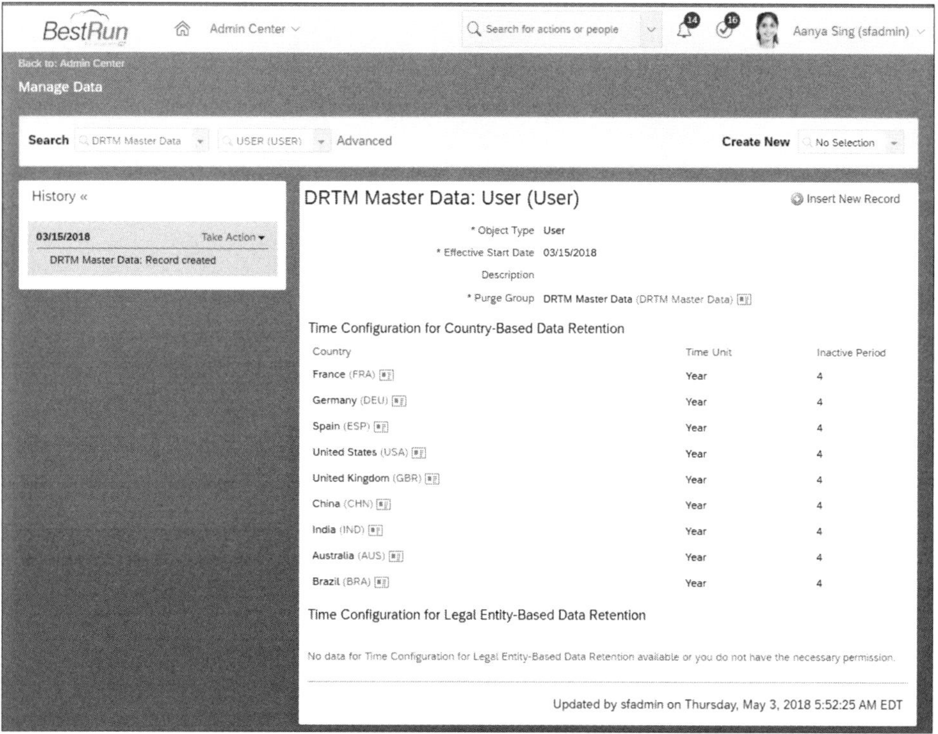

Figure 17.27 Setting Up a Data Retention Period

Depending on the data purge rule object you are configuring, the retention period is configured for an active period and an inactive period. This means, for example, that a mentoring program can be purged after a period when active and also after a different period when inactive.

The date from which data is considered to be inactive differs from application to application and from object to object. For example, in Employee Central the termination date is used, while for a compensation statement the statement creation date is used.

Data purging is performed using Data Retention Time Management (DRTM) in SAP SuccessFactors. It requires a user (which in most cases would be the super admin) to submit a purge request that, upon approval, is executed. Purge requests can also be scheduled to run automatically.

Data purge requests are created and approved in **Data Retention Management** in the Admin Center. Click **Create New Purge Request** (see Figure 17.28), and select the appropriate type of data purge to initiate.

BestRun
Admin Center
Search for actions or people
Aanya Sing (sfadmin)
Admin Center
Back to Admin Center
Data Retention Management
Use this page to manage purge requests.
Create New Purge Request
User Permanent Purge
Items per page 10
Page 1 of 1
Name
Type
Last Modified
Status
Actions
Purge Inactive User [62]
Purge Inactive User
12/12/2017 05:24:08 AM CET
Not Scheduled
Launch Immediately
More Actions

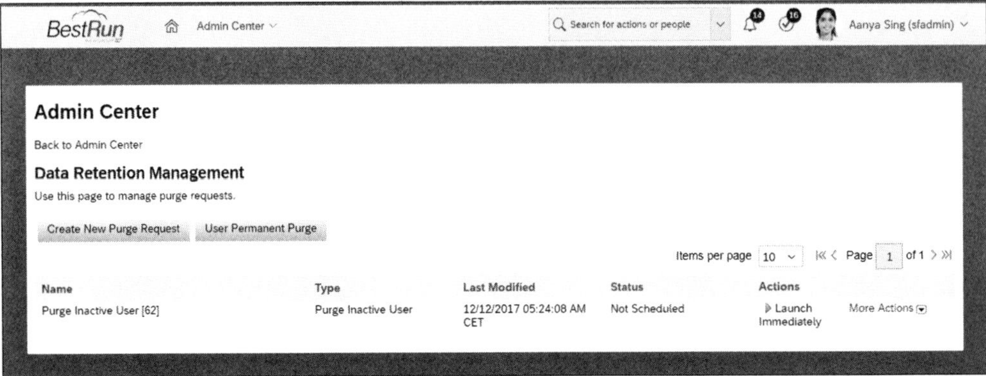

Figure 17.28 Data Retention Management Home Page

After clicking the type of data purge, you are requested to name the data purge request, fill out any relevant criteria for filtering, and identify one or multiple approvers for this request, as shown in Figure 17.29. Unless otherwise selected to do so, the purge request will automatically use the data retention period configured in the system.

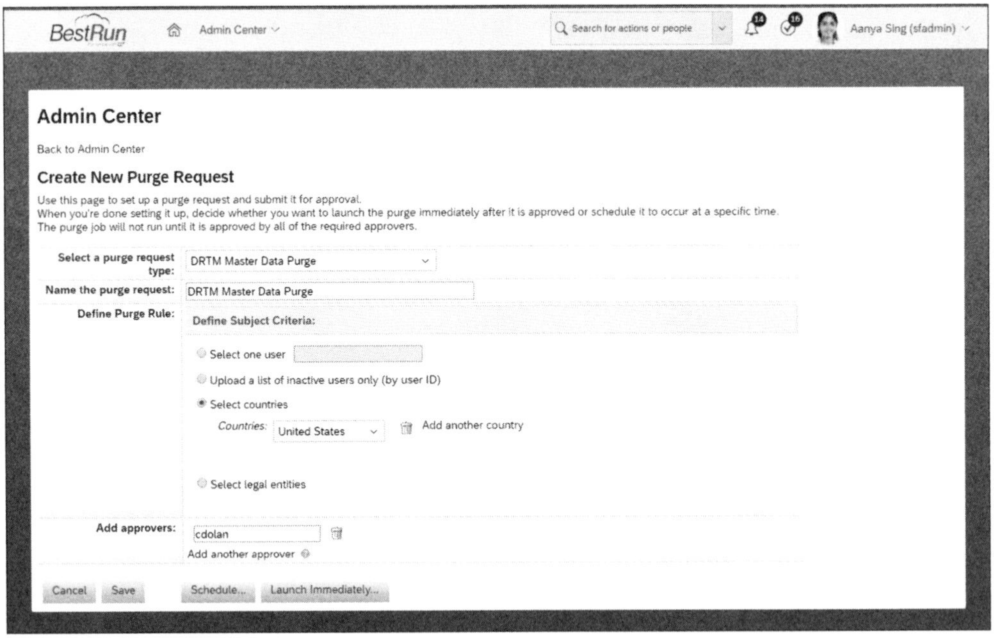

BestRun
Admin Center
Search for actions or people
Aanya Sing (sfadmin)
Admin Center
Back to Admin Center
Create New Purge Request
Use this page to set up a purge request and submit it for approval.
When you're done setting it up, decide whether you want to launch the purge immediately after it is approved or schedule it to occur at a specific time.
The purge job will not run until it is approved by all of the required approvers.
Select a purge request type:
DRTM Master Data Purge
Name the purge request:
DRTM Master Data Purge
Define Purge Rule:
Define Subject Criteria:
Select one user
Upload a list of inactive users only (by user ID)
Select countries
Countries:
United States
Add another country
Select legal entities
Add approvers:
cdolan
Add another approver
Cancel
Save
Schedule...
Launch Immediately...

Figure 17.29 Purge Request Criteria Setup

Upon submitting the data purge request for this data purge request, administrators that have approval rights are notified through email that the request is ready for approval.

To view any data purge requests awaiting approval or approved requests, navigate to **Purge Request Monitor** in the Admin Center, as shown in Figure 17.30.

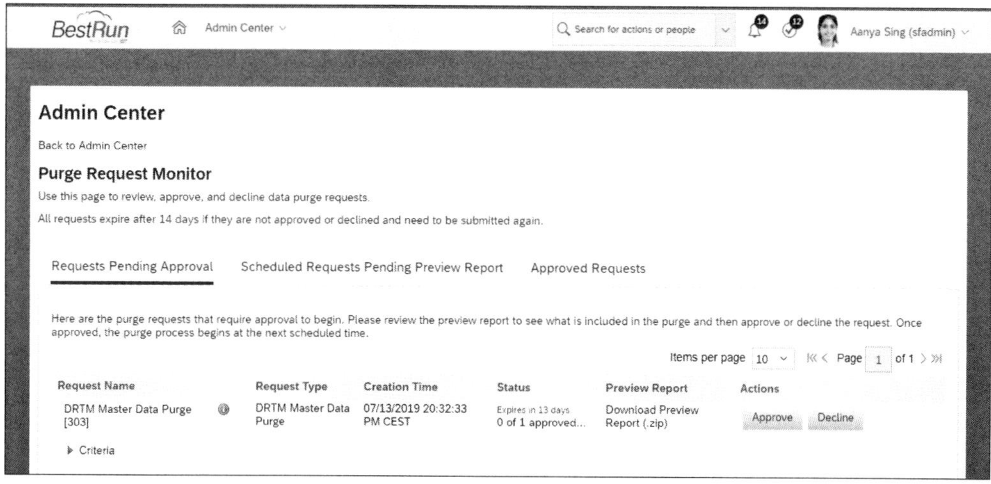

Figure 17.30 Purge Request Monitor

An administrator can download the preview report and ensure that valid objects are being requested to be purged. Once a request is approved or declined, the action cannot be reversed.

17.10.2 Data Blocking

Data blocking provides the capability of enabling data that has to be retained for different periods for different purposes to be blocked from access by those whose access is outside of the retention period of the data.

Let's look at an example to better understand what this means. Say the social security number of an employee may need to be retained in payroll for seven years, but HR must purge the data after five years. In this case, the data would be retained for seven years, but HR and other non-payroll users would be blocked from accessing the data after five years. After seven years, the data would be purged.

Note

Data blocking is only available in Employee Central and Reporting (at the time of writing, fall 2019).

Both ad hoc reporting (for Employee Central subdomain schemas) and Employee Central advanced reporting (all data) support data blocking. Note that data blocking does not apply to ad hoc reports that use the **Group By** function.

Data blocking is applied through permission roles in the system. When granting a permission role, the restriction period can be assigned by scrolling down to the **5: Data Access Period Settings** section, selecting the **Restricted** radio button next to the appropriate data type, and then entering the restriction period in months in the **Period** column. The period entered is effective as of the day it is configured. If 0 is entered, then no data can be accessed from the day it is configured.

17.10.3 Change Audit

The change audit capability enables the tracking of changes in the system audit logs. This includes not only data, but also system configuration changes and other data in the system, such as RBPs or proxy assignments. Change audit reports can be generated to view the changes and are available for 48 hours after generation.

A change audit report can be generated for changes made to a specific user's data or for changes made by a specific user. The report provides information on what data was changed, when it was changed, and who changed it. A change audit report can be run for any given 7-day period. Depending on the module and scope of data, reports can take up to 72 hours to generate.

Further Resources

At the time of writing (fall 2019), there are some limitations for some modules as per what data is logged by the change audit functionality. You can find more information on these limitations in the guide *Setting Up and Using Data Protection and Privacy* found on the SAP Help Portal under the SAP SuccessFactors HCM Suite product page.

Change audit reports are generated in the Admin Center in **Change Audit Reports**, as shown in Figure 17.31.

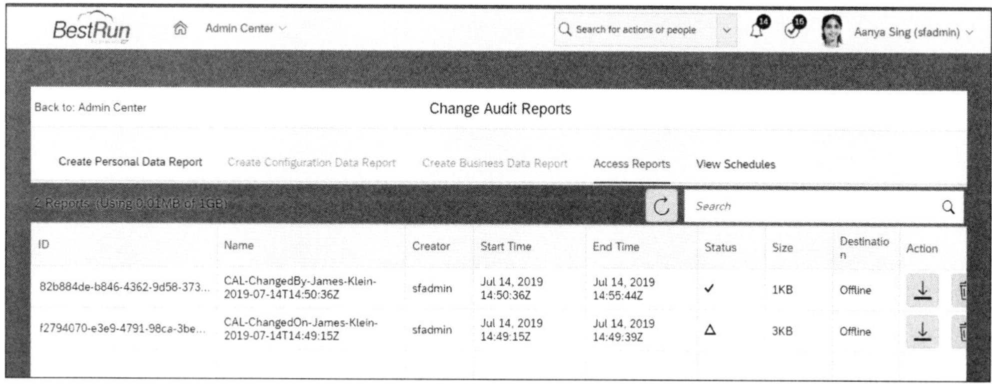

Figure 17.31 Change Audit Reports Transaction Screen

Three different types of change audit report can be generated by selecting the appropriate tab:

- **Create Personal Data Report**
  Creates a report on changes to personal data for employees, external candidates, or onboardees (creating a personal data report can be seen in Figure 17.32).

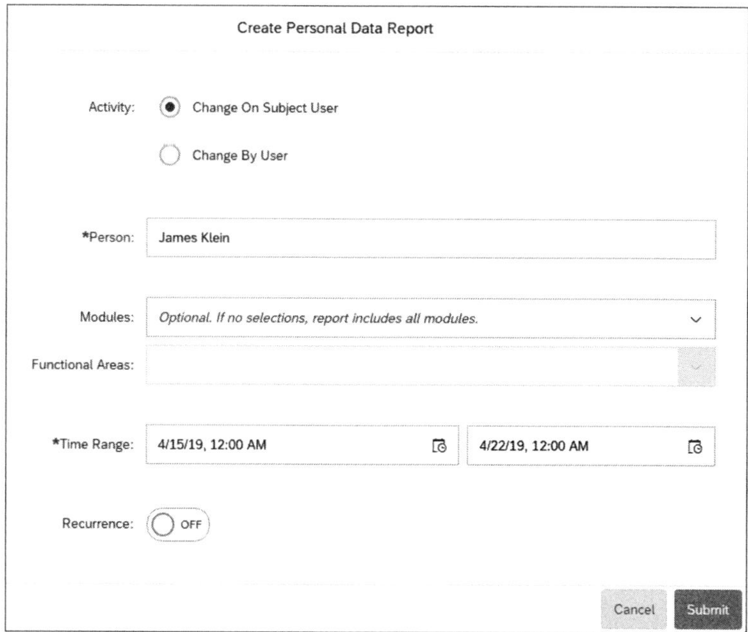

Figure 17.32 Creating a Change Audit Report for Personal Data

- **Create Configuration Data Report**
  Creates a report on changes to system configurations.
- **Create Business Data Report**
  Creates a report on changes to other data.

A *change audit report* contains a variety of data. For the overall report, the report includes the user ID of the report creator, subject of the data, modules, functional areas, and the start and end dates of the reporting period. For each data change, the report includes:

- The user that made the change
- The logged-in user, if it was a proxy that made the change
- Secondary user provisioner ID and email (if the user accessed via Provisioning)
- Subject user of the change
- Module
- Functional area and subarea
- Context key and value (tells you what change was made or how the change was made)
- Field name
- Old value and new value
- Operation performed (inserted, updated, or deleted)
- Timestamp
- Effective start date and sequence

An example of a change audit report for personal data is shown in Figure 17.33.

17.10.4 Information Report

Under the law in some countries, it is mandated to provide a report upon request of an employee on what data is stored about them in your HR system. The Data Subject Information report in SAP SuccessFactors provides such a capability.

The Data Subject Information report is configured and generated through **Data Subject Information** in the Admin Center. The home page of the Data Subject Information transaction is shown in Figure 17.34.

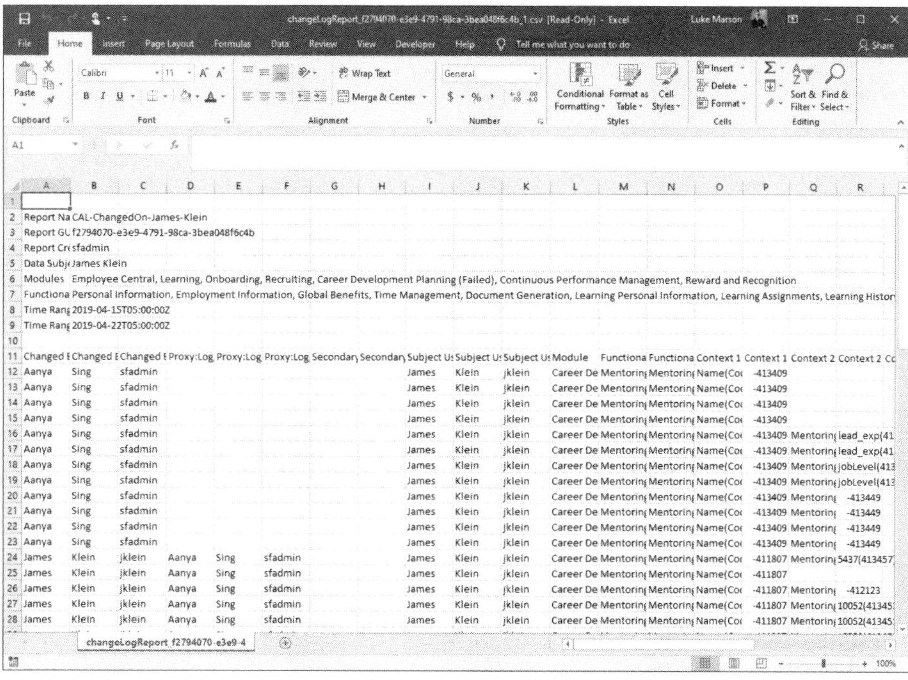

Changed E	Changed E	Changed E	Proxy:Log	Proxy:Log	Proxy:Log	Secondary	Secondary	Subject U	Subject U	Subject U	Module	Functiona	Functiona	Context 1	Context 1	Context 2	Context 2
Aanya	Sing	sfadmin						James	Klein	jklein	Career De	Mentorin	Mentorin	Name(Co	-413409		
Aanya	Sing	sfadmin						James	Klein	jklein	Career De	Mentorin	Mentorin	Name(Co	-413409		
Aanya	Sing	sfadmin						James	Klein	jklein	Career De	Mentorin	Mentorin	Name(Co	-413409		
Aanya	Sing	sfadmin						James	Klein	jklein	Career De	Mentorin	Mentorin	Name(Co	-413409		
Aanya	Sing	sfadmin						James	Klein	jklein	Career De	Mentorin	Mentorin	Name(Co	-413409	Mentorin	lead_exp(41
Aanya	Sing	sfadmin						James	Klein	jklein	Career De	Mentorin	Mentorin	Name(Co	-413409	Mentorin	lead_exp(41
Aanya	Sing	sfadmin						James	Klein	jklein	Career De	Mentorin	Mentorin	Name(Co	-413409	Mentorin	jobLevel(41
Aanya	Sing	sfadmin						James	Klein	jklein	Career De	Mentorin	Mentorin	Name(Co	-413409	Mentorin	jobLevel(41
Aanya	Sing	sfadmin						James	Klein	jklein	Career De	Mentorin	Mentorin	Name(Co	-413409	Mentorin	-413449
Aanya	Sing	sfadmin						James	Klein	jklein	Career De	Mentorin	Mentorin	Name(Co	-413409	Mentorin	-413449
Aanya	Sing	sfadmin						James	Klein	jklein	Career De	Mentorin	Mentorin	Name(Co	-413409	Mentorin	-413449
Aanya	Sing	sfadmin						James	Klein	jklein	Career De	Mentorin	Mentorin	Name(Co	-413409	Mentorin	-413449
James	Klein	jklein	Aanya	Sing	sfadmin			James	Klein	jklein	Career De	Mentorin	Mentorin	Name(Co	-411807	Mentorin	5437(413457
James	Klein	jklein	Aanya	Sing	sfadmin			James	Klein	jklein	Career De	Mentorin	Mentorin	Name(Co	-411807		
James	Klein	jklein	Aanya	Sing	sfadmin			James	Klein	jklein	Career De	Mentorin	Mentorin	Name(Co	-411807	Mentorin	-412123
James	Klein	jklein	Aanya	Sing	sfadmin			James	Klein	jklein	Career De	Mentorin	Mentorin	Name(Co	-411807	Mentorin	10052(41345
James	Klein	jklein	Aanya	Sing	sfadmin			James	Klein	jklein	Career De	Mentorin	Mentorin	Name(Co	-411807	Mentorin	10052(41345

Figure 17.33 A Change Audit Report for Employee Data

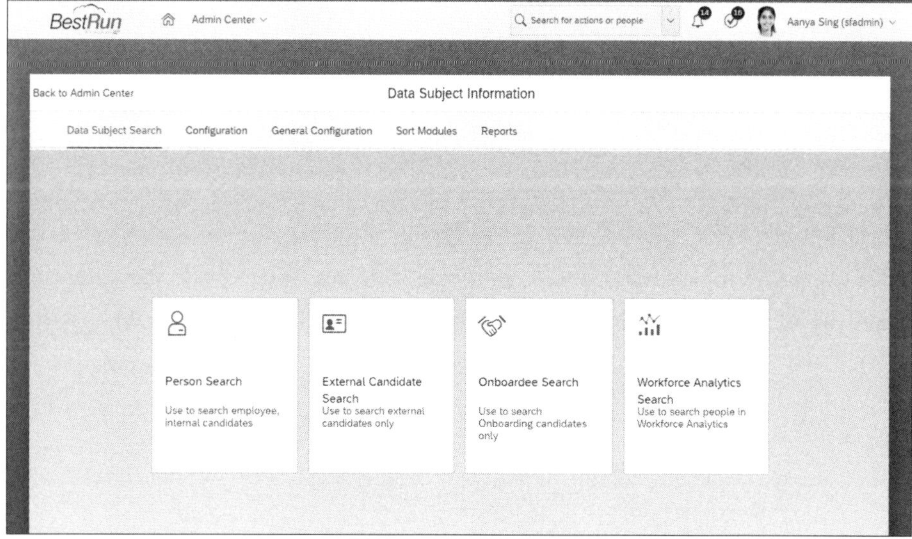

Figure 17.34 Data Subject Information Transaction

You can configure which fields appear in the Data Subject Information report and for what purpose that data is stored. Figure 17.35 shows some fields being configured on the report.

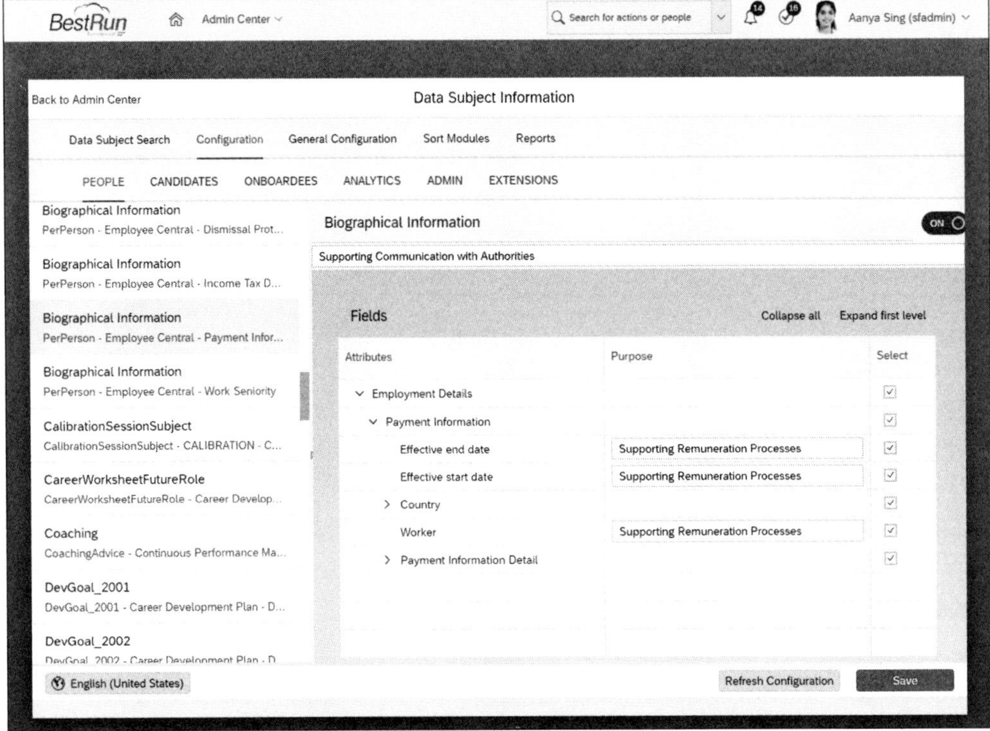

Figure 17.35 Configuring Fields on the Data Subject Information Report

To generate a report, navigate to the **Data Subject Search** tab, select the type of report you want to run (employee, external candidate, onboardee, or Workforce Analytics data), select the employee and appropriate selection data, and execute the generation of the report. While the report is generating and after it has generated, it is listed in the **Reports** tab.

Note

The data in a Data Subject Information report will only contain data that the person generating the report has permission to see.

Once a report has been generated, it can be downloaded. The report can be downloaded either as a PDF or Excel file, which is downloaded in a ZIP file. Figure 17.36 shows an example of a downloaded PDF report.

Page 1 of 137

Employee Central

Biographical Information

Supporting Communication with Authorities

Data Field Name	Field Value	Data Purpose Category
Country Of Birth	USA	*Supporting Communication with Authorities*
Date Of Birth	1956-01-31 00:00:00	*Supporting Communication with Authorities*
Person Id	802984	*Supporting Communication with Authorities*
Email Information		
Email Information - 1		
Email Address	james.klein@bestrun.com	*Supporting Communication with Authorities*
Email Type	Business	*Supporting Communication with Authorities*
Is Primary	Yes	*Supporting Communication with Authorities*
Primary Emergency Contact		
Primary Emergency Contact - 1		
Name	Margaret Klein	*Supporting Emergency Situations*
Phone	(732) 555-0099	*Supporting Emergency Situations*
primaryFlag	Y	*Supporting Emergency Situations*
Relationship	Spouse	*Supporting Emergency Situations*
National ID Information		
National ID Information - 1		
National Id Card Type	ssn	*Supporting Communication with Authorities*
Territory		
territory Name	United States	*Supporting Communication with Authorities*

Figure 17.36 A Data Subject Information Report

Reports that are too big for the system default file size will be split into multiple files in the ZIP file.

17.10.5 Consent Agreements

Consent agreements give employees and other users the opportunity to provide or decline consent to have their data stored and enables you to inform those users why data is being stored.

In SAP SuccessFactors, the Data Privacy Consent Statement (DPCS) is the consent agreement that can be configured for logging into the system and for specific aspects of the following modules:

- Recruiting
- Onboarding
- Learning
- Performance Management

For Recruiting and Onboarding, both internal and external candidates can be configured. For Performance Management, you can only configure the Ask for Feedback functionality.

A DPCS is configured in the Admin Center in **Data Privacy Statement**. Here, multiple DPCSs can be configured for different countries and in different languages. It is possible to create a draft and leave it inactive until you are ready to publish it. Figure 17.37 shows the home page of the **Data Privacy Statement** transaction.

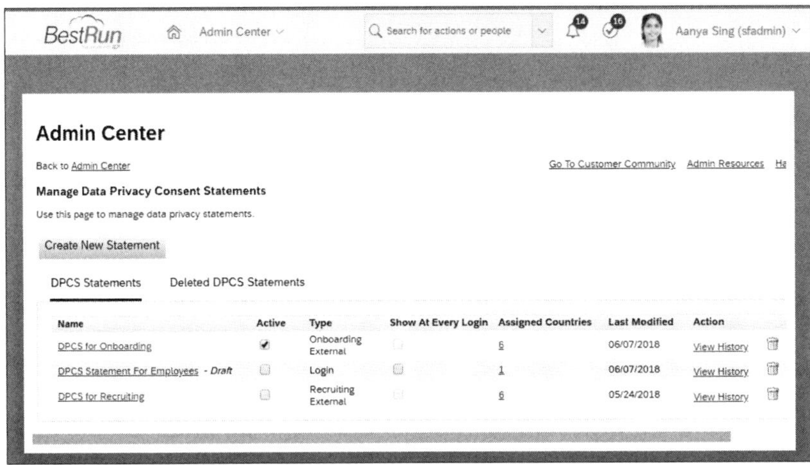

Figure 17.37 Managing Data Privacy Consent Statements

Once a DPCS is published, it will display for each employee that is accessing the specific functionality for which the DPCS is configured. Figure 17.38 shows a DPCS for an employee logging into SAP SuccessFactors for the first time.

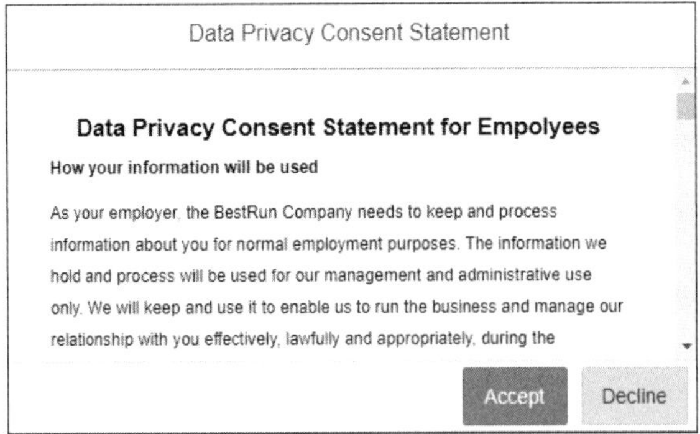

Figure 17.38 A Data Privacy Consent Statement

An audit log is provided so that an administrator can view the activity and changes for each DPCS.

By using the transaction **Set DPCS Statement Status** in the Admin Center, you can review and change the acceptance of the DPCS for each employee, as shown in Figure 17.39.

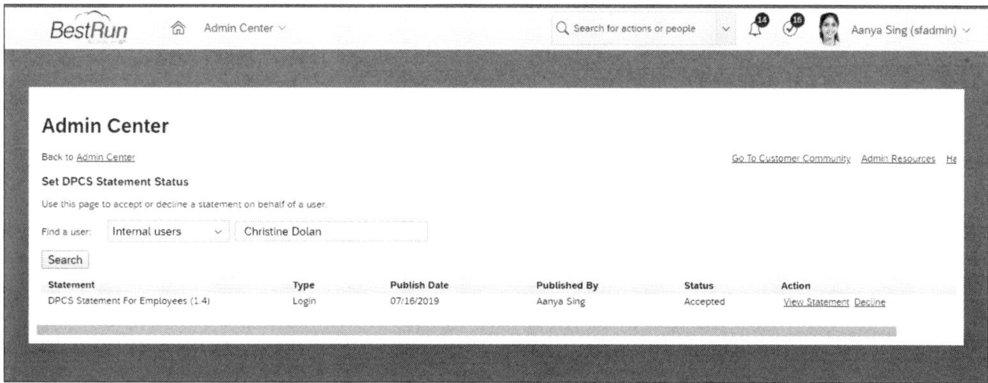

Figure 17.39 The Set DPCS Statement Status Transaction

After our discussion of auditing data, we'll now turn our attention to synchronizing data between different SAP SuccessFactors instances and refreshing instances.

17.11 Instance Management

In order to manage your instance, SAP SuccessFactors provides two key features:

- Configuration copy (instance synchronization)
- Full copy (instance refresh)

These features are both accessed in the **Instance Management** screen (shown in Figure 17.40), which you can reach via **Instance Synchronization Wizard** or **Instance Refresh** in the Admin Center. Here you are presented with the two options that are mentioned in the previous bulleted list.

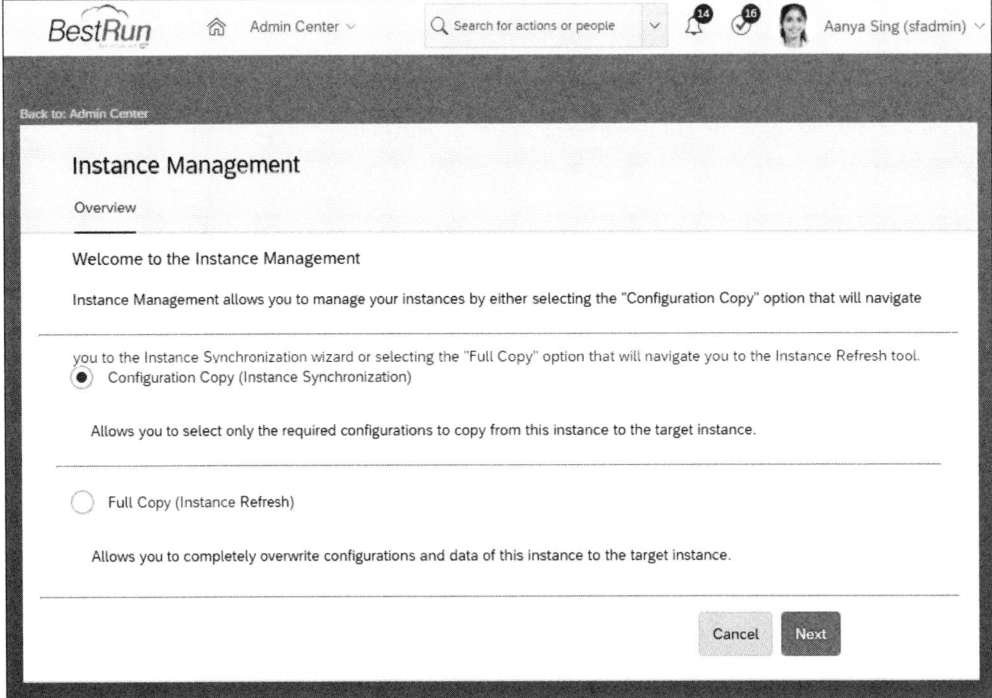

Figure 17.40 Instance Management

We'll take a look at these two options now.

17.11.1 Instance Synchronization

This feature allows for synchronization of configuration objects between two SAP SuccessFactors instances. Essentially, this provides you with a way of copying your configuration from one instance to another. The feature behaves as a push model from the source instance to the target instance.

To launch the sync wizard, click **Configuration Copy (Instance Synchronization)** in the **Instance Management** screen, as was shown in Figure 17.40.

To initiate the sync, select the target instance (the first time you use the Instance Sync tool you need to pair the instance with your target instance) and the configuration objects (called *artifacts*) that you wish to synchronize in the target instance (shown in Figure 17.41). In the next step of the wizard you must define a name for the sync job, add an optional description, and then select a username in the target instance that has the permissions to write the data that is being synchronized. The sync wizard then takes you through a series of criteria selection and confirmation screens for each artifact and then presents a final summary of the instance sync request, as shown in Figure 17.42. Here it is possible to save the selection of artifacts for synchronization as a *sync package* that can be reused in a future synchronization.

Once the details have been reviewed and you are ready to synchronize, you can choose to run the sync in test mode (which allows you to preview the results of the sync process in a report format) or go ahead and execute the synchronization.

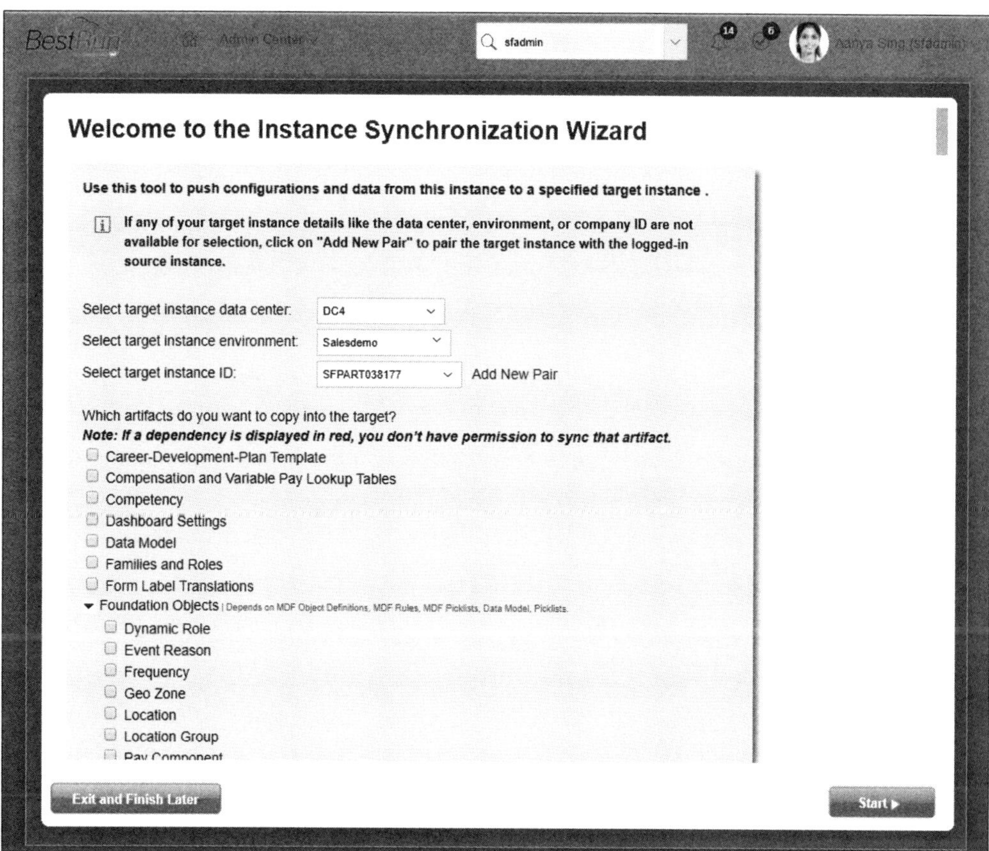

Figure 17.41 Selecting Artifacts to Synchronize

Once a configuration object sync is initiated in live or test mode, customers can monitor the progress of the sync process by going to **Instance Synchronization Monitor Tool** in the Admin Center, as shown in Figure 17.43.

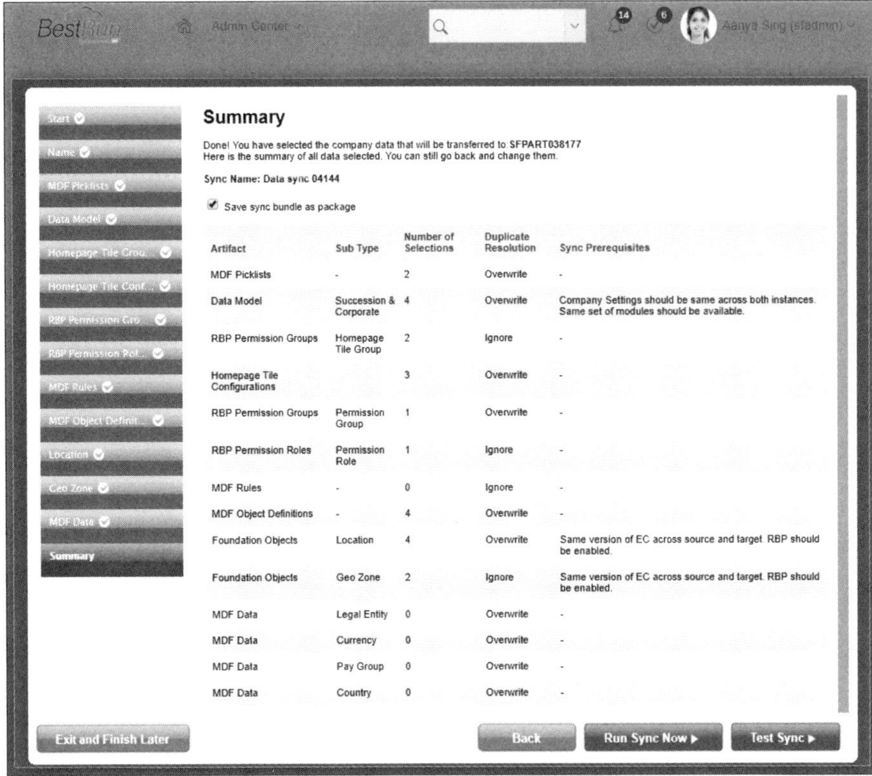

Figure 17.42 Summary of the Artifacts to Be Synchronized

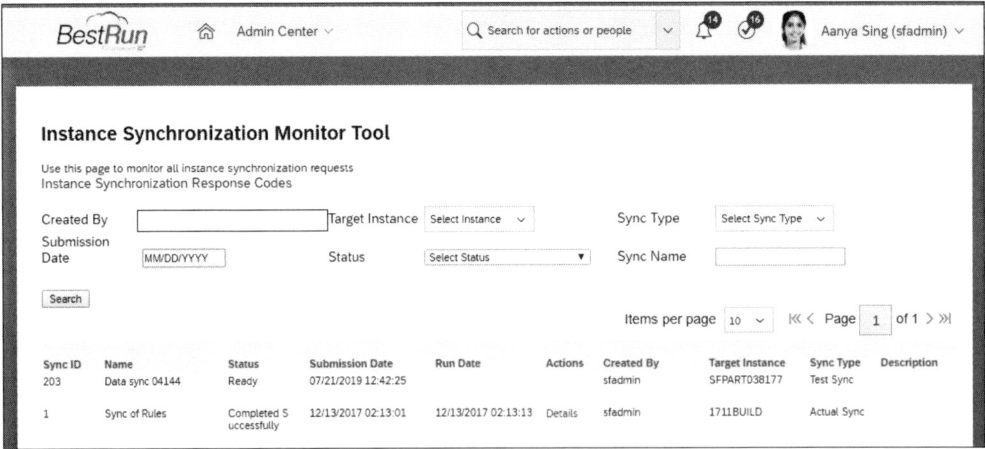

Figure 17.43 Instance Synchronization Monitor Tool

The sync monitoring tool allows for downloading of a detailed report of all actions that will be performed. Also, the tool has a hyperlink of the **Instance Synchronization Response Codes** that provide a detailed explanation of the response code generated as part of the sync process.

By using **Manage Sync Packages**, it is possible to modify or delete sync packages.

Further Resources

You can find more information on the instance synchronization feature in the guide *Instance Sync: Implementation and Administration* found on the SAP Help Portal under the SAP SuccessFactors HCM Suite product page.

17.11.2 Instance Refresh

Instance refresh allows you to request a full refresh of the instance from another instance in your landscape, without impacting the integrations in the target instance that you are refreshing to. Refreshes can only be performed in instances in the same data center. Instance refresh allows you to perform the following activities for refreshing an instance:

- Create refresh request on a preferred date
- View all requests that have been initiated from the current instance
- View and track the status of requests that have been submitted but not yet completed
- Cancel any requests that are not yet in progress
- Download the error log for requests that failed or errored out
- Receive email notifications and alerts for each step of the refresh process

Note

An instance refresh is a nonreversible action.

The instance refresh functionality provides the ability to refresh the following instances between each other, as shown in Table 17.1.

Source Instance	Target Instance
Preview (test instance)	Production (development or productive/ live instance)
Preview (test instance)	Preview (test instance)
Production (productive/live instance)	Preview (test instance)
Production (development instance)	Preview (test instance)

Table 17.1 Instances That Can Be Refreshed

For Learning, instance refresh allows you to request a refresh from production (productive/live instance) to preview (test instance).

Note

At the time of writing (fall 2019), Onboarding instances cannot be refreshed using the instance refresh functionality. You need to raise a ticket with SAP Support to refresh an Onboarding instance.

The diagram shown in Figure 17.44 displays these combinations visually.

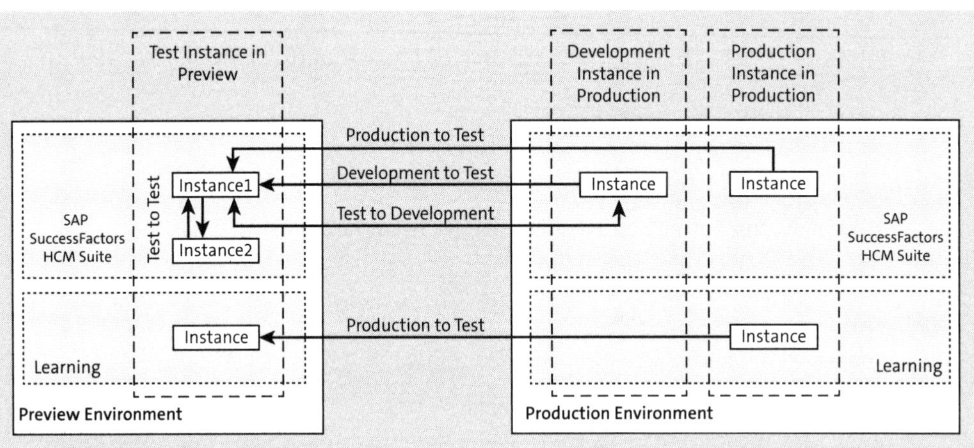

Figure 17.44 Instances That Can Be Refreshed

Note

During the blackout period (the period between a quarterly release being made into a preview instance and the same quarterly release being made into production), it is not possible to refresh from the preview instance to a production instance. You must wait until the blackout period has finished and the quarterly release is in the production instance.

To launch the instance refresh wizard, click **Full Copy (Instance Refresh)** in the **Instance Management** screen, as was shown in Figure 17.40. You'll be taken to the **Instance Refresh Center** screen (shown in Figure 17.45), where you can see any target instances that have been paired with the instance for refreshing and a list of the instance refresh requests in the **OVERVIEW** tab. You can also view the status workflow overview diagram by selecting **View Status Workflow**, and create a new request by selecting **Create New Request**.

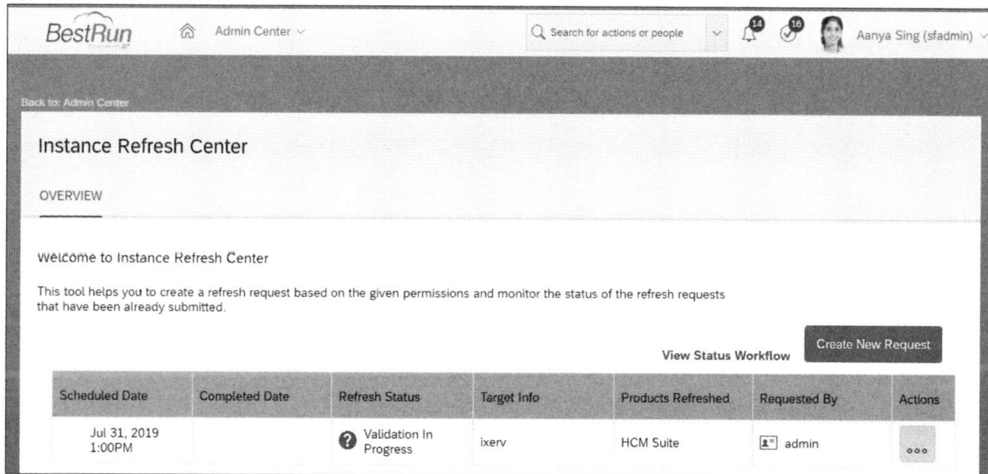

Figure 17.45 Instance Refresh Center

In the **OVERVIEW** tab, the following details are displayed for each instance refresh request:

- Scheduled date of the refresh
- Completed date of the refresh
- Status of the refresh

- Target instance ID
- Products refreshed
- User ID of the user that requested the refresh

When creating a new request, you select a paired target instance, the modules to refresh, the date on which you want the refresh to occur, and a dummy email address to be assigned to employees if you do not wish to have real email addresses used (this step is optional), as shown in Figure 17.46.

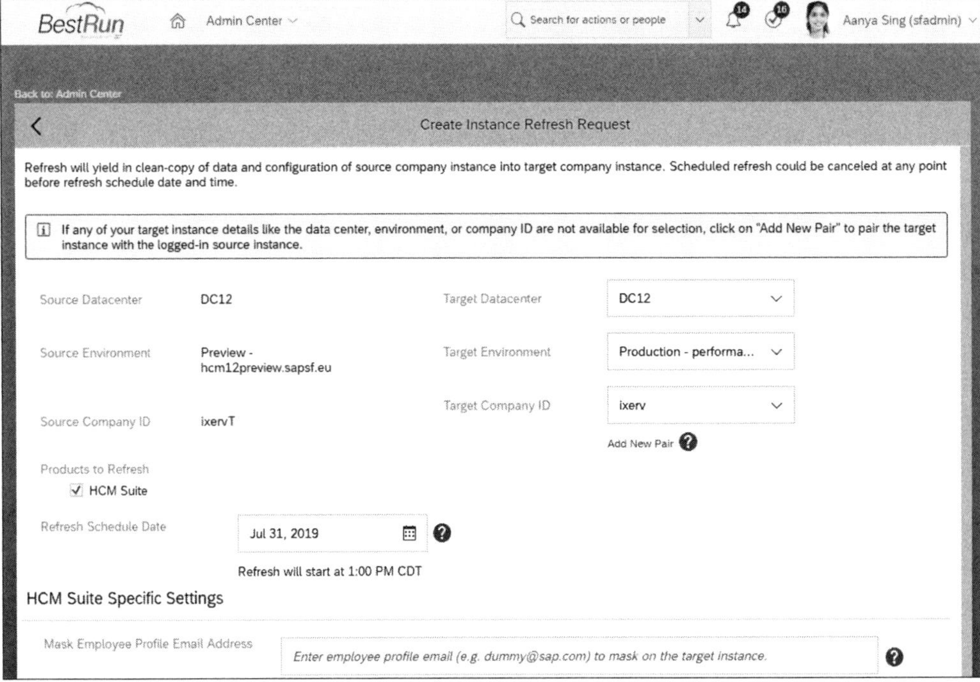

Figure 17.46 Creating a Refresh Request

Once the refresh request has been created, it can be seen in the **OVERVIEW** tab on the **Instance Refresh Center** screen. From here you can track the status of the request.

Further Resources

You can find more information on the instance refresh feature in the guide *Instance Refresh* found on the SAP Help Portal under the SAP SuccessFactors HCM Suite product page. Additionally, knowledge base article (KBA) 2277508 should also be consulted.

17.12 Managing Provisioning Access

Provisioning—as we discussed in Section 17.1—provides implementation consultants and SAP with the ability to enable features and provides some basic configurations. As part of your instance management strategy, it is important to be able to manage exactly who has access to Provisioning for your instance. This is done in **Manage Provisioning Access** in the Admin Center.

Manage Provisioning Access provides a list of all users who have Provisioning access to your instance (shown in Figure 17.47) and enables you to add and delete users. Users are "added" using the **Add** (plus) button, while to delete any users, simply select them in the list and click the **Delete** (trashcan) icon. When a user is added, they are sent an email with details of the instance that they can submit directly to SAP SuccessFactors operations to have access granted. The user is not automatically granted access.

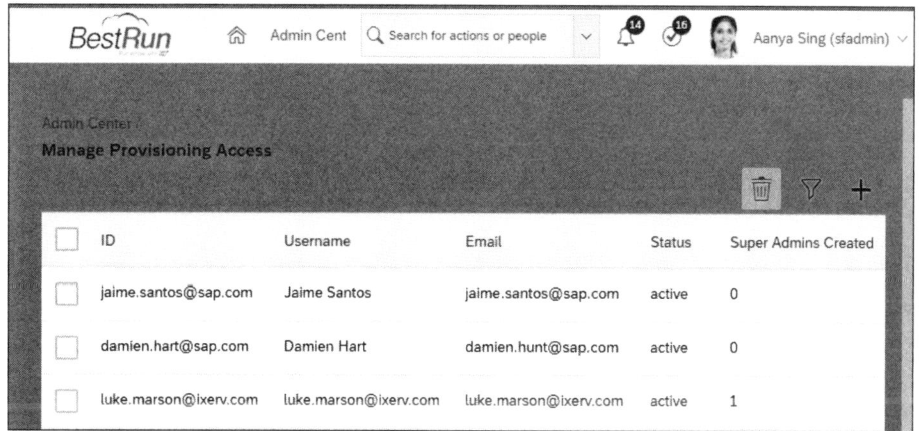

Figure 17.47 Manage Provisioning Access

Access can be provided for users on a long-term basis (i.e., without an end date) or short-term basis (i.e., with a fixed end date). Typically, short-term access would be provided to support users to review, investigate, or fix specific issues.

Further Resources

You can find more information on managing Provisioning access in the guide *Managing Instance Access* found on the SAP Help Portal under the SAP SuccessFactors HCM Suite product page.

17.13 Managing Support Access

If required, it is possible to provide someone with support access to the instance. This is a special type of access that is typically requested by SAP Support. Support access is provided and removed via **Manage Support Access** in the Admin Center, as shown in Figure 17.48.

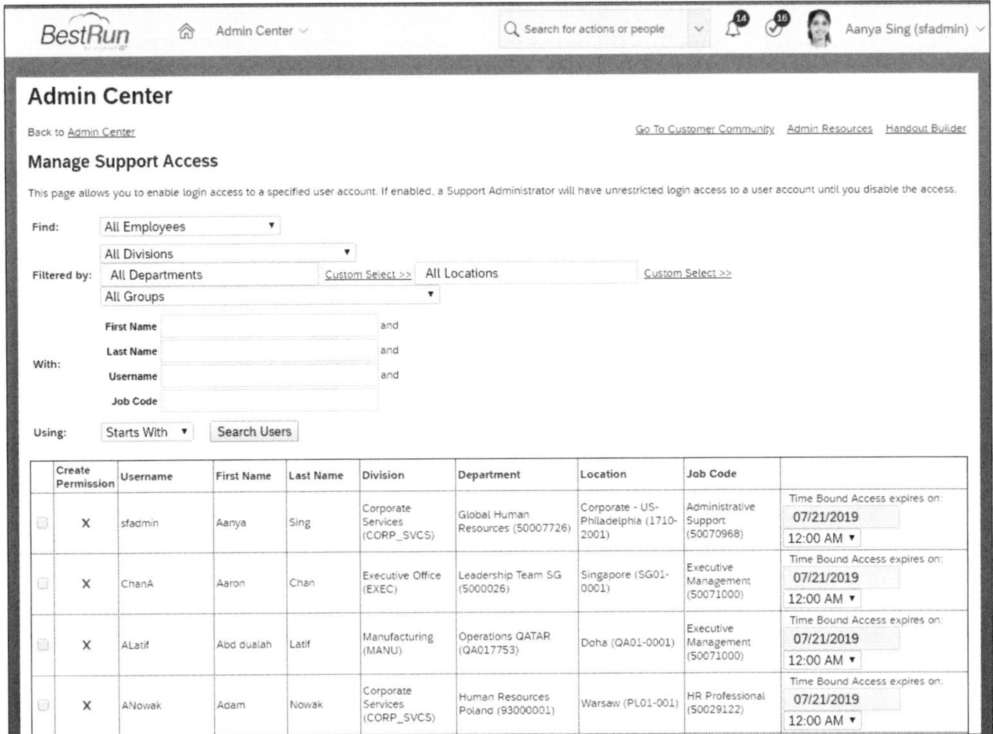

Figure 17.48 Manage Support Access

Access is granted by searching for a user, selecting them, selecting the end date of the access, and selecting **Grant a Support Administrator Access to the Account**. To remove access, search for a user, select them, and select **Disable Support Access**.

17.14 Managing Business Configuration

Being able to make changes to fields in Employee Central and People Profile is one of the key components of a system that needs to evolve along with your business.

The Manage Business Configuration application, shown in Figure 17.49, enables you to do just that. It is accessed in the Admin Center via **Manage Business Configuration**.

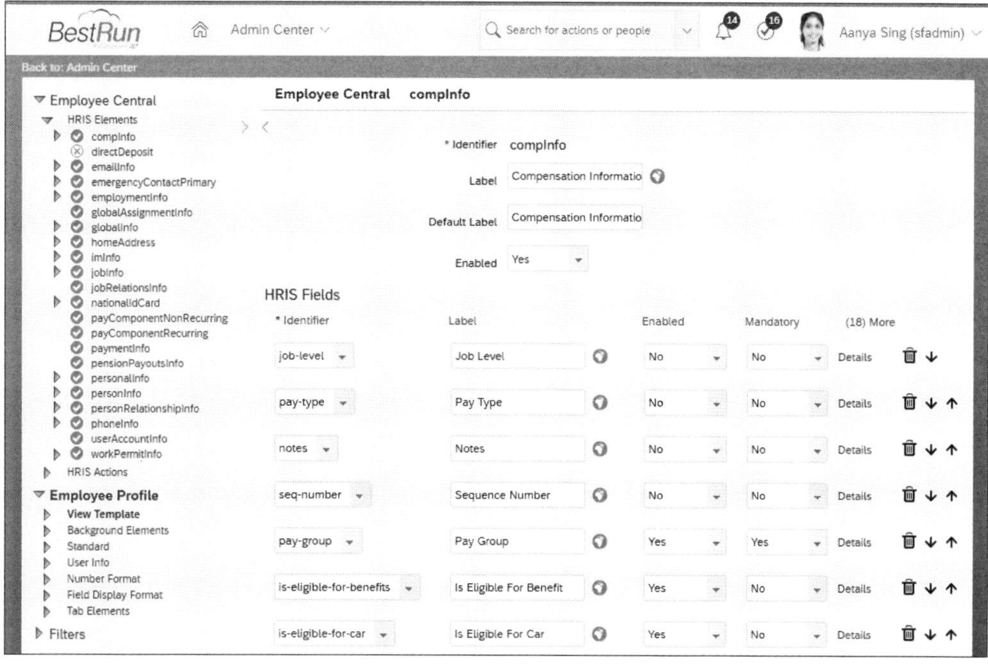

Figure 17.49 Manage Business Configuration

The application enables each of the blocks in Employee Central and both standard and user info element blocks of the Employee Profile to be configured using a simple UI. For Employee Central portlets, the portlet label and visibility can be changed, and fields can be added, removed, enabled or disabled, renamed, made required, changed to a picklist, be masked, and so on. Rules can also be assigned. Figure 17.50 shows the types of changes that can be made to the job-level field on the **Compensation Information** portlet.

For the Employee Profile elements, the label, visibility, picklist, required, length, reportable, and masked attributes can all be set. For **User Info** elements, the field type (**Text**, **Decimal Number**, **Number**, **Boolean**, or **Date**) can also be configured. You can also create new **User Info** elements here by clicking the **Create New** button at the bottom of the **User Info** list.

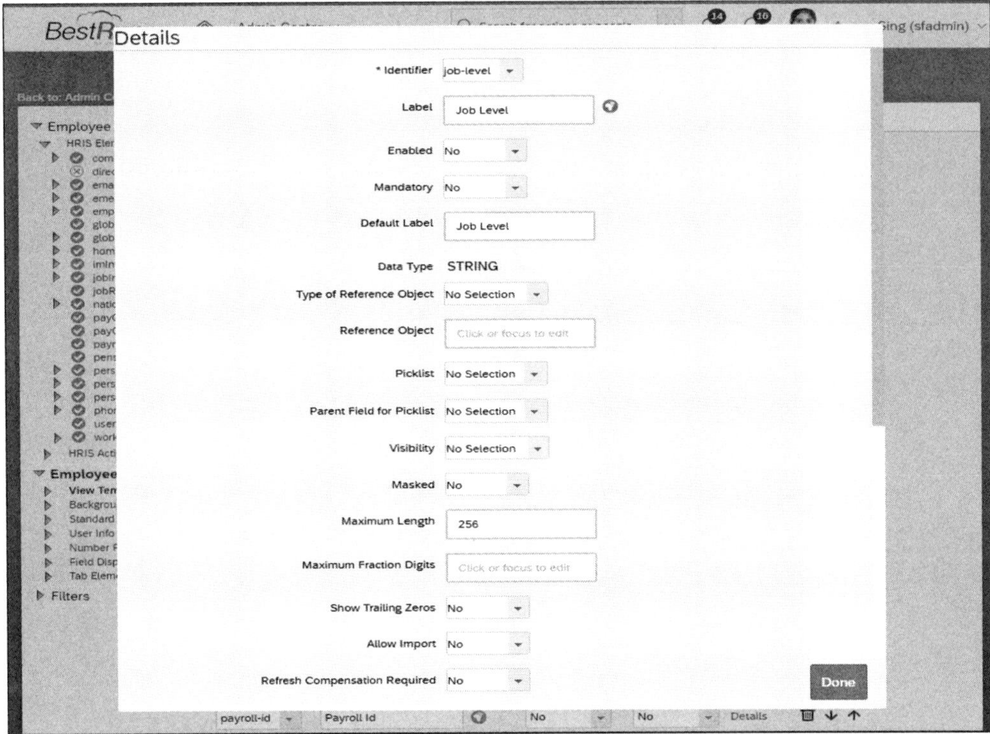

Figure 17.50 Editing a Field in Manage Business Configuration

17.15 Monitoring Execution of Business Rules

Business rules that are set to trigger in your system can be monitored and debugged using the **Business Rule Execution Log**, which is accessed in the Admin Center. The Business Rule Execution log enables you to set up a rule trace for a specific business rule or all business rules and download the log of the executing rule(s).

The **Business Rule Execution Log** user interface (UI) is the same as the **Manage Data** UI; you select **Rule Trace** in the **Search** dropdown and then the rule trace you want to view in the adjacent dropdown. To create a new rule trace, select **Rule Trace** in the **Create New** dropdown. Figure 17.51 shows a rule trace in **Business Rule Execution Log**.

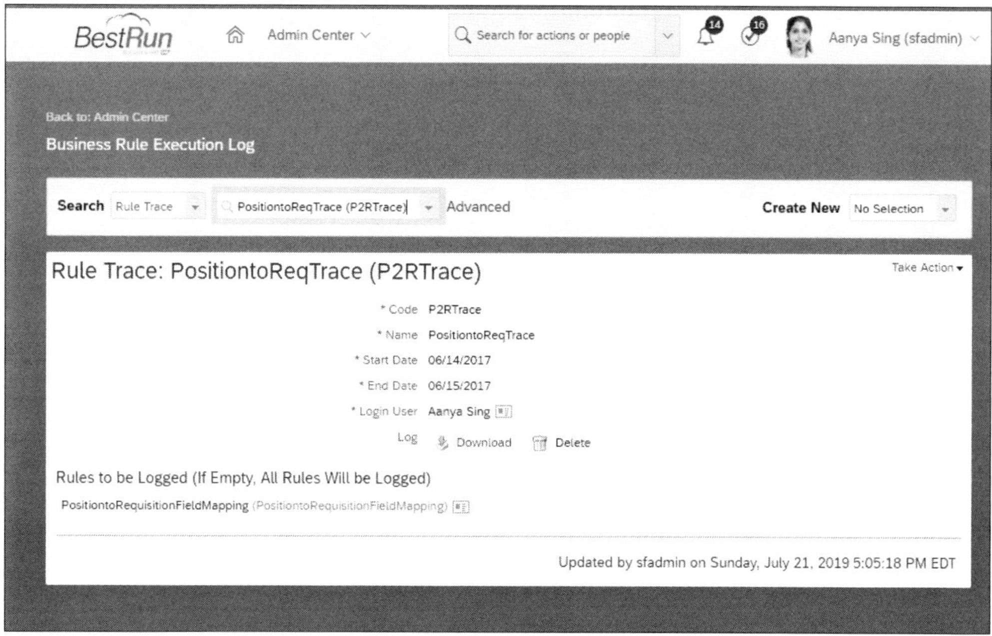

Figure 17.51 A Trace Rule in the Business Rule Execution Log

A rule trace logs the actions of each executed business rule that you've configured in the rule trace. A rule trace is configured with a code, name, start date, end date (a maximum of two days after the start date), a login user who will execute the rule, and then one or more rule that will be logged when they execute (if left blank then every rule that executes will be logged), as shown in Figure 17.51.

Once the rule trace has been configured and saved, it will run and log the rules automatically. During the configured dates, any time that any of the business rules configured in the rule trace execute, they will be logged. At any point, you can download the log by navigating to the **Business Rule Execution Log**. You can also delete the log at any point. The log file has a maximum size of 1MB, so at this point the log file will delete entries within the file. It is recommended to configure as few rules in the trace rule as possible, so that the log file can store all entries.

The Business Rule Execution log logs various types of steps and actions for each rule. It logs actions such as:

- Start and end of a rule executing
- Beginning and ending of a rule block executing

- Result of a condition is found
- The value of a field is retrieved
- The value of a field is set
- A value is compared to another value

Figure 17.52 shows an example log file.

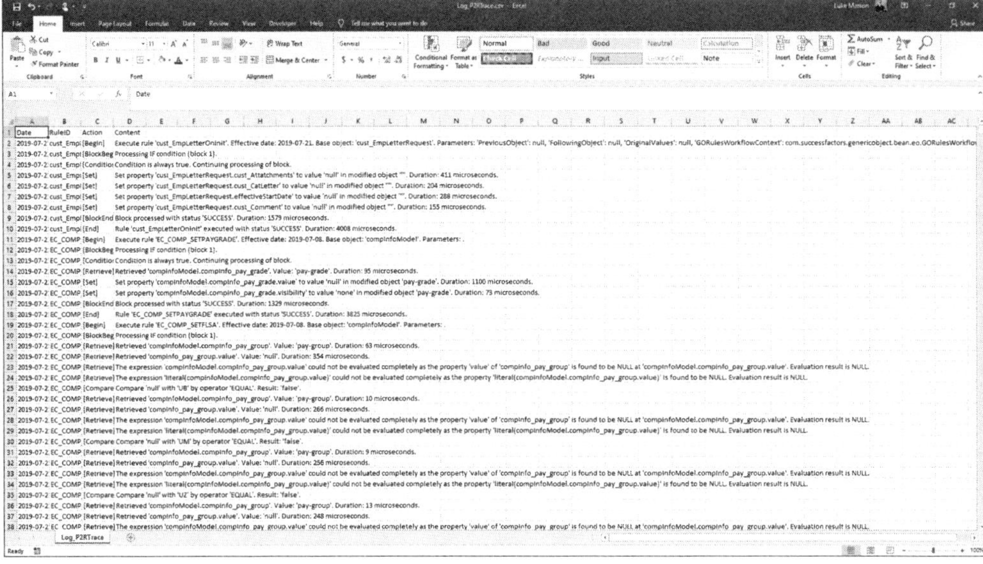

Figure 17.52 A Log File from Business Rule Execution Log

If the log file is empty, then none of the rules assigned in the rule trace have executed for the user configured in the rule trace.

Further Resources

You can find more information on the Business Rule Execution log in the guide *Implementing Business Rules in SAP SuccessFactors* found on the SAP Help Portal under the SAP SuccessFactors HCM Suite product page.

17.16 Managing Documents

Inevitably as part of the day-to-day use of SAP SuccessFactors, you will need to store documents in the system. There are a few activities available to you as an administrator:

- Set document and storage settings
- View documents stored in the system
- Upload documents to be display on a tile on the home page

We'll look at each of these now.

17.16.1 Document and Storage Settings

You can configure document attachment settings in **Company System and Logo Settings** in the Admin Center. Here you can configure the following:

- **Attachment Storage Allocation**
  Sets the maximum total attachment storage allocated in your instance. This can be 1 GB, 2 GB, 5 GB, 10 GB, 50 GB, 100 GB, 200 GB, 500 GB, or 1 TB.
- **Attachment User Limit**
  The maximum total attachment storage allocated to each user in the instance. This can be 5 MB, 10 MB, 20 MB, 50 MB, 100 MB, or no limit.
- **Attachment Max File Size**
  The maximum file size allowed for an attachment. This can be 5 MB or 10 MB.
- **Attachment Limit Notification Monitor Period**
  The frequency in which notifications are sent to users with access to Document Management once 75 percent of the total storage allocation is reached (the allocation defined in the **Attachment Storage Allocation** setting). This can be 1 day, 3 days, 7 days, or never.
- **Retention Period for Purging Deleted Attachments**
  The period for which purged attachments are retained in the system. This can be 30 days, 90 days, 180 days, or 365 days.

17.16.2 View Stored Documents

Any documents stored in the documents can be searched for and viewed in **Manage Documents** in the Admin Center, which can be seen in Figure 17.53. By default, all documents in the instance are listed, but it is possible to filter documents by name, uploader, internal or external, size, active or deleted, and type. You can also download one or more files.

Files cannot be deleted in **Manage Documents**.

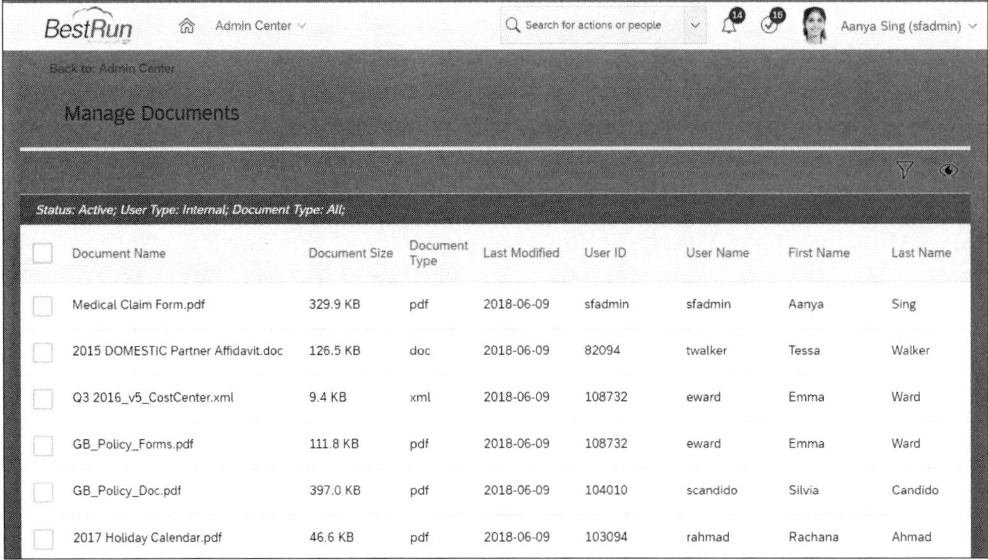

Document Name	Document Size	Document Type	Last Modified	User ID	User Name	First Name	Last Name
Medical Claim Form.pdf	329.9 KB	pdf	2018-06-09	sfadmin	sfadmin	Aanya	Sing
2015 DOMESTIC Partner Affidavit.doc	126.5 KB	doc	2018-06-09	82094	twalker	Tessa	Walker
Q3 2016_v5_CostCenter.xml	9.4 KB	xml	2018-06-09	108732	eward	Emma	Ward
GB_Policy_Forms.pdf	111.8 KB	pdf	2018-06-09	108732	eward	Emma	Ward
GB_Policy_Doc.pdf	397.0 KB	pdf	2018-06-09	104010	scandido	Silvia	Candido
2017 Holiday Calendar.pdf	46.6 KB	pdf	2018-06-09	103094	rahmad	Rachana	Ahmad

Figure 17.53 Manage Documents

17.16.3 Company Documents Tile

Documents can be uploaded in **Manage Documents** to display on the **Company Documents** tile on the home page. This could be documents such as a company handbook, corporate policy, how-to guide, or other documents relevant to all employees that have the **Company Documents**.

When documents are uploaded, you can define a description for the document, the category of the document, and the country it will display for.

> **Further Resources**
>
> You can find more information on document management in the guide *Document Management and Attachment Storage* found on the SAP Help Portal under the SAP SuccessFactors HCM Suite product page.

17.17 Reporting

Reporting on data in the system is critical to the ongoing operation of the business. The Report Center in SAP SuccessFactors is a one-stop shop for reporting on data in different formats across all modules in the suite. It is accessed from the **Reporting** option in the navigation menu.

The Report Center—shown in Figure 17.54—enables you to create, run, and share different types of reports. All users will see the **My Reports** tab. Admins will also see the **All Reports** tab. Within these tabs, a user has several options, including:

- Create a report
- Import a report
- Toggle between grouped reports and a flat list of reports
- Search for reports
- Filter and sort the list of reports

Reports can be grouped by labels in the list, such as **Payroll Reports** or **Recruiting Reports**.

Below the options, the user will see all reports that they have created or have been shared with them. In the **All Reports** tab, they will see all reports available in the instance. The name, author, last modified date, type of report, and **Action** button are shown for each report. The **Action** button (three horizontal dots) allows a user to perform several actions, such as run, edit, delete, share, duplicate, export, and add to one of the existing labels.

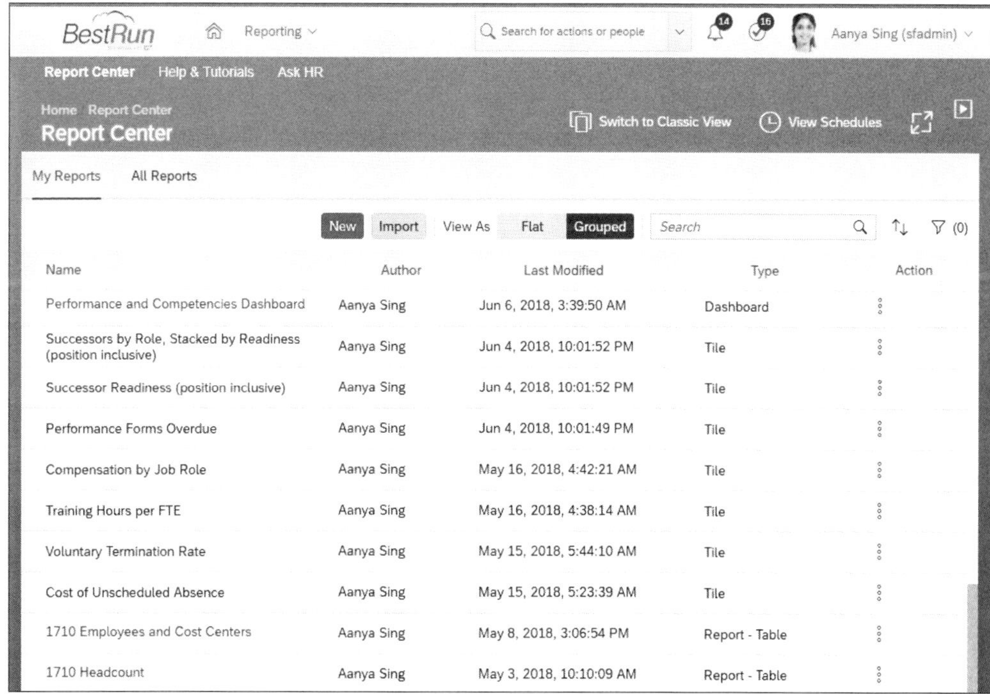

Figure 17.54 The Report Center Home Page

To run a report, a user simply clicks on the report. Figure 17.55 shows an example of a report that has been run.

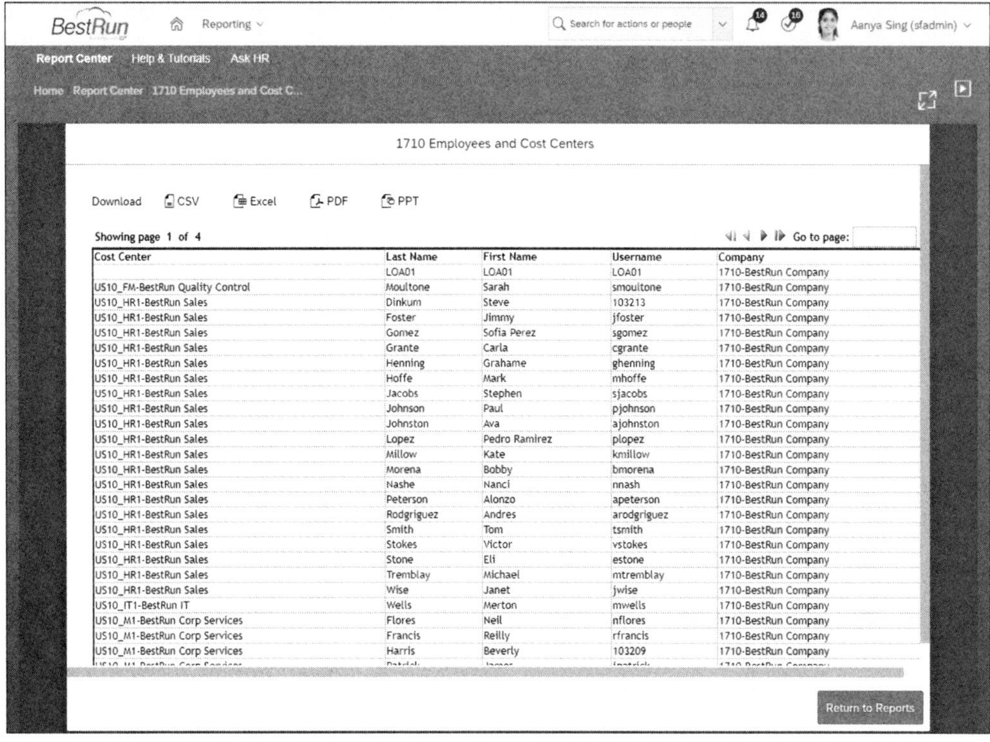

Cost Center	Last Name	First Name	Username	Company
	LOA01	LOA01	LOA01	1710-BestRun Company
US10_FM-BestRun Quality Control	Moultone	Sarah	smoultone	1710-BestRun Company
US10_HR1-BestRun Sales	Dinkum	Steve	103213	1710-BestRun Company
US10_HR1-BestRun Sales	Foster	Jimmy	jfoster	1710-BestRun Company
US10_HR1-BestRun Sales	Gomez	Sofia Perez	sgomez	1710-BestRun Company
US10_HR1-BestRun Sales	Grante	Carla	cgrante	1710-BestRun Company
US10_HR1-BestRun Sales	Henning	Grahame	ghenning	1710-BestRun Company
US10_HR1-BestRun Sales	Hoffe	Mark	mhoffe	1710-BestRun Company
US10_HR1-BestRun Sales	Jacobs	Stephen	sjacobs	1710-BestRun Company
US10_HR1-BestRun Sales	Johnson	Paul	pjohnson	1710-BestRun Company
US10_HR1-BestRun Sales	Johnston	Ava	ajohnston	1710-BestRun Company
US10_HR1-BestRun Sales	Lopez	Pedro Ramirez	plopez	1710-BestRun Company
US10_HR1-BestRun Sales	Millow	Kate	kmillow	1710-BestRun Company
US10_HR1-BestRun Sales	Morena	Bobby	bmorena	1710-BestRun Company
US10_HR1-BestRun Sales	Nashe	Nanci	nnash	1710-BestRun Company
US10_HR1-BestRun Sales	Peterson	Alonzo	apeterson	1710-BestRun Company
US10_HR1-BestRun Sales	Rodgriguez	Andres	arodgriguez	1710-BestRun Company
US10_HR1-BestRun Sales	Smith	Tom	tsmith	1710-BestRun Company
US10_HR1-BestRun Sales	Stokes	Victor	vstokes	1710-BestRun Company
US10_HR1-BestRun Sales	Stone	Eli	estone	1710-BestRun Company
US10_HR1-BestRun Sales	Tremblay	Michael	mtremblay	1710-BestRun Company
US10_HR1-BestRun Sales	Wise	Janet	jwise	1710-BestRun Company
US10_IT1-BestRun IT	Wells	Merton	mwells	1710-BestRun Company
US10_M1-BestRun Corp Services	Flores	Neil	nflores	1710-BestRun Company
US10_M1-BestRun Corp Services	Francis	Reilly	rfrancis	1710-BestRun Company
US10_M1-BestRun Corp Services	Harris	Beverly	103209	1710-BestRun Company

Figure 17.55 The 1710 Employees and Cost Centers Report

Users can create a report by clicking the **New** button. They will then be presented with the following different types of reports that they can create, as shown in Figure 17.56:

- Report – Canvas
  Build freeform reports by dragging and dropping report components (such as tables or charts) onto a canvas. This was previously called Online Report Designer.
- **Report – Table**
  Ad hoc reports that enable you to report on one or more types of data. This was previously called **Ad-Hoc Reporting**.

- **Tile**
  A chart with drill-to-detail.
- **Dashboard**
  A collection of tiles.

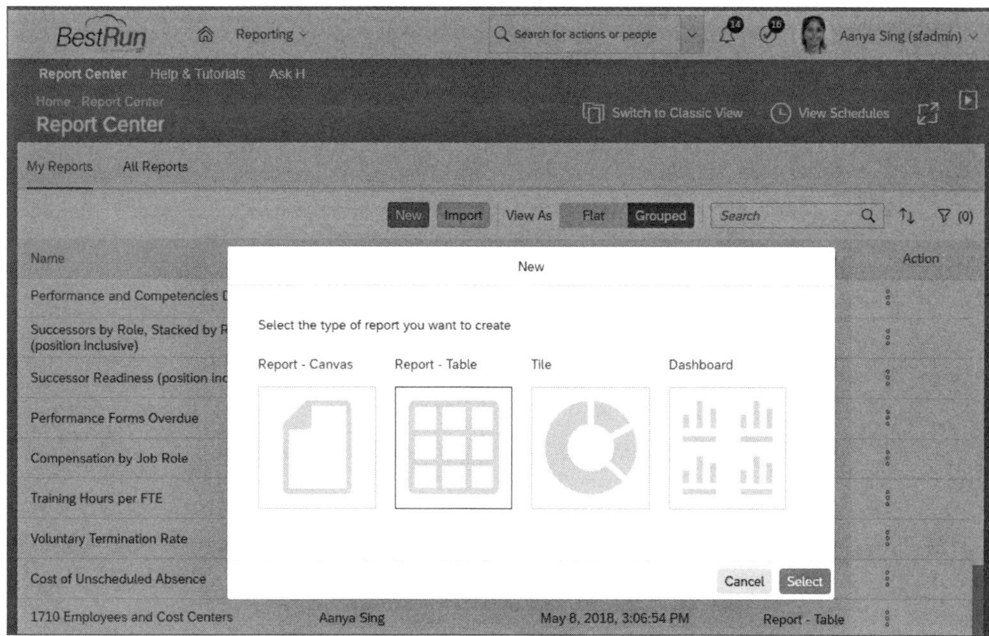

Figure 17.56 The Types of Reports That Can Be Created

When a user runs a report, RBPs are effective, as they are in any other part of the system.

Further Resources

You can find more information on the Report Center and the different types of report in the guides *Using Report Center*, *Managing Report Center*, and *SAP SuccessFactors Analytics Reporting Directory* found on the SAP Help Portal under the SAP Success-Factors Workforce Analytics product page.

17.18 Summary

We've taken a look at a number of administrative activities that are required to continuously support the SAP SuccessFactors system. After reading this chapter, you should be familiar with the different types of activities that administrators can perform to keep the system working. Here, we've looked at user management and authentication, email notifications, picklists, data imports, data retention and purging, instance synchronization, business configuration, and some of the various Employee Central administrative activities.

Appendix A
Further Resources

In light of the continuous innovation in SAP SuccessFactors software, constant development of strategy, and changes within the market, it is important to ensure that you stay abreast of all the latest information available. A number of resources and channels are available to do this.

With the software-as-a-service (SaaS) delivery model, the SAP SuccessFactors HCM Suite of software is enhancing on a regular basis. Along with that continuous innovation, SAP is also constantly remodeling how they deliver resources to customers and partners.

Since the last edition of the book, there have been many changes in the resources available to customers and partners. There is now a wealth of information available for customers and partners that was not available before, and SAP is continuing to provide more and more resources. We strongly recommend that you stay as up-to-date and as well informed as possible because the pace of change is quick.

This chapter will recommend reliable channels of information for your ongoing research and education. We have split the content into those resources that are useful for both customers and partners, and those that are specific for partners, implementation, social media resources, publications, conferences, and user groups.

A.1 Resources for Customers and Partners

SAP continues to improve the release and distribution of information to customers and partners. We recommend several outlets of information that are maintained by SAP.

SAP's sales and presales executives, as well as production management, are a source of the latest information on products, integration, and roadmaps. Although information from this channel can have a strong marketing feel, it's nevertheless a good starting point to understand the capabilities of the SAP SuccessFactors HCM Suite and the integration content and technology that SAP offers.

A.1.1 SAP Website

The SAP website offers a plethora of information on SAP's offerings, but it is also where the SAP product and solution roadmaps can be found. Additionally, you can find the SAP SuccessFactors roadmap and the SAP Trust Center on the SAP website.

The SAP SuccessFactors roadmap can be found by navigating to the product roadmaps URL (*http://s-prs.co/v485805*) and selecting **SAP SuccessFactors HCM Suite** in the **Products** dropdown.

The SAP Trust Center provides information on security, privacy, and compliance for SAP's range of Cloud solutions. You can check the status of SAP's cloud services, review security and compliance standards, explore privacy policies, explore data centers, and more. The SAP Trust Center is accessed via the URL *http://s-prs.co/v485806*.

A.1.2 SAP Support Portal

The SAP Support site is your one-stop shop for access to product support, SAP Notes, knowledge base articles (KBAs), product downloads, service availability, and more. Here you can also do the following:

- Search for answers to questions, queries, or product issues
- Report and view incidents for product issues
- Download software (for example, integration add-ons)
- View the service availability
- View the latest news (called "Spotlight News")

Most of these capabilities are delivered via the SAP ONE Support Launchpad, which we will cover in the next section of this chapter. Additionally, you can navigate to SAP

Community, SAP SuccessFactors Community, and the SAP Help Portal from here. We will also cover these three portals in the following sections of this chapter.

Figure A.1 shows the home page of the SAP Support Portal.

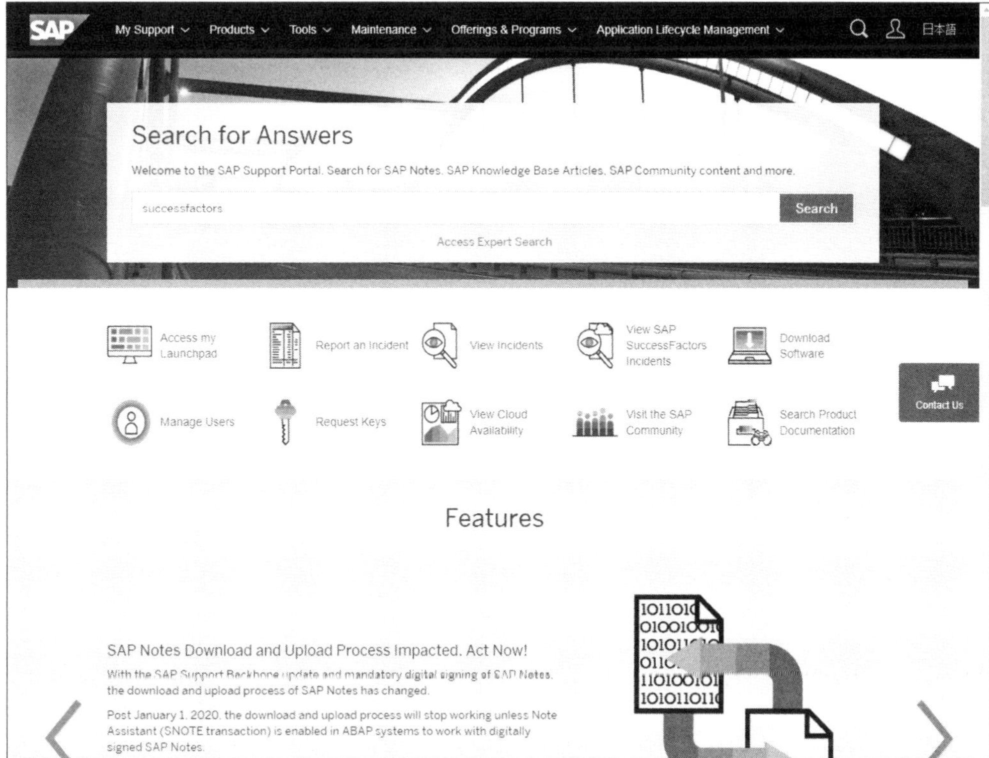

Figure A.1 SAP Support Portal Home Page

A.1.3 SAP ONE Support Launchpad

The SAP ONE Support Launchpad is the gateway to your core support needs. Along with the SAP Support Portal, this platform replaced much of the functionality and service offered through the now retired SAP Service Marketplace. Figure A.2 shows the home page of the SAP ONE Support Launchpad.

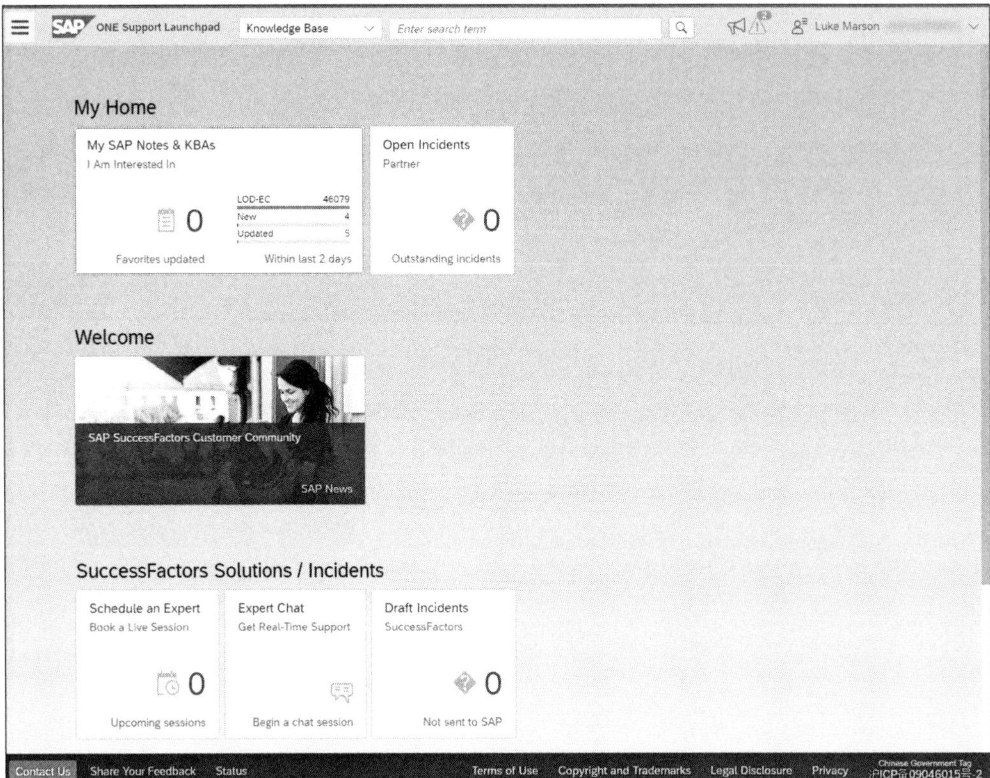

Figure A.2 SAP ONE Support Launchpad Home Page

Let's take a quick look at some of the key activities you can perform here.

Incidents

When you discover issues or bugs with the SAP SuccessFactors software, you can report these incidents through a ticketing system. Incidents can be created and worked on through the SAP ONE Support Launchpad. Existing SAP customers should be familiar with this process of creating, viewing, and working with tickets in this environment. New customers should become familiar with this system over time, depending on the regularity in which they need to create incidents.

SAP Notes and KBAs

SAP regularly release advice on bugs and issues with their software. These are called SAP Notes. SAP Notes can also be information notes, how-tos, or corrections. KBAs describe SAP Notes that are information notes and how-tos instead of product bugs, issues, or corrections. KBAs are included in the SAP Notes search by default. Figure A.3 shows an SAP Note for SAP SuccessFactors Employee Central.

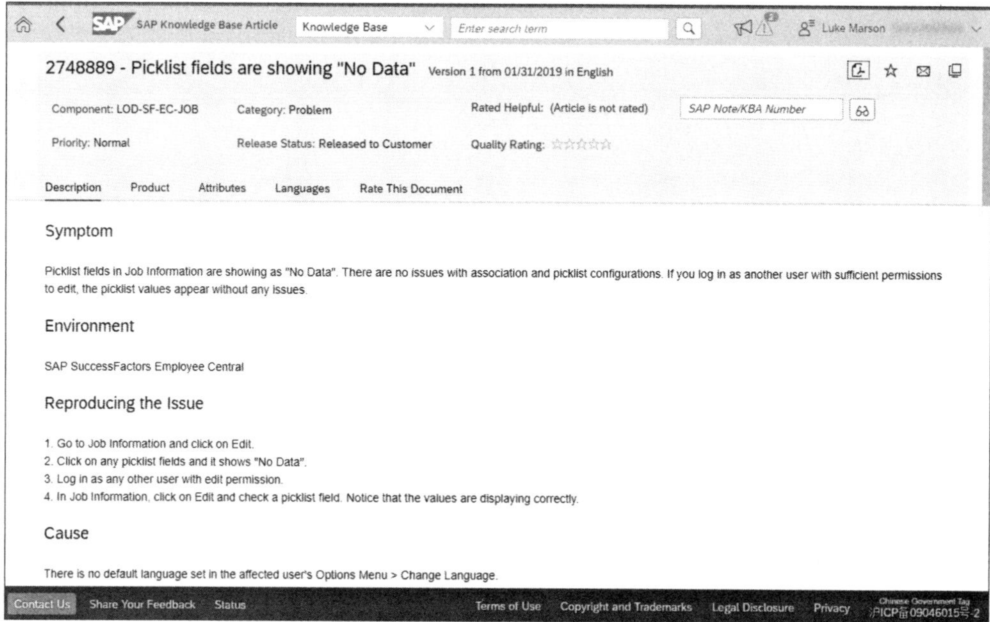

Figure A.3 An SAP Note for Employee Central

Unlike with SAP ERP Human Capital Management (SAP ERP HCM) on-premise, SAP Notes are not imported into SAP SuccessFactors to resolve product bugs or issues.

SAP Notes cover all of the SAP SuccessFactors HCM Suite products, as well as the prepackaged integrations that they offer. Each product and any sub-areas of each product have their own code; these are called *components*. When you create an incident in the SAP ONE Support Launchpad, you select one of these components as the product area for your incident.

Cloud Availability Center

The Cloud Availability Center enables you to view the service availability for SAP Cloud applications. It provides a status of cloud applications and a day-by-day event calendar, and latest news on service availability and disruptions. Figure A.4 shows the status of SAP SuccessFactors in the Cloud Availability Center.

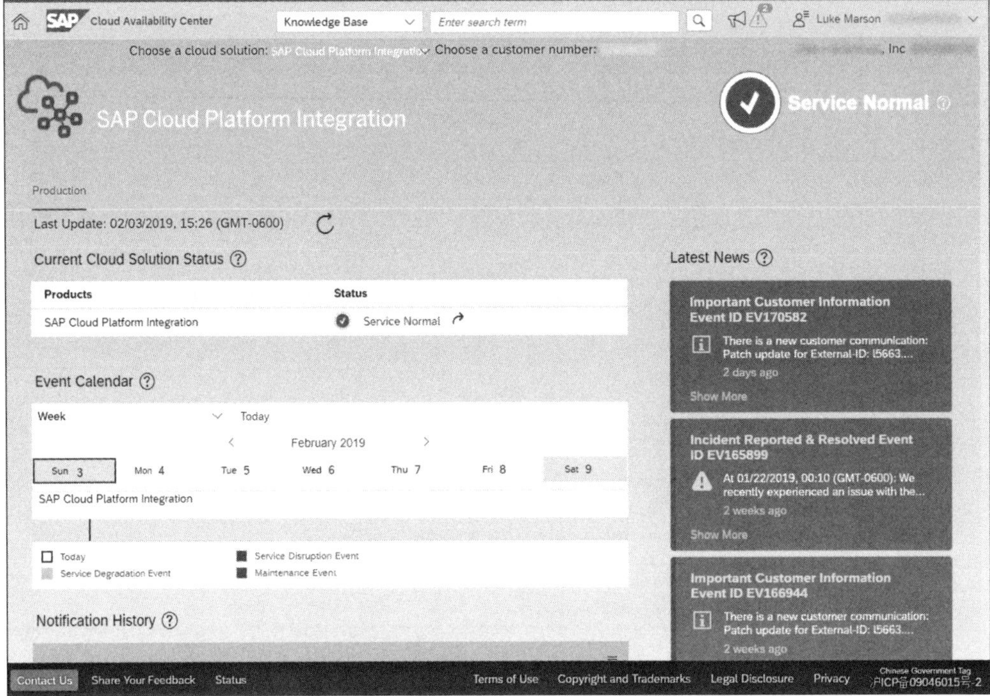

Figure A.4 The Cloud Availability Center Showing the Status of SAP SuccessFactors

Software Download

In SAP ONE Support Launchpad you can download the integration add-on's to install in the SAP ERP on-premise system in order to integrate SAP ERP with SAP SuccessFactors (no matter which deployment model you are using or planning to use). Here you can download the integration add-ons for the following:

- Employee Central and SAP ERP (full cloud, core hybrid, and side-by-side models)
- SAP ERP HCM and SAP SuccessFactors talent modules (talent hybrid model)
- SAP Finance and Employee Central (cost center replication)

The add-on for integration Employee Central and SAP ERP includes Infoporter (data migration application for migrating data from SAP ERP HCM to Employee Central).

Schedule an Expert

The Schedule an Expert feature in the SAP ONE Support Launchpad allows you to set-up a 30-minute call directly with an SAP Support engineer. You simply schedule the appointment with three or more days' notice and provide your support-related question. SAP will then set up the call with the engineer for you to work through your issue.

Expert Chat

Expert Chat is a real-time chat with an SAP Support operator. This can be useful for talking through more basic issues with support, such as how to raise an incident or where to find a specific resource.

A.1.4 SAP Help Portal

The SAP Help Portal (*http://help.sap.com*) is a useful resource for getting detailed and technical information on SAP's products, including the SAP SuccessFactors HCM Suite. It features product pages for all products in the suite, plus the following pages:

- SAP SuccessFactors HCM Suite
- SAP SuccessFactors Release Information
- SAP SuccessFactors Employee Central Integration to SAP Business Suite
- SFIHCM (also known as the integration add-on for SAP ERP HCM and SAP SuccessFactors HCM Suite)
- SAP Localization Hub, social media integration service for China for SAP SuccessFactors Recruiting

Each product page contains information about what is new with each product, documentation on configuration, implementation, development, and more. In Figure A.5 we can see the product page for the SAP SuccessFactors HCM Suite.

All of the implementation handbooks are available in the product pages. These had previously been housed on SAP Service Marketplace.

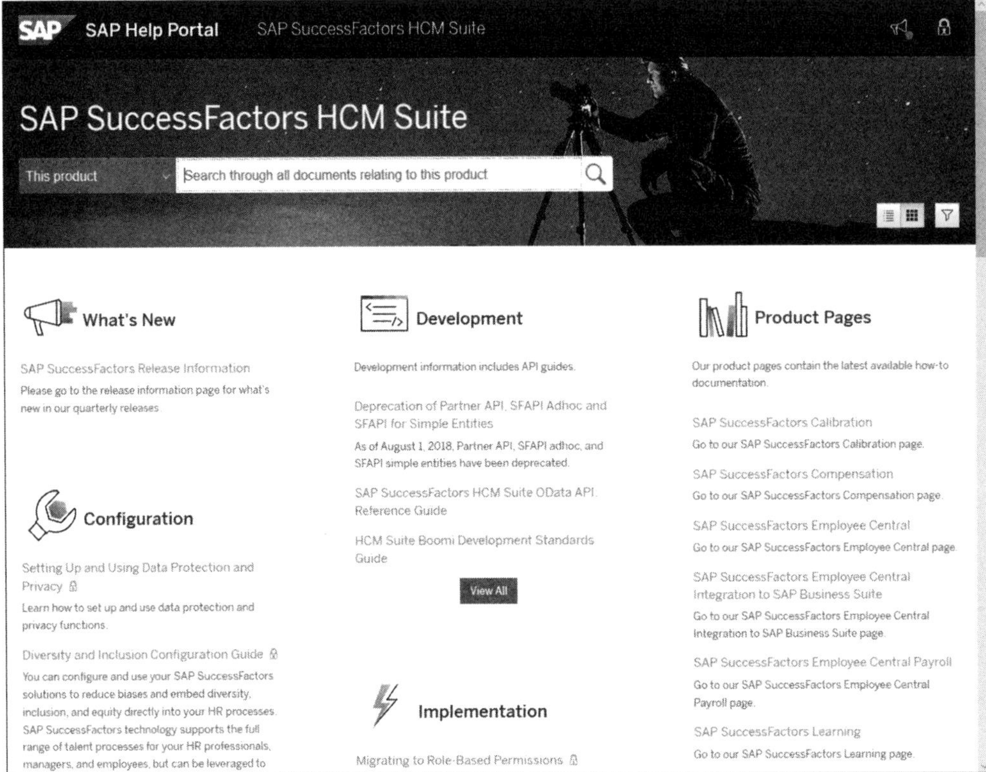

Figure A.5 SAP SuccessFactors HCM Suite Product Page on the SAP Help Portal

A.1.5 SAP SuccessFactors Community

The SAP SuccessFactors Community (*http://community.successfactors.com*) is the central point for SAP SuccessFactors customers. It is the place to find the latest information, post questions for fellow users to answer, check the release schedule, watch videos, download resources, take training, partake in forums, access webinars and events, read blogs, research certified partners, and much more. From the SAP SuccessFactors Community home page (shown in Figure A.6), you can see the amount of days left to the next release and you can navigate to topics of interest.

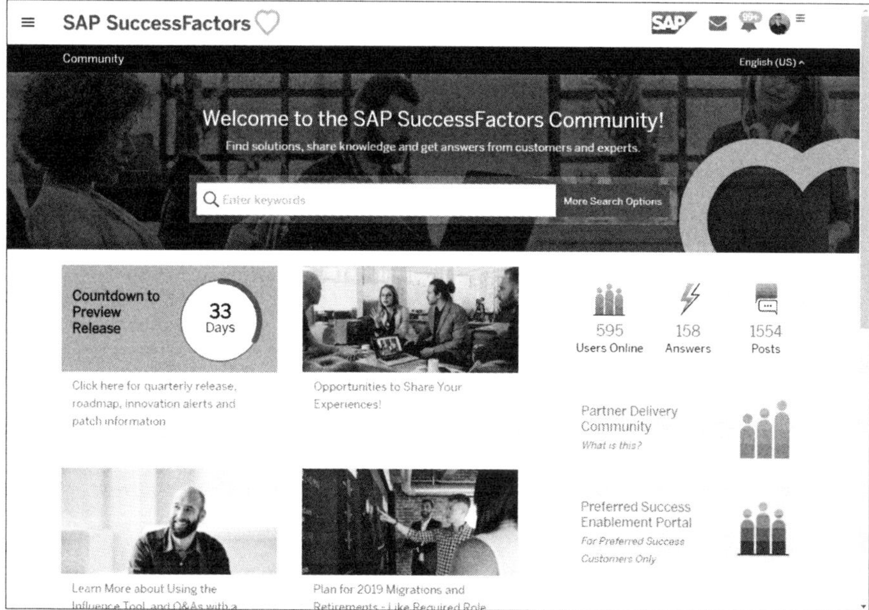

Figure A.6 The SAP SuccessFactors Community Website

A.1.6 SAP Community

SAP Community is the official user community of SAP and has more than two million members. It contains a wide range of spaces covering different SAP areas and disciplines, with content largely focused around blogs and forum discussions.

Although not as popular as it once was, SAP Community still has a significant amount of content posted there regularly and is worth visiting weekly.

SAP Community hosts one of the most comprehensive and popular collections of blogs and articles on SAP SuccessFactors, the *SAP SuccessFactors—Useful Resources and Documents* document (*http://s-prs.co/v485807*).

A.1.7 SAP SuccessFactors Customer Empowerment Newsletter

The SAP SuccessFactors Customer Empowerment Newsletter provides a wealth of information to customers on a monthly basis. The newsletter summarizes important announcement, release information, news, webinars, videos, useful resources, and more.

You can subscribe at the URL *http://s-prs.co/v485808*.

A.1.8 Customer Influence

SAP's Customer Influence program allows customers and partners to submit ideas and enhancement requests ("improvement requests") for SAP SuccessFactors products. Customers and partners can review and vote on these ideas/enhancement requests, and SAP will respond to requests to confirm their intentions or thoughts on development of the idea.

To access the Customer Influence program, go to *http://s-prs.co/v485809* and select **Log in to view current projects** under **SAP Customer Engagement Initiative**. Expand **Lines of Business** and select **Human Resources** to see the list of requests. Figure A.7 shows some enhancement requests for Recruiting.

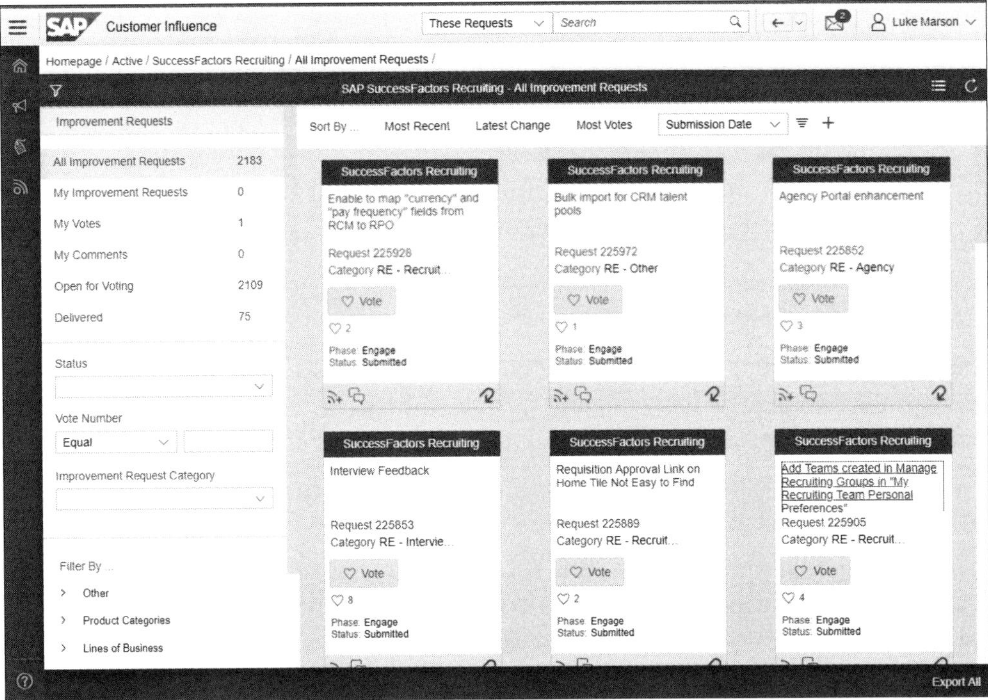

Figure A.7 Improvement Requests for Recruiting

A.1.9 openSAP

openSAP (*https://open.sap.com/*) is a massive open online course (MOOC) platform to provide free training and educational courses to the public, free of charge. At the time of writing (fall 2019), there are eight SAP SuccessFactors courses available on openSAP, most of which you can take at your own pace in your own time. While some courses have a little bit of a marketing feel, all of the courses are fairly educational and provide useful information on the SAP SuccessFactors HCM Suite.

A.1.10 SAP API Business Hub

SAP API Business Hub (*https://api.sap.com/*) is an application programming interface (API) repository for customers and partners looking to build integration to and from SAP cloud applications. More than 20 APIs are accessible for SAP SuccessFactors, with most of the APIs supporting SAP SuccessFactors Employee Central integrations.

SAP API Business Hub provides details on each API, including downloadable definition, entity paths and commands, sandbox and production server URLs, API key, software development kit (SDK), and version number, along with other information. In Figure A.8, you can see the entity details for the EmployeePayrollRunResultsItems API.

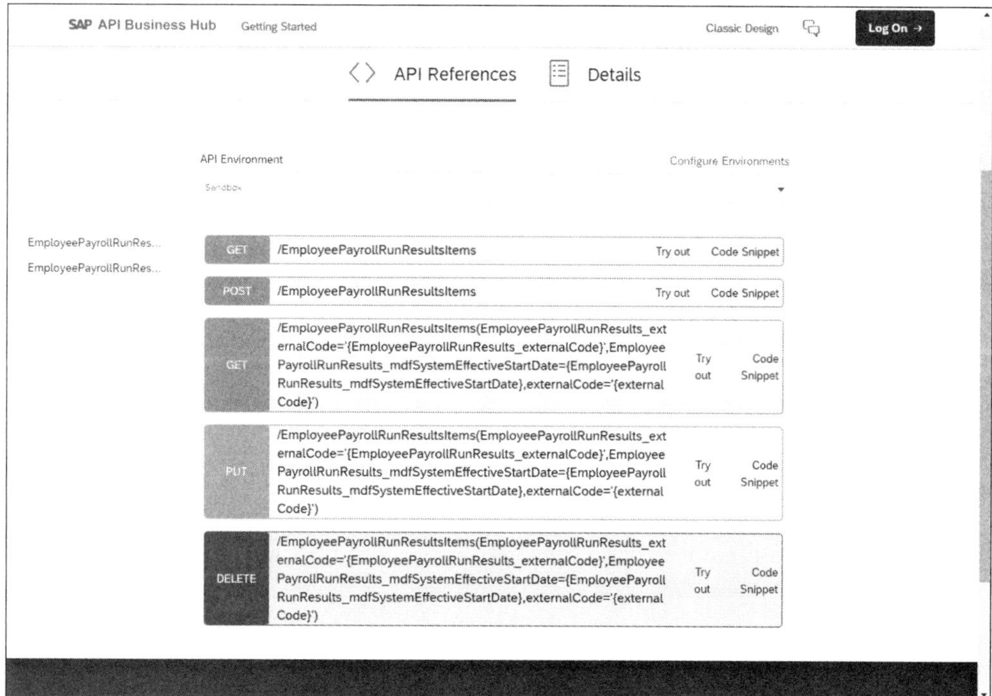

Figure A.8 Entity Details for the EmployeePayrollRunResultsItems API

A.1.11 SAP App Center

The SAP App Center (*https://www.sapappcenter.com*) is where customers can browse and purchase applications and packages built by SAP and their partners to use in conjunction with their SAP applications. There are a variety of SAP SuccessFactors extension applications, such as the Job Descriptions Made Simple app shown in Figure A.9.

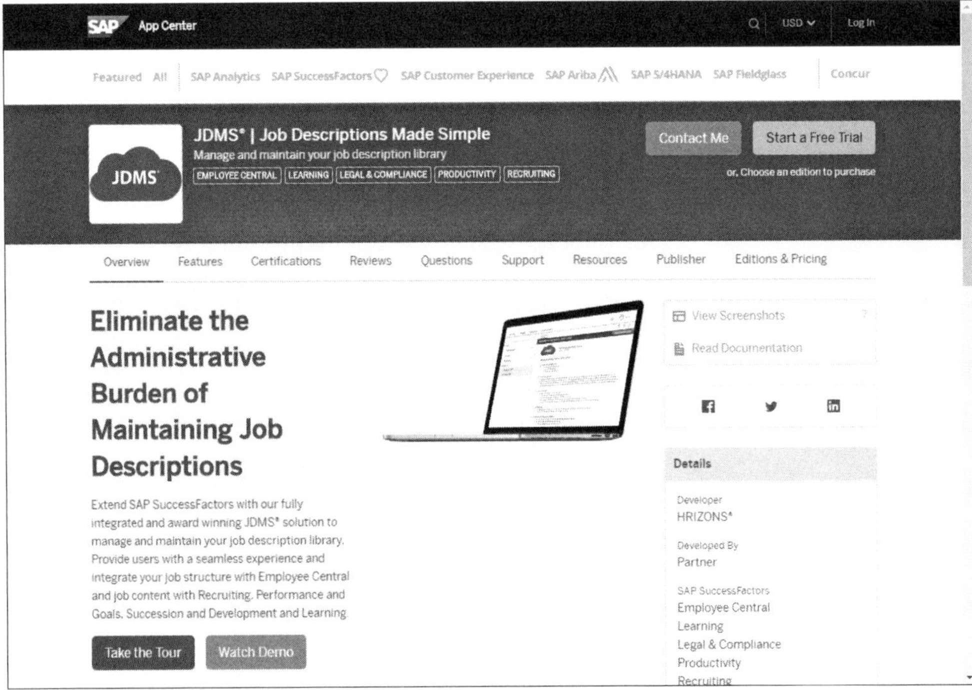

Figure A.9 An Application in the SAP App Center

You can purchase these applications from here, start a free trial, or be put in touch with the vendor sales team to find out more information.

Applications available here cover all sorts of HR domains, such as time management, job description management, org charting and org restructuring, health and wellbeing, employee surveys and assessments, rapid deployment packages, and more.

A.1.12 SAP Best Practices Explorer

The SAP Best Practices Explorer (*https://rapid.sap.com*) is where SAP's rapid-deployment solutions (RDS) and SAP Best Practices can be viewed. SAP Best Practices are SAP's standard-delivered processes and configuration to run business processes using the SAP technology you choose.

For SAP SuccessFactors (at the time of writing, *http://s-prs.co/v485810*) the SAP Best Practices Explorer provides the SAP Best Practices and RDS solutions for Employee Central, Employee Central Service Center, Payroll Control Center, Performance & Goals, Compensation, Learning, Recruiting, Succession & Development, integration between Employee Central and SAP ERP (core hybrid or full HCM cloud), and integration between SAP ERP HCM and SAP SuccessFactors talent solutions (talent hybrid).

A.1.13 WhatsApp

SAP Support provides a WhatsApp channel for SAP SuccessFactors customers to get real-time information on product updates, KBAs, wikis, guided answers, SAP Notes, and "hot tips" on the SAP SuccessFactors HCM Suite applications that you choose. You can choose any number of SAP SuccessFactors HCM Suite applications to subscribe to.

Visit the URL *http://s-prs.co/v485811* to see a video on how to get access to the WhatsApp Channel for SAP SuccessFactors. You can also visit this SAP Community blog for more information: *http://s-prs.co/v485812*.

A.2 Resources for Partners

SAP provides a number of resources exclusively for its partners. In the past, SAP SuccessFactors had the partner portal for partners, but these resources are now part of the various different systems we cover in this chapter.

We'll now go through each of the key resources available to partners.

A.2.1 Cloud Operations Portal

The Cloud Operations Portal provides partners with tools to request the following:

- Demo systems
- Access to customer system provisioning
- Provisioning of certain customer instances
- Secure File Transfer Protocol (SFTP) account password reset

Partners can also raise support tickets for the operations team in relation to instance and access issues.

A.2.2 SAP SuccessFactors Partner Delivery Community

The SAP SuccessFactors Partner Delivery Community (PDC) is the partner equivalent of the SAP SuccessFactors Community. Partners can access a variety of information on products, training, implementation, sales, and marketing. SAP SuccessFactors make partner announcements here, and there are also forums for partner consultants to ask questions of fellow consultants in the community (see Figure A.10).

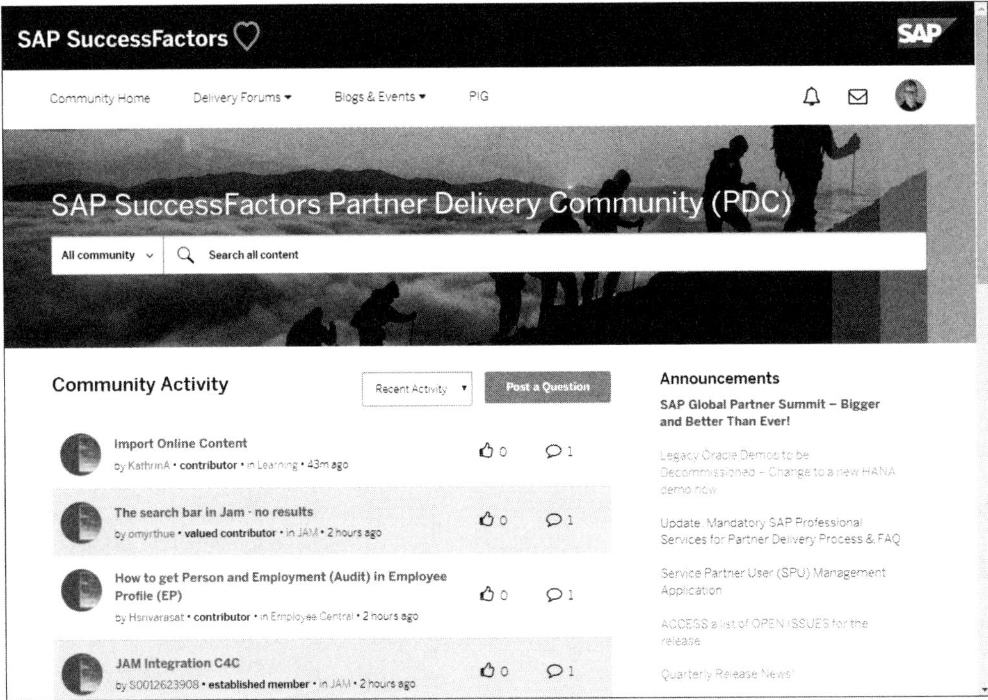

Figure A.10 The PDC Home Page

The PDC is split into three main areas:

- **Delivery Forums**
  The **Delivery Forums** are where consultants can post questions and respond to questions. This is a great place to learn about real-life situations and understand

how to solve real implementation problems. There are forums for each SAP SuccessFactors HCM Suite solution, as well as integration and SAP Jam.

- **Blogs & Events**
  In **Blogs & Events**, both SAP SuccessFactors and consultants can write blogs on any topic. Typically, SAP SuccessFactors will use this platform to write about announcements or upcoming changes, for example.
- **Partner Implementation Guide (PIG)**
  One of the best resources for consultants is the Partner Implementation Guide (PIG). The home page can be seen in Figure A.11. The PIG provides partners with resources and tools to help consultants successfully implement SAP SuccessFactors HCM Suite solutions, such as information on training and certifications, the support transition process, mandatory SAP Professional Services needed, tips and tricks, and more.

The PIG is a must-read for any consultants who have not yet read it.

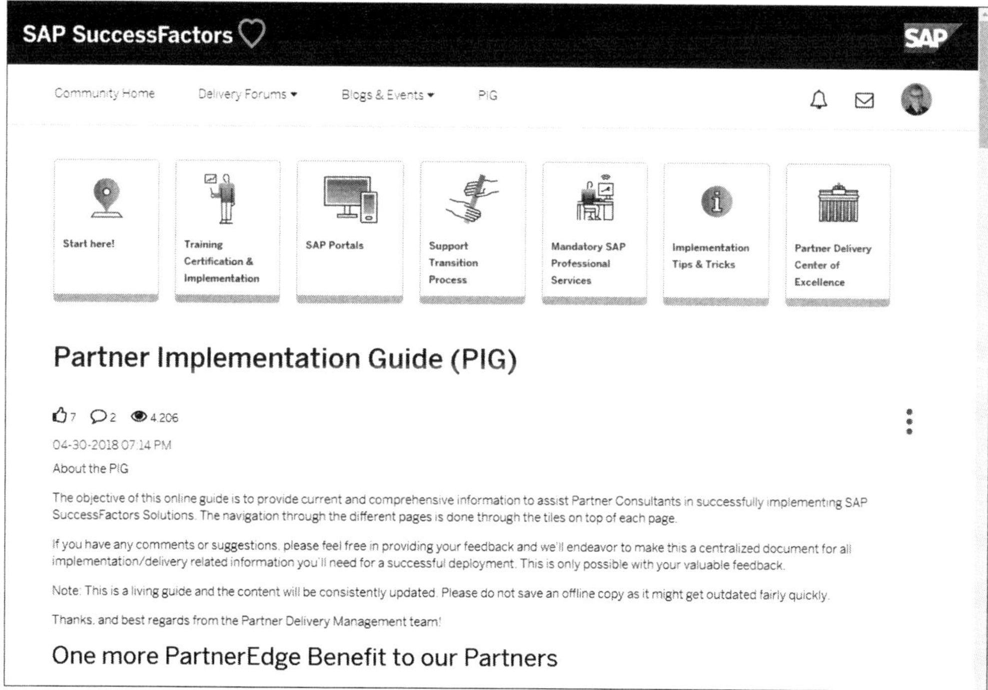

Figure A.11 The Partner Implementation Guide (PIG)

A.2.3 SAP PartnerEdge

SAP PartnerEdge (*http://partneredge.sap.com*) is SAP's core partner portal and home to resources for partners for sales, training, solution brochures, and general information. It also hosts specific program resources for partners that participate in SAP programs to build products or offer managed services. And naturally, it hosts a section for SAP SuccessFactors HCM Suite solutions, as shown in Figure A.12.

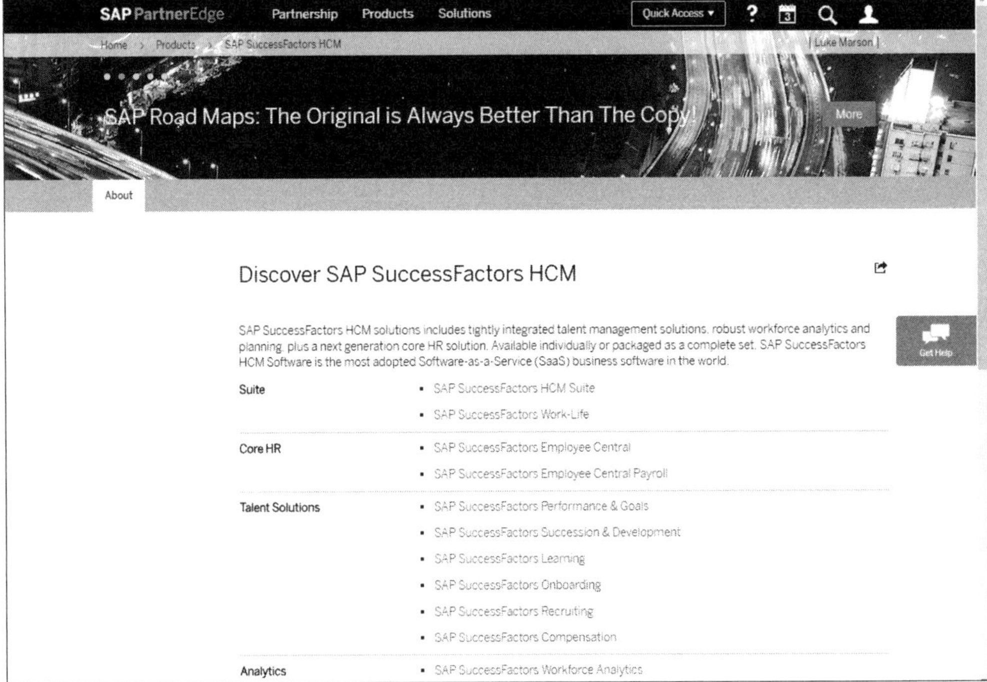

Figure A.12 The SAP SuccessFactors HCM Suite Page on SAP PartnerEdge

Partners can access assets such as product overviews, videos, presentations, white papers, roadmaps, materials to support sales and marketing, quarterly release webinars and information, demo videos, data models, useful links, and more.

All of the quarterly release Internal Release Readiness (IRR) sessions can be found here.

A.2.4 SAP Jam

SAP and SAP SuccessFactors leverage SAP Jam for social collaboration and knowledge sharing and host a number of groups for partners. As a partner, you automatically get access to SAP Jam, and a number of SAP SuccessFactors product-specific groups are automatically available.

For consultants who have completed application training, an application-specific group may be available. The following groups are available to some or all partner consultants, irrespective of the certifications held:

- SAP SuccessFactors Quarterly Releases for Partners
- SAP Activate Methodology for Cloud
- SAP SuccessFactors Partner Newsflash
- SAP SuccessFactors Integration For Partners

When you become certified in any given SAP SuccessFactors HCM Suite application, you can gain access to any SAP Jam groups that exist for that application.

A.2.5 SAP Learning Hub

The SAP Learning Hub (*https://training.sap.com/*) is SAP's training and education platform. Here you can take virtual training courses on SAP SuccessFactors HCM Suite applications (including integration) and the certification exams needed to become certified in SAP SuccessFactors HCM Suite solutions.

SAP Learning Hub offers a feature called *Live Access*. Live Access enables users to practice on an actual system.

The SAP SuccessFactors Learning Rooms are where the training courses can be located. The SAP SuccessFactors Learning Rooms leverage SAP SuccessFactors Learning technology to provide a great platform for taking training courses and getting educated on SAP SuccessFactors HCM Suite solutions. Delta certifications (quarterly exams that all certified consultants are required to take) are taken in the SAP Learning Room.

In Figure A.13 we can see the SAP SuccessFactors Employee Central Certified Associate Exam on the SAP Learning Hub.

At the time of writing (fall 2019), anyone who wants to subscribe to these courses must purchase a subscription to HUB077. Depending on your country of residence, this offering is called either *SAP Learning Hub, Edition for Human Resources* or *SAP Learning Hub, Edition for People Engagement*. This course gives unlimited access for one year to all training courses available on the SAP Learning Hub.

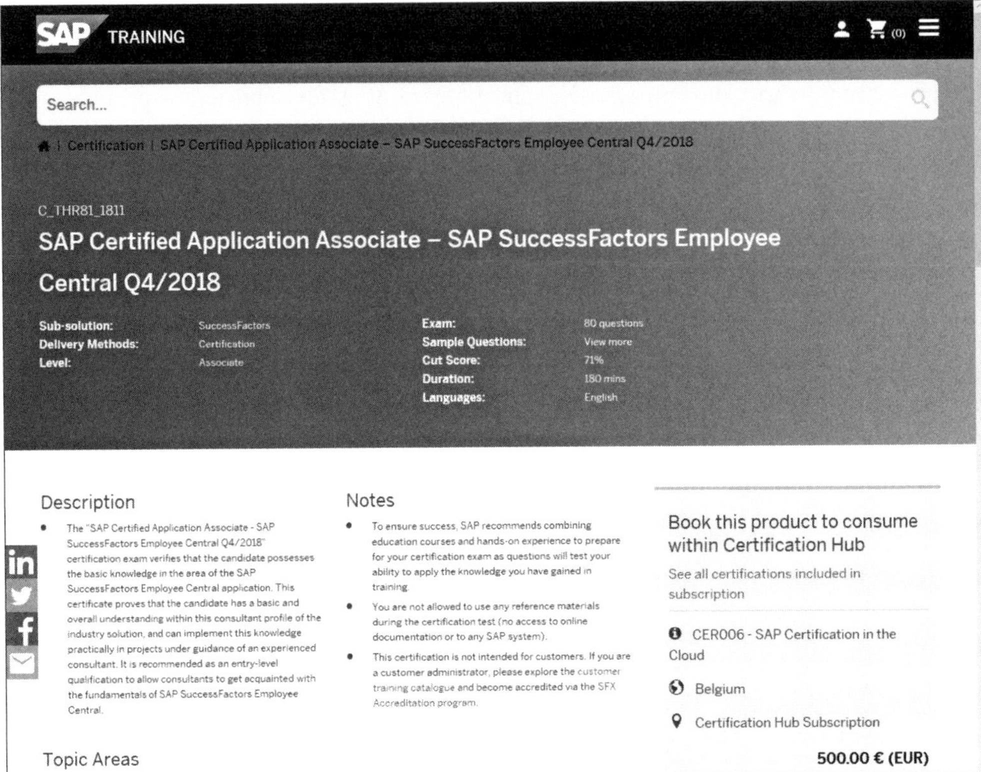

Figure A.13 The Employee Central Certified Associate Exam on the SAP Learning Hub

A.3 Implementation Resources

To help customers have a successful delivery of their implementation, SAP provides a range of resources that both customers and partners can refer to and use during the project. These include:

- SAP SuccessFactors Process Library
- Implementation Design Principles (IDPs)
- Architectural Leading Practices (ALPs)
- SAP Best Practices
- SAP Activate methodology templates
- Implementation guides

We've covered some of these already in this chapter, so for now we will just take a look at the first three.

A.3.1 SAP SuccessFactors Process Library

The SAP SuccessFactors Process Library contains a set of documentation for a number of processes across the SAP SuccessFactors HCM Suite. Each of these process sets have three documents:

- **Leading practice definitions**
  These provide definitions for what SAP SuccessFactors define as "leading practices" including a description, prerequisites, benefits/outcomes, and out-of-scope items for each process.
- **Process summaries**
  Process summaries contain a summary of each process, including the following sections of information for each:
  - Start event
  - Input
  - Prerequisites
  - Process participants
  - Purpose
  - Dependencies
  - End event
  - Output
  - Success criteria
  - Use cases
- **Process diagrams**
  The process diagrams provide a swim-lane diagram for each process.

Each of these provide a package of processes that can be used to build your business processes. At the time of writing (fall 2019), the SAP SuccessFactors Process Library contains processes for organizational management, HR administration, recruiting, onboarding, performance and goals, compensation, succession and development, and learning.

The practices contained in the SAP SuccessFactors Process Library form the basis of the SAP Model Company, referenced in Chapter 2, Section 2.3.

The SAP SuccessFactors Process Library can be found on the SAP SuccessFactors Community website.

A.3.2 Implementation Design Principles (IDPs)

The Implementation Design Principles (IDPs) are expert-level documents that complement the existing implementation guides by addressing real-life implementation design and strategy challenges, as well as answering frequently asked questions. They provide structured guidance to address challenges via product configuration and/or provide workarounds to avoid typical implementation pitfalls. Additionally, they try to provide guardrails to safeguard decision-making during implementation.

The format of each IDP varies by the topic and/or problem that needs to be overcome. Some are structured, detailed documents listing the problem statement, solution design approach, detailed solution, and any assumptions and exclusions. Other IDPs come in a presentation format.

At the time of writing (fall 2019), IDPs are available for Employee Central (including integration to the SAP Business Suite and data migration), Employee Central Payroll, and the Integration Center. SAP is planning to release many more IDPs in the future.

The IDPs can be found on the SAP SuccessFactors Community website and SAP PartnerEdge.

A.3.3 Architectural Leading Practices (ALPs)

Architectural Leading Practices (ALPs) are similar to IDPs insomuch as they provide customers and partners with expert-level documentation to support implementation design. The key difference between IDPs and ALPs is that ALPs focus on technical and architectural aspects, as the name suggests. They also provide guardrails to safeguard design decisions and technical setup.

At present, the available ALPs include:

- Instance strategy
- Localization strategy
- Test strategy
- Mobile strategy
- Permission framework
- Translation strategy

- Job architecture strategy
- Deployment and rollout strategy
- Data migration strategy
- Global assignments and concurrent employment strategy
- Integration strategy

These typically come in presentation format and are available to partners on SAP PartnerEdge.

A.4 Social Media

Social media plays a large role in disseminating information, and a number of high-profile contributors and influencers are involved in this posting or sharing content. You can use several different social media platforms to source the latest information on SAP SuccessFactors. We'll look at a few of the most prominent channels now.

A.4.1 LinkedIn

LinkedIn hosts a number of groups focused on SAP SuccessFactors. The most prominent of these groups are:

- Global SuccessFactors and SAP Community (*http://s-prs.co/v485813*)
- Global SAP and SuccessFactors Community (*http://s-prs.co/v485814*)
- SAP SuccessFactors Employee Central (*http://s-prs.co/v485815*)

These groups have more than 40,000 members between them and are updated almost daily with new content. A majority of the experts and industry influencers are members of one or more groups.

A.4.2 Twitter

If you are a Twitter user, then you can follow the SAP SuccessFactors Twitter account (*@successfactors*). SAP Cloud Support also has a Twitter account (*@SAPCloudSupport*) that provides various support information, including service updates and KBAs. The #SuccessFactors hashtag is also worth following, as most tweets on SAP SuccessFactors use this hashtag.

There are a number of SAP SuccessFactors employees, consultants, partners, and influencers on Twitter whom you can follow to keep up-to-date. You can find most of these individuals from the #SuccessFactors hashtag.

During conferences, you can follow hashtags to hear the latest information as it is announced. For example, attendees at the SAPPHIRE show used the hashtag #SAPPHIRENOW. Similarly, the #ASUG hashtag is used for the ASUG annual conference. For the annual SuccessConnect conferences, #SuccessConnect is the official hashtag to use.

A.4.3 YouTube

SAP SuccessFactors maintains a channel on the video-hosting platform YouTube at *http://s-prs.co/v485816*. Additionally, SAP SuccessFactors also has a playlist of videos about its SAP SuccessFactors Community website that can be accessed by selecting the **Playlists** tab on its channel.

A.4.4 Slack

A group of leading industry experts have created and run the SAP and SAP SuccessFactors group on Slack (*http://s-prs.co/v485817*). This is a truly social platform that enables you to connect with other consultants and individuals interested in SAP SuccessFactors. Slack acts as an easily accessible forum for SAP SuccessFactors-based discussions.

A.5 Publications

There are a number of professional publications that regularly publish books, articles, and reports on SAP SuccessFactors, including:

- SAP PRESS (*http://s-prs.co/v485818*)
- SAPexperts (*http://s-prs.co/v485819*)
- SAP Insider (*http://s-prs.co/v485820*)
- SearchSAP (*http://s-prs.co/v485821*)

A.6 Conferences

The regular SAP conferences serve as another great source of information. Informal networking provides an opportunity for customers to talk to other customers or have off-the-record conversations with experts, consultants, and SAP executives. The following are some of the popular conferences:

- SuccessConnect
- SAPPHIRE NOW and the ASUG Annual Conference
- Mastering SAP
- ASUG chapter meetings
- Upgrade2Success

A.7 User Groups

User groups are country-based organizations that are composed of companies using SAP and SAP partners, such as consulting partners or software developers. They provide a valuable channel of information to members and provide SAP an opportunity to work with SAP users to improve its software and services.

There are a number of these groups globally, including the following:

- Americas' SAP Users' Group (ASUG)
- German SAP User Group (DSAG)
- UK & Ireland SAP User Group (UKISUG)
- SAP Australian User Group (SAUG)

These groups often hold events or provide information to members about SAP ERP HCM topics that include SAP SuccessFactors. ASUG also hosts its annual conference in conjunction with SAPPHIRE and has a strong influence within SAP. You can check locally with SAP to see there if there is a user group in your region.

Appendix B
The Authors

Amy Grubb is a principal consultant and solution architect for human capital management (HCM) processes and technologies, a conference speaker, and a published author. She has consulted in the SAP SuccessFactors space for more than 12 years, and holds three professional certifications. She is the coauthor of *SAP SuccessFactors Recruiting and Onboarding: The Comprehensive Guide*.

Luke Marson is an experienced HR transformation leader and expert in SAP SuccessFactors technology across multiple industries, countries, and cultures. As a C-level leader, architect, and principal consultant for SAP SuccessFactors HCM solutions—being a certified professional in Employee Central—Luke works with multiple customers, advising them on HR strategy, implementation, governance, and success strategies. In addition to being an author, writer, speaker, and go-to individual on HCM and SAP SuccessFactors topics, he is also part of SAP SuccessFactors' Influencer Program and an alumni of the SAP Mentor program.

In his current role, Luke delivers strategy, advisory, roadmap, and consulting services to customers across the world. He has delivered more than 50 projects across the Americas, Europe, the Middle East, South Africa, and Asia to organizations of various sizes and types in different industries and sectors, including automotive, defense, manufacturing, media, oil and gas, public sector, retail, and telecommunications. Luke has worked with multiple customer that have 100,000 employees or more.

Luke is an author of multiple books, articles, and blogs on SAP SuccessFactors. He has presented at a number of conferences, featured in several different podcasts, videos, and webinars, and worked with SAP on multiple customer, product, and educational engagements. Luke can be found on Twitter at @lukemarson.

Contributors

Mick Collins is a global vice president for SAP SuccessFactors Workforce Analytics and Workforce Planning. In this capacity, he oversees presales strategy and execution, with specific responsibilities including go-to-market messaging, commercialization strategy, sales enablement, prospect and customer engagement, alliance management, and product thought leadership. With more than 15 years of experience in analytics and planning, Mick has delivered hundreds of presentations and workshops to public- and private-sector organizations on how to build their capabilities for data-driven decision making in HR.

Eliza Dash is an SAP SuccessFactors professional consultant in Recruiting and Onboarding. She has successfully managed and delivered 18 SAP SuccessFactors Recruiting and Onboarding implementations. She has been in the HR and HRIS space for more than 15 years. Eliza was associated with several strategic projects earlier in her career, including HRIS system analysis. She has an immense interest in learning about HRIS and industry trends, and she believes in facilitating companies towards making informed HR system decisions. With her added experience in HR management and SAP SuccessFactors product knowledge, she also brings a unique user perspective in implementing business technology solutions.

In her spare time, Eliza loves reading books and watching science fiction movies. She is also an amateur astronomer and an eclipse chaser, and loves sky gazing in her telescope from her backyard.

Sven Ringling currently works for the Adessa Group (*www.adessa-group.com*) as a digital HR consultant, where he leads their Qualtrics team. He has worked as an HR technology and process consultant with SAP's HR solutions since 1996. Since 2010, he's built experience in cloud solutions, including SAP Concur, Workday, SAP SuccessFactors, and most recently Qualtrics. He loves sharing his experience with various target audiences, for example, as a coauthor of several SAP PRESS books and as a speaker at a variety of conferences across four continents. You can contact him by email, LinkedIn, or Twitter (*@svenringling*).

Joelle Smith is a learning solutions expert with more than 17 years of consulting, implementation, and pre-sales expertise. Joelle provides thought leadership, strategic direction, and functional implementation support to clients who are looking to invest in learning, collaboration, and talent management solutions. She has successfully led many learning management system implementations in various industries, including electrical energy, oil and gas, health care, retail, manufacturing, and government. In addition to LMS expertise, Joelle has provided guidance with the selection and setup of third-party vendor content, online content authoring tools, and content management strategies.

Index

B

C

D

E

F

M

P

Q

R

S

U

V